Encyclopedia of
American Literature of
the Sea and Great Lakes

"Stowing a Topsail," 1893
Frank Brangwyn (1867–1956), illustrator
Charles Wesley Chadwick (1861–?), engraver
Reprinted with permission from Mystic Seaport Museum, Inc.

Encyclopedia of
American Literature of the Sea and Great Lakes

Edited by
JILL B. GIDMARK

Greenwood Press
Westport, Connecticut • London

Library of Congress Cataloging-in-Publication Data

Encyclopedia of American literature of the sea and Great Lakes / edited by Jill B. Gidmark.
    p. cm.
    Includes bibliographical references and index.
    ISBN 0–313–30148–4 (alk. paper)
    1. American literature—Encyclopedias. 2. American literature—Great Lakes
  Region—History and criticism. 3. Sea in literature—Encyclopedias. 4. Seafaring life in
  literature—Encyclopedias. 5. Ocean travel in literature—Encyclopedias. 6. Great
  Lakes—In literature—Encyclopedias. I. Gidmark, Jill B.
  PS169.S42E53 2001
  810.9'355—dc21   00–025112

British Library Cataloguing in Publication Data is available.

Library of Congress Catalog Card Number: 00–025112
ISBN: 0–313–30148–4

First published in 2001

Greenwood Press, 88 Post Road West, Westport, CT 06881
An imprint of Greenwood Publishing Group, Inc.
www.greenwood.com

Printed in the United States of America

The paper used in this book complies with the
Permanent Paper Standard issued by the National
Information Standards Organization (Z39.48–1984).

10 9 8 7 6 5 4 3 2 1

Copyright Acknowledgments

The editor and the publisher gratefully acknowledge permission for use of the following
material:

Excerpts from poems reprinted by permission of the publishers and the Trustees of Amherst
College from *The Poems of Emily Dickinson*, Thomas H. Johnson, ed., Cambridge, Mass.: The
Belknap Press of Harvard University Press, Copyright © 1951, 1955, 1979, 1983 by the President and Fellows of Harvard College.

Excerpts from a letter reprinted by permission of the publishers from *The Letters of Emily
Dickinson* edited by Thomas H. Johnson, Cambridge, Mass.: The Belknap Press of Harvard
University Press, Copyright © 1958, 1986 by the President and Fellows of Harvard College.

Excerpts from *The Complete Poems of Emily Dickinson* by T. H. Johnson, Copyright 1929, 1935
by Martha Dickinson Bianchi; copyright © renewed 1957, 1963 by Mary L. Hampson. By
permission of Little, Brown and Company.

To the memory of **Joseph T. Flibbert** (1938–1999),
editorial board member, scholar, friend:

A very high and noble nature, and better worth immortality than most of us.
—Nathaniel Hawthorne of Herman Melville

Death is at all times solemn, but never so much so as at sea. . . . [A]t sea, the man is near you—at your side—you hear his voice, and in an instant he is gone, and nothing but a *vacancy* shows his loss. Then, too, at sea—to use a homely but expressive phrase—you *miss* a man so much. A dozen men are shut up together in a little bark, upon the wide, wide sea, and for months and months see no forms and hear no voices but their own and one is taken suddenly from among them, and they miss him at every turn. It is like losing a limb. There are no new faces or new scenes to fill up the gap. There is always an empty berth in the forecastle, and one man wanting when the small night watch is mustered. There is one less to take the wheel and one less to lay out with you upon the yard. You miss his form, and the sound of his voice, for habit had made them almost necessary to you, and each of your senses feels the loss.

—Richard Henry Dana Jr.,
Two Years before the Mast

Contents

Preface

This reference work of maritime literature has been designed to appeal to scholars and to casual readers alike; it seeks to get concise, factual information into the hands of the hobbyist at the same time that it provides a useful tool for the academic researcher. Its aim is to deepen awareness of the value of the sea environment and the sea experience in American life and letters by identifying and surveying works of imaginative literature that were "inspired" one way or another by the great bodies of water known as the Atlantic, the Pacific, the Caribbean, and the Arctic Oceans and the Great Lakes.

Although the encyclopedia selections have doubtless been influenced by a number of subjective factors, the members of my editorial board and I have tried to steer a course along pragmatic lines. We first surveyed highly regarded maritime scholarship: Jeanne-Marie Santraud's *La Mer et le Roman Américain dans la Première Moitié du Dix-Neuvième Siècle* (1972), Thomas Philbrick's *James Fenimore Cooper and the Development of American Sea Fiction* (1961), Haskell Springer's *America and the Sea: A Literary History* (1995), Myron J. Smith Jr. and Robert C. Weller's *Sea Fiction Guide* (1976), Bert Bender's *Sea-Brothers: The Tradition of American Sea Fiction from* Moby-Dick *to the Present* (1988), among others. The final list of 459 entries was culled, in large part, from bibliographies within these sources. The entries, which vary in length from under 50 words to over 2,000, consider American literature of all periods and genres: fiction, creative nonfiction, drama, and poetry. I have also included naval history and autobiography where there has been a compelling literary link, and I have aimed to balance entries on early established works of literary merit with recent publications that seem capable of standing the test of time.

The categories included are authors, published works, characters, themes, vessels, ports, and geographical regions. In author entries I sought neither complete biography nor exhaustive publication citations but aimed instead to highlight maritime experience and to survey those works that referred to the sea in significant ways. I have included some well-known authors who are not usually considered writers of the sea, such as Robert Frost, Gary Snyder, and Stephen King, to acknowledge their attention to the maritime. Title entries focus on the role that the sea plays within a work of literature, tracking the sea as setting, theme, or motif. Most title entries situate a work within a larger literature-of-the-sea context. Literary character entries explore the maritime significance of those figures. Entries on themes, vessels, ports, and geographical regions discuss the symbolic and representational import of major literary references.

While Derek Walcott has defined "America" as the territory from Greenland to Tierra del Fuego, we have used instead the more commonly held definition of America as the United States and its waters, expanding the locus by drawing from bordering Canadian and Caribbean literary sources published in English. Mexican and Central and South American non-English writings are excluded. A few entries on themes with a broader global sweep, such as Women at Sea and Ghosts and Ghost Ship Legends, include some European references for contextual and/or historical perspective; British Influences on American Sea Literature intentionally reaches outside American shores. In keeping with Rudyard Kipling's assessment of the Great Lakes as a "fully accredited ocean," I have featured these waters in several entries but have not considered other American lakes or rivers. Acknowledging that the seagoing enterprise has traditionally been the domain of white male privilege, the historical picture is fleshed out by including ethnic and gender perspectives with entries on African American, American Indian, Asian American, and Latino/a Literatures of the Sea and a focused entry on Women at Sea.

Aiming for more breadth than depth, I opted for a greater number of short entries over a smaller number of lengthy ones. I strove for consistency among entries and to that end encouraged all 159 contributors to present their information with as little critical bias or theoretical interpretation as possible. I have not attempted, however, to homogenize the contributors' unique voices, styles, or perspectives.

Entries are arranged alphabetically. Cross-references are indicated by an asterisk following the name of another entry; further reading citations are provided for the more significant entries. A literary/historical timeline appears in the back matter to illuminate the context of the entries, and a selective general bibliography has been provided.

Acknowledgments

A project of this design and scope is the collaboration of many hands and minds. Chief among these are the members of my editorial board, who assisted me from the beginning on all aspects of the form and content of the encyclopedia: Mary K. Bercaw Edwards, Attilio Favorini, Joseph Flibbert, Robert Madison, Mary Malloy, and Haskell Springer. Our survey of 459 entries includes some that we wrote ourselves and others for which we targeted knowledgeable colleagues, grad students, friends, and, in a few cases, family members. Their eyes and minds were indispensable to my editing process; I could not have wished for a more collegial or dedicated crew on this five-year voyage. To Mary K. Bercaw Edwards, above all, heart-deep gratitude for acting as my assistant editor. To all 159 contributors, many of whom provided more than one revision to meet our wishes and constraints, some of whose entries I had to shorten or modify at the eleventh hour, your professionalism and good humor buoyed us up: deep thanks for your scholarship and participation.

Many others made our lives bearable and even pleasant during the process. With apologies for overlooking an effort or a kindness, I acknowledge the following with a glad heart: George Butler, Greenwood Press, who first envisioned the project and asked me to woman the helm; Phil Greasley, who advised early stages of my process even as he was compiling his own *Dictionary of Midwestern Literature*; Dennis Lien, University of Minnesota librarian, and Peter McCracken, University of Washington librarian, for reference assistance par excellence; Vicki Neau and Doug Robertson for technical expertise and assistance with manuscript preparation; Barry Stehlik for secretarial services; Dana L. Peterson and Mira Dock for research assistance; Heidi Straight for fine copyediting; and the professional indexing services;

To institutions and organizations that offered funding support: the University of Minnesota for a Grant-in-Aid of Scholarship, Research, and

Artistry; the Minnesota Humanities Commission for a Works-in-Progress Grant; and the Munson Institute at Mystic Seaport for my 1998 Paul Cuffe Memorial Fellowship, and special thanks to Lori-Anne Williams, John B. Hattendorf, and Katrina Bercaw; the General College at the University of Minnesota, for necessary research and secretarial support and particularly to Director Terry Collins and Dean David Taylor for making adjustments in my teaching schedule when I desperately needed it;

For uncommon hospitality, lodging, and collegiality during our board meetings at SUNY-Maritime—Karen Markoe and Esther Carstensen; for so cheerfully opening your homes to us for meetings, overnights, and meals— Marilyn Sallack in Reading, Massachusetts; Ellen Madison in Westerly, Rhode Island; Carl and Janet Edwards in Glencoe, Maryland, Jim Millinger in Woods Hole, Massachusetts; Susan Beegel and Wesley Tiffney for breathtaking space and days and nights at the University of Massachusetts-Boston Nantucket Field Station during a series of autumn board meetings on the island; North American Society for Oceanic History, local arrangements people, and the U.S.S. Constitution Museum staff for meeting accommodations in Boston;

Stuart Frank, Kendall Whaling Museum, for collegiality during my research there and lodging at the Scholars Quarters, and Michael P. Dyer for his uncommon expertise; Victoria Brehm, Grand Valley State University, for helping to identify a short list of entries on the Great Lakes; Peggy Tate-Smith and the Photo Archives Department at Mystic Seaport Museum for generous permission to use "Stowing a Topsail" for our frontispiece and for processing and donating a photograph of the engraving; Robert Del Tredici for use of his "Meditation and Water" illustration; Don Sineti for use of his "Sperm Whale" illustration; Tina Furtado, New Bedford Free Public Library; Daniel Finamore, Peabody Essex Museum; Lawrence Moe, Metropolitan State University; Glenn Grasso, Mystic Seaport Museum; Ellen R. Nelson, Cape Ann Historical Association; Eleanor Reynolds, Salem State College Library; Vincent Ferrini, Gloucester, Massachusetts; Dianne M. Gutscher, Bowdoin College Library; William Watterson, Bowdoin; Lee Heald and Judith Downey, New Bedford Whaling Museum; Kevin Cole, University of Sioux Falls; and Clive Cussler.

Thanks are also due for kindnesses and occasions not necessarily connected with the project but that continue to inspire me in nautical and literary directions: Mary Malloy for getting me aboard the S.S.V. *Westward* for an entire week one January to cruise the West Florida Shelf as a deckhand and for pointing out the Southern Cross to me while I stood dawn watch at the bow; Lisa Norling, University of Minnesota, for our shared maritime enthusiasm and collaboration; Chris Sten, Robert Lewis, Roger Bresnahan, and Doug Robillard for valued collegiality; Tony Hunt for our pleasurable work together on Derek Walcott; Bob Del Tredici for generous imagination, lambent vision and friendship; Mary Ellen Caldwell for encouragement and love.

To John, Benjamin, and Nicholas, thank you, when shoals of this project threatened to wreck me and calms stalled and parched me, for giving me safe harbor.

Yes, as every
one knows,
meditation and water
are wedded
forever.

"Meditation and Water," 1966.
Robert Del Tredici (b. 1938).
Reprinted with permission.

Introduction

Only the sea is like a human being; the sky is not, nor the earth. But the sea is always moving; always something deep in itself is stirring it. It never rests; it is always wanting, wanting, wanting.
—Olive Schreiner, *The Story of an African Farm*

The voice of the sea is seductive; never ceasing, whispering, clamoring, murmuring, inviting the soul to wander for a spell in abysses of solitude; to lose itself in mazes of inward contemplation. The voice of the sea speaks to the soul. The touch of the sea is sensuous, enfolding the body in its soft, close embrace.
—Kate Chopin, *The Awakening*

I

Both Olive Schreiner's South African perspective and Kate Chopin's Louisiana reflection attest to the sea's power to pull at, and charm, human thought and action. Schreiner's simile binds the sea to humanity; Chopin's personification gives the sea human voice and limb. Such linkage has given rise to literary outpouring of a wide spectrum of moods and genres from earliest times to the present. The sea swells with praise and keens in lamentation; in its simultaneous constancy and movement the sea provides both impetus and object for extended contemplation. Writing in the middle of the twentieth century, Charles Olson, Melville scholar and Black Mountain poet, makes vital the long-standing connection between humankind and the sea: "The beginning of man was salt sea, and the perpetual reverberation of that great ancient fact, [is] constantly renewed in the unfolding of life in every human individual" (13). At the heart of Olson's thought is Herman Melville's certainty: "Yes, as everyone knows, meditation and water are wedded forever" (ch. 1).

In his fine introduction to *America and the Sea: A Literary History*, a thoroughgoing discourse on the sea's seminal influence on the history and literature of America from early development to modern times, Haskell Springer begins with an elemental contradiction: "[W]ater is the joiner of human beings and the center of their communities . . . also the separator, the border, the dangerous boundary" (1). These two poles define the range of human interaction with the sea, from passive water-gazing from the shore or a safe vantage on a calm sea, to active navigating under harrowing conditions. In this insightful survey of ways in which American authors have responded to the sea both as meditative water-gazers and as voyagers living out literal and archetypal journeys, Springer metaphorically searches the sea for its "voices" of enchantment, death, and life; he reveals the sea in its many guises, its motion and movement, its complex gender associations. As if to match the richness of this imaginative and enduring literature, articulating the sea has historically taken varied forms: oral legends, myths of creation and hardship, sagas of endurance and sacrifice, narratives of log-books and journals and diaries, poetry, plays and chamber dramas, sermons and broadsides, chanteys and ballads, essays, short stories, and novels.

Springer surveys the powerful effects that exploring, slaving, whaling, fishing, shipping, trading, and waging war have had on sea literature produced in early and recent America. To take a single outstanding example, the debt that the vitality of the New England coast owes to the sea is enormous; it is manifest in the largest and most luminous maritime literary outpouring of any region of America. Springer also notes the shift at the dawn of the twentieth century "from business to pleasure" (12) in human associations with the sea, and he demonstrates how literary reflections parallel that shift. Herman Melville, James Fenimore Cooper, Nathaniel Hawthorne, Washington Irving, Edgar Allan Poe, Richard Henry Dana Jr., Walt Whitman, Eugene O'Neill, Sarah Orne Jewett, Celia Thaxter, and numerous additional authors all relay personal seagoing experience and/or create enduring visions of the many ways the sea transforms the human psyche.

II

Four years after becoming an American citizen, W. H. Auden analyzed maritime iconography in Cervantes, Coleridge, Poe, and Melville to explore the nature of the romantic spirit in three essays collected under the title *The Enchafèd Flood*. The act of putting to sea, says Auden, "separates or estranges" (7) as one moves from land, severing ties to home, fleeing from memory, freeing the spirit. It is at sea where decisive events happen, those "moments of eternal choice" (13); occurrences on land seem transient by comparison. Such are fine validation and recommendation for studying literature of the sea. A place of freedom and independence, of potentiality, perpetual motion, and hidden life, the sea also signifies for Auden a condition of loneliness and alienation, as many American sea authors confirm.

The privations of an actual sea voyage are perhaps nowhere better expressed than in Stephen Crane's metaphorical short story "The Open Boat." The story is drawn from Crane's experience as a correspondent aboard the steamship *Commodore*, just prior to the Spanish-American War. The vessel, with its cargo of arms and munitions, was illegally bound for Cuba. When engine trouble caused her to sink, Crane and three of the crew spent a harrowing thirty hours afloat in a ten-foot dinghy. First published as "Stephen Crane's Own Story," Crane transformed the episode into myth with "The Open Boat," a story with the barest of plotlines that pits the wrath of a bitter January sea against the vulnerability of weakened humans. The unnamed men in the story are incapable of meditatively appreciating the "glorious . . . play of the free sea, wild with lights of emerald and white and amber" (pt. 2) because they are preoccupied with the life-or-death labors of bailing the boat and pulling the oars. The "subtle brotherhood" (pt. 3) that develops among the men is their only hedge against the blank indifference of Fate and the "diabolical punishment" that she metes out: tumultuous wind and formidable waves, cryptic gestures from a man on shore, and the bitter irony of the strongest swimmer drowning when the men jump for shore before the dinghy swamps. Only at a physical and temporal remove, after having survived the agony, do the three survivors feel they are able to become "interpreters" of the sea, finally able to gaze across it and face its meaning in their lives. As the writings of Poe and Melville and Cooper and London attest, being at sea is, more often than not, life-threatening: the interpretation comes at a price.

While navigating the sea can be physically demanding and downright dangerous, it can also be emotionally and spiritually clarifying. Melville knew this better than anyone. His character Bulkington from *Moby-Dick*, having just returned from a four-year voyage, restlessly signs aboard the *Pequod* for another term at sea; because "land seemed scorching to his feet," he sought "all the lashed sea's landlessness again" (ch. 23). He is the archetypical water-gazer, a "deep, earnest" thinker who craves "the open independence of . . . [the] sea" and for whom "in landlessness alone resides the highest truth, shoreless, indefinite as God" (ch. 23).

The craving for the clarifying, healing properties of water can lead to self-discovery. Thomas Farber's *On Water*, a pastiche of literary and scientific musings on the maritime, brings together the kinds of water-gazing, water-reading, and physical immersion to which poets, novelists, philosophers, and naturalists have aspired in attempting to interpret the "highest truth" of landlessness. Early in the work, Farber offers the only statement recorded by the pre-Socratic philosopher Thales, in which all other quotations and observations in his book become suspended: " 'Everything is water, water is all' " (9).

The sea's impact upon the human imagination is also the subject of British author James Hamilton-Paterson's *The Great Deep: The Sea and Its Thresholds*. The sea, he says, is "reservoir of private imagery and public myth. . . . We are full of its beauty, of that strange power it gives off which echoes through our racial history and fills our language with its metaphors" (9). Sensing the human insignificance that was so apparent to Crane adrift in his open boat, Hamilton-Paterson remarks that a man alone in the deep, "in this wide salt world . . . is nothing" (247). He comments, too, on the sea's "special melancholy and . . . power to haunt," as shown in "a capacity to conceal, [in] the ability to stand for time and the quality of erasure" (143), and in the mythic power behind the very notion of "the Deep" (165). The sea retains, says Hamilton-Paterson, "its psychic force, its sonorous and chilling stateliness, its amalgamation of height and depth, of gulfs of space and of time" (193). Some water-gazers, of course, become literally overwhelmed: Edna Pontellier in Kate Chopin's *The Awakening* and Owen Browne in Robert Stone's *Outerbridge Reach* both seek immersion in the sea as their death.

Derek Walcott, 1992 recipient of the Nobel Prize in literature, is a modern-day water-gazer whose stance before his native St. Lucia sea is anything but passive. Plumbing the meaning of the sea with urgency, he illuminates what the sea can erase and how it can bless. Some of his best poetry and drama capture his personal and ethnic Caribbean identification with the sea and the profoundly liberating sea change that called him to celebrate his native people in their own voice. An early poem, "The Schooner *Flight*," affirms the sea's necessity in his life and art and asserts that his true theme is "the bowsprit, the arrow, the longing, the lunging heart" (361). The sea is the primal flow and force within his 324-page epic *Omeros*; it unites distant shores of ancient Greece with modern Caribbean beaches, levels great empires, and generates a visceral aesthetic. The title of the poem is the Greek word for Homer; Geert Lernout is among critics who have hailed the epic as a modern version of the *Odyssey* (96). The title also refers to the poem's shape-shifting protagonist, elusive as the sea's many moods, whose multiple guises include Homer, Proteus, Dante, the sea, a white marble statue, a foam-headed old man called Seven Seas with a dog perpetually nipping at his heels, and a poet-narrator who bears an uncanny resemblance to Derek Walcott.

Three years after *Omeros* appeared, Walcott published a stage version of *The Odyssey*, another Aegean/Caribbean celebration, this time of the world's most famous sailor-wanderer, "that man against whom the sea still rages,/ Who escaped its terrors, that despair could not destroy" (160). Physically and emotionally ravaged by the sea and its monsters but now secure in the comforting arms of Penelope, Odysseus, when pressed, confides that he will continue to long for, to gaze toward, the sea. Whatever meaning he will be able to draw from it for his life is, as with Crane's survivors, a matter for later contemplation.

III

Maritime inspiration in America arises from the Great Lakes as well as from the Pacific, the Atlantic, the Caribbean, and the Polar seas. Citing Rudyard Kipling's assertion that the freshwater seas of the Great Lakes are each a " 'fully accredited ocean' " (2), Springer comments on the literature inspired by those waters in Native American and in European traditions. In fact, in terms of depth and breadth, industry and economy, and the potential for meteorological or technological disaster, the Great Lakes far more resemble a sea than they resemble other waters; in Kipling's words, the Lakes "engulf . . . and wreck . . . and drive . . . ashore" (159). Moreover, as Victoria Brehm proposes in her essay "Great Lakes Maritime Fiction," these bodies of water figure into two significant traditions within the larger context of sea literature: as an unchanging "presence bent on destruction" (231) and as a myth of conquest limited by technology (232). Brehm suggests further that Lakes fiction is unique in illustrating a truth not shared by most American fiction: the fact of "our own frailty in the face of nature, and our fear" (232). But the most eloquent and persuasive argument for linking the Great Lakes with the ocean is recorded in America's greatest sea novel, *Moby-Dick*:

For in their interflowing aggregate, those grand freshwater seas of ours,—Erie, and Ontario, and Huron, and Superior, and Michigan,—possess an ocean-like expansiveness, with many of the ocean's noblest traits. . . . [T]hey float alike the full-rigged merchant ship, the armed cruiser of the State, the steamer, and the beech canoe; they are swept by Borean and dismasting blasts as direful as any that lash the salted wave; they know what shipwrecks are, for out of sight of land, however inland, they have drowned full many a midnight ship with all its shrieking crew. (ch. 54)

For all of these reasons, literature of the Great Lakes has a place within, and is included in, the present survey of American literature of the sea.

In addition to these inland waters, the interior landscape of America partakes of the myths of the sea. In *The Great Prairie Fact and Literary Imagination* Robert Thacker explores how maritime sensibilities affect human nature even in the landlocked grasslands/farmlands of North America. It is noteworthy, but not uncommon, that a book concentrating on the relationship between the human psyche and the earth should use sea imagery as a touchstone. Early geographers tended to represent the uncharted North American interior as what Thacker calls a "vast inland sea" (52) and to characterize the appearance of the prairie lands themselves as a "level sea of grass" (52).

Thacker evokes nineteenth-century geographer Sir William Francis Butler, who, charting the Canadian Northwest, first encountered the "prairie" traveling northwest from central Minnesota. Significantly, Butler's narrative of prairie travel begins with an Atlantic crossing during which he observes an "unruffled" sea: "as evening came down over the still tranquil ocean and the vessel clove her outward way through phosphorescent water, the lights along the iron coast grew fainter in distance till there lay around only the unbroken circle of the sea" (*Great Lone Land* 11). Butler, in fact, several decades prior to Kipling's use of the metaphor, had termed Lake Superior an "inland-ocean" (*Great Lone Land* 74) and the Great Lakes themselves "immense inland seas" (*Great Lone Land* 18). Though his travel narrative does not attain the status of imaginative literature, something about the land and its geography draws Butler meditatively seaward; something in his quest of the soil seeks imagery of the sea for inspiration and validation:

The great ocean itself does not present more infinite variety than does this prairie-ocean of which we speak. . . . No ocean of water in the world can vie with its gorgeous sunsets. . . . This ocean has no past—time has been nought to it; and men have come and gone, leaving behind them no track, no vestige, of their presence. (*Great Lone Land* 199–200)

Butler's later American travel narrative, *Wild North Land*, is, in part, more symbolic than descriptive; here the Great Prairie, "the vast rigid ocean of the central continent," is "ocean-like in everything save motion" (49); here the westward migrations of bison are characterized as "the waves of the ocean roll[ing] before the storm" (53). Predating Butler by four decades, William Cullen Bryant had compared billowing Illinois grasslands to an ocean in "The Prairies"; writing fifty years after Butler, an obscure poet of the Red River Valley named Eva K. Anglesburg described the winter prairie of her native North Dakota as being "sculpted like the sea" with "fiery-crested, black-troughed billows roll[ing]." Bryant, Butler, Anglesburg, and other prairie authors who use sea imagery are in venerable company: Melville in the first chapter of *Moby-Dick* compares the Pacific Ocean to the prairie.

Charles Olson echoed the same sensibility more recently in *Call Me Ishmael*; for him it was important "to understand the Pacific as part of our geography, another West, prefigured in the Plains, antithetical" (13). In the 1990s Jonathan Raban, author and seafarer, opens his book about Montana homesteaders with nautical imagery: "Breasting the regular swells of land, on a red dirt road as true as a line of longitude, the car was like a boat at sea" (3). In *Landscape and Memory*, art critic and prize-winning author Simon Schama discusses the ways in which geography shapes mythology, how "place . . . exposes its connections to an ancient and peculiar vision" (16). His observation that landscape is "a work of the mind, a repository of the memories and obsessions of the people who gaze upon it" (back cover) can apply as well to the sea's power and potential; he gives the title "Water" to the second of four parts of his book (and titles subsections "Streams of

Consciousness" and "Bloodstreams"). Indeed, one need not be near or on the sea to resonate to it.

IV

Exploring human purpose regarding the open sea is an endeavor that transcends time, place, genre, and discipline. While the kaleidoscope of maritime literature from colonial America to the present is the substance of this encyclopedia, the sea as an intellectual pursuit, it must be acknowledged, also resonates meaningfully into nonliterary disciplines. Two recent books are masterfully representative of how sea literature richly extends, for example, into the fields of art and astronomy: Elizabeth Schultz's *Unpainted to the Last: Moby-Dick and Twentieth-Century American Art* and Brett Zimmerman's *Herman Melville: Stargazer.*

Throughout the encyclopedia, I have flagged some disciplinary crossovers by citing film or musical adaptations that complement the literature. Other entries, while illuminating literary references, are rooted primarily in non-literary disciplines—natural science, environmental studies, and history: entries, thus, are included on the naturalist William Beebe, the anthropologist Loren Eiseley, and the environmentalist Rachel Carson. Entries rooted firmly in history include *Monitor* and *Merrimack* and other vessel entries, *The Red Record*, Slave Narratives, and U.S. Exploring Expedition. There are other entries on artistic expression, the broader humanities, and serial publication. Some entries are devoted to art or music: artists Gilbert Wilson and Rockwell Kent, composer Dominick Argento, Philip Glass' opera *The Voyage*. Discrete entries on playwrights and plays are complemented by the thematic convergence of drama and the maritime: Drama of the Sea, Melville Dramatizations, Ocean Liner Drama, and Shore Leave Musicals. An entry entitled Nineteenth-Century Periodicals reveals the pervasive voice of the sea within the popular print media of the previous century.

This survey aims to immerse the reader in the world of maritime literature; it also prompts the reader to seek the sea in prairie and city as well as on the coast or in the deeps. Contemporary culture in recent years is experiencing a maritime resurgence. Sessions on literature of the sea are being hosted at conferences of the Modern Language Association, the American Culture Association/Popular Culture Association, and the College English Association, among other academic venues. Art exhibits celebrating the sea have been mounted from Ketchikan, Alaska, to New Bedford, Massachusetts. An experimental theatre piece, "Ahab's Wife or The Whale," premiered in Snug Harbor Cultural Center in 1998, and in 1999 composer Laurie Anderson toured from New York to California with her avant-garde rendition of "Songs and Stories from *Moby-Dick.*" Performing and recording technomusician Moby claims to be a blood relative of Herman Melville. Recent films—*Deep Blue Sea, Titanic, Amistad, Jaws,* and *White Squall*—help make the sea an enduring cinematic icon. Remountings of Benjamin

Britten's *Billy Budd* by the Metropolitan Opera, Orson Welles' *Moby-Dick Rehearsed* by the Theatre Workshop of Nantucket and the Berkshire Theatre Festival, and realizations of Rudyard Kipling's *Captains Courageous* by the Manhattan Theatre Club and Arthur Miller's *A View from the Bridge* by Chicago's Lyric Opera infuse new musical and dramatic interest in the nautical classics.

Given constrictions of our publication length and production schedule and the ever-swelling ranks of contemporary literary and artistic expression, the works that are described within this volume should be taken more as a representative than as a definitive account of the American maritime literary scene. Worth further examination are many new titles that were either published too recently to be surveyed here or are in some way tangential to our purpose; bibliographic information for these is provided in the further reading list.

Some of these new books fictionally embellish the lives of established authors (Frederick Busch's *The Night Inspector*, Larry Duberstein's *The Handsome Sailor*, Stephen Marlowe's *The Lighthouse at the End of the World*, Roger McDonald's *Mr. Darwin's Shooter*) and familiar characters (Sena Jeter Naslund's *Ahab's Wife or, The Star-Gazer*); some extend the historical record (Antonio Benítez-Rojo's *A View from the Mangrove*, Robert D. Ballard and Will Hively's *The Eternal Darkness*). Reflective narratives of experiences at sea or on the coast are being published: Peter Nichols' *Sea Change: Alone across the Atlantic in a Wooden Boat*, Steve Callahan's *Adrift: Seventy-Six Days Lost at Sea*, Linda Greenlaw's *The Hungry Ocean: A Swordboat Captain's Journey*, Gordon Chaplin's *Dark Wind: A Survivor's Tale of Love and Loss*, and Jennifer Ackerman's *Notes from the Shore*. New histories, some illustrated, are appearing: Benjamin Labaree's *America and the Sea: A Maritime History*, John Szarkowski and Richard Benson's *A Maritime Album: 100 Photographs and Their Stories*, Patrick Dillon's *Lost at Sea: An American Tragedy*, Warren F. Spencer's *Raphael Semmes: The Philosophical Mariner*, Donald A. Petrie's *The Prize Game: Lawful Looting on the High Seas in the Days of Fighting Sail*, Timothy J. Runyan's *Ships, Seafaring and Society: Essays in Maritime History*, Peter Maas' *The Terrible Hours*. New printings of old biographies, such as Joseph C. Hart's *Miriam Coffin or, The Whale-Fishermen*, keep significant ideas before us. Other authors are reimagining legends: Richard Ellis' *Imagining Atlantis*, Janet Lembke's *Skinny Dipping: And Other Immersions in Water, Myth, and Being Human*, Lena Lencek and Gideon Bosker's *The Beach: The History of Paradise on Earth*. Some escape novels appropriate sea themes: Philip Caputo's *The Voyage*, Paul Garrison's *Fire and Ice*, James Powlik's *Sea Change*, Robin Beeman's *A Minus Tide*, Gene Hackman and Daniel Lenihan's *Wake of the Perdito Star*, and Marge Piercy and Ira Wood's *Storm Tide*. Children's literature, too, continues to draw minds seaward: Bruce Balan's *Buoy: Home at Sea*, Kimberley Knutson's *Beach Babble*, Debra Fraisier's *Out of the Ocean*, Cynthia Rylant's *The Islander*, Susan Shreve's *Jonah the Whale*, Michael McCurdy's *The Sailor's Alphabet*.

"When he left the beach, the sea was still going on" (*Omeros* 325); so says Derek Walcott of his protagonist Achilles and the Caribbean Sea in the line that closes his maritime epic. These are reassuring words: no human mind will have the final vision, and no human voice will speak the final word about the sea. This encyclopedia is but one attempt to gather together the most meaningful of what literary America has thought, sensed, and imagined about this fluid and potent element. I await the next.

Jill B. Gidmark

WORKS CITED

Anglesburg, Eva K. "Prairie Murals: Flame Phantasy." *For Many Moods*, Bismarck, ND: Cairn, 1938, 20.

Auden, W. H. *The Enchafèd Flood: or The Romantic Iconography of the Sea*. 1950. New York: Vintage, 1967.

Brehm, Victoria. "Great Lakes Maritime Fiction." *America and the Sea: A Literary History*. Ed. Haskell Springer. Athens: U of Georgia P, 1995, 224–32.

Bryant, William Cullen. "The Prairies." *Poems*. 3rd ed. New York: Harper, 1836, 50–54.

Butler, William Francis. *The Great Lone Land: A Narrative Tale of Travel and Adventure in the North-West of America*. London: Sampson, Low, Marston, Low, and Searle, 1874.

———. *The Wild North Land: The Story of a Winter Journey, with Dogs, across Northern North America*. London: Sampson, Low, Marston, Low, and Searle, 1874.

Chopin, Kate. *The Awakening*. New York: Capricorn Books, 1964.

Crane, Stephen. "Stephen Crane's Own Story." *New York Press*, January 7, 1897: 1–2.

———. *The Open Boat and Three Other Stories*. New York: Franklin Watts, 1968.

Farber, Thomas. *On Water*. Hopewell, NJ: Ecco, 1994.

Hamilton-Paterson, James. *The Great Deep: The Sea and Its Thresholds*. New York: Henry Holt, 1992.

Kipling, Rudyard. *Letters of Travel, 1892–1913*. Garden City, NY: Doubleday, 1920.

Lernout, Geert. "Derek Walcott's *Omeros*: The Isle Is Full of Voices." *Kunapipi* 14.2 (1992): 90–104.

Melville, Herman. *Moby-Dick or The Whale*. Ed. Harrison Hayford, Hershel Parker, and G. Thomas Tanselle. Evanston and Chicago: Northwestern UP and Newberry Library, 1988.

Olson, Charles. *Call Me Ishmael*. Baltimore: Johns Hopkins UP, 1997.

Raban, Jonathan. *Bad Land: An American Romance*. New York: Pantheon, 1996.

Schama, Simon. *Landscape and Memory*. New York: Knopf, 1995.

Schultz, Elizabeth A. *Unpainted to the Last: Moby-Dick and Twentieth-Century American Art*. Lawrence: UP of Kansas, 1995.

Shreiner, Olive. *The Story of an African Farm*. Chicago: Academy Press/Cassandra, 1977.

Springer, Haskell. "Introduction: The Sea, the Land, the Literature." *America and the Sea: A Literary History*. Athens: U of Georgia P, 1995, 1–31.

Stone, Robert. *Outerbridge Reach.* New York: Ticknor and Fields, 1992.

Thacker, Robert. *The Great Prairie Fact and Literary Imagination.* Albuquerque: U of New Mexico P, 1989.

Walcott, Derek. *Omeros.* New York: Noonday, 1990.

———. "The Schooner *Flight.*" *Collected Poems, 1948–1984.* New York: Noonday, 1992, 345–61.

———. *The Odyssey.* New York: Noonday, 1993.

Zimmerman, Brett. *Herman Melville: Stargazer.* Montreal: McGill-Queen's UP, 1998.

FURTHER READING

Ackerman, Jennifer. *Notes from the Shore.* New York: Viking, 1995.

Balan, Bruce. *Buoy: Home at Sea.* New York: Delacorte, 1998.

Ballard, Robert D., and Will Hively. *The Eternal Darkness: A Personal History of Deep-Sea Exploration.* Princeton, NJ: Princeton UP, 2000.

Beeman, Robin. *A Minus Tide.* Washington, DC: Chronicle, 1995.

Benítez-Rojo, Antonio. *A View from the Mangrove.* Amherst: U of Massachusetts P, 1998.

Busch, Frederick. *The Night Inspector.* New York: Harmony, 1999.

Callahan, Steve. *Adrift: Seventy-Six Days Lost at Sea.* New York: Ballantine, 1987.

Caputo, Philip. *The Voyage.* New York: Alfred A. Knopf, 1999.

Chaplin, Gordon. *Dark Wind: A Survivor's Tale of Love and Loss.* New York: Atlantic Monthly, 1999.

Dillon, Patrick. *Lost at Sea: An American Tragedy.* New York: Dial, 1998.

Duberstein, Larry. *The Handsome Sailor.* Sag Harbor, NY: Permanent P, 1998.

Ellis, Richard. *Imagining Atlantis.* New York: Alfred A. Knopf, 1998.

Fraisier, Debra. *Out of the Ocean.* Orlando: Harcourt Brace, 1998.

Garrison, Paul. *Fire and Ice.* New York: Avon, 1998.

Greenlaw, Linda. *The Hungry Ocean: A Swordboat Captain's Journey.* Boston: Hyperion, 1999.

Hackman, Gene, and Daniel Lenihan. *Wake of the Perdito Star.* New York: Newmarket, 1999.

Hart, Joseph C. *Miriam Coffin or, The Whale-Fishermen.* Introduction by Nathaniel Philbrick. Nantucket, MA: Mill Hill, 1995.

Knutson, Kimberley. *Beach Babble.* New York: Marshall Cavendish, 1998.

Labaree, Benjamin, et al. *America and the Sea: A Maritime History.* Mystic, CT: Mystic Seaport Museum, 1999.

Lembke, Janet. *Skinny Dipping: And Other Immersions in Water, Myth, and Being Human.* New York: Lyons and Buford, 1996.

Lencek, Lena, and Gideon Bosker. *The Beach: The History of Paradise on Earth.* New York: Viking, 1998.

Maas, Peter. *The Terrible Hours: The Man behind the Greatest Submarine Rescue in History.* New York: Harpercollins, 1999.

Marlowe, Stephen. *The Lighthouse at the End of the World.* New York: NAL/Dutton, 1995.

McCurdy, Michael. *The Sailor's Alphabet.* Boston: Houghton Mifflin, 1998.

McDonald, Roger. *Mr. Darwin's Shooter*. New York: Grove Atlantic, 1999.

Naslund, Sena Jeter. *Ahab's Wife or, The Star-Gazer*. New York: William Morrow, 1999.

Nichols, Peter. *Sea Change: Alone across the Atlantic in a Wooden Boat*. New York: Viking, 1998.

Petrie, Donald A. *The Prize Game: Lawful Looting on the High Seas in the Days of Fighting Sail*. Annapolis, MD: Naval Institute P, 1999.

Philbrick, Nathaniel. *Away off Shore: Nantucket Island and Its People, 1602–1890*. Nantucket, MA: Mill Hill, 1995.

Piercy, Marge, and Ira Wood. *Storm Tide*. New York: Fawcett Columbine, 1999.

Powlik, James. *Sea Change*. New York: Delacorte, 1999.

Runyan, Timothy J. *Ships, Seafaring and Society: Essays in Maritime History*. Detroit: Wayne State UP, 1987.

Rylant, Cynthia. *The Islander*. New York: Richard Jackson/DK, 1998.

Shreve, Susan. *Jonah the Whale*. New York: Arthur A. Levine/Scholastic, 1997.

Spencer, Warren F. *Raphael Semmes: The Philosophical Mariner*. Birmingham: U of Alabama P, 1996.

Szarkowski, John, and Richard Benson. *A Maritime Album: 100 Photographs and Their Stories*. New Haven, CT: Mariners' Museum and Yale U, 1997.

Encyclopedia of
American Literature of
the Sea and Great Lakes

"Sperm Whale, *Physeter macrocephalus*," 1984.
Donald A. Sineti (b. 1943).
Reprinted with permission.

A

ADAMS, BERTRAM MARTIN [BILL ADAMS] (1879–?). Bill Adams was born in England to American parents. He left college to go to sea at age seventeen in a career that lasted four or five years and logged seven passages around Cape Horn.* Before his sailing career was ended by ill health, he had attained the rank of mate. After retiring from the sea, he lived in the San Francisco area, where he became involved in the socialist movement and found inspiration in Jack London's* writings of the sea.

In 1921 Adams began a modest literary career of his own, culminating in 1937 with an autobiography, *Ships and Women*. His early sea stories were collected in *Fenceless Meadows* (1923), and he published a volume of sea verse, *Wind in the Topsails*, in 1923. In the late 1920s and early 1930s he published several good sea stories. Although they appeared in such excellent magazines as *The Atlantic Monthly* and *Esquire*, and there were enough for another volume of stories, he never collected them. At least three of his stories appeared in O. Henry collections of best short stories of the year: "Jukes" (1927), "Home Is the Sailor" (1928), and "The Lubber" (1933). "The Foreigner" appeared in *Best Short Stories of America* (1932). As expressions of his socialist values, his stories often celebrate the lives of working sailors, and they are notable for their frequent inclusion of sea songs.

Bert Bender

[ADAMS, WILLIAM TAYLOR], "OLIVER OPTIC" (1822–1897). Using the pen name "Oliver Optic," William Taylor Adams spent twenty years as a teacher in Boston schools and wrote popular children's fiction in the nineteenth century. The publication of *The Boat Club: or, The Bunkers of Rippleton* (1855) gave Adams the status of major author of children's literature. He left teaching in 1865 to write full-time and over the next thirty-two years published 126 novels and almost 1,000 short stories for young people, most often for boys. Many of his works were written in the "series" format, each series consisting of six related, but not chronologically linked, narratives. In addition to his writing, Adams edited several children's magazines, including *Student and Schoolmate, Oliver Optic's Magazine,* and *Our Little Ones Magazine.*

Adams set many of his stories and books on the sea or inland waters. Even some of his Civil War stories featuring young Union heroes are set in the navy, such as *The Sailor Boy: or, Jack Somers in the Navy* (1863). *Outward Bound; or, Young America Afloat* (1867) was one of his most popular series. In the first narrative, a boarding school tries to reform some of its troublesome students by putting them on a ship to learn discipline and teamwork through their exposure to the elements. Though criticized by Louisa May Alcott and others for sensationalism in his narratives, Adams maintained in the preface to *The Boat Club* that his goal was to "combine healthy moral lessons with a sufficient amount of exciting interest" for young readers. Self-discipline, instruction, moral righteousness, adventure, patriotism, and the love of God and family are the chief characteristics of an Oliver Optic book. The sea often provides a fitting background in which these virtues can be learned by young Americans. [*See also* CONFEDERATE NAVAL FICTION; JUVENILE LITERATURE]

Frank Rotsaert

THE ADMIRAL (first perf. 1924; pub. 1927). Although best known for the religious allegory *The Servant in the House* (1902), Charles Rann Kennedy (1871–1950) also wrote a series of theatrical exercises that used well-known historical events to explore contemporary issues and to refocus theatrical attention on the actor and the playwright and away from overly elaborate spectacle. This series of nine plays, each written for three actors, focused on such figures as Dante, Job, King Arthur, and Jesus. One of these, *The Admiral,* hailed by George Bernard Shaw as a magnificent play, explores the price and profit of discovering new worlds. The characters are the Sailor, later identified as Christopher Columbus*; the Queen, revealed as Isabella and depicted as the first modern woman and a staunch defender of religious freedom; and the Girl, an unnamed young woman who is Columbus' adviser, mistress, and mother of his four-year-old son.

As the play opens, the Girl tells the Queen, not realizing who she is, about how the King has thwarted the Sailor's grand plans. Columbus enters, denouncing the popinjays who stand in his way. He tells the women of his glorious plans for using the resources of the New World and for bringing Christ to the natives. Enthralled by his vision and by the story of how he conquered his childhood fear of the sea, the women decide to do what they, as women, can do for him. The Girl will wait patiently, a beacon for him to steer home by. The Queen will sell her jewels to outfit his expedition. The Sailor will bring civilization to the New World and riches to the old.

The play ends with all three looking into the future, lost in dreams of glory and visions of Columbus' journey across the sea and his discovery of great lakes and rivers that will unify nations. [*See also* DRAMA OF THE SEA]

Brian T. Carney

THE ADVENTURES OF ROBIN DAY (1839). *The Adventures of Robin Day* was the final work of long fiction written by playwright, poet, and novelist Robert Montgomery Bird (1806–1854). Bird was born in Delaware but spent much of his life in and near Philadelphia working as a doctor, farmer, scientist, musician, politician, editor, and writer. Although Bird also wrote history, poetry, and drama, he is remembered as the author of historical novels, including *Calavar* (1834), *The Hawks of Hawk-Hollow* (1835), *Sheppard Lee* (1836), *Nick of the Woods* (1837), and *Robin Day*.

Originally conceived as a satire on various aspects of American life, *Robin Day* is actually more a picaresque adventure novel, highly derivative of similar efforts by more accomplished writers such as Sir Walter Scott and James Fenimore Cooper.* The novel is organized around the first-person narrative of a young castaway orphan named Robin Day. The book tells the story of Robin's many adventures, which include being sold to a sea captain for a keg of rum, accidentally fighting on the British side in a battle of the War of 1812, escaping capture by Indians on the southern frontier, being taken prisoner by the Spanish in Florida, becoming a pirate in the waters off Cuba, and being cast away at sea with a young woman with whom he is in love and who, he finally discovers, is his long-lost sister.

Although the plot of *Robin Day* is convoluted and improbable, the many nautical adventures in the book make it an important contemporaneous example of the more developed sea fictions of such writers as Cooper and Herman Melville.*

Michael P. Branch

AFRICAN AMERICAN LITERATURE OF THE SEA. Although African American literature centers predominantly on the American landscape, rural and urban, when it does allude to the sea, it is usually associated with the historical memory of slavery. Consequently, in this literature, including folk materials, the sea is represented paradoxically, through the vicissitudes of the Middle Passage and the loss of a homeland as well as through possibilities for liberation and the re-creation of a new homeland. African American spirituals reflect this duality, voicing, on one hand, the slave community's consciousness of the sea's perils in songs concerning Noah and the Ark, Jonah and the whale, Moses and the Red Sea, or Jesus on the Sea of Galilee and, on the other, belief in the sea's power, as a manifestation of God's will, to destroy their enemies and belief in the capacities of righteous and courageous individuals to triumph over hardships at sea and in life.

Olaudah Equiano* in his 1789 narrative presents a graphic description of his terrifying, dehumanizing personal experiences during the Middle Passage, a description that is repeatedly evoked throughout the twentieth century in such diverse works as Melvin Tolson's epic poem *Libretto for the Republic of Liberia* (1935), Robert Hayden's* long, symbolic poem "The Middle Passage" (1962), Alex Haley's* fictionalized family history *Roots: The Saga of an American Family* (1976), Paule Marshall's Caribbean* novels *The Chosen Place, the Timeless People* (1969) and *Praisesong for the Widow* (1983), and Charles Johnson's National Book Award-winning *Middle Passage** (1990).

As the sea historically provided slaves the opportunity to leave the South and, both before and after the Civil War, the opportunity for employment, it came to be associated with escape. In the nineteenth century both Frederick Douglass* in "Heroic Slave" (1853) and Martin Delaney in *Blake: Or, The Huts of America** (1859, 1861–1862), drawing on such incidents as the 1839 *Amistad** revolt, imagine the heroic endeavors of brilliant African American men to organize shipboard slave mutinies. Another factual narrative of escape on shipboard is John Thompson's *Life of John Thompson, a Fugitive Slave* (1856). Narratives of working sailors include Native/African American Paul Cuffe Jr.'s *Narrative of the Life and Adventures of Paul Cuffe, a Pequot Indian: During Thirty Years Spent at Sea* (1839) and James H. Williams' papers, edited by Warren F. Kuehl in *Blow the Man Down! A Yankee Seaman's Adventures under Sail* (1959). Louise Meriwether's historical novel *Fragments of the Ark* (1994) tells the story of a ship pilot and slave who commandeers a Confederate gunboat and delivers it with a group of escaped slaves to the Union navy. Harlem Renaissance writers Claude McKay, in novels *Home to Harlem* (1928) and *Banjo* (1929), and Langston Hughes,* in several poems and his autobiography *The Big Sea* (1940), as well as late twentieth-century novelists Toni Morrison in *Tar Baby* (1981), Ntozake Shange in *Sassafrass, Cypress & Indigo* (1982), and Johnson in *Middle Passage*, propose the open sea, with its options for contemplation, travel, and the democratic fraternity of sailors, as an alternative for black men to the limited options for work and civil rights in the United States. Racism may persist on shipboard, but Shine, in a well-known African American folk poem, forced to perform degrading work in the *Titanic*'s* boiler room, has the last laugh as he swims to safety while his abusers drown. Shine's story is told in many places; the version that Hughes purportedly heard in Harlem in 1956 appears with the title "Sinking of the *Titanic*" in *Book of Negro Folklore*, a collection that was edited by Hughes and Arna Bontemps (1958).

From the end of the nineteenth century, African American writing assigns to the sea symbolic, mythic, and psychological interpretations. In Paul Laurence Dunbar's* turn-of-the-century, nondialectic poems, the sea becomes the projection of the poet's romantic despair. For the Harlem Renaissance poets McKay, Hughes, and Countee Cullen, the sea is equated with romantic yearning for Africa and the Caribbean, for mystery and love. In her fiction, "John Redding Goes to Sea" (1921) and *Their Eyes Were Watching God* (1937), both of which draw extensively on black folk culture, Zora Neale Hurston associates the sea with the pursuit of individual desires, doomed if they are not mitigated by love. Increasingly, African American writers, including modern poets Hayden and Michael S. Harper,* have joined an awareness of the sea's historical significance with its symbolic, mythic, and psychological possibilities. Late twentieth-century fiction, including Morrison's *Tar Baby*, Shange's *Sassafrass, Cypress & Indigo*, Johnson's *Middle Passage*, Gloria Naylor's *Mama Day* (1988), and Marshall's *Chosen Place, Praisesong*, and *Daughters* (1991), presents the sea as the immediate source of renewal through the characters' memory of the Africans who suffered and died during the Middle Passage and their mystical reincarnation and celebration in memory. Derek Walcott's* poem "The Schooner *Flight*" (1979) and his epic *Omeros* (1990) render this theme evocatively, biographically, and racially. [*See also* CARIBBEAN LITERATURE OF THE SEA; SLAVE NARRATIVES]

FURTHER READING: Bolster, W. Jeffrey. *Black Jacks: African American Seamen in the Age of Sail*. Cambridge: Harvard UP, 1997; Born, Brad. "Writing on the 'Restless Billows': Black Mariners and Mutineers in Selected Works of Antebellum American Literature." Diss., University of Kansas, 1993; Malloy, Mary. *African Americans in the Maritime Trades: A Guide to Resources in New England*. Sharon, MA: Kendall Whaling Museum, 1990; Schultz, Elizabeth. "African American Literature." *American Literature and the Sea: A Literary History*. Ed. Haskell Springer. Athens and London: U of Georgia P, 1995, 233–59.

Elizabeth Schultz

AHAB. The captain of the Nantucket whaleship *Pequod** in Herman Melville's* novel *Moby-Dick** (1851), Ahab is identified by a scar running down his face, his ivory leg, replacing the leg taken by Moby Dick, and his fixed, seaward gaze. Soon after his first appearance in Melville's novel, he proclaims to the *Pequod*'s crew, hypnotized by the urgency and eloquence of his rhetoric, his intention to seek and to slay Moby Dick. Resisted only by his first mate, Starbuck, Ahab legitimates this quest by implying that the white whale is the embodiment of evil. To the task of discovering one whale in all the world's seas Ahab brings extraordinary intellectual concentration and physical courage. However, he becomes increasingly isolated from his crew and from gams with other whaleship captains and increasingly hubristic, projecting the illusion of an intellectual and spiritual power over nature, through technological tricks and black magic. Finally confronting Moby Dick, Ahab sees the whale sink the *Pequod* and dies, snared in his own harpoon line.

Numerous antecedents have been suggested as sources for Captain Ahab, whose namesake is an idolatrous Hebrew king, including other Old Testament figures Adam, Jonah, and Job; the classical Prometheus; Shakespeare's Macbeth and King Lear; as well as Johann Goethe's Faust, John Milton's Satan, and Lord Byron's Manfred. Through association with such tragic figures, who, in their suffering, defiance of human limitations, and challenge to God's authority, become heroic, Melville ennobles his American whaling captain.

Critics, however, considering the devastating impact of Ahab's quest on his crew, also perceive him as a reflection of nineteenth-century imperialism and industrialism and a precursor of twentieth-century fascism. Caricatured since the 1950s in cartoons, adventure novels, and science fiction as the archetypal, driven madman, Melville's Ahab remains an enigmatic, complex, and moving character. Enduring contemporary interest with a feminist orientation is demonstrated by two creative endeavors: Ellen Driscoll and Tom Sleigh's "Ahab's Wife or the Whale," a multimedia theatrical production that premiered in 1998, and Sena Jeter Naslund's novel *Ahab's Wife or, The Star-Gazer* (1999).

Elizabeth Schultz

[AIKEN, CONRAD POTTER], "SAMUEL JEAKE JR." (1889–1973). A friend and contemporary of T. S. Eliot,* Conrad Aiken divided his time between England and the United States before settling in Massachusetts in 1947. He used the pen name "Samuel Jeake Jr." during 1934–1936 as the London correspondent for the *New Yorker*, although he never published a book under that name; the original Samuel Jeake was a seventeenth-century astrologer.

Aiken's poems, novels, short stories, plays, and nonfiction employ nautical imagery as well as sea settings, often reflecting biographical and psychological concerns. "Landscape West of Eden" (1934) is a poetic sea voyage in a dream-boat with Adam and Eve; the narrative voice (and humankind) moves toward death. *Blue Voyage* (1927) is a novel whose main character, William Demarest ("de mare est" meaning "he is from the sea"), is on a sea voyage, hoping to discover his true identity. Implicit in the story is Aiken's own horrific childhood, dominated by his father's murder of his mother and his father's subsequent suicide. Demarest's "identity" has been forged by Aiken's trauma, affecting his relations with women and shaping his sense of self. He returns to his bunk each day, recording its events and contemplating the next. His "night-sea journey" to Europe to reach Cynthia, a former lover, is mythically aborted when she turns up as a passenger, engaged to be married. A phantasmagoria, enhanced by the ship setting, pervades the novel and turns the mother/lover loss into nightmare as the sea tosses the ship about.

This same Demarest is the "D" of "Ushant: An Essay" (1952); Ushant is a dragon-shaped rock on the French side of the English Channel, a point of embarkation from Europe. The essay provides a moment in his ship bunk for D to hope for escape over that same sea from evils connoted by the dragon shape of "You shan't."

"Mr. Arcularis," published as a short story in 1934, was produced as a play titled *Fear No More* in London in 1946 and in Washington, D.C. in 1951. It was later published as *Mr. Arcularis: A Play* (1957). Again the oedipal theme of *Blue Voyage*—love/hate of father, loss of mother/lover— dominates the way that the sea, for Arcularis, rolls with highs and lows, calms and tempests. Arcularis' "throbbing" is the "throbbing" of the ship (himself) over the sea of life to try to reach finally and safely his father's home (both psychologically his father and metaphorically God). His name indicates the set of little boxes that confine him emotionally and psychologically and also the ship's alleged destination, Arcturus, the star in Boötes that guards the constellation Ursa Major and signifies tempestuous weather and rough seas.

John T. Shawcross

ALABAMA. A Confederate cruiser under the command of Raphael Semmes,* the C.S.S. *Alabama* (built 1862) traveled the major shipping lanes, capturing sixty-six Northern vessels and destroying fifty-two. Almost all of the *Alabama*'s conquests were merchantmen. She engaged the Union navy only twice: the first time she sank the *Hatteras*; the second she was sunk by the *Kearsarge* in a spectacular engagement off the coast of Cherbourg, France.

As a famous privateer, the *Alabama*'s story is told by Confederate and Union naval officers in written reminiscences as well as by naval historians. The most complete and compelling account of the cruiser's adventures is given by her captain, Raphael Semmes, in his *Memoirs of Service Afloat during the War between the States* (1869). Semmes' *Memoirs* relates not only the encounters of a Confederate privateer but also exciting experiences of storms at sea, as well as clear explanations of the effect of weather and ocean currents upon seamanship. Because Semmes was the only captain of the *Alabama*, his *Memoirs* remains one of the most thorough and intriguing accounts of her career, although her fame ensures that she will figure in any naval history of the Civil War. [*See also* CONFEDERATE NAVAL FICTION]

Anna E. Lomando

ALBEE, EDWARD (1928–   ). A leading contemporary playwright, Edward Albee made his early reputation writing spare, psychological dramas, of which his most acclaimed and widely known remains *Who's Afraid of Virginia Woolf* (first perf. 1962; pub. 1962). An early one-act, *The Sandbox* (first perf. 1960; pub. 1960), employing such stylistic conceits as allegorical characters, rhythmic dialogue, and expressionist theatricality, owes much to the absurdist style of Irish playwright Samuel Beckett. Using a beach setting for its literal and metaphorical backdrop, Albee explores in *The Sandbox* themes that also preoccupy his later work: spiritual insularity, familial dysfunction, and the power relations embedded within language.

Seascape (first perf. 1975; pub. 1975), which won for Albee the 1975 Pulitzer Prize, is also set on an indeterminate beach. Mixing realistic detail with fantasy, this play dramatizes the intrusion of two sea lizards, one male and the other female, into the lives of a middle-aged married couple on vacation. Serving as metaphor for the individual and collective unconscious, the sea becomes the site of rite of passage and regeneration for both the reptilian and human couples. For Nancy and her spiritually depleted husband, Charlie, encountering the alien sea creatures allows for the reemergence and maturation of repressed psychic energies. Similarly, the surfacing of the lizards from the primordial ocean depths represents an evolutionary development in the lizards' acquisition of social, linguistic, and emotional capacities. Ultimately, the seascape functions as artifice, as well as setting and metaphor. Just as Nancy busies herself painting the seascape that is her and the play's immediate reality, the play itself unfolds on a ritual site, upon which language and image coalesce in both panoramic and intimate detail.

Although a lesser work, *Finding the Sun* (first perf. 1983; pub. 1983) reconfirmed Albee's interest in the sea as a metaphor for psychosexual and social passages. In this one-act play, eight characters, most of them related, sit on a sunny New England beach and converse about themselves and their tangled interrelationships. Here, Albee is most concerned with infusing the play's structure and language with the dramaturgical equivalent of the ocean's sensory, particularly aural, properties. [*See also* DRAMA OF THE SEA]

David R. Pellegrini

ALDRICH, THOMAS BAILEY (1836–1907). Thomas Bailey Aldrich, known chiefly as the author of *The Story of a Bad Boy* (1869), edited *Every Saturday* (1866–1874) and *The Atlantic Monthly* (1881–1890) and also wrote poems, short stories, and five novels. Born in Portsmouth, New Hampshire, Aldrich lived for brief periods in the seaports of New York and New Orleans, finally settling in Boston. The sea was important to Aldrich and recurs as a minor topic in some of his writings. In her book *Crowding Memories* (1920), his wife describes her husband as a "fair-weather sailor" (65) and recounts how he was seasick for eleven days on his first ocean crossing in 1875.

The Story of a Bad Boy is an account of Aldrich's youth in Portsmouth, called Rivermouth in the novel. He recounts his seasickness when sailing from New Orleans to Rivermouth and in a later chapter, "The Cruise of the *Dolphin*," narrates how he and three friends row to Sandpeep Island, the last island in the Piscataqua River before the open sea. After hours of exploring and playing, they send Binny Wallace back to the boat for food, and he is accidentally set adrift without oars in the midst of an approaching squall. Townspeople later find his drowned body.

Aldrich's strong affection for the sea is glimpsed in his poem "Sea Longings" (1896), where he acknowledges that the first sounds he heard were from the sea and that inland "life languishes." He wrote about twenty sea poems in all, which fall into three categories: those celebrating his natural ties to the sea ("Piscataqua River" [1861], "In Youth, beside the Lonely Sea" [1896]), those that use the sea as the start for musings not necessarily about the sea ("On Lynne Terrace" [1896]), and miscellaneous poems dealing with some sea event ("Seadrift" [1863], "Lost at Sea" [1896], "Alec Yeaton's Son" [1896]).

Frank Rotsaert

THE ALGERINE CAPTIVE (1797). Royall Tyler (1757–1826) grew up in Boston in the ferment of pre-Revolutionary activities. His best-known work is *The Contrast* (1787), which was the first professionally produced American comedy in New York City. In addition to the novel *The Algerine Captive*, Tyler wrote several dramas, a number of essays and sketches, and a considerable body of poetry. At his death in 1826 most of his published writings did not attribute authorship to him.

The Algerine Captive (1797), a picaresque narrative with strong antislavery sentiment, is the only work in which Tyler uses maritime imagery. In two central chapters Updike Underhill, the novel's hapless central figure, relates his experiences as surgeon aboard the slave ship *Sympathy*. The shipboard section links the two disparate books of the novel and prefaces Underhill's own captivity narrative, which reverses the structure of white masters and black slaves. [*See also* SLAVE NARRATIVES]

Joan Tyler Mead

ALL THE BROTHERS WERE VALIANT (1919). The first published novel by Ben Ames Williams (1889–1953), *All the Brothers Were Valiant* chronicles the lives of a family of whalers in an unnamed harbor of New England, perhaps the Buzzard's Bay region of Massachusetts. Joel Shore, youngest of five brothers, gains command of the whaling bark *Nathan Ross* when his brother Mark, its former captain, disappears. Found by his brother in the South Seas, Mark tells Joel an incredible story of smuggling diamonds and murder and offers to split the treasure if Joel will abandon duty and use the *Nathan Ross* to recapture the diamonds. When Joel refuses, Mark spreads rumors that sway the crew to mutiny.* Joel's steady courage, however, rekindles Mark's sense of family honor. Mark dies defending Joel against the mutineers, thus earning the traditional family epithet: "All the brothers were valiant."

Williams, a midwesterner whose adopted home was rural Searsmont, Maine, built his early fame on tales of the sea such as the popular *All the*

Brothers Were Valiant, a work published by seven different firms in Williams' lifetime and adapted into films of the same title in 1923 and 1953. Williams builds a solid, believable background that gives credence to the plot of intrigue and adventure. Following his belief that setting influences character, Williams creates in his protagonist Joel Shore a man who has been molded by sea and shore; his courage is steadfast as the New England coast, while his patience reflects the varying fortunes of whaling and weather. The logbook of the *House of Shore*, quoted within the novel, further demonstrates the influence of the ocean on this aptly-named family, for each entry begins by describing the conditions of the sea.

Carolyn Adele Gardner

ALONGSHORE (1994). *Alongshore* offers a thought-provoking and informative examination of an aspect of the sea that typically goes unnoticed in literature: the littoral. This coast, which establishes the border of every league of pounding surf, every harbor, embayment, estuary, and marsh, is a vital part of the sea itself. *Alongshore* considers the many faces of the landscape and seascape along the shore and their place within American culture.

Author John R. Stilgoe (1949–   ) is a professor of the history of landscape at Harvard University. His previous books have offered important observations on elements of the American scene, such as suburbs and railroads, and their interaction with the natural world. Much of the value of *Alongshore* draws from the interplay between historical analysis and Stilgoe's personal observations. A resident of Norwell, Massachusetts, Stilgoe has spent innumerable hours exploring his section of the Massachusetts shore in small boats. He brings to this work both the enthusiasm of the youthful explorer and the considered reflections of the senior scholar.

Chapters with intriguing titles such as "Glim," "Guzzle," "Treasure," "Quaintness," and "Bikinis" examine both physical settings and the use of language as a reflection of American culture and its changing relations with the littoral boundary. Stilgoe's personal observations of salt creeks and marshes authenticate his presentation. He also draws on a variety of literary and historical sources, including John Milton, Henry David Thoreau,* and Herman Melville,* as well as late nineteenth- and early twentieth-century popular imprints, serials, guides, and manuals.

Glenn S. Gordinier

AMERICAN INDIAN LITERATURE OF THE SEA AND THE GREAT LAKES. The coasts of the Northeast Atlantic and the Northwest* Pacific, as well as the shores of the Great Lakes,* sparked the imagination of the early American Indians who resided in these regions. An abundance of literature in the form of legends, myths, prayers, poems, and songs shows the significance that the sea and the Great Lakes played in their lives.

The myths and legends told by the Micmac, Passamaquoddy, and Penobscot tribes of the coastal northeast focus on the mythical demigod Glooskap, whose name, ironically, means "the Liar." In one Passamaquoddy story, Glooskap's antics result in the waters of the sea and the Lakes becoming stagnant. Other legends dealing with Glooskap's escapades include turning giant sorcerers into fish (Penobscot); sailing across the sea to England and France (Passamaquoddy); and cheating a whale, as well as providing a pipe for the whales to smoke (Micmac). Not all Atlantic coastal tales feature Glooskap as the main character; the tale of the mermaid* Ne Hwas, the story of two girls who are changed into mermaids, and the myth of a flying canoe figure into the legends of the Passamaquoddy oral tradition, and there is the Penobscot myth of the First Mother, whose son is created from the water's foam.

The literary expression of the coastal tribes of the Northwest relied heavily on allusions to the sea, particularly salmon fishing and whaling. The trickster tales of the Chinook emphasize Coyote's blunders as he herds, catches, kills, and distributes the salmon among the people. In a prayer to a dead killer whale (Kwakiutl), a tribesman prays that he may inherit the whale's qualities and protection. The story of a man who marries a killer-whale woman (Haida) chronicles the whale woman's life as she leaves her husband, enters the waters of the West Coast, and turns into a reef. Another tale involving a whale pertains to the marriage of a woman to a merman (Coos). After becoming impregnated, the woman leaves her tribe and lives with her merman husband in the ocean. The woman does not forget her land-bound kinsmen, however; every summer and winter she leaves a whale on the shore as a gift to her brothers. Other stories associated with the sea include the *chetco* monster, whose roars from the ocean portend the weather (Chinook) and the marriage of South Wind to Ocean's daughter (Nehalem Tillamook).

Early stories describing the Great Lakes and the treacherous canoeing experiences on the waters were related orally among the American Indians in the winter months when they believed the spirits of the Lakes were living underground. A common tale among these tribes pertains to manidog, the guardian of the Lakes. Accounts of watery disasters related to manidog pervade the tales of the Chippewa, Menomini, and Fox. Other myths include the Winnebago adventures of Wak-chung-kaka (the Foolish One), who was sent by the Earth-Maker to rid the world of evil. These stories tell of Wak-chung-kaka's mistaking a burned tree stump for a chief pointing across the water and the village people's mistaking Wak-chung-kaka for a water spirit after he rises out of the lake wearing an elk's head. Other cyclical tales that significantly refer to the Great Lakes region include the Ojibwa accounts of the mythical character Winabojo and his exploits. Songs of the Chippewa likewise hold an important place in the American Indian literature of the Great Lakes; one song poignantly tells of a maiden who mistakes the sound of her departing lover's splashing oar for the cry of a loon. Another song relates how the beating of a drum calms the waters.

The American Indian literature of the sea and the Great Lakes is both vast and rich in its description of the ever-present waters that played such a vital role in the lives of its coastal inhabitants.

FURTHER READING: Astrov, Margot. *The Winged Serpent: An Anthology of American Indian Prose and Poetry.* New York: John Day, 1946; Least Heat-Moon, William. *River-Horse*: A Voyage across America.* Boston: Houghton Mifflin, 1999; Leland, Charles G. *The Algonquin Legends of New England.* Detroit: Singing Tree, 1968; Ramsey, Jarold, ed. *Coyote Was Going There: Indian Literature of the Oregon Country.* Seattle: U of Washington P, 1977; Swann, Brian, ed. *Coming to Light: Contemporary Translations of the Native Literatures of North America.* New York: Vintage, 1996.

Melinda F. Williams

AMES, NATHANIEL (1805–1835). Son of the Federalist statesman Fisher Ames and grandson of a famous colonial almanac publisher, Nathaniel Ames was a blueblood who went to sea and later wrote about it. In this way he served as a literary forerunner of Richard Henry Dana Jr.,* Herman Melville,* and others. Like Dana, Ames went from Harvard University to the forecastle; he wrote humorously of how he preferred the "seminary" of a man-of-war to Harvard and how his status as a self-sufficient able seaman was superior to the occupation of authorship. As had Melville in his early novels, Ames combined a genteel, picaresque style with trenchant analyses of foreign missionaries and the inhumane treatment of sailors. He is best known for his nonfiction *A Mariner's Sketches* (1830) and *Nautical Reminiscences* (1832), which recount his experiences in naval and merchant vessels across the globe. Written in a casual, almost offhand manner but with an eye toward startling and realistic detail, these works were among the first to depict the everyday rhythms of a sailor's existence, its tedium, and its danger. Ames notes in passing, for instance, how a man swimming between vessels is consumed by sharks. His descriptions of landscape and harbor often attain a pictorial eloquence. Impatient with romantic renderings of sea life, Ames was a particularly bitter critic of James Fenimore Cooper's* early sea novels. In *A Mariner's Sketches* he claims to have read Cooper's *The Pilot** (1823) out loud to the crew of a naval vessel and records their disgust with it. In *Nautical Reminiscences,* he ridicules the "nonsensical gibberish" spoken by Cooper's sailors but claims nothing better can be expected from an author who "came in at the cabin windows" (25).

Ames wrote fictional tales of the sea as well, collected in *An Old Sailor's Yarns* (1835); many of these are concerned with the love of a sailor for a beautiful woman. Genteel and whimsical, they are very much in the tradition of Washington Irving's* *Sketch-Book.* In the novella-length *Morton,* Ames pairs the first mate of an American whaler with the niece of a Spanish governor. In this story of love, battle, imprisonment, and disguise, romantic stratagems are wittily compared to tactics at sea. Together with William Leggett,* Ames helped build a tradition of popular, sentimental sea tales that found their way into East Coast literary magazines during the 1830s.

Ames' reputation, however, rests upon his autobiographical writings, especially *A Mariner's Sketches*, which provided fellow sailor-authors with a model for conveying the unvarnished realities of sea life. Dana mentions this book on the first page of *Two Years before the Mast** (1840) as the only previous work in which nautical life is presented from a sailor's point of view. *A Mariner's Sketches* also served as a sourcebook for Melville as he wrote his novel *White-Jacket** (1850). Melville borrowed a number of details from Ames, most importantly a description of a fall overboard that serves as the climax of *White-Jacket*. Ames' work helped to initiate a major shift in American sea literature from Cooper's romantic novels, to more factual accounts told from the point of view of the common sailor. [*See also* NINETEENTH-CENTURY PERIODICALS]

FURTHER READING: Philbrick, Thomas. *James Fenimore Cooper and the Development of American Sea Fiction*. Cambridge: Harvard UP, 1961; Springer, Haskell, ed. *America and the Sea: A Literary History*. Athens: U of Georgia P, 1995; Vincent, Howard P. *The Tailoring of Melville's* White-Jacket. Evanston, IL: Northwestern UP, 1970.

Hugh Egan

AMISTAD. In the early morning darkness in a stormy sea off the coast of Cuba on 2 July 1839, the enslaved Africans carried as cargo aboard the Spanish schooner *Amistad* revolted against their captors. Led by fellow captives Cinqué and Grabeau, the fifty-three slaves managed to overpower their captors, killing the captain and cook but sparing the two slave owners and the cabin boy so that they could navigate the ship eastward back to Africa. For sixty-three days the ship zigzagged up the Atlantic coast as the Spaniards sailed east by day and covertly altered course toward the north by night. In a desperate search for provisions, Cinqué made a landfall on Long Island. There the schooner, the blacks, and the cargo were seized by the U.S.S. *Washington*. The *Amistad* was first brought into New London, Connecticut, and the Africans were imprisoned.

The ensuing legal proceedings pitted the abolitionist interest in the fundamental principles of personal liberty against the Spanish owners' claims that the mutinous, murderous slaves were their rightful property. The antislavery movement saw the trial as an opportunity to bring into focus the issues troubling the country and dividing its people. As the case progressed, the abolitionists convinced former president John Quincy Adams of the righteousness of their cause; he ultimately argued the case before the Supreme Court, contending that Cinqué, Grabeau, and the surviving Africans were neither slaves nor criminals but "self emancipated" free persons. The

Court agreed, finding that the Spaniards had no property rights over their former captives and that the U.S. government had no obligation to compensate the claimants.

This decision had lingering aftereffects that complicated diplomatic relationships between the United States and Spain, while the abolitionists came perilously close to exploiting the Africans as individuals for the larger cause of abolishing slavery. Finally, on 27 November 1841, the thirty-five survivors of the original fifty-three "Amistaders" were returned to Sierra Leone, nearly three years after they had left their homeland. A contemporary play, *The Black Schooner or the Private Slaver* Amistad (first perf. 1840), ran several evenings in New York at four theatres.

The *Amistad* story, the "mutiny"* itself, and the landmark legal case gathered dust in historical limbo until resurrected in the mid-twentieth century by creative artists such as Robert Hayden* ("Middle Passage" [1945]) and modern scholars such as Mary Cable (*Black Odyssey* [1971]) and Howard Jones (*Mutiny on the* Amistad [1987]). Most recently, Steven Spielberg retold the story as a major motion picture (*Amistad* [1997]), for many *the* venue of our national consciousness and conscience. Alexs Pate's novel *Amistad* (1997) was based on the screenplay of Spielberg's movie and contains color photographs from the film; David Pesci also published his novel *Amistad* in the same year. Composer Anthony Davis and his librettist cousin Thulani Davis turned the story into an opera that premiered at the Lyric Opera in Chicago in 1997. A replica of the schooner *Amistad* was built in the shipyard of Mystic Seaport: The Museum of America and the Sea, Mystic, Connecticut, launched on 25 March 2000, and made her maiden voyage in OpSail 2000 in New York Harbor on 4 July 2000.

Fred M. Fetrow

ANTARCTICA. The last continent to be visited by human beings, Antarctica figured largely in the European and American imagination through the whole age of exploration. In the last decades of the eighteenth century, British, Russian, and French expeditions were sent to the southern polar regions to locate what was then called "terra incognita." Not until the second decade of the nineteenth century, however, did American sealers begin to reach the edge of the Antarctic continent, and their efforts were first described in Benjamin Morrell's* *Narrative of Four Voyages* (1832) and Edmund Fanning's* *Voyages round the World* (1833).

The lack of solid scientific information made it possible to project onto the South Pole romantic and mysterious literary notions, as well as specious theories about its geography and geology. One of the most popular authors on the subject was John Cleves Symmes, who in 1818 began to write about his theory that the earth was hollow and that the interior could be accessed through "Holes in the Poles." His writings were collected and published in 1826 by James McBride. Symmes' theories inspired the novel *Symzonia**:

A Voyage of Discovery. By "Captain Adam Seaborn" (1820). Edgar Allan Poe,* who had experimented with an Antarctic theme in his short story "MS. Found in a Bottle" in 1833, was inspired by Symmes to write his novel *The Narrative of Arthur Gordon Pym of Nantucket** (1838).

Using Symmes' theory as a launching point, Jeremiah N. Reynolds* began in 1825 to promote the idea of a U.S. Exploring Expedition* to the southern high latitudes. The resulting expedition of 1838–1842, under the command of Charles Wilkes, investigated the Antarctic continent during a circumnavigation* of the globe. The scientific information published in Wilkes' five-volume *Narrative of the United States Exploring Expedition* (1844) directly influenced both popular discourse about the Antarctic and literary themes. James Fenimore Cooper,* especially, began to work almost immediately with material drawn from it. Cooper had earlier written about the southern polar regions in *The Monikins* (1835), but in *The Sea Lions** (1849) he actually incorporated descriptions of Antarctica from Wilkes' *Narrative.* Cooper's Antarctic voyage is the antithesis of Poe's—the former could not have been written before the Wilkes Expedition; the latter could not have been written after. The eyewitness accounts of Wilkes' scientists filled in unknown areas of the globe and in the process changed them from mysterious places of fantastic possibilities to rock, ice, and snow.

Though one of the men aboard the Wilkes Expedition, assistant surgeon James Croxall Palmer, later wrote a novel, *Thulia: A Tale of the Antarctic* (1843), the bulk of the next century's Antarctic literature was either scientific or narrative accounts of attempts to reach the South Pole itself. The notion of the Antarctic continent as "the last place on earth" was not lost, though. In 1983 John Calvin Bachelor's *The Birth of the People's Republic of Antarctica* once again introduced the southern polar region as a place of mysterious possibilities for voyagers.

FURTHER READING Collier, Graham, and Patricia Graham Collier. *Antarctic Odyssey: Endurance and Adventure in the Farthest South.* New York: Carroll and Graf, 1999; Lenz, William E. *The Poetics of the Antarctic: A Study in Nineteenth-Century American Cultural Perceptions.* New York: Garland, 1995.

Mary Malloy

THE ARCTIC. From Samuel Hearne's 1795 travel account to Dean Koontz's 1995 best-seller *Icebound,* the Arctic regions have provided a stark, yet fertile, setting for various literary genres: fiction, travel accounts, essays, and occasional verse. Geographically defined, the Arctic covers the Arctic Ocean and lands within Arctic waters to latitude 66° N. Norsemen explored the region as early as the ninth century, and the quest for the Northwest Passage* to China lured both British and Dutch explorers to the Arctic during the sixteenth and seventeenth centuries. Beginning in the nineteenth century, Arctic expeditions shifted from the commercial to the scientific, and published accounts of the explorations began to appear.

Of the literary genres, the travel account is most prevalent, beginning with Samuel Hearne's *A Journal from Prince of Wale's Fort, in Hudson's Bay to the Northern Ocean in the Years 1769, 1770, 1771, and 1772* (1795). Several American imprints appeared after the turn of the century, many of which were published by the Washington, D.C., Government Printing Office, including scientific accounts by Michael Healy (1887 and 1889), Adolphus W. Greely (1888), Admiral Charles H. Davis (1876), Calvin L. Hooper (1884), John Murdoch (1892), Joseph E. Nourse (1879), Orray T. Sherman (1885), and Winfield Scott Schley (1884). As with most of these travel logs, the primary purpose was to report scientific discoveries on expeditions financed by the federal government.

Likewise, there were also numerous commercially published travel accounts. The lost expedition of Sir John Franklin of 1845 was the subject of several books that documented the search for signs of Franklin's ship and crew, including books by Elisha Kent Kane (1856), William Godfrey (1857), William H. Gilder (1881), and Adolphus Washington Greely (1885). More recent books on the ill-fated Franklin Expedition include *Frozen in Time* (1987) by physical anthropologist Owen Beattie and journalist John Geiger, who conclude lead poisoning was the cause for the demise of the men. In *Unraveling the Franklin Testimony* (1991), David Woodman disputes the Beattie/Geiger thesis using Inuit testimony. Scott Cookman's *Ice Blink* (2000) faults naval stores as a source for botulism, which killed many of the crew.

Other Arctic travel accounts include those of Alexander W. Habersham (1857), Isaac Israel Hayes (1861), Charles Francis Hall (1865), and George W. Melville (1885). Two of the more interesting books on Arctic exploration are William Wellman's book on airships over the region (1911) and Matthew Alexander Henson's *A Negro Explorer at the North Pole* (1912). Henson was a member of the Robert E. Peary expeditions from 1886 to 1909. Peary himself wrote four books and countless articles on his travels, and the Peary expedition generated several additional books. A more recent title is *When the Whalers Were Up North* (1989) by Montreal freelance writer Dorothy Eber, who relates the whaling experience from the Inuit view. Common to the vast majority of these publications is their description of harsh conditions: the difficulties of seasonal navigation, the stark landscape and environment of the Arctic, and the personal sacrifices and heroic efforts of the hardy explorers.

Arctic fiction is limited in quantity, yet the setting makes for some unique literary contributions. The earliest is a brief fictional account of the Franklin expedition entitled *The Extraordinary and All-Absorbing Journal of William N. Seldon: One of a Party of Three Men Who Belonged to the Exploring Expedition of Sir John Franklin, and Who Left the Ship* Terror, *Frozen Up in Ice, in the Arctic Ocean, on the 10th Day of June, 1850* (1851). The aforementioned expeditions provide the background for *Call of the Arctic* (1960) by Robert Stedman, about a young Harvard man who joined the Hall expedition (1860–1873). More recently, William T. Vollmann's* *The Rifles* (1994) is set during Franklin's last expedition (1845–1848), where a 1980s traveler to the Arctic imagines he is Franklin. Richard Woodman's *Arctic Treachery* (1987) is also historical fiction; Rudy Wiebe's *A Discovery of Strangers: A Novel* (1994) is yet another fictional account of the Franklin expedition. James Houston's* *The Ice Master: A Novel of the Arctic* (1997) is an action-filled historical novel of the 1870s by a prolific Canadian* author who lived among Arctic Inuits from 1948 until 1962.

The majority of Arctic fiction fits into several categories: social relations, exploration and settlement, adventure and intrigue, and coming-of-age stories. Phillip Pullman's *Northern Lights* (1946) is science fiction later published as *The Golden Compass* (1996). A few novels focusing on the relations between Eskimos and whites were published during the 1970s. First among these was Alan Fry's *Come a Long Journey: A Novel* (1971), followed by Harold Horwood's *White Eskimo: a Novel of Labrador* (1972). Finn Schultz-Lorentzen's *Arctic* (1976) deals with an Eskimo–white clash, while *Where the Mountain Falls* (1977) by David Keenleyside focuses on a less hostile relationship.

Fictional stories of hardship and adversity and coming-of-age offer another view of the Arctic. Published in 1885, Thomas W. Knox's *The Voyage of the* Vivian *to the North Pole and Beyond* is a tale of two youths on a voyage on the open polar sea. Adolph P. Lerner's *The Moose Call* (1938) is a story of love and adventure involving a trapper, and C. W. Nicol's *The White Shaman: A Novel* (1979) tells of a young white man who learns to survive in the North. *The Iceberg Hermit* (1974) by Arthur Roth is another tale of Arctic survival. Perhaps the best-known author of Arctic fiction is Britain's E. M. Forster, whose posthumous *Arctic Summer and Other Fiction* was published in 1980, ten years after his death. Begun in 1911 and not completed until 1951, *Arctic Summer* is the fictional account of a young man's experiences in the Arctic after the turn of the century. *The Doomed Ship, or The Wreck of the Arctic Regions* (1864), by dime novelist "Harry Hazel" [Justin Jones*], is an exciting tale of adventure and romance. Peter Freuchen's *Sea Tyrant* (1943) is the tale of an Arctic whaling ship.

Certainly, the most popular fictional theme is adventure or intrigue. Two of Alistair MacLean's works are set in the Arctic: *Ice Station Zebra* (1963) is the story of an American nuclear submarine crew's efforts to rescue a British scientific team, and *Bear Island* (1971) is about a movie production crew on a journey to the northern Arctic. In *The Devil's Lighter; A Novel* (1973), John Ballem utilizes the theme of exploitation of Arctic natural resources; he followed that success with *The Moon Pool* (1978), about oil drilling in the Beaufort Sea. Basil Jackson's *Rage under the Arctic* (1974) is about the world's first submarine oil tanker to suffer an oil spill. Richard Rohman wrote still another novel of intrigue, *Ultimatum* (1973), about

Americans and Canadians clashing over access to northern oil resources; the book was reissued the following year as *Exxoneration*. Roger Hurst's *Status ISQ* (1979) is a thriller about a submarine trapped under the Arctic cap. *Icebound* (1995), by popular novelist Dean Koontz, is about attempts to utilize Arctic resources to relieve agricultural droughts in North America. Andrea Barrett combines fact and fiction in *The Voyage of the* Narwhal* (1998), in which a scholar-naturalist joins an expedition on a search for an open polar sea. Finally, Peter Nichols' *Voyage to the North Star* (1999), a fog-bound and tempest-tossed maritime adventure, is technically authentic even as it tackles the large themes of morality and justice.

Stories from the Canadian North (1980) is a collection of short stories by some of Canada's most renowned writers, including Farley Mowat,* Houston, and Rudy Wiebe. Another selection of short stories is *Stories from the Pacific & Arctic Canada* (1974), as is Mowat's *The Snow Walker* (1975). Poetry collections with an Arctic theme include Cheryl Morse's *Loonlark: Orca Anthology of Poems and Prose* (1983), a collection of thirty-four poems, and *Arctic Heart: A Poem Cycle* (1992) by Gretel Ehrlich. Thomas York's *The Musk Ox Passion* (1978) is a satirical novel about attempts to civilize the North.

The two most prominent authors of children's books about the Arctic are Houston and Mowat, and the list also includes such names as Bonnie Turner, Nick Burns, Anna Rokeby-Thomas, Bessie Marchant, Violet Irwin, and Charles S. Strong. Houston, who has won numerous book awards for his children's works, is also an accomplished illustrator, sculptor, and film producer. His juvenile* fiction includes *Frozen Fire* (1977), *Long Claws* (1981), *Black Diamonds* (1982), *Ice Swords* (1985), *The Falcon Bow* (1986), and *Drifting Snow* (1992). Mowat's Arctic books include *Lost in the Barrens* (1956). The aforementioned Beattie wrote *Buried in Ice* (1992), a young readers' book on the Franklin Expedition.

FURTHER READING: Berton, Pierre. *The Arctic Grail.* New York: Viking, 1988; Caswell, John Edwards. *Arctic Frontiers: United States Explorations in the Far North.* Norman: U of Oklahoma P, 1956; Moss, John. *Enduring Dreams: An Exploration of the Arctic Landscape.* Concord, Ontario: Anansi, 1994.

Boyd Childress

ARGENTO, DOMINICK (1927–   ). Son of Sicilian immigrant parents, Dominick Argento won a Pulitzer Prize in music in 1975 for his mezzo-soprano song cycle *From the Diary of Virginia Woolf.* Argento has lived near water, and his works are inspired occasionally by the sea and frequently by literature. His chamber opera *Postcards from Morocco* (1971) uses the symbol of a ship resembling the *Flying Dutchman*, which carries a seeker forth on his quest for the meaning of life. He fashioned the monodrama for male voice *A Water Bird Talk* (1977) after John James Audubon* and his opera *The Aspern Papers* (1988) after Henry James. His song cycle *To Be Sung* *upon the Water: Barcarolles and Nocturnes* (1974) is based on eight poems of William Wordsworth.

For his sacred oratorio *Jonah and the Whale* (1974), Argento used *The Book of Jonah*, II: 2–9, the fourteenth-century medieval English poem "Patience, or Jonah and the Whale," and traditional work songs and sea chanteys of the nineteenth century. This creates intentional anachronisms, such as when Jonah, sailing to the biblical port of Tarshish, breaks out in a traditional whaling song, "The Greenland Fishery." Because Argento considers the Whale, not Jonah, to be the hero of the piece, he gives the Whale the best tune in the work (in a trombone solo).

The suspenseful opera *The Voyage of Edgar Allan Poe* (1976) casts a phantasmagoric maelstrom of Poe's* nightmarish life as a final voyage. In the first scene, Poe stands at a dock in Richmond, Virginia, awaiting a ghostly vessel commanded by Rufus Griswold; he goes aboard, where hallucinatory scenes involve Poe's mother and the Allans. His child-bride Virginia Clemm sails by in a small boat, which Poe boards; another boat glides by, bearing Poe's mother, who is seducing Griswold. Characters from Poe's life transform into other characters amid a full-blown gale. Virginia sings "Annabel Lee" and dies. Appearing to Poe after death, she tells him of the otherworld, where "gold and silver fish swim through the river of silence" (II: 9). Poe, on a wharf in Baltimore, dies by her side in delirium, thinking that he has boarded a vessel, though no ship departs. [*See also* GHOSTS AND GHOST SHIP LEGENDS; SEA MUSIC]

Jill B. Gidmark

THE ARK OF THE MARINDOR (1998). This novel by Barry Targan (1932–   ), who has published poetry and other prose, is his maiden voyage into the realm of maritime literature. The narrative is an inverted *Odyssey*: a woman sails away from the memory of an unfaithful spouse and a dead son. Incorporating flashbacks, Targan's book details the concluding leg of a picaresque journey by middle-aged protagonist Katherine Dennison, from the steaming jungle of Southeast Asia to the foggy coastline of northeast America. Dennison is a seafarer's daughter born at sea, a wartime photojournalist turned children's writer, and, most importantly, a skilled sailor. She comes to realize that she has always believed in mythic creatures and sought mythic resolutions. In her search for sunken treasure (in the modern-day form of a valuable computer disk), the all-too-human characters with whom her argosy crosses paths include a powerful magus, a witless satyr, a violated sea nymph, and an amoral demon.

Like Ulysses, Dennison survives the deadly fury of nature and the calculating treachery of man by her wits, demonstrating a mastery of ship and self, eventually finding an epiphanic release from the vessel that has served as the lifelong incarnation of both her freedom and her restriction.

Victor Verney

ASHTON'S MEMORIAL (1725). One of the most remarkable sea narratives of early American print culture, *Ashton's Memorial* narrates the extraordinary adventures of Philip Ashton (1703–17??) from 5 June 1722, when he was captured by pirates,* until 1 May 1725, when he unexpectedly returned to his parents' home in Marblehead, Massachusetts. The *Memorial* was actually written by John Barnard (1681–1770) from Ashton's oral narrative and published together with a brief account of one Nicholas Merritt (apparently captured at the same time) and with a sermon on Daniel 3:17.

While fishing off the coast of Nova Scotia, the nineteen-year-old Ashton was captured by the infamous Ned Low and his pirate crew. During the nine months he spent with Low, he was pressured to sign pirate articles and beaten for his refusal. When the pirates stopped for water at an uninhabited island off the coast of Honduras, Ashton escaped into the jungle, and for the next nine months he lived alone, without any comforts of civilization. Nearly dead from starvation and injury, his life was saved when an old woodcutter stopped off at the island, leaving him food, powder, flint, and a knife. After another seven months he was rescued by a group of Englishmen from the mainland.

Within a week of his return, John Barnard, the minister of Marblehead, preached a special sermon on divine providence, using Ashton's deliverance as an example. In response to the great demand for a narrative, Barnard and Ashton collaborated over the next two months, and by the beginning of August *Ashton's Memorial* was completed. Barnard was no mere amanuensis; the text combined the words of both minister and mariner.

Barnard fashioned Ashton's experiences into a narrative of remarkable providence, a textual form familiar to most New England readers. The apparently random kidnapping of a young fisherman by pirates seems to fulfill God's intentions and display his sovereignty. Thus, all of Ashton's adventures are related as a Job-like struggle to overcome evil. At the same time, the narrative is a highly detailed, realistic account of remarkable adventure. Although barely known today, the text was popular and went through several editions, including a 1726 London edition that influenced Daniel Defoe's *The Four Years Voyages of Capt. George Roberts* (1726). [*See also* SEA DELIVERANCE NARRATIVES]

Daniel E. Williams

ASIAN AMERICAN LITERATURE. A theme common to Asian American literature is immigration and migration. *Island: Poetry and History of Chinese Immigrants on Angel Island, 1910–1940*, edited by Him Mark Lai, Genny Lim, and Judy Yung (1980), documents the plight of would-be immigrants detained at Angel Island in San Francisco Bay. While they awaited decisions about their entry into America or deportation back to China, many of the male inmates carved and ink-brushed more than 135 poems onto their barracks walls. Some described the seasickness they suffered in overcrowded steerage during their voyage. Others lamented their imprisonment while government bureaucracy prevented their passage to the mainland, their sense of isolation exacerbated by the encircling waters of the bay.

Midway through the novel *Jasmine* (1989), author Bharati Mukherjee recounts the measures taken by refugees desperate to get to North America as the title character describes her odyssey, first in tiered bunks on a trawler out of Europe, then on a Caribbean* shrimper, hiding for days under a tarp on deck. Similarly, Mei Oi, the female protagonist in Louis Chu's *Eat a Bowl of Tea* (1961), undergoes a sea change from innocent young schoolgirl to vamp during her Pacific Ocean crossing. Vinh Liem's poem "Ko Kra" in *War and Exile* (1989) recalls one of the worst atrocities of the exodus of the so-called boat people from Vietnam, the rape of hundreds of women and female children and the subsequent mass murders on a remote Thai island in 1980. David Mura's poem "Huy Nguyen: Brothers, Drowning Cries" in *After We Lost Our Way* (1989) gives wider voice to a Vietnamese student who, assigned a comparison-contrast paper, has written of his experience as a refugee on the South China Sea.

Canadian* Joy Kogawa in *Obasan* (1981) recalls the sufferings of the Japanese immigrants who settled on the coast of Vancouver. Her immigrant grandfather had prospered as a boatbuilder and salmon fisherman. But in 1941, in an extensive confiscation of Japanese boats by the Canadian government, the Royal Canadian Mounted Police (RCMP) seized a beautiful fishing vessel designed by her father. Soon afterward, her uncle and neighboring Japanese fishermen were forcefully relocated inland, eventually to Alberta. That same year, Kogawa and her family watched as a boat carried her mother away. They never saw her again. A recurrent image contrasts the prairie of their exile with the sea of their longing.

Two poems in *War and Exile* carry similar themes. "Tonight I Go Out to the Sea" by Cao Tan reprises the experience of an exile dangling his feet in the Pacific Ocean in California as he dreams of returning to Vietnam. "When I Die, Take My Body to the Sea" by Du Tu Le reveals a similar motif, the realization that the ocean separating Vietnam and the United States in life joins them in death. Mei-mei Berssenbrugge's *Summits Move with the Tide: Poems and a Play* (1982) contains several poems concerned with the sea, as well as a play, *One, Two Cups,* in which the sea itself is a character.

In his memoir *Running in the Family* (1982), Toronto author Michael Ondaatje chronicles his late 1970s return to Sri Lanka in the Indian Ocean, where he exults in the fishing vessels and luxury liners as he rides on a tug with his brother, a harbor pilot. Ondaatje's novel *In the Skin of a Lion* (1987) is set in 1920s Toronto, where workers dig forty feet under Lake Ontario, building a tunnel to collect lake water as recreational boats ply the surface.

With the literature of Hawai'i, a distinction is generally made between

Hawaiian writing, which properly denotes works in the Hawaiian language, and what is called "local." As might be expected in an island society, Hawaiian writing is deeply imbued with sea images and references, particularly in traditional works like the hula songs. Many of these may be found in *Na Mele o Hawai'i Nei: 101 Hawaiian Songs* (1970), collected by Samuel H. Elbert and Noelani Mahoe. Most notable is the plaintive "Aloha 'Oe," composed in 1877 by then-Princess Lili'u-o-ka-lani. In the days of the steamers, passenger ships were serenaded with this song, which speaks of "fragrance in the blue depths." "Local" literature, largely written in English, deals extensively with the sea. Julie S. Kono's poem "Surfer" in *Hilo Rains* (1988) contrasts the experience and values of a seventeen-year-old absorbed in the sport of surfing with his great-grandfather from Japan, who at the same age had "crossed the same ocean that mesmerizes" the grandson.

In his poetry collection *The River of Heaven* (1988) and in *Volcano: A Memoir of Hawai'i* (1995), Garrett Kaoru Hongo writes largely of the inland town of Volcano, his birthplace; in "The Pier" (1988) and several poems in *Yellow Light* (1982) his perspective is a California beach. "The Pier" is a meditation upon his father's death that locates the transpacific voyage as the origin of the Japanese experience in Hawai'i. Numerous poems focusing on boats, the sea, and the seashore may be found in the anthology edited by Eric Chock and Darrell H. Y. Lim, *The Best of Bamboo Ridge: The Hawaiian Writers' Quarterly* (1986).

In Amy Tan's *The Joy Luck Club* (1989), one of the four daughters, Rose Hsu Jordan, recalls a family outing at the beach that culminates in the drowning of a four-year-old brother. Eric Chock's "Poem for George Helm: Aloha Week 1980" in *Last Days Here* (1990) memorializes a friend who drowned in "that vast ocean from which we all come."

The Filipino immigrant author N. V. M. Gonzalez focuses several short stories on seafarers, fisherfolk, and shipboard travelers in the Philippines, in and around the island of Mindoro. In "Far Horizons" (*Seven Hills Away* [1947]), a seafarer sails home to bring news of his brother's death at sea. "The Old Priest," also in *Seven Hills Away*, contrasts an aging priest who delights in sailing to villages along the seacoast with a visiting young priest who fears sailing and the sea. Several stories written much earlier and collected in *The Bread of Salt and Other Stories* (1993) highlight themes of migration, inter-island travel, fishing, and the perils of the sea. In "A Warm Hand" the passengers of the *Ligaya* (happiness) must go ashore to seek refuge in a fisherman's hut during a violent storm. A pregnant woman wandering on the beach in "The Morning Star" finds a boat; later, in a nearby hut, a sailor and an old man deliver her baby. "The Sea Beyond" features a dying stevedore who has fallen off the reconverted minesweeper *Adela*. "On the Ferry" takes a group of people on a rough crossing of the straits that separate Mindoro from the principal island of Luzon. "Crossing Over" describes a young Filipino student's freighter trip and arrival in Oakland, California.

FURTHER READING: Cheung, King-Kok, ed. *An Interethnic Companion to Asian American Literature*. New York: Cambridge UP, 1997; Lim, Shirley Geok-lin, and Amy Ling, eds. *Reading the Literatures of Asian America*. Philadelphia: Temple UP, 1992; see also the extensive annual bibliographies in *Amerasia Journal*, published by the Asian American Studies Center at UCLA.

Roger J. Jiang Bresnahan and Sally C. Hoople

AUDUBON, JOHN JAMES (1785–1851). Born in Haiti and raised in France, John James Audubon became the world's premier bird artist with the publication of *The Birds of America* (1827–1838). Audubon accompanied his life-size drawings with five volumes of text, the *Ornithological Biography* (1831–1839). In the first three of these volumes, Audubon varied his bird biographies by interspersing what he called "Delineations of American Scenery and Character." These sketches, many of them maritime in character, sit firmly in the tradition of southwest humor but range widely in subject matter, moving from the floodwaters of the Mississippi valley to the Florida Keys to the wastes of Labrador. As in the sketches of Washington Irving* and Nathaniel Hawthorne,* the distinction between accurate journalism and fiction is frequently blurred. The sketches were collected and given separate publication by Francis Hobart Herrick in 1926.

As a science writer, Audubon's maritime observations are equally interesting: his "Labrador Journal," published posthumously by Maria R. Audubon in 1897, records the difficulties of pursuing science and art under shipboard conditions and imaginatively captures the sea-dependent culture of the Maritime Provinces of Canada.* A recent representative sampling of Audubon's writings is *Selected Journals and Other Writings*, edited by Ben Forkner (1996). [*See also* KEY WEST LITERATURE]

R. D. Madison

AVERILL, CHARLES (1825?–1868). Charles Averill wrote around a dozen adventure and romance novels between 1847 and 1850, about half of which take place wholly or mostly at sea. *The Pirates of Cape Ann* (1848) is representative. Here, "Paul Perril, the Pirate," scourge of postcolonial Cape Ann, Massachusetts, is estranged from his family but watches over them from afar. Though ruthless at sea, Perril has a pure heart and returns to assure his mother that he is still alive. Paul eventually rescues and wins the heart of Bertha, whose cousin Ned has fallen in love with Paul's sister. Paul returns to society, changes his name, and becomes "Paul Jones, the Patriot" and naval hero.

The Corsair King (1847) tells the story of the noble and honorable Conrad, leader of the "Piratical Empire" in the West Indies. Other novels focus on the ship-plunderers of the Jersey coast (*The Wreckers*, 1848) and the Mexican-American War at sea (*The Secret Service Ship*, 1848) and on land (*The Mexican Ranchero*, 1847). Details about Averill's life remain obscure. [*See also* JONES, JOHN PAUL; PIRATE LITERATURE]

Peter H. McCracken

AWAY ALL BOATS (1954). Kenneth Dodson (1907–1999) wrote *Away All Boats*, perhaps the best novel on amphibious warfare, at the personal encouragement and friendship of poet Carl Sandburg.* Sandburg, who had seen letters Dodson wrote home to his wife from the Pacific during World War II, was intrigued by their descriptive quality.

The detail of boats, rigging, debarkation beachmasters, and kamikazes found in *Away All Boats* is authentic. The protagonist of the novel closely mirrors Dodson, a former merchant mariner who is not entirely happy about having given up his lucrative maritime profession but who grows to love his ship and its crew. The fictional U.S.S. *Belinda*, like the U.S.S. *Pierce* (Dodson's ship), participates in most of the major landings of the Central Pacific drive toward Japan and undergoes trouble with its unbalanced skipper, Captain Hawks. Hawks has the ship's carpenter build him a personal sailboat with lumber meant for the ship's boats and sails it with red sails through the fleet in the sunsets of Pacific anchorages, just as Dodson's own captain had done. In the crisis the captain dies, but the ship survives a kamikaze hit due to the expertise of the protagonist.

The novel succeeds largely because the author knows his material. The book focuses on the small stories of dozens of humble individuals and follows them to the end of the war as they become an expert amphibious crew. A film adaptation in 1956 starred Jeff Chandler.

Robert Shenk

B

"**BALDWIN, BATES.**" *See* [JENNINGS JR., JOHN EDWARD].

[**BALLOU, MATURIN MURRAY**], "**LIEUT. MURRAY**," "**FRANK FORESTER**" (1820–1895). An influential publisher of American periodicals, Maturin Murray Ballou was born in Boston. He traveled extensively and entered the literary world by writing descriptive letters of his adventures for publication in local newspapers. The editor and/or publisher of ten periodicals, including the *Boston Globe* (1872–1874) and *Ballou's Pictorial Drawing-Room Companion* (1854–1859), Ballou was a pioneer in producing the kind of popular genre material that would eventually flourish in dime novels. As the author of forty-two books, more than half of them under the pseudonym "Lieut. Murray," Ballou specialized in exotic locales, dangerous situations, and broadly drawn characters. He circumnavigated the globe in 1882, and the trip provided much of his material.

Under his own name, Ballou's work was mostly straightforward travel: *Due West; or Round the World in Ten Months* (1884) and *Under the Southern Cross; or Travels in Australia, Tasmania, New Zealand, Samoa and Other Pacific Islands* (1888) are examples. Among the nautical romances he wrote as "Lieut. Murray" are *Fanny Campbell; or, The Female Pirate Captain* (1844); *Red Rupert, the American Buccanier* (1845); *Roderick the Rover* (1847); *The Cabin Boy; or, Life on the Wing* (1848); *The Adventurer; or, The Wreck on the Indian Ocean* (1848); *The Naval Officer; or, The Pirate's Cave: A Tale of the Last War* (1849); *The Sea-Witch; or, The African Quadroon: A Story of the Slave Coast* (1855); *The Pirate Smugglers; or, The Last Cruise of the* Viper (1861); and *Captain Lovell; or, The Pirate's Cave; A Tale of the War of 1812* (1870). He also apparently wrote two books under the pseudonym "Frank Forester," including *Albert Simmons; or, The Midshipman's Revenge: A Tale of Land & Sea* (1845).

Ballou's nautical romances are informed not only by his own extensive sea travel but also by knowledge he gained as a young man when he was employed as deputy navy-agent in the Boston Custom House. Ballou sometimes positioned the pseudonymous Murray as a historical personage, and the confusion he generated has continued for a century and a half. The heroine of *Fanny Campbell*, for instance, who could "row a boat, shoot a panther, ride the wildest horse in the province, or do almost any brave or useful act . . . and could write poetry too," is still described by some scholars as a historical figure. The illustration of Fanny on the cover of the book was ideal in size and subject matter for transfer to a sperm whale's tooth, consequently becoming one of the most popular subjects of nineteenth-century whalemen's scrimshaw. [*See also* CIRCUMNAVIGATIONS AND BLUE-WATER PASSAGES; NINETEENTH-CENTURY PERIODICALS]

Mary Malloy

BARKER, BENJAMIN (1817–18??). Beyond birth records in Salem, Massachusetts, the only documents that survive of Benjamin Barker are twenty short novels published under that name between 1845 and 1847 and one in 1855. Those with authors' prefaces all indicate that he was living in Salem at the time of their composition. Barker, who in one preface described himself as a contributor to "the world of cheap literature," wrote in the popular genres of his day: historical romance, patriot's story, frontier tale, South Sea island adventure. Barker wrote five novels under the pseudonym "Seafarer," all published roughly a century after his death; among them are *Bold Buccaneer* (1955), *The Cook's Cruise* (1960), and *The Haunted Ship* (1958).

Almost half of his literary output is sea adventure that, like that of such Barker contemporaries as Joseph Holt Ingraham,* "Ned Buntline" (Edward Zane Carroll Judson*), and Maturin Murray Ballou,* exploits the more sensational aspects of the genre popularized by James Fenimore Cooper* a generation earlier: piracy, military battles, mythical sea creatures, and ghost* ships. Barker's main contribution to sea fiction is the creation of the female pirate,* best represented by the figure of Ernestine in his last novel, *The Bandit of the Ocean: or The Female Privateer* (1855), published under the pseudonym "Harry Halyard."* The female pirate reiterates a theme that runs throughout Barker's fiction: the ambivalent position of the willful woman in a patriarchal society. To exercise their will, characters such as Ernestine become outlaws. [*See also* WOMEN AT SEA]

Dean DeFino

BARNES, JAMES (1866–1936). Author of books about naval history and naval wartime campaigns, as well as juvenile works on naval leaders, Colonel James Barnes was a prolific writer, historian, journalist, and naval officer. His depiction of seafaring individuals is characterized by what he called "hard service" in peace and war.

Born in Annapolis, Maryland, on 19 September 1866, Barnes graduated from Princeton University in 1891, received an honorary master of arts degree in 1894, and launched a successful career in journalism. He was a staff writer at *Scribner's Magazine* (1891–1893), then an assistant editor at *Harper's Weekly* (1894–1895). In 1898 Barnes served as an active lieutenant (junior grade) in the First Battalion of the New York State Naval Militia during the Spanish-American War. Following six years as a war correspondent in South Africa and in Venezuela, Barnes became literary editor at the publishing firm of D. Appleton and Company from 1905 to 1908, working the following year at Joseph Pulitzer's *New York World*. His journalistic career molded his later terse, concise style.

For the remainder of his life, in both active and reserve service, Barnes pursued a naval career that would also have a significant impact on his writing. Barnes authored many informative and entertaining works on sea warfare and naval leaders. In addition, his so-called boys' books met with wide audiences. Now out of print, these portray the heroic exploits of naval leaders whose actions and character serve as models for young readers. In *The Hero of Erie* (1898), Barnes details the actions taken by naval officer Oliver Hazard Perry in defeating the British fleet on Lake Erie in 1813. In *Drake and His Yeomen* (1899), Barnes offers an appreciative, if idealized, depiction of British navigator Sir Francis Drake. Also published in 1899, Barnes' biographical *David G. Farragut* stands as one of his best works: a concise, detailed, well-researched work on the life and naval career of the first admiral of the U.S. Navy. Using diaries, letters, and reports written by Farragut, Barnes' engaging portrayal spans the admiral's birth in 1801 in Tennessee to his recognized campaigns and victories during the Civil War. A highlight of the text is Barnes' portrayal of Farragut's defeat of the Confederate fleet in August 1864, a victory that epitomized, as Barnes states in his preface, Farragut's "manliness" and "character."

Barnes' other works include *For King or Country* (1895); *Naval Actions of 1812* (1896); *Midshipman Farragut* (1896), which focuses on the earlier part of Farragut's career, including his first cruise as a midshipman in 1811; *Yankee Ships and Yankee Sailors* (1897); *Ships and Sailors* (1898); *The Great War Trek* (1901); *With the Flag in the Channel* (1902); *The Blockaders* (1905); *Commodore Perry* (1912), another biography; *Through Central Africa from Coast to Coast* (1915); and *The Story of the American Navy* (1919), a history. Barnes' focus is usually celebrated seamen who demonstrate heroism, valor, and patriotism. Barnes died in Portsmouth, New Hampshire, two years after completing his own life's story, *From Then till Now* (1934). [*See also* CONFEDERATE NAVAL FICTION; JUVENILE LITERATURE; PERRY, COMMODORE MATTHEW]

Richard J. Williamson

BARTH, JOHN [SIMMONS] (1930–   ). There is a great deal of water in the fiction of John Barth, as one would expect of a writer who was born in Cambridge on the eastern shore of Maryland, was educated at Johns Hopkins University in Baltimore, and lived and taught on the shores of the Chesapeake and sailed its waters. From his first novel, *The Floating Opera* (1956), through the recent *Once upon a Time: A Floating Opera* (1994), rivers and seas, chiefly the great Chesapeake Bay as it divides Maryland, often furnish settings and catalysts for action. Large bodies of water also play vital roles in *The Sot-Weed Factor* (1960), *Sabbatical: A Romance* (1982), *The Tidewater Tales: A Novel* (1987), and *The Last Voyage of Somebody the Sailor* (1991). Although less central to the works, oceans, lakes, marshes, and other waters provide memorable settings in *Lost in the Funhouse* (1968), *Chimera* (1972), and *LETTERS: A Novel* (1979). His recent collection of essays and other nonfiction from 1984 to 1994, titled *Further Fridays* (1995), boasts a cover portrait of the author perched high in the rigging of a sailing craft. Like other elements in Barth fiction, watery settings commonly appear as much for their metaphorical significance as for their decorative function, no matter how convincing the latter may seem. The first novel, several short fictions in *Lost in the Funhouse*, and *The Tidewater Tales* exemplify the usages Barth makes of various waters.

The title *The Floating Opera* denotes the old showboat that provides the setting for the scene to which the novel builds and that emerges immediately as a metaphor for human life. Todd Andrews, the narrator, amplifies the showboat into a *mirror* of life—that is, a metaphor for the novel—as well as a mirror of the way life commonly works, one emphasizing the gaps in our perceptions of the world, the consequent relativity of our knowledge, and the role that imagination plays in filling the blanks.

Such gaps appear again in the note in a bottle that concludes the story "Water-Message" in *Lost in the Funhouse*, a note that seems to the boys in the tale to come from past their river and bay, in fact, from distant continents. Such blanks leave the protagonist, young Ambrose Mensch (meaning "Immortal Man"), a space in which to write the story of his life and are the gift that oceans and seas often provide in Barth's fiction. They are a treasure that a number of his adult narrators, like the blocked author in the collection's title story, most earnestly require. Such narrators and protagonists learn to look into the blank spaces that waters afford and use them, as Tiresias in "Echo" contemplates doing when he wonders whether the best way to involve one's self with another may be to start with what is immediately at hand, that is, to become beguiled with the other through self-knowledge. With this sanguine view of narcissism, the mirroring, liberating, fecundating powers of water enter the awareness of Barth's characters. As the poet-narrator of "Anonymiad" discovers, the sea has the power to fertilize us as though with our own seed. There are whole other worlds to be discovered by staring through the surface of water, not only the microscopic world through which the sperm of life travels in "Night-Sea Journey" but the vast, nobly narcissistic cosmos of human imagination that may require the mirror of open spaces if it is to flow free.

Already in *The Sot-Weed Factor*, Barth had allowed the great blanks in the Atlantic Ocean, the Chesapeake, and the history of Maryland to free his powers of invention when he created the remarkable encounters of Ebenezer Cooke. The creative gain of putting to sea Barth foregrounds in his more recent megafiction, *The Tidewater Tales*, by making the imaginative freedom of sailing the premise of the novel. While offering one of Barth's finest sailing stories, this novel demonstrates the remarkable metaphorical powers that the seas and other waters bring to his fictions.

FURTHER READING: Bowen, Zack R. *A Reader's Guide to John Barth.* Westport, CT: Greenwood, 1994; Harris, Charles B. *Passionate Virtuosity: The Fiction of John Barth.* Champagne: U of Illinois P, 1938; David Morrell, *John Barth: An Introduction.* University Park: Penn State UP, 1976; Tobin, Patricia D. *John Barth and the Anxiety of Continuance.* Philadelphia: U of Pennsylvania P, 1992.

Julius Rowan Raper

BATES, MARTHA E. CRAM (1839–1905). Scant biographical detail exists concerning M.E.C. Bates. She was born in Northville, Michigan, and attended the State Normal School, now Eastern Michigan University. It appears that she taught school for at least two years in the 1860s in Traverse City, Michigan, where she met and married Thomas T. Bates. Upon her husband's acquiring ownership of the *Grand Traverse Herald* in 1876, Bates became editor of the Home and Sunshine departments of that paper. She was also instrumental in organizing both the Traverse City Ladies' Library Association in 1896 and the Michigan Woman's Press Association in 1890.

A writer of verse, Bates is better known for her book of ten stories, co-authored with Mary Knezik Buck, *Along Traverse Shores* (1891). The pieces in this collection all use the Grand Traverse Bay area and surrounding waters for evocative, romantic settings. The book evidently was a vehicle to promote the region as a destination for vacationers, as a portion is given over to advertisements for local resorts and emporia in addition to ship and rail timetables. [*See also* GREAT LAKES LITERATURE]

Robert Beasecker

THE BAY PSALM BOOK (1640). As the first book printed in America, *The Bay Psalm Book* is one of the most important works in American print culture. Originally published as *The Whole Booke of Psalmes Faithfully Translated into English Metre*, *The Bay Psalm Book* either directly or indirectly touched the lives of New Englanders throughout the seventeenth and eighteenth centuries, and thus its unique tropes and images were crucial in forming the collective imagination of the Puritans. Since references to the sea and men in ships abound, *The Bay Psalm Book* played an important part in helping New Englanders perceive and interpret the maritime world around them.

Since psalm singing was such an important part of the Reformation and since publication itself was a symbolic act, the Puritan ministers published their own translation of the psalms as a means of distinguishing themselves from both Anglicans in England and Pilgrims in Plymouth. In 1639 the chief ministers of the Bay Colony divided up the Hebrew Psalms among themselves for translation and versification. In particular, John Cotton, Richard Mather, Thomas Weld, and John Eliot are thought to have collaborated in preparing the new text. Sensing that current translations had departed too far from the original Hebrew and intending to remain as close to the original language as possible, in the closing paragraph of the "Preface," believed to have been written by either Cotton or Mather, they stated: "If therefore the verses are not alwayes so smooth and elegant as some may desire or expect: let them consider that Gods Altar needs not our pollishings . . . we have respected rather a plaine translation . . . and soe have attended Conscience rather than Elegance, fidelity rather than poetry" (12).

Most people of the seventeenth century viewed the seas as a realm distinct from land. Accepting the biblical story of creation, they believed that God had brought order to chaos by separating land from sea. At several points in *The Bay Psalm Book*, the oceans are referred to as one of three distinct areas of the universe: heaven, earth, and sea. As heaven was God's domain, and earth was man's, the sea was perceived as a vast and strange environment that was both unknowable and unpredictable and as such was referenced with tropes to illustrate something beyond human comprehension and control. Moreover, as a symbol of chaos, the sea was also often used to dramatize God's dominion over all creation. As the psalms often celebrate God's great deeds, the biblical stories of the flood and the parting of the Red Sea are referred to several times as examples of God's omnipotence.

For the Puritans who crossed the Atlantic to settle in New England, the sea had a special significance. Surviving the arduous voyage was interpreted as a sign of their special covenant with God and as a physical manifestation of their conversion. Thus, a successful transatlantic voyage had both spiritual and physical import. One of the most often quoted passages, particularly in sermons directed toward those embarking on sea voyages, came from Psalm 107:32: "They that goe downe to th' sea in ships:/ their busines there to doo/ in waters great. The Lords work see,/ in th' deep his wonders too." [*See also* "PIETAS IN PATRIAM"; SEA-DELIVERANCE NARRATIVES]

FURTHER READING: Foote, Henry Wilder. *An Account of the Bay Psalm Book.* Fort Worth, TX: Hymn Society of America, 1940; Haraszti, Zoltan. *The Enigma of the Bay Psalm Book.* Chicago: U of Chicago P, 1956; Haraszti, Zoltan, ed. *The Bay Psalm Book: A Facsimile Reprint of the First Edition of 1640.* Chicago: U of Chicago P, 1957; Stackhouse, Rochelle A. *The Language of the Psalms in Worship: American Revisions of Watts' Psalter.* London: Scarecrow, 1997.

Daniel E. Williams

BEACH, EDWARD LATIMER [JR.] (1918–   ). As his father had done, Edward L. Beach [Jr.] spent a career as a naval officer and wrote many books on naval topics. Three of these are excellent novels about submarines.

Beach graduated from the U.S. Naval Academy and then entered submarine school in New London, Connecticut. He spent most of World War II conducting war patrols against Japan. Moved by the loss of the *Trigger* (in which he had served for over two years, the last year as executive officer), Beach wrote some recollections for the families of that vessel's crew members and eventually stiched these stories and other true-life accounts of submarine duty into his popular *Submarine!* (1952).

Later, while serving as naval aide to President Eisenhower, Beach drafted a novel about the submarine war against Japan, *Run Silent, Run Deep* (1955). Based on Beach's own experience, this novel accurately portrays the technical environment of a World War II submarine and various tactical challenges of submarine duty. It also believably presents the difficulties of a skipper with a subordinate and the submarine's battles with a brilliant Japanese antisubmarine captain. In 1972 Beach published a sequel, *Dust on the Sea*, which narrates additional gripping accounts of attacks on Japanese shipping and the challenge of working under an older commodore plagued with mounting mental problems.

Beach also served in, and wrote about, the nuclear navy. In 1960 he captained the *Triton* in the first underwater circumnavigation of the world, about which he wrote the comparatively prosaic *Around the World Submerged* (1962). In *Cold Is the Sea* (1978), Beach's protagonist undergoes nuclear training and commands a nuclear submarine.

Beach retired as a captain in 1966, then wrote naval history and other books. A recent title is *Scapegoats* (1995), in which he argues that Admiral Kimmel and General Short were wrongly blamed for being caught by surprise at Pearl Harbor. [*See also* NAVAL FICTION]

Robert Shenk

BEACH, EDWARD LATIMER, SR. (1867–1943). Edward Latimer Beach Sr., novelist, was born 30 June 1867 in Toledo, Ohio. Graduating from the U.S. Naval Academy in 1888, he took part in the Battle of Manila Bay on 1 May 1898 and in the capture of Manila 13 August 1898. Beach was captain of the cruiser U.S.S. *Memphis* when, on 29 August 1916, while at anchor with a recreation baseball party ashore, she was engulfed, grounded, and wrecked by a sudden tidal wave off Santo Domingo.

Between 1907 and 1922 Beach wrote thirteen juvenile* novels, all with naval settings. Most of these might be said to have the common theme of "how to become a naval officer." The *Annapolis* series (1907–1910) includes one novel (*An Annapolis Plebe . . .*) for each of the four years that midshipmen spend at the Naval Academy. The four Ralph Osborn books (1909–1912) (*Ralph Osborn: Midshipman at Annapolis . . .*) follow Osborn from midshipman, to ensign, to lieutenant. His *Roger Paulding* novels (1911–1914), on the other hand, show the protagonist rising through the enlisted ranks to a direct commission. Finally, *Dan Quin of the Navy* (1922) conveys the trials and success of a seaman. Retiring from his final duty station as commandant of Mare Island Navy Yard in California with the rank of captain in 1922, Beach served as city clerk and assessor of Palo Alto, California, until 1938. Beach died in Oakland, California.

C. Herbert Gilliland

BEEBE, WILLIAM [CHARLES] (1877–1962). William Beebe was born in Brooklyn and attended Columbia University, where he earned his B.S. in 1898. He led more than sixty scientific expeditions, many of them intentionally maritime. Influenced especially by the writings of Jules Verne, Rudyard Kipling, and H. G. Wells, he participated in the development of the bathysphere and was a pioneer in both shallow and deep-sea diving.

More than a scientist, Beebe published a series of narratives marked by literary and illustrative elegance, capturing the pattern and color of undersea fauna in the design of books such as *Galápagos*: World's End* (1924) and *The Arcturus Adventure* (1926). Later works include *Beneath Tropic Seas* (1928), *Nonsuch: Land of Water* (1934), and *Half Mile Down* (1934). He was widely read in the previous literature of science and the sea, from the touted Charles Darwin, to the neglected (for the time) Herman Melville.*

Curator of ornithology at the New York Zoological Society, Beebe spent much of his later life at his field station in Trinidad, where he died.

R. D. Madison

BEHRMAN, S[AMUEL]. N[ATHANIEL]. (1893–1973). The prolific playwright S. N. Behrman was born in Worcester, Massachusetts, into dire poverty; his entry into professional theatre was rapid, and by the mid-1920s he was already a notable literary figure. He remained a significant presence in the American theatre until the early 1960s; some of his important efforts use the sea in significant ways.

Behrman wrote the dialogue for the 1930 film adaptation of Jack London's* *The Sea-Wolf*.* Behrman also wrote *The Pirate* (first perf. 1942; pub. 1943), a melodrama of romance and intrigue, which he freely adapted from *Die Seerauber*, an obscure German melodrama of the 1890s written by playwright and producer Ludwig Fulda. Set in a small village on an unnamed West Indian island, *The Pirate* dramatizes the truth and illusion in the legend of Estramudo, the "Robin Hood of the Seas." Manuela, marooned in a loveless marriage, dreams of the legendary hero, only to discover, with the help of a rogue posing as Estramudo, that he is, in fact, both her husband and the rogue. In this play, which mixes carnivalesque elements and songs, the Gulf Stream casts an enchanting spell on the island's inhabitants, while the far-off ocean represents the expansiveness of desire and the duplicitous nature of truth and illusion at the core of the romance genre.

Behrman also coauthored with Joshua Logan the book for the Broadway musical *Fanny* (first perf. and pub. 1954) based on the "Cesar Trilogy" of films by Marcel Pagnol (*Marius*, 1931; *Fanny*, 1933; *Cesar*, 1936). The musical, with music and lyrics by Harold Rome, follows the fortunes of two families in the port of Marseilles. Marius impregnates Fanny and then takes off on a long voyage. The elderly and wealthy sailmaker Panisse marries Fanny and claims the child as his own. The story comes to a bittersweet "Gallic" ending when Marius returns, and Panisse, on his deathbed, urges Fanny to marry her true love. The production features evocative seaside locations and a square-rigger traversing the stage under full sail. [*See also* DRAMA OF THE SEA]

David R. Pellegrini

BENCHLEY, PETER [BRADFORD] (1940–). Born in New York City, Peter Benchley earned a B.A. at Harvard in 1961 and took up a career in travel writing, journalism, and government. He served in the U.S. Marine Corps Reserve from 1962 to 1963 and as a White House aide from 1967 to 1969. He turned to fiction with *Jaws* (1973), a novel that became director Steven Spielberg's first blockbuster movie (1975). *Jaws* set the pattern for Benchley's subsequent nautical thrillers: ordinary people encountering the terrors and mysteries of the deep—a great white shark, pirates*, a giant squid—and, after a series of gruesome and violent deaths, discovering a new respect for the sea's unfathomable horrors.

In *Jaws*, a latter-day version of *Moby-Dick*,* a vengeful great white shark preys on summer visitors to a Long Island coastal village. Neither Quint, a brutal fisherman and the book's Ahab*-figure; Martin Brody, the town's police chief; nor Matt Hooper, an icthyologist from Woods Hole, Massachusetts, can stop the immense fish. Local officials, concerned about the shark's effect on tourism, refuse to acknowledge the threat, which only compounds the problem and provides more opportunities for bloody descriptions of shark attacks. In an apocalyptic finale, the shark devours both Quint and Hooper and swims off, presumably to kill again. Benchley's most thrilling and tightly written novel, *Jaws* exploits traditional human fear of sea monsters with modern knowledge of shark behavior to lend credibility to its fast-paced narrative.

Benchley has had trouble replicating the success of *Jaws*, despite writing five more sea novels. *The Deep* (1976) describes a struggle for sunken treasure in Bermuda, with drug runners fighting honeymooning scuba divers over gold, jewels, and morphine ampules. *The Island* (1979) somewhat improbably imagines descendants of seventeenth-century pirates preying on modern tourists in the Turks and Caicos Islands. Both of these novels were made into movies (1977, 1980), with Benchley sharing in the screenplays, an activity he continued with the screenplay for the movie *Jaws 3-D* (1983). Benchley tried his hand at juvenile* sea fiction in *The Girl of the Sea of Cortez* (1982), the story of a Mexican teenager who learns to live in communion with the animals of the sea. Simply told, as touching as a John

Steinbeck* parable, and sensitive to the beauty and fragility of marine ecology, this book contrasts sharply with Benchley's usual emphasis on maritime terrors.

With *Beast* (1991) and *White Shark* (1994), Benchley returned to the sea-monster myths and plot formula of *Jaws*. In *Beast*, a giant squid preys on human beings around Bermuda. Overfishing and pollution have weakened its natural enemies and allowed it to grow larger and more voracious. In *White Shark*, a humanoid amphibian fabricated by Nazi scientists revives from fifty years of ocean hibernation to terrorize people and marine life in Block Island Sound. Although brave heroes eventually kill both monsters, the creatures' mere existence shows how human interference with the marine environment has upset the balance of nature.

Benchley grounds his novels in history, scientific research, and personal travel, which provide a measure of realism even to his tales of sea monsters. During his boyhood, he spent several summers on Nantucket* Island, not far from the setting of several of his novels. He credits Jacques Cousteau, the treasure diver Kip Wagner, and numerous acquaintances for the maritime details in his fiction. His contributions to popular science publications and numerous appearances in television documentaries reveal his familiarity with the sea and ballast his fantastic plots with personal experience and fact.

Dennis Berthold

"BENITO CERENO" (1856). "Benito Cereno" is a long story by Herman Melville* (1819–1891) that was first published in three parts in *Putnam's Magazine* (1855) and then included in *The Piazza Tales* (1856). It is based on the true-life experiences of Captain Amasa Delano* of Duxbury, Massachusetts, which Delano had recounted in *A Narrative of Voyages and Travels in the Northern and Southern Hemispheres* (1817). Melville retained the historical characters' names but added his characteristic mixture of irony and mystery to the account of a slave rebellion aboard a ship traveling off the coast of South America. He concludes his story with excerpts from the legal deposition of Don Benito Cereno, which add chilling insight to his fiction.

Melville's story is set in the year 1799. At a small island on the southern coast of Chile, Captain Delano observes the *San Dominick*, badly in need of repairs, approach the harbor. He boards the vessel in an attempt to find out what has happened and to offer aid. The *San Dominick*'s captain, Benito Cereno, a strangely subdued and nervous young man, supplies him with a singular account. Cereno had started out from Buenos Aires bound for Lima in the company of his slave-owner friend, numerous other crewmen, and his friend's group of slaves. Strange calms and fevers had reduced the crew to only a few, although the slaves had not fared as badly. During the course of the day, Captain Delano notices with suspicion the strange behavior of many of the slaves, particularly Cereno's personal slave, Babo, and the unsettled and melancholy behavior of Cereno himself. These mysterious signs prompt Delano to suspect that Cereno and his slaves are plotting against the Americans. Not until Delano disembarks to return to his own ship, however, does he learn anything of the truth: that the slaves have gained control of the ship. Cereno unexpectedly leaps from his own ship into Captain Delano's boat, and the slaves attempt to escape in the *San Dominick* but are captured by Delano's men. During the course of the ensuing voyage to Concepción, Delano learns that Cereno's friends, including the slaves' master, Don Alexandro Aranda, had been killed by the slaves in a mutiny, and the remaining men were forced to attempt to sail the ship to Senegal. Cereno dies in a monastery in Lima after the mutineers, including ringleader Babo, are executed.

The story makes a penetrating statement on racial and political conditions of the time, prophetically figuring the institution of slavery as a masquerade threatening to break out of control. More than a century later, poet Robert Lowell,* recognizing the story's rich potential for social commentary, adapted "Benito Cereno" into drama as part of his trilogy of plays *The Old Glory* (1964), which also makes use of stories by Nathaniel Hawthorne.* Lowell reset Melville's story in the year 1800, cast it in free verse, and used it as a medium for discussion of such current events as the Vietnam War and the civil rights struggle. The production of Lowell's play won five Obie Awards. [*See also* SLAVE NARRATIVES]

FURTHER READING: Buckholder, Robert, ed. *Critical Essays on Herman Melville's "Benito Cereno."* New York: O. K. Hall, 1992; Gross, Seymour Lee. *A Benito Cereno Handbook.* Belmont, CA: Wadsworth, 1965; Levine, Robert S. *Conspiracy and Romance: Studies in Brockden Brown, Cooper, Hawthorne, and Melville.* New York: Cambridge UP, 1989; Sundquist, Eric J. *To Wake the Nations: Race in the Making of American Literature.* Cambridge: Harvard UP, 1993.

Christopher Lee

BERRYMAN, JOHN (1914–1972). Born John Smith in Oklahoma, John Berryman assumed the name of his stepfather after his own father committed suicide. Berryman's best-known work is the poetic sequence of *77 Dream Songs*, published in 1964, for which he won the Pulitzer Prize. *His Toy, His Dream, His Rest* (1968) continued the *Dream Songs* and won the National Book Award and a share of the Bollingen Prize for Poetry in 1969. These poems exemplify Berryman's characteristic use of a persona or alter ego to explore the concerns with guilt and death that inform much of his work. That work is often overtly Freudian in its allusions and consistently rooted in the illusion and depression that colored much of the poet's own life.

Berryman has scant credentials as a poet of the sea; the only recurrent marine reference in his poetry is his preoccupation with suicide by drowning. See, for example, the last stanza of "Henry's Understanding" in the "Scherzo" section of *Delusions, Etc.* (1972). Berryman committed suicide in 1972 in Minneapolis by jumping off a bridge into the Mississippi River. [*See also* SEA IMAGERY IN MODERN AND CONTEMPORARY PO-ETRY]

Thomas R. Brooks

BESTON [SHEAHAN], HENRY (1888–1968). Born Henry Beston Sheahan in Quincy, Massachusetts, Henry Beston is the author of about a dozen books, including *The Outermost House. A Year of Life on the Great Beach of Cape Cod* (1928). In 1925 Beston built a two-room cottage on the dunes in Eastham about twenty feet from the high-water mark. In September 1926 he went for a brief visit but decided to stay for the year, remaining until the end of the following summer. His account of the experience includes descriptions of shipwrecks* along the Cape Cod* coast in the worst winter in fifty years and of his interactions with his closest neighbors, the coastguardsmen stationed a mile away. But the work is especially notable for its commentary on the natural environment—permanently displaying, Beston emphasizes, a primeval beauty, harmony, and mystery amid the continual seasonal changes in such things as the texture and colors of the sea and the sand and the life forms of the sea, the sky, and the land. Beston's close observation of the natural world, his preoccupation with the human connection to the sea environment, and his organization of the book according to the cycle of the seasons have led many to compare it to Henry David Thoreau's* *Walden* (1854). Declared a national literary landmark in 1954, the house itself was swept out to sea during the blizzard of February 1978. Beston spent the last four decades of his life on a farm in Nobleboro, Maine, where he continued to write. Among his later publications, *White Pines and Blue Water* (1950) includes observations on the seacoast of Maine.

Joseph Flibbert

THE BETHELS. The word "bethel" comes from Hebrew and is translated "House of God." Seamen's bethels were floating or land-based churches, sometimes affiliated with a particular denomination, that specifically catered to sailors and their families. In American literature, the most famous bethel scene is the sermon delivered by Father Mapple in the Whaleman's Chapel, or Seamen's Bethel, in New Bedford, Massachusetts, which takes place in Herman Melville's* *Moby-Dick** (1851).

"Maritime mission" is the phrase most often used by scholars to describe the whole array of religious and benevolent work directed toward seafarers, of which the bethel was central. After the War of 1812, maritime mission efforts in New York soon overshadowed the infant works in Boston and Philadelphia, and in 1817 the Marine Bible Society of New York was founded; in 1820 Presbyterian minister Ward Stafford founded twenty-three Marine Bible Societies in New England.

Also in 1820 the world's first shore-based Mariner's Church was built on Roosevelt Street in New York. Seamen's Friend chapters, women's auxiliaries, Marine Bible Societies, and mariners' churches, banks, and boardinghouses sprang up all along the Atlantic coast at this time. In 1826 many of the diverse efforts to reach seafarers from Maine to New Orleans with the Protestant Christian gospel were brought together under the national leadership of the American Seamen's Friend Society (ASFS). The ASFS published *The Sailor's Magazine* in New York, attempting to keep an individual from each chapter on the board and to represent progress being made all over the world on behalf of seafarers in their literature.

The American Bethel Society was founded in Buffalo to minister to mariners on the Great Lakes,* canals, and western rivers. The ASFS chaplain to the Sandwich Islands, the Reverend Samuel C. Damon, published a temperance newspaper for mariners, *The Friend*, for almost all of his forty-two years in Honolulu.

Mariners' bethels supported asylums for aged seafarers, schools for their daughters, savings banks, temperance boardinghouses, proto-workers'-compensation arrangements, and provisions for widows. However, the service with which most sailors were familiar was the loan library. Although loan libraries were put on some ships before 1840, the release of Richard Henry Dana's* *Two Years before the Mast** spurred the public to do more to help alleviate the boredom and lack of constructive pastimes available to the crews of American merchant vessels. Also, as crews were less likely to be native-born Americans by midcentury, libraries represented a way to help Americanize the men in the forecastle with works that could be read aloud. By the time of the Civil War, loan libraries were being placed in a systematic way on ships, and many times they were entrusted to a converted crew member, thereby shifting the burden of ministry from elites to common sailors. The practice of placing loan libraries on ships continued well into the twentieth century, although the books became more secular in their content.

Twentieth-century technology forever changed the methods of maritime ministry. Rapid methods of loading and unloading cargo mean that seafarers remain in port for ever shorter periods of time. Although missions exist in some 900 ports, chaplains may assist sailors for only a few hours, taking them to the store, providing telephone usage, or conducting a communion service. Modern-day seafarers may still suffer from the loneliness of their earlier predecessors, but they have less time in port. Therefore, much modern-day Christian maritime ministry incorporates training lay seafarers how to minister to their shipmates while at sea.

FURTHER READING: French, Thomas E. *The Missionary Whaleship*, New York: Vantage, 1961; Kverndal, Roald. *Seamen's Missions: Their Origin and Early Growth*. Pasadena: William Carey Library, 1986; Seymour, Jack M. *Ships, Sailors and Samaritans: The Woman's Seamen's Friend Society of Connecticut, 1859–1976*. New Haven,

CT: Eastern, 1976; Skallerup, Harry R. *Books Afloat and Ashore: A History of Books, Libraries, and Reading among Seamen during the Age of Sail.* Hamden, CT: Archon, 1974; Webster, George Sidney. *The Seamen's Friend: A Sketch of the American Seamen's Friend Society.* New York: American Seamen's Friend Society, 1932.

Steven H. Park

BILLY BUDD (1924). The novella *Billy Budd, Sailor (An Inside Narrative),* Herman Melville's* (1819–1891) last work, was written between 1886 and 1891, left unfinished in manuscript, and published posthumously.

The narrative action takes place in 1797, during England's war with Revolutionary France. As the story begins, foretopman Billy Budd, a foundling of unknown parentage, travels homeward on a merchantman, the *Rights-of-Man.* When the British navy impresses him into service, the merchantman's captain laments the loss of Billy, his "peacemaker." Billy bears his impressment on the H.M.S. *Bellipotent* easily, and his hard work and amiable appearance and behavior commend him to his captain, the Honourable Edward Fairfax Vere.

John Claggart, the master-at-arms, takes an immediate aversion to "the handsome sailor." Claggart seeks Billy's downfall and, after the unsuccessful pursuit of a French frigate, falsely accuses the young sailor of mutiny.* Billy tries to protest his innocence; when his stuttering prevents him from defending himself verbally, he strikes out physically. With a single blow, his fist knocks Claggart down dead. Captain Vere believes Billy to be innocent of mutiny and knows that Claggart's death is unintentional. Still, a reluctant drumhead court, urged on by Vere, convicts Billy and sentences him to be hanged.

The complicated textual history of Melville's novella began with Raymond Weaver's publication of *Billy Budd, Foretopman* in corrupt editions (1924, 1928). Weaver included three sections omitted by Melville, one entitled "Lawyers, Experts, Clergy" and another, a rejected chapter on Admiral Nelson. Most famously, Weaver inserted part of a rejected chapter as a "Preface." Subsequent editions of *Billy Budd, Foretopman* by F. Barron Freeman in 1948 and 1950 editions based on Freeman's work, corrected a few of Weaver's errors. Still, an accurate, critical edition did not exist until the one published by the University of Chicago in 1962. Editors Harrison Hayford and Merton M. Sealts Jr. presented Melville's draft "Genetic Text," as well as his final version, entitled *Billy Budd, Sailor (an Inside Narrative).* In 1975 an edition by Milton Stern appeared, based on Melville's "Genetic Text." While general readers may not care about this text's intricate editorial history, they should be aware that the *Billy Budd'*s to which readers, professors, and critics refer are not necessarily identical.

Beyond the editorial controversies, *Billy Budd* has generated a wealth of critical attention, containing, as it does, many layers of political, philosophical, and religious symbolism. Furthermore, there are, essentially, four *Billy Budd'*s.

First is the novella itself; then there is the character Billy Budd, who has popularly come to symbolize pure innocence unjustly persecuted, though this interpretation flattens out the ironic complexity. A third "Budd" emerged in 1947, when Louis Osborne Coxe* and Robert Chapman adapted Melville's novella for the theatre in a play originally titled *Uniform of Flesh*. Finally, a four-act opera based on *Billy Budd*, with music by Benjamin Britten and book and lyrics by E. M. Forster, premiered at London's Covent Garden Theatre in 1951. A revised version, which more accurately resembles Melville's story, premiered in 1964. A film was made by Peter Ustinov in 1962. Claire Denis' film *Beau Travail* (1999) is loosely based on *Billy Budd*; it includes a soundtrack comprised of Britten's opera, loud disco, and strange sound compositions. [*See also* MELVILLE DRAMATIZATIONS]

FURTHER READING: Johnson, Barbara. *The Critical Difference: Essays in the Contemporary Rhetoric of Reading*. Baltimore and London: Johns Hopkins UP, 1988; Parker, Hershel. *Reading Billy Budd*. Evanston, IL: Northwestern UP, 1990; Sedgwick, Eve. *Epistemology of the Closet*. Berkeley and Los Angeles: U of California P, 1990; Weaver, Raymond M. *Herman Melville, Mariner and Mystic*. New York: Doran, 1921.

Arnold Schmidt

BINNS, ARCHIE [FRED] (1899–1971). Archie Binns, novelist and historian of the northwestern United States, is best known for his critically acclaimed novel *Lightship* (1934). Based partly on Binns' own experiences at age eighteen aboard the *Umatilla Reef Lightship* off Cape Flattery, Washington, the story brings together the diverse lives of nine sailors as they struggle to save the ship, which has broken loose from its moorings in a deadly storm.

Binns was born and raised in the Puget Sound area to a family steeped in seafaring: his mother was born outside New York aboard a ship that her father commanded, and Binns' grandfather, who died at sea when he was thirty-one, was renowned as a cotton blockade runner during the Civil War. After serving nine months aboard the *Umatilla*, Binns spent six years alternating college studies ashore with seafaring abroad, including voyages throughout the Atlantic, Pacific, and Indian Oceans as well as the Arabian Sea and rivers within India. He then worked as a journalist in New York for several years before publishing his first novel, *The Maiden Voyage* (1931), a collaborative effort with Felix Riesenberg.*

In his prolific career, Binns wrote several novels centered around the Pacific Northwest* and set against the backdrop of the Puget Sound wilderness, including *Backwater Voyage* (1936), *Mighty Mountain* (1940), *You Rolling River* (1947), and *The Headwaters* (1957). He completed several historical and scholarly studies of the northwestern coastal regions, including *Northwest Gateway* (1941), *The Roaring Land* (1942), and *Sea in the Forest* (1953). Binns also wrote several successful juvenile* works based on sailing adventures, including *The Secret of the Sleeping River* (1952), *Sea Pup* (1954), and *Enchanted Islands* (1956). He died in Sequim, Washington, near the coastal wilderness he had chronicled throughout his life.

Matthew Evertson

BISHOP, ELIZABETH (1911–1979). Elizabeth Bishop, American poet for whom the coastlines of North and South America served as powerful sources of inspiration, was born in Worcester, Massachusetts. Her father died when she was eight months old, and her mother, after suffering mental breakdowns, was permanently institutionalized by the time Bishop was five. An only child, Bishop was raised alternately by her maternal grandparents in Nova Scotia and by relatives of her father in Worcester and Boston. She remembered these households fondly, but her childhood of ill health, transience, and emotional loss instilled in Bishop a lasting reminder of how provisional is one's sense of "home."

In her senior year at Vassar College, Bishop was befriended by Marianne Moore,* who encouraged her in the writing of poetry. After graduating in 1934 with a degree in English, Bishop led a genteel, but nomadic, existence throughout her adult life, living for substantial periods in New York, Key West,* Brazil, and Boston; her poems record the perceptual flux experienced by the lifelong traveler. The sea and its margins provided almost a laboratory environment to investigate these "questions of travel" (this phrase became the title of one of Bishop's volumes), and her poetry is rich with the vocabulary of bay, cape, port, wharf, quay, bight, sand, and swamp. Adept in the use of traditional metrical forms, Bishop more often gave her poems flexible and elastic dimensions, gaining resonant effects through alliteration, repetition, and the use of colloquial language. Steeped in the scenic and visual, well over a third of her 100 or so poems make significant reference to the sea.

Bishop displays an initial debt to Herman Melville* in her sea poems, but her distinctiveness emerges as nameless oceans become domestic sites that resist the speculations of the romantic. The speaker of "The Unbeliever" (1946) sits Ishmael*-like atop the mast, dreading a fall into the ocean; "The Imaginary Iceberg" (1946), similar to Melville's "The Berg" (1888), posits the iceberg as an image of impenetrable sublimity. Poised against this early attraction to the sea as a Melvillean arena of philosophical assertion, however, is a clear-eyed modernist skepticism about the very nature of that attraction. In this way, Bishop's poems often engage in a psychic sifting and refinement; her speakers test and question in essential ways. In this process, land and sea serve as the poles of a subliminal argument, with the back-and-forth dynamic leading Bishop's speakers from a comfortable surface of received wisdom or romantic declaration into indeterminate depths of qualified insight and elusive psychological control.

Defining the precise relation of earth to water was, in one sense, a career-long endeavor for Bishop. In "The Map" (1946), the first poem in her first published volume of verse, Bishop begins with a simple statement—"Land lies in water; it is shadowed green"—but she insistently undermines it in the course of the poem. Her final published work, *Geography III* (1976), begins by quoting a nineteenth-century school primer ("*Of what is the earth's surface composed?* Land and water") and raising questions that once again erode objective, maplike representations.

For the most part, Bishop's sea, unlike Melville's, is never very far from shore; earth and water give scale and temporary sense to one another. In the long, lush opening of "The Moose" (1976), Nova Scotia tides serve as an avenue into a deepening meditation. The poem "Questions of Travel" (1965) begins with a scenic contrast of Brazilian waterfalls and mountains; with these sites established, the poem expands into a consideration of what "home" means. In "The Fish" (1946), Bishop's speaker holds a creature from the sea "half out of water" and attains a qualified epiphany by letting it go. Similarly, the seashore serves as an environment conducive to psychic revision in "Seascape" (1946), "Florida" (1946), "The Bight" (1955), "Cape Breton" (1955), "Sandpiper" (1965), "The End of March" (1976), "Santarem" (1979), and "Pleasure Seas" (1979).

Bishop's most complete sea poem is "At the Fishhouses" (1955), which revisits Marianne Moore's poem "A Grave" (1924). A figure for knowledge itself, "a transmutation of fire," the icy sea in Bishop's poem takes one beyond the normal registers of sensation, memory, and sequential thinking. The speaker's awareness of the sea's informing, indifferent power is poignantly combined with a sense of her own inability to *know* the knowledge the sea has to offer.

Bishop's volumes of poetry include *North and South* (1946), *A Cold Spring* (1955), *Questions of Travel* (1965), and *Geography III* (1976). Her *Complete Poems* was published in 1979. Her *Collected Prose* (1984) also contains some seaborne sketches. [*See also* KEY WEST LITERATURE; MELVILLE'S POETRY OF THE SEA; SEA IMAGERY IN MODERN AND CONTEMPORARY AMERICAN POETRY]

FURTHER READING: Costello, Bonnie. *Elizabeth Bishop: Questions of Mastery*. Cambridge: Harvard UP, 1991; Fast, Robin Riley. "Moore, Bishop, and Oliver: Thinking Back, Re-Seeing the Sea." *Twentieth Century Literature* 39 (1993): 364–79; Millier, Brett C. *Elizabeth Bishop: Life and the Memory of It*. Berkeley: U of California P, 1993.

Hugh Egan

BISHOP, JOHN PEALE (1892–1944). A colleague and friend of such literary giants as F. Scott Fitzgerald,* Edmond Wilson, Ernest Hemingway,* Edna St. Vincent Millay, and Allen Tate, John Peale Bishop was a secondary figure in letters, writing essays, fiction, and poetry. He was a member of the Princeton circle that featured Wilson and Fitzgerald, was associated with the expatriate group in Paris that included Hemingway and Ezra Pound,* and circulated with the Nashville agrarians. Remembered more for whom he knew than for what he wrote, Bishop's place in literature has been partially resurrected since his death.

Bishop was born in Charleston, West Virginia, on 21 May 1892. As a youth he suffered from a psychosomatic illness but was able to attend Princeton, graduating in 1917. *Green Fruit,* his first volume of poetry, was published that year. He served in the U.S. Army in Europe in World War I and, returning to the States, became active in New York's literary culture. From 1920 to 1922 Bishop was a contributing editor of *Vanity Fair.* Over the next dozen years, he traveled in Europe, worked in New York, and spent seven years in Ongeral, France. In 1933 Bishop returned to the United States, living first in Connecticut and New Orleans, then moving to an oceanside home on Cape Cod* in 1938 that he named "Sea Change."

Bishop turned to the sea for material and inspiration for his poems. Primary among his late poems was "A Subject of Sea Change" (1942), a despairing verse focusing on death. The parallel between the sea and death is striking in such later poems as "The Submarine Bed," "Ghouls' Wharf," and "The Parallel" (all 1944), works that reflect Bishop's seclusion overlooking the sea. He died 4 April 1944 at Hyannis, Massachusetts.

Boyd Childress

BLAKE; OR, THE HUTS OF AMERICA (1859). In this novel by early black nationalist Martin Robison Delany (1812–1885), the title character, an experienced seaman, ships out from Cuba aboard an American slave ship to advance an international insurrection against slavery. En route to Africa, Blake and fellow black sailors sing a mutinous chantey celebrating the unfettered ocean as an inspiration for the liberation of slaves. Later, during the voyage, a mutiny* and tempest erupt simultaneously, the slaves belowdecks unleashing a storm of rebellion that mirrors the hurricane raging above. The revolt is quelled as the seas calm, and a promising rainbow greets the ship's arrival. Ensuing chapters use sea imagery metaphorically as they recount Blake's continuing inland efforts to orchestrate a slave rebellion and thereby realize on land the freedom of the fetterless main. [*See also* AFRICAN AMERICAN LITERATURE OF THE SEA; SLAVE NARRATIVES]

Brad S. Born

BLATCHFORD, JOHN (1762–1794). John Blatchford's account of his voyages is one of the more extraordinary sea narratives from the American Revolution. First published in 1788 and soon republished in at least half a dozen other editions, Blatchford's *Narrative of Remarkable Occurrences in the Life of John Blatchford* relates his experiences from 1777, when he sailed out of Boston as a fifteen-year-old cabin boy on an American privateer, to

1783, when he returned to his father's house on Cape Ann, Massachusetts. During the six years of his absence, Blatchford journeyed throughout the world, including Nova Scotia, the West Indies, England, France, Spain, Gibraltar, and even Java and Sumatra. His travels, however, were not of his own volition. Just a month after shipping out on the *Hancock*, Blatchford was taken as a prisoner on 8 July 1777, when his ship surrendered to two British warships. A nautical microcosm of the Revolution, the *Narrative* relates Blatchford's persistent efforts to regain his freedom while held by the British.

Blatchford was first taken to Halifax, Nova Scotia, where he was imprisoned with the rest of his crew but was soon pressed into service on board a British warship and cruised to Antigua, New York, and Philadelphia before returning to Halifax. When put ashore, he attempted escape and in the ensuing struggle killed a guard. Sent to England to stand trial, he was acquitted on the grounds of self-defense. Instead of being returned to Halifax, however, Blatchford was put on board an Indiaman of the East India Company and sent to Sumatra, where he arrived in June 1780. First pressed into service as a common soldier, he was soon sent into the pepper gardens and forced to pick peppers from morning till night because of his obstinacy.

Blatchford and two other Americans ran off into the jungle but were soon recaptured. All three were condemned to death; Blatchford and one other were pardoned and escaped again in December 1780. Halfway through their 800-mile journey, Blatchford's companion died after eating poisoned fruit, leaving Blatchford to wander alone along the coast. He eventually fell into a delirium, but a native woman helped him reach the Dutch settlement. More than half of the roughly twenty-five-page text focuses on Blatchford's Sumatran experiences, particularly his arduous journey along the coast.

There were actually two Blatchfords, the historical figure and the literary character. The former left his home in 1777 to become a cabin boy on an American privateer and returned six years later to settle down as a coastal trader and fisherman. While on a voyage to Port-au-Prince, he died in 1794, leaving a widow and three children. The latter was created for a popular audience out of the materials provided by the former. Although some American prisoners were indeed sent to the East Indies, Blatchford's ordeal in Sumatra was obviously embellished. More important than separating fact from fiction are the basic literary facts in the text's print history. Blatchford and his unknown writer carefully combined elements from both sea narratives and Revolutionary prisoner-of-war accounts to create a text designed to appeal to readers of the new nation.

Daniel E. Williams

BLESS ME, ULTIMA (1972). Set in New Mexico during the period of profound social changes following World War II, this novel by Rudolfo Anaya (1937–   ) focuses on the coming-of-age of Antonio Márez, a sensitive boy whose parents' backgrounds pull him in two different directions. Whereas his mother's family compels him to consider a stable life in the Mexican American community as either priest or farmer, his father urges him to remember his ancestors—men as free and restless as the sea. Mitigating this conflict for Antonio is Ultima, a *curandera*, herbalist and healer, who teaches him to recognize the connections between all living beings and all places that support life—land, sea, and rivers. Antonio must also come to accept Ultima's pantheism, which simultaneously endorses a Christian God, Native American religious practices, and folk beliefs concerning mysterious mermaids* and a great golden carp, all committed to the well-being and survival of humanity. [*See also* AMERICAN INDIAN LITERATURE OF THE SEA; LATINO/A LITERATURE OF THE SEA]

Elizabeth Schultz

THE BOAT OF LONGING (1921 as *Længselens Baat*; Eng. trans. 1933). The fourth novel of Norwegian American Ole Edvart Rølvaag (1876–1931) and his personal favorite, *The Boat of Longing* preceded Rølvaag's better-known tale of immigrant life on the midwestern plains, *Giants in the Earth: A Saga of the Prairie* (1927). Fellow sailor and friend Lincoln Colcord* assisted Rølvaag with the translation of this later masterpiece into English.

The Boat of Longing is a melancholy tale framed with ocean crossings and infused with prose poems about the sea. It follows a Scandinavian legend about a phantom boat that foretells death and signifies a deep, painful longing for something unattainable in this life. Protagonist Nils Vaag, as had Rølvaag, spends twenty years eking out a meager existence on Lofoten Island, Norway, following the family tradition of fishing, before his own dreams and disenchantment with the provincialism of his homeland lure him to America. When his family rescues a wild and enigmatic shipwrecked* Dutch girl, Nils falls in love with her. His parents become increasingly disturbed by the couple's growing attachment, and they contrive to have the girl sent home in an ineffectual ploy to hold on to Nils. At the same time as the boat on which she departs eludes Nils' frantic rowing attempts to gain her back, his nets swell mysteriously with a bounteous catch of herring.

Amid the squalor Nils finds in the slums of Minneapolis, his violin repeatedly offers him solace, particularly when he plays a folk melody called "The Boat of Longing." After his letters back to Norway cease, his desperate father, Jo, crosses the ocean to find him, only to be turned back at Ellis Island for lack of supporting documents. Heartbroken, Jo allows himself to believe an unconvincing story from a fellow steerage passenger that she has seen Nils, and he offers this slim delusion to his wife upon his return home. One sunset, his son seems to glide in a golden vision on the waters ahead of him, and Jo rows after it; neither he nor any trace of his boat is seen again. He has followed the phantom Boat of Longing, even as Nils had pursued the woman who had enchanted him.

Jill B. Gidmark

BONHOMME RICHARD. Early in 1779 the king of France arranged for the purchase of the French-built Indiaman *Duc de Duras*, as part of a squadron of vessels to be put temporarily at the disposition of John Paul Jones.* Thus, the vessels remained French, although they were to sail under the American flag. The old-fashioned *Duras*, renamed *Bonhomme Richard* in honor of Benjamin Franklin's "Poor Richard," was quickly, but illy, fitted out. She carried guns on three decks, although the lowest tier of six old eighteen-pounders was nearly useless. Her armament was roughly that of a thirty-two-gun frigate.

The *Richard*'s short career as a commerce raider is not without interest, but the vessel's primary engagement was her close combat with the *Serapis** off Flamborough Head on 23 September 1779. During the famous battle, undertaken at night, several of the *Richard*'s guns burst, and the tangled vessels fought unequally—the *Serapis* tearing the *Richard* apart below, while the *Richard* commanded the upperworks of the *Serapis*. With the *Richard* on fire and sinking, victory seemed clear for the *Serapis* until an American seaman dropped a grenade from one of the *Richard*'s yardarms through the main hatchway of the *Serapis*. The grenade ignited loose powder on the gundeck, setting off a huge explosion that killed or disabled nearly sixty of the English.

Several times the English commander called out to know if the Americans had surrendered; each time Jones answered in the negative. Finally, in the name of humanity, the English commander lowered his flag with his own hands—the men fearing to go on deck. At daybreak the *Richard* was a wreck, her men unable to control the fire or keep up at the pumps. She lasted through that day and the next night, but at about ten the next morning the *Richard* rolled heavily and sank bow foremost into the sea.

The *Richard*'s sea fight has been celebrated in Nathaniel Fanning's* *Narrative* (1806), by James Fenimore Cooper* in *The History of the Navy* (1839) and "John Paul Jones" in *Lives of Distinguished American Naval Officers* (1846), by Herman Melville* in *Israel Potter* (1855), and by Walt Whitman* in *Leaves of Grass* (1855), among major authors, each taking his cue from the report of Jones himself, who was no mean writer. More recently, William Gilkerson* treated the vessel in *The Ships of John Paul Jones* (1987).

R. D. Madison

BOWDITCH, NATHANIEL (1773–1838). Mathematician, navigator, and astronomer, Nathaniel Bowditch authored the book that since 1802 has been the standard reference for celestial navigators worldwide. Schooled only to age ten, Bowditch taught himself mathematics and several foreign languages in the course of his academic pursuits. While on a voyage to Manila in 1796, Bowditch used his time to correct and supplement information contained in the standard navigation text of the day, John Hamilton Moore's *The Practical Navigator* (London, 1772; first American ed. 1799).

Bowditch published two updated editions of this work (1799, 1800) and then in 1802 released revised tables and instructions under his own name as *The New American Practical Navigator*. This reference immediately became the most frequently consulted text on the subject, selling 30,000 copies in ten editions during his lifetime; it is still in print today.

Bowditch further authored twenty-three scientific papers and an English translation of Pierre Simon de LaPlace's *Traite de Mécanique Céleste* (five vols., 1798–1825; Bowditch's trans., 1829–1839). As the secretary of Salem's East India Marine Society, he transcribed and disseminated information contained in logs of voyages conducted by society members. The name Bowditch is still synonymous with scientific navigation instruction, bolstered by several biographies for juvenile* readers, including *Nat the Navigator* (1870) and *Carry on, Mr. Bowditch* (1955). At his death, one eulogy stated that "every American ship crosses the ocean more safely for his labors."

Daniel Finamore

BOYER, DWIGHT (1912–1977). A journalist, photographer, and feature writer for the *Toledo Blade*, 1944–1954, and the *Cleveland Plain Dealer*, 1954–1977, Dwight Boyer grew up and spent his professional life on the south shore of Lake Erie. He turned his personal and professional interest in the history, legends, and folklore of the Great Lakes* into a productive writing career that resulted in five volumes of Great Lakes history and legend. His interest was kindled, as he recounted in the preface to *Great Stories of the Great Lakes* (1966), by long "yarning" sessions in the darkened pilothouses of Great Lakes freighters and tugs in the Toledo harbor. The tales in that volume and the four succeeding volumes, *Ghost Ships of the Great Lakes* (1968), *True Tales of the Great Lakes* (1971), *Strange Adventures of the Great Lakes* (1974), and *Ships and Men of the Great Lakes* (1977), range from the familiar, such as the wreck of the *Edmund Fitzgerald** (built 1958) of 10 November 1975 and that of the legendary "Christmas tree ship," the schooner *Rouse Simmons* (built c. 1889), which disappeared on her pre-Christmas run from Manistique to Chicago in 1912, to such little-known near legends as those of the workship *Andaste* (built 1892), lost on 9 September 1929, and the odyssey of the U.S.S. *Wolverine*, formerly the U.S.S. *Michigan* (built 1843), ignominiously destroyed, together with a century of Great Lakes history, in 1948. All volumes are illustrated with photos, etchings, and maps and include bibliographies and indexes.

Boyer writes well, and his works are meticulously researched, but he has the voice of an oral storyteller and the ear of a mythmaker. His works are valuable additions to the rich historical and legendary past of the Great Lakes.

David D. Anderson

BRACKENRIDGE, HENRY MARIE (1786–1871). Henry Marie Brackenridge, writer, lawyer, legislator, and diplomat, was born in Pittsburgh, the son of well-known writer and jurist Hugh Henry Brackenridge. Most of Brackenridge's career was devoted to legal work and wide-ranging writings on U.S. political, territorial, and economic expansion into the trans-Appalachian South and West. His most influential writings, however, stem from his interest in South American affairs.

In 1817 President Monroe made Brackenridge the secretary of a U.S. delegation commissioned to travel to South America and report on political affairs there. His account appeared in 1819 as *A Voyage to South America, Performed by Order of the American Government, in the Years 1817 & 1818, in the Frigate* Congress. The work is both a fascinating narrative of oceanic and landgoing exploration and a detailed and philosophically inflected survey of the political, economic, cultural, military, and educational institutions of the South American republics. Throughout *Voyage*, great emphasis is placed on republican institutions and values. But the economic engine behind republican freedoms, in keeping with Brackenridge's liberal-progressive vision, is the maritime commerce and the gradual increase in living standards and opportunities that it creates. Noting that Spanish colonial policy monopolized the benefits of commerce, thereby impeding social progress, he observes that improved maritime commerce is essential to the political health of the South Americans.

Brackenridge appears in these works as a proponent of closer South American political and commercial relations and an advocate of liberal doctrines of maritime commerce as a key factor in social improvement and political progress. While he ended his career inland, retiring to his native Pennsylvania, where he died in 1871, his most important political achievements are linked to his literary rendering of his voyage of naval diplomacy and exploration.

Philip Barnard

BRADBURY, RAY [DOUGLAS]

BRADBURY, RAY [DOUGLAS] (1920–   ). Ray Bradbury, prolific author of twenty story collections and eight novels evolving out of more than 340 published short stories, was born in Waukegan, Illinois. He has lived in Los Angeles since 1934. His work as a writer of fantasy, science fiction, horror, mystery, and juvenile* fiction spans nearly six decades and includes *The Martian Chronicles* (1950; film 2000), *The Illustrated Man* (1951; film 1969), *Fahrenheit 451* (1953; film 1966), *Dandelion Wine* (1957; film 1997), and *Something Wicked This Way Comes* (1962; film 1983). His childhood on Lake Michigan and his many years on the Pacific coast have had a long-abiding influence on his work. Throughout his career, Bradbury has drawn on the sea as a significant source for his fantasies, and this creative focus has resulted in a body of sea literature that includes some of his best stories as well as his most famous treatment of the sea, the screenplay for John Huston's film *Moby Dick** (1956).

In 1944, just two years after the sale of his first story, Bradbury published "The Lake," a tale of a young man who returns to the shore where his childhood love was taken by the water, only to find that the lake has returned her body (and their castle of sand) as if time had never passed. It is widely regarded as Bradbury's breakthrough into mature fiction. "The Beast from 20,000 Fathoms" (1951; reprinted as "The Fog Horn") describes the last of the leviathans, a creature drawn to the beacon and fog horn of a California lighthouse* in search of companionship; Bradbury wrote the screenplay for the film adaptation. Other sea tales of merit include "The Women" (1948), "In a Season of Calm Weather" (1957; reprinted as "Picasso Summer"), and "Forever Voyage" (1960; reprinted as "And the Sailor, Home from the Sea"). Bradbury's water reveries can also become dark tales. In *Death Is a Lonely Business* (1985), Bradbury invents an underwater killer who tracks victims through the ocean surf and abandoned canals of Venice, California.

During the fall and winter of 1953–1954, Bradbury joined John Huston and his preproduction crew in Ireland to write the *Moby Dick* screenplay. He was able to tap into Herman Melville's* biblical and Shakespearean roots to develop a treatment that was faithful to the power of language (if not to the plot) of the original work. For Bradbury, Ahab's* gold doubloon and all that it implies about power and control become the central metaphor, diminishing Melville's philosophical framework and shifting the film to an action-adventure structure. Although dual credit appears on-screen, the writing is almost entirely Bradbury's. His tempestuous working relationship with Huston provides the plot for his novel *Green Shadows, White Whale* (1992). He would later go on to write a play, *Leviathan 99*, transplanting the Moby Dick myth into science fiction; the play became a libretto to an opera of the same name.

"The Ardent Blasphemers," Bradbury's introduction to the 1962 Bantam edition of *Twenty Thousand Leagues under the Sea*, develops significant comparisons between Jules Verne's Nemo and Melville's Ahab; even more important, it includes his major critical statements on literature of the sea.

Jonathan R. Eller

BRADY, CYRUS [TOWNSEND] (1861–1920). Author of some seventy volumes of fiction and nonfiction, some having to do with seagoing or naval heroes, Cyrus Brady was born 20 December 1861 in Allegheny, Pennsylvania. Graduating from the U.S. Naval Academy in June 1883, he resigned from the navy that October. Employed by railroads in Missouri and Nebraska, Brady in his spare time took up religious studies and became an Episcopal priest. He then held a series of clerical posts in the Indian Territory and various western and eastern states.

Brady's first novel, written in 1897, was very successful, and others quickly followed. He became a full-time writer in 1901, continuing church work as an avocation. Often drawing upon his naval background and his experiences in the American West, Brady produced a steady stream of novels and nonfiction with considerable popular appeal at the time, though, with the exception of *When the Sun Stood Still* (1917), about the biblical hero Samson, they are little read today. A number were adapted to the stage or motion pictures. Works related to the sea include the biographies *Commodore Paul Jones* (1900) and *Stephen Decatur* (1900) and the novels *A Midshipman in the Pacific* (1904), *For the Freedom of the Sea* (1899), and *Sir Henry Morgan, Buccaneer* (1903). *Under Tops'ls and Tents* (1901) is an autobiography with anecdotes of his time at the Naval Academy. He died in Yonkers, New York. [*See also* JONES, JOHN PAUL]

C. Herbert Gilliland

BREWER," "LUCY. Lucy Brewer is the pseudonym of either Nathaniel Coverly Jr. (1775?–1824), an early nineteenth-century Boston broadside and pamphlet publisher, or a writer in his employ, Nathaniel Hill Wright (1787–1824). "Brewer's" *The Adventures of Louisa Baker* (1815) is purportedly a "true" tale of Brewer/Baker's seduction, pregnancy, abandonment, life of prostitution, escape in sailor disguise, and service aboard the frigate U.S.S. *Constitution*.

Between 1815 and 1818, the story went through nineteen editions, including two sequels. Better known as *The Female Marine*, Brewer/Baker's tale of her heroic service as a marine aboard *Constitution* in the War of 1812 went unchallenged into the twentieth century. The battle descriptions, however, are nearly verbatim accounts culled from contemporary newspapers, and the alias "George Baker" that Louisa adopted appears nowhere on *Constitution* muster rolls. [*See also* WOMEN AT SEA]

Margherita M. Desy

BRIDGE, HORATIO (1806–1893). A naval officer, Horatio Bridge is most famous for his close friendship with Nathaniel Hawthorne,* for whom he found a publisher for *Twice-told Tales* (1837) and to whom Hawthorne dedicated *The Snow Image* (1851). Born in Augusta, Maine, Bridge graduated from Bowdoin College in 1825 with Hawthorne. Upon graduation, Bridge attended Northampton Law School and practiced law for several years. After being financially ruined in a dam-building project on the Kennebec River, he joined the navy as a paymaster in 1838.

His first cruise was under the command of Commander John Percival, in the sloop of war U.S.S. *Cyane* on her maiden voyage to the Mediterranean in 1838–1841. After a period ashore, he was assigned in 1843–1844 to the newly built sloop of war U.S.S. *Saratoga*, under Commander Josiah Tatnall. Serving with the Africa Squadron under Commodore Matthew Calbraith Perry,* *Saratoga* was one of three ships protecting American citizens and commerce, while suppressing the slave trade on the west coast of Africa. During this voyage, Bridge kept a detailed account, which Hawthorne edited for him as *Journal of an African Cruiser* (1845, 1853).

After serving a year at the Portsmouth Navy Yard, Bridge returned to the Mediterranean and the West African coast in 1846–1849 as paymaster of the frigate U.S.S. *United States*, flagship of Commodore George Read. From 1849 to 1851 he served again at Portsmouth before returning to sea in the sloop of war U.S.S. *Portsmouth* on the Pacific Station. Ordered to Washington in 1854, he became chief of the Bureau of Provisions and Clothing and was in charge during the period when the navy expanded sevenfold during the Civil War. In 1869 he became chief inspector of provisions and clothing until retirement in 1873. Bridge lived until his death in Athens, Pennsylvania, where in 1892 he wrote his *Personal Recollections of Nathaniel Hawthorne*.

John B. Hattendorf

BRIGGS, CHARLES FREDERICK (1804–1877). Born a Nantucket* Yankee (his mother was a Coffin), Charles Frederick Briggs was a real sailor before he became a professional writer. Though he would later turn to the magazines to earn a living, Briggs began his career as a sea novelist. *The Adventures of Harry Franco, a Tale of the Great Panic* (1839) is the tale of a boy from Albany, New York, who goes to sea as a green hand when his family falls on hard times. This novel, both successful and influential, was followed by *The Haunted Merchant* (1843), the story of a New York merchant who goes bankrupt, and by *Working a Passage: or Life in a Liner* (1844), another picaresque adventure by "Harry Franco," telling of a young man's voyage to Liverpool.

In 1846 Briggs posed as Fernando Mendez Pinto in a series of letters for the *New York Evening Mirror*, satirizing literary humbug and affectation. In *The Trippings of Tom Pepper, or the Results of Romancing*, again by "Harry Franco" (2 vols., 1847–1850), Briggs used an urban backdrop to lampoon the New York literati, notably Edgar Allan Poe,* who had coedited the *Broadway Journal* with Briggs in 1845. Starting in 1848, Briggs edited *Holden's Dollar Magazine*, in the 1850s, as editor of *Putnam's Monthly Magazine*; he solicited and published the short fiction of Herman Melville.* In the early 1860s, between various other editing jobs, Briggs worked at the New York Customs House. *Seaweeds from the Shores of Nantucket* (1853) is a volume of miscellaneous short pieces celebrating the island of Briggs' birth. In *The Raven and the Whale* (1956), Perry Miller places Briggs in the New York scene and explores parallels between Briggs and Melville.

Gail H. Coffler

BRINKLEY, WILLIAM CLARK (1917–1993). Two of William Clark Brinkley's books, *Don't Go Near the Water* (1956) and *The Ninety and Nine* (1966), are based on his four years of experience in the U.S. Navy during World War II. *Don't Go Near the Water* is not a "sea" story exactly, but it is a navy story: a hilarious tale of incompetence, bureaucratic bumbling, and a touch of romance in the life of a public information officer on a Pacific Island during World War II. It was made into a movie of the same title in 1957 starring Glenn Ford. *The Ninety and Nine* thoughtfully presents the tragic story of the lives and loves of the officers and crew of a landing ship tank (LST) in the Mediterranean during the Italian campaign.

A third novel by Brinkley, *The Last Ship* (1988), is a masterful tale of suspense set on the last existing U.S. naval vessel after the nuclear war. With echoes of Neville Shute's *On the Beach* (1957), Brinkley weaves a masterful story of the hopes and fears of the surviving crew of 152 men and twenty-six women aboard the *Nathan James*, their voyage past the blighted coasts of Europe and Africa, and their strange encounter with a submarine, the last existing naval vessel of the Soviet Union.

James F. Millinger

BRITISH INFLUENCES ON AMERICAN SEA LITERATURE. By the time that Shakespeare's *The Tempest* was published in the "First Folio" in 1623, William Bradford had already been governor of the Plymouth colony for two years, and the "brave new world" theme had already begun to shape literature in English. Richard Hakluyt's *Principal Navigations* (1589, 1598–1600) helped to create and then satisfy the demand for voyage literature—a form so attractive to readers throughout the following century that the form was followed by Jonathan Swift in his satire *Gulliver's Travels* (1726) and by Daniel Defoe in his early and enormously successful fiction *Robinson Crusoe* (1719). In turn, the shipwreck* motif of the latter must have contributed to William Falconer's preromantic poem "The Shipwreck" (1762). Falconer's popular poem fused elements of the sublime as recently analyzed in Edmund Burke's *A Philosophical Inquiry into the Sublime and Beautiful* (1757), while elaborately retaining technical accuracy. In the following decades J. Hawkesworth shaped the public perception of James Cook in *An Account of a Voyage round the World* (1773). Hawkesworth, a protégé of Samuel Johnson, painted an idyllic picture of South Seas life and created an audience for Cook's subsequent journals: *A Voyage towards the South Pole* (1777) and *A Voyage to the Pacific Ocean* (1784). Cook's exploration of the unfrequented Pacific and skirting of the Antarctic* continent provided Samuel Taylor Coleridge with an imaginative setting for his "Rime of the Ancient Mariner" (1798), which itself expressed the complete romanticization of the sea. The second great age of English exploration may be said to have come to an end with Cook's death (in an altercation with natives of Hawai'i in 1779), but a recession of the ice caps encouraged even further polar exploration. The voyages themselves, watchfully chronicled in *The Quarterly Review* and *The Edinburgh Review*, provided for the earliest maritime adventures of Horatio Nelson, whose career and character would be celebrated in Robert Southey's *Life of Nelson* (1813). Southey's book had the additional effect of rescuing the portrait of the British tar from the eighteenth-century sentimentalization of songwriter Charles Dibdin and novelist Tobias Smollett. That portrait itself was paralleled by the "Byronic" treatment of maritime character in George Gordon, Lord Byron's *The Corsair* (1813) and *Lara* (1814). William Parry in *Journal of a Voyage to Discover a North-West Passage* (1821) and especially William Scoresby in *An Account of the Arctic* Regions, with a History and Description of the Northern Whale Fishery* (1820) demonstrated the sublimity and utilitarian aspects of these forays of exploration and industry.

If the birth of American sea fiction is to be dated from the publication of James Fenimore Cooper's* *The Pilot** in 1824—a fair assumption—the foregoing summary (with perhaps the exception of Hakluyt) might represent a list of Cooper's reading as he undertook to become the first successful professional American novelist—and the first novelist of the sea. But the initial spur to Cooper's writing came immediately from Sir Walter Scott's *The Pirate* (1821) with its misleading scenes of whale-catching set in the Shetland Islands. Scott's historical fiction would continue to be more predictive of the American sea novel than that of Cooper's contemporary Frederick Marryat, whose *Frank Mildmay* (1829) and subsequent novels continued to be based largely on the caricatures of British seamen originated by Smollett.

Near midcentury two nonliterary events, one briefly influential and the other far-reaching, contributed to shaping the future of sea literature. In 1845 Sir John Franklin, who had previously published accounts of one disastrous expedition and one successful expedition to the north, began his third voyage of Arctic exploration, one that was to end in tragedy and the loss of his own life. The solution to the mystery of Franklin's disappearance was not made public until the publication of Sir Francis McClintock's *Voyage of the* Fox *in the Arctic Seas* (1859). The same year Charles Darwin published *The Origin of Species*, a work based largely on observations Darwin had made while a seagoing naturalist and published as *Journal of Researches into the Geology and Natural History of the Various Countries Visited by H.M.S.* Beagle (1839). Darwin's earlier work was coincidentally published the same year as Thomas Beale's *The Natural History of the Sperm Whale*, a work that was not only immediately recognized as exhaustive and authoritative but one that may also have become the single most important sourcebook in the history of sea literature when Herman Melville* ordered a copy in the spring of 1850.

While Melville and his generation were intimately familiar with the tradition of British sea literature, following the Civil War, Darwin (modified and popularized by Herbert Spencer and T. H. Huxley) exerted probably the greatest influence on American literature of the sea, especially through the works of Frank Norris,* Stephen Crane,* and Jack London.* That this influence most likely was secondhand does not lessen its importance. For these proponents of naturalism, the conflict of romanticism and realism found a challenge in the works of Rudyard Kipling, whose *Captains Courageous** (1897) was a romantic-revival treatment of a Darwinian theme, and resolution in the modernism of Joseph Conrad, whose career as a master of fiction followed a career as an officer in the merchant service. Conrad's *Nigger of the* Narcissus (1897) added depth of characterization and theme to the conventional storm piece previously best exemplified by Melville's correspondent William Clark Russell in *The Wreck of the* Grosvenor (1877). *Lord Jim* (begun in 1898 but not completed until 1900) expanded the role of the narrator Marlow, who meanwhile appeared in "Youth" (1898) and would appear again in "Heart of Darkness" (1898–1899) and *Chance* (1913). Conrad's *Typhoon* (1902) extended a literary form closely associated with the age of sail into the age of steam. Conrad's final sea novel, *The Rescue* (1920), took twenty years to write and is no less a product of the romantic revival than Kipling's *Captains Courageous.* Nevertheless, Conrad's work as a whole indicated a new direction and new level of sophistication not only for sea literature but for all literature in English.

FURTHER READING: Philbrick, Thomas. *James Fenimore Cooper and the Development of American Sea Fiction*. Cambridge: Harvard UP, 1961.

R. D. Madison

BROADSIDES. Broadsides were the most versatile and thus the most popular form of publication in early America. Throughout the eighteenth century, thousands of broadsides were published and distributed for many reasons, and often their content directly pertained to the sea and maritime life. From broadsides readers along the coasts learned about naval battles, pirates,* shipwrecks,* shipping news, trade regulations, and even the latest imported goods for sale.

The broadside itself was a convenient vehicle for printers to publish a variety of news expeditiously. Although the size varied, broadsides were usually a single large sheet that averaged ten by fifteen inches. Since newspapers were published only once a week for much of the eighteenth century, and since they often contained little space for extended description, broadsides conveyed news, advertisements, proclamations, and ballads when immediacy, directness, and amplification were required; thus some of colonial America's most interesting and important narrative accounts were published as broadsides. Once printed, they were hawked in streets, posted on walls, and passed around in taverns and coffeehouses. With the exception of a few determined balladmongers, notably Jonathan Plummer of Newburyport, Massachusetts, few authors ever bothered to sign their names. Because of their fragility and popularity, broadsides are the most ephemeral of early American publications.

The first broadside in colonial America was "The Oath of a Free-Man," printed in Cambridge in 1639. Throughout the seventeenth century, broadsides were used primarily to publish official proclamations, including trade regulations. Some of the more interesting examples are proclamations seeking the arrest of pirates, such as William Stoughton's 1699 broadside calling for the capture of a group of pirates who had scuttled their ship off Block Island and the earl of Bellomont's 1700 broadside calling for the seizure of a group of pirates who had dispersed after arriving in New York. These were the first "wanted posters" in America.

During the early eighteenth century, broadsides became more commercial and less political, and thus their subjects and styles became more varied and diverse. Merchants used broadsides to announce the arrival of their latest cargoes, and ship owners used them to celebrate the launching of a new ship and to recruit crews. As a literary marketplace began to develop, printers increasingly produced broadsides to publish news that was lurid and sensational. Benjamin Franklin's first two publications were broadside ballads (dates unknown); the first is "Lighthouse* Tragedy," an account of a shipwreck, and the second is "Sailor's Song on the Taking of the Famous Teach, or Blackbeard the Pirate." Although Franklin reported that his "Lighthouse Tragedy" sold remarkably well, he escaped being a balladmonger after his father convinced him that poets were generally beggars.

Many eighteenth-century broadsides that dealt with the sea fall into three general categories: maritime disasters, pirates and piracy, and naval battles. Of disasters at sea, any calamity or catastrophe resulting in sudden death was liable to be printed as a broadside as soon as the news reached shore. Accounts of drownings, hurricanes, and shipwrecks were often published in broadside form, and at times fires, explosions, and even outbreaks of disease were reported as broadsides. Like Franklin, printers published and sold such broadsides while the tragic news was new and while readers were still hungry for details, though the factual accuracy of these accounts was not always reliable.

Similarly sensational, pirates inevitably became the stuff of broadsides. From the beginning of the eighteenth century, broadsides were often used to announce the last words and dying speeches of condemned pirates; it was not unusual for such broadsides to be sold to the spectators as they gathered around the gallows. In 1704 one of the earliest of all American pirate publications was published as a broadside, "An Account of the Behavior and Last Dying Speeches," describing the final, defiant words of John Quelch and five of his crew. Notorious pirates such as William Kidd and Edward Teach often became the subject of several cheap broadside collections that competed for readers.

By far the most numerous group of broadsides concerned battles at sea. Although newspapers began to supplant broadsides as the most popular medium for the dissemination of news during the latter half of the eighteenth century, a remarkable number of broadsides described naval engagements from the Revolution and the War of 1812. Both the Boston Tea Party and the burning of the *Gaspee* in Narragansett Bay were celebrated as broadside ballads in 1773; a year later the British responded with a broadside salvo of their own by having the Intolerable Acts distributed around Boston on a single sheet. John Paul Jones'* career resulted in a flurry of broadsides, beginning in 1777, when a Boston printer published a recruitment poster announcing the launching of Jones' first command, the *Ranger*, and offering a bounty of forty dollars. Jones' attacks along the English coast and the famous battle between the *Bonhomme Richard** and the *Serapis** were memorialized on broadsides, thus contributing much to his popularity as a Revolutionary War hero.

When the United States again went to war with Great Britain, broadsides were used to announce battles and recruit sailors. After the U.S. frigate *Constitution* defeated the British frigate *Guerriere* off the coast of Massachusetts on 19 August 1812, half a dozen different broadsides were published announcing the victory and celebrating "Old Ironsides." Similarly, when Oliver Hazard Perry wrote his fateful words after the Battle of Lake Erie, "We have met the enemy and they are ours," several broadside ballads were soon printed describing the victory. Other successful American naval engagements were equally memorialized as broadsides, including Stephen Decatur's victory over the British ship *Macedonian* and the defeat of the British flotilla on Lake Champlain.

As printing technology rapidly improved during the first half of the nineteenth century, the need for broadsides declined. The few broadsides that were published served more as commemorative issues or commercial announcements than news reports. Due to their fragile, ephemeral nature, broadsides have been difficult to collect and preserve. Those that have been collected offer invaluable insight into early American maritime history. [*See also* SEA MUSIC]

FURTHER READING: Bumgardner, Georgia B. *American Broadsides.* Barre, MA: Imprint Society, 1971; Ford, W. C. *Broadsides, Ballads, & c. Printed in Massachusetts 1639–1800.* Boston: Massachusetts Historical Society, 1922; Winslow, Ola Elizabeth. *American Broadside Verse.* New Haven, CT: Yale UP, 1930.

Daniel E. Williams

BROOKS, KENNETH F., JR. (1921–   ). Kenneth F. Brooks Jr., a decorated World War II pilot living near Washington, D.C., spent his childhood summers on his uncle's sailboat in the Chesapeake Bay and continues to sail. In *Run to the Lee* (1965) Brooks recounts a voyage made by his great-uncle John Talbott in 1904 on a ninety-foot schooner, the *Albatross*, from Baltimore to Solomons Island, fifty miles south. When the crew fell ill from spoiled oysters, Talbott battled a storm alone at the helm, reaching safe harbor. *Chesapeake Sleighride* (1970) is a fictionalized, illustrated version of the same story written for juvenile* readers. Here the author narrates from the viewpoint of one of the crew, a fictional fourteen-year-old boy who did not eat the spoiled oysters and who assists the captain in sailing through the storm.

Mira Dock

BROWNE, JOHN ROSS (1821–1875). Author of *Etchings of a Whaling Cruise* (1846), J. Ross Browne was born in Beggars Bush, Ireland, and emigrated to America when he was twelve years old. In 1838 Browne journeyed on a trading boat from Louisville to New Orleans. Lacking funds to take a grand European tour, he shipped out of New Bedford, Massachusetts, in July 1842 as a common sailor on a whaler. Unhappy with shipboard conditions and the captain's cruelty, he negotiated his release from duty and stayed in Zanzibar until he secured a berth on a brig, which arrived in Salem harbor on 19 November 1843.

Etchings of a Whaling Cruise is Browne's autobiographical account of those travels. Herman Melville,* one of Browne's reviewers, praised the graphic, authentic writing and incorporated some of the details into *Moby-Dick** (1851). An effective antidote to romantic notions of seafaring, *Etchings* not only describes vividly the implements and process of whaling but also exposes the cruelty of some nineteenth-century sea captains. Browne states, for example, that the forecastle is much filthier than pigsties in Kentucky. While the captain and officers dine royally, he has learned to settle for hard biscuits, greasy pork, and fat, mutilated cockroaches in his molasses. Browne attacks the captain for requiring hard labor from desperately ill sailors and condemns the inhumane practice of flogging. He concludes that the system is authoritarian and tyrannical.

Browne's *Etchings of a Whaling Cruise* has been compared with Richard Henry Dana's* *Two Years before the Mast** (1840). In the introduction to *Etchings*, Browne acknowledges his indebtedness to Dana for realistic descriptions of shipboard life. [*See also THE RED RECORD*]

Sally C. Hoople

BRYANT, WILLIAM CULLEN (1794–1878). William Cullen Bryant was born and raised in the back country of western Massachusetts, where an early talent for versifying displayed in religious, sentimental, and satiric poems culminated in the publication in the *North American Review* of his best-known poem, "Thanatopsis" (1817). Thereafter, editions of his poems appeared regularly, and he soon became America's first internationally prominent poet. He moved to New York in 1825, joined the *New York Evening Post* in 1827, first as associate editor and, two years later, as editor-in-chief and part-owner, remaining in that position for the rest of his life. Although he continued to write poetry until the year of his death, his position with the *Evening Post* involved him increasingly in social causes such as abolition, workers' rights, and free trade, and his poetic output declined after the early 1840s.

Bryant's five ocean voyages to Europe and the Near East, as well as several trips to South America, gave him considerable firsthand experience of the sea. Fugitive references to the discomforts and potential perils of sea voyaging appear in his accounts *Letters of a Traveller* (1850, 1859) and *Letters from the East* (1869). In one of his sea poems, "A Day Dream" (1860), inspired by his travels abroad, the narrator bemoans the decline of myth in a rational age as he looks out from the shores of Naples at the fading image of sea nymphs, only occasionally evoked by the poets of his time.

Other poems explore the sea metaphorically. The vast expanse of billowing grasses that he saw on a trip to Illinois in 1832 is compared to a motionless sea in "The Prairies" (1833). In "A Hymn of the Sea" (1842), the immense power of the sea in both its creative and destructive manifestations becomes an emblem of divine power. In "The Tides" (1860), the upward motion of the rising tide is a metaphor for human spiritual aspiration. Herman Melville,* Nathaniel Hawthorne,* and Oliver Wendell Holmes* listened to Cornelius Matthews read Bryant's "Monument Mountain" (1824) at the top of that mountain on the occasion of a famous literary picnic on 5 August 1850.

Bryant's most significant sea poem—more than 500 lines long—is a fanciful tale titled "Sella" (1862). In the poem, the maiden Sella, thwarted by gender boundaries that restrict her ability to explore distant lands, finds a pair of magical slippers that transport her to the depths of the sea, where she returns repeatedly to investigate its mysteries until her brothers throw the slippers away. Although devastated by this loss, she spends the rest of her life teaching people how to harness the power of water.

Bryant's blank verse translations of the *Iliad* and the *Odyssey* (1870–1872) were well received in his time. [*See also* SEA IMAGERY IN MODERN AND CONTEMPORARY POETRY]

Joseph Flibbert

BUCKLEY, WILLIAM F[RANK]., Jr. (1925–   ). William F. Buckley Jr., prolific journalist, author, and editor of *National Review*, is also a passionate sailor. Those two worlds join in a trilogy of narratives about monthlong ocean cruises he has taken in yachts he either owned or chartered: *Airborne: A Sentimental Journey* (1970), *Atlantic High: A Celebration* (1982), and *Racing through Paradise: A Pacific Passage* (1987). There is plenty of nautical substance in these volumes for serious blue-water sailors as well as for general readers, if they can tolerate or ignore the parenthetical name-dropping of celebrities, most of which is not essential to the fabric of the voyages.

In the first volume, Buckley attempts to demystify ocean sailing for his uninitiated readers by including long sections on mechanical problems and celestial navigation. The narrative is replete with accounts of failures of gear and near disasters, both past and present, so much so that it is difficult to imagine such an experienced sailor getting into that many scrapes with boats. The second volume, like the first, begins with a series of digressions— cruises to Mexico and the Fiji Islands—before it eventually addresses crossing the Atlantic; the passage is uneventful, apart from some hard slog- ging on the final leg from the Azores to Spain. The third volume sets aside the digressive voyages taken in the interval between books into a separate section, continues the detailed analysis of navigational gear, and follows the Buckley practice of excerpting from his crew's journals. The voyage is again uneventful, but a chatty and sometimes witty style as well as magnificent photographs propel the reading.

Buckley wrote the foreward to Titanic* *Adventure: One Woman's True Life Voyage Down to the Legendary Ocean Liner* (1999) by Jennifer Carter and Joel Hirschhorn, a book about the 1987 French/American diving ex- pedition to the wreck. [*See also* CRUISING LITERATURE]

Robert C. Foulke

"BUNTLINE, NED." *See* [JUDSON, EDWARD ZANE CARROLL].

BURLAND, BRIAN [BERKELEY] (1931–   ). Born in Bermuda, edu- cated in England and Canada,* and living a good part of his life in the United States, Brian Burland has written several maritime novels. Son of a yacht builder, Burland went to sea when he was twelve aboard a vessel of the British merchant marine. He is perhaps best known for *A Fall from Aloft* (1968), part of his series of novels called "The Bermudians."

James Berkeley, the main character of *A Fall from Aloft,* is a teenage boy who leaves Bermuda for school in England on a British freighter during World War II. The *Empire United* sails to Halifax, where it joins a large convoy to Great Britain, encountering an aggressive storm on the last leg of the trip. While living with the crew, James recalls his life in Bermuda. Burland relates the actions, fears, and thoughts of a teenage boy with em- pathy and candor, while demonstrating the callousness of war. Other novels in "The Bermudians" series include *A Few Flowers for St. George* (1969), *Love Is a Durable Fire* (1986), and *Whatwanderwith* (1987).

Surprise (1974) is about an accomplished black sailor named Surprise, who builds his own magnificent sloop and attempts to establish a free black colony on the Caribbean* island of Barbuda. Surprise valiantly defends his settlement against the Royal Navy. *Stephen Decatur, the Devil and the En- dymion* (1975) is a work of historical fiction centered on Commodore Ste- phen Decatur's loss of the U.S. frigate *President* to the British on Long Island Sound in 1815. Burland also wrote the novels *Undertow* (1971), *The Sailor and the Fox* (1973), and *The Flight of the Cavalier* (1980). Burland includes poetry, shifting points of view and time, sexual undertones, and accurate historic settings in most of his writing.

Richard J. King

BURTS, ROBERT (17??–1839). Robert Burts was born in Maryland and entered the navy in 1833 as a midshipman. He sailed to the Mediterranean on the sloop *Ontario*, but upon return in 1836 he began a string of extended leaves. After fourteen months of continuous leave he was assigned to the Navy School in New York and then, briefly, to the *Brandywine*. After spending several days in a naval hospital in September 1839, Burts received three months' leave and joined his family in Cincinnati, where he died in December. Burts probably wrote much of his fiction while on leave, drawing on his experiences in the Mediterranean.

Burts' melodramatic stories, such as *The Scourge of the Ocean* (1837), feature piracy, naval battles, and forbidden—but eventually requited—love. Burts' heroes, like himself, serve in the navy, though in *The Scourge of the Ocean* New York colonist George Everett quickly turns to patriotic piracy after striking his tyrannical first lieutenant. The British lieutenant is engaged to a young woman with whom Everett is in love, but in the end Everett wins the woman and national acclaim following the Revolution.

Burts' best-known work is *The Sea-King: A Nautical Romance* (1851). The book's hero, Harry Sutherland, leaves home and joins the navy, moving rapidly through the ranks following exemplary service during the War of 1812. Sutherland finds himself battling against the famed privateer Manly, who had successfully wooed Sutherland's mother from his father, apparently ruining the reputation of his beloved Anna Hamilton, and Frederick Montgomery, who resented being forever in Sutherland's shadow. Burts died before *The Sea-King* was completed; Frank Marryat, the son of Frederick Marryat, finished the work for the publishers.

Peter H. McCracken

BYLES, MATHER (1707–1788). Congregational minister, sermonizer, and poet, Mather Byles was the grandson of Increase Mather. Among his publications are two notable volumes, *Poems on Several Occasions* (1744) and *Poems. The Conflagration . . . The God of Tempest and Earthquake* (1755). The first collection includes his major piece, "Hymn at Sea," which was set to music by William Billings and published in the *New England Psalm-Singer* (1770). Addressed to the "Great God, thy Works our Wonders raise," the hymn is in five numbered tetrameter quatrains dealing with such matters as day, night, tempest, calm—as the mariner follows his compass.

"The Conflagration," which also appears in the first volume, is an early version of "The God of Tempest," appearing in the second. Byles' frequent sea imagery is particularly connected with storms at sea and relates these dark natural occurrences to the hand of God, signifying his wrath and judgment or, with their dissipation, signifying his benevolence. Two significant examples are "Old Ocean with presaging Horror rores" ("The Conflagration") and "Th'attending Sea thy Will performs" ("The God of Tempest"). [*See also* SEA-DELIVERANCE NARRATIVES]

John T. Shawcross

C

CADWELL, CLARA [GERTRUDE] (c.1856–1???). Other than the two facts that Clara Cadwell was born in Jefferson, Ohio, and later lived in Cleveland, almost nothing is known of her life. Her single published literary work, a novel titled *De Barr's Friends, or Number Seventeen; Trip to Lake Superior with a Romance* (1881), may contain autobiographical elements. The story tells of a young man traveling aboard an excursion steamer from Lake Erie to Lake Superior, specifically en route to Duluth, Minnesota, where he meets and falls in love with an attractive farm girl from Cleveland with a hint of a mysterious and perhaps unsavory past. In a florid, romantic style, Cadwell provides colorful descriptions of the ship, the scenery, and the ports typical of the Great Lakes.*

Robert Beasecker

CALM AT SUNSET, CALM AT DAWN (1989). The second novel of Paul Watkins (1964–) tells of one man's coming-of-age at sea. Despite the wishes of his fisherman father, twenty-year-old James Pfeiffer, newly expelled from college, signs aboard a decrepit scallop trawler out of Newport, Rhode Island, hoping to discover the lure that the sea has for his father and other men. There he performs backbreaking, often dangerous work with men, each of whom reveals some sort of sordid past or secret and is using the sea as a personal escape or as therapy. He suffers physically, emotionally, and mentally as he attempts to fit in and discover what meaning the sea has for him. The often brutal lessons are revealed in graphic, frequently gory, first-person detail as the reader comes to know life aboard a scallop trawler.

Son of Welsh parents, Watkins writes from firsthand experience. His father, an oceanography professor, introduced him early to Narragansett Bay when the family lived in Saunderstown, Rhode Island. As a child, Watkins, who had attended school in England, gloried in life on the water and the absence of uniforms. While a student at Yale, Watkins spent summer vacations working out of Newport, first on a trapboat that made daily trips tending semipermanent fixed nets and later mostly on scallop trawlers. Throughout his trips, he kept a diary and took notes, which he incorporated into this book two years later.

Calm at Sunset, Calm at Dawn was awarded Britain's 1989 Encore Prize for best second novel and was made into a Hallmark Hall of Fame movie, *Calm at Sunset*, in 1996.

Ellen L. Madison

CALVIN, JACK (1901–1985). Jack Calvin was well acquainted with the Pacific coast from Monterey north. His first two novels, *Square-Rigged* (1929) and *Fisherman 28* (1930), are based on his experience sailing from San Francisco to the Bering Sea. After leaving his position as a writing instructor at Stanford University, he and his wife, Sasha (Kashevaroff), the daughter of a Russian Orthodox bishop in Juneau, settled in Carmel, California. In the early 1930s they became members of a Monterey intellectual circle that included his former student, Ritchie Lovejoy (who married Sasha's sister, Natalya), Carol and John Steinbeck,* Joseph Campbell, and Edward F. Ricketts.* Calvin described a trip that he and Sasha took in a seventeen-foot canoe from Tacoma up the inland passage to Juneau in an article published in the July 1933 issue of *National Geographic.*

In the summer of 1932, Ricketts and Campbell sailed with the Calvins on their thirty-three-foot boat, the *Grampus*, from Tacoma to Juneau on a marine specimen-collecting trip for a long-term project. Calvin collaborated on the literary aspects of the text and took photographs for *Between Pacific Tides* (1939), coauthored by Ricketts and Calvin, a classic work in ecology that achieved five editions by 1985, including those revised by Joel W. Hedgpeth and David W. Williams. In the mid-1930s the Calvins moved to Alaska, where Calvin wrote *Sitka* (1936), a history of that Russian settlement in Alaska, ran a printing business, and became an advocate of conservation and wilderness preservation.

Kenneth A. Robb

CANADIAN LITERATURE OF THE SEA. As with the majority of its literature, Canada's works about the sea can be divided geographically into three major categories: the Atlantic/Maritimes, the Arctic*/Northwest Territories, and the Pacific. What unites all three areas in the literature is the recurrent theme of exploration on both a national and an individual scale.

A great deal of Canada's best writing about the sea is either autobiography or nonfiction. This has set the tone for many of its creative works, as noted by critic Northrop Frye. To Frye, beginning with tales of the early French and English sailors, these stories establish what he describes as his nation's particular documentary style of narrative. Among the major influences are the exploits of such Arctic explorers as Samuel Hearne, Sir Alexander Mackenzie, and Captain John Franklin from the 1770s to the 1820s. The narrative style was still evident in stories of World War II North Atlantic convoys, such as William Howard Pugsley's *Saints, Devils, and Ordinary Seamen* (1945). From the 1950s through the 1970s, Farley Mowat* reissued many of the explorers' journals, including Hearne's. He followed them with a study of the easternmost province in the northern Atlantic Ocean, *New Founde Land* (1989).

The Atlantic Maritime Provinces are the oldest of the European-speaking settlements and speak in the most diverse literary voices. The first storytellers were the aboriginal people of Canada, often referred to as the First Nations, who met and joined voices in print with the French. New France stretched from present-day New Brunswick westward down the St. Lawrence River; this colony was also known as Acadia and was the initial setting for Henry Wadsworth Longfellow's* *Evangeline* (1847). The stories of the Acadians' battles with the English, including colonists from New England, appear in recent historical fiction such as Victor Suthren's *The Black Cockade: Paul Gallant's Louisbourg Command* (1977), which focuses on attacks on the French settlement in Nova Scotia during the 1740s. Many contemporary Francophone writers of Acadian literature continue to explore the relationship between French Canadians and the sea, including poet Ronald Despres in *Paysages en contrebande* (1979) and fiction writer Louis Hache in *Toubes jersiaises* (1980). Toronto-based poet Robert Finch, who died in 1995, was an avid sailor whose evocative collection of sea poems, *Sail-boat and Lake* (1988), was introduced by Robertson Davies.

A whimsical work from Nova Scotia in the mid-nineteenth century, *The Letterbag of the* Great Western (1840) is by legendary humorist T. C. Haliburton, who uses letters of fictional passengers to poke fun at American, British, and Canadian travelers on the famous ship. A more adventurous style belongs to Norman Duncan and his stories of life in Newfoundland and Labrador, *The Way of the Sea* (1903). Poet E. J. Pratt in his first collection, *Newfoundland Verse* (1923), established his strength in narrative verse. He followed with other books, including *The* Roosevelt *and the* Antinoe (1930) about the heroic rescue of a ship's crew in the mid-Atlantic. Pratt used irony in his epic poem *The* Titanic* (1935), often called a classic of Canadian literature, on the tragic pride of people who believed that they could conquer the sea.

Sir Charles Roberts, sometimes called the father of Canadian literature, also took up the power of the sea late in his career with *The Iceberg and Other Poems* (1934). Following Pratt's example of the epic, historically based narrative poem is Frederick Watt's sixty-page documentary poem of the North Atlantic convoys, *Who Dare to Live* (1943). Many of the convoys, as had many luxury liners before the war, used Halifax as a main port. Fred

Gogswell, Alden Nowlan, Robert Gibbs, and other so-called Fiddlehead Po-
ets explore life in an environment dominated by the sea, as exemplified in
Gibbs' poems "The *Manes P.* Aground off Fort Dufferin" (1971) and
"Travels: Eastbound/Westbound" (1985).

Canadian sea drama is marked by two high points: the performance of
the masque *Le Theatre de Neptune* on the water facing Port Royal in Acadia,
arguably the first dramatic work performed in North America (1606), and
Michael Cook's Newfoundland Plays, a cycle that includes *Quiller* (1975),
about a provincial outpost; *On the Rim of the Curve* (1977), showing the
demise of the Beothuk, Newfoundland's aboriginal people; and *The Gayden
Chronicles* (1979), telling the story of a Royal Navy rebel hanged in 1812.
Newfoundland's conflict over accepting confederation into the rest of Canada, which lasted from the late nineteenth century into the middle of the
twentieth, is told in Tom Cahill's *As Loved Our Fathers* (1974).

As for more contemporary Maritime prose, there are Mowat's entertaining
tales for juvenile* readers, among them *The Boat Who Wouldn't Float*
(1968) and *The Black Joke* (1974). Alistar MacLeod's collection *The Lost
Salt Gift of Blood* (1976) tells of life on and off the coast of Cape Breton
in such pieces as "The Boat" and the title story. These narrative explorations
continue with works such as Jane Urquhart's* *Away: A Novel* (1993), with
settings reaching out to the Irish Sea, with her short story "The Boat"
(1996), and with Howard Norman's historical novel *The Bird Artist* (1994),
which has a Nova Scotia location and features a lighthouse.*

The St. Lawrence River and its modern incarnation as the St. Lawrence
Seaway have always been important in politics, society, and economics. A
popular novel of its time, *Altham: A tale of the Sea* (1848) follows the main
character, paralleling author John Swete Cummins' own life, from Great
Britain, to the ocean, to the Gulf of St. Lawrence. The War of 1812, much
of which was fought along the St. Lawrence and the Great Lakes,* appears
in the works of well-known writer and commentator Pierre Berton. A multiple winner of the prestigious Governor General's Award, Berton wrote *The
Invasion of Canada* (1980) and *Flames across the Border* (1981), colorful
histories of the people and the geography. The waterways are central in
Charles Sangster's collection *The St. Lawrence and the Saguenay and Other
Poems* (1856), especially the title piece. Sangster is sometimes referred to as
the poet laureate of colonial Canada. The Gulf of St. Lawrence is the setting
for a popular novel of a later time, *The Sacrifice of the* Shannon (1903) by
W. Albert Hickman, about an icebreaker and her crew.

There are some stories handed down by the First Nations' peoples about
the coast and Vancouver Island, including the stories and poems of E. Pau-
line Johnson, who took the name Tekahionwake in 1886. Her "Deep Water" appears in Suthren's *Canadian Stories of the Sea* (1993). Because of the
many nearly mythic, real-life adventures that occurred in connecting the
Pacific coast region to the rest of Canada, many writers use it as a metaphoric

location that can represent ideas such as hope, perseverance, or salvation. This happens in Jack Hodgins' *Spit Delaney's Island* (1977), a book of parables, many redemptive, set on Vancouver Island. In his novels about the Barclay family, particularly *The Resurrection of Joseph Bourne* (1980), in which a tidal wave brings both a lost ship and a magical woman to the island, Hodgins promotes a world in which the characters can create and re-create their lives. A more recent work of fiction is William Gaston's *Deep Cove Stories* (1989), also set along the Pacific coast. Sharon Pollock's play *The Komagata Maru Incident* (1978) is based on a 1914 clash, when Sikh immigrants were not allowed to disembark in Vancouver. Highly imaginative, Gothic poems constitute Susan Musgrave's *Songs of the Sea-Witch* (1970) and *The Impstone* (1976).

Among fanciful works of children's literature on sea themes are George H. Griffin's *At the Court of King Neptune: A Romance of Canada's Fisheries* (1932) and *Legends of the Evergreen Coast* (1934). *The Boatman* (1957; revised 1968) by Jay Macpherson is a collection of poetic recastings of classic and religious parables, often compared to the work of William Blake. Pratt's humorous fantasy *The Witch's Brew* (1925) is a Prohibition satire about a drunken fish and other creatures of the deep. [*See also GAFF TOPSAILS*; KENT, ROCKWELL; SNIDER, CHARLES HENRY; VOLLMANN, WILLIAM T.; *THE VOYAGE OF THE* NARWHAL]

FURTHER READING: Gair, Reavley, ed. *A Literary and Linguistic History of New Brunswick*. Fredericton: Fiddlehead Poetry and Goose Lane, 1985; New, W. H. *A History of Canadian Literature*. Basingstoke: Macmillan Education, 1989; Suthren, Victor, ed. *Canadian Stories of the Sea*. Toronto: Oxford UP, 1993; Toye, William, ed. *The Oxford Companion to Canadian Literature*. Toronto: Oxford UP, 1983.

Michael W. Young

CAPE COD. Extending farther east into the Atlantic Ocean than any other portion of the United States, Cape Cod is the peninsula that forms the so-called arm of southeastern Massachusetts. It begins at the Bourne and Sagamore bridges that span the Cape Cod Canal, continues thirty-five miles east to Chatham, then curves north and northwest to Truro and finally to Provincetown at its tip.

With Nantucket* Sound to the south, the Atlantic to the east, and the Cape Cod Bay to the north and west, Cape Cod has inspired many writers to document their sea-related experiences on its shores. The most famous literature concerning the area consists of personal narrative and nature writing. Henry David Thoreau's* *Cape Cod* (1865) chronicles his three week-long excursions on the cape. Thoreau describes the area's towns, residents, landscape, and folk culture, investigating the local phenomenon of "wrecking," which refers to both the searching for treasure along cape beaches and the deliberate wrecking of ships by luring them with false lights to rocky shores. To that end, he opens his text with a passage on the *St. John*, a brig that wrecked at Cohasset just over a mile from shore one day before his first visit to the cape.

Joel Porte examines Thoreau's fascination with water in his critical essay "Henry Thoreau and the Reverend Poluphloisboios Thalassa," included in *The Chief Glory of Every People* (1973), and Thoreau's renowned journal inspired other nature writers to share their own experiences on Cape Cod. Henry Beston's* *The Outermost House* (1928) describes his solitary year on the dunes of the Eastham bar, thirty miles from mainland Massachusetts, offering extended descriptions of the sea, its wrecks, and its wildlife, especially seabirds. More recently, Robert Finch shared his view of the modern transformation of Cape Cod's landscape in *The Primal Place* (1983). Much of Finch's text revolves around the cape's seas, as he describes the acts of "clamming" and "scratching" (digging for shellfish and quahogs, respectively), the stranding of ducks, seals, dolphins, and whales along the bay's beaches, and the effects of winter and tidal movements on beach erosion and marine wildlife.

Daily life on Cape Cod also has led to the publication of cape-related memoirs. In *I Retire to Cape Cod* (1944), Arthur W. Tarbell presents a history of the ships that have traveled the cape and its canal, focusing in particular on clipper ships. He notes the continued influence of wrecking (also called, according to Tarbell, "scow-banging"), citing the value and prevalence of quarterboards (boards bearing the names of wrecked ships) proudly displayed by cape residents on homes, woodsheds, and garage doors.

One of the cape's most prolific writers of fiction, poetry, and memoir was Joseph Crosby Lincoln.* Much of Lincoln's work centers on the sea, ships and crew, weather, and wrecking. *Fair Harbor* (1922) details the escapades of a sea captain and a ship's cook at a home for mariners' women, and *Storm Signals* (1935) finds a disabled captain returning home to the cape after a shipwreck.* His earlier novel, *Partners of the Tide* (1905), which concerns two successful wreckers on the cape, was released as a Hollywood movie in 1916 and 1921.

Cape Codder Henry C. Kittredge also documented his perspective of the area. *Cape Cod: Its People and Their History* (1930) examines the history of the cape from the era of exploration and settlement to the twentieth-century construction of the canal, while *Shipmasters of Cape Cod* (1935) tracks neglected voyages of cape sea captains along the East Coast, to the Northwest* Territories, and to Liverpool, China, and the Mediterranean. *Mooncussers of Cape Cod* (1937) examines the cape's wreckers, who "cuss the moon" for shedding light that prevents the scavenging of potential nighttime wrecks. In the same year, *Cape Cod Pilot* was published as part of the Federal Writer's Project; this compilation includes "The Sea Witch of Billingsgate" by Jeremiah Digges, pseudonym of Joseph Berger, who moved to Provincetown from New York following the crash of 1929.

Other novels concerning or set on Cape Cod include William Martin's*
Cape Cod (1991) and William Carpenter's *A Keeper of Sheep* (1994). Poetry
by cape writers includes Charles H. Philbrick's *Wonderstrand Revisited: A
Cape Cod Sequence* (1960), John V. Hinshaw's anthology, *East of America:
A Selection of Cape Cod Poems* (1969), and Conrad Aiken's* *Collected Poems*
(1970). Marge Piercy, who lives in Wellfleet, uses cape imagery notably in
her novel *Summer People* (1990) and in her poetry collections *Living in the
Open* (1976) and *Mars and Her Children* (1992). Truro writer Maria Flook
published *Open Water* (1994), about a wayward sailor discharged from the
navy for petty thievery. Norman Mailer's murder mystery *Tough Guys Don't
Dance* (1984) is set on the cape.

Shorter fiction, essays, and poetry are compiled in *A Place Apart: A Cape
Cod Reader* (1993), edited by Robert Finch. *Cape Cod Stories* (1996), edited by John Miller and Tim Smith, offers reminiscences of the cape, of
Nantucket, and of Martha's Vineyard by an array of famous authors such as
Edna St. Vincent Millay, Sylvia Plath, John Updike,* and John Cheever.*
Richard Adams Carey's *Against the Tide: The Fate of the New England Fisherman* (1999), a work containing natural and local history and literature,
chronicles one season with four cape fishermen struggling to succeed in a
threatened way of life.

Melanie Brown

CAPE HORN. Both a geographical location and a literary symbol, rugged
Cape Horn represents the ultimate test of nautical skill. The cape itself is
located on Horn Island, a 1391-foot-high rock at the southernmost tip of
South America. More broadly, Cape Horn constitutes the whole area from
fifty degrees south in the Atlantic to fifty degrees south in the Pacific. Willem
Cornelisz Schouten and Jacob le Maire, on an expedition to discover a new
route from the Atlantic to the Pacific in 1616 for the Dutch East India
Company, were the first Europeans to sight Horn Island. It was visited
infrequently until the nineteenth century, when "rounding the Horn" became the primary route to the South Seas whaling grounds and the California goldfields. The completion of the Panama Canal in 1914 largely
ended the Horn's commercial significance, though oil tankers must still
round the Horn since they are too large for the Panama Canal.

Cape Horn has the most dangerous waters in the world, with 100-foot
waves, relentless, gale-force winds, fifty-mile-long icebergs, and treacherous
currents. In 1905 alone, over 400 ships perished there.

Many fine descriptions of the Cape Horn passage exist, including James
Fenimore Cooper's* in *The Sea Lions,* Richard Henry Dana's* in *Two Years
before the Mast,* and Herman Melville's* in *White-Jacket.* Warwick M.
Tompkins sailed around the Horn with a crew that included his two small
children, as described in his *Fifty South to Fifty South: The Story of a Voyage
West around Cape Horn in the Schooner* Wander Bird (1938). Today the

cape is usually rounded only for adventure, as described, for example, in David and Daniel Hays' *My Old Man and the Sea* (1995). [*See also* CIR-CUMNAVIGATIONS AND BLUE-WATER PASSAGES; CRUISING LITERATURE; VOYAGE NARRATIVES]

Dennis Berthold

CAPTAINS COURAGEOUS (1897). *Captains Courageous,* written by Rudyard Kipling (1865–1936), was published serially in November 1896 by *McClure's Magazine* and in book form in 1897. Harvey Cheyne, the dissolute fifteen-year-old son of a multimillionaire, falls off a steamer bound from New York to Europe and is presumed dead. He is rescued by the Gloucester* fishing schooner *We're Here,* commanded by Disko Troop, an expert fisherman and a just man. Kipling is interested in the life of the fishermen rather than in the transformation of Harvey, and he concentrates on Harvey's acquisition of the fishermen's skills. After a season fishing on the Grand Banks, the *We're Here* is the first vessel back to Gloucester, Massachusetts, therefore commanding the highest prices for its fish. Harvey sends a telegram to his father, a captain of industry (hence, the plural "Captains" of the title), and his parents cross the United States in a record-setting trip in a private railroad car. Through the influence of both captains, Harvey achieves maturity and understanding.

Kipling, the Anglo-Indian son of a sculptor, was born in Bombay, spent his childhood in England, did not even visit the United States until 1889, yet seven years later wrote a fine novel of Gloucester fishing, *Captains Courageous.* In London Kipling had met Wolcott Balestier, an American writer working as a publisher's agent. Together, they wrote *The Naulahka, a Novel of the East and West* (1892). Kipling married Balestier's sister on 18 January 1892, and they set off on their round-the-world honeymoon voyage, arriving eventually at her family home near Brattleboro, Vermont. Dr. James Conland, who assisted at the birth of Kipling's daughter, introduced him to Gloucester fishing, as Kipling later explained in his autobiography, *Something of Myself for My Friends Known and Unknown* (1937). Kipling made three visits to Gloucester and one to Boston to observe and absorb details of the fishermen and their lives. His part was the writing, Kipling later explained, and Conland's the details. Conland showed him how to split cod and sent him out on a pollock-fisher, where Kipling was "immortally sick." Kipling also got charts of the Grand Banks and information on the American cod fisheries from the Washington lawyer William Hallett Phillips.

In *Captains Courageous,* Kipling captures the danger and the heroism of fishermen's lives. During the sixty-eight years between 1830 and 1897, 668 Gloucester schooners and 3,755 Gloucester men were lost. In 1879 alone, Gloucester lost 29 schooners and 249 fishermen, including thirteen vessels and 143 men who died in a single gale on the night of 20 February. During this period, Gloucester rarely had a population larger than 10,000. The memorial service at the end of *Captains Courageous,* when the names of 117 dead from that year alone are to be read out, one of the most powerful scenes in the novel, tears Harvey Cheyne apart and makes him feel "all crowded up and shivery" (ch. 10).

Kipling thought he'd written a great story. He wrote to Conland, after the book had begun to appear serially, "I tell you that tale will be a snorter" (Letter of 8–24 November [1896]). Just before he died, Kipling sold the film rights to the novel, and it was made into a film directed by Victor Fleming and starring Spencer Tracy (1937). The use of authentic footage of actual fishermen and fishing schooners at work on the Grand Banks makes the film an invaluable document. A musical based on the Kipling novel, with music by Frederick Freyer and book and lyrics by Patrick Cook, enjoyed moderate success in a run that opened at the Manhattan Theatre Club in February 1999.

FURTHER READING: Bercaw Edwards, Mary K. " 'That Tale Will Be a Snorter': The Writing of *Captains Courageous,*" *The Log of Mystic Seaport* 48 (1996): 16–21; Garland, Joseph E. *Down to the Sea: The Fishing Schooners of Gloucester.* Boston: David R. Godine, 1983; McAveeney, David C. *Kipling in Gloucester: The Writing of Captains Courageous.* Gloucester, MA: Curious Traveller, 1996.

Mary K. Bercaw Edwards

CARIBBEAN LITERATURE OF THE SEA. An island is defined by its surrounding waters, and so the Caribbean Sea has shaped and delimited the Caribbean archipelago, often reflecting the region's history. The sea brought Christopher Columbus,* whose expedition from Spain ultimately doomed the native Taino Indians; the sea brought centuries of European expansionism and imperialism. Later, the sea brought Africans through their perilous Middle Passage to slavery. Although the sea provided economic opportunity through migration to England in the 1940s and 1950s, the result was the separation of families and isolation for West Indians in London. The terrifying flight of Haitian refugees to Miami has emerged as the most recent defining sea journey.

Not surprisingly, then, the canon of Caribbean literature contains a paucity of purely positive images of the sea. Jean Rhys, in her "prequel" to Charlotte Brontë's *Jane Eyre* (1847), takes the title *Wide Sargasso Sea* (1966) for her novel, referring to an area of the Atlantic Ocean choked with sea grass, to symbolize human lethargy and entrapment. Indeed, most Caribbean writers, including Derek Walcott,* approach the sea with ambiguity at best. Caribbean literature seems, in fact, to be dominated by the powerful, overarching association of the sea as an instrument of exploitation, most profoundly the nightmare of the Middle Passage.

One of the strongest indictments of the sea occurs in the recent novel by Guyanese writer Fred D'Aguiar, *Feeding the Ghosts* (1997). The novel centers on a ship captain's brutal decision to throw 132 dead or dying slaves into the sea; D'Aguiar describes how their lives were so easily and thoroughly swallowed up by the sea as if it were complicit in the slavery itself.

Jamaica Kincaid, from Antigua, writes of both rivers and the sea in her works. In *A Small Place* (1988) she imagines a tourist's excitement at seeing the beautiful Caribbean Sea, then undercuts that with images of contaminated sewage flowing into the sea, and, finally, reminds the reader of the slaves who died in the very same waters.

Slave imagery appears as well in *The Chosen Place, the Timeless People* (1984), where Paule Marshall, of Barbados, imagines the sounds of the ocean as the lament of doomed slaves. Yet the sea facilitates a journey back to Africa in her *Praisesong for the Widow* (1983), when a proper, middle-class American is driven by self-doubts and the urgings of a strange and ancient man to abandon a luxury cruise and embark on a voyage of an altogether different sort. During this symbolic return to her roots, she is violently ill but recovers, purged and reborn, with newfound enthusiasm for her lost African heritage.

Haitian-born Edwidge Danticat, writing about the hardships Haitians endure to reach Miami, connects their sea journey to both the Middle Passage *from* Africa and a return *to* Africa in "Children of the Sea" from her collection *Krik? Krak!* (1995).

George Lamming, in Barbados, follows the migration patterns of an earlier generation in *The Emigrants* (1954), which tells of several men who voyage from the West Indies to England. He foreshadows their fate by describing the oil-laden, sinister darkness of the sea as it surrounds their ship in port. Nearly twenty years later, Lamming uses an allegorical sea voyage in *Natives of My Person* (1972). In the section entitled "The Middle Passage," he records an excursion aboard the ship *Reconnaissance*, which sails from the corrupted Old World to the New World in an idealistic, but doomed, attempt to found a new society.

A journey from the Old World to the New is also the subject of Trinidadian-born V. S. Naipaul's travel book *The Middle Passage* (1962). Here, Naipaul returns home to the Caribbean for a visit after years of absence and offers his acerbic assessment not only of Trinidad but also of other Caribbean islands.

Barbadian poet and editor Frank Collymore concedes the sea's beauty, but in "Return" from *Collected Poems* (1959) writes of its "dark embrace" and likens the sea to a "mother vomiting her living and her dead" (47). Also from that volume, in "Hymn to the Sea," Collymore identifies the sea as the source of love, sustenance, and even philosophical musings but concludes with its integral contradictions of life-giver and destroyer (48). Collymore mentored many poets, fellow Barbadian Kamau Brathwaite among them, and the sea appears frequently in Brathwaite's work. While images of boys frolicking and playing cricket on the beach are frequent, for Brathwaite, the sea also carries the weight of history, as numerous examples from his canon would indicate. For example, in "The Cracked Mother" from *Islands* (1969), Brathwaite first imagines "three nuns"—Columbus' boats—and later refers to slave ships sailing to the New World.

Slavery is also connected to the sea, at least initially, in *Return to My Native Land* (1938) by Martiniquan Aimé Césaire. Early in this book-length poem, Césaire compares the sea to an aggressive boxer and a "great dog licking and biting the shins of the beach" (48) and refers to his people as "we, vomit of the slave ships" (67). Eventually, though, he envisions a transformed future.

The sea is more personal for such poets as Marvin E. Williams (St. Croix), Christopher Laird (Trinidad), and Geoffrey Philp (Jamaica), yet it remains more often than not connected with drownings or grief. Philp records his father-fisherman's death in "Bull Bay" from *Exodus and Other Poems* (1990).

The enticements of swimming and recreational sailing are generally the province of the nonnative writer. The early poems of Laurence Lieberman,* a midwestern poet who focuses on the Caribbean, for instance, extol undersea life. Twentieth-century novelists such as Graham Greene and Alec Waugh detail the British expatriate life by the Caribbean Sea. An exception is American writer Ernest Hemingway,* who took as his hero a Cuban fisherman and sensitively portrayed his experiences in the Pulitzer Prize-winning novella *The Old Man and the Sea** (1952).

For the most part, indigenous writers have opted to reveal the breadth and depth of Caribbean society, to describe its people, politics, and heritage. Thus, for a great number of native-born Caribbean writers, the waters surrounding the Caribbean, however beautiful and compelling, must bear the curse of history.

FURTHER READING: Brown, Lloyd W. *West Indian Poetry.* Boston: Twayne, 1980; Burnett, Paula, ed. *The Penguin Book of Caribbean Verse in English.* New York: Penguin, 1986; Dance, Daryl Cumber: *New World Adams: Conversations with Contemporary West Indian Writers.* Leeds: Peepal Tree Books, 1992; King, Bruce, ed. *West Indian Literature.* 2d ed. London: Macmillan, 1995; Markham, E. A., ed. *Penguin Book of Short Stories.* New York: Penguin, 1996; Waters, Erika J., ed. *The Caribbean Writer.* Vols. 1–12. St. Croix: University of the Virgin Islands, 1987–1999; Waters, Erika J., ed. *New Writing from the Caribbean.* London: Macmillan, 1994.

Erika J. Waters

CARLISLE, HENRY COFFIN (1926–   ). Born in San Francisco, Henry Coffin Carlisle served in the U.S. Naval Reserve from 1944 to 1946, earned a B.A. and M.A. at Stanford University in 1950 and 1953, and entered the book trade as an editor in New York City. He now lives in San Francisco and maintains a summer home on Nantucket.*

He began writing nautical fiction with *Voyage to the First of December*

(1972), which retells the story of the 1842 *Somers** mutiny* from the perspective of the ship's surgeon, Robert Leacock. The novel explores the event's psychological undercurrents and sympathizes with the three men who were precipitately executed.

The Jonah Man (1984, repub. 2000) is a fictional autobiography of George Pollard, the Nantucket whaleman who captained the *Essex** when it was rammed by a whale in 1820. Along with part of his crew, he escaped in a whaleboat, where he survived by resorting to cannibalism before he was rescued by another ship. His next voyage also ended in shipwreck,* forever marking him as a doomed man, a "Jonah." The *Essex* disaster inspired the final chapters of *Moby-Dick** (1851) and a short section of *Clarel* (1876), where Herman Melville* characterizes Pollard as a Jonah. Carlisle's novel mentions both sources. By presenting Pollard's experiences autobiographically, Carlisle adds psychological and spiritual depth to the story, along with credible descriptions of life at sea and in nineteenth-century Nantucket. [*See also* MUTINIES; NICKERSON, THOMAS; SEA-DELIVERANCE NARRATIVES]

Dennis Berthold

CARSE, ROBERT (1902–1971). A Great Lakes* sailor at seventeen, Robert Carse later worked salt water, attaining the position of chief mate. He sailed most of the world and developed a reputation as an expert seaman and maritime historian. Carse claimed to have spent half of his life on water, and he must have spent the other half writing about it. In short stories, serials, articles, and nearly fifty books, Carse wrote for both children and adults. In *There Go the Ships* (1942) and *A Cold Corner of Hell* (1969), Carse drew from his own experiences as a merchant seaman in the Murmansk Convoy, which lost half its ships during its 1942 run. *The Beckoning Waters* (1953) recounts a fictional immigrant's struggle to become a Great Lakes captain around the turn of the century. Other works include *Deep Six* (1946), *The Twilight of Sailing Ships* (1965), and *The Great Lakes Story* (1968).

Donald P. Curtis

CARSON, RACHEL [LOUISE] (1907–1964). Though Rachel Carson's fame as an environmental writer rests on the warnings about pesticide pollution in her last book, *Silent Spring* (1962), her previous three books on the sea established her reputation. *Under the Sea Wind: A Naturalist's Picture of Ocean Life* (1941), *The Sea around Us* (1951), and *The Edge of the Sea* (1955) offer an enduring picture of the ocean and its inhabitants, presented by a writer who not only understood the science involved but could also express research findings in exquisite prose. Carson's work revealed the current state of scientific knowledge while at the same time conveying her own sense of the wonder and the majesty of her subject.

Born into a rural setting outside Pittsburgh, she showed an early aptitude for writing and entered what is now Chatham College, planning to major in English, but she shifted to biology and attended the Marine Biological Laboratory at Woods Hole, Massachusetts, in 1929. Writing a thesis on catfish, she earned an M.S. degree in zoology from Johns Hopkins University and in 1935 was hired by the government agency that later became the U.S. Fish and Wildlife Service, rising eventually to the position of biologist and editor in chief of the service's publications.

Under the Sea Wind uses the point of view of marine creatures, notably a seabird, a mackerel, and an eel, to present a broad picture of ocean life. Though the book was well received by critics, not until *The Sea around Us* ten years later did Carson attain wide recognition. *The Sea around Us* encapsulated geology, physical oceanography, and the history of human interactions with the ocean in Carson's characteristic visionary prose. It was a runaway success, winning major awards and becoming the basis of a feature film of the same title (1953).

The success of *The Sea around Us* enabled Carson to leave the Fish and Wildlife Service and build a cottage overlooking the sea in Maine, where she spent summers exploring coastal tide pools. *The Edge of the Sea* covered the rocky coasts, beaches, and reefs of the Atlantic coast and was, like its predecessor four years earlier, a best-seller. It was a tribute to Carson's vision and prose style that she could manage to create enthusiasm in the general public with a book that is essentially a nature guide to coastal ecology. One of her great gifts to American literature was the demonstration that there is no necessary conflict between art and science: her roles as author, scientist, and environmental activist reciprocated and supported one another. The 1961 revision of *The Sea around Us* incorporated new scientific findings and sounded a warning about the dumping of nuclear wastes in the oceans.

In 1962 Carson published the work for which she is currently most famous, *Silent Spring*, which alerted the public to the poisonous dangers of uncontrolled pesticide use. Savagely attacked by chemical companies and other critics and already severely ill with the cancer that would eventually kill her, Carson fought for pesticide regulation until her death, continuing her speaking engagements and correspondence.

Though the historic importance of *Silent Spring* as an early environmental warning continues to overshadow Carson's books on the oceans and sea life, her presentation of lucid scientific knowledge informed by a lyrical vision has continued to attract appreciative readers. As she pointed out in her acceptance speech for the National Book Award in 1952: "If there is poetry in my book about the sea, it is not because I deliberately put it there, but because no one could write truthfully about the sea and leave out the poetry."

FURTHER READING: Brooks, Paul. *The House of Life: Rachel Carson at Work.* Boston: Houghton Mifflin, 1972; Carson, Rachel. *Always, Rachel: The Letters of*

Rachel Carson and Dorothy Freeman, 1952–1964. Ed. Martha Freeman. Boston: Beacon, 1994; Lear, Linda. *Rachel Carson, Witness for Nature.* New York: Holt, 1997.

Betsy S. Hilbert

CATHERWOOD, MARY HARTWELL (1847–1902). Mary Hartwell Catherwood began her career with realistic stories of the midwest frontier but focused on stories of the French in early America after her novel *The Romance of Dollard* (1888). This interest merged with her love for Mackinac Island, where she spent her summers from 1892 to 1899, resulting in several works of fiction.

The White Islander (1893) tells melodramatically of Alexander Henry's escape from Fort Michilimackinac during "Pontiac's conspiracy." Catherwood probably relied on Francis Parkman's historical work here, as she often did, but the love for Mackinac Island expressed through her descriptions is distinctly her own. The stories in *Mackinac and Other Stories* (1899) are based on both historical research and folklore. For example, "Marianson" tells how a beautiful French widow saved a Canadian* deserter from the British and Sioux forces as they were about to attack the Americans in the Mackinac fortress during the War of 1812. She fell in love with him and arranged for his escape but, upon returning to the cave where he was hidden, found that the Sioux had discovered, killed, and scalped him. "The Penitent of Cross Village" ends happily when a Chippewa fisherman discovers that his partner is not lying drowned at the bottom of St. Mary's River, where he thought he had left him after a drunken quarrel, but is still alive and able to marry his wife's cousin. Some stories in *The Chase of Saint-Castin and Other Stories of the French in the New World* (1894) further portray the French in the St. Lawrence River and Great Lakes* regions.

Kenneth A. Robb

CHASE, OWEN (1796–1869). Author of *Narrative of the Shipwreck* of the Whale-Ship* Essex,* of Nantucket* (1821), Owen Chase was first mate if the *Essex* when it was stove and sunk by a whale in the Pacific Ocean, 20 November 1820. The unprecedented whale attack and the three-month survival at sea of some of the crew made the event a legend. In Chapter 45 of *Moby-Dick* Herman Melville* says that he saw Owen Chase (apparently a faulty recollection on Melville's part), met Owen's son at sea, and read a copy of the *Narrative* borrowed from Owen's son. The *Narrative* is the main dramatic source for the ending of *Moby-Dick*.

A native of Nantucket, Chase was one of five brothers to serve as whaling captains. His first ship after the *Essex* was the *Winslow* in 1825, and his next command the *Charles Carroll*. Chase was married four times and is buried on Nantucket next to three of his wives.

Thomas Farel Heffernan

CHEEVER, HENRY T[HEODORE]. (1814–1897). Editor of the *New York Evangelist* (1849–1852), Henry T. Cheever was born and educated in Maine. In the early 1840s he voyaged as a passenger on the whaleship *Commodore Preble* and in late 1849 or early 1850 published *The Whale and His Captors*, a major source for Herman Melville's* *Moby-Dick** (1851).

Like Richard Henry Dana, Jr.,* Cheever began his book of maritime experience with a reference to Virgil's *Aeneid* and claimed daguerreotypical realism for his work. Cheever did not hesitate to weave "moral hints" into his work, and thus *The Whale and His Captors* became exactly the kind of work the brothers Harper sought as they attempted to provide the country with inspirational reading. The book was instantly reprinted in England as *The Whaleman's Adventures* (part of the American subtitle) with an introduction by William Scoresby the younger, Melville's "Captain Sleet."

Cheever's book was advertised in *The Literary World* when Melville returned from England early in 1850. Howard Vincent's observations in *The Trying-out of* Moby-Dick (1949) do not suggest that Melville turned to the work for any structural guidance: instead, he seems to have gleaned from the work metaphors, definitions, and occasional bursts of nationalism or piety that Melville would rework late in the process of composition. Perhaps Cheever's diction was more important to Melville than his subject matter. But except for J. Ross Browne's* *Etchings of a Whaling Cruise* (1846), which Melville already owned, Cheever's book may have been the most readily available of Melville's major sources. From Cheever's preface onward Melville would have read of the delights of sea meditations, Matthew Fontaine Maury's* study of whale migration, Samuel Taylor Coleridge's "Rime of the Ancient Mariner" (1798), and the piety of the younger William Scoresby, who had himself at one time served as the chaplain of the mariners' church at Liverpool. Even Cheever's running heads read like the chapter titles of *Moby-Dick*.

Cheever also published *Life in the Sandwich Islands* (1851) and edited the travel books of Chaplain Walter Colton of the U.S. Navy. He died in Worcester, Massachusetts.

R. D. Madison

CHEEVER, JOHN (1912–1982). John Cheever, a writer of predominantly short fiction, uses seaside cottages and beaches as backgrounds for many of his stories. Sometimes Cheever's depiction of the sea is more significant, however, with references to the sea possessing curative, erotic, and even redemptive powers.

A belief in the spiritually curative benefit of the sea is expressed by several of Cheever's characters. In "Brimmer" (1959), the narrator suggests that relationships filled with tension on the land can be escaped in the water. In "Goodbye, My Brother" (1951), swimming in the sea allows members of a family to suppress dislike of their brother; when they emerge from the waters, their words are filled with kindness for him. The narrator of the story suggests that the act of swimming in the sea has an effect like baptism, cleansing human spirits of negativity.

Cheever combines the erotic and the religious through nudity in his stories. In *The Wapshot Chronicle* (1957), the sea's properties are claimed by Venus, an erotic figure of worship. In "The Seaside Houses" (1961), the narrator believes that people approach the sea as lovers. Cheever includes the scents of the seawater and women's breasts among life's perfumes in "A Miscellany of Characters That Will Not Appear" (1960). Ocean landscape evokes the erotic in "The Trouble of Marcie Flint" (1957), where the sea islands are compared to a woman's thighs, and in "The Golden Age" (1959), the hills of the shore are compared to women's breasts. In *Bullet Park* (1969), the nakedness of swimmers on ordinary beaches is compared to religious images of eternity and the apocalypse, which also depict naked figures. In "Montraldo" (1964), a typical beach scene is compared to a mythical paradise.

A famous image of naked women and the sea appears at the conclusion of "Goodbye, My Brother" when the narrator sees his wife and sister walk out of the sea. The nudity of the women recalls Venus' birth from the sea and the nakedness in Eden. The image of women walking out of the sea, which is repeated in *The Wapshot Chronicle*, is consistent with Cheever's view of the sea as possessing both the erotic and redemptive qualities of paradise.

Robert Imes

CHOPIN, KATE [O'FLAHERTY] (1850–1904). Born in St. Louis, Missouri, Kate Chopin had no experience of the sea until her three-month European honeymoon in 1870. On her return to the United States, she moved with her husband to the coastal city of New Orleans, the setting of her best-known novel, *The Awakening* (1899). Like Chopin's other fiction, *The Awakening* can be aligned with nineteenth-century local color and regional works; however, its complex representation of the sea and the protagonist's response to it align it with symbolic, psychological, and philosophical literature.

At the upper-middle-class seaside resort where the novel opens, Edna Pontellier, a wife and mother, expresses a new consciousness of her senses and of unlimited possibilities by learning to swim in the sea. In describing Edna's awakening, Chopin writes with a lyrical prose that reflects the sensuous whispering of waves. Aware of the sea's danger, Edna nevertheless defies that danger just as she increasingly defies social conventions in accordance with her own impulses. Chopin points to potential problems in Edna's romantic attitude when, charmed by Creole folktales regarding hidden pirate* treasure and a Gulf Spirit's search for a lovely mortal, Edna leaves her family for a day to sail away with a young man to a provincial island. (In her only story concerning the sea, "At Chênière Caminada" [1894], which is set on this same island, Chopin recounts the nearly tragic infatuation that a young island man develops for a sophisticated New Orleans woman when he takes her sailing on the enchanted Gulf waters.) In *The Awakening*'s conclusion, Edna, alienated from society and family, returns to the seaside resort, symbolically removes her incumbering bathing suit, and takes her final swim. Readers of Chopin's novel continue to debate whether Edna's suicide is narcissistic or liberating, self-destructive or self-fulfilling.

Elizabeth Schultz

CIRCUMNAVIGATIONS AND BLUE-WATER PASSAGES. In 1876 Alfred Johnson singlehandedly crossed the Atlantic in his twenty-foot dory *Centennial* from Gloucester, Massachusetts, to Abercastle, Wales, which took fifty-nine days. Johnson was a handline Banks fisherman completely familiar with dories. Thus began the age of singlehanded sailing. The first person to make a singlehanded circumnavigation was Nova Scotia-born Joshua Slocum,* a professional sea captain who built the thirty-six-foot, nine-inch sloop *Spray* from the remains of an old oyster sloop. Slocum's dry wit and nautical competence made *Sailing Alone around the World the* classic circumnavigation account, first published in 1900 and still in print. The smallest American sailboat to round Cape Horn* as of 1985 was sailed by a father-and-son team, David and Daniel Hays, in a twenty-five-foot Vertue, a fiberglass replica of a proven blue-water design. The two Hays present their nautical and psychological account in *My Old Man and the Sea* (1995).

The Venturesome Voyages of Captain Voss (1913) by John Claus Voss is a classic in the Slocum tradition. Voss, like Slocum, was a professional sea captain at the end of the age of sail. Voss hoped to follow in Slocum's wake but believed his written account would be profitable only if his vessel were smaller and unique. Accordingly, he decked over a large Indian dugout canoe and stepped three small masts. *Tilikum* was thirty-eight feet overall, including the figurehead, five feet, six inches wide, and drew two feet when completely loaded. Voss sailed from Victoria, B.C., to London (1901–1904). Although not a technical circumnavigation, the tip of Africa was rounded, and the narrow and shallow vessel survived many gales, which fortune Voss attributed to his sea anchor, a cone-shaped canvas bag streamed from the bow. Voss lost his crew member overboard and sailed alone for 1,200 miles. Unlike Slocum, Voss offers technical advice to small-boat voyagers, including an account of surviving a typhoon in the twenty-five-foot, eight-inch yawl *Sea Queen*.

Following World War I, sailors from many nations went to sea. Among these was Harry Pidgeon, born on an Iowa farm, who built the thirty-four-foot yawl *Islander*, an enlarged *Sea Bird*-type similar to Voss' *Sea Queen*. Pidgeon, an amateur boat builder and sailor, solo-circumnavigated twice, 1921–1925 and 1932–1937. His well-written account, *Around the World*

Single-Handed (1933), inspired other amateurs with limited means and skills.

Vito Dumas, an Argentine rancher, made a remarkable circumnavigation 1942–1943, rounding the great capes and making only three landfalls. Captain Raymond Johnes translated *Alone through the Roaring Forties* (1960), enabling English-speaking readers to learn how Dumas singlehanded his thirty-one-foot, six-inch double-ended ketch *Legh II* over the planet's heaviest seas. John Guzzwell built the twenty-foot, six-inch yawl *Trekka* and singlehandedly circumnavigated, leaving from Victoria, B.C. (1953–1957). Guzzwell's Trekka *round the World* (1963) demonstrated what a well-designed and superbly sailed microcruiser could do; his clear, honest, and unmelodramatic style is both informative and inspiring.

Dumas and Guzzwell were both experienced blue-water sailors prior to circumnavigating. Perhaps copy editor Robert Manry's Atlantic crossing (1965) in the thirteen-foot, six-inch sloop *Tinkerbelle* captivated the public precisely because of Manry's apparent nautical innocence. He seemed to have gone out for an afternoon's sail and stayed out long enough to cross an ocean. *Trekka* and *Tinkerbelle* set "smallest" records, *Trekka*'s lasting until 1980. Manry's book, *Tinkerbelle* (1966), reveals that he had carefully studied the history of ocean crossing in midget sailboats, but his knowledge was mostly theoretical; he first learned how to deploy his sea anchor and learned that *Tinkerbelle* was indeed self-righting while in passage.

Hugo S. Vihlen, a pilot living in Florida, had his six-foot boat designed and built for an Atlantic passage. In 1968 his eighty-five-day second attempt from Casablanca to just off the coast of Florida was successful. *April Fool* (1971) reveals what a resolute amateur can accomplish. In 1993 Vihlen sailed the five-foot, four-inch *Father's Day* from St. John's, Newfoundland, to Falmouth, England, in 105 days. Minnesota schoolteacher Gerry Spiess designed, built, and sailed the ten-foot *Yankee Girl* from Chesapeake Bay to Falmouth, Cornwall, in 1979, taking 54 days. The voyage is presented in *Alone against the Atlantic* (1981), written by Spiess with Marlin Bree. Spiess subsequently crossed the Pacific in *Yankee Girl* from California to Australia in 1981. In 1999 Tori Murden was the first American and the first woman to row solo across the Atlantic, a feat she accomplished in eighty-one days beginning in the Canary Islands and ending in Guadeloupe.

Two single-handed circumnavigations are noteworthy because of the young age of the sailors. Robin Lee Graham was sixteen when he departed in 1965. With Derek L. T. Gill he wrote *Dove* (1972; the story first appeared as three *National Geographic* articles [1968, 1969, 1970]; the Gregory Peck-produced film, *The* Dove, appeared in 1974). Tania Aebi, who was eighteen when she departed in 1985, wrote *Maiden Voyage* (1989) with Bernadette Brennan.

Among notable ocean races was the 1960 initiation of the *Observer*'s Singlehanded Transatlantic Race (OSTAR), won by Francis Chichester. The

OSTAR spawned similar events, including the Golden Globe nonstop, sin-glehanded race around the world in 1968. At age sixty-five, American Philip S. Weld won the 1980 OSTAR in *Moxie*, a fifty-foot trimaran. An experi-enced multihull racer, Weld describes the race and the events leading to it in *Moxie* (1981). Dodge Morgan set the record for the fastest singlehanded, nonstop circumnavigation eastabout via the capes in 1985–1986; his ac-count is presented in *The Voyage of* American Promise (1989).

The epic account of poet Webb Chiles appears in his *Storm Passage* (1977). Chiles sailed three-quarters of the way around the world before being imprisoned and his boat confiscated by a Red Sea nation whose of-ficials could not believe he was *yachting* around the world in an eighteen-foot boat. Chiles tells of storms, shipwreck, and physical and psychological suffering, and he offers joy and triumph as well in *Open Boat across the Pacific* (1982) and *The Ocean Waits* (1984).

Bill Pinkney was the first African American solo circumnavigator (1990–1992); departing and arriving at the Charlestown Navy Yard, Boston, he rounded all of the most challenging and the stormiest capes, including Cape Horn, the Cape of Good Hope, and Cape Leeuwin. Pinkney sailed in a forty-seven-foot cutter named the *Commitment* and produced a packet for schoolchildren called "The Middle Passage Project." Hundreds of sailboats now circumnavigate in relative safety made possible by electronic aids to steering, navigating, weather forecasting, and communications. The sea re-mains open, but an electronic umbilical cord connects current sailors to shore. A comprehensive bibliography that includes the preceding works not individually listed in the following can be found in Henderson. [*See also* CRUISING LITERATURE; *DARING THE SEA*]

FURTHER READING: Borden, Charles A. *Sea Quest*. Philadelphia: Macrae Smith, 1967; Clarke, Derrick H. *Blue Water Dream*. New York: David McKay, 1981; Do-herty, John Stephen, *The Boats They Sailed In*. New York: Norton, 1985; Henderson, Richard. *Singlehanded Sailing*. 2d ed. Camden: International Marine, 1988; Holm, Don. *The Circumnavigators*. Englewood Cliffs, NJ: Prentice-Hall, 1974.

Lee F. Werth

CLANCY, TOM (1947–   ). *The Hunt for Red October* (1984) was Tom Clancy's first published novel, catapulting him to celebrity. Fast-paced ac-tion, subtle character development, and accurate and abundant technical information make this a suspenseful and convincing story, one more focused on the sea than this popular author's other novels. It is a tale of the surren-der of the largest, most threatening Soviet supersubmarine ever manufac-tured, commanded by Marko Ramius, who leads the defection. The stakes are high for both Cold War superpowers, as is always the case in post–World War II versions of this genre: the technology that Ramius controls is of critical strategic importance to the Soviets and Americans. A 1990 film ad-aptation starred Sean Connery and Alec Baldwin.

Other Clancy novels, such as *The Cardinal of the Kremlin* (1988), which involves another submarine, and *Clear and Present Danger* (1989), which develops the character of Jack Ryan—formidable Central Intelligence Agency (CIA) agent, Vietnam veteran, and navy SEAL (SEa-Air-Land)— are set partially on water, the latter on Chesapeake Bay, where the search for drugs and their lords and peddlers drives the action. The 1994 film adaptation of *Clear and Present Danger* starred Harrison Ford.

Precluded by poor eyesight from serving in the military, Clancy has acquired his wide-ranging, sophisticated knowledge of technology and military and foreign affairs strategies from unclassified public documents, a fact he again demonstrated in *Submarine: A Guided Tour inside a Nuclear Warship* (1995).

Donald Yannella

[CLEMENS, SAMUEL LANGHORNE], "MARK TWAIN" (1835– 1910). Though more widely known for his writing on the Mississippi River, Samuel Clemens traveled extensively at sea, experiences that find their way into a number of the writings he published under the name Mark Twain. His prose accounts of sea voyages contain much that is typical of Twain's acute observations, social commentary, and wry humor.

Twain's first sea literature can be found among the letters detailing his voyage to the Sandwich Islands printed in 1866 in the *Sacramento Union* and published in a revised form in *Roughing It* (1872). Among the passages of Hawai'i and its culture are some describing his fellow passengers, his sense of exhilaration and irritation at being at sea, and his graphic account of dashing through the waves in a native canoe. For Clemens, this voyage initiated a lifelong love of Hawai'i.

These qualities describe Twain's later travel writings as well. *Innocents Abroad* (1869), culled like *Roughing It* from reports written to newspapers, records Twain's voyage to and around Europe and the Holy Land. The narrative begins with a lively and extensive description of the preparations and the voyage, Twain again lauding the excitement and camaraderie of life on a pleasure cruise, with its dancing, playing games, and swapping stories. Twain also devotes some of his best prose to the beauties of the seascapes and the islands sighted. Following this opening section, Twain's rambles through the Mediterranean countries are punctuated by only brief passages at sea, and he ends with a very short account of the monotony of the voyage home.

Later in his career, Twain undertook an even more ambitious cruise, an around-the-world lecture tour recorded in *Following the Equator* (1897). Although most of the narrative concerns travels on land, mainly in Australia and India, the passages at sea again reveal Twain's love of sea voyages, and again he presents lush descriptions, interesting characters, and humorous stories, here even more comic and unstructured than in the previous narratives. Twain's exuberant accounts of sea life are, however, in marked contrast to his condemnations of the imperialism he witnesses on land.

At the time of writing *Following the Equator*, Twain also produced three unfinished sea-disaster stories (later collected in *Which Was the Dream*, a volume written in 1897 but unpublished until John F. Tuckey's 1966 edition), considered but rejected for inclusion in the narrative. "The Enchanted Sea-Wilderness," a short fragment, records the trials of sailors who, forced to abandon ship, drift into a circle of currents between the Cape of Good Hope and the South Pole. "The Great Dark" injects elements of fantasy into the sea-disaster motif, as it describes a family's microscopic voyage in a drop of water. Finally, "An Adventure in Remote Seas" expands the motif developed in "The Enchanted Sea-Wilderness" and involves a sealing expedition to an island in the Antarctic* Sea.

FURTHER READING: Neider, Charles, ed. *The Travels of Mark Twain*. New York: Coward-McCann, 1961; Tuckey, John S., ed. *The Devil's Race-Track: Mark Twain's Great Dark Writings, The Best from "Which Was the Dream?" and "Fables of Man."* Berkeley: U of California P, 1966; Tuckey, John S., ed. *Mark Twain's "Which Was the Dream?" and Other Symbolic Writings of the Later Years*. Berkeley: U of California P, 1967.

John Samson

[CODMAN, JOHN], "CAPTAIN RINGBOLT" (1814–1900). John Codman, a well-traveled sea captain and writer, was born in Dorchester, Massachusetts, in 1814. A pastor's son, he enjoyed listening to lengthy theological discussions with visiting clergymen, but he realized that, like his maternal grandfather, the sea was his true calling. After two years at Amherst College (1832–1834), Codman put to sea on a clipper ship, the first of many voyages for him. During his long career he traveled to China and the East Indies, commanded the troop ship *William Penn* during the Crimean War, was the captain of the supply ship *Quaker City* in the Civil War, and ran coastal traders in Brazil.

Drawing on his vast experience at sea, Codman wrote *Sailors' Lives and Sailors' Yarns* in 1847, a work that was reviewed by Herman Melville* in the first issue of the *Literary World* (1847). In this context his persona became one "Captain Ringbolt," who waxes eloquent with opinions on life at sea, ranging from advice to passengers and types of construction, to the concerns of captains and the problems of sailors.

After the Civil War Codman resumed his writing, publishing sea-related works such as *Ten Months in Brazil* (1867) and *An American Transport in the Crimean War* (1896). Codman then became an Idaho ranch owner, writing about his experiences in the American West in *The Round Trip* (1879) and *Winter Sketches from the Saddle* (1888). An activist as well as a storyteller, Codman published numerous pamphlets that favored free ships and materials for shipbuilders and opposed subsidies for the merchant marine. Codman was married to Anna G. Day of New York, who accompanied him on many of his journeys. He died at his daughter's home in Boston.

Lisa Franchetti

COKER, DANIEL (1780–1846). The son of a white servant and a black slave, Daniel Coker was born in Maryland as Isaac Wright, changing his name when he escaped to New York. After buying his freedom, he moved to Baltimore to be a minister, teacher, and abolitionist. Coker helped create a separate Methodist church for blacks, later named the Bethel African Methodist Episcopal Church. He wrote several pamphlets, including *A Dialogue between a Virginian and an African Minister* (1810). In 1816 the newly formed African Methodist Episcopal Church elected Coker its bishop, but he resigned the next day. Coker sailed to Sierra Leone in 1820, settling in Africa as part of the American Colonization Society's effort to establish a colony for the emigration of free blacks and to provide support for ships working against the slave trade.

In 1820 Edward J. Coale published the *Journal of Daniel Coker, a Descendant of Africa: from the Time of Leaving New York in the Ship* Elizabeth *Capt. Sebor on a Voyage for Sherbo in Africa in Company with Three Agents and about Ninety Persons of Colour . . . with an Appendix*. Coker writes with a devoted, religious tone. He describes a storm that separates the *Elizabeth* from the ship of war meant to accompany her. The next day they discover a wrecked and deserted vessel with all hands apparently lost. After thirty-four days at sea, the *Elizabeth* drops anchor in Freetown, Sierra Leone. Coker chronicles his experiences ashore and sailing the coast, including observations of the slave trade. He hears a story about an illegal Spanish slaver who poisoned 400 Africans when the vessel was discovered by an English ship; only 6 survived. [*See also* AFRICAN AMERICAN LITERATURE OF THE SEA; SLAVE NARRATIVES]

Richard J. King

COLCORD, JOANNA CARVER (1882–1960). Born aboard the *Charlotte A. Littlefield*, a vessel commanded by her father, Joanna Carver Colcord spent her first eighteen years at sea. She went ashore to attend the University of Maine and graduated in 1906 with a degree in chemistry. Colcord had a successful career as a social worker and was the author of numerous works on the subject, but her interest in seafaring culture never waned. In 1924 she compiled the first comprehensive collection of American sea songs, *Roll and Go: Songs of American Sailormen*, which was revised and reissued as *Songs of American Sailormen* (1938). *Sea Language Comes Ashore* followed in 1945, as did several articles in *The American Neptune* on family life at sea. When she was posted to the Virgin Islands by the American Red Cross, Colcord undertook a study of West Indian songs and corresponded on the subject with folklorists John and Alan Lomax at the Library of Congress.

"Storm Along: An American Sea Anthology," an unpublished manuscript that presents a timeline of American history illustrated with relevant sea poetry, was deposited at the Peabody Essex Museum in Salem, Massachusetts, in 1947.

Though she spent almost two decades at sea, Joanna Colcord was concerned that her gender would make hers a less acceptable voice of the seafaring community, and she considered publishing *Roll and Go* under her initials only. Her brother (and shipmate), the poet Lincoln Colcord,* convinced her otherwise. [*See also* SEA MUSIC; WOMEN AT SEA]

Mary Malloy

COLCORD, LINCOLN ROSS (1883–1947). Lincoln Ross Colcord, author of sea fiction and maritime historian, was born at sea aboard the bark *Charlotte A. Littlefield*, commanded by his father, Lincoln Alden Colcord of Searsport, Maine. Colcord spent much of his first fourteen years aboard deepwater vessels, an experience that instilled in the boy an abiding love of the sea and strongly influenced his interests and pursuits of later years. Fifth-generation seafarers, Colcord and his sister are the subjects of Parker Bishop Albee Jr.'s *Letters from Sea, 1882–1901: Joanna and Lincoln Colcord's Seafaring Childhood* (1999).

By 1916 Colcord emerged as an important literary figure. Macmillan had published three of his books, and some twenty sea stories and several poems had appeared in magazines such as *American, Bookman, McClure's,* and *Hampton.* Bert Bender wrote in *Sea Brothers: The Tradition of American Sea Fiction from* Moby-Dick* *to the Present* (1988) that the typhoon scene that appears in Colcord's sea novel *The Drifting Diamond* (1912) would have been appreciated even by Herman Melville.* In reviewing Colcord's first book of short stories of the sea, *The Game of Life and Death* (1914), the *New York Times* (1 November 1914) compared him favorably with Joseph Conrad, suggesting that "the spirit of the sea and the mystery of the Orient" infuse the works of both authors.

Following another book of sea stories, *An Instrument of the Gods* (1922), Colcord turned increasingly to the research and writing of maritime history. He assisted his sister, Joanna Carver Colcord,* with her collection of chanteys, *Roll and Go: Songs of American Sailormen* (1924). Colcord also compiled *Record of Vessels Built on Penobscot River and Bay* (1932).

In 1926 he became acquainted with Ole Edvart Rølvaag, a novelist who had spent his youth at sea as a fisherman off the coast of Norway. Working closely with the author, Colcord translated Rølvaag's first book, *Giants in the Earth: A Saga of the Prairie* (1927), from the Norwegian. The friendship between these two sailors led to Colcord's biographical article, "Rølvaag the Fisherman Shook His Fist at Fate" (*The American Magazine* [March 1928]).

The late 1920s found Colcord reviewing maritime and naval books for the *New York Herald Tribune*. In this capacity he reviewed a purported autobiography, *The Cradle of the Deep* (1929), by actress Joan Lowell, who claimed to have spent her first seventeen years at sea; Colcord's review exposed her work as fiction. His exposé caused a sensational literary controversy, and he emerged more firmly established than ever as a preeminent authority on the sea. In 1936 he proved instrumental in founding the Penobscot Marine Museum in Maine. *The American Neptune* was in part Colcord's creation, and he served as an editor and contributor until his death.

Parker Bishop Albee Jr.

COLUMBUS PLAYS. Christopher Columbus (1451–1506) was an Italian explorer who sailed under the auspices of Spain in an attempt to reach Asia voyaging west from Europe and who, in 1492, laid claim to discovering America. In all, he made four voyages.

The earliest stage version of the Columbus story is likely *El Nuevo Mundo*, a comedy in verse by the sixteenth-century Spanish playwright Lope de Vega and not published until 1950 in English and 1963 in Spanish. The first version staged in English was by the British playwright Thomas Morton, *Columbus: Or, The Discovery of America. An Historical Play*, first performed at the Theatre-Royal Covent Garden in 1792, thereafter playing in several American theaters (pub. England, 1792; America, 1794). Few American productions on a Columbus theme are known in the first half of the nineteenth century, though in France a popular melodrama by R. C. Guilbert de Pixérécourt (*Christophe Colomb: ou, La découvert du Nouveau monde*) opened at the Théâtre de la Gaîté on 5 September 1815 and was published that year. One of the first satiric treatments of the story is credited to John Brougham, who opened *Columbus el Filibustero!! A New and Audaciously Original Historica-Plagiaristic, Ante-National, Pre-Patriotic, and Omni-Local Confusion of Circumstances, Running through Two Acts and Four Centuries* at the Boston Theatre in 1858. Brougham, known for his lampoons of heroic dramas, toured his Columbus spoof throughout the United States and Great Britain.

Late nineteenth-century productions were mostly burlesques and spectacles. In England, entertainments based on the story were produced in 1869 at London's Gaiety Theatre and in 1889 by George Dance. New York's Windsor Theatre staged Webster Edgerly's *Christopher Columbus or, The Discovery of America* in 1890, and Imre Kiralfy, a popular producer and director of spectacles, offered *Columbus and the Discovery of America* in 1893. Chicago's Columbian Exposition of 1893 was to be the site of one of the largest theatrical spectacles ever imagined; Steele MacKaye's *The World-Finder*, which he dubbed a "spectatorio," was to be staged in its own massive, specially built theater with a 100,000-square-foot "ocean," telescopic stages, and special effects to simulate ocean waves, sunrises, sunsets, and rainstorms. MacKaye's theater was neither completed, nor was the play published, and his Columbus story was never seen except in a much scaled-down version after the exposition closed.

One of the best-regarded of all Columbus plays is Paul Claudel's *Christophe Colomb*. Originally written in 1930, its revival by Jean-Louis Barrault in 1953 is famous, and it became the basis of an opera by Darius Milhaud in the same year. Also well known is *Christopher Columbus* by the Belgian playwright Michel de Ghelderode, which premiered at the Théâtre Art et Action in Paris in 1928 (pub. in French, 1950; in English, 1964). Adapted by Lyon Phelps in English, it was revived several times in the United States, including productions at the Provincetown Playhouse (1961), New York's Jean Cocteau Theatre (1971), and Chicago's Goodman Theatre (1973). Dario Fo's satire of the Columbus voyage is called *Isabella, Three Ships and a Shyster* (first perf. 1963; pub. in Italian 1966, French 1971, German 1986, no Eng. trans.).

Several plays on the Columbus theme appeared in the 1990s, some reflecting Columbus in heroic and others in nonheroic terms. Don Nigro's *Mariner* (first perf. 1991; pub. 1991) sets the two received images of Columbus as adventurer-hero and colonialist-villain against each other and concludes that Columbus was a bit of both. *The Voyage*,* an opera with music by Philip Glass and text by David Henry Hwang, appeared at the Metropolitan Opera in 1992. That same year the Royal Shakespeare Company staged Richard Nelson's *Columbus and the Discovery of Japan* (pub. 1992), which focused on the explorer's creative character. Richard Epp's *Japango* (first perf. 1992; not pub.) has a similar emphasis on Columbus the man. Vermont's Bread and Puppet toured the United States with *Christopher Columbus: The New World Order* (first perf. 1992; not pub.), a two-part play developed by Peter Schumann that juxtaposed Columbus' voyage with conflict between environmental groups and a northern Quebec power company. *Terra Incognita*, a theater piece by Maria Irene Fornes and composer Roberto Sierra, premiered at New York's INTAR Hispanic Arts Center in May 1992 and has not been published.

Lynn Jacobson's essay "The Columbus Conundrum," published in the October 1992 issue of *American Theatre* (18–22), discusses the performance of Columbus plays. Donald L. Hixon's *Nineteenth-Century American Drama: A Finding Guide* (1977) cites English and American plays, operas, and librettos on a Columbus theme by little-known playwrights in the 1890s, such as Henry Peterson, George Lansing Raymond, John J. Harden, and Rev. M.M.A. Hartnedy, some of these writing for amateur groups. A prose treatment of this theme is *The Memoirs of Christopher Columbus*, by Stephen Marlowe (1987). [*See also THE ADMIRAL*; DRAMA OF THE SEA]

Paul Kosidowski

CONFEDERATE NAVAL FICTION. The exploits of Confederate naval forces have been captured in fictional form, and, although not as popular as ground battles and the turmoil of southern life, these sea or river tales represent a significant body of adult and juvenile* literature.

Confederate naval fiction has its roots in two titles published just before the turn of the twentieth century, and the battle of the ironclads was the subject of each. Warren L. Goss wrote the first book, *In the Navy* (1898), and Charles E. Banks and George C. Cooke followed the next year with the more successful *In Hampton Roads: A Dramatic Romance* (1899), a love story combined with the classic engagement of the ironclads *Monitor* and *Merrimack.** In 1906 Jesse Frothingham published *Running the Gauntlet: The Daring Exploits of Lieutenant Cushing, U.S.N.*, one of many works of fiction that, by focusing on the U.S. Navy, necessarily included an account of Southern ships and seamen.

Confederate naval fiction was dormant for the next twenty years until James Stuart Montgomery published an exciting tale of Confederate blockade running, *Tall Men* (1927). In 1939 Bruce Lancaster and Lowell Brentano utilized the same theme in *Bride of a Thousand Cedars*, the best-selling of these books to date. In 1944 James Howell Street's *By Valour and Arms* was published by the Dial Press and, through several later printings (the latest in 1964), has enjoyed almost as much success as any novel set in the Civil War. The book centers on the battle for Vicksburg through the eyes of a gunner on the C.S.S. *Arkansas.*

By 1951, following on his successful use of the American Revolution for fictional settings during the decade of the 1940s, Francis van Wyck Mason* began to use the Civil War for a setting and over the next fifteen years wrote dozens of Civil War novels, many of them using the Confederate navy in some way. The Civil War centennial resulted in a surge of novels centered around the "tragic era." Mason wrote four historical novels on naval action during the war, three with a distinctly Southern setting: *Proud New Flags* (1951), the story of building a Confederate navy; *Our Valiant Few* (1956), about blockade running and war profiteering; and *Blue Hurricane*, a 1957 sequel to *Proud New Flags*. Mason drowned off Bermuda in 1978; his last work, *Armored Giants* (1980), about life on the *Monitor* and *Merrimack*, was published posthumously.

Nearly a dozen novels of Confederate naval action appeared from 1956 to 1966, among them works by several popular fiction writers, including Frank Yerby, James D. Horan, John Claggett, Showell Styles, and Garland Roark.* Yerby's *The Rebel* (1956) centers on a blockade runner, while Roark uses Confederate and Union ships as settings in *The Outlawed Banner* (1956). Claggett's *Rebel* (1964) is the tragic story of a Southern naval hero who kills a close friend and falls in love with a spy. Horan and Styles follow history more closely. In one of the most popular Confederate novels, *Seek Out and Destroy* (1958), Horan uses experiences on board the Confederate raider *Shenandoah* at the close of the war in an exciting tale. Styles follows the raider *Alabama** in a similar style in *Number Two-Ninety* (1966). Still another novelist, Willard Wallace, utilized the daring adventures of the crew of the *Alabama* in *The Raiders: A Novel of the Civil War at Sea* (1970).

Lee Willoughby's two novels, *The Caribbeans* (1983) and *The Raiders* (1984), also follow the Confederate naval theme. More recently, four additional novelists have turned to Southern life at sea. The most intriguing of these is Louise Meriwether, the only woman and African American* to use the theme. Her *Fragments of the Ark* (1994) follows the historical attempts of runaway slaves* to take over a Confederate gunboat. Paul Williams wrote *The* Shenandoah *Affair* (1992), a historical romance in the vein of *Gone with the Wind*. Finally, Ireland's Harry Harrison, who now lives in the United States, contributed *Stars & Stripes Forever* (1998), a new book on joint British-Confederate naval action.

Juvenile books are fewer in number but include several interesting titles. *On the Old* Kearsage (1919) was one of several titles in the Scribner Series for Young People and one of several books by Cyrus Townsend Brady.* The book is a tale of two young boys and their encounters during the war. Western writer Gordon Shirreffs published four books with a Civil War focus for young readers, three with a naval theme. *The Gray Sea Raiders, The Mosquito Fleet*, and, especially, *Powder Boy of the* Monitor (all 1961) were centennial books that sold fairly well. The same is true for Robert B. Alter's *Day of the* Arkansas (1965), a story of the Vicksburg campaign on the Mississippi River. Arthur Mokin's *Ironclads: The* Monitor *and the* Merrimack (1992) is classified as a title for young readers.

FURTHER READING: Gerhardstein, Virginia. *Dickinson's American Historical Fiction*. 5th ed. Metuchen, NJ: Scarecrow, 1986; Menendez, Albert J. *Civil War Novels: An Annotated Bibliography*. New York: Garland, 1986.

Boyd Childress

CONNELL, EVAN S[HELBY]., JR. (1924–   ). Born in Kansas City and educated at Dartmouth, Columbia, and Stanford, Evan S. Connell Jr. remains best known for his novels *Mrs. Bridge* (1959) and *Mr. Bridge* (1969). Connell wrote the screenplay of the 1990 film adaptation that combined these two titles; it was directed by James Ivory and starred Paul Newman. He has also written several works about the sea, including two volumes of poetry, *Notes from a Bottle Found on the Beach at Carmel* (1963) and *Points for a Compass Rose* (1973). A Naval Air Force veteran, Connell criticizes the military in *The Patriot* (1960), the story of Melvin Isaacs, a misfit in the air force who finally crashes his plane and is discharged. At the end of the novel, Isaacs refuses to fight in the upcoming war between the United States and the Soviet Union, a pacifist in defiance of his father's militarism.

Connell describes the Antarctic* expeditions made by Apsley Cherry Garrard, Sir Douglas Mawson, Roald Amundsen, and Robert Scott in *The White*

Lantern (1980), a collection of nonfiction travel accounts. The title refers to Antarctica's great ice sheets, which radiate light into space, a phenomenon that astronauts term a "white lantern." In the same collection, Connell describes Norse journeys to America, as well as King Gustavus Adolphus' fated dreadnought *Vasa*, the intended flagship for his armed forces that sank only one mile out of port.

Connell has also written war stories about navy bombers, including "Crash Landing" and "The Yellow Raft," as well as sea-related stories like "The Caribbean* Provedor," "The Cuban Missile Crisis," and "The Fisherman from Chihuahua," all reprinted in *The Collected Stories of Evan S. Connell* (1995). "The Fisherman from Chihuahua," in fact, glosses Connell's method in his two collections of poetry. As Pendleton, the story's principal character, suggests, the beach attracts the detritus of ocean currents. Connell uses "beach" and "compass" as metaphors for serendipity; hence, his epic-length poems are the repositories for historical and cultural artifacts that randomly wash up on the shore, for which readers are invited to construct their own narrative.

Jeffrey Cass

COOMER, JOE (1958–   ). A transplanted Texan, Joe Coomer married into a boating family and has spent a great deal of time off the Maine coast becoming adept at sailing. In 1992 Coomer purchased a wooden motor boat and recounted his adventures in his journal, *Sailing in a Spoonful of Water: A Man, a Family, and a Vintage Wooden Boat* (1997). He recalls several incidents involving seasick guests, failing engines, and ensnared seagulls.

Of greater interest is his haunting novel *Beachcombing for a Shipwrecked God* (1995), the story of Charlotte, whose husband, Jonah, has recently died in a car wreck, perhaps a suicide. Charlotte flees her husband's clinging, grieving parents in Kentucky and makes her way to Portsmouth, New Hampshire. There she whimsically decides to rent a room on a boat with Grace, an aging widow who owns the boat, and Chloe, an overweight young woman who works in a novelty shop and who becomes pregnant by an abusive, exploitative young man. The three women work through their individual problems collectively. In particular, for Charlotte, their bond forces her to confront the difficult truth that her husband never really loved her, although she desperately loved him. The pain of this awakening realization motivates her to sift through her past and that of her shipmates in an effort to reclaim emotional balance. An archaeologist, Charlotte literally digs her way through a seventeenth-century cemetery in an effort to recover Portsmouth's lost history and bury her own lingering memories.

When Grace's memory fails after a stroke, Charlotte must also become a sailor because Grace's daughter wishes to sell the boat and put Grace into a nursing facility. Charlotte and Chloe steal Grace's boat, the *Rosinante*, and embark upon a quixotic journey, hoping that Grace's memory returns before the authorities apprehend them. Charlotte and Chloe sail from the port where Grace has doggedly tied her boat since the death of her husband, "Sweet George." The women happen across marked charts for Prince Edward Island and head there. They discover that Grace had compiled the charts because she had long intended to visit the island, the setting of George's favorite book. Through Chloe's latent seamanship, inherited from her fisherman father, the women evade the Canadian* police for a time but are finally captured and imprisoned. When Grace fortuitously recovers her memory, they maintain their sorority, nurturing each other and the baby that Chloe eventually delivers.

Jeffrey Cass

COOPER, JAMES FENIMORE (1789–1851). With *The Pilot** (1824) James Fenimore Cooper invented the sea novel, for the first time employing the dominant literary form of the nineteenth century as the vehicle for a fiction in which the sea and the ship provide the principal settings, and seamen become the chief characters. In some dozen subsequent books, he explored and expanded the possibilities of the new genre, establishing it as a popular and versatile expression of the interest romanticism had engendered in the interaction of the natural world and human experience. In making maritime life an effective literary subject, Cooper inspired an armada of imitators in Europe and America and pointed the way for such later major writers as Herman Melville* and Joseph Conrad, both of whom acknowledged their debt to him.

Like all successful writers of the sea, Cooper himself had been a sailor. Growing up in the inland fastness of his father's settlement at Cooperstown, New York, he first came in contact with sailors and shipping as a passenger in the sloops that plied the Hudson River between Albany and Manhattan, virtually the only means of access to the outside world in the days before railroads. In the summer of 1806, expelled from Yale University for disciplinary reasons and bored and restless on his return to Cooperstown, the sixteen-year-old Cooper apparently used the Hudson as an escape route, running away from home in pursuit of adventure. Frustrated in his attempt to join a filibustering expedition to Venezuela, he shipped before the mast in the merchantman *Stirling*, bound for England. After clearing New York in early September, the ship stopped at Cowes for orders and then proceeded to London, arriving there in mid-October. In early November she sailed for Spain, returning to London in early May 1807. At last the *Stirling* set sail for the United States in late July and made her landfall off Delaware on 15 September, Cooper's eighteenth birthday.

Cooper's boyhood voyage surely provided the adventure that he had sought. To the ordinary hazards of forecastle life—of storms in the Bay of Biscay and near-hurricanes in the Gulf Stream—had been added the dangers imposed by the belligerents in the Napoleonic Wars, including close encounters with British press-gangs and French privateers. But the voyage served a practical purpose as well, qualifying the young man for an appointment as a midshipman in the U.S. Navy. Entering the navy on 1 January 1808, he saw service in the bomb-ketch *Vesuvius* in New York harbor, then at the wilderness outpost of Oswego on Lake Ontario, and finally in the sloop-of-war *Wasp*, once again at New York. In May 1810 he left the navy in order to marry, but throughout the rest of his life his interest in naval affairs remained intense. He kept up his acquaintance with the officers with whom he had served, above all, with his closest friend, William Branford Shubrick, periodically visited various naval installations and vessels, and wholeheartedly joined in every major naval controversy of his time. In incidental ways, too, Cooper kept in touch with the sea. In 1819, just before he discovered that he could support himself by writing, he purchased the whaling ship *Union*, overseeing her fitting-out and commanding her on short coastal passages in the intervals between her three voyages to the Brazil banks. He took delight in his passage to England in 1826 in the packet ship *Hudson*, as he and his family crossed the Atlantic to begin a seven-year residence in Europe, the happiest moments of which occurred when he chartered and commanded a felucca on the Mediterranean.

It is ironic that a writer whose experience and interests were so focused upon maritime life should be remembered today almost exclusively as the author of the Leatherstocking Tales, those narratives of the inland frontier. But in Cooper's own day he was celebrated at least as much for his sea novels as for his wilderness tales. Indeed, within the corpus of his thirty-two works of fiction, the sea novels outnumber the Indian novels as well as the novels of social criticism. Only the accident of history by which the continental frontier came to displace the maritime frontier in the American memory and imagination accounts for the fact that Cooper's fiction is now popularly associated with the wilderness rather than with the ocean.

The core of Cooper's achievement as a writer of the sea consists of nine novels. The first three—*The Pilot, The Red Rover** (1827), and *The Water-Witch* (1830)—are tightly related in subject, theme, and tone. Written in the most exuberant phase of Cooper's literary career and at the height of his international popularity, they are intensely romantic works, employing central characters who are at once superb seamen and Byronic rebels against the constraints of conventional society. For them the ship is the graceful and responsive instrument of her commander's will; the ocean is the arena of freedom and self-realization. In all three books the aura of glamour is enhanced by the distancing provided by their eighteenth-century settings.

In *Mercedes of Castile* (1840), *The Two Admirals* (1842), and *The Wing-and-Wing* (1842), Cooper again chose to set his fictions in the past, but for wholly different purposes. In these novels the past becomes the center of interest, not merely a device for thickening an exotic atmosphere. No longer operating in the never-never land of romance, maritime characters and action serve to illustrate and comment upon a succession of grand historical panoramas, from the first voyage of Christopher Columbus* in *Mercedes*, to great fleet actions of the Royal Navy in the eighteenth century in *Two Admirals*, to naval warfare in the Mediterranean in the Napoleonic era in *Wing-and-Wing*. Here the novelist borders on the historian, as he adopts the sober tone and the documentary concerns appropriate to his materials, all drawn from the grand maritime past of Europe.

In his last three sea novels—*Afloat and Ashore* (1844), *Jack Tier* (1846–1848), and *The Sea Lions** (1849)—Cooper carried the genre into entirely new areas. He was now writing for an audience no longer entranced by the pageantry of Sir Walter Scott but by the familiar comedy and pathos of Charles Dickens, an audience, moreover, whose view of maritime life had been revolutionized by the realism and reforming zeal of Richard Henry Dana's* enormously influential *Two Years before the Mast** (1840). Responding to these changes in the taste and expectations of his readers and surely responding as well to his own darkening view of life, Cooper abandoned both romantic glamour and historical pomp for a far more intimate, realistic, and somber mode. The result in the double novel *Afloat and Ashore* is a first-person account of a young American's progress from the forecastle to command of a merchantman, a nautical career that ends in shipwreck and debtor's prison. In the serially published *Jack Tier* he turned the materials of his early sea romances inside out, writing a bitter tale of betrayal and cruelty that is set not in a shimmering past but in a grimy present. In *The Sea Lions*, which Melville reviewed, Cooper curiously anticipated the design of *Moby-Dick** (1851) by shaping a tale of metaphysical discovery and spiritual renewal from the humble materials of the southern seal fishery.

Beyond these nine novels, Cooper's writings make frequent and important reference to the sea. Nautical action and characters figure prominently in the allegorical satire *The Monikins* (1835); in *Homeward Bound* (1838), a book that Cooper planned as a social satire but that turned into a sea tale; in the terraqueous *The Pathfinder** (1840), in which he combined the materials of his Leatherstocking Tales with those of the sea novels; and in *The Crater* (1847), his powerful and visionary allegory of an America given over to greed and demagoguery.

Cooper's contribution to maritime literature does not end with his fiction. His polemic writings *The Battle of Lake Erie* (1843) and his "Review" (1844) of the court-martial of Alexander Slidell Mackenzie,* commander of the *Somers,** are vigorously argued and authoritative. His *History of the Navy of the United States of America* (1839), the first extended and responsible treatment of that institution, and his *Lives of Distinguished Naval Officers* (1846) are both invaluable for their author's firsthand acquaintance with many of their subjects. The same is true of his life of a not-so-distinguished seaman, *Ned Myers* (1843), the account of the career of a broken-down old sailor who as a boy had been Cooper's shipmate in the *Stirling*.

But his highest achievement as a writer of the sea remains his fiction, in which he succeeded in making maritime experience serve as a magnified and intensified image of all experience. Contrasting Cooper with his predecessors and many of his contemporaries, Joseph Conrad observed in his *Notes on Life and Letters* (1921) that in Cooper's sea novels "nature was not the framework, it was an essential part of existence"; in them, he said, "the sea inter-penetrates with life" (55).

FURTHER READING: Beard, James Franklin. *The Letters and Journals of James Fenimore Cooper.* 6 vols. Cambridge: Harvard UP, 1961–1968; Philbrick, Thomas. *James Fenimore Cooper and the Development of American Sea Fiction.* Cambridge: Harvard UP, 1961; Santraud, Jeanne-Marie. *La Mer et le roman américain.* Paris: Didier, 1972; Taylor, Alan. "James Fenimore Cooper Goes to Sea," *Studies in the American Renaissance* (1993): 43–54.

Thomas Philbrick

CORWIN. The U.S. revenue steamer *Thomas Corwin* (built 1876) embarked from San Francisco on 4 May 1881 on its most famous expedition to northern Alaskan waters. Although the normal duties of the *Corwin* included the control of contraband trade in the far north, the 1881 voyage, under the command of Captain Calvin L. Hooper, was charged with three additional goals: to examine the condition of Eskimo peoples, imperiled after a particularly severe Arctic* winter; to locate the *Mount Wollaston* and the *Vigilant*, two American whaleships missing in the Chukchi Sea since 1879; and, most importantly, to search for traces of Captain George W. De Long's *Jeannette* expedition, lost since 1879 in a celebrated attempt to reach the North Pole through the Bering Strait.

Among the crew of the *Corwin*'s 1881 voyage was John Muir, American naturalist, conservationist, and nature writer. Muir's talents as adventurer, glaciologist, and author ideally suited him to accompany the ship as a journalist and naturalist, and Muir's literary account immortalized the 1881 voyage. In journals and in letters published in the *San Francisco Evening Bulletin*, Muir recorded the events of the journey, described the customs and condition of Chukchi, Tlingit, and other northern Indians, and narrated the discovery that the crews of the *Mount Wollaston* and the *Vigilant* had all died. From Muir, in a letter published in the *Bulletin*, 29 September 1881, the world learned that the *Jeannette* had been crushed by ice and sunk in the Arctic Ocean and that De Long and nineteen others of the ship's crew of thirty-three had died of exposure and starvation. Muir's writings concerning the *Corwin* expedition, edited by William F. Badè, were published posthumously as *The Cruise of the* Corwin (1917).

Michael P. Branch

COXE, LOUIS O[SBORNE]. (1918–   ). Louis O. Coxe was a student in Allen Tate's Creative Arts program at Princeton when Pearl Harbor occurred. Having grown up in Salem, Massachusetts, Coxe joined the navy. He came to regard his wartime service at sea as the central experience of his life.

Coxe's naval service involved strenuous duty aboard small patrol vessels convoying cargo and amphibious ships to landings in the central Pacific. During the war Coxe wrote poetry about his experiences, sometimes meeting with fellow naval officer and poet William Meredith* to discuss their poetry. After leaving the service, Coxe published *The Sea Faring and Other Poems* (1947). This volume is dominated by poems with naval subjects, such as "The Sea Faring," "Red Right Returning," and "Convoy," although New England and its literary seafarers also find their place in this and (more often) in later books. Among Coxe's later naval poetry is "The Strait," the concluding poem in *The Last Hero and Other Poems* (1965). This long poem memorably elegizes the death of the cruiser *Houston* during the 1942 Battle of the Java Sea. Other Coxe poems, such as "Nuns on Shipboard" and "The Navigator Contemplates Heaven," use naval metaphors to affirm orthodox Christian values.

Much of Coxe's writing is not based on personal experience but still has seafaring as a central subject. Coxe and Robert Chapman collaborated in writing *Billy Budd** (1951), a play based on Herman Melville's* novella that ran on Broadway for four months after receiving good reviews when it premiered at the Experimental Theatre. This version featured Lee Marvin in his Broadway debut. *The Middle Passage* (1960), perhaps Coxe's best single work, is a long narrative poem about the slave trade in New England. Based on a personal narrative of the slaver Theodore Canot, this poem narrates in gripping detail the brutal transport of slaves to America aboard a Salem whaling vessel. The poem condemns New England mercantilism and racism and also offers a poetic reprise of the fall of humankind. [*See also* SEA IMAGERY IN MODERN AND CONTEMPORARY POETRY; MELVILLE DRAMATIZATIONS; SLAVE NARRATIVES]

Robert Shenk

COZZENS, JAMES GOULD (1903–1979). Born in Chicago, James Gould Cozzens lived for a time on Staten Island. Educated at the Kent School and at Harvard, he left college after completing a first work, *Confusion: a Novel* (1924). After several immature novels, Cozzens found his stride in the 1930s with a controlling theme of societies operating under a reasonable system of rules and authority frequently challenged by human defects and misbehavior. *The Just and the Unjust* (1942) offers full and careful descriptions of locale and occupations, informing and giving body to his plot, in this case the legal profession. *Guard of Honor* (1948), a carefully plotted story of the air corps during wartime, received the Pulitzer

Prize. *By Love Possessed* (1957) delineates the public and private life of a lawyer and outlines life in the small town where he practices; film adaptations were 1961, starring Lana Turner, and 1983.

A brief novel, *S.S. San Pedro* (1931), set aboard an ocean liner, is usually considered Cozzens' first mature story. The maritime disaster that sinks the S.S. *San Pedro* is the result of human flaws in the face of implacable natural forces. The ship sails with a list to port, an error in judgment that will cost dearly. The captain is ill and should not be in command. As the troubles of the ship mount, discipline begins to break down, and members of the crew disobey orders, so that a workable and necessary system of order and authority cannot hold the fabric of the social group together. Ironically, a ship that could have saved passengers and crew sails by within easy reach, unaware of the ship's distress, while other ships notified of the tragedy are too far away to help.

Another novel, *Castaway* (1934), can be seen as an allegory that parodies a common theme in sea fiction, the castaway marooned* on a desert island. The protagonist, a Robinson Crusoe figure, is "marooned" in a large department store, deserted, and without human contact. His search for arms and food, his building of a fort for protection, and his ineffectual attempts at survival allow Cozzens to play upon an important motif in sea literature.

Douglas Robillard

CRANE, [HAROLD] HART (1899–1932). Critical opinion remains divided about the quality of Hart Crane's best-known and longest poem, *The Bridge* (1930), but it appears that it will continue to hold a solid place in the canon of American literature. Ten of the fifteen separate poems that constitute *The Bridge*, its most vital section, were written during the summer of 1926 that he spent at his grandmother's home on the Isle of Pines, Cuba. Composed over several years, it is epic in aspiration and best understood and appreciated if seen from a mythopoetic vantage point, even though Crane possessed firsthand knowledge of the sea, principally from his Caribbean* experiences.

The poem's focus is on the remarkable and enduring engineering and architectural feat, the Brooklyn Bridge, completed in 1883 to link Brooklyn and Manhattan shortly before the borough annexations that formed modern New York City. Opening and closing with a paean to this bridge and gazing on seabirds and harbor life, the complex poem also traces Christopher Columbus'* voyage and moves back and forth through history and time. Clearly influenced by Walt Whitman's* writing—particularly "Crossing Brooklyn Ferry" (1856), the East River transportation mode replaced by the span—*The Bridge* is an emblem of industrialism that contrasts with the pastoral setting.

The paradigms useful in comprehending Crane's statement and judging its success are familiar to cultural and intellectual historians: modernity's threatened aridity in contrast to tradition's proven and comfortable fecundity, desert and water, urban and pastoral, civilized and primitive, corrupt and innocent, materialistic and spiritual. Crane's strategy is to journey back in time and west in space, juxtaposing the simpler, more virtuous pre-Columbian or frontier epoch with the more complex and sullied modernity that Western civilization has forged.

Crane connects with romantics such as Ralph Waldo Emerson and Henry David Thoreau,* Herman Melville,* Whitman, Emily Dickinson,* and others. The river symbolizes the same renewal for Crane that it does for Samuel Clemens* and for countless other artists, and the subway (underground) and bestial sailors, for example, clearly conjure up the opposite pole. Other bodies of water such as Columbus' Atlantic suggest similar voyaging in the quest to recover lost innocence, which is implicit in other modernist works, for example, T. S. Eliot's* *The Waste Land* (1922) and F. Scott Fitzgerald's* *The Great Gatsby* (1925).

Facets of Crane's vision in *The Bridge* are also present in other works such as "Voyages" (1926) and "Key West"* (1933). His tribute "At Melville's Tomb" (1926) uses maritime imagery of waves, wrecks, shells, compass, quadrant, and sextant. Crane committed suicide when returning to New York from a Guggenheim Fellowship in Mexico by jumping off the ship that was carrying him. A recent biography is Paul Mariani's *The Broken Tower: A Life of Hart Crane* (1999). [*See also* SEA IMAGERY IN MODERN AND CONTEMPORARY POETRY]

Donald Yannella

CRANE, STEPHEN (1871–1900). Stephen Crane's first extended trip at sea ended in a shipwreck* less than thirty-five hours after he left the Florida coast, forcing Crane and three other crew members to struggle toward land for almost thirty hours, crammed into a small dinghy, inches removed from the rough and chilly seas. Nearly all of Crane's writing about the sea was inspired by this incident, and although Crane's sea experience and his writing about the subject were limited, his impact on American sea fiction has been significant. Many critics and scholars consider his mythical story "The Open Boat" (1898) one of the best examples of American sea fiction and American short fiction ever written.

Crane was born in the port city of Newark, New Jersey, and moved to Port Jervis, New York, when he was seven and to the ocean resort of Asbury Park when he was twelve. When he was seventeen, Crane began writing about the coastal life of Asbury Park during the summer resort season, contributing the stories to his brother's news reporting agency for the *New York Tribune*. During this period Crane also wrote several short works that illustrate an almost prophetic interest, as biographer R. W. Stallman has put it, in disasters at sea.

In the waning hours of New Year's Eve, 1896, Crane joined the crew of the S.S. *Commodore* as the ship left Jacksonville, Florida, for Cuba, loaded with weapons and supplies to support the Cuban insurrection against Spain. Twenty-four hours later, the ship began taking on water, and by seven the following morning the *Commodore* was at the bottom of the sea, sixteen miles outside of Mosquito Inlet on the Florida coast. Crane (a news reporter), an injured Captain Edward Murphy, Charles B. Montgomery (the ship's steward), and William Higgins (an oiler) were among the last to abandon ship, making use of the ten-foot dinghy, the only "life boat" left. Over the next thirty hours, Crane and Higgins faced the delicate task of changing positions in the nearly submerged boat so that they could take turns rowing toward a safe landing point. During much of the ordeal, the four crew members were in sight of land, sometimes even spotting and signaling toward people on shore. The tidal waters along the coast were too harsh, however, to attempt a landing until the early morning hours of 3 January, just off of Daytona Beach, Florida. Due, in part, to the political intrigue of the failed covert operation, the mysterious circumstances surrounding the sinking, and the fact that a well-known writer was a surviving eyewitness, newspapers across the United States featured accounts of the incident, including Crane's own widely syndicated article, "Stephen Crane's Own Story," which appeared in the *New York Press* on 7 January 1897.

Many survivors recounted flattering, almost heroic images of Crane's composure and bravery throughout the ordeal. In a *New York Press* article written two days after the sinking, Captain Murphy praised the novice seaman, claiming that Crane had behaved like a "born sailor" who wasn't affected by the pitching waves that had sickened many of the *Commodore*'s more experienced sailors. Despite the rough seas, Murphy claimed, Crane remained on deck at the captain's side and later was instrumental in helping to ready and launch lifeboats from the foundering vessel. The captain also praised Crane for his efforts in helping to row and direct their dinghy to land and his calm behavior in the final seconds when their boat swamped, and they were forced to swim to shore. Crane enjoyed this fame, especially the favorable accounts of his behavior throughout the disaster. When a nine-year-old asked Crane, recovering from the ordeal in a Jacksonville hotel, to sign her autograph book, he inscribed, "Stephen Crane: Able Seaman, S.S. *Commodore*."

After having recovered, Crane carefully composed his short story "The Open Boat," now recognized as a masterpiece for its methodical, detailed depiction of four men stuck in a tiny boat and how they perceive the hostile world around them as they fight for survival. As the men come to realize that God, nature, fate, and even other human civilization fail to sympathize with, or even to recognize, their plight, they turn to each other in a bleak solace of brotherhood. The correspondent questions the meaning of his life with the famous refrain: "If I am going to be drowned—if I am going to be drowned—if I am going to be drowned, why, in the name of the seven mad gods who rule the sea, was I allowed to come thus far and contemplate sand and trees?" Crane's ironic answer is dramatized in the disastrous landing when the Oiler, clearly the strongest and most fit of all on board, drowns, his body discovered face down, just inches from dry land. When *The Open Boat and Other Tales of Adventure* appeared in 1898, it was greeted with much critical acclaim by writers such as Harold Frederic, Joseph Conrad, and H. G. Wells.

Crane's dramatic experiences inspired him to write works about the sea, including a syndicated article of 2 May 1897, "The Filibustering Industry," the short story "Flanagan: And His Short Filibustering Adventure" (1897), and many poems, notably "A Man Adrift on a Slim Spar" in *War Is Kind* (1899). After 1898, Crane contributed little more to sea fiction, though his few remaining years were filled with sea experiences. He logged many hours sailing to and from the shores of battle zones as a war correspondent, first in Turkey and Greece, where he wrote about the awesome power of modern navies, and later in Puerto Rico and Cuba, where he observed and wrote about the landing of troops at Guantánamo Bay.

Crane's limited time at sea affected him deeply, and in the final weeks of his brief life, his sea experiences continued to grip his mind. While waiting to cross the English Channel for treatment of his chronic tuberculosis at a German sanitarium, the bedridden Crane is said to have spent hours watching the boats sailing back and forth from Dover. In his final conscious hours before he died, Crane experienced feverish dreams taking him back to the *Commodore* incident, as recorded in a letter written by his common-law wife, Cora: "My husband's brain is never at rest. He lives over everything in dreams and talks aloud constantly. It is too awful to hear him try to change places in the 'open boat'!" (*Crane Log* 442). [*See also* LIFESAVING LITERATURE]

FURTHER READING: Bender, Bert. *Sea Brothers: The Tradition of American Sea Fiction from* Moby-Dick *to the Present.* Philadelphia: U of Pennsylvania P, 1988; Covert, James B. *Stephen Crane.* San Diego: Harcourt Brace Jovanovich, 1984; Stallman, R. W. *Stephen Crane: A Biography.* New York: George Braziller, 1968; Wertheim, Stanley, and Paul Sorrentino, eds. *The Crane Log: A Documentary Life of Stephen Crane 1871–1900.* New York: G. K. Hall, 1994.

Matthew Evertson

CREELEY, ROBERT [WHITE] (1926–   ). Robert Creeley's most sustained and important piece of sea writing is his 1963 novel *The Island.* Although his work only infrequently focuses on the sea or even uses it as background, the center section of the poem "Here" (1969) is a crafted and compressed articulation of some central ideas in *The Island.*

This novel, somewhat autobiographical, is set in Banalbufar, Mallorca, Spain, where the author lived for a short period in the early 1950s. John, the protagonist, and his spouse, Joan, are psychologically alienated, as are

the lonely people with whom they come in contact. The island itself is
fraught with significance: most of the visitors are themselves islands, struggling to alter their conditions or at least to come to terms with them. Although he is perhaps incapable of human touch, John yearns for it and yet
fears it, as does Joan. As divorced from humanity as her husband is, Joan
has an affair with Rene, a French Ishmael,* and during that brief interlude,
a bid for connection, all three watch, detached and unemotional, as another
visitor almost drowns; only at the last moment do they save him from being
battered to death.

One passage employs the healing qualities of water, alluding to Mallorca's
involvement in the whaling industry, in a reference resonating with the sug-
gestiveness of Herman Melville's* *Moby-Dick* (1851), the book so central
to the thought and artistry of Creeley's friend and Black Mountain colleague
Charles Olson.* The shore is the threshold to the renewing sea, but those
who even contemplate reaching it or for it are precluded from doing so by
the stasis of existential suspension. Appalled by the virtual murder of sea
creatures by scuba-diving visitors who "invade" the sea near the end of the
story, John and Joan buy and repair a boat in order to reach the healing
waters. The tale ends, however, with the prospect of further isolation.

Creeley is known chiefly as a poet of the short lyric. In his *Collected Poems*
(1982) he uses the sea's surging tides and its fluid, formless condition to
depict strong states of feeling that never seem to be adequately communi-
cated. See, for example, "The Surf," "The Sea," "An Obscene Poem," "The
Innocence," "The," and "Sea." Although the sea is often associated with
creativity, the circumscribed and ordinary nature of the seashore scene in
"Mazatlan: The Sea" fails to provide inspiration. [*See also* SEA IMAGERY
IN MODERN AND CONTEMPORARY POETRY]

Donald Yannella

CRUISING LITERATURE. In the long time-span of sea literature, tales
of yacht cruising and passage-making over the oceans of the world are relatively recent. Conditions were not ripe for the emergence of this genre
until late in the nineteenth century, when the economic decline of sailing
ships coincided with shifts in attitude about going to sea for pleasure. Just
as commercial billets for those trained in sail became scarce, yachtsmen, who
had generally hugged the shore, began to venture on long ocean passages
that would have been unthinkable a few decades earlier. Thus, cruising literature began in England as a new form of a much older genre, travel literature.

Since captains' wives at sea had been writing journals that far surpassed
their husbands' logs in interest for generations, it is not surprising that the
best-seller of this new genre was written by Lady Anne Brassey, daughter
of Lord Thomas Brassey, a yachtsman and licensed master mariner, editor
of the *Naval Annual,* and the member of Parliament most responsible for

significant reforms in the British Merchant Service. Her *Around the World in the Yacht* Sunbeam: *Our Home on the Ocean for Eleven Months* (1878) soon became the classic of British cruising literature, with many editions published both in England and in the United States through the next three decades. Their yacht, a 531-ton, three-masted topsail schooner with a steam auxiliary, had a complement of thirty-two crew members and eleven passengers for the circumnavigation in 1876–1877. A few years later, E. F. Knight, a young and adventurous barrister, took up crossing the Atlantic with a much smaller entourage—a sailing friend, two gentlemen greenhorns, and a cabin boy—and sailed to South America in a 28-ton yawl in 1880–1881. The resulting book, *The Cruise of the* Falcon (1884), was so successful that Knight took up writing about his adventures as a profession.

Two decades later the genre reached America in an improbable way, through the journalistic ventures of an experienced sailing-ship captain down on his luck in a dying trade. During the same decade that Joseph Conrad came ashore to begin his writing career, Joshua Slocum* proposed syndicating travel letters from ports as he sailed around the world alone. He had already written accounts of his remarkable voyages from Brazil to Washington, D.C., in an open boat with his wife and two sons after the wreck of his ship, self-published as *The Voyage of the* Liberdade (1890), as well as a brief account of another voyage on John Ericsson's 130-foot torpedo boat, *The Voyage of the* Destroyer *from New York to Brazil* (1894). Rebuilding the *Spray*, a derelict 36-foot oyster sloop, Slocum set out from Boston in 1895 on the first single-handed circumnavigation* of the world, returning to Newport three years later. His venture had attracted worldwide coverage by newspapers, and the resulting book, *Sailing Alone around the World* (1900), was immediately successful. It became the archetype of cruising literature in America and a required text in many schools; the book has remained in print continuously, in many editions, for nearly a century.

Within a year after its publication, Slocum's book had inspired the first of many imitations, J. C. Voss' attempt to circumnavigate the world in a less substantial vessel than *Spray*, the thirty-eight-foot log canoe *Tilikum*. Like Slocum's voyage, this one had publication as a rationale, suggested to Voss by Norman Luxton, a journalist who sailed with him as mate on the first leg of the voyage until they fell out, and Luxton left. Departing across the Pacific from Victoria, British Columbia, Voss managed to sail 40,000 miles in three oceans but abandoned the circumnavigation in London. This voyage, along with two others, was eventually published in *The Venturesome Voyages of Captain Voss* (1913).

These two tales of ocean adventure in small sailing vessels at the turn of the twentieth century opened the floodgates to cruising literature, which issues in a steady stream from publishers, fills the shelves of maritime book dealers and collectors, and sustains nautical book clubs to this day. Although much of this prolific genre is written by British wanderers, a good part records voyages of all kinds undertaken by Americans. Jack London* entered the stream with *The Cruise of the* Snark (1911), an account of the misadventures of a voyage from San Francisco to the Solomon Islands in his new, untested fifty-five-foot ketch. One early classic is Harry Pidgeon's *Around the World Single-Handed: The Cruise of the* Islander (1933). Pidgeon is often portrayed as an inexperienced landlubber before he undertook this repetition of Slocum's circumnavigation by sailing the other way from California, but that is a half-truth. He had built a canoe and used it in the white-water rivers of Alaska, and he had also built a flatboat in Minneapolis and floated down the course of the Mississippi to the sea. He adapted the design of the thirty-four-foot *Islander* from plans published in *Rudder*, edited by Thomas Fleming Day, who had written an earlier voyage account praising the seaworthiness of the type, *Across the Atlantic in* Sea Bird (1911). After building the boat on the shore of Los Angeles harbor, he sailed westward across the Pacific in 1921 and returned to the same port in 1925.

Other circumnavigators chose larger vessels and fuller crews. Donald C. Starr's *The Schooner* Pilgrim*'s Progress: A Voyage around the World, 1932–1934* (pub. posthumously, 1996) recounts the westward voyage of his eighty-five-foot Alden schooner, beginning and ending in Boston. During the same era Warwick Tompkins and his wife began crossing and recrossing the Atlantic in an old pilot schooner of the same size with young people as crew, including renowned future circumnavigators Electa and Irving Johnson.* One voyage rounded Cape Horn* on the path of the California clippers, as recounted in *Fifty South to Fifty South: The Story of a Voyage West around Cape Horn in the Schooner* Wander Bird (1938). Continuing the Tompkins tradition of sailing with a crew of young amateurs who would share the expense of the voyages, the Johnsons began the first of their seven circumnavigations in *Yankee,** a North Sea pilot schooner, and Electa wrote its account in *Westward Bound in the Schooner* Yankee (1936). After the war they continued these voyages in another ninety-six-foot North Sea pilot schooner, renamed *Yankee* and rerigged as a brigantine, and continued to write more books about their world cruises.

Restlessness and dissatisfaction with shore life took many others to sea on long voyages in smaller vessels. Among these was William A. Robinson, a young engineer who set out from New York in 1928 on a westward circumnavigation in the thirty-two-foot ketch *Svaap* and returned in 1932, recounting his voyage in *10,000 Leagues over the Sea* (1932). A year later Rockwell Kent* sailed on board Arthur Allen's thirty-three-foot cutter *Direction* to the coast of Greenland, where the adventure he sought turned into a disaster as the vessel was blown ashore and wrecked. The resulting book, *N by E* (1930), is a classic of cruising literature, both for its finely wrought text and for Kent's dramatic woodcuts; *Voyaging Southward from the Strait of Magellan* (1924) chronicles several boat voyages and land journeys that Kent took.

Yet others sought to escape problems ashore by putting to sea, as Sterling Hayden* did when he abandoned Hollywood and a broken marriage, loaded his children on board his old pilot schooner, and took off for Tahiti, a tale he told in *Wanderer* (1963). After a divorce, Webb Chiles determined to be the first to circumnavigate the world in an open boat; the story of his successes and failures at sea and ashore is told in two volumes, *Open Boat: Across the Pacific* (1982) and *The Ocean Waits* (1984).

As the world put itself together again after World War II, a new urge for breaking records brought circumnavigators into the limelight. The impulse struck first in Britain, where Sir Francis Chichester succeeded in making the fastest solo passage around the world in his fifty-three-foot yawl by heading for the justly feared roaring forties of the Southern Ocean and making only one stop in Sydney; he was rewarded with a knighthood and told his tale in a best-seller, Gipsy Moth *Circles the World* (1968). This feat enticed other British sailors to undertake their own circumnavigations and write books: Sir Alec Rose, also knighted, *My* Lively Lady (1969); Robin Knox-Johnston, winner of the first Golden Globe Race, *A World of My Own: The Single-Handed, Non-Stop Circumnavigation of the World in* Suhaili (1969).

By this time the quest for speed in circumnavigations had become institutionalized in races like the Golden Globe for single-handers and the Whitbread for full racing crews, with many Americans participating but fewer writing about the experience. Among those who did is Skip Novak in *One Watch at a Time: Around the World with* Drum *on the Whitbread Race* (1988). More characteristically, American circumnavigators set out to break records in their own way. Dodge Morgan wanted to make the fastest non-stop, single-handed passage around the world and succeeded, recording the experience in *The Voyage of* American Promise (1989), while Robin Lee Graham set out at age sixteen to become the youngest circumnavigator; his story, ghosted by Derek Gill, is told in *Dove* (1972). Equally ambitious on the smaller scale of crossing a single ocean is Robert Manry's transatlantic voyage in the smallest boat, a 13 1/2-foot, rebuilt Old Town dinghy, described in *Tinkerbelle* (1966). One of the few chronicles to focus on a circumnavigation by an American woman is Tania Aebi's *Maiden Voyage* (1989), ghostwritten by Bernadette Brennan.

Those less interested in breaking records than in enjoying the cruising life continued to write good books. Among them are volumes by couples who have made cruising and writing about it a way of life, notably the Smeetons, a British couple who emigrated to Canada before they took to the sea for good in their forty-foot double-ended ketch; the Pardeys, who left California to cruise worldwide in their twenty-four-foot cutter; and the Roths, who have circumnavigated the Pacific Basin and rounded Cape Horn in their thirty-five-foot sloop. The Herron family voyaged from Florida to Africa and produced *Voyage of the* Aquarius (1974). The profusion of American cruising literature, which began with journalistic schemes, continues to marry the pleasures of sailing with the writing life. [*See also* WOMEN AT SEA]

FURTHER READING: Anderson, J. R. L. *The Ulysses Factor: The Exploring Instinct in Man*. New York: Harcourt Brace Jovanovich, 1970; Barton, Humphrey. *Atlantic Adventures: Voyages in Small Craft*. 2d ed. New York: de Graff, 1962; Borden, Charles A. *Sea Quest: Global Blue-Water Adventuring in Small Craft*. Camden, ME: International Marine, 1975; Holm, Don. *The Circumnavigators: Small Boat Voyagers of Modern Times*. Englewood Cliffs, NJ: Prentice-Hall, 1974; Lloyd, Harvey, and Jay Clarke. *Voyages: The Romance of Cruising*. New York: Dorling Kindersley, 1999; Toy, Ernest W., Jr. *Adventures Afloat: A Nautical Bibliography*. 2 vols. Metuchen, NJ: Scarecrow, 1988.

                                                                    Robert C. Foulke

CUFFE, PAUL (1759–1817). Seaman, captain, shipowner, businessman, author, and African colonizer, Paul Cuffe was born 17 January 1759, on Cuttyhunk Island, Massachusetts, the seventh child of his African-born father and Ruth Slocum, a Wampanoag Indian. Cuffe went to the sea in the 1770s as an ordinary seaman, first aboard a whaler and then a West Indies trader. Captured by the British in 1776 or 1777 aboard another ship, perhaps the *Charming Polly*, Cuffe was soon released. He shipped out on several more voyages before 1779, when he and a brother built a small boat that they manned for commercial activities in Narragansett Bay and Long Island Sound and possibly used for running the British blockade as well. Beginning with this open boat, Cuffe invested his profits to build ever-larger vessels, ending with the 162-ton brig *Hero* and the 268-ton sloop *Alpha*.

Commonly sailing with an all-black crew, Cuffe traded along the Atlantic coast and in the West Indies. To encourage trade with Africa, Cuffe sailed the 109-ton brig *Traveller* for Sierra Leone in 1810, a voyage he recounted in his *Brief Account of the Settlement and Present Situation of the Colony of Sierra Leone in Africa* (1812). Although this journal provides scant detail, it is valuable as sea literature, for it describes such matters as sailing conditions, ship provisions, and the London docks. To encourage commercial alternatives to the slave trade, Cuffe sailed from Sierra Leone to Liverpool in 1811 with a cargo produced by free African labor. A promoter of African commerce on this first voyage to Sierra Leone, Cuffe next sailed there as a supporter of African colonization. In 1815 he pioneered black-initiated emigration from the United States in his Back to Africa movement, transporting thirty-eight passengers aboard the brig *Traveller*.

Paul Cuffe founded a dynasty of African American captains, including his sons, sons-in-law, nephews, and grandsons. His daughters inherited shares in the *Traveller*. His son, Paul Cuffe Jr., documented his own life at sea in the *Narrative of the Life and Adventures of Paul Cuffee* [sic], *a Pequot Indian: During Thirty Years Spent at Sea, and in Travelling in Foreign*

Lands (1839). [*See also* AFRICAN AMERICAN LITERATURE; SLAVE NARRATIVES]

Brad S. Born

CURWOOD, JAMES OLIVER (1878–1927). James Oliver Curwood, born in Owosso, Michigan, was a popular writer of nonfiction, romance and adventure fiction, and scripts for silent films. Although much of his fiction is set in the Canadian* wilderness, his important early work is focused on Great Lakes* freighters. While working as a reporter for the *Detroit News-Tribune*, he met dockworkers, sailors, and ship captains. His frequent travel on freighters between Detroit and Thunder Bay at the western end of Lake Superior led to a series of stories and articles, including "Fourteenth Floater o' Jacob Strauss" (1901), "The Wreck of the *Winsome Winny*" (1903), "Captain of the *Christopher Duggan*" (1904), "The Copper Ship" (1905), "The Lake Breed" (1905), "The Fish Pirates" (1909), and "Salvage" (1909). Most of these early stories relied on dialect and viewed Lake shipping as thrilling—similar to that depicted in popular stories of ocean travel—with romantic, long-haired women and adventurous men, mutinous crews, pirates* and smugglers, and sinking freighters. Fourteen of these early Great Lakes stories were collected in *Falkner of the Inland Seas* (1931). Curwood's first novel, *The Courage of Captain Plum* (1908), was based on "King" Strang's Mormon colony on Lake Michigan's Beaver Island. His non-fiction work, *The Great Lakes: The Vessels That Plough Them, the Owners, the Sailors, and a Their Cargoes* (1909), includes maps, photographs, and a brief history of the Lakes.

Ed Demerly

CUSSLER, CLIVE [ERIC] (1931–   ). As a boy Clive Cussler immersed himself in the literature of the American Civil War and the writings of C. S. Forester. Describing himself as "the kid that stared out the window," he entered the air force after two years at Pasadena City College.

While creative director for an advertising agency in the early 1960s, Cussler began writing fiction. His initial idea was to write a series of books that continued the career of a single villain, but he had such success with his protagonist Dirk Pitt that the original project was abandoned. Pitt, who first appeared to the public in the *Mediterranean Caper* (pub. in 1973 as *Mayday!*), continued to appear as the central character in nearly a dozen more novels, including a revision of *Pacific Vortex!* (1982), the first Pitt novel actually written. Cussler's breakthrough novel was *Raise the* Titanic!* (1976), a work that in many ways anticipated the oceanographic discoveries of Woods Hole, Massachusetts, scientist Robert Ballard and that was adapted into film in 1980. The craftsmanship and tautness of this work were carried over into *Vixen 03* (1978) and *Night Probe!* (1981), in which Dirk Pitt confronts an aging James Bond.

In his more recent novels, Cussler himself appears as a character, and his fictional agency NUMA (National Underwater & Marine Agency), of which Dirk Pitt was the special projects director, has assumed reality as the name of a group founded by Cussler to locate historical shipwrecks.* His efforts in this area are chronicled in *The Sea Hunters* (with Craig Dirgo, 1996). Dirgo and Cussler also collaborated on a handbook to the fiction, *Clive Cussler and Dirk Pitt Revealed* (1998).

R. D. Madison

D

DANA, RICHARD HENRY, JR. (1815–1882). Son of a genteel poet and member of a prominent Boston family, Richard Henry Dana Jr. gained literary fame by turning his back on his Brahmin upbringing, sailing aboard a merchant vessel, and subsequently describing the life of a common sailor in *Two Years before the Mast** (1840). While this departure from class and culture was only temporary, a "parenthesis," as he called it, Dana's experience as a nineteen-year-old sailor served as a continuing touchstone of memory throughout a professional career marked by both moderate success and frustrated ambition.

Dana's father, Richard Henry Dana Sr.,* was a prominent New England poet who helped found the *North American Review* and pioneer literary romanticism in America. Against a background of rarified intellectual discussion and declining family fortune, young Dana left Harvard University and took to sea. He secured a berth aboard the hide carrier *Pilgrim* and departed Boston on 14 August 1834, for a trip around Cape Horn* to California. Anchoring in Santa Barbara the following January, Dana spent the next year and a half collecting and curing hides up and down the coast of California. He returned to Boston aboard the *Alert* on 22 September 1836, and promptly reentered Harvard, eventually graduating with his original class.

He wrote *Two Years before the Mast* while in law school and allowed his father and the poet William Cullen Bryant* to negotiate a contract with Harpers for a flat rate of $250 rather than one that would have given him a percentage of the sales. Published in 1840, *Two Years* was immediately popular, acclaimed by Bryant, Ralph Waldo Emerson, and others for the truth it told about the life of the common sailor. Framed by the scenic rendering of the voyages out and back, the book also attains a symbolic coherence as the story of a young man's education at sea. *Two Years* helped turn the course of American sea literature away from the Byronic romanticism made popular by James Fenimore Cooper* and toward realistic, firsthand accounts told from the point of view of the sailor. It had a particularly lasting influence on Herman Melville,* who called Dana his "sea brother" in an 1849 letter.

Perhaps the most powerful scene in *Two Years* is a description of a flogging, after which the young narrator vows to help redress the grievances suffered unjustly by common sailors. Upon his return to Boston, Dana kept his promise by representing numerous sailors in claims against captains and shipping companies. In 1841 he wrote a manual, *The Seaman's Friend* (kept in print throughout the century and reprinted in 1979 and 1997), to explain nautical vocabulary and procedures at sea. A passionate and committed lawyer, Dana also championed the rights of fugitive slaves. He was involved in a number of famous cases in Boston, including the "Rescue Trials" of 1851 and the trial of Anthony Burns in 1854. For his efforts, he was at one point knocked unconscious by a street thug and boycotted by supporters of slavery.

In 1876 Dana was nominated by President Grant to become ambassador to England, a post that would have capped his career in admirable fashion, but his candidacy was unsuccessful. He had hoped that President Hayes might appoint him to a federal post, but nothing came of this, either, and eventually Dana and his wife retired to Europe. Dana died in Rome.

In a life that Dana himself characterized as one of repeated disappointments, he saw the irony that his "boy's book" would outlast any of his other achievements. Following periods of stress and overwork, Dana often took enforced vacations; these intervals of rest and physical exercise would bring back the memory of his two-year parenthesis. In 1869 Dana appended a "Twenty Four Years Later" chapter to *Two Years* after he revisited California, and this along with his short book *To Cuba and Back* (1859) demonstrate that Dana retained his eye for scenic maritime description throughout his life. [*See also THE RED RECORD*; SLAVE NARRATIVES]

FURTHER READING: Adams, Charles Francis. *Richard Henry Dana: A Biography.* 2 vols. Rev. ed. Boston and New York: Houghton Mifflin, 1891; Gale, Robert. *Richard Henry Dana, Jr.* Boston: Twayne, 1969; Shapiro, Samuel. *Richard Henry Dana, Jr.: 1815–1882.* East Lansing: Michigan State UP, 1961.

Hugh Egan

DANA, RICHARD HENRY, SR. (1787–1879). Richard Henry Dana Sr. was born into a prominent Cambridge, Massachusetts, family. He was educated at Harvard, leaving without a degree in 1807. He studied law and passed the bar in 1811 but showed little interest in practicing law. In 1814 he collaborated with others to establish the *North American Review*, where he first expressed what would become a lifelong devotion to the romantic ideology of William Wordsworth and Samuel Taylor Coleridge.

The author of numerous essays and four brief novels, Dana wrote about the sea only in his poetry. Aside from two brief lyrical poems, his chief contribution is "The Buccaneer" (1827), a narrative poem of more than 700 lines that remained popular throughout the 1830s. Strongly influenced in its themes and imagery by Coleridge's "Rime of the Ancient Mariner" (1798), the poem details the retribution exacted on a murderous pirate,* Matthew Lee, haunted and finally ridden to his death in the sea by the spirit of his victim's steed.

Dana spent summers in his later years at his seaside home in Manchester, on the south side of Cape Ann. He was the father of Richard Henry Dana Jr.,* author of *Two Years before the Mast** (1840).

Joseph Flibbert

"DANFORTH, HARRY." *See* PETERSON, CHARLES JACOBS.

DARING THE SEA: THE TRUE STORY OF THE FIRST MEN TO ROW ACROSS THE ATLANTIC OCEAN (1998). Written by David W. Shaw (1961–), *Daring the Sea* is the true story of George Harbo (1864–1908) and Frank Samuelsen (1870–1946), two Norwegian immigrants who in 1896 successfully rowed from New York City to La Havre, France. The pair left Manhattan on 6 June 1896 and arrived in La Havre two months later, having endured exhaustion, starvation, near collision with steamships, and near drowning when a monstrous wave capsized their eighteen-foot boat, the *Fox*, in midocean. Against all odds, the pair persevered and survived, expecting that their daring feat would bring them fame and wealth on the lecture circuit. Though they set the record for being the first men to row across the Atlantic nonstop, they failed to gain much public acclaim, and the truth of their story has become obscured by legend and supposition.

Their crossing has attained nearly mythic proportions over the last 100 years; they were rumored, for example, to have been offered a $10,000 prize on completion of their venture. Shaw effectively replaces such rumors with the facts of the voyage, having gained access to descendants, Harbo's personal log, and a later history that Harbo dictated. The contemporary "Ballad of Harbo and Samuelsen" (1985), written by Jerry Bryant, has been sung in folk and sea music* circles for years. *Daring the Sea* is the first published work about this legendary voyage.

Glenn Grasso

DAVIS, REBECCA HARDING (1830–1910). Although best known for her gritty depiction of factory life in her story "Life in the Iron-Mills" (1861), Rebecca Harding Davis frequently used vivid sea imagery in her writings. Intimately familiar with marshes, sand dunes, shipwreck* legends, and the moods of the sea through summers spent vacationing with her family at Point Pleasant, New Jersey, Davis uses indeterminate coastal settings in exploring ambiguities of gender and class. In the story "Out of the Sea" (1865), for instance, urbanite Mary Defourchet travels through the primal seascape of the New Jersey coast, where she observes the quiet mannerisms of its inhabitants. While watching the spectacle of a shipwreck, Mary witnesses a vision of redemption through disaster as the aged Phebe Trull rescues her long-absent son, who happens to be Mary's fiancé. "Earthen Pitchers" (1873–1874), set in Lewes, Delaware, questions how urban and rural characters define artistic and natural aesthetics in relation to a protean coastal environment. The sea, with its rejuvenating characteristics as well as thundering surf, quicksand, and buried wreck victims, serves as a vehicle through which Davis explores social, cultural, and gender constraints and obligations.

In two of her journalistic essays, "The House on the Beach" (1876) and "Life-Saving* Stations" (1876), Davis narrates the adventures of tourists as they explore a section of New Jersey coast. "The House on the Beach" documents the efforts to reduce shipwreck and storm damage through the systematic study of weather patterns by the Signal Service. Likewise, in "Life-Saving Stations," Davis blends melodramatic action with descriptions of life-saving equipment and the efficiency of lifesaving crews to respond to shipwreck. By linking the specific locality to an analysis of heroism and technology, tempered by accounts of morally corrupt wrecking endeavors, Davis not only replaces the highly romanticized view of heroic lifesaving with a more balanced realism but also elevates local geography to national prominence.

Other Davis writings in which the sea figures prominently include "Natasqua" (1870–1871), "A Faded Leaf of History" (1873), and "On the Jersey Coast" (1900). [*See also* DAVIS, RICHARD HARDING]

Daniel W. Lane

DAVIS, RICHARD HARDING (1864–1916). Born in Philadelphia, Richard Harding Davis was the first child born to the journalist L. Clarke Davis and the fiction writer Rebecca Harding Davis.* He soon followed in his parents' footsteps as a newspaperman and later the author of short stories, novels, and plays. Davis was not content to report only local, regional, or national events, however, and rapidly established himself as a superb war correspondent, traveling by ship to many exotic locales. He sailed to Cuba on the *Oliviette* in 1886 to cover the insurrection, returning on the same vessel.

In 1895 he published *Three Gringos in Venezuela and Central America*, which includes an account of his travels by steamer, open boat, and cargo boat. He sailed to England, then on to Greece in 1897 to cover the Greco-Turkish War. The explosion of the U.S.S. *Maine* in Havana harbor in 1898 brought Davis home from Europe; from Key West* he watched American warships head for Cuba. Securing passage on a mail boat, Davis managed to get aboard the flagship *New York*. His coverage of the Spanish-American War in *The Cuban and Porto Rico Campaigns* (1898) was very well received.

Several of Davis' fictional works take place on ships, including the short stories "A Derelict" (1901), set on a press boat during a naval battle, and "On the Fever Ship" (1899), set on a transport converted to a hospital ship. Though these ships serve principally as setting, the transport of "On the Fever Ship" is personified briefly as unsympathetic to the heroic, sickly, human cargo she was not designed to carry. Ships figure prominently in Davis' plays as well, such as *The Dictator*, set partly on the *Bolivar*, a passenger steamer, and *The Galloper*, whose second act is set on a wharf with ships in the background and several characters ascending and descending the gangways. Both plays were published along with *Miss Civilization*, in *Farces* (1906). [*See also* DRAMA OF THE SEA]

Linda Ledford-Miller

DEAN, HARRY [FOSTER] (1864–1935). Published in 1929 in Boston, Berlin, and London, Harry Dean's unique sea narrative and remarkable autobiography was entitled *Umbala* in Britain and *The Pedro Gorino* in the United States.

Dean was born in Philadelphia in 1864, a descendant of Paul Cuffe,* the first noted black sea captain, and was educated briefly at Philadelphia's Institute for Colored Youth. Between 1876 and 1879 he sailed around the world with his uncle Silas Dean, visiting South Africa, Ethiopia, and ports of the Far East, including Japan. Between 1880 and 1900 he purchased the *Pedro Gorino* and again traveled the seas. In 1900 he visited London, where he met W.E.B. Du Bois; at about this time Dean proposed an "Ethiopian Empire" and espoused his ideas on black nationalism. He spent several years on the African continent and in 1909 was in Liberia promoting a merchant fleet. He sat out World War I in Chicago, avoiding the war at sea. Dean traveled to California in 1921, where he met with associates of Marcus Garvey and in 1924 chartered the Dean Habashi Nautical College of Almeda, a school to train African American sailors. When this venture failed, Dean attempted to promote black agricultural communities in Washington state.

Dean began his autobiography in 1928, when two University of Chicago professors introduced the aging seaman to Sterling North, a university student with literary aspirations. Over that year, North assisted Dean in preparing his recollections for publications, and early the next year *The Pedro Gorino* was published. Dean died in the summer of 1935. His rare account of a black sea captain was reprinted in 1989 in the United States. [*See also* AFRICAN AMERICAN LITERATURE]

Boyd Childress

THE DEATH SHIP (*Das Totenschiff* 1926; Eng. trans. 1934). Ascribed to B. Traven (1882? 1890?–1969), *The Death Ship* was first published in Germany in 1926 and translated into English in 1934. A scathing indictment of bureaucracy, privilege, and social class, *The Death Ship* follows the life of a fictional American sailor named Gerard Gales. Distracted by a night of drinking and a newfound female companion, he misses the departure of his ship. With neither passport nor sailor's card to prove his identity, European authorities pass him from country to country. While the rich and powerful quickly navigate the bureaucratic morass established after World War I, Gales, a common sailor, is shuffled between consulates and police stations.

Failing after considerable effort to identify himself legally, he settles for a berth on the *Yorikke*, an illegal steamship involved in smuggling arms to various revolutionary groups. Gales is a coal-drag, hauling coal from the bunkers to the firemen stoking the boilers, the lowest position on the ship. He endures horrid working conditions: brutes for officers, an agonizing watch schedule, and nearly catastrophic equipment failure. Working in the boiler room, Gales is perpetually burned, scalded, and scorched by hot coals, leaking steam, and the grate-bars that fall from the furnace.

The *Yorikke* appears to be the "death ship" of the novel's title in both physical condition and mission. On board, Gales gives up the identity that he has tried so hard to establish and becomes known as Pippip. Nonetheless, he comes to love the old *Yorikke* just as he is shanghaied* on the *Empress of Madagascar*, a supposedly "civilized" British vessel. This vessel is about to be scuttled for the insurance money, and it is the real "death ship." Gales and his companion come to a frantic end, delirious and hallucinating, as the ship finally sinks. How Gales apparently survives to tell the tale remains a mystery.

Identity is a theme relevant to both the work and its author. Traven admits that Gales, who tries to prove his identity before accepting the anonymity of a tramp sailor, is his closest biographical character. Likewise, Traven's personal identity is enigmatic. He was deliberate in his attempts to mislead investigators, reporters, and researchers and was known to have used over twenty-five aliases crossing seven nationalities. For his trouble, he succeeded in drawing even more attention to himself, creating one of the greatest literary mysteries of the twentieth century.

Researchers have hotly debated whether "B. Traven" was Rex Marut, actor, author, revolutionary, and alleged illegitimate son of Kaiser Wilhelm II, born 25 February 1882, in San Francisco, or Otto Feige, born 23 February 1882, in Schwiebus, Germany. Once Traven began publishing from post office boxes in Tampico, Mexico, records and references to Marut and Feige disappear. His identity was then traced to one Traven Torsvan, born 5 March 1890, in Chicago. Traven's claims to being an American seemed confirmed, but there is no birth record for Torsvan in Chicago. A final alias, Hal Croves, the writer's "agent," appears late in the author's life. In his will, Traven states that all the names are indeed his. Perhaps the only certainty is that the author known as B. Traven died 26 March 1969.

FURTHER READING: Chankin, Donald O. *Anonymity and Death: The Fiction of B. Traven*. University Park: Pennsylvania State UP, 1975; Guthke, Karl S. *B. Traven: The Life behind the Legends*. Frankfurt am Main: Buchergilde Gutenberg, 1987, Eng. trans. Brooklyn, NY: Lawrence Hill Books, 1991; Stone, Judy. *The Mystery of B. Traven*. Los Altos, CA: William Kaufmann, 1977; Wyatt, Will. *The Man Who Was B. Traven*. London: Jonathan Cape, 1980.

Glenn Grasso

DELANO, AMASA (1763–1823). Amasa Delano, whose *Voyages and Travels* (1817) was the source for Herman Melville's* "Benito Cereno"* (1855), was born in Duxbury, Massachusetts. After serving briefly in the Continental army during the American Revolution, Delano began a lifelong career as sailor, ship captain, and occasional shipbuilder, often in conjunction with his brother Samuel.

Voyages and Travels focuses on his experiences in the Pacific and Indian Oceans from 1790 until 1807, during which time Delano several times circumnavigated the globe. In *Voyages and Travels* Delano clearly wants to be both informative and entertaining. He offers advice on what supplies to take on a voyage, how best to approach specific islands and landfalls, and where to find water and other supplies. He describes not only such well-known places as Canton, Bombay, Calcutta, and Lima but also the Palau Islands, New Guinea, and other relatively unexplored areas. Finally, Delano likes to tell a good story: a battle with the natives of New Guinea, the mutiny* on the *Bounty* and its aftermath, a near drowning. Delano clearly wonders whether civilization is best for the natives of the islands he visits. He ordinarily thinks well of the islanders and believes that European exploitation has caused most of the antagonism he encounters.

Delano gave significant space to an account of his capture of the Spanish ship *Tryal* off the coast of Chile in 1801 and to the events subsequent to the capture. Seeing the ship in apparent difficulty, Delano went aboard, was told that the ship was long without provisions, remained on board while a boat went for food and water, and learned that the slaves had revolted and captured the ship only when its captain, Benito Cereno, jumped into his boat as it was leaving. Melville's rewriting of that account is one of his most famous narratives, "Benito Cereno." Melville's character Amasa Delano much resembles the historical author of *Voyages and Travels*. Both figures desire to be helpful and are filled with advice for others; both are generally sympathetic to the slaves but consider themselves superior and are strict disciplinarians; both are deceived by the situation until Cereno leaps into the boat. Melville, however, at once enlarges the scope of his Delano to be more nearly a representative American and diminishes him into a character somewhat less acute than the real person. [*See also* CIRCUMNAVIGATIONS AND BLUE-WATER PASSAGES]

James L. Gray

DESROSIERS, LÉO-PAUL (1896–1967). Léo-Paul Desrosiers was born in Berthier-en-Haut, Quebec, a village on the banks of the Saint Lawrence River northeast of Montreal. His happy childhood provided him with material for his first work, *Ames et Paysages* (1922), and a job as a government news editor gave him the time he needed to write *Nord-Sud* (1931). *Les Engagés du Grand Portage* (1938), generally considered his best-written novel, tells of the ambitions and hardships of fur-trading voyageurs paddling canoes through calm and storm on the Great Lakes* and connected waters in the early 1800s. Vacations in his beloved Gaspé, a small fishing village on the Gulf of Saint Lawrence, inspired him to use this locale as a setting for his psychological novel *L'Ampoule d'or* (1951), for which he won the Prix Duvernay. Other works include *Commencements* (1939), *Les Opiniâtres* (1941), *Sources* (1942), *Iroquoisie* (1947), and the trilogy *Vous Qui Passez* (1958–1960). [*See also* CANADIAN LITERATURE OF THE SEA]

Donald P. Curtis

DICKEY, JAMES [LAFAYETTE] (1923–1997). James Dickey, noted poet, novelist, and critic, was born in Atlanta, Georgia. During World War II, he served in a night-fighter squadron in the South Pacific. In the late 1940s he attended Vanderbilt University, during which time he also began writing and publishing poems. He received a master's degree from Vanderbilt and taught at Rice University in Houston from 1950 to 1954, taking a two-year leave of absence to serve in the Korean War. After successfully forging a second career as an advertising copywriter and executive, Dickey returned to poetry full-time in 1960 and became a professor and poet-in-residence at the University of South Carolina in 1968.

As a poet, Dickey has been labeled a romantic modernist. He is primarily concerned with the rapturous possibilities of nature, as in "The Movement of Fish" (1961) and "The Heaven of Animals" (1961), and with the life-awakening experiences of war and violence as contrasted to the deadening effects of the suburban milieu. His poetry, which appeared throughout the 1950s, 1960s, and 1970s in various literary journals and magazines, has been collected in several volumes: *Into the Stone* (1960), *Drowning with Others* (1962), *Buckdancer's Choice* (1965), and *The Strength of Fields* (1979).

In a prose-poem meditation on fishing, "Pursuing the Grey Soul" (1978), Dickey characterizes the sea as an otherworldly setting that nourishes man's "wished-for vastness of spirit." While this and many of his other works focus on the creek-fed wilderness of Dickey's youth, the sea remains an important setting for his explorations of the brutal aspects of nature. Dickey displays a particular fascination with sharks in such poems as "The Shark at the Window" (1951), which centers on the image of a shark behind aquarium glass, and "The Shark's Parlor" (1965), a humorous, yet stirring, account of a shark-and-fisherman tug-of-war on Cumberland Island, Georgia. Dickey's other sea-related poems include "The Ax-God: Sea-Pursuit" (1978), "Undersea Fragments in Colons" (1979), and "Below the Lighthouse"* (1959). [*See also* SEA IMAGERY IN MODERN AND CONTEMPORARY POETRY]

Brian Anderson

DICKINSON, EMILY [ELIZABETH] (1830–1886). Although the great American poet Emily Dickinson is frequently quoted as saying she "never saw the Sea" (P 1052), it seems probable that the reclusive native of Amherst, Massachusetts, may have glimpsed the Atlantic coast on her occasional girlhood trips to Boston or when she and her sister visited their congressman father in Washington. Whether or not she physically witnessed the ocean, however, she knew it through reading the Bible, Henry Wadsworth Longfellow,* Ik Marvell, Elizabeth and Robert Browning, and other favorite writers. She also knew it through reports of European travel by family friends, especially Samuel Bowles.

Geographic allusions to the Caspian Sea, the Red Sea, the Spice Isles, and other exotic places reached in her time only by ocean voyages reveal Dickinson's excited response to explorations widely reported in the magazines and newspapers to which her family subscribed. So, too, her ability to imagine the pine tree at her bedroom window as "Just a Sea—with a Stem—" (P 797) demonstrates the power of her imagination to transcend landlocked circumstances. Her poems reflect Dickinson's ability to imagine the mountain-born sailor's exultant joy when first venturing upon ocean (P 76) or the diver's pride in emerging with a pearl (P 84), but they also sketch more idiosyncratic and disturbing fantasies involving a hot-air balloon plummeting into the sea (P 700), a tiny boat spinning and slipping into its abyss (P 723), a brook engaging in subtle negotiations with the sea (P 1210), or a drop of river water's confused response to ocean's obliterating seduction (P 284).

Although a lyric poet, Dickinson sometimes distilled into her poems narrative elements about disasters at sea. "Glee—The great storm is over—" (P 619), for example, contrasts ways in which people relate and receive stories about shipwreck:* adult narrators celebrate the survival of four mariners while their children silently wonder about the forty who died. Although "Adrift! A little boat adrift!" (P 30) ends with angels welcoming a sunken craft, "The waters chased him as he fled" (P 1749) takes a starkly naturalistic approach to man's unequal battle with the sea.

Most often, however, the sea figures symbolically in Dickinson's poems. She often ascribes erotic force to this symbol, as in "I started Early—Took my Dog—" (P 520), in which the child-speaker retreats from the tide pursuing her, and "Wild Nights—Wild Nights!" (P 249), in which the turbulence of a storm at sea provides dramatic backdrop to the ecstasy of lovers

who experience their private bliss as "Rowing in Eden—." Dickinson's
" 'Master' Letters" also deploy sea imagery to express the wildness of sensual
and/or spiritual passion.

It is as a symbol of the fascinating and frightening unknown, however,
that the ocean appears most characteristically in Dickinson's writings. Analogous to death, her circumferential "Crescent in the Sea" figures as the
mystery to be confronted between mortal life and immortality, while the
soul pursues its dizzying voyage between Eternity behind it and Immortality
ahead (P 721). Taking a venturesome approach to life as quest, Dickinson
apparently maintained through life the attitude she expressed in an 1850
letter to a girlhood friend: "The shore is safer, Abiah," she wrote, "but I
love to buffet the sea" (L 39).

FURTHER READING: *The Letters of Emily Dickinson*. Ed. Thomas H. Johnson
and Theodora Ward. 3 vols. Cambridge: Belknap-Harvard UP, 1958; *The Poems of
Emily Dickinson*. Ed. Thomas H. Johnson. 3 vols. Cambridge: Belknap-Harvard UP,
1955; Eberwein, Jane Donahue. *Dickinson: Strategies of Limitation*. Amherst: U of
Massachusetts P, 1985; Eberwein, Jane Donahue. *An Emily Dickinson Encyclopedia*.
Westport, CT: Greenwood P, 1998; Farr, Judith. *The Passion of Emily Dickinson*.
Cambridge: Harvard UP, 1992; Patterson, Rebecca. *Emily Dickinson's Imagery*. Ed.
Margaret H. Freeman. Amherst: U of Massachusetts P, 1979.

Jane Donahue Eberwein

DISTURNELL, JOHN (1801–1877). A printer and book dealer, as well
as librarian of the Cooper Union, John Disturnell, who lived most of his
life in New York City when he was not traveling, was a prolific writer of
travel books and guides to travel in North America. His first and his last
books focus on travel in New York and the East, but *The Western Traveller*
(1844) describes travel by canal boat to Buffalo and by steamer from Buffalo
to Detroit and Chicago and is essentially a guide to shipping lines and
routes. In 1857, with *A Trip through the Lakes of North America*, Disturnell
writes in the tradition of Thomas Jefferson's *Notes on the State of Virginia*
(1787). Here, within the framework of the description of an apparent single
journey, Disturnell combines statistical information on the economy and
information on the development of the Great Lakes* with descriptions of
points of interest and historical events, human interest anecdotes, and observations on the sociology and geography of the region. The work provides
a vivid portrait of the Lakes region as it was taking its place as part of the
national whole, and it remains a valuable source of information.

Disturnell followed *A Trip through the Lakes of North America* with two
other books on the Lakes, *The Great Lakes or Inland Seas of America*
(1865), a shorter, revised version of the former, and *Island of Mackinac*
(1875). He concluded his concern with travel on the Lakes with *Sailing on
the Great Lakes and Rivers of North America* (1874) and broadened his
venue with *Around the Continent and around the World* (1873). It is some-

times difficult to tell exactly how much of the last book is based on his own travels, and at times it threatens to become a steamer schedule and railroad timetable.

In a great age of travel writing, Disturnell was a prolific leader; his works remain valuable sources of information about that age, as noted in David D. Anderson, "John Disturnell Introduces the Great Lakes to America," *Inland Seas* 18 (Summer 1962): 96–106.

David D. Anderson

DONER, MARY FRANCES (1893–1985). Mary Frances Doner set many of her books near her birthplace, Port Huron, Michigan. She supplied around 250 short stories for pulp magazines early in her career and in the 1930s began producing novels and nonfiction, over twenty-eight books altogether. Her Great Lakes* novels include *Fool's Heaven* (1932), *Some Fell among Thorns* (1939), *Chalice* (1940), *Not by Bread Alone* (1941), *Glass Mountain* (1942), *O Distant Star* (1944), *Ravenswood* (1948), *The Wind and the Fog* (1963), and *Not by Appointment* (1972). They focus on the people who sailed the freight and passenger ships on the Lakes, their ambitions and joy in their work, and the drama of storms and accidents; and on the wives, girlfriends, and children who awaited them in the cities and small towns on the shores. *While the River Flows* (1962) also treats ecological matters, such as the influence of the Soo Locks on the water level and hence on values of shoreline property and of industry on the wildlife of the rivers and lakes; *Thine Is the Power* (1972) discusses stored power like that provided by a plant at Ludington, Michigan. A biography, *The Salvager: The Life of Captain Tom Reid on the Great Lakes* (1958), describes shipwrecks* and their aftermath in the late nineteenth and early twentieth centuries.

Mary DeJong Obuchowski

D[OOLITTLE]., H[ILDA]. (1886–1961). H. D., a poet, novelist, dramatist, and translator whose works often incorporate sea imagery, was born in Pennsylvania. Childhood visits to the seacoasts of Rhode Island and Maine first inspired H. D., best known for her imagist poetry, to write about the sea. "Hermes of the Ways" (1913), one of her earliest published poems, imagines the god of the crossroads standing at the tide line, the shifting boundary between sea and sand. Images of stormy beaches and seaside gardens link the poems collected in *Sea Garden* (1916), her first book of poetry. Poems such as "Sea Rose" (1915), "Sea Iris" (1915), and "Sea Violet" (1916) celebrate the strength and beauty of the flowers that thrive in the harsh conditions at the water's edge. In "Sheltered Garden" (1916) the poet rejects the oppressive peace of an inland orchard protected from the wind and waves in favor of the freedom of the coastline. Other books by H. D. voice this fascination with the sea, including *Hymen* (1921), a collection of poems; *Hippolytus Temporizes* (1928), a play; *Heydlus* (1928), a novel; and

Red Roses from Bronze (1931), a volume of poetry. She died in Switzerland in 1961. [*See also* SEA IMAGERY IN MODERN AND CONTEMPORARY POETRY]

Gregg Allen Walker

A DOOR INTO OCEAN (1986). Joan Slonczewski (1956–   ) brings an ecofeminist perspective to her science fiction novel set on Shora, a moon comprised of ocean and peopled by women wholly adapted to living in this watery realm. Committed to sustaining and understanding life, the women of Shora exist in harmony, acknowledging individual differences within their community and appreciating the diverse fantastic sea creatures and oceanic forces of their moon. Outside galactic powers, however, seek to colonize Shora and to exploit its human and natural resources, and when the women, in their desire to acknowledge and to learn from all life, permit interaction, Slonczewski's narrative becomes a melodrama, with Shora's community, represented by the organic and fluid sea, set in opposition to a technological and hierarchical patriarchy, represented by dead stone.

Elizabeth Schultz

DOUGLASS, FREDERICK (1818–1895). Abolitionist, orator, social reformer, editor, author, and consul general to Haiti, Frederick Douglass was born into slavery as Frederick Augustus Bailey. He spent the early years of his childhood in Talbot County, Maryland, on the eastern shore of Chesapeake Bay. Separated in infancy from his black slave mother, Harriet Bailey, Douglass was raised by his grandmother, Betsy Bailey. The identity of his white father remains unknown. His first master, Aaron Anthony, was manager for the Lloyd Plantation, a large concern employing hundreds of slaves to grow tobacco, corn, and wheat. Douglass' early memories of the sea included fishing in the Chesapeake estuaries, watching sailing vessels plying the bay, and listening to stories about Annapolis and Baltimore told by the privileged slaves who worked on board the plantation's sloop, *Sally Lloyd*.

When Frederick was between seven and eight years old, he was sent to Baltimore to serve as a house boy. He later regarded this escape from the enforced ignorance and harshness of plantation labor for the enlarged horizons and opportunities of a bustling port city to be the most fortunate occurrence of his life. On the docks he encountered worldly black sailors, both slave and free, the black intellectuals of their day, able to tell him about the abolitionist movement in the North, Britain's pursuit of slave ships on the high seas, shipboard slave revolts, black insurrections in Jamaica, and the revolutionary black nation of Haiti.

Despite opposition, Douglass taught himself to read by auditing the lessons of white children and borrowing their primers. At age twelve, he purchased with hoarded pennies Caleb Bingham's *The Columbian Orator* (1802), a collection of historic speeches on behalf of liberty, which he read repeatedly and practiced delivering. At the black Dallas Street Methodist Church, he attended Sunday school, read the Bible, heard stirring sermons, and met role models such as Dr. Lewis G. Wells, black physician and lecturer. At fourteen, Douglass began teaching in the Sunday school.

In 1832 he was forced to return to the plantation for work as a field hand. Insubordinate, articulate, and physically powerful, the teenaged Douglass was sent to a slave-breaker by his intimidated owner. Yet Douglass remained defiant: striking the slave-breaker, organizing an underground Sunday school for slaves, teaching them to read, and plotting with friends to run away. Douglass had noted the direction taken by steamboats going to Philadelphia, and the men planned to follow the shoreline north to freedom. In 1836, on the verge of escape, Douglass and his comrades were betrayed and imprisoned. To protect Douglass, the recognized ringleader, from angry slaveholders, his master returned him to Baltimore.

Hired out as a caulker, Douglass was reimmersed in the subversive black subculture of Baltimore's shipyards. By 1838 he was ready to escape from slavery. Dressed in sailor's clothing, well versed in nautical jargon, and carrying the customary Seaman's Protection Certificate (proof of citizenship for all sailors and one that essentially protected free black sailors from enslavement in southern ports), he took the train north to freedom, exchanging the name Bailey for Douglass to disguise his fugitive status. Anna Murray, his free black fiancée, followed. In the whaling port of New Bedford, the newlyweds found a thriving free black community involved in the maritime trades. Organized white labor prevented Douglass from working as a caulker, but he found employment as a stevedore. A mainstay of New Bedford's African Methodist Episcopal Zion chapel, Douglass began preaching and became involved with the abolitionist movement.

In 1841 Douglass addressed an antislavery convention on Nantucket.* His educated demeanor, practiced oratory, compelling voice, and poignant testimony riveted the white audience, and the Massachusetts Anti-Slavery Society hired him as a lecturer. His reputation as an orator grew, and in 1845 he published his now classic *Narrative of the Life of Frederick Douglass*, recounting the physical and emotional trials of his bondage and escape. Widely read in its own time, the narrative is rich with maritime metaphor, including one of its virtuoso passages, his apostrophe to the Chesapeake's ships, calling them "freedom's swift-winged angels."

Between 1845 and 1847 Douglass made a speaking tour of Great Britain, becoming internationally famous. British friends purchased his freedom, and Douglass returned to the United States to begin his own abolitionist weekly, *The North Star*. There he published his novella, *The Heroic Slave* (1853), a fictionalized account of a historic slave ship revolt. In 1841, 134 slaves led by Madison Washington mutinied* and took command of the vessel *Creole*, carrying them from Virginia for sale in the New Orleans market. The slaves sailed *Creole* to Jamaica and received asylum from the British government.

In Douglass' novella, Washington is a high-minded statesman-hero, to be honored with Thomas Jefferson for upholding the principles of 1776. The sea offers opportunities for freedom that encirclement on land does not: "You cannot write the bloody laws of slavery on those restless billows."

Douglass continued his life story in two more autobiographies, *My Bondage and My Freedom* (1855) and *Life and Times of Frederick Douglass* (1881, rev. 1892). He participated in the first woman's rights convention, harbored John Brown while he planned the Harpers Ferry raid, and recruited black troops for the Union army. After the Civil War, he fought for black suffrage and civil rights. In 1883, after his first wife's death, he married white suffragist Helen Pitts. Douglass held several presidential appointments and in 1891 was made consul general to Haiti, this hemisphere's only independent black nation. Active to the last, he died of a heart attack after speaking at a woman's rights meeting.

Although much of his life was spent far from the sea, Douglass' education by the black cultures of maritime Baltimore and New Bedford empowered him to become one of America's most influential black political leaders. A made-for-television biography, *Frederick Douglass: When the Lion Wrote History*, was released in 1994. Douglass appears as a very minor character in Sena Jeter Naslund's *Ahab's Wife, Or the Star-Gazer* (1999). [*See also* AFRICAN AMERICAN LITERATURE; SLAVE NARRATIVES]

FURTHER READING: Bolster, W. Jeffrey. *Black Jacks: African American Seamen in the Age of Sail*. Cambridge: Harvard UP, 1997; Malloy, Mary. *African Americans in the Maritime Trades: A Guide to Resources in New England*. Sharon, MA: Kendall Whaling Museum, 1990; McFeely, William S. *Frederick Douglass*. New York: Norton, 1991.

Susan F. Beegel

DRAMA OF THE SEA. According to the lyrics of *Oklahoma!* (1945), Americans supposedly know "the land we belong to is grand." American drama of the sea sometimes matches such buoyant, national optimism, but many playwrights have turned to the sea as a metaphor to express doubts about the American enterprise as drifting, mutinous, or in danger of sinking altogether. Still others have used the endlessly changing seascape to reflect philosophically on human aspiration and folly, on intimacy and drifting apart, on coming-of-age and wrecked lives, on romantic quest and metaphysical query.

Nautical themes had already permeated the eighteenth-century pantomime, to judge from *Robinson Crusoe: or, the Genius of Columbia* (1790) and *Harlequin Shipwreck** (1795). More substantially, the nineteenth-century tradition of American maritime drama, though not so rich as its English counterpart, presents a mirror of aspiration and adventure reflecting the American face as if from the glassy surface of the sea. Although virtually all sea plays written by Americans during the nineteenth century may be mustered under the flag of nautical melodrama, they form a diverse, even motley crew.

A wave of Barbary Coast pirate* plays, inspired by Susannah Rowson's* phenomenally popular novel *Charlotte Temple* (1791), which had 160 printings, rose in the 1790s with Rowson's own dramatization, *A Struggle for Freedom* (1794). The Barbary Coast continued to fascinate playwrights and audiences through the 1840s with such popular vehicles as Maria H. Pinckney's *The Young Carolinians; or, Americans in Algiers* (1818); *The Siege of Tripoli* (1820) by Mordechai Noah; Jonathan S. Smith's *The Siege of Algiers; or, The Downfall of Hadgi-Ali-Bashaw, a Political, Historical and Sentimental Tragi-Comedy* (1823) and *Naval Glory, or Decatur's Triumph* (1844). Less long-lived were plays born of American sea battles during the War of 1812, including William Dunlap's* *Yankee Chronology* (1812), celebrating the victory of the *Constitution* over the *Guerrière*, or *The Triumph of Plattsburgh* (1830) by Richard Penn Smith, based on Thomas Macdonough's victory at Plattsburgh Bay in September 1814. As in English nautical melodrama, the stock character of "Jolly Jack Tar" made numerous appearances in American sea plays, among them *American Tars in Tripoli* (1805); *The Constitution, or American Tars Triumphant* (1812); *The Naval Frolic, or A Tribute to American Tars* (1812). These and/or other presentations of Jack Tar* may have distantly influenced Herman Melville* in his creation of the "Handsome Sailor," Billy Budd.*

Reputable American authors of the nineteenth century occasionally tried a hand at sea drama. James Nelson Barker wrote two sea plays of topical interest: *The Embargo; or, What News?* (1808) and *The Armourer's Escape, or Three Years at Nootka Sound* (1817), the latter based on the adventure of John Jewitt.* James Fenimore Cooper's* modern editor Kay Seymour House notes that *The Pilot** (1824) had been transformed into a "nautical burletta" as early as 1826 by the Englishman Edward Fitzball. By 1828 Cooper's *The Red Rover** (1827) had already been adapted for the stage and performed in Philadelphia by the English actor Samuel Chapman, just a year after its initial publication. Other adaptations of these two novels held the stage until late in the century. Near the end of the century, William Dean Howells'* *A Sea Change, or, Love's Stowaway* (1884) reached the stage, albeit unsuccessfully.

Far more commonly, nautical melodrama ruled the canvas seas in America's nineteenth-century playhouses. Melodramatists celebrated Jean Lafitte* and John Paul Jones* and other sea captains. By midcentury, potboilers featuring the highly popular Laura Keene included such titles as *The Sea of Ice; or, A Mother's Prayer* and *Young Bacchus; or, Spirits and Water* (1857–1858). As the century wore on, there appeared lighthouse* plays, seamonster plays, Commodore Matthew Perry* plays, and plays commemorating Christopher Columbus,* including Steele Mackaye's *The World Finder*, intended for performance at his ill-fated Spectatorium at the Columbian

Exposition of 1893. The popularity of nautical melodrama and farce is testified to in the scores of plays written by George Melville Baker (apparently no relation to Herman Melville) for amateur players in the 1860s, 1870s, and 1880s. Such forgettable efforts as *Down by the Sea, Messmates*, and *My Uncle, the Captain* (all c. 1868) feature salty old storytellers, damsels saved from drowning, "darky" cabin stewards, sea chanteys, and roaring gales. Toward the end of the century, James Herne* made tentative moves toward naturalism with *Hearts of Oak* (1879), *Drifting Apart: or, Mary, the Fisherman's Child* (1888), *Shore Acres* (1892), and *Sag Harbor* (1899). Herne's plays bespeak a genuine love of the sea, firsthand knowledge of maritime and fishing lore, and a talent for enlivening melodramatic format with vivid local color.

Eugene O'Neill* both built upon and changed all this with the S.S. *Glencairn** plays (first presented together in 1924), *The Hairy Ape* (1922), *Anna Christie* (1922), and others where the sea figures centrally or crucially as setting and metaphor. One might say that O'Neill was haunted both by the sea and by the melodramatic tradition virtually incarnated in his famous actor father, James. The sea surely freed O'Neill from the worst of the latter's effects, and he used it as a marvelously varied theme in his work to explore freedom, coming-of-age, courage, despair, loneliness, death, and transcendence.

Many of the finest American dramatists of the twentieth century have waded in after O'Neill, if none so deeply. Laurence Stallings and Maxwell Anderson (*The Buccaneer* [1925]), Elmer Rice,* Don Marquis (*Out of the Sea* [1927], a dramatic retelling of the Tristan and Isolde legend), Robert Sherwood (who wrote the book for the unsuccessful Irving Berlin musical *Miss Liberty* [1949]), Susan Glaspell,* Paul Green,* S. N. Behrman,* Tennessee Williams,* Arthur Miller, Edward Albee,* John Guare, Israel Horovitz, Terence McNally,* Tina Howe,* Steven Dietz, and David Mamet have all written at least one play suffused with the atmosphere of sea and seashore or set aboard a ship or steeped in maritime lore and legend or simply employing the sea as a convenient metaphor and special effect. For some, the Atlantic crossing symbolized the overcoming of class boundaries. For others the seashore is a version of American pastoral—or antipastoral. For still others the sea is both cradle and grave for the dreams of drifters, misfits, adventurers, and antiheroes.

Other high-water marks for twentieth-century nonmusical plays with nautical settings include Paul Osborn's adaptation of Richard Hughes' *A High Wind in Jamaica* (1929; film adaptation, 1965) as *The Innocent Voyage* (1943), *Mister Roberts** (1948), the dramatization of *Billy Budd** (1951), *The Caine Mutiny Court Martial* (1954; film 1954), and Robert Lowell's* adaptation of *Benito Cereno** (1965, frequently produced in regional theatres thereafter). Lesser lights have frequently followed O'Neill's misty and moody models, though various maritime locales have spawned different and quasi-generic dramatic situations. Lighthouses invite tragedy born of isolation, eccentricity, and sexual frustration. Freighters are the scene of melodramatic intrigue. Fishing boats produce tales of American enterprise. Ferry boats are often captained by characters given to unfocused dreaming. Yachts breed farce; ocean liners, romance. Seaside dives inspire philosophical speculation and soul-searching; beaches and seashores incite intimacy.

The sheer volume of such efforts, irrespective of their merit as dramatic literature, may be surprising. Samuel Leiter records sixty-eight plays appearing on Broadway between 1920 and 1950 that use seafaring characters or that take place on boats or ships. Long before the enthusiasm for the *Titanic** story, ocean liners were the setting for at least a score of American plays. Just as an early performance of the 1997 Broadway musical was canceled because the ship refused to sink, technical mishaps regularly afflicted ocean liner drama.* During the 1897 Broadway season, Harrison Grey Fiske's *The Privateer* was doomed to failure when the canvas "water" refused to operate properly, conveying the impression that the hero was floating on a raft rather than swimming furiously to save his friend's life.

The Broadway and Hollywood phenomenon *Titanic* is only the latest in a line that includes shore leave musicals,* vaudevilles, or reviews set on shipboard, musicals and operettas featuring pirates and sailors, and seagoing romances. Among these are such excellent examples of the American musical tradition as *Hit the Deck!* (1927; films 1930, 1955), *Anything Goes* (1934; films 1936, 1956), *Gentlemen Prefer Blondes* (1949; films 1928, 1953), *South Pacific** (1949; film 1958), and *The Unsinkable Molly Brown* (1961; film 1964). [*See also LAKEBOAT*; MELVILLE DRAMATIZATIONS; NANTUCKET CYCLE; *TEN NOVEMBER*]

FURTHER READING: Bordman, Gerald Martin. *American Musical Theatre: A Chronicle.* New York: Oxford UP, 1992; Bordman, Gerald Martin. *American Theatre: A Chronicle of Comedy and Drama, 1869–1914.* New York: Oxford UP, 1994; Leiter, Samuel L. *The Encyclopedia of the New York Stage, 1920–1950.* 3 vols. Westport, CT: Greenwood, 1985–1992; Meserve, Walter J. *An Emerging Entertainment: The Drama of the American People to 1828.* Bloomington: Indiana UP, 1977; Quinn, Arthur Hobson. *A History of the American Drama from the Civil War to the Present Day.* Rev. ed. New York: Appleton-Century-Crofts, 1964.

Attilio Favorini

DREAMING IN CUBAN (1992). The sea, like Cuba, connects the lives of three generations of women in this novel by Christina Garcia (1958–   ), which spans, politically, the Batista and the Castro years and, geographically, Cuba and the United States. Described in the novel as an "island-colony," Cuba is rendered vulnerable by the sea, which the pro-Castro Celia also blames for stimulating restlessness in her family and for separating her from her anti-Castro husband and daughter, who have escaped to New York with her beloved granddaughter, Pilar.

However, throughout *Dreaming in Cuban* the sea is referred to not only realistically and historically, bringing diverse cultures to Cuba and uniting them by touching all of their shores, but also surrealistically and magically, prompting imagination, memory, and desire. Thus, while Celia serves Castro by keeping a lookout for foreign invaders from her beach house at Santa Teresa del Mar, she envisions her dead husband walking across the sea to return to her. Part of Pilar's legacy from her grandmother is her love of the sea and the smoothness of pearls. At the novel's conclusion, when Celia takes her last swim out to sea, her death by water restores her to the romantic Cuba of her youth—lovely and liberating. [*See also* CARIBBEAN LITERATURE OF THE SEA]

Elizabeth Schultz

DUNBAR, PAUL LAURENCE (1872–1906). Best known for the dialect poetry suggested by the titles of his four published volumes, Paul Laurence Dunbar, the son of former slaves, also wrote a number of short stories and novels. His interest in the sea as a metaphorical medium is best exemplified in a half dozen of his celebratory poems, a subgenre perhaps justifiably ignored by most critics. While these works are typical neither of Dunbar's major modes nor of his artistic successes, they do illustrate the ocean's potential for mythic perspective in an active imagination.

Dunbar's "Columbian Ode" (1896) patriotically celebrates man's impulse toward discovery and his conquest of natural barriers. "The Mystic Sea" (1899) describes the inspirational mystique of the sea for its own sake; "On the Sea Wall" (1899) presents the ocean as both an avenue to the past and a resonator of the human heart. More lighthearted poems evoke joy, such as "A Sailor's Song" (1899); others lament the sorrows of isolation or alienation, such as "Ships That Pass in the Night" (1895). The poet's most "seaworthy" poem in terms of content and quality of verse portrays the sea as a natural phenomenon symbolically expressing the vagaries of the human condition. "The Wind and the Sea" (1896) may be one long exercise in psychological projection, but the close correlation between seascape and emotion transcends the triviality of other Dunbar poems of this ilk. If little else, Dunbar's poetic canon further reveals the proclivity of so many poets for viewing the sea as both a source and an object of poetic perspectives. [*See also* SEA IMAGERY IN MODERN AND CONTEMPORARY POETRY]

Fred M. Fetrow

DUNLAP, WILLIAM (1766–1839). William Dunlap, born in Perth Amboy, New Jersey, showed considerable artistic aptitude at an early age and in 1784 was sent to England to study painting under Benjamin West. There, however, he became fascinated with the theater and, upon his arrival in New York three years later, soon abandoned his art career for the stage. He wrote, adapted, or translated between fifty and sixty-five plays, some of which are lost or misattributed. His later writings included histories and biographies, and he ultimately returned to painting.

His *Yankee Chronology; or, Huzza for the* Constitution! *A Musical Interlude, in One Act. To Which Are Added, the Patriotic Songs of the Freedom of the Seas, and Yankee Tars* (1812) was written to celebrate the naval victory of the American frigate *Constitution* over its English counterpart, *Guerriere*, earlier that year. This short musical drama begins with an American sailor, a veteran of that engagement, returning to his home and recounting the battle to his friends. The sailor sings several patriotic songs that Dunlap had actually written a few years earlier in reaction to the British impressment of American seamen. The production was a rousing success.

Of Dunlap's numerous plays, which were mainly popular potboilers with European themes and scenes, *Yankee Chronology* is the only one to feature the sea or the Great Lakes,* with one minor exception. His final play, *A Trip to Niagara; or Travellers in America: A Farce* (1830), uses Niagara Falls in the final scene, where an English tourist, heretofore anti-American, proclaims the greatness of the United States.

Significant collections of Dunlap's manuscripts are held by the New York Public Library and Virginia Historical Society. [*See also* DRAMA OF THE SEA; SEA MUSIC]

Robert Beasecker

E

EBERHART, RICHARD [GHORMLEY] (1904–   ). Richard Eberhart is the author of some twenty-six volumes of poetry, from *A Bravery of Earth* (1930), to *Maine Poems* (1989). Throughout his career he has utilized nautical images and themes, many of which derive from his immediate experience of the sea. A precise observer for whom the natural world offers moral lessons, Eberhart often uses the sea to represent human powerlessness in the face of natural forces. In his first, largely autobiographical volume, for example, his experience in 1927 as a deckhand on freighters crossing the Pacific heightens his sense of the paradoxical loneliness and exhilaration of life at sea. In the sonnet "Fear of Death by Water" (*The Long Reach* [1984]), he writes that the sight of a bay filled with boats "Argues that man controls the ocean," but that this isn't really the case, and that poems will not save one from drowning.

Later in his career, his experiences as the owner of the thirty-six-foot sailing cruiser *Reve* on the coast of Maine supply the settings and substance for much of his poetry. He owned a cottage at Undercliff on the Penobscot Bay and often took fellow poets sailing. "How to Make Something of the Rocks," "Sea Bells," "Sea Storm," "Fog I" and "Fog II" (there are two sequences with these titles), and a host of other poems from *The Long Reach* that also appear in *Maine Poems* continue to use Eberhart's straightforward perception of the sea as a powerful force and a compelling image for the expression of moral concerns. "The implications of fog are enormous," he reminds us in typical fashion in "Fog II." The sea bell in "Sea Bells" tolls the ocean's character, effects, and meaning, from silence, to repetition, to salvation. [*See also* SEA IMAGERY IN MODERN AND CONTEMPORARY POETRY]

Thomas R. Brooks

EDMUND FITZGERALD. The Great Lakes* bulk freighter *Edmund Fitzgerald* (built 1958) has assumed an unparalleled position in the folklore of the inland seas. Throughout the history of the navigation of the Great Lakes, ships have been lost with all hands under conditions that were seemingly inexplicable. The *Edmund Fitzgerald* is the most recent example.

At 7:00 P.M., 10 November 1975, the 729-foot *Edmund Fitzgerald* sank approximately fifteen miles northwest of Whitefish Point, Lake Superior. The freighter was bound from Superior, Wisconsin, to Detroit, with a cargo of iron ore pellets. The weather was horrible, with some mariners describing it as hurricane conditions. On the open Lake, winds exceeded ninety miles per hour, and waves crested at thirty-five feet. The *Fitzgerald* plunged so quickly that there was not even time for a radio distress call. Search and rescue efforts were fruitless. There were no survivors or witnesses to the tragedy; twenty-nine men perished with the vessel. Only a small amount of wreckage was found, and none of the victims' bodies were recovered. Detailed investigations by both the U.S. Coast Guard and National Transportation Safety Board failed to satisfactorily explain the loss.

The wreck of the *Edmund Fitzgerald* has become the best known of an estimated 9,000 Great Lakes shipwrecks.* Canadian* folksinger Gordon Lightfoot wrote of it in his popular ballad "The Wreck of the *Edmund Fitzgerald*" (1976). It is the subject of a novel by Joan Skelton, *The Survivor of the* Edmund Fitzgerald (1985), as well as the topic of *The Gales of November* by Robert J. Hemming (1981), a book combining the factual account of the loss with fictionalized crew interplay during the final trip. The evocative play *Ten November** (1986) by Steven Dietz also takes the *Fitzgerald* as its main subject. The *Fitzgerald* has been the topic of numerous nonfiction books, periodical articles, and videotapes. Several expeditions using high-technology diving equipment have filmed the wreck extensively, and there has been considerable controversy regarding not only the actual cause of loss but also the issue of leaving the wreck as an underwater grave site.

Fitzgerald has become part of the fabric of Great Lakes legend and lore. When sailors gather and talk of the Lakes, invariably the *Fitzgerald* will come up, with the question of where they were the night she sank. To the men and women of the Lakes, *Fitzgerald* is still a current event, not something to be considered history. To them, it is a chilling reminder of the ever-present danger of sailing the Great Lakes.

Frederick Stonehouse

EISELEY, LOREN C[OREY]. (1907–1977). Loren C. Eiseley, anthropologist, educator, and author, was born in Lincoln, Nebraska. He collected fossils as a child and began speculating on the evolution of humankind and the universe. His early books, *The Immense Journey* (1957) and *Darwin's*

Century: Evolution and the Men Who Discovered It (1958), are histories of modern science, with particular focus on the theory of evolution. In *Darwin's Century* Eiseley offers a close reading of both *The Voyage of the* Beagle (1839) and *On the Origin of Species* (1859). *The Immense Journey* is a collection of essays that speculate on the origins and future of humans and the universe. The ebb and flow of the sea and the flow of the river are primary images in these essays. In "The Slit," "The Flow of the River," "The Great Deeps," and "The Snout," Eiseley explores the mystery and magic of water as the source of all life. "The Star Thrower" in *The Unexpected Universe* (1969) muses on shells and starfish washed ashore and again contemplates the place of humanity in the universe.

The "missing link" in Eiseley's speculations on evolution became a metaphor for the physical/spiritual nature of humanity. Eiseley considered himself a naturalist in the tradition of Henry David Thoreau,* Francis Bacon, Sir Thomas Browne, and Izaak Walton. Living up to that tradition, Eiseley became a literary naturalist and a poet. The last two volumes published in his life were collections of poetry, *Notes of an Alchemist* (1972) and *The Innocent Assassins* (1973). Images of the sea are as prevalent in the poetry as in the prose. For example, "The Lost Plateau" from *Notes of an Alchemist* traces a tumultuous body of running water backward to an arid and lost plateau. In "The Rope," from the same collection, the fraying of a rope is an analogy for following the evolution of the present-day universe backward to its source in the sea and its creatures. In *The Innocent Assassins*, lifestyles of creatures such as the dolphin, tortoise, fish, and beaver are examined for what they can teach humanity about revering nature.

William A. Sullivan

ELIOT, T[HOMAS]. S[TEARNS]. (1888–1965). T. S. Eliot, perhaps the greatest poet of the twentieth century, was born on the banks of the Mississippi River in St. Louis, Missouri. Educated at Harvard, the Sorbonne, and Oxford, he became a British subject in 1927 and received the Nobel Prize in literature in 1948. Though he is best known for his great poem of dryness, *The Waste Land* (1922), poetry alluding to water spans his entire career. He became an avid sailor in his youth while summering on the Massachusetts coast, and his memories of the Mississippi and of the New England coastline infuse the later poems "Marina" (1930) and "The Dry Salvages" (1941), one of the *Four Quartets* (1942), his final long poem and crowning poetic achievement.

Eliot's poetry shifts in tone after his conversion to Anglicanism in 1927. In the earlier poems, specifically *The Love Song of J. Alfred Prufrock* (1917), *The Waste Land*, and *The Hollow Men* (1925), there is either dryness or death by, and dread of, water. In the later poems, water suggests mystery and divinity, where the interaction of river and sea is an image of humanity within eternity, an idea Eliot takes from Herakleitos and applies in *The Dry*

Salvages. Most significantly, Eliot redeems the image of the sea in his later poetry, buying it back from modernist nihilism, and his thoughts also come back to America, the homeland that he had purposely fled. [*See also* SEA IMAGERY IN MODERN AND CONTEMPORARY AMERICAN POETRY]

Matthew D. Childs

ELLIS, EDWARD SYLVESTER (1840–1916). A prolific, versatile author, Edward Sylvester Ellis was born in Geneva, Ohio, near Lake Erie. While young, he moved to New Jersey, only later to return to the Great Lakes* in his writing. Ellis wrote during stints as a schoolmaster, school superintendent, and editor. He became a full-time writer in 1874, publishing hundreds of books under his own name and using numerous pseudonyms. His successful early work, *Seth Jones* (1860), helped establish the genre of dime novels. His dime-novel Indian tales, all published under the name Colonel H. R. Gordon, included such titles as *Jim: A Tale of the Minnesota Massacre* (1864), *The Hunter's Escape: A Tale of the Northwest in 1862* (1864), *Pontiac: Chief of the Ottawas* (1897), and *Tecumseh: Chief of the Shawanoes* (1898). These generally use the Great Lakes setting merely as a plot expedient, although in *Black Partridge, or the Fall of Fort Dearborn* (1906) the chain of Lakes is given more poetic treatment. Ellis also wrote school texts, biographies, and histories, such as his popular six-volume *History of the United States* (1896). [*See also* AMERICAN INDIAN LITERATURE OF THE SEA]

Donald P. Curtis

ELLMS, CHARLES (1805–1851). The elusive Charles Ellms was a Boston stationer who, after 1830, turned to popular writing and compiling almanacs. Little is known of Ellms, his birth, education, or even his death. Before he turned to writing a series of books on pirates* and shipwrecks,* Ellms operated a stationery business, most likely in association with Samuel N. Dickinson, a printer. He published a "comic" almanac in 1831 and then both comic and more traditional almanacs from 1833 to 1837. It was, however, through four popular books that Ellms left his mark on sea literature.

Ellms published *The Pirates Own Book* in 1837. Printed by his associate Dickinson, this was his most popular book. Reprinted in 1841, 1859, 1924, 1993, and 1996, the work also appeared under the title *The Pirates: Authentic Narratives of the Lives, Exploits, and Executions of the World's Most Infamous Buccaneers, including Contemporary Eyewitness Accounts, Documents, Trial Transcripts, and Letters*. It is a collection of pirate narratives that highlight swashbuckling corsairs during the "golden age of piracy," 1690–1725. In 1836 Ellms published *Shipwrecks and Disasters at Sea*, a set of highly exciting shipwreck and nautical tragedies. In 1841 *The Tragedy of the Seas* was published, another collection of highly popular stories of disasters on lakes and rivers, as well as at sea. Ellms followed the success of his other books in 1842 with *Robinson Crusoe's Own Book* (with later printings in 1846 and 1848), seizing upon Daniel Defoe's best-seller, *Robinson Crusoe* (1719).

While Ellms' books are all based in history, the author did not hesitate to embellish the lives of pirates or details about the shipwrecks. Some later critics conclude that it is difficult to determine where accuracy ends and Ellms begins. The fact remains that the mysterious Ellms did much to preserve exciting sea stories and tales of pirates. [*See also* MAROONED LITERATURE]

Boyd Childress

ELLSBERG, EDWARD (1891–1983). Edward Ellsberg was a naval officer, diver, expert in ship salvage, and captivating storyteller. Graduating from the Naval Academy in 1914, Ellsberg served as a naval officer until 1926, when he went into the naval reserve and became chief engineer for Tide Water Oil. Before becoming a civilian, he had helped to salvage the submarine *S-51*, for which work he won the Distinguished Service Medal and was promoted to commander by special act of Congress. Ellsberg's first book, *On the Bottom* (1929), is an account of the raising of this submarine. In late 1927 Ellsberg volunteered his services for the failed rescue attempt on the submarine *S-4*, an operation he later described in *Harper's* ("When the *S-4* Went Down," May 1936, pp. 643–55).

While a civilian engineer, Ellsberg wrote other books on diving; a novel about World War I submarines called *Pigboats* (1931), which was later made into the movie *Hell Below* (1933); and a long novel about John Paul Jones,* *Captain Paul* (1942). He also wrote a series of four juvenile* books on treasure hunting, beginning with *Thirty Fathoms Deep* (1930) and ending with *Treasure Below* (1940).

Ellsberg's most important book of this period is *Hell on Ice* (1938), a gripping account of the fortunes of the *Jeannette*, a 142-foot bark that attempted to sail to the North Pole by way of the Bering Sea and western Arctic* Ocean. The *Jeannette*'s captain, Lieutenant Commander George Washington DeLong, had conceived the venture under the mistaken belief that the warm Japan current was deflected up the coast of Alaska and would provide closer access to the pole by boat than from the Atlantic. Obtaining civilian backing, he gathered a crew of officers and men from the U.S. Navy and a few civilian scientists and sailed from San Francisco on 8 July 1879. For almost three years, nothing was heard of the vessel. A handful of survivors finally reported that the vessel had been frozen in ice for two years and then sank. Its half-crazed, starved crew had then dragged three small boats across 500 miles of ice floes to Siberia; two-thirds of the remaining men were lost just upon reaching the coast.

Originally moved by curiosity about a monument to the *Jeannette* on the Naval Academy grounds, a stone cross frosted with marble icicles, Ellsberg did three years of research into diaries and historical records to find the ship's story, which he narrates as though from the log of the *Jeannette*'s chief engineer. *Hell on Ice* is a novel of beauty and compassion as well as adventure, hardship, and tragedy.

Ellsberg resigned his naval reserve commission in 1940 and volunteered for active service on 7 December 1941. Pearl Harbor had made the navy desperate for salvage expertise, and, though he was over fifty, Ellsberg was ordered to Massawa, Ethiopia, where rested the greatest collection of sunken wrecks in the world. The previous year, the Italians had systematically scuttled some forty Italian and German ships and two invaluable floating steel dry docks, destroying all the machinery in the port. Ellsberg raised the dry docks and several ships. He also got the port operating again, in time to help the British against General Rommel, the "Desert Fox," in North Africa.

After the war Ellsberg told the story of this experience in *Under the Red Sea Sun* (1946), which describes well the months of exhausting salvage work in the face of blistering temperatures and a virtual lack of technical and moral support. The sequel, *No Banners No Bugles* (1949), traces Ellsberg's second assignment, salvage in the Mediterranean in 1943. The second book is even more dramatic than the first, particularly the episode in which Ellsberg saves a torpedoed British cruiser from sinking despite her captain and crew's having completely abandoned her. Ellsberg's tone sometimes borders on the magisterial, but his confidence and vivid, firsthand descriptions are not quite like anything else in sea literature.

Robert Shenk

"THE ENCANTADAS" (1854). This collection of ten short sketches written by Herman Melville* (1819–1991) is set in the Galápagos Islands,* a volcanic archipelago lying along the equator 600 miles off the coast of Ecuador and otherwise known in the nineteenth century as the Encantadas or Enchanted Isles. Melville visited the Galápagos in the 1840s; his whaleship, the *Acushnet*, cruised among the islands for three weeks in the fall of 1841 and returned in early January 1842. He wrote "The Encantadas" during a period devoted to producing stories for magazines, after receiving a mixed reception for *Moby-Dick** (1851) and after the failure of *Pierre or the Ambiguities* (1852). The ten loosely connected sketches are based on Melville's visits to the islands and on his reading, especially of William Cowley, David Porter,* James Colnett, and Charles Darwin. These sketches are difficult to categorize, partaking of several genres such as travel writing, journalism, and fiction but conforming neatly to none of them. Stylistically, they are held together, in part, by a consistent point of view, that of a sailor aboard a whaling ship speaking to the reader, telling what he sees and what he thinks, and relating various anecdotes that he has collected. He describes the islands as desolate and cursed, giant heaps of black cinders and clinkers looking as the world might after "a penal conflagration" (Sketch First).

The first four sketches are devoted mostly to description of the islands, the next five to anecdotes telling of human tragedy and depravity in the Encantadas, and the last sketch, "Runaways, Castaways, Solitaries, Grave-Stones, Etc.," functions as an epitaph succinctly memorializing the islands as hellish sites of wretchedness. In contrast to the blasted islands are ships and the sea. While the islands initially seem a respite from the monotony of long voyages, they prove an evil from which the sea offers escape. On these lands the various characters find drought, isolation, and enslavement; the sea is their only hope of deliverance. The work first appeared in 1854 in three installments in *Putnam's Monthly Magazine*; in 1856 it was collected in Melville's *The Piazza Tales*.

Capper Nichols

EQUIANO, OLAUDAH (1745–1797). Olaudah Equiano, an Igbo of noble birth, grew up in the area of West Africa that is present-day Nigeria. At age eleven, he was kidnapped into slavery and eventually sold to a British sea captain. While on board naval vessels, two sailors, Richard Baker and Daniel Queen, helped Equiano adjust to life at sea and encouraged his conversion to Christianity. Equiano served under various captains, and ultimately, Captain Thomas Farmer convinced Equiano's master to sell the slave his manumission in 1766. When Farmer died at sea, command temporarily fell to Equiano, who navigated the ship to Antigua and then safely to port in Montserrat.

During the Seven Years' War, Equiano saw action on various warships of the Royal Navy. Serving under Vice-Admiral Boscawen, he participated in General Wolfe's 1758 attack against the French in Louisbourgh and in 1759 carried powder for gunners during a battle between Boscawen and the French under Le Clue. In 1761 he accompanied Commodore Keppel on the successful siege of Belleisle and subsequently served under such prestigious leaders as Commodores Stanhope, Dennis, and Lord Howe. Surviving the shipwreck* of a slave ship on which he worked in 1767, Equiano set out on the *Race Horse* with Constantine John Phipps (later Lord Mulgrave) on his 1773 expedition in search of the Northeast Passage, which Equiano took on one of the earliest explorations to the Arctic.* A year later, while on a merchant voyage to Smyrna, Equiano rescued another free black sailor from reenslavement through the help of abolitionist attorney Grenville Sharp. In between various merchant voyages, in 1776 Equiano lived in Central America with the Miskito Indians.

All told, Equiano's experiences made him one of the most-traveled men of his time. Equiano wrote about those travels and his experiences of slavery in his autobiography, whose subscription list included the Prince of Wales and other members of Britain's social elite. Published in 1789, *The Inter-esting Narrative of the Life of Olaudah Equiano, or Gustavus Vassa, the Af-rican (Written by Himself)* is one of the first and most popular slave narratives,* running through nine editions in his lifetime and appearing in posthumous translations into German and Dutch. [*See also* AFRICAN AMERICAN LITERATURE OF THE SEA]

FURTHER READING: Allison, Robert J., ed. *The Interesting Narrative of the Life of Olaudah Equiano Written by Himself.* Boston: Bedford, 1995; Bolster, W. Jeffrey. *Black Jacks: African American Seamen in the Age of Sail.* Cambridge: Harvard UP, 1997; Davis, Charles T., and Henry Louis Gates Jr., eds. *The Slave's Narrative.* Oxford/New York: Oxford UP, 1985; Malloy, Mary. *African Americans in the Mar-itime Trades: A Guide to Resources in New England.* Sharon, MA: Kendall Whaling Museum, 1990.

Arnold Schmidt

ESSEX. The Nantucket* whaleship *Essex* (built 1799) is the first ship defi-nitely known to have been sunk by a whale. Built in Amesbury, Massachu-setts, the 238-ton ship had made at least six whaling voyages by 1819 when she sailed from Nantucket under Captain George Pollard for the Pacific. On 20 November 1820, when a few miles south of the equator at longitude 119° W, she was rammed twice and sunk by an eighty-five-foot sperm whale. The twenty men from the ship drifted in three boats for a month before reaching Henderson (which they thought was Ducie) Island; three of them elected to stay on the island, while the rest after a week set out eastward. One boat was lost, and five men had survived in the other two boats when they were rescued off the coast of South America three months after the wreck; the three left on Henderson Island were picked up by an Australian captain who had been told about them.

The ship's story is recounted by the first mate, Owen Chase,* in his *Nar-rative of the Shipwreck of the Whale-ship* Essex *of Nantucket* (1821), which Herman Melville* discusses at length in Chapter 45 of *Moby-Dick*,* and which was the main dramatic source for the ending of that novel. Thomas Farel Heffernan includes contemporary accounts of the sinking of the *Essex* in his book *Stove by a Whale: Owen Chase and the* Essex (1981). The other authorities are Nathaniel Philbrick, *In the Heart of the Sea: The Tragedy of the Whaleship* Essex (2000) and Thomas Philbrick and Nathaniel Philbrick, eds., *The Loss of the Ship* Essex, *Sunk by a Whale: First Person Accounts* (2000). Although the names are identical, the whaleship *Essex* should not be confused with the frigate *Essex*, on which David Porter* sailed. [*See also* NICKERSON, THOMAS]

Thomas Farel Heffernan

F

FANNING, EDMUND (1769–1841). Captain Edmund Fanning of Stonington, Connecticut, was the younger brother of naval officer Nathaniel Fanning.* In a memorial to the U.S. Congress in 1833, Edmund Fanning urged the legislature to support funding for an exploring expedition to the high southern latitudes and the Pacific Ocean. He gave vent to the patriotic sentiment that for the past thirty-three years he had engaged in trade with China and various Pacific islands for the benefit of the nation. He affirmed that his exertions initiated the extremely lucrative development of trade with China, whereby fur-seal skins, beche-de-mer, sandalwood, mother-of-pearl, and other commodities were obtained from the islands of the Pacific and South Atlantic. He petitioned Congress so earnestly because the 1830s saw a radical decline in seal populations, as the rookeries at Juan Fernandez Island, Masafuera, the Falkland Islands, and other regions of fur-seal resort had been heavily exploited.

Fanning was something of a pioneer. Not only was he engaged in the seal fishery and the China trade at an early date, but he wrote books about it. In the opening paragraphs of his first book, *Voyages round the World; with Selected Sketches of Voyages to the South Seas, North and South Pacific Oceans, China, etc . . . 1792–1832* (1833), he describes his first sealing voyage in 1792 as promising an auspicious beginning, which idea, as soon becomes apparent, was mistaken, as there were few people available with any experience in the seal fisheries of the South Atlantic. While this first voyage was not a particular success, his subsequent efforts became landmarks in sealing history. By 1797, when he commanded the brig *Betsey*, of New York, he had gained such experience in the fur-seal fishery and the China trade that the voyage cleared $52,000 in profit.

Fanning was among the first to publish voyage narratives* regarding these aspects of the China trade. He wrote two books, the first dealing with his early voyages and sealing experiences. The second, *Voyages to the South Seas, Indian and Pacific Oceans, China, North-west Coast, Feejee Islands, South Shetlands, &c. &c . . . 1830–1837* (1838), includes historical material such as a narrative description of the massacre in 1811 of the crew of the ship *Tonquin*,* Lieutenant Jonathan Thorn, U.S. Navy, master, by the native peoples of Vancouver Island on the Northwest Coast.* He also includes a description of American whaling, detailing the cutting-in and trying-out of right whales. He discusses the discovery of some small islands in the Pacific, one of which, Fanning Island, located at 3° 51' north, 159° 12' west, about 1,200 miles south of Hawai'i, still bears his name. He gives good accounts of the particulars of trade with the Fiji Islanders and the curiosities, dangers, ethnographic observations, and other features of importance to future traders with these people.

The importance of Fanning's voyages and writings is reflected in his influence upon such mariners as Captain Nathaniel B. Palmer, for whom Palmer's Land in Antarctica* is named; Captain Benjamin Pendleton, who commanded the exploring expedition that ended ignominiously in mutiny* upon the Araucanian coast in the late summer of 1830; and Charles Wilkes, who was to command the very successful and important U.S. Exploring Expedition* of 1838 to 1842. Fanning was able to convince Congress of the importance of his ideas, which speaks to his authoritative knowledge of the position of the United States in the maritime merchant trade at the turn of the eighteenth century and the early years of the nineteenth.

Michael P. Dyer

FANNING, NATHANIEL (1755–1805). Nathaniel Fanning's *Narrative of the Adventures of an American Navy Officer* (1806) is one of the most reliable, graphic, and extensive eyewitness accounts of the famous battle between the *Bonhomme Richard** and the *Serapis.** Following the four-hour battle, in which both ships were devastated, and half of both crews were killed or wounded, the twenty-four-year-old Fanning realized that something of great consequence had taken place, and over two decades later while preparing his journal for publication he carefully chronicled both the battle and his place in it.

The eldest of eight sons, Fanning was born in Stonington, Connecticut, and went to sea at an early age. When the Revolution broke out, he sailed on several privateers, and on 31 May 1778, he and his ship were captured by the British. Fanning and his shipmates were carried to England, where they were detained at Forton Prison near Portsmouth. After a harsh imprisonment, he was eventually exchanged and sent to France, where he met John Paul Jones* and agreed to sail on the *Bonhomme Richard* as a midshipman and as the commodore's private secretary. When the famous battle took place on 22 September 1779, Fanning was captain of the maintop, remaining aloft during the whole battle with four sailors and fifteen marines.

According to Fanning, his marines were responsible for emptying the main-tops of the *Serapis* of marksmen and then for sending those on deck scurrying for cover. Once the two ships were grappled together, one of his men crawled out on a yardarm and dropped a grenade onto the *Serapis*. Intended for a group of British sailors huddled between the gundecks, the grenade fell through an open hatchway, where it exploded a large quantity of loose powder, killing twenty men and resulting in the American victory.

Fanning sailed with Jones on the *Ariel* for another year, but in December 1780 he and most of the other officers refused to serve under the commodore's command any longer. In his narrative, Fanning cataloged a series of Jones' abuses, including cruelty, corruption, and conceit. His depiction of Jones sharply contrasts the popular mythic figure that became immediately legendary after the battle. Although Fanning documented Jones' bravery during the encounter with the *Serapis*, he also described the commodore as kicking his men and cheating them of their prize money. Because his description ran counter to the popular image of Jones, the first 1806 edition of Fanning's narrative was published anonymously and then withheld from general circulation.

For the rest of the war, Fanning served on several French privateers, becoming a naturalized French citizen and finally a lieutenant in the French navy. While privateering, he was captured by the British three more times but quickly released, and in 1782 he made two trips to England carrying informal peace proposals for the French court. When the war ended, he resigned his commission and returned to America, where he married. Little is known of his life after the Revolution except that he resided in both New York and Stonington and that he continued to follow the sea. Presumably during 1801, after Jefferson and the Republicans came into power, he wrote his narrative from the journals he had kept during the Revolution. On 5 December 1804, Fanning was commissioned as a lieutenant in the U.S. Navy and was given command of the naval station at Charleston, South Carolina, where he died ten months later from yellow fever.

A year after his death in 1805, Fanning's narrative was published by his brother Edmund Fanning,* the famous explorer. Three years later, in 1808, Edmund published a second edition, changing the title to *Memoirs of the Life of Captain Nathaniel Fanning*. The narrative was published four more times during the early nineteenth century and three times in the twentieth century. In addition to its firsthand account of the famous battle and the unfavorable depiction of Jones, the narrative provides remarkable insight into the privateering of the Americans and the French.

Daniel E. Williams

FAR TORTUGA (1975). An experimental novel by Peter Matthiessen* (1927–   ), *Far Tortuga* is perhaps as notable for its unusual narrative technique as for its plot. Matthiessen uses a combination of succinct narration and description, phonetically rendered Caribbean* dialect, symbols and ink-blots, drawings of the rigging and phases of the moon, blank space, meteorological detail, and a ship's manifest to tell the tale of nine Cayman Islanders on a doomed turtle-fishing expedition through the Caribbean Sea aboard the *Lilias Eden*, a sixty-foot commercial schooner.

Cop'm (Captain) Raib Evers, an "old-time wind sailor," is displeased from the outset with his "modern time" crew of motor-sailors, drunks, and assorted misfits as they sail toward Far Tortuga on the Mysteriosa Reef, near Nicaragua. During the voyage, the *Eden* encounters a rival boat (captained by Raib's half brother Desmond and his dying father, Cop'm Andrew), sharks, Jamaican pirates,* and finally a gale, which is described more with pictures than with words. The *Eden* evades a second pirate attack by attempting to sail over Far Tortuga at night during the gale but strikes the reef and sinks. Only one crew member survives the days spent in two cat-boats.

Amid the action in *Far Tortuga* lurks a fear of the sea by all except Cop'm Raib, who attempts a kinship with the captains of lore with his bold night sail over the reefs, but in "modern time" the old-wind sailor forgets some timeless lessons: that bravado leads to catastrophe at sea and that those who ignore the Conradian "fellowship of the craft" are doomed.

Far Tortuga received a *New York Times Book Review* "Editor's Choice" citation and was praised heavily by such authors as James Dickey* and Thomas Pynchon. Matthiessen has stated that the book was consciously conceived and plotted from a Zen Buddhist perspective; many critics have noted the similarities between his naturalist writings and Zen concepts of the physical world. Matthiessen has written further about his connection to Zen thought in *Nine-Headed Dragon River: Zen Journals 1969–1982* (1986).

Joseph Navratil and Eric G. Waggoner

FAREWELL TO THE SEA (1986). A novel by Cuban author Reinaldo Arenas (1943–1990), who was exiled to the United States in 1980 as part of the Mariel boat lift, *Farewell to the Sea* was written in Cuba and first published in Spain as *Otra Vez el Mar* (1982), meaning "once more the sea." The novel, a vivid representation of Arenas' bitterness over the Castro regime's restriction of free expression and repression of homosexuality, details the brief seaside vacation of a young married couple. The first half is told from the perspective of the wife, who watches with quiet desperation as her secretly homosexual husband begins a sexual liaison with a young boy vacationing in a neighboring beach house. The novel then switches to the perspective of the husband, a disillusioned supporter of Castro's revolution and a writer whose voice has been stymied by his policies. The novel's emphasis is not on plot events but rather on the turmoil of the couple's inner lives, represented by an experimental and at times chaotic narrative style that alternates between stream of consciousness, flashback, surrealistic hallucination, and poetry.

The sea is a constant in the characters' lives and a witness to their desperation and entrapment. It is invested with an almost overwhelming metaphorical weight, suggesting, at times, oblivion and forgetfulness, escape from the drudgery of everyday life, an infiniteness associated with a sense of cosmic indifference to the lives of Cubans, the dissolution of physical and psychic boundaries, the unrealizable possibility of escape from Cuba, and the uncontrollable force of repressed desire. [See also LATINO/A LITERATURE OF THE SEA]

Marta Caminero-Santangelo

FATHER MAPPLE. Herman Melville* identifies the powerful preacher of the Whaleman's Chapel in *Moby-Dick** (1851) as "the famous Father Mapple," a former sailor and harpooner and a favorite among seamen. Prior to going whaling, Ishmael,* the novel's narrator, visits the chapel and listens to Father Mapple preach. Although Melville may have based the character of Father Mapple on the Reverend Enoch Mudge, pastor of the New Bedford Seaman's Bethel* during the time of Melville's visit to New Bedford, the characterization is enriched through reference to the better-known Father Edward Taylor of the Boston Seaman's Bethel, whose eccentric and invigorating sermons were praised by such writers as Richard Henry Dana Jr.,* Catherine Maria Sedgwick, Charles Dickens, Walt Whitman,* and Ralph Waldo Emerson.

Mapple notwithstanding, Melville's description of the Whaleman's Chapel and of Mapple's sermon appear largely imagined. Melville places Mapple in a lofty pulpit resembling a ship's prow and reached by a rope ladder, suggesting not only his elevated position as a spiritual leader but also his aloofness and isolation. With dramatic rhetoric, descriptions of the sea's terror, and analogies of the sea to extreme psychological states, Mapple's mesmerizing sermon takes the Book of Jonah as its text, focusing on Jonah's refusal to obey God and his consequent encounter with the Leviathan. Interpreted for many years as a testament of Christian faith and a foreshadowing of Captain Ahab's* audacious, defiant behavior later in *Moby-Dick*, the sermon has been interpreted by critics since the 1950s to be an ironic commentary on the difficulties of knowing the truth.

Elizabeth Schultz

FAULKNER, WILLIAM [CUTHBERT] (1897–1962). William Faulkner, who lived and wrote in the hills of north Mississippi, often visited the Gulf coast. From April to June 1925, he resided in New Orleans, frequently sailing on yachts and riverboats. Years later he spoke of sailing the waters beyond New Orleans to traffic in the liquor trade. He admitted to running a launch out into the gulf to a sand spit where raw alcohol from Cuba was buried, though his brother has questioned the veracity of this sea experience. True or not, Faulkner turned the episode into fiction in an early story about gulf rumrunners, "Once aboard the Lugger" (1932). The story describes an expedition to an island in the gulf where the crew braves wild cattle and mosquitoes to dig up illicit alcohol.

From New Orleans on 7 July 1925, Faulkner boarded the freighter *West Ivis* and sailed to Genoa, Italy, for a tour of Europe. On the second day of the voyage, Faulkner appeared on deck and disposed of a manuscript about four inches thick by tearing up the pages in batches and throwing them overboard. Possibly inspired by his voyage on the freighter during his stay in Paris, Faulkner wrote "Yo Ho and Two Bottles of Rum" (1925), published in the 27 September issue of the *Times Picayune*. The action of this brief piece takes place aboard a freighter in the Pacific: in a drunken rage, a British mate "accidentally" murders a Chinese mess boy. Taken altogether, the sketch exposes the baselessness of the British officers' feelings of racial superiority to their patient, inscrutable Chinese crew. Faulkner returned from Europe aboard the S.S. *Republic*, which docked in New Jersey 19 December 1925 after a stormy crossing.

For several weeks during the summers of 1925, 1926, and 1927, Faulkner vacationed with friends, the Stone family, in a cabin some 100 yards from the bay in the gulf town of Pascagoula, Mississippi. Faulkner spent the days swimming, sailing, and taking long walks on the tidal flats. Often he was accompanied by the Stone children, to whom he told stories of pirate* treasure. In Pascagoula in the summer of 1926, he completed his second novel, *Mosquitoes* (1927), which is based on his experiences with the literati of New Orleans and is set aboard a yacht afloat in Lake Pontchartrain. In 1929 he returned to Pascagoula with his wife, Estelle, for a honeymoon at a beachside cottage. During this inauspicious honeymoon, Estelle attempted to commit suicide by walking out into the gulf. Faulkner called to a neighbor, who ran out into the shallow water and caught Estelle almost where the shelf of the beach dropped away into the channel. He drew on his experiences in this seaside town for *The Wild Palms* (1939). In this novel images of the ocean recur as Charlotte Rittenmeyer dies of a botched abortion in Pascagoula.

One other Faulkner work, "Turnabout" (1932), also features the sea. Faulkner seems to have drawn on his own experience in 1918 training to be a Royal Air Force pilot in this World War I story, which pits American airmen against British seamen. At first, the American pilot, Bogard, feels immensely superior to Hope, a young British naval officer. But when Bogard accompanies Hope and his mate, Ronnie, on a dangerous torpedo mission, Bogard is deeply moved by the British seamen's spectacular courage.

Doreen Fowler

FERRINI, VINCENT (1913–   ). Vincent Ferrini was born into a blue-collar, immigrant family struggling to earn a living in the shoe factories of Lynn, Massachusetts. His first volume of poems, *No Smoke* (1941), records the depression-era deprivations of his early years. A reluctant graduate of high school, Ferrini read voraciously from the public library collection until World War II brought him work in a General Electric plant. Drawn by the beauty of its harbor and by the Italian fishing community, he moved to Gloucester* in 1948 as his fifth book of poems on working-class life, *Plow in the Ruins*, was being published. Since then, his writings have focused on the changing destiny of America's first fishing port. His first collection of verse on Gloucester, *Sea Sprung* (1949), evokes scenes of the port, its vessels, and its fishing community.

In 1950 he began a lifelong friendship with Charles Olson,* who wrote the first Maximus poem as a letter to Ferrini. In the same year, declaring his hands extensions of his poems, he began a career as a picture-frame maker, pioneering the use of driftwood as a framing material for the seascapes and harbor scenes of local artists. Among the thirty volumes of poetry he has published, the seven volumes of *Know Fish* (1979–1991) chronicle most effectively his portrait of the decline of the fishing industry in his adopted home. With Whitmanesque verve and a consistently proletarian voice, Ferrini chides government bureaucracies for their inept management policies in such poems as "Fresh Fish Industry Thrown a Bone" (1976) and "The Savior" (1979) and local business interests for their shortsighted greed ("Gloucester: Why It Is As It Is," "Squid" [both 1979], "Gloucester Aroused" [1986]). In other poems, he celebrates the glories of its seagoing past ("The Flood Time of Fishing" [1979]), the resilient strength of its Italian fisherpeople ("Da Family Dragga" [1979], "At Sea" [1984]), and the achievements of its more visionary citizenry ("Brahma" [1984], on Philip Weld, "Gus Foote: At the Fo'c'sle of City Hall" [1991], "The Luminist of Gloucester" [1991], on Fitz Hugh Lane).

In *Sea Root* (1959), the son of a sea captain returns from twenty years at sea to release his family from the guilt and anguish of incestuous bonds. *Undersea Bread* (1989) contains two relevant verse plays: *Nightsea Journey*, in which a fisherman whose boat sinks in a blizzard leaves behind a son struggling with a heroin addiction in a sinking fishing economy; and *The Fisherwomen*, in which the wives and daughters of drowned fishermen discover inner resources of strength without their men. Ferrini's second verse play, *Telling of the North Star* (1954), uses the tradition of the returning ghost ship as a commentary on the ethical compromises forced upon fishermen faced with a depleted stock. The play is the text for a one-act chamber opera composed by John Corina and performed at the University of Georgia in 1981.

Ferrini, who considers himself a "deepsea Fisher of Words and Souls," continues to write from his conviction of the unity of life and art out of his home in East Gloucester. [*See also* GHOSTS AND GHOST SHIP LEG-ENDS; SEA IMAGERY IN MODERN AND CONTEMPORARY PO-ETRY]

Joseph Flibbert

FINAL PASSAGES (first perf. as *Derelict*, 1982; pub. 1992). Written by Tony award winner Robert Schenkkan (1953–   ), *Final Passages* is a play based on an incident that occurred off the coast of Nova Scotia in 1878, when the *Elizabeth Watson* discovered the *San Cristobal* adrift and appar-ently abandoned. In the play, a boarding party determines the cargo to be intact, although the crew are dead, most of them on deck around a table. By reading the journal left by Tom, the cabin boy of the *San Cristobal*, Captain Craig discovers a story of a crew undone by an attractive woman. The mysterious Countess had seduced Lieutenant Brand, a father figure to Tom, while Tom watches through a peephole into her cabin. She then sleeps with Tom. It is a sexual initiation for him, but for her it is only a fling before marrying Brand. When the Countess, in emotional turmoil over her two lovers, accuses Tom of stealing from her, Tom is flogged, and the Countess marries Brand. Tom puts rat poison in the wine, murdering everyone on board, and disappears.

The sea in *Final Passages* is both a male domain and a jealous lover. In marrying the Countess, Brand threatens to abandon not only Tom but also the sea. The sea is a place of mystery and dreams, in different ways for Tom, the Countess, and Captain Craig. The play's structure follows that of many maritime ghost* stories, where a sailing ship encounters a ghost ship, jeop-ardizing its own course. There are references to the *Flying Dutchman* legend and to sailors' superstitions and habits, and a sea chantey is included for musical accompaniment. [*See also* DRAMA OF THE SEA]

Gwen Orel

FITZGERALD, F[RANCIS]. SCOTT (1896–1940). Although not an author of sea fiction, F. Scott Fitzgerald used water as a setting and em-ployed water imagery and related symbolism in his most important work, *The Great Gatsby* (1925), and to a lesser degree in *Tender Is the Night* (1934), set, in part, on the French Riviera.

Most of the action of *The Great Gatsby* occurs on Long Island's North Shore, near Long Island Sound. The first-person narrator, Nick Carraway, is the next-door neighbor of Jay Gatsby, a mysterious westerner who has suddenly appeared on the East Coast during the extravagant and euphoric post–World War I 1920s. Incredibly wealthy and evidently involved in Pro-hibition crime, he is profoundly in love with Nick's relative, Daisy, who lives across the bay in an area called East Egg. Gatsby had met Daisy when he was in the army, but Daisy had married Tom Buchanan, and they are leading unsavory, materialistic, careless lives on New York's fast track. At Gatsby's insistence Nick arranges a meeting between Daisy and her obsessed admirer. After a wild summer night in New York City, Daisy, driving Gatsby's luxurious automobile back to the island, accidentally strikes and kills Myrtle, her husband, Tom's, mistress. Myrtle's aggrieved husband, thinking it was Gatsby at the wheel, shoots and kills him. Significantly, Gatsby is in a swimming pool, and his body continues to float after his death.

The period's gross and barbarous materialism and its want of worthy values, symbolized by the wastelandish ash heap opposite the Wilsons' garage, contrast to the New World's "fresh, green breast" that greeted the early European discoverers, the Dutch sailors. The New Eden, the hopeful and bountiful promise of the new continent, was, from the moment it was discovered, doomed to be metamorphosed from an object of wonder into a commodity. The book shows a capacity for "wonder" at this New World and not at the sea itself.

The fictionally compressed art of *Gatsby* shares some views and fundamental emblems of that other modernist masterpiece, T. S. Eliot's* *The Waste Land* (1922). For example, water can renew and cleanse, even nourish, but as Phlebas the Phoenician learned, it can also bring death to the postwar civilization. *Gatsby* had three film adaptations: 1926, 1949 (based on the play version by Owen Gould Davis Sr., also 1949), and 1974, starring Mia Farrow and Robert Redford. The Metropolitan Opera premiered John Harbison's opera adaptation in December 1999.

Donald Yannella

"FORESTER, FRANK." *See* [BALLOU, MATURIN MURRAY]; HERBERT, HENRY WILLIAM.

FRENEAU, PHILIP [MORIN] (1752–1832). An "occasional" poet born in New York City, Philip Freneau during his long life wrote lyric and narrative poems on a wide range of subjects. Since he spent many years working on ships, a sizable number of these concern the sea.

Freneau in 1768 entered the College of New Jersey (now Princeton University), where fellow students James Madison and Hugh Henry Brackenridge encouraged his penchant for intellectual speculation. Later, during the war against England, Freneau wrote political poetry and was tagged "the Poet of the American Revolution." Some of Freneau's earliest poems deal with the sea, including collegiate verses such as "The History of the Prophet Jonah" (written in 1768) and "Columbus to Ferdinand" (1770), the latter depicting Christopher Columbus* as both an adventurer and a champion of reason who sought to prove that the other side of the earth was not all water. One of Freneau's best-known collegiate poems, "The Rising Glory of America" (1771), cowritten with Brackenridge in response to the unpopular Stamp Act, predicted the emergence of a Utopian political entity extending "from the Atlantic to the Pacific shores."

Between 1776 and 1778 Freneau avoided the chaos in the wartime colonies by working as a sailor on trading vessels in the Atlantic and Caribbean* and by serving as the secretary of a sugar plantation on the island of Santa Cruz. A major poem from this period, "The Beauties of Santa Cruz" (1776), features, alongside highly romanticized descriptions of the island's tropical landscape, Freneau's identification with the plight of slaves. The poet's disdain for the institution of slavery was most memorably expressed in a later poem set in the West Indies, "To Sir Toby" (1784). In 1778 Freneau returned home to enlist in the New Jersey militia, spending the next two years leading trading and privateering expeditions. In 1780 Freneau's ship *Aurora* was captured by the British navy; the poet was imprisoned in New York harbor, an experience that inspired his important protest poem, "The British Prison Ship" (1780).

Between 1781 and 1783 Freneau was based in Philadelphia, where he contributed both poetry and prose to the anti-British periodical *Freeman's Journal*. Although living inland, he continued to write about the sea. For example, in "On the Late Royal Sloop of War *General Monk*" (1782), the poet lauded the April 1782 victory of *Hyder Ally* over the British ship *General Monk*. Freneau's "On the Memorable Victory" (1781) celebrated patriot John Paul Jones'* heroic 1779 conquest of a fleet of British warships.

Freneau captained numerous trading expeditions from 1785 to 1790, probably to earn money for his marriage to Eleanor Forman. Living apart from the woman he loved, Freneau composed elegiac poems—including "Philander: Or the Emigrant" (c. 1788), "To Cynthia" (1789), and "Florio to Amanda" (1789)—modeled on early eighteenth-century British neoclassical poetry; all of these poems depict lovers separated by the sea. During this period he also composed descriptive poems evoking the natural environment of the Caribbean and the Atlantic, including "The Hurricane" (1785) and "The Bermuda Islands" (1788).

By the early 1800s the difficulty of making a living in publishing and the need to support his family convinced Freneau to return to the sea to work as a trader. Poems from this period of sea-voyaging are more reflective and less descriptive than earlier efforts; the poet now favored romantic revelry ("Lines Written at Sea" [c.1800]) and perceptive characterizations of island people ("The Nautical Rendezvous" [1800]). About 1807 Freneau returned to New Jersey, struggled to support his family by farming, and never ventured to sea again.

In 1815 Freneau published a collection of War of 1812 poems that largely commemorate naval warfare, including "The Battle of Lake Erie" (1813), "The Terrific Torpedoes" (1814), and "On the Naval Attack near Baltimore" (1814). Although a house fire destroyed many of his manuscripts, papers, and letters in 1818, Freneau continued to write poems until his death. He was the most prolific colonial American poet, with over 550 poems and many prose pieces preserved in print. [*See also* SEA IMAGERY IN MODERN AND CONTEMPORARY POETRY]

FURTHER READING: Bowden, Mary W. *Philip Freneau*. Boston: Twayne, 1976; Leary, Lewis, ed. *The Last Poems of Philip Freneau*. New Brunswick, NJ: Rutgers UP, 1945; Pattee, Fred Lewis, ed. *The Poems of Philip Freneau: Poet of the American Revolution*. New York: Russell and Russell, 1963; Vizthum, Richard C. *Land and Sea: The Lyric Poetry of Philip Freneau*. Minneapolis: U of Minnesota P, 1978.

Ted Olson

FROST, ROBERT [LEE] (1874–1963). Though Robert Frost was not a nautical writer, he did treat the sea as a subject in several poems. Best known among these are "Once by the Pacific" (1926), "Neither Out Far nor in Deep" (1934), and "Sand Dunes" (1926), and they also include "The Discovery of the Madeiras" (1949), "Does No One at All Ever Feel This Way in the Least?" (1952), "America Is Hard to See" (1951). These poems, to one degree or another, take iconoclastic views of famous seafarers and, most significantly, of the sea itself, contesting or denying its often exalted, revered, or feared properties. "America Is Hard to See" faults Christopher Columbus* for his bad navigation; "Sand Dunes" claims that despite the sea's sinking of ships and then transforming itself into dunes so as to destroy habitations, human beings will only be freed thereby to think more largely, more freely.

In "Neither Out Far nor in Deep" those on the beach all look at the sea, turning their backs on the land on which they rest. Frost seems to imply a critique of the tradition of looking for deep meanings in the sea, which, in this poem, is obscure and dull. Also antitraditional is "Once by the Pacific," in which a sea-gazer stands on shore contemplating the approach of a violent storm on the ironically named ocean and seems to believe in its apocalyptic possibilities. Frost undercuts the apparent connection between the sea storm and God's wrath, however, by having the speaker reiterate that it "looked" as if the storm was to be seen this way. In addition, the voice in the poem distances itself from the meanings it has evoked by saying that "Someone" (implicitly not the speaker) had better get ready for the putative coming end. Both these poems undercut the notion that the sea can mean or reveal very much to us—though many, if not most, continue to look to it for transcendent meaning.

Frost's poems involving the sea all speak with the voices of landlubbers. His speakers never go to sea, though they imagine activities conducted there. Whether he is expressing an ironic version of Teiresias' advice to Odysseus to put an oar on his shoulder and travel inland until the oar is mistaken for a winnowing fan ("Does No One . . .") or saying that a storm from the east evokes thoughts of the antediluvian sea ("A Line-Storm Song"

[1913]), where human meaning is concerned, for Robert Frost, Earth is earth. [*See also* SEA IMAGERY IN MODERN AND CONTEMPORARY POETRY]

Haskell Springer

FULLER [MCCOY], IOLA (1906–   ). Born in Marcellus, Michigan, Iola Fuller worked both as a librarian and a teacher at Ferris State College before engaging in writing full-time. She won an Avery Hopwood award at the University of Michigan in 1939 for her first novel, *The Loon Feather* (1940), which deals with the relationships among the Ojibways of Mackinac Island and the trappers, traders, and militia who encroach upon their territory. In *The Gilded Torch* (1957), Fuller traces René Robert Cavelier, de la Salle on his route along the present-day Saint Lawrence Seaway, through the Great Lakes* and down the Mississippi to claim the Louisiana Territory. The novel focuses on the hardships of the trip and suggests the effects of the explorers, missionaries, and settlers on the Great Lakes and other parts of the North-west Territories and on the Native Americans there. [*See also* AMERICAN INDIAN LITERATURE OF THE SEA]

Mary DeJong Obuchowski

FULLER, [SARAH] MARGARET (1810–1850). Born in Cambridge-port, Massachusetts, Margaret Fuller was the eldest of nine children. Her father, a lawyer and congressman, educated her at home, and under his demanding regimen she developed her remarkable intellectual gifts. She later taught school in Boston, where she met Ralph Waldo Emerson and entered the circle of the transcendentalists. She became the first editor of their short-lived, but influential, journal, *The Dial*, and her association with this group ultimately led to the writing of her most famous work, *Woman in the Nine-teenth Century* (1845), a reasoned examination and promulgation of femi-nism. The next year she traveled to Europe and by 1848 had settled in Rome, where she met and secretly married Giovanni Angelo, Marchese Os-soli. Returning to America in 1850, their ship was wrecked off New York, and they were drowned, along with their infant son.

Fuller's first significant book, *Summer on the Lakes, in 1843* (1844), is a record of a journey she undertook to the Great Lakes* to witness the rapid settlement of that area and its effect on the land as well as the resulting displacement of the Native Americans. Her narrative, somewhat rambling and episodic, contains her observations of Niagara Falls, Chicago, the Illinois prairies, Milwaukee, Mackinac Island, and Sault Ste. Marie and the contrast between encroaching civilization and its corrupting influence upon indige-nous peoples. She also includes bits of poetry, a short story, and some other unrelated writings. Although a modest success when it appeared, *Summer on the Lakes* remains not as well known as other contemporary travel nar-ratives.

Important collections of Fuller's manuscripts reside at Boston Public Library and at the Houghton Library, Harvard University. Fictionalized Margaret Fuller and Ralph Waldo Emerson appear as minor characters in Sena Jeter Naslund's *Ahab's Wife, Or The Star-Gazer* (1999). [*See also* AMERICAN INDIAN LITERATURE OF THE SEA]

Robert Beasecker

G

GAFF TOPSAILS (1996). *Gaff Topsails* is set in a small coastal Newfoundland town during the Feast of St. John the Baptist, 24 June 1948. Local mountain peaks known as Gaff Topsails loom over the town; a melting iceberg looms at the cove's mouth. The characters are depicted serially as each relates to the ocean: a drunken war hero mans the lighthouse* and lives in delusions of heroically rescuing fellow sailors; a woman awaits the return of her husband lost at sea; a teenaged boy concludes a fishing trip with a seal-killing on the iceberg.

Author Patrick Kavanagh (1950–) was raised in a Newfoundland town resembling his novel's setting. He sailed and fished as a youth, encountering both storms and icebergs. [*See also* CANADIAN LITERATURE OF THE SEA]

Mira Dock

GALÁPAGOS ISLANDS LITERATURE. The Galápagos Islands, despite their remoteness and inhospitality to travelers, have been a subject of meditation for many writers, including several Americans, over the past four and a half centuries. Located 600 miles west of Ecuador and straddling the equator, the archipelago was first discovered for the European world accidentally in 1535 by the bishop of Panama, Father Tomás de Berlanga, who wrote to Charles V, emperor of the Spains, of the strange fauna he stumbled upon there and the difficulties of finding water. Three hundred years later, in 1836, not long after the first settlement, a penal colony, was established on Floreana (1832), Charles Darwin conducted his scientific research there into some of those very same plants and animals. Darwin's findings, reported informally in *Journal of Researches into the Geology and Natural History of the Various Countries Visited by H.M.S.* Beagle (1839), led eventually to the revolutionary theory of natural selection announced in *On the Origin of*

Species (1859), establishing the islands as one of the most important research sites in the history of science.

In the intervening centuries, the mysterious islands became a refuge for buccaneers and other adventurers and a frequent stopping place for whalers, who eventually decimated the tortoise population of the islands in their search for fresh meat and water. The navigator William Dampier, whose *The New Voyage around the World* (1697) includes the first description of the islands by an Englishman, is the most famous of the pirate* adventurers, a man with a scientific cast of mind and a rich prose style that left its mark on several prominent writers of the eighteenth century, including Daniel Defoe. Herman Melville,* whose sketches "The Encantadas,* or Enchanted Isles" (1854) capture the volcanic desolation and shape-shifting of the archipelago, is the most famous whaler and along with Darwin, whose *Beagle* narrative Melville owned, is the most famous author ever to write about the islands. Originally published serially under the pseudonym Salvator R. Tarnmoor, Melville's sketches portray a fallen world of hissing reptiles, diabolical hermits, and tragic castaways trapped in changeless misery.

The first Americans known to visit the Galápagos were ship captains. Amasa Delano,* author of *A Narrative of Voyages and Travels* (1817), stopped there three times starting in 1800, commenting on the islands' distinctive natural history, especially the land tortoises and iguanas. George Little, captain of a merchant ship and author of *Life on the Ocean, or Twenty Years at Sea* (1843), touched on Chatham and James Islands in 1808 in search of turtles, terrapin, and water, while seeking to avoid the predations of Spanish men-of-war. Benjamin Morrell* in *Narrative of Four Voyages to the South Seas* (1832) reported saving several starving castaways from one of the islands. David Porter,* author of *Journal of a Cruise Made to the Pacific Ocean in the Frigate* Essex (1815), made several stops at various islands during the War of 1812, spectacularly fulfilling orders to destroy British whaling in the area. Porter's skills at scientific observation led him to anticipate several of the findings regarding species differentiation and the geological history of the islands later investigated by Darwin. His work also proved an important source for several scenes in Herman Melville's* "The Encantadas"* (1854).

In the years after the Civil War, American scientists, following the lead of Darwin, began to explore the islands in a series of scientific expeditions. Elizabeth Cabot Cary Agassiz, wife of Harvard geologist Louis Agassiz, published "A Cruise through the Galápagos" in *The Atlantic Monthly* (1873), while their son, Alexander, wrote a "General Sketch of the Expedition of the *Albatross* from February to May 1891; The Galápagos Islands," for the *Bulletin of the Museum of Comparative Zoology* (1892). At about the same time, Professor George Baur published his "On the Origins of the Galápagos" in *American Naturalist* (1891). Early in the twentieth century came the most ambitious scientific excursion to the islands, the California Academy of Sciences Galápagos Expedition (1905–1906), led by Rollo H. Beck and captured memorably by Joseph R. Slevin in his *Log of the Schooner Academy* (1931). Other expeditions, by Americans and others, have followed with regularity almost every decade since then, spawning a rich scientific and historical literature.

One of the most important of these expeditions was engaged by William Beebe* of the New York Zoological Society, who in 1924 published a massive, colorful study, *Galápagos, World's End.* This provocative work enjoyed great popularity in the United States and abroad and inspired a rash of informal tours of the islands and even a few efforts at settlement. One notable settlement, dating from the 1930s on Floreana and involving a series of mysterious murders unsolved to this day, is captured by John Traherne in *The Galápagos Affair* (1983). A related work by a remarkable German, Margret Wittmer's *Floreana: A Woman's Pilgrimage to the Galápagos* (first pub. in German [1959]; Eng. trans. 1961; rpt. 1989), gives a close-up account of these events and tells the story of a lifetime of struggle and adventure on the island. Significant recent work by Americans inspired by the mysterious archipelago includes Kurt Vonnegut's* fantasy novel *Galápagos* (1985), Cathleen Schine's novel *The Evolution of Jane* (1998), and a haunting composition for chamber orchestra, narrator, and dancers, *The Encantadas* (1983), by Tobias Picker. [*See also* MAROONED LITERATURE]

FURTHER READING: Beebe, William. *Galápagos, World's End.* New York: G. P. Putnam's Sons, 1924; Darwin, Charles. *The Voyage of the* Beagle. London: John Murray, 1845; Darwin, Charles. *On the Origin of Species by Means of Natural Selection, or, The Preservation of Favored Races in the Struggle for Life.* London: John Murray, 1859; Melville, Herman. *The Encantadas, or The Enchanted Islands* (1854). Rpt. in *The Piazza Tales and Other Prose Pieces, 1839–1860.* Evanston, IL, and Chicago: Northwestern UP and the Newberry Library, 1987; Porter, David. *Journal of a Cruise Made to the Pacific Ocean in the Frigate* Essex (1815). Rpt. Annapolis: Naval Institute P, 1986; Slevin, Joseph R. *Log of the Schooner* Academy *on a Voyage of Scientific Research to the Galápagos Islands, 1905–1906.* San Francisco: California Academy of Sciences, 1931; Traherne, John. *The Galápagos Affair.* New York: Random, 1983.

Christopher Sten

GALLERY, DANIEL V[INCENT]. (1901–1977). Admiral Daniel V. Gallery, termed a "true original" by his friend Herman Wouk,* was a brilliant career naval officer who published widely both during and after his naval duty. A 1920 Naval Academy graduate, Gallery first served on battleships and later volunteered for naval aviation. At the outbreak of World War II, he commanded an Icelandic antisubmarine base; in 1943 he directed the boarding and capture of the German submarine *U-505* on the high seas while commanding the antisubmarine carrier *Guadalcanal* and her task group, the first American capture of an enemy warship on the high seas since the War of 1812.

At the end of the war, while serving in the Pentagon from 1946 to 1949, Gallery began writing. He described the *U-505* episode and the Iceland duty in articles for the *Saturday Evening Post*; he wrote humorous short stories for the *Post* and other magazines; and he penned several articles on important naval subjects of the day. An official document, the fabled "Gallery Memorandum," which leaked to the pen of journalist Drew Pearson, played a minor role in the 1949 "revolt of the admirals" about the planned denigration of naval aviation.

Gallery retired from the navy in 1960. His collected short stories, *Now Hear This* (1965) and *Stand By-y-y to Start Engines* (1966), were successful enough to encourage Gallery to write two short "epics" about his favorite main character, the best of which was titled *Cap'n Fatso* (1969). A comic figure without much depth, Fatso nevertheless possesses the ingenuity, bravado, and enlisted "wisdom" to make him an ideal vehicle for Gallery's wit. Fatso shared with Gallery a deep knowledge of navy prerogatives and a refined ability to get around the regulations.

Noteworthy among Gallery's other books are his polemic, *The* Pueblo *Incident* (1970), and his engaging autobiography, *Eight Bells and All's Well* (1965).

Robert Shenk

GALLOWAY, LES [EDWARD WILLIAM] (1919–1990). A commercial fisherman for most of his life, Les Galloway also wrote fiction, publishing short sea stories in several periodicals. *Of Great Spaces* (1987), shared with Jerome Gold, collects and reprints five Galloway stories, the most intellectually ambitious of which is "Last Passenger North, or the Doppelganger," in the "mysterious stranger" genre. In this long story, set on an old Pacific coast steamer, an old captain looking forward to his imminent retirement has a long and complex conversation with a mysterious passenger who proves to be more metaphysical than human. In the surprise ending, which to an attentive reader is not truly a surprise, the captain has died. "The Albacore Fisherman" shows the ease with which a deadly accident can occur in the notoriously dangerous world of commercial fishing.

Galloway's only longer work, and his best, is *The Forty Fathom Bank* (1994), privately published earlier (1984). This novella, set in the San Francisco area, is told in retrospect by a tormented ex-fisherman. The German conquest of Scandinavia in World War II has meant a shortage of vitamin A from fish livers, and it is discovered that the livers of nurse sharks, plentiful in the area, are sixteen times richer in the vitamin than are cod livers. The price by the buyers quickly goes up to an astonishing $1,800 a ton. The author-narrator belatedly buys an old fishing boat and tries to cash in. He hires as crewman Ethan May, a quiet, odd-looking, strangely prescient man who advises him to fish in forty fathoms, though no one else has gone that deep. It's the end of the season, and there's not much chance of getting more than a few fish, but Ethan proposes the unusual bargain that the first three tons caught be the captain's and anything above that the crewman's. They agree.

When the narrator, failing to catch anything much by the usual methods, finally agrees to listen to May, they catch five tons on their first forty-fathom set, making him more money than he had ever thought possible. But over his exhaustion and exhilaration he realizes that from then on all the additional fishing they do will be solely for the benefit of his crewman. Irrationally but understandably, he inwardly rebels at their bargain and begins speculating about May's possibly being other than the innocent loner he seems.

In the next day's fishing they do even better, and then Ethan proposes one last short set, to which the narrator agrees, though he feels an awful sense of foreboding. As the line goes out, a hook snags one of Ethan's boots; the narrator momentarily freezes; the crewman is dragged under and disappears. Ethan's death is terrible, inevitable, swift, and believable. After it occurs, it leaves the narrator picturing his own mental torment to come.

Haskell Springer

GANN, ERNEST K[ELLOGG]. (1910–1991). Known primarily for his books in the field of aviation literature, Ernest K. Gann wrote about seafaring in *Twilight for the Gods* (1956) and *Song of the Sirens* (1968). *Twilight for the Gods* is an engaging tale of the passage on an overaged barquentine, *Cannibal*, carrying copra from Suva in the Fiji Islands to Mexico in the 1920s, the "twilight" of the era of sailing cargo vessels. The *Cannibal* carries people from many walks of life who have been less than "successful," and Gann reveals much about their characters, especially that of the captain, as the *Cannibal* begins to sink en route.

While waiting out a gale in a Danish port, Gann reminisces about the seventeen vessels that have been in his life in the *Song of the Sirens*. His "sirens" range from *Liberty*, which sank on its first trip out on a lake, to two commercial fishing boats that Gann once owned and operated on the Northwest* Pacific coast. The centerpiece of the *Song of the Sirens* is the *Albatross*, like the *Cannibal* a "middle-aged maid of fading beauty" (3), which he owned for four years. Gann takes us on his actual sailing voyage from Holland to San Francisco, then into the South Pacific and back to England.

On both the fictional and the actual vessels, the "principal cargo was dreams" (*Song of the Sirens* 158). Gann's skills as a storyteller result in stories of adventure and romance. They are nautically informed and are made particularly interesting by his thoughtful comments and observations about life at sea and its meanings and his obvious love for his vessels. *Twilight for the Gods* was made into a movie of the same title in 1958 starring Rock Hudson.

James F. Millinger

GARDNER, JOHN [CHAMPLIN] (1933–1982). The son of a dairy farmer, John Gardner had no important personal connection with the sea. Indeed, his maritime novella, *The King's Indian* (1972, in a volume of the same name), a modern Ancient Mariner story about a Captain Dirge and the whaler *Jerusalem* seeking the Vanishing Islands, projects a constant desire to return to land or perhaps even to convert the sea into land. Still, the sea figures pervasively in some of Gardner's works, from metaphors about mental activity in *The Wreckage of Agathon* (1970), to the fictional police chief Fred Clumly's reveries about serving on the S.S. *Carolina* and the thief Walter Boyle's memories of unloading Great Lakes* freight in *The Sunlight Dialogues* (1973).

The ocean figures most prominently in the narrative poem *Jason and Medeia* (1973) and in the novel *October Light* (1977). As Gardner says in his introduction, *Jason* is roughly based on Apollonios Rhodios' *Argonautica* (1546) (with liberal sprinklings from the *Odyssey*). Gardner carefully researched the construction, planking, binding, tarring, and rigging of the *Argo*, the ship that Athena sponsors on Jason's quest for the Golden Fleece. As in tradition, the ship often speaks in Athena's voice. Gardner also pays great attention to coastal names, real and imagined, from Achaea in the Gulf of Corinth, past Thrace, through the Propontis, the Bosporus, and the Bithynian Sea, to the estuary of Phasis (modern Rion) at the end of the Black Sea in Colchis (modern Mingrelia in Georgian Russia).

October Light takes place in landlocked Bennington, Vermont, where an old woman discovers a "dirty" paperback sea novel that her brother's grandson has hidden in a pigsty. The narrative of the paperback, which occupies about a third of the novel, chronicles the adventures of two competing twentieth-century drug smugglers, the captains of the *Indomitable* and the *Militant*, who traffic in marijuana between the Pacific coast of Mexico and San Francisco. The tragicomic plot places a would-be suicide from the Golden Gate Bridge as the skipper of the *Indomitable*. For transacting their marijuana deal, the ships land at Lost Souls' Rock, which is probably a fictional locale; given details in the ship's log, however, the landing may be Isla Roca Partida in the Revillagigedo Islands. There a flying saucer may rescue the skippers from a deadly earthquake.

William Crisman

"GARNETT, CAPT. MAYN CLEW." *See* [HAINS, THORNTON JENKINS].

GHOSTS AND GHOST SHIP LEGENDS. Beginning with the oldest yarns of the sea, authors and storytellers have described, largely in oral tradition, ghosts and ghost ships that appear and reappear in many different forms. Some of these legends assert that ghosts bedevil a ship until their wants are recognized and satisfied. They appear as cold, but corporeal, people, as wraiths upon the water or in the air, as voices or sounds, and as transmigrated beings assuming the form of a bird, fish, or sea mammal. They can guard treasure and occupy lighthouses* and the ships in which they went down. Although generally feared by seamen in the lore of the sea, ghosts are, for the most part, benevolent, warning sailors of impending danger, effecting rescues, or conveying useful messages.

Unhelpful ghosts, according to legend, are those for whom the ship is responsible. Should a man be killed during construction or launching or by falling from the rigging, his shade will not rest until the vessel is wrecked. If a ghost takes the crew with her, so be it.

Sailors believe that the sea seeks to claim the wicked and will take the good to get them. Hence, in the midst of great storms, the ghost of a murdered person will appear and identify the killer. He is thrown overboard, the storm abates, and the ship is saved. Sailors also believe that their best friend will be loyal even after death and that drowned sailors sometimes take the form of birds. If a gull drove a particular sailor out of the rigging just before the mast fell, and if other people were killed, for example, it meant that his long-dead friend had saved him.

Ghosts often appear in numbers. The schooner *Haskell* ran down the *Johnson* in a gale on Georges Bank with the loss of all hands. When the *Haskell* returned to the scene, she was boarded by the drowned crew. She went back to Gloucester* and became derelict, for no one would go in her. The *Northern Light* is said to have been saved from disaster by a dripping crew of sailors who came aboard in a raging gale on Georges Bank and took over the schooner, sailing her safely back to Gloucester.

Sailors believe in the supernatural and have reported frequent sightings of ghost ships in the Gulf of Saint Lawrence and the Bay of Chaleur. Most observations occur in high latitudes off great capes and reefs where visibility is poor, temperature low, currents strong, and storms frequent. Some such visions happen only once, such as the vessel loaded with Puritans that left New Haven, Connecticut, bound east, its specter reappearing bound west a few days later; all hands were dressed in black, singing hymns.

Ghost ships have been preserved in a wide range of literature that depicts a variety of circumstances. A vessel might sink with loss of life and without proper rites being performed, or ships and crews might be destroyed by mutiny,* wreckers, or inhuman acts of the captain. Ghosts sail ships of their own accord or travel aboard vessels to return to their place of rest. Some never sink but roam the sea forever, particularly if the captain committed sins against humanity or defied either God or ocean. A few vessels, like the *Merry Dun*, were said to have been built by Satan, manned by fiends, and sent to search for drowned souls to haul to hell.

Traditionally, ghost ships move across a windless sea. They sail backward with the sails trimmed forward or sail directly into the wind. Some carry sail when no sail can be borne. Some burn. Some ghost ships are so sea-worn that their planks have fallen off, the sun shines through their ribs, and only the bolt ropes of the sails remain. The crews are often skeletons. Satan's vessels might show red and blue running lights. While the *Quedah Merchant* plies Long Island Sound for no apparent purpose, most ghostly ships predict coming events. The *Teaser* and the *Palatine** burn before a storm; the *Dash* foretells a death on Harpswell Island, Maine. To meet some ghost ships such as the *Flying Dutchman* augurs immediate death.

An influential English ghost story is *The Rime of the Ancient Mariner* (1798) by Samuel Taylor Coleridge. The ballad has a Latin epigraph by Thomas Burnet, a seventeenth-century theologian, which translates: "I readily believe that there are more invisible beings in the universe than visible." *The Rime of the Ancient Mariner* includes earthly and heavenly spirits, Death and Life-in-Death, and a skeleton ghost ship. The Ancient Mariner wonders if he is a ghost himself. According to John Livingston Lowes in *The Road to Xanadu* (1927), *The Rime of the Ancient Mariner* likely collects many of the oral tales of ghosts at sea told during Coleridge's time.

In America, Richard Henry Dana Sr.,* in the poem "The Buccaneer" (1827), writes of a burning ghost ship and a white horse that rises from the water. The ship and the horse avenge the massacre of the passengers. In the short story "MS. Found in Bottle" (1833), Edgar Allan Poe* gives the text of a manuscript written by a shipwrecked* man whose vessel collides with a ghost ship. The man is hurled on board the ghost ship. The ancient sailors cannot see him as they sail their massive black ship toward the South Pole.

Many ghost stories of the sea are influenced by real events. The 1738 wreck of the *Princess Augusta* inspired William Gilmore Simms'* poem "The Ship of the Palatines" (1843) and John Greenleaf Whittier's* poem "The Palatine" (1867). Whittier also wrote "Death Ship of Harpswell" (1866), which describes a ghost ship that haunts the coast of Maine. She is sailed by the Angel of Death, sails against the tide, and never comes into port.

Washington Irving* published "The Haunted Ship: A True Story as Far as It Goes" (1835) about a ship adrift in the Bahamas. In 1850 Henry Wadsworth Longfellow* wrote "The Phantom Ship," inspired by the disappearance at sea of the *Fellowship*, which sailed from New Haven, Connecticut, in 1646 on a voyage to England. In "The Phantom Ship" the ship makes one appearance only, unlike other reappearing legends. Longfellow shows the people of New Haven observing a "Ship of Air" that sails against the wind. They see the faces of the crew as the sails blow away and the masts fall one by one, until the ship has completely disappeared.

In 1886 Celia Thaxter* published "The Cruise of Mystery," a poem about a slave* vessel that turns into a ghost ship. The captain kills all the slaves by locking them in the hold during a storm. He forces the crew to throw the dead overboard when the weather improves. The captain turns the ship around to get more slaves, and eventually the corpses swim back to the vessel and lash him to the mast. The rest of the crew escapes, but the *Mystery* still sails, and presumably will forever, always followed closely by misfortune.

Joshua Slocum's* nonfiction classic *Sailing Alone around the World* (1900) describes a ghost from Christopher Columbus'* crew who boards his vessel, *Spray*, and steers while Slocum is ill, conning her through a storm. In another legend, a man named Seymour Harnish saw a green and dripping sailor climb in over his ship's bow. The ghostly mate shook Harnish's hand and walked off the stern. Harnish opened the throttle for home, arriving just before the outbreak of a storm. A more contemporary use of the ghost ship is Ole Rølvaag's *The Boat of Longing** (1921). In Vincent Ferrini's* *Telling of the North Star* (1954), a ghostly crew disembarks to claim an eager young woman who has become obsessed with reading her grandfather's logbooks in the attic.

Though not American, universally the best-known and most dreaded ghost ship is the *Flying Dutchman*, which is said to haunt Cape Horn* and the Cape of Good Hope. According to this tale, a Dutch sea captain named Vanderdecker, or the Cloaked One, once attempted to round the Horn in his ship, the *Voltigeur*, but was held back by head winds. In a rage, he swore he would go around no matter how long it took "or be damned." God appeared and ordered him to recant. The Dutchman refused and ordered him off the quarterdeck, in desperation shooting at God. The bullet bounced back, wounding Vanderdecker in the hand. God then pronounced his fate: he would never reach land, never receive or send mail, always be wet, always have head winds, have only vinegar to drink, chew molten iron, and never rest. Any vessel he spoke would become accursed and go down in a storm with all hands. Many seamen claim to have sighted the vessel; always she is seen driving hard in the murk before a hurricane off one of the two great capes.

Several variations of the nineteenth-century *Flying Dutchman* legend exist, with the captain and ship known by different names and with the story set in different places. Some trace the story back to the crucifixion and the tale of the Wandering Jew. According to sixteenth-century German lore, a man named Ahasuerus laughed at Christ on the way to the cross, and Christ promised that the man would wander until his return. From that time, Ahasuerus could be identified by a large black hat and black cloak, fated to walk the world unceasingly, homeless and solitary. Others claim the story derives from a Norse legend of the Viking Stöte. German composer Richard Wagner wrote the opera *Der fliegende Holländer*, or *The Flying Dutchman*, in 1841. British author Captain Frederick Marryat wrote the novel *The Phantom Ship* in 1839. In 1888 W. Clark Russell published a three-volume account in *The Death Ship*.

Visions of ghosts and ghost ships in maritime lore can be rationalized by fatigue, cold, bad food, poor visibility, anxiety, and especially a subliminal response to minute atmospheric and oceanic changes, which can lead to a dreamlike trance where fantasy and reality merge. Today, sailors and landsmen still report ghosts on vessels, in lighthouses, and at sea all over the world, including aboard the U.S.S. *Constitution* in Boston and aboard the *Charles W. Morgan* in Mystic, Connecticut. [*See also FINAL PASSAGES;* GREAT LAKES MYTHS AND LEGENDS; *MARY CELESTE*]

FURTHER READING: Baker, Margaret. *Folklore of the Sea.* North Pomfret, VT: David and Charles, 1979; Bassett, Wilbur. *Wander-Ships: Folk Stories of the Sea with Notes upon Their Origin.* Chicago: Open Court, 1917; Beck, Horace. *Folklore and the Sea.* Middletown, CT: Wesleyan UP, 1973; Beck, Horace. *The Folklore of Maine.* Philadelphia: J. B. Lippincott, 1957; Behrman, Cynthia Fansler. *Victorian Myths of the Sea.* Athens: Ohio UP, 1977; Goss, Michael, and George Behe. *Lost at Sea: Ghost Ships and Other Mysteries.* Amherst, NY: Prometheus, 1994; Snow, Edward Rowe. *Strange Tales from Nova Scotia to Cape Hatteras.* New York: Dodd, Mead, 1949; Snow, Edward Rowe. *Unsolved Mysteries of Sea and Shore.* New York: Dodd, Mead 1963.

Horace Beck and Richard J. King

GILKERSON, WILLIAM (1936–   ). William Gilkerson has written nine books, most of which relate directly to maritime history. His first book, *Gilkerson on War—From Rocks to Rockets* (1964), is an exception, as it only touches upon maritime history in the larger context of naval warfare, which, in turn, appears only in the larger context of warfare in general. *The Scrimshander* (1975, rev. 1978) and *Maritime Arts by Wm. Gilkerson* (1981) portray Gilkerson as scrimshander and painter: *Maritime Arts* is an exhibition catalog of such artwork displayed at the Peabody Museum of Salem, Massachusetts, in 1980. Gilkerson illustrated *American Whalers in the Western Arctic* (1983), written by Arctic whaling expert John Bockstoce. Its companion volume, *An Arctic Whaling Sketchbook* (1983), is a collection of related drawings, some of which appeared in *American Whalers in the Western Arctic. The Ships of John Paul Jones* (1987) is a scholarly examination of the career of John Paul Jones* and of the naval architecture of the vessels that he commanded. Gilkerson's attention to historical exactitude is nowhere more apparent than in his representations of Jones' famous ship the *Bonhomme Richard** and other vessels. He has also written a two-volume reference book about shipboard small arms entitled *Boarders Away—With Steel* (1991) and *Boarders Away—With Fire* (1993).

All of these books are progressions toward his novel *Ultimate Voyage. A Book of Five Mariners* (1998). A sailor since boyhood, Gilkerson frames the action of his novel in a maritime context, but there is nothing fictitious in his narrative description. From the viewpoint of a sailor, shipwright, or naval architect, the genius of this book is in the details. *Ultimate Voyage* is a philosophical treatise very loosely based in any actual historical period or circumstance but firmly grounded in the principles of maritime history. It takes the reader on an exploration of the author's perception of the human condition through the metaphor of a voyage under sail, the metaphysical ramifications of which seem cunningly applicable to everyday life. [*See also* VOYAGE NARRATIVES; WHALING NARRATIVES]

Michael P. Dyer

GLASPELL, SUSAN [KEATING] (1876–1948). Associated with the Provincetown Players, a group that included Eugene O'Neill,* Jig Cook, and Floyd Dell in the early years of their illustrious collaboration (1916–1922), Susan Glaspell is best known for her novels and the play *Trifles* (1916). The only one of her plays in which the sea figures prominently is the one-act *The Outside* (first perf. 1917; pub. 1920), set at a former life-saving station between the open sea beyond Cape Cod* and the curve of land that creates the natural harbor of Provincetown. The setting symbolizes the allegorical pull of the play between life force, symbolized by the harbor, and death force, symbolized by the treacherous seas. Glaspell's language expressionistically evokes the sea and dunes. In the minimal action, two men have dragged a drowned man into what is now a home occupied by a woman and her housekeeper, both recluses. The men fail in an attempt to revive him, but their efforts and that of the anonymous Captain serve to encourage one of the women to abandon her solitude. This woman is the housekeeper, Allie Mayo, a role performed by the playwright in the original production. [*See also* DRAMA OF THE SEA; LIFESAVING LITERATURE]

Attilio Favorini

GLENCAIRN. The S.S. *Glencairn* is a fictional British tramp steamer, scene of Eugene O'Neill's* *The Moon of the Caribees* (first perf. 1918; pub. 1919), *Bound East for Cardiff* (first perf. 1916; pub. 1919), and *In the Zone* (first perf. 1917; pub. 1919). The crew from the *Glencairn* also appear in the shore-based play of the group, *Long Voyage Home* (first perf. 1917; pub. 1917), which is set in a London waterfront dive. The ship is likewise the scene of *Children of the Sea*, an earlier unpublished version of *Bound East for Cardiff*. In *Moon of the Caribees*, the ship is anchored in the West Indies, while in *Bound East* and *In the Zone* it sails eastward in the North Atlantic. The *Glencairn* cycle was made into a successful film with the title *Long Voyage Home* (1940), directed by John Ford. [*See also* DRAMA OF THE SEA]

Attilio Favorini

***GLOBE* MUTINY.** The *Globe* (built 1815) of Nantucket* might have been remembered as the first ship to return more than 2,000 barrels of whale oil, but that distinction was eclipsed by its being the stage of the bloodiest mutiny* in the history of the whale fishery.

The *Globe* sailed on its fourth voyage December 1822 for the Pacific, worked the Japan ground, and stopped at Oahu in the Hawaiian Islands in December 1823, where it lost seven crew members (six by desertion) and signed on six new hands, two of whom, Silas Payne and John Oliver, were to be key players in the mutiny and its sequel. The vessel left Honolulu 29 December 1823; a month later on the night of 26 January 1824, while off Fanning* Island (3° 49' N/158° 29' W), boatsteerer Samuel Comstock, the organizer of the mutiny, aided by Payne, Oliver, and William Humphries, broke into the cabin and killed Captain Thomas Worth, Mate William Beetle, Second Mate John Lombard (or Lumbert), and Third Mate Nathaniel Fisher. Two days later the mutineers hanged one of their own number, Humphries, of whose loyalty Comstock claimed to be suspicious.

The motive of the killings seems to have been not so much grievances about discipline (a flogging, insufficient time for meals) as the peculiar psychopathology of Comstock, whose earlier life had been marked by dramatic outbursts of idiosyncratic, often violent behavior.

Under Comstock's command the ship sailed first to the Kingsmill Islands, where the natives were hostile, and then to the Marshalls and the Mulgraves, where the mutineers landed on Mili Island. There the natives were unthreatening, but the *Globe* settlement was not destined to be the island kingdom that Comstock, according to some reports, hoped to establish. Within days of their landing, Comstock was murdered by Payne and Oliver, who suspected him of squandering the ship's stores on the natives to put himself in an alliance with them at the expense of the rest of the crew. Soon thereafter Gilbert Smith, Comstock's fellow boatsteerer, enlisted five of the seamen who were not mutineers (Stephen Kidder, Peter Kidder, George Comstock, Anthony Hanson, and Joseph Thomas) in an escape attempt. George Comstock was the younger brother of the chief mutineer; some suspicions hung about the role of Joseph Thomas in the mutiny.

Under cover of night the six sailed the *Globe* out to sea and reached Valparaiso four months later on 7 June 1824. Bad relations between the natives and the nine remaining *Globe* people on the island, attributable mainly to Payne's abusive treatment of the natives, led to a massacre of all the remaining seamen except for William Lay and Cyrus Hussey, who came under the protection of friendly natives. The dead included not only Payne and Oliver but Thomas Lilliston, who had been recruited by Comstock for the killings but turned back and did not participate, and the innocent seamen Columbus Worth, Rowland Jones, Rowland Coffin, and Joseph Brown.

Lay and Hussey, who were to become the primary chroniclers of the *Globe* story, lived almost two years among the Mulgrave natives before they were rescued. Under orders from the secretary of the navy transmitted to Commodore Isaac Hull, the schooner *Dolphin* was dispatched under the command of Captain John Percival to find the *Globe* remnant, arrest the mutineers, and rescue the rest. A perilous rescue of Lay was accomplished

e bear the names of two families caught in a furious storm in
oastal voyage from Newbury to Marblehead. Thacher's Island is
r Anthony Thacher, who lost his four children in the shipwreck.*
account was first published in Increase Mather's *Essay for the Il-
Recording of Providence (1684). Avery's Rock, where the vessel
memorializes the minister John Avery and his family of ten, who
ed in the disaster. John Greenleaf Whittier's* "The Swan Song of
n Avery" (1860) draws on the text of Thacher's description of Avery's
iction that spiritual deliverance awaits him in the aftermath of his in-
able death. Henry Wadsworth Longfellow,* Whittier's contemporary,
ew loosely on several newspaper reports of storms in December 1839 for
etails in perhaps the best-known Gloucester poem, "The Wreck of the
Hesperus" (1839), which Longfellow situates on a reef in Gloucester's outer
harbor called Norman's Woe.

Fictional recitals of Gloucester's fishing activities abound. One of the earliest, J. Reynolds' *Peter Gott, the Cape Ann Fisherman* (1856), claims historical accuracy but presents an idealized portrait of the work life of a typical
Gloucester fisherman. The most famous Gloucester work of fiction is Rudyard Kipling's *Captains Courageous** (1897), the story of Harvey Cheyne,
a boy who comes of age through the challenges of working on a Gloucester
schooner.

James Brendan Connolly—who saw action in Cuba in the Spanish-
American War, served briefly in the American navy, and fished in his early
years with the Gloucester, North Sea, and Baltic fleets, as well as in the
Arctic*—remains the most admired of Gloucester's fictional chroniclers.
The author of twenty-five books, most of them about the sea, Connolly
vividly portrays swaggering seamen defiant of the dangers of their trade,
appealing to a reading public recently enchanted by the virile fiction of Jack
London.* His publications include *Out of Gloucester* (1902), a collection of
five tales, and *The Seiners* (1904), a novel on mackerel fishing. Gloucester
stories continued to appear throughout his writing career, including the
novella *The Trawler* (1914). *Gloucestermen. Stories of the Fishing Fleet*
(1930) is a collection of twenty-seven of those stories. *The Book of the
Gloucester Fishermen* (1927) laments the decline of the all-sail fishing fleet.
The Port of Gloucester (1940) tells the story of Gloucester's connections to
the sea from the first settlements to the last sailing schooners.

Edmund Gilligan authored nine novels centered on various aspects of the
Gloucester fisheries, including *White Sails Crowding* (1939), a story of winter halibut fishing and shipwreck on the Grand Banks; *The Gaunt Woman*
(1943), in which the Gloucester halibut vessel *Daniel Webster* engages a
square-rigger serving as a weapons supply ship for German U-boats; and
Voyage of the Golden Hind (1945), a tale of intrigue and treachery on a
Grand Banks dory schooner.

Raymond McFarland presents a firsthand account of the labor of the

29 November 1825; Hussey, who ha'
from Lay, was found shortly ther
cued after a show of force. The t
the *Dolphin* and returned to New
arriving 22 April 1827.

The six crewmen who had escaped
examined by U.S. consul Michael Hogan i
on their return to the United States. One
tried for complicity in the mutiny and acquitte

Accounts of the *Globe* events contain minor dis
eral complementary. Lay and Hussey produced the
but the later telling of the story by William Comstock,
mutineer, is a remarkably engaging piece of writing.
participants and other official documents are noted by Ed
cited in the following.

FURTHER READING: Comstock, William. *The Life of Samuel Coms*
rible Whaleman. Containing an Account of the Mutiny, and Massacre of
of the Ship Globe, *of Nantucket; With His Subsequent Adventures, and His B*
at the Mulgrave Islands. Also, Lieutenant Percival's Voyage in Search of the Sur
By His Brother, William Comstock. Boston: James Fisher, 1840; Lay, William,
Cyrus M. Hussey. *A Narrative of the Mutiny on Board the Whaleship* Globe.
Nantucket, *in the Pacific Ocean, Jan. 1824. And the Journal of a Residence of Two*
Years on the Mulgrave Islands; With Observations on the Manners and Customs of the
Inhabitants. By William Lay, of Saybrook, Conn. and Cyrus M. Hussey, of Nantucket,
The Only Survivors from the Massacre of the Ship's Company by the Natives. New
London: Wm. Lay and C. M. Hussey, 1828 [rpt. New York: Corinth, 1963]; Stack-
pole, Edouard. "Mutiny at Midnight," *The Sea-Hunters.* Westport, CT: Greenwood,
1972.

Thomas Farel Heffernan

GLOUCESTER. A port city on the Cape Ann peninsula in northeastern
Massachusetts, Gloucester has been noted for its fishing enterprise since the
first English fishermen settled there in 1623 and for the hardiness and courage of its fishermen, more than 10,000 of whom have perished at sea. Although it rose to become one of the most productive fishing ports of the
world by the end of the nineteenth century, more than a century later, with
fish stocks depleted, its fishing industry is in serious decline.

Accounts of experiences along the Cape Ann coast have inspired poetical
re-creations. Among the earliest narratives, Francis Higginson's *New-*
Englands Plantation (1630) notes the abundance of mackerel as his vessel
approaches Cape Ann on its voyage from England. Higginson's description,
filled with expressions of wonder at the bounty and beauty around him,
prompted Ann Stanford to re-create the experience in her poem "The Rev.
Higginson's Voyage" (1981). Prominent, but perilous, features of the Cape

mackerel fishery in *The Masts of Gloucester* (1937) and celebrates the heroic qualities of the "high-liners," the elite seamen whose reputations for courage and competence were legendary in the community. A teacher and scholar, McFarland also wrote *A History of the New England Fisheries* (1911), a survey of the development of the fishing industry from the early seventeenth to the late nineteenth centuries, with emphasis on the herring, shellfish, cod, and mackerel fisheries and with an account of the evolution of the New England fishing schooner. Sterling Hayden's* autobiography, *Wanderer* (1963), includes, among numerous other seagoing experiences, an account of working in his youth as a deckhand on Gloucester schooners. Joseph Garland's *Lone Voyager* (1978) is a tribute to Gloucester's most famous dory fisherman, Howard Blackburn, who survived savage wintry seas for three days when lost in the fog by freezing his hands to the oars of his dory and rowing ashore. A noted local historian, Garland has also written a history of the coastal section of Gloucester known as *Eastern Point* (1973) and *Down to the Sea: The Fishing Schooners of Gloucester* (1983), an illustrated history of the men and schooners of the period between 1870 and 1930, commonly known as "Gloucestermen."

Notable among early American poets associated with the Gloucester area are Richard Henry Dana Sr.,* author of a well-known sea poem, "The Buccaneer" (1827); Epes Sargent,* the son of a Gloucester sea captain whose *Songs of the Sea with Other Poems* (1847) includes the popular song "A Life on the Ocean Wave"; and Lucy Larcom,* whose *Wild Roses of Cape Ann, and Other Poems* (1880) contains a nine-poem cluster devoted to the sea and the fishing fleet. James Davis *Pleasant Water: A Song of the Sea and Shore* (1877) is a long, narrative portrait idealizing Gloucester fishermen. Clarence Manning Falt presents a more realistic picture of the Gloucester fisherman's activities, often in the vernacular, in *Gloucester in Song* (1894) and *Wharf and Fleet: Ballads of the Fishermen of Gloucester* (1902). T. S. Eliot's* "Cape Ann" (1936), "Marina" (1930), and "The Dry Salvages" (1941) reflect the influence of the summers he spent on Cape Ann in his youth.

More recently, Vincent Ferrini* uses Italian American dialect in his poetry to remind his contemporaries of Gloucester's immigrant maritime heritage in a period when the city seems to be losing its seagoing identity. In *Know Fish* (1979), Ferrini chides Gloucester's political and commercial powers for undermining the way of life of the city's working-class "fisherfolk." Inspired by Ferrini, Charles Olson* takes up the theme of Gloucester's changing maritime destiny in *The Maximus Poems* (1983). More literary and less proletarian than Ferrini's poetry, Olson's verse epic surveys Gloucester's past and present in the context of an American history removed from its communal and spiritual roots.

In his plays of working-class life, especially *North Shore Fish* and *Henry Lumper* (*Gloucester Plays*, 1992), Israel Horovitz captures the economic and moral decline that Ferrini had predicted. Horovitz's *Captains and Courage* (1997), a centennial adaptation of *Captains Courageous*, interweaves the destinies of Rudyard Kipling's principal characters with their struggling descendants 100 years later: Ben Cheyne, one of the last Gloucester fishermen; Roland Troop, whose sense of impending doom makes him a reluctant crew member; and Manny Shimma, a neglected, abused, homeless juvenile. Troop's portentous mood may have been influenced by the enormously popular retelling of the actual sinking in 1991 of a Gloucester swordfishing vessel, the *Andrea Gail*, in Sebastian Junger's *The Perfect Storm** (1997). [*See also* GHOSTS AND GHOST SHIP LEGENDS; SEA DELIVERANCE NARRATIVES]

FURTHER READING: Bartlett, Kim. *The Finest Kind*. New York: Norton, 1977; Boeri, David. *"Tell It Good-Bye, Kiddo": The Decline of the New England Offshore Fishery*. Camden, ME: International Marine, 1976; Connolly, James Brendan. *The Port of Gloucester*. New York: Doubleday, Doran, 1940; John F. Brown Marine Collection, Cape Ann Historical Association; Kenny, Herbert A. *Cape Ann, Cape America*. Philadelphia: Lippincott, 1971; McFarland, Raymond. *The Masts of Gloucester*. New York: Norton, 1937.

Joseph Flibbert

GOODRICH, MARCUS [AURELIUS] (1897–1991). Novelist Marcus Goodrich was born 28 November 1897, in San Antonio, Texas. Enlisting in the navy in 1916, he served initially in the Philippines aboard the destroyer U.S.S. *Chauncey*. With the outbreak of World War I, the *Chauncey* was sent to the Atlantic, and Goodrich was aboard on 19 November 1917, when she collided with a merchant ship while escorting a convoy and went down with the loss of twenty-one men, including the captain. Serving throughout World War I, Goodrich became a naval aviator before leaving the service in 1920. After attending Columbia University while working as a Broadway stage manager and newspaperman, Goodrich became a professional journalist.

In 1926 he began, in earnest, work on his novel *Delilah* (1941), based on his experiences aboard the *Chauncey* in the Philippines and ending as World War I begins. Writing *Delilah* took him fourteen years, during which he supported himself with newspaper work, advertising copywriting, and writing "treatments" for Hollywood movies. His treatments include *Navy Born* (1936) and *It's a Wonderful Life* (1947). Finally published on the eve of America's entry into World War II, *Delilah* became a best-seller. Goodrich returned to active duty in World War II, serving in the Mediterranean and Pacific and ending the war as a lieutenant commander. *Delilah* was his only novel, though for the rest of his life he indicated that he was polishing the sequel. The last of Goodrich's five marriages (1946–1952) was to actress Olivia de Haviland. He died in Richmond, Virginia.

C. Herbert Gilliland

29 November 1825; Hussey, who had been kept for most of the time apart from Lay, was found shortly thereafter thanks to Lay's directions and rescued after a show of force. The two survivors were taken to Valparaiso by the *Dolphin* and returned to New York in the U.S. frigate *United States*, arriving 22 April 1827.

The six crewmen who had escaped with the *Globe* were confined and examined by U.S. consul Michael Hogan in Valparaiso and examined again on their return to the United States. One of them, Joseph Thomas, was tried for complicity in the mutiny and acquitted.

Accounts of the *Globe* events contain minor discrepancies but are in general complementary. Lay and Hussey produced the most popular version, but the later telling of the story by William Comstock, brother of the chief mutineer, is a remarkably engaging piece of writing. The depositions of participants and other official documents are noted by Edouard Stackpole, cited in the following.

FURTHER READING: Comstock, William. *The Life of Samuel Comstock, the Terrible Whaleman. Containing an Account of the Mutiny, and Massacre of the Officers of the Ship* Globe, *of Nantucket; With His Subsequent Adventures, and His Being Shot at the Mulgrave Islands. Also, Lieutenant Percival's Voyage in Search of the Survivors. By His Brother, William Comstock.* Boston: James Fisher, 1840; Lay, William, and Cyrus M. Hussey. *A Narrative of the Mutiny on Board the Whaleship* Globe. *Of Nantucket, in the Pacific Ocean, Jan. 1824. And the Journal of a Residence of Two Years on the Mulgrave Islands; With Observations on the Manners and Customs of the Inhabitants. By William Lay, of Saybrook, Conn. and Cyrus M. Hussey, of Nantucket, The Only Survivors from the Massacre of the Ship's Company by the Natives.* New London: Wm. Lay and C. M. Hussey, 1828 [rpt. New York: Corinth, 1963]; Stackpole, Edouard. "Mutiny at Midnight," *The Sea-Hunters.* Westport, CT: Greenwood, 1972.

Thomas Farel Heffernan

GLOUCESTER. A port city on the Cape Ann peninsula in northeastern Massachusetts, Gloucester has been noted for its fishing enterprise since the first English fishermen settled there in 1623 and for the hardiness and courage of its fishermen, more than 10,000 of whom have perished at sea. Although it rose to become one of the most productive fishing ports of the world by the end of the nineteenth century, more than a century later, with fish stocks depleted, its fishing industry is in serious decline.

Accounts of experiences along the Cape Ann coast have inspired poetical re-creations. Among the earliest narratives, Francis Higginson's *New-Englands Plantation* (1630) notes the abundance of mackerel as his vessel approaches Cape Ann on its voyage from England. Higginson's description, filled with expressions of wonder at the bounty and beauty around him, prompted Ann Stanford to re-create the experience in her poem "The Rev. Higginson's Voyage" (1981). Prominent, but perilous, features of the Cape

Ann coastline bear the names of two families caught in a furious storm in 1635 in a coastal voyage from Newbury to Marblehead. Thacher's Island is named after Anthony Thacher, who lost his four children in the shipwreck.* Thacher's account was first published in Increase Mather's *Essay for the Illustrious Recording of Providence* (1684). Avery's Rock, where the vessel struck, memorializes the minister John Avery and his family of ten, who perished in the disaster. John Greenleaf Whittier's* "The Swan Song of Parson Avery" (1860) draws on the text of Thacher's description of Avery's conviction that spiritual deliverance awaits him in the aftermath of his inevitable death. Henry Wadsworth Longfellow,* Whittier's contemporary, drew loosely on several newspaper reports of storms in December 1839 for details in perhaps the best-known Gloucester poem, "The Wreck of the *Hesperus*" (1839), which Longfellow situates on a reef in Gloucester's outer harbor called Norman's Woe.

Fictional recitals of Gloucester's fishing activities abound. One of the earliest, J. Reynolds' *Peter Gott, the Cape Ann Fisherman* (1856), claims historical accuracy but presents an idealized portrait of the work life of a typical Gloucester fisherman. The most famous Gloucester work of fiction is Rudyard Kipling's *Captains Courageous** (1897), the story of Harvey Cheyne, a boy who comes of age through the challenges of working on a Gloucester schooner.

James Brendan Connolly—who saw action in Cuba in the Spanish-American War, served briefly in the American navy, and fished in his early years with the Gloucester, North Sea, and Baltic fleets, as well as in the Arctic*—remains the most admired of Gloucester's fictional chroniclers. The author of twenty-five books, most of them about the sea, Connolly vividly portrays swaggering seamen defiant of the dangers of their trade, appealing to a reading public recently enchanted by the virile fiction of Jack London.* His publications include *Out of Gloucester* (1902), a collection of five tales, and *The Seiners* (1904), a novel on mackerel fishing. Gloucester stories continued to appear throughout his writing career, including the novella *The Trawler* (1914). *Gloucestermen. Stories of the Fishing Fleet* (1930) is a collection of twenty-seven of those stories. *The Book of the Gloucester Fishermen* (1927) laments the decline of the all-sail fishing fleet. *The Port of Gloucester* (1940) tells the story of Gloucester's connections to the sea from the first settlements to the last sailing schooners.

Edmund Gilligan authored nine novels centered on various aspects of the Gloucester fisheries, including *White Sails Crowding* (1939), a story of winter halibut fishing and shipwreck on the Grand Banks; *The Gaunt Woman* (1943), in which the Gloucester halibut vessel *Daniel Webster* engages a square-rigger serving as a weapons supply ship for German U-boats; and *Voyage of the* Golden Hind (1945), a tale of intrigue and treachery on a Grand Banks dory schooner.

Raymond McFarland presents a firsthand account of the labor of the

GOULD, JOHN W. (1814–1838). John W. Gould was born in Litchfield, Connecticut, the seventh son of influential judge and educator James Gould. He was christened "John Gould" but added the middle initial "W." in 1835 to avoid confusion.

Gould's health was always poor; he sailed from New York in 1833 before the mast, bound for Canton via Cape Horn,* in an attempt to improve his health. The captain's behavior forced Gould to leave the ship in Valparaiso, and he returned to New York in 1834 with his health completely restored. Despite minimal formal education, which was limited to a failed attempt at study for a life in the ministry, Gould began writing about his experiences at sea. All of his sea stories were based on his single voyage to Valparaiso and back, and all were written between the ages of nineteen and twenty-two. He published several fiction and nonfiction articles in the *New York Mirror*, the *Knickerbocker Magazine*, and the *American Monthly Magazine*. His works feature extensive use of nautical metaphors and speak of those places he visited or heard about from others. His stories describe sailors' views of mutiny,* piracy, naval engagements, and the trials of life at sea. His writings were compiled and edited by his brother Edward, also an author, in *Forecastle Yarns* (1845).

In 1837 Gould became sick again and tried to repeat his cure at sea. He sailed for Rio de Janeiro in 1838 as a passenger. He was very weak throughout the voyage, and despite some convalescence in Rio, he died on the return trip. His journal of the voyage, along with his correspondence and writings, appeared in another volume edited by his brother, *John W. Gould's Private Journal* (1838).

Peter H. McCracken

GREAT LAKES BALLADS. The history of ballad-making, reciting, and singing in the Great Lakes region began after the Battle of Lake Erie on 10 September 1813, itself the subject of a number of Great Lakes ballads, when the Lakes became American-dominated, and shipping grew rapidly. That history and its ensuing ballad-making continues today, incorporating such events as the wreck of the *Edmund Fitzgerald** (built 1958) on 10 November 1975, which gained fame in the song by Gordon Lightfoot.

Like other ballads, those of the Great Lakes usually become anonymous in their authorship as they are transmitted orally or in informal print. They are usually of four-line ballad stanzas, alternating four-stress and three-stress lines, and they are often set to simple, familiar tunes, frequently with a simple, sometimes meaningless refrain. Their language is almost always colloquial. Peculiar to Great Lakes ballads is that most of them are concerned with Great Lakes tragedies, usually shipwrecks,* and many of them were originally published in port-town newspapers near the locations of the tragedies. They were usually the work of local poets, often of the school of Julia A. Moore, the "Sweet Singer of Michigan," who was so sharply caricatured by Mark Twain as Emmeline Grangerford in *Adventures of Huckleberry Finn* (1884). In some cases, no records of the subject shipwrecks exist outside of the ballads, and these subjects themselves may be fictitious, but many of them, real or not, have become the substance of Great Lakes legend, myth, and folklore.

Such a ship was the schooner *Antelope*, which, late in the season, probably in 1894, was bound for Chicago from the Upper Lakes, loaded with grain. Lines from the ballad, apparently written by a survivor, describe the course of events that doomed her in the storm: "With our canvas gone, both anchors out,/ We were drifting on the shore./ . . . Our mainmast by the deck was broke,/ Our mizzenmast was gone!/ . . . And only one of that gallant crew/ Was in life once more to stand."

Countless other ballads mark the deaths of Great Lakes schooners during the three-quarters of a century when sail dominated Great Lakes shipping: the *City of Green Bay*, sunk off South Haven, Michigan, in the 1880s; the *Gilbert Mollison*, sunk with all hands off North Manitou Island late in 1873; the *Oriole*, wrecked with all hands off the Pictured Rocks, date unrecorded. With the coming of steam, the tradition continued, and ballads commemorate the collision of the steamer *Lady Elgin* with the schooner *Augusta* on Lake Michigan on 8 September 1860, with the loss of 287 lives, including the entire Union Guard and a Milwaukee Democratic group returning from a rally in Chicago for Stephen A. Douglas. Other ballads record the loss of the *City of Alpena* off Holland, Michigan, on 17 October 1880; the *Erie*, lost in Lake Erie in 1841 with 180 as her boiler exploded; the *Atlantic*, which took 250 lives on the night of 20 August 1895. With the domination of steam over sail, the casualty lists grew and lost their anonymity as the wrecks entered recorded history.

Not all of the ballads record the tragedies of shipwreck. Others record steamer races that sometimes ended tragically, and some record the daily lives of the sailors and of the peculiar relationship between steamers and the geography of the Lakes. One such, still heard in Great Lakes bars, records the experiences of the trade that dominated Great Lakes shipping for much of the twentieth century: that of the ore shipments from the Upper Lakes, where the great Mesabi Range provided iron ore for the then-dominant steel industry, to Lower Lake ports—Cleveland, Lorain, Ashtabula, and others— for refinement and steelmaking there or transshipment to Pittsburgh. One such ballad, "Red Iron Ore," excerpted next, records in detail the course of the down-lake journey:

> The tug *Escanaba*, she towed out the *Minch*,
> The *Roberts*, she thought, had been left in a pinch,
> And as they passed by us, they bid us goodbye,
> Saying, "We'll meet you in Cleveland next Fourth of July."
>
> The *Roberts* rolled on across Saginaw Bay,
> And over her bow splashed the white spray,

And bound for the rivers the *Roberts* did go,
Where the tug *Kate Williams* took us in tow.

Now we're down from Escanaba, and my two hands are sore
From pushing a wheelbarrow; I'll do it no more.
I'm sore-backed from shoveling, so hear my loud roar,
Now I'm ashore in Cleveland, I'll shake iron ore.

This ballad, like many of the others, exists in several versions. In this case the text is appropriate for sail (another extant version records a steam voyage); in both cases the ballads record a way of life and a pattern of work that have vanished as mechanization and unionization have come to the Lakes.

Other ballads celebrate historical events, significantly the 10 September 1813 Battle of Lake Erie, in which Captain Oliver H. Perry "met the enemy and they are ours" in an American victory that was the turning point in the war in the Northwest. "Perry's Victory" is a rousing patriotic air that began life as a penny broadside* and was widely sung during the Perry Centennial celebrations in 1913. Another ballad records the last journey and the death of Dr. Douglas Houghton, who made Michigan's Upper Peninsula known to science and to the nation.

Both the writing and singing of Great Lakes ballads have enjoyed a resurgence in recent years as Great Lakes tragedies continue to occur, and ballad singers, amateur and professional, make their voices heard in the cities and towns of the Lakes and beyond. But the century between Perry's victory in 1813 and the Great Storm of November 1913, in which nineteen vessels were destroyed or sunk and twenty stranded, at a cost of 248 lives, marked the richest period of Great Lakes ballad writing and singing. [*See also* CLEMENS, SAMUEL LANGHORNE; GREAT LAKES CHANTEYS; GREAT LAKES MYTHS AND LEGENDS; SEA MUSIC]

FURTHER READING: No anthologies of Great Lakes ballads are in print, but the ballads themselves are found in folklore anthologies and collections, as well as in the repertoires of Great Lakes singers. The ballad tradition remains an oral one, passed on to me by my grandfather, William E. Foster (1896–1951). An important contemporary singer is Lee Murdock, who appears in concert and whose recordings include "Folk Songs of the Great Lakes," "Freshwater Highways," and others, available from Depot Recordings, Kaneville, IL 60144–0011. The Bentley Historical Library has a good collection of ballads, some of which are recorded in David D. Anderson, "Songs and Sayings of the Lakes," *Midwest Folklore* 12 (Spring 1962): 5–16.

David D. Anderson

GREAT LAKES CHANTEYS. Commercial sailing on the Great Lakes made its short-lived beginning with the launching of the *Griffon*, built near Niagara Falls in 1679 by René Robert Cavelier, de la Salle, known to history as La Salle, for fur trade to the Upper Lakes. The ship made its first voyage that year, wintering at Green Bay, Wisconsin, and vanished the next year on its return voyage loaded with furs, thus giving rise to numerous myths and legends. However, the Battle of Lake Erie on 10 September 1813, a major American victory over the British, opened up that part of the Northwest Territory, including the northern part of Ohio, a state since 1803, and what were to become Indiana (1816), Illinois (1818), Michigan (1837), and Wisconsin (1848) to settlement, both by Americans and by new immigrants from Northern Europe.

The result was an active sailing packet service, especially after the opening of the Erie Canal in 1825 permitted passage by water from the East Coast to increasing numbers of Great Lakes destinations. The discovery of iron ore and copper in Michigan's Upper Peninsula in 1844 contributed to the accelerated construction of hundreds of a relatively standard three-masted schooner for both passenger and commercial trade. That construction was further accelerated by the growing lumber industry in Michigan and, later, Wisconsin.

Although steam came to the Lakes as early as 1818, when the *Walk-in-the-Water* was launched near Buffalo, commercial traffic was dominated by the schooners until near the end of the nineteenth century. With the decline of the lumber trade and the emergence of the modern Lakes-style bulk carrier, commercial sailing went into an irreversible decline. It ended in the fall of 1930, when the last commercial schooner, *Our Son*, a pulpwood carrier built in Lorain, Ohio, in the 1870s, was wrecked on the Michigan shore of Lake Michigan.

During the three-quarters of a century when schooner traffic dominated the Lakes, a chanteying tradition emerged. Strongly influenced by the saltwater tradition and undoubtedly brought to the Lakes by saltwater sailors, Great Lakes chanteys quickly took on characteristics unique to the circumstances of Great Lakes sailing. As was true of sea chanteys during the nineteenth century, Great Lakes chanteys were work songs. Like their saltwater counterparts, the verses of Great Lakes chanteys were generally of anonymous, perhaps collective evolutionary authorship, with the chanteyman (often but not always a petty officer) singing the verses, often to traditional tunes, and the rest of the men singing the alternating chorus. The combination provided the spirit as well as the rhythms by which lines were hauled, capstans turned, and windlasses and pumps worked, as demanded not only by the operation of the ship but by the peculiar geography of the Lakes themselves.

The geography of the Lakes is defined by the five individual lakes—Superior, Michigan, Huron, Erie, and Ontario—joined by narrow connecting bodies of water of varying lengths with a variety of hazards. Lake voyages are traditionally short, marked by a limited sailing season, and further restricted by a limited number of points of departure and destination. Storms on the Great Lakes, particularly at the end of the shipping season, can be intense. All of these elements found their way into the verses and choruses of Great Lakes chanteys.

One typical chantey tells the story of a long haul up-lake from Buffalo to Chicago. First the schooner gets under way as the chanteyman sings: "When the mate calls up all hands/ To man the capstan, walk 'er round,/ We'll heave 'er up lads with a will,/ For we are homeward bound." Then the crew at the capstan takes up the chorus, an echo of the saltwater version, which replaces "Chicago" with "New England" in the penultimate line: "Rolling home, rolling home,/ Rolling home across the sea,/ Rolling home to old Chicago, Rolling home, old town, to thee!" Clearing Buffalo harbor, the schooner tacks up-lake across Lake Erie against the wind. Then, entering the Detroit River for transit via Lake St. Clair and the St. Clair River to Lake Huron, it is taken in tow by a steam tug, as many schooners were in the last years of sailing on the Lakes. Then, after another chorus, the schooner is again under sail. Through the straits and down the long length of Lake Michigan, chorus and verse are strong: "Soon, my boys, the trip is done,/ And there is no more to say,/ We'll go down to old Black Pete's,/ And spend our whole damned pay."

In another chantey, the chanteyman takes a three-masted schooner up-lake as he recounts the shortcomings of the captain, the mate, the food, and the weather, finally concluding as the ship turns back down the Lakes: "And now we're bound down the Lakes, let 'er roar,/ Hurrah, boys, heave 'er down!/ And on this old scow we'll never ship more,/ Way down, laddies, down!"

Chanteymen on Lakes schooners, like their counterparts at sea, were valuable crewmen, providing leadership and spirit as they sang from their repertoire and improvised freely on subjects ranging from the weather and the food, to the virtues or lack of virtues of young ladies in port towns from Buffalo, New York, to Duluth, Minnesota. A unique feature of Great Lakes chanteying was the fact that the chanteys were often heard ashore, not only as the schooners entered or cleared port but also as the sailors made or took in sail in the narrow waterways between the Lakes. Often, too, at night, schooners were warned of others nearby by the sound of chanteys echoing over the water.

The decline in sailing and the subsequent decline in chanteying were rapid after 1890. Not only did donkey engines increasingly power capstans and raise sails, but many schooners were converted to barges, ending their days ignominiously in tow by steam tugs. The great storms, especially that of 8 November 1913, took a heavy toll, and many Lakes schooners were pressed into the Atlantic coastal trade during World War I. By 1930, with the wreck of *Our Son*, commercial sailing and chanteys passed from the Lakes. [*See also* CLEMENS, SAMUEL LANGHORNE; GREAT LAKES BALLADS; GREAT LAKES MYTHS AND LEGENDS; SEA MUSIC]

FURTHER READING: Few chanteys or studies of chanteys have found their way into print. See David D. Anderson, "Songs and Sayings of the Lakes," *Midwest Folklore* 12 (Spring 1962): 5–16. Chanteying remains an oral tradition, passed onto me by my grandfather, William E. Foster (1869–1951), who sailed the Lakes as a young man. The oral tradition is best preserved today by Lee Murdock, whose recordings of chanteys and ballads of the Lakes include "Songs of the Sweetwater Seas," "Voices across the Water," "Cold Winds," "Safe in the Harbor," and others, available from Depot Recordings, Kaneville, IL 60144–0011. The Bentley Historical Library at the University of Michigan houses the best collection of sources of chanteys.

David D. Anderson

GREAT LAKES LITERATURE. An accident of geology, the abandoned scourings of the Wisconsin glacier, the Great Lakes have made possible a maritime commerce that began before Native Americans first traded with Europeans for furs in the sixteenth century. The Algonquian word *odawa* first meant "trader" before it was applied to an artificially created tribal unit, and these precontact mariners ferried copper and furs to trade with tribes distant from the Lakes. The *odawa* perfected the first long, lean, indigenous Lakes vessel—the birchbark canoe—the ancestor of modern, 1,000-foot bulk carriers. Native culture created the first literature of the Great Lakes as well, stories about a unique underwater monster, a spiny lynx known as *Micipijiu* (Missipeshu), who ruled this world of waters by raising storms that endangered everyone who traveled there. His malevolence undiminished by time or marine engineering, *Micipijiu* survives in rock paintings on the Precambrian Shield on the north shore of Lake Superior, in the texts of ethnologists such as Henry Rowe Schoolcraft,* in the folklore of freshwater sailors, and in contemporary novels. His work offers a fitting representative of waters classed among the most dangerous on earth.

European American history and literature on the Lakes, which began as early as the Puritan settlements in New England, have always been linked inextricably with commercial and industrial expansion. Father Louis Hennepin, who accompanied René Robert Cavelier, de la Salle in 1679 on the first ship to sail the upper Lakes, immediately recognized their potential for development into another Mediterranean basin. The furs ferried east in long *maître* canoes were the prizes of the French and Indian War (1756–1763) and the War of 1812 (1812–1815) that defined the fledgling United States as a nation. Immigrants who later sailed through the Lakes seeking economic prosperity in the Northwest Territories, which were rich in copper, iron, salt, limestone, lumber, and prairie land, followed routes developed by Native Americans and extended by the great drive for economic and national expansion that characterized the nineteenth century. They created a concentration of agriculture, industry, and urban enterprise that defined American and Canadian* business and inspired what is commonly thought of as Great Lakes literature: the novels of freshwater merchant marine culture.

This literature, initiated by an anonymous novel titled *Scenes on Lake Huron** in 1836 and by James Fenimore Cooper's* *The Pathfinder** in 1840, began as a response to class and cultural conflicts on the emerging frontier. When Cooper pits Jasper, the young captain of a Lakes vessel, against Cap, a tradition-bound saltwater mate, their encounter epitomizes the North American experience of western expansion: survival demanded new skills and a willingness to break with centuries-old traditions. Herman Melville* joined this contest with "The Town-Ho's Story" in *Moby-Dick** (1851), describing the Lakes there as "swept by Borean and dismasting blasts as direful as any that lash the salted wave" (ch. 54) and creating another Lakes sailor who triumphs over a traditional saltwater captain.

Once frontier culture was superseded by industrialization, however, the romantic cast of Lakes fiction could no longer be sustained except in historical novels. The industrialization of the Great Lakes in the nineteenth century coincided with the rise of realism in the United States; therefore, the fiction created was a proletarian, working-class literature such as Richard Matthews Hallet's* *Trial by Fire* (1915) and Jay McCormick's* *November Storm* (1942), novels that attempt to make sensible experiences that were harrowing but still misunderstood because they took place on freshwater "lakes." Hurricane-force storms, few harbors of refuge, technological obsolescence, disastrous deflation, and the vertical integration of shipping led only to death or failure for many who thought to participate in the dreams of independence first delineated by Cooper. As the twentieth century progressed, Lakes merchant marine literature became a culturally contested site once more, this time divided between realist and postrealist indictments of industrialization, such as David Mamet's play *Lakeboat** (1970), and historical romances that attempted to re-create a past free of the class, gender, and racial conflicts that still prevailed.

Women's literature, however, charts a different course. When the Great Lakes were a maritime frontier with the concomitant fluidity of gender roles, women participated in the world outside the home, working as cooks on ships, sailing to remote outposts as missionaries, and keeping lighthouses.* Women writers could board a boat in Buffalo, New York, and within a few days be at the edge of the wilderness, then return home and write about their experiences in travel narratives, one of the most salable genres of the nineteenth and early twentieth centuries. Others who grew up on the Lakes were able to develop lucrative careers as writers after the Civil War, when the conjunction of widespread literacy, mass-circulation magazines such as *Harper's* and *The Atlantic*, and eastern readers' desire to escape the problems of the Industrial Revolution and urban immigration created a market for escapist local-color fiction. Mary Hartwell Catherwood* and Constance Fenimore Woolson,* among others, began their careers publishing short stories set on the Lakes. Although writers often portrayed their women characters' lives as difficult, they also described the freedom that the Lakes allowed them: to work, to achieve, to be free in the small boats and canoes they treasured.

This freedom and the self-respect that accompanied it were frequently linked with the example of American Indian women. European American women early recognized that Indian women had great freedom and respect in their societies: they could own property, divorce their husbands and retain custody of their children, and participate in community decisions. Nineteenth-century white women writers had few models of feminine achievement in their own culture, and on the Great Lakes, where Indian and white cultures had lived together for centuries, the example of Indian women was powerful, particularly after capitalistic industrialization diminished women's opportunities to participate outside the home.

Thus, the legacy of Indian life on the Great Lakes survives not only in the texts collected by ethnologists but in the fiction of white writers as well, particularly in the late twentieth century, when the themes of Great Lakes fiction change once again. No longer a site of contention about the traditions of sailing or the exploitation of workers, recent maritime literature such as Joan Skelton's *The Survivor of the* Edmund Fitzgerald* (1985) critiques the ideologies of the postindustrial cultures of the Lakes. This fiction suggests that unrestrained development and resource extraction reflect a nineteenth-century viewpoint that is no longer viable and that mythic creatures such as *Micipijiu*, who becomes a character in Skelton's novel, may reflect earlier cultures' acknowledgment of the limits of technology and human ability.

As Cooper pointed out in *The Pathfinder*, new places require new ideas. Only by recognizing the contending forces that created the regional maritime literature of the Great Lakes can readers understand its complexity. Because the development of the Lakes coincided with the Industrial Revolution in the United States and the collateral rise of the realistic mode in literature, much of the imaginative literature portrays English-speaking, white, working-class lives, the culture that dominated the Lakes after 1776, and the decline of French and Indian influence. Although African Americans* were early drawn to the Lakes because the Northwest Ordinance of 1787 outlawed slave trading, and the historical record offers tantalizing glimpses of black shipping operations, no literature of their lives on the Lakes has been discovered.

Thus, readers must approach Great Lakes literature from multiple perspectives: as a classic literature of the sea celebrating a way of life that was dangerous and difficult but sometimes rewarded those with luck and courage; as a literature of resistance written by women and who made their own place on the frontier and later in the industrialized world that followed it; and as a fragmented record that seldom includes natives and other people of color. Without this complicated viewpoint, readers risk reducing the maritime literature of the Great Lakes to a story of men before the mast, a shorter story than it was. [*See also* AMERICAN INDIAN LITERATURE OF THE SEA; BATES, MARTHA E. CRAM; CADWELL, CLARA GERTRUDE; CARSE, ROBERT; CURWOOD, JAMES OLIVER; DESROSIERS, LÉO-PAUL; DONER, MARY FRANCES; ELLIS, EDWARD SYLVESTER; ELLSBERG, EDWARD; FULLER, IOLA; FULLER, MARGARET; GREAT LAKES MYTHS AND LEGENDS; HAVIGHURST, WALTER; HURLBUT, FRANCES; LANE, CARL DANIEL; MACHARG; WILLIAM; MERWIN, SAMUEL; PARETSKY, SARA; *RIVER-HORSE*; SNIDER, CHARLES HENRY JEREMIAH; VUKELICH, GEORGE; WOMEN AT SEA]

FURTHER READING: Brehm, Victoria. *Sweetwater, Storms, and Spirits: Stories of the Great Lakes*. Ann Arbor: U of Michigan P, 1990; Brehm, Victoria. *"A Fully Accredited Ocean": Essays on the Great Lakes*. Ann Arbor: U of Michigan P, 1997; Brehm, Victoria. *The Women's Great Lakes Reader*. Duluth, MN: Holy Cow!, 1997; Havighurst, Walter. *The Great Lakes Reader*. New York: Collier Macmillan, 1966; White, Richard. *The Middle Ground: Indians, Empires, and Republics in the Great Lakes Region, 1650–1815*. New York: Cambridge UP, 1991.

Victoria Brehm

GREAT LAKES MYTHS AND LEGENDS. The Great Lakes are as rich in maritime myth and legend as are the oceans. From the 1840s on, Great Lakes navigation expanded dramatically due to the westward movement of population and the resulting increase in commerce. The Lakes provided the natural highway to carry the vast numbers of immigrants and resulting trade on to the new lands. Originally, saltwater sailors crewed the large fleets of sailing craft and steamers. Eventually, homegrown men sailed the fleets. Pay and working conditions were considerably better on the inland seas, and the saltwater men were eager to sail freshwater. There were no bucko mates or cat-o'-nine-tails. Trips were shorter, and the food better. Doubtless, many of the ocean myths and legends followed the sailors to the Great Lakes, changing somewhat in the transition. Others, perhaps, are unique to the Lakes.

The Great Lakes are often beset by thick and persistent fog. In the spring and fall, blinding snowstorms race over the water. Freezing temperatures can cause thick ice to coat a ship's topsides, spars, rigging, and sails, making them unmanageable. In the fall, storms raging out of the North can bring hurricane-force winds and house-size waves of great power. The seas themselves are steeper and closer together than on the ocean, presenting saltwater sailors with conditions far different from what they are used to experiencing. It is an environment that lends itself well to maritime myth and legend.

Ghost ships are perhaps the most common legend on the Lakes. Unlike the famous *Flying Dutchman* of Cape Horn* fame, sighting a Great Lakes ghost ship does not necessarily foretell disaster. The earliest ghost ship is René Robert Cavelier, de la Salle's *Griffon* (built 1679). On her return trip from Green Bay, Lake Michigan, to Lake Erie in 1679, she disappeared with all hands. Some said she was the victim of the curse of a Native American chief. Ever since, Great Lakes sailors have reported briefly seeing her ghostly form scudding through storm and gale. The steamer *Bannockburn* (built 1893) was said to have reappeared numerous times after her 1902 disappearance on Lake Superior. James Oliver Curwood* cites her tale in his book *Falkner of the Inland Seas* (1905). The legend of the ship grew when it was claimed that one of her oars was found on a north shore beach with the name scraped crudely into the wood. To assure visibility, each letter was filled with what was claimed to be a dead sailor's dried blood.

Seeing some ghosts ships, like the *Hamilton* (built 1809) and the *Scourge* (built 1811), meant death. Both vessels were part of the American fleet on Lake Ontario during the War of 1812. As the American and British fleets lay becalmed within sight of each other on the predawn of 8 August 1813, a sudden squall burst on them. The *Hamilton* and *Scourge*, both converted merchant vessels and top-heavy with cannon, capsized with the loss of at least fifty lives. Legend claims that both vessels periodically appear in the clouds and re-create their death scene. Should these ships be sighted, one of the crew of the sighting would die within a day. The big steamer *Chicora* (built 1892) was lost with all hands in a terrible Lake Michigan storm in 1895. For years afterward, Lake Michigan car-ferry sailors reported seeing her ghostly image again, usually foretelling a bad storm. In 1926 a steamer captain in northern Lake Michigan sighted her blowing distress signals in a gale and nearly lost his license when he reported the incident to the Coast Guard. They thought him either drunk or crazy.

The infamous "three sisters" legend is rooted in both fact and fiction. Old sailors believed that during especially big storms giant waves traveled in groups of three with a pause between the groups. To observation, this is true. The legend part is the number of ships supposedly lost to the three sisters, surviving the first two waves only to be overwhelmed by the monstrous third. In modern times some sailors blame the 1975 loss of the *Edmund Fitzgerald** (built 1958) on the three sisters.

A long-held sailor's myth is that Lake Superior never gives up its dead. Many examples can be cited to support this belief. In November 1918, the French navy minesweepers *Inkermann* (built 1918) and *Cerisoles* (built 1918) disappeared in a Lake Superior storm while down-bound from their Thunder Bay, Ontario, shipyard. Not a single body of the seventy-two sailors aboard was ever found. Great Lakes sailors expected none would be. Once a sailor disappears beneath the waves, he is gone forever. While there are exceptions, there is much truth to this old legend. The water temperature is often so cold, especially in the open Lake, that bacteria cannot grow, and consequently gas does not form in the tissue. Without the buoyancy of the gas, the bodies remain on the bottom. The Lake truly does not give up her dead; not a single body has been recovered from the *Edmund Fitzgerald*.

Old-timers believed that those areas where many shipwrecks* occurred and numerous sailors drowned were haunted. When sailing near them, they could hear the cries of the drowning men and see the ghostly forms of the wrecks happening again. Although Lake Superior's Whitefish Point has often been called the Graveyard of the Lakes because of the large number of ships wrecked in the area, other locations can lay equal claim. Long Point on Lake Erie, Point aux Barques on Lake Huron, and Death's Door Passage on Lake Michigan are all notorious ship traps and equally haunted by their victims.

There are also legends of captains going down with their ships rather than abandoning them. A case in point is the steamer *Arlington* (built 1913), lost in a gale in the middle of Lake Superior in 1940. As the steamer sank, the captain was said to have waved a final farewell to his crew in the lifeboat from his pilothouse door. He would not leave his ship. Lighthouses* also are the stuff of legends. A popular example involves old Presque Isle Light on Lake Huron. Although abandoned in 1870, there are claims that a mysterious glow continues to be seen from its stone tower. White River Light on Lake Michigan is said to be haunted by both Captain William Robinson, a former keeper, and his wife, Sarah.

Legends of sea monsters also abound on the lakes. In Ojibwa lore, Mishi-Peshu, a large lynxlike creature, lives underwater waiting to seize an unwary canoe. In 1812 Northwest Fur Company voyageurs claimed to have seen a "merman" near Thunder Bay Island, Lake Superior. Local Native Americans claimed it was Manitou Niba Nibas, also known as the god of lakes and waters. Other voyageurs claimed to have sighted the creature in the same area on later trips. Sailors have reported sea serpents on all of the Great Lakes. In 1895 the captain of the steamer S.S. *Curry* off Whitefish Point watched one with a neck fifteen feet long keep pace with his ship for five minutes. Two years later, a group of Detroit yachtsmen stated they were attacked by a giant squid off Duluth, Minnesota. Reports of sea serpents near Kingston, Ontario, on Lake Ontario are so numerous that the creature is known locally simply as "Kingstie."

Legend and myth on the Great Lakes continue to grow. Ships still sink under unexplained circumstances, and bizarre phenomena continue to puzzle sailors. [*See also* AMERICAN INDIAN LITERATURE OF THE SEA; GHOSTS AND GHOST SHIP LEGENDS; MERMAIDS]

FURTHER READING: Boyer, Dwight. *Ghost Ships of the Great Lakes.* New York: Dodd, Mead, 1968; Dorson, Richard M. *Bloodstoppers and Bearwalkers: Folk Traditions on the Upper Peninsula.* Cambridge: Harvard UP, 1952; Floren, Russell, and Andrea Gutsche. *Ghosts of the Bay, a Guide to the History of Georgian Bay.* Toronto: Lynx Images, 1994; Stonehouse, Frederick. *Haunted Lakes, Great Lakes Ghost Stories, Superstitions and Sea Serpents.* Duluth, MN: Lake Superior Port Cities, 1997.

Frederick Stonehouse

GREEN, PAUL [ELIOT] (1894–1981). A prolific playwright and poet whose literary career spanned several decades and genres, Paul Green is remembered chiefly for his dramatizations of southern folklore and customs and the plight of the African American* in particular, in such plays as *In Abraham's Bosom* (first perf. 1927; pub. 1927) and *The House of Connelly* (first perf. 1931; pub. 1931).

With American history and folklore among his main thematic concerns, Green wrote *The Lost Colony* (first perf. 1937; pub. 1937), a panoramic drama commemorating the 350th anniversary of the establishment of Sir Walter Raleigh's colony on Roanoke Island, intended to be performed outdoors. In this "Symphonic Drama in Two Acts," Green employs music, pantomime, dance, and scores of actors, singers, and dancers to portray the hardships of the early colonists, their encounters with Native Americans, and their neglect by the British Crown. The ocean, on which the settlers experienced hardships and death, comes to represent the brutality of nature, hope, and the formation of group identity, as the colony is forced, at the play's end, to flee from invading Spanish troops. This play, which became a popular annual attraction, was commissioned by the North Carolina Historical Commission as a site-specific environmental production and benefited from the assistance of the Federal Theatre Project of the Works Progress Administration.

With *The Founders* (first perf. 1957; pub. 1957), Green once again turned to American colonial history, this time with a more overtly pageantlike approach. Here he tells the story of the earliest years of the Jamestown settlement and its chief personalities—John Rolfe, Sir Thomas Dale, and Pocahontas—with the land disputes between the colonists and Native Americans as its primary conflict. The watery environment of the York River near Jamestown and the Atlantic Ocean functions as a sort of deus ex machina, upon which the fate and well-being of the colonists depend. Above all, the ocean represents the vast social and political distance, primarily between tyranny and freedom, symbolized by the founders' crossing. Although Green's biased account of the colonists in their land disputes with the Indians and Pocahontas' uncritical embrace of colonial ideologies are problematic by contemporary standards, his emphasis on thrilling spectacle and authentic pageantry renders this an exemplary document of environmental, community-based, and site-specific historical drama. [*See also* AMERICAN INDIAN LITERATURE OF THE SEA; DRAMA OF THE SEA]

David R. Pellegrini

GUTERSON, DAVID S. (1956–). Born in Seattle, and residing on Bainbridge Island in Puget Sound, David S. Guterson is well aware of the nuanced lives of his fellow islanders. His haunting novel *Snow Falling on Cedars* (1994) vividly captures both the hard agrarian work of inland strawberry farmers and the gritty marine labors of the salmon fishermen. The omnipresence of the sea is the central fact in this, Guterson's principal work. He argues in his essay "The Citizens of Paradise" (1996) that a divided island psychology develops from the realization that one is "surrounded by water" and that one feels both imprisoned and secure at the same time. This paradox underwrites the emotional undercurrents of *Snow Falling on Cedars*.

The novel's action centers on the trial of Kabuo Miyamoto, grandson of a samurai warrior who had committed ritual *seppuku*. Miyamoto, a salmon fisherman who has been accused of murdering a man on his boat, embodies the strong desire to achieve the American Dream, even as he struggles against antiassimilation sentiment. The novel's characters individually assess Miyamoto's guilt or innocence in light of their past experiences with him, his family, and the island's Japanese residents. Of particular interest is Ishmael* Chambers, a war veteran and Amity Harbor's newspaper publisher, who has been in love with Miyamoto's wife most of his life and whose penetrating analysis of Coast Guard lighthouse* logs saves Miyamoto's life. A psychic healing both liberates Ishmael from the past's imprisoning grip and mends emotional wounds of the town's intimately-connected populace. The novel won the Faulkner/PEN prize in 1995 and was adapted into film in 1999.

Guterson's short story "The Drowned Son" (1996) presents a man, not unlike Ishmael Chambers, who must confront his grief and guilt after his son drowns at sea. Guterson's Seattle roots keep him in touch with the Northwest's* coastal and seascape beauty, which infuse the lives of his gently philosophical characters.

Jeffrey Cass

H _____

[HAINS, THORNTON JENKINS], "CAPTAIN MAYN CLEW GARNETT" (1866–?). Named for his maternal grandfather, Admiral Thornton Jenkins, U.S.N., Thornton Jenkins Hains had a career of indefinite length as a working seaman and was licensed in both England and the United States as a navigator for large oceangoing vessels. He began a writing career in 1889 and had gained enough fame as a sea-writer to be the subject of a front-page article in the *New York Times* on 16 December 1903. Titled "Author Rescued at Sea," the article recounts the sinking of Hains' yacht *Edna* in a hurricane that struck on his voyage from North Carolina to the Bahamas. By then he had published at least two collections of sea stories, *Tales of the South Seas* (1894) and *The Wind-Jammers* (1899), and one novel, *The Wreck of the* Conemaugh (1899). Of his several other books, three are especially notable: a collection of stories mostly of sea animals, *The Strife of the Sea* (1903), and the novels *The Black Barque* (1905) and *The Voyage of the* Arrow (1906).

Tales of the South Seas, published in the same year as Jack London's* *Call of the Wild*, presents a unique, Darwinian view of sea life. The handsome, illustrated volume attracted London's attention, as did *The Voyage of the* Arrow, which features an interesting, self-conscious narrator and Hains' typically engaging, plain style. *The Black Barque* is a novel about the slave trade, presented in a balanced, realistic way. The title story of a later collection, *The White Ghost of Disaster* (published in 1912, the year of the *Titanic** disaster, under the name "Captain Mayn Clew Garnett") is a memorable tale of a captain who kills himself after sinking his speeding passenger liner in a collision with an iceberg.

Bert Bender

HALE, EDWARD EVERETT (1822–1909). Born in Boston, Edward Everett Hale belonged to an old New England family. His great-uncle, Captain

Nathan Hale, uttered the memorable cry, "I only regret that I have but one life to lose for my country," just before the British hanged him as a spy during the Revolutionary War. A prolific writer of fiction and nonfiction, Hale was by vocation a Unitarian minister. His essays include "The Naval History of the American Revolution" (1888) and "Paul Jones* and Denis Duval" (1857), an account of "the father of the American Navy."

The work for which Hale is best known is his historical short story "The Man without a Country" (1863), first published in *The Atlantic Monthly*, later appearing in a collection of Hale's fiction, *If, Yes, and Perhaps...* (1868), and adapted into three films of the same name (1917, 1925, 1937). The story's narrator is a retired navy captain, Frederic Ingham, who with the same name but in different guises narrates a number of Hale's stories. Ingham traces the career of Philip Nolan, an army officer whom Aaron Burr entices into joining his treasonous plot. At his court-martial, Nolan rejects the United States and is sentenced to a life of exile aboard American ships where he will never again see or hear of his native land. Metaphorically, Nolan is doomed to be forever adrift, forever at sea with himself.

An officer named Philip Nolan did exist, but he bore only superficial resemblance to Hale's protagonist. Nevertheless, many have assumed Hale's fictional narrative to be rooted in fact: a sermon on patriotism, on nationalism, and even (through incidents such as an encounter with a ship bearing enchained Africans) on the evil of slavery. The numerous references to actual people and events, as well as the absence of traditional techniques, such as a turning point or plot surprises, create this verisimilitude. [*See also* NAVAL MEMOIRS]

Norman E. Stafford

HALEY, ALEX (1921–1992). Alex Haley joined the Coast Guard as a "mess boy" at seventeen after two years of college. During World War II, aboard the cargo ship U.S.S. *Murzim*, he sent story after story to national magazines, with no luck. But an illiterate first-class steward's mate set Haley to writing love letters for fellow blacks on the mess decks, with considerable reported success. After the war, Haley continued to write and eventually, eight years later, had some articles accepted. Admiral "Iceberg" Smith noticed an article of his, and soon Haley became the Coast Guard's first chief journalist.

Haley retired from the Coast Guard in 1959 and wrote some articles for men's magazines about historic maritime adventures. In 1961 he published an article in *Reader's Digest* about the unforgettable first-class steward on the *Murzim*. The cofounder of the magazine, Mrs. Dewitt Wallace, very much liked the article and asked Haley to let her know if he ever needed help. Much later, when Haley wrote her about his genealogical interests, she convinced *Reader's Digest* editors to help fund him.

A significant part of the twelve years of effort that was to result in *Roots: The Saga of an American Family* (1976) was research into maritime records of the slave trade. Haley also took passage in a modern steamer, lying stripped to his underwear in the ship's cargo hold for ten nights to help visualize what his ancestors' experience had been. The description of slaves' experience during this "middle passage" from the Gambia River in Africa to Annapolis, Maryland, is one of the book's more compelling narratives. A 1977 miniseries for television starred Maya Angelou and Le Var Burton.

After the success of *Roots*, Haley would often book passage on international cargo ships for several months in order to write. He spoke highly of his Coast Guard experience and often remarked that he loved the sea. [*See also* AFRICAN AMERICAN LITERATURE OF THE SEA; SLAVE NARRATIVES]

Robert Shenk

HALL, JAMES NORMAN. *See* NORDHOFF, CHARLES, AND JAMES NORMAN HALL.

HALL, LAWRENCE SARGENT (1915–1993). Lawrence Sargent Hall was born in Haverhill, Massachusetts. Following completion of his Ph.D. at Yale University in 1941, he served for four years as an officer in the U.S. Navy, including three years of sea duty. In 1946 Hall took a teaching position at his undergraduate alma mater, Bowdoin College, Brunswick, Maine, where he was to remain until his retirement in 1986. While at Bowdoin, he resided at Orr's Island, the setting for Harriet Beecher Stowe's* *The Pearl of Orr's Island* (1862), where he operated a boatyard for some years.

Hall's short story "The Ledge" (1959) was awarded first place in the 1960 O. Henry competition. Its principal character, a fisherman overconfident of his seagoing skills, commits a foolish and fatal blunder during a winter hunt for sea ducks on the outer ledges of the coast, resulting in the drowning of the fisherman, his son, and his nephew.

Hall's only novel, *Stowaway* (1961), takes place on a World War II freighter named *Belle*, used as a liberty ship delivering supplies in escorted convoys to England. The disillusioned crew on this derelict vessel, outcasts of a war they didn't want to be involved in, wander aimlessly at war's end from port to port, eventually falling into a drunken lethargy on the open sea on a purposeless voyage to Australia. Their revolt against an irrational and dissolute authority, said to be in the name of human solidarity, reflects the influence of Joseph Conrad on Hall.

In 1962 Hall sailed down the Mississippi River in a Grand Banks dory. His account of this experience appeared in articles he published in three consecutive issues of the magazine *The Skipper* (November 1964–January 1965).

Joseph Flibbert

HALLET, RICHARD MATTHEWS (1887–1967). In 1912, at age twenty-five and with both a B.A. and LL.B. from Harvard University, Richard Matthews Hallet abandoned the practice of law in search of adventure and a career as a sea-writer. A New Englander from Maine who drew inspiration from relatives involved in Maine shipbuilding and seafaring, he was well aware of the literary opportunities that Richard Henry Dana* and Herman Melville* had found in their sea experiences. He quite self-consciously sought a position in one of the few remaining commercial sailing ventures in his time.

Signing on as an able seaman aboard the iron bark *Juteopolis*, in the employ of Standard Oil, he worked a single passage of four months from Boston to Sydney, Australia. From there he signed on as a fireman aboard the *Orvieto* for a stint of thirty-five days through the Indian Ocean to England. Later he worked for a few months as a fireman on the Great Lakes* iron ore freighter, *James A. Jenks*, and at the outbreak of World War I he returned to Harvard briefly in order to earn a degree in navigation. This enabled him to serve first as a junior officer aboard the *Wittekind* (later renamed *Iroquois*) hauling horses to Europe and then aboard the army transport ship *Westland*, hauling locomotives.

Hallet quickly exploited the literary possibilities of his brief career at sea, and his career as a significant sea-writer was equally brief, centering in the years 1915 and 1916. In 1915 he published his best novel, *The Lady Aft*, based on his adventure aboard the *Juteopolis*; in 1916 he published *Trial by Fire*, based on his experiences as a fireman in the Indian Ocean and Great Lakes; also in 1916 his sea story, "Making Port," based on the *Orvieto* experience, was selected as the best American short story of the year by Edward J. O'Brien. Hallet's autobiography, *The Rolling World* (1938), is a very readable account of his adventurous years and sheds light on the relationship between his experiences at sea and his fiction.

Hallet's two novels are notable for several reasons. *The Lady Aft* was well received, demonstrating that in those very last days of sailing ships there was an audience for such stories, but Hallet did not write a nostalgic tale of the golden days of sail. He was keenly aware not only of the historic anomaly of his enterprise but, partly because he had studied modern philosophy with George Santayana,* of the seeming absurdity of the human place in a universe that seemed adrift. Consequently, the novel is marked with an ironic style and vision that sometimes resemble Stephen Crane's* and that will seem dated to many readers of today. But even though Hallet sometimes uses mock-heroic tones for describing such experiences as going aloft, he also provides a record that has considerable dramatic and historic interest. Much of the plot develops around the idea suggested in its title, one that seemed obligatory in sea novels of that time, such as Jack London's* *The Sea-Wolf** and Frank Norris'* *Moran of the* Lady Letty, that of the woman aboard ship. Like London and Norris, Hallet seems quite aware that the woman's presence focuses attention on the Darwinian theme of sexual selection and the larger evolutionary implications of the voyage.

Hallet's other novel, *Trial by Fire*, is virtually unknown today, and even

Hallet ignored it in his autobiography. But it deserves to be remembered for two very good reasons. First, it is still one of the most important novels of the Great Lakes maritime experience; second, Hallet's portrait of the sailor-fireman as an exploited laborer in a chaotic modern universe is memorable not only in its own right but for having exerted a powerful, but still largely unrecognized, influence on Eugene O'Neill's* *The Hairy Ape*, which appeared six years later.

FURTHER READING: Bender, Bert. *Sea-Brothers: The Tradition of American Sea Fiction from* Moby-Dick *to the Present.* Philadelphia: U of Pennsylvania P, 1988, 149–60; Cary, Richard. "Richard Matthews Hallet: Architect of the Dream," *Colby Library Quarterly* 7, no. 10 (1967): 417–65.

Bert Bender

"HALYARD, HARRY" (dates unknown). "Harry Halyard" is the pseudonym of the unknown author of twelve novels published in the mid-nineteenth century. Five of them were intended to exploit public interest in the Mexican War: *The Chieftain of Churubusco* (1848), *The Heroine of Tampico* (1847), *The Mexican Spy* (1848), *The Ocean Monarch* (1848), and *The Warrior Queen* (1848). Others have a vague association with sensational historical events such as the Salem witch trials of 1692 (*The Haunted Bride* [1848]), the American Revolution (*The Rover of the Reef* [1848]), or the French Revolution (*The Heroine of Paris* [1848]).

All are exactly 100 pages long and reflect the emphasis on glib dialogue and fast-paced action characteristic of the emerging "dime novel" tradition. They were published by F[rederick]. Gleason, whose stable of hack authors during this period included Maturin M. Ballou,* Benjamin Barker,* and "Ned Buntline," pseudonym of Edward Zane Carroll Judson.* Any or all of these authors may have ghostwritten the "Harry Halyard" series, although the emphasis upon women as the works' heroes may suggest a woman author. The novel *The Bandit of the Ocean; or The Female Privateer, a Romance of the Sea* (1855) uses Halyard as the pseudonym and includes Barker's name on the cover as the presumed author. As the "Halyard" tag and some of the titles suggest, all of the books are principally or partly set on the sea. The other four Halyard titles are *The Doom of the Dolphin* (1848); *Geraldine* (1848); *The Peruvian Nun* (1848); and *Wharton the Whale-Killer!* (1848), presumably a source that Herman Melville* used for *Moby-Dick** (1851).

Joseph Flibbert

HARLOW, FREDERICK PEASE (1856–1952). Frederick Pease Harlow was born in Mount Morris, Illinois, on 12 December 1856. He was the youngest son of Frances Ann Winsor and William T. Harlow, an educator and Methodist minister originally from Duxbury, Massachusetts.

Harlow's first experience at sea was on board the coasting schooner *David*

G. Floyd in 1875. The captain of the *Floyd* was a neighbor, and Harlow's father had privately requested that the captain make the experience as "disagreeable" as possible, in a vain effort to dissuade his youngest son from following in the footsteps of his three older brothers. Aboard the *Floyd*, the young Harlow learned the ways of a sailing craft from the deck up. The customary hazing of a greenhorn, an anchor-dragging storm, and a near collision with another schooner all challenged Harlow on his first voyage. He became skilled enough to leave the vessel an "ordinary seaman."

Undeterred by his father's meddling, Harlow sailed on board the full-rigged ship *Akbar* in December 1875. The voyage gave him firsthand knowledge of deepwater sailing. His experiences in the Far East trade on board the *Akbar* furnished him with the basis for his book *The Making of a Sailor or Sea Life aboard a Yankee Square-Rigger* (1928), republished in 1988 by Dover.

This volume, written when Harlow was over seventy, offers an enlightening account of shipboard life and politics. Harlow kept a detailed journal of his experiences aboard the *Akbar*. With journal in hand and over fifty years to reflect on the varying events of the voyage, he relates the square-rig experiences of his youth. Included are music and lyrics to dozens of chanteys. Also included are detailed technical descriptions of the mechanics of square-rig sail. *The Making of a Sailor* is the most readable of all similar works, on a par with Richard Henry Dana's* *Two Years before the Mast** (1840).

In 1878 Harlow sailed on the bark *Conquest* from Boston to Barbados, West Indies, where he observed the African connection to sea music.* He settled in Seattle in 1890 and held jobs with the Occidental Fish Company, the Washington Shipping Bureau, and the Puget Sound Navigation Company. After retiring, he traveled around the world, built ship models, and continued to write.

The *Conquest* voyage provided much of the material for his second work, *Chanteying aboard American Ships* (1962). It contains more than 110 chanteys with musical notation drawn from nineteenth-century singers, other researchers, and expanded music from *The Making of a Sailor*. Completed by 1945, the work first appeared in installments in *The American Neptune* in 1948 and was published posthumously in its entirety. Today it is considered one of the principal sources for nineteenth-century sea music.

Glenn Grasso

HARPER, MICHAEL S[TEVEN]. (1938–   ). Few of Michael S. Harper's challenging poems draw upon the sea for either setting or theme, but when his strong interest in history intersects with even stronger feelings about racial justice, he infrequently employs sea imagery for thematic impact. For example, one of his most quietly dramatic works, simply titled "American History" (1970), through deft allusion compares the Birmingham church bombing that killed four little girls in the early 1960s with the unconscionable cruelty of the slave trade. His image of several hundred black slaves submerged "in a net, under water," whether historically true or artistically imagined, resonates timelessly with the same moral outrage of more recent murders. With "The White Whale," also from the 1970 *Coltrane* collection, Harper co-opts Herman Melville's* presumed symbol of evil for one more modern, yet equally subtle and specific, application. In that same volume "Lookout Point: U.S.S. *San Francisco*" invites comparison with Robert Hayden's* "Veracruz" (1962), both introspective imaginings prompted by seascape description and revery.

Both past and recent history figure in later poems dealing indirectly with sea themes. Harper's visit to Bristol, England, in the 1970s inspired his "Bicentenary Remembrance of Trade" (1977) in the British seaport during the nineteenth century. Later, as poet laureate of Rhode Island (1988–1993), he wrote a piece to commemorate the launching of a nuclear submarine christened after his home state. In the latter poem, formally titled "*Rhode Island* (SSBNT740): A Toast" (1993), Harper correlates the uncommon common majesties of sleek technology, unseen seascape, and the "zone of freedom" that depend on such military machinery and its dedicated crew. [*See also* AFRICAN AMERICAN LITERATURE OF THE SEA; SEA IMAGERY IN MODERN AND CONTEMPORARY POETRY; SLAVE NARRATIVES]

Fred M. Fetrow

THE HARRIMAN ALASKA EXPEDITION. The Harriman Alaska Expedition of 1899 was the last great Alaska expedition of the nineteenth century. Sponsored entirely by American railroad magnate and philanthropist Edward H. Harriman and organized by C. Hart Merriam, then head of the U.S. Biological Survey, the eight-week voyage from Seattle to Alaska (31 May to 30 July 1899) was made aboard the *George W. Elder*, a steamship that had been refitted as a scientific luxury liner. The *Elder*'s 126-member crew constituted a "floating university" that consisted of eminent American scientists, artists, photographers, and writers. Although the geographical discoveries of the expedition were not particularly significant, the carefully orchestrated voyage of so many important naturalists and writers drew national media attention both to the landscape of Alaska and to the importance of American literary and scientific natural history.

Among the literary members of the expedition were John Burroughs (1837–1921), nature writer and ornithologist; John Muir (1838–1914), author, conservationist, and glaciologist; George Bird Grinnell (1849–1938), essayist and editor of *Forest and Stream*; and Charles Keeler (1871–1937), poet and director of the Museum of the California Academy of Sciences. The scientific discoveries of the expedition were published by the Smithsonian Institution in the thirteen volumes titled *Harriman Alaska Expedi-*

tion (1901–1914); the first two volumes, published by Doubleday, Page and Company in 1901, are usually considered the "narrative set" of the expedition.

Literary accounts of the voyage are more dispersed. Among the most significant of these are Muir's in *Edward Henry Harriman* (1912), in *Travels in Alaska* (1915), and in his journals (*John of the Mountains: Unpublished Journals of John Muir*, 1938); and Burroughs' "In Green Alaska" in *Far and Near* (1904), in *My Boyhood* (1928), and in his journals (*The Heart of Burroughs' Journals*, 1938). [*See also* THE ARCTIC]

Michael P. Branch

HARRY MARTINGALE: OR, ADVENTURES OF A WHALEMAN IN THE PACIFIC OCEAN (1848).

This melodramatic novel by an elusive Dr. Louis A. Baker (18??–18??) tells the story of Harry Martingale, a young man from the Pennsylvania hills who turns to the sea for adventure. On his second voyage, Harry is tricked into serving a year on a pirate* ship with storyteller Bill Longyarn but later finds a better position on a whaler, the *Albatross*, under Captain Hawser, where Harry works his way from foremast hand to first mate. On an early voyage the crew battles a notorious white-spotted whale, later killed by an English whaler. In Valparaiso Harry falls in love with Margita, a devout Catholic. Harry and some crew are abandoned on an island when the *Albatross* drifts away, but they are reunited in New York; on a later voyage a whale tows Harry and a whaleboat away from the *Albatross*, and the crew eventually makes its way to Payta (now Paita), Peru. There it rejoins the *Albatross*, which is later taken off Dominica by natives. Baker devotes a scant phrase to conveying the massacre of all the crew but Harry. Harry's life is spared due to the intervention of the chief's daughter; he eventually escapes in an open boat and is picked up at sea. After five years away from Margita, Harry finally returns to Chile, where he enters a church moments before Margita is about to join a convent, and they are happily reunited.

Though not a source for Herman Melville's* *Moby-Dick** (1851), Baker's novel represents, as Howard Vincent suggests in *The Trying-Out of* Moby-Dick (1949), an outgrowth of whaling legend in the same vein.

Peter H. McCracken

HART, JOSEPH C. (1798–1855).

A New Yorker whose mother's family came from Nantucket* Island, Joseph C. Hart is known today as the author of *Miriam Coffin, or The Whale-Fishermen* (1834), a novel that was an important source for *Moby-Dick** (1851).

An attorney, school principal, and author of several widely used geography textbooks, Hart traveled to Nantucket sometime prior to 1834, where he collected material for *Miriam Coffin*, a "semi-Romance of the Sea" based on the rise and fall of the notorious whaling merchant Kezia Coffin (1723–1798). In addition to information about the Quakers and Indians of Nantucket Island during the Revolutionary War period, Hart's novel provides detailed (albeit anachronistic) descriptions of the Pacific whale fishery. Published anonymously, Hart's novel was well received and reprinted within a year.

His subsequent book, *The Romance of Yachting* (1848), is known chiefly today for the savage review it received from Herman Melville,* who deemed this loose collection of musings on Shakespeare, the Puritans, Europe, music, and sailing "an abortion." In 1854 Hart was appointed American consul at Santa Cruz de Tenerife in the Canary Islands, where he died soon after his arrival.

Nathaniel Philbrick

HARTE, [FRANCIS] BRET[T] (1836–1902). Born in Albany, New York, Bret Harte rose to literary prominence as editor of the *Overland Monthly* (first pub. 1868), a San Francisco-based magazine of western lore. In this forum Harte produced his best sketches, stories, and poems, including "The Luck of Roaring Camp" (August 1868), "The Outcasts of Poker Flat" (January 1869), and the satirical poem "Plain Language from Truthful James," better known as "The Heathen Chinee" (September 1870). Following his return to the East Coast in 1871, Harte lectured extensively about the Pacific coast and eventually produced his best-known novel, *Gabriel Conroy* (1876). The tepid reception of his novel, a sign of ebbing interest in his stories, convinced Harte to accept a consulate in Prussia in 1878 and later in Scotland in 1880. He remained in Europe, where interest in his writing continued throughout his lifetime.

Harte romanticized the hardy souls who settled California and the hardships they endured, using themes and metaphors drawn from the sea. In "The Luck of Roaring Camp" and in "Notes by Flood and Field" (1870), in which various rural settlements along estuaries of the Pacific Ocean are inundated with floodwaters from the Sierra Mountain range, Harte depicts nature as unpredictable and wild. In a similar vein, "High-Water Mark" (1870) is the tale of a woman whose home is consumed by the rising tide of the nearby Pacific Ocean and of her struggle for survival aboard a fallen tree. The power of the wild waters rushing to the sea symbolizes the adversity faced by the inhabitants of this new frontier, generating awe and respect for both sea and westerners.

In "The Outcasts of Poker Flat," a story evoking thoughts of the ill-fated Donner party, swells of snow that consume a band of refugees are equated metaphorically with the sea. "The Man of No Account" (1860), an easterner whose failed California experiment left him with the title, is returning home aboard a passenger steamer, which is lost at sea. "By Shore and Sedge" (1885) is the story of Abner McNott, an entrepreneur who converts the

Pontiac, a ship abandoned on the California shore by early gold-seekers, into lodging rooms. In "The Right Eye of the Commander" (1870), a mysterious sailor named Peleg Scudder from Salem, Massachusetts, is given safe harbor at a Spanish fort during a storm. By the next morning he has disappeared, leaving the commander of the fort with a seemingly possessed right eye, striking fear in those around him.

A rare story not involving California, "Mr. Midshipman Breezy" (1867) chronicles a young English sailor's journey across the Atlantic Ocean and through the Caribbean* Sea. In a lecture delivered in the Martin Opera House in Albany, New York, in 1872, Harte referred to the early settlers of California as "Argonauts" whom he respected for their adventurous optimism in settling the Pacific coast.

Nathaniel T. Mott

DE HARTOG, JAN (1914–   ). Born in Holland, Jan de Hartog ran off to sea when he was ten years old. Six years later he enrolled in Amsterdam Naval College and became a junior mate in the Dutch oceangoing tugboat service. Escaping to London under the German occupation, he served as war correspondent for the Dutch merchant marine. An early play, *Skipper next to God* (1947), is a dramatic tale about a religious captain who quells a near mutiny* and scuttles his ship to bring 146 Jews onto American soil during the annual Hatteras Cup race in 1938. De Hartog was made an officer of the French Academy in 1953, settled in the United States, and in 1983 was nominated for the Nobel Prize in literature.

De Hartog's nautical experiences range from working in the Dutch fishing fleet in the North Sea to serving on oceangoing salvage tugs during World War II, and his published works reflect his experiences. His first novel, *Captain Jan: A Story of Ocean Tugboats* (1947), is a humorous story of a boy's career in the merchant navy. *The Lost Sea* (1951) is de Hartog's story of his coming-of-age as a stowaway on a Dutch fishing vessel. *The Distant Shore* (1952) presents two short stories. The first, "War," was originally published as *Stella* in 1950 and, after being made into the movie *The Key* (1958), was published in that year with the movie title. It revolves about one particular sailor and his female companion while on his shore leaves, presenting a poignant story of human relationships in the uncertainties of wartime shipping. The second part, "Peace," portrays the life of the working waterfront and the maritime scene in the coastal Mediterranean after the close of World War II.

A Sailor's Life (1956) is a collection of very short, reflective vignettes of pre–World War II life at sea by different members of the crew of a vessel identified by their job descriptions and positions. The vignettes comment on the routine of shipboard life, ships and shipping, the sea; it is an assemblage of sailors' thoughts at sea about the world in which they live, the world they left behind, and the world to which they will be returning. It is a major contribution to our ability to envision life on board merchant vessels in the first half of the twentieth century. *The Lost Sea, The Distant Shore,* and *A Sailor's Life* were published in one volume, *The Call of the Sea* (1966), for which de Hartog wrote a six-page preface.

The Captain (1967) presents life at sea on a wartime oceangoing salvage tug. Its work was rescuing vessels damaged by German submarines, surface ships, or airplanes or by the heavy winds and seas in the North Atlantic from Nova Scotia to Murmansk, Russia. De Hartog's Captain Martinus Harinxma emerges as a thoughtful observer of the passing human and inhuman scene. Harinxma's saga is continued in *The Commodore: A Novel of the Sea* (1986) and *The Centurion* (1989) and completed in *The Outer Buoy: A Story of the Ultimate Voyage* (1994).

James F. Millinger

HAVIGHURST, WALTER [EDWIN] (1901–1994). Walter Havighurst is known primarily as a historian of the Midwest, but he also wrote fiction, much of it influenced by his experiences at sea in the 1920s. Havighurst worked as a deckhand on Great Lakes* freighters and Pacific lumber schooners before going to college and served in the merchant marine before completing graduate school. His first novel, *Pier 17* (1935), is about a young sailor with ambitions of writing fiction who gets caught up in a shipping strike in Seattle. *The Quiet Shore* (1937) and *Signature of Time* (1949) both describe life on Lake Erie. *No Homeward Course* (1941) concerns a German sea raider. *The Long Ships Passing* (1942), a regional history of the Great Lakes for which he is best known, draws on his deckhand experiences aboard Great Lakes freighters.

Peter H. McCracken

HAWTHORNE, NATHANIEL (1804–1864). Born in Salem, Massachusetts, when the town was still one of the most active seaports in America, Nathaniel Hawthorne spent most of his youth within sight of the town's busy wharves. His grandfather, Daniel, had been a shipmaster and achieved minor distinction as a privateer during the Revolutionary War. Daniel's two sons both went to sea: the older of the two, Nathaniel's uncle, was lost at sea in the year of Hawthorne's birth; the younger, Hawthorne's father, died of yellow fever on a sea voyage four years later.

In his adult years, Hawthorne held three jobs that exposed him to many facets of the maritime world. As measurer of salt and coal at the Boston Custom House, he supervised the unloading of cargoes at Boston's Long Wharf from January 1839 to January 1841. For more than three years, he served as surveyor of customs at the Salem Custom House (1846–1849). When his Bowdoin College friend Franklin Pierce was elected president of the United States in 1851, Hawthorne was rewarded for writing Pierce's campaign biography with the consulship of Liverpool, where virtually all his responsibilities for the next four years involved activities of American maritime trade. His diplomatic correspondence during this period, as well as his personal notebooks and letters, include detailed commentary on issues and problems of the American merchant marine.

Hawthorne maintained friendships with a number of authors who had a close association with the sea. He edited *Journal of an African Cruiser* (1845) for his college classmate Horatio Bridge,* who pursued a career in the navy. He responded enthusiastically to the publications of another college acquaintance, Henry Wadsworth Longfellow,* whose lyrics, ballads, and narrative poems often reflect the influence of his youth in the seaport of Portland, Maine. His inspirational effect on Herman Melville* during the period of the composition of *Moby-Dick** (1851) is suggested in Melville's dedication of the book to him.

Despite these associations with the sea, Hawthorne's tales, sketches, and romances make only scant reference to nautical themes and subjects. In his most sustained description of the sea's influence, "Foot-prints on the Sea-shore" (1838), a young man drawn to the shore in search of solitude muses on the power and majesty of the sea. The apparent drowning of a sailor at sea figures prominently in "The Wives of the Dead" (1832). "Chippings with a Chisel" (1838) focuses on an elderly woman whose first love was killed by a whale forty years earlier. "The Custom House," significant for its role in introducing some of the themes of *The Scarlet Letter* (1850), is also a vivid portrait of a mid-nineteenth-century seaport in decline. Less central references in *The Scarlet Letter* include the location of Hester's cottage by the sea and the appearance of a sea captain in the final chapters. A sea captain also has a minor role in "Night Sketches" (1838). In "Drowne's Wooden Image" (1844), a sea captain's request for a figurehead for his ship inspires an ordinary carver to temporary artistic heights.

FURTHER READING: Flibbert, Joseph. "Hawthorne, Salem, and the Sea." *Sextant* 5.1 (1994): 1–9; Flibbert, Joseph. "Nathaniel Hawthorne: Salem Personified." *Salem: Cornerstones of a Historic City.* Ed. Joseph Flibbert et al. Beverly, MA: Commonwealth Editions, 1999, 85–103; Hawthorne, Nathaniel. *The Centenary Edition of the Works of Nathaniel Hawthorne.* Ed. William Charvat et al. 23 vols. Columbus: Ohio State UP, 1964–1996; Mellow, James R. *Nathaniel Hawthorne in His Times.* Boston: Houghton Mifflin, 1980; Miller, Edwin Haviland. *Salem Is My Dwelling Place: A Life of Nathaniel Hawthorne.* Iowa City: U of Iowa P, 1991; Turner, Arlin. *Nathaniel Hawthorne: A Biography.* New York: Oxford UP, 1980.

Joseph Flibbert

HAYDEN, ROBERT [EARL] (1913–1980). A long-neglected African American* poet, Robert Hayden (born Asa Bundy Sheffey) climaxed his career with two successive terms as consultant in poetry to the Library of Congress (1976–1978), the position now known as poet laureate. His ten volumes of poetry show a consistent interest in African American history and culture, as well as a transcendent concern for humane issues. While neither his biography nor his canon suggests a knowledge of, or an affinity with, the sea, his works do include significant metaphorical uses of sea imagery for thematic emphasis.

Perhaps most notable among these is his epic in miniature, "Middle Passage," a montage of voices and historical swatches in description of the horrors of the slave trade era, with a central theme exalting the timeless human aspiration for personal freedom. First published in 1945, the poem directly invokes the sea as an irresistible, natural force in concert with, and in support of, the human quest for freedom. This modern epic quest includes a truncated version of the *Amistad** rebellion of 1839, with its hero, Cinqué, and his natural ally, the stormy sea. Hayden thus locates the sea on the side of moral justice, suggesting that the forces of nature take vengeance upon those who pervert nature by enslaving others. Hayden combines authenticity of historical research with almost archetypal symbolism of the sea setting to establish and confirm the role of nature in the timeless epic quest for human freedom.

Other poems are more personal, applying sea settings and symbolism in autobiographical allegories of the poet's life experiences or psyche. A typical example is "The Diver" (1966), an introspective account of a personal emotional crisis presented as a descent to the ocean's floor by a scuba diver. Other poems such as "Veracruz" (1962) and "Aunt Jemima of the Ocean Waves" (1970) include the sea as both literal setting and symbolic extension of theme, but neither is dependent on either aspect for full disclosure. His poem in honor of Malcolm X, "El-Hajj Malik El-Shabazz" (1970), compares the black leader to Ahab* as both being of the same "tribe" and borrows a line from *Moby-Dick** (1851): " 'Strike through the mask!' " These and other poems by this "poet of perfect pitch" show his interest in the timeless potential of the sea for enhancing human expression and enlightenment. [*See also* HARPER, MICHAEL S.; SEA IMAGERY IN MODERN AND CONTEMPORARY POETRY; SLAVE NARRATIVES]

Fred M. Fetrow

HAYDEN, STERLING [RELYEA WALTER] (1916–1986). Born in Upper Montclair, New Jersey, Sterling Hayden quit school at sixteen to join the crew of a sailing ship. He served as seaman aboard fishing vessels and sailing ships out of New England ports from 1932 to 1936, was first mate on Irving Johnson's* circumnavigation* on the schooner *Yankee** (1936–1938), became captain of the brigantine *Florence Robinson* out of Gloucester* in 1938, and owned and captained ships out of eastern ports during the late 1930s and early 1940s. He served in the U.S. Marine Corps beginning in 1942 and acted in over fifty Hollywood films (*Bahama Passage* [1941] and *The Eternal Sea* [1955], as maritime titles).

Wanderer (1963) is the personal story of Sterling Hayden's flight from

Hollywood to sea and eventually to Tahiti on the schooner *Wanderer*. Although his account of the sea passage is interrupted by many asides about his life as a movie star and the custody battle over his four children, whom he took with him on the ocean voyage to the South Pacific, his maritime experience and his fine writing make *Wanderer* a meaningful story of seafaring as well as a story of escape.

Voyage: A Novel of 1896 (1976) is a re-creation of the days of the big wooden "down-easters" built on the coast of Maine in the final decades of the nineteenth century and early years of the twentieth. These vessels carried the bulk cargoes of the United States on the oceans of the world. Hayden takes advantage of the literary license of the 1970s to write dialogue using the gritty, uncensored language that was most likely spoken on those vessels eighty years earlier.

James F. Millinger

"HAZEL, HARRY." *See* [JONES, JUSTIN].

HEARN, [PATRICIO] LAFCADIO [TESSIMA CARLOS] (1850–1904). Lafcadio Hearn was born in Greece and migrated to the United States, where he drifted from New York, to Cincinnati, to New Orleans. In New Orleans he wrote *Chita: A Memory of Last Island* (1888), a fictionalized account of a hurricane in 1850 that decimated lle Dernière, a resort island in the Gulf of Mexico. The sea's moods, from destructive and death-destroying, to calm, provide the tone and structure for the book, which first appeared serially in *Harper's Magazine*.

Hearn then toured the Caribbean,* settling for a while in Martinique, where he worked on stories about Americans in the tropics and Creoles emigrating to the north. *Martinique Sketches* (1890) includes such portraits of Caribbean life as "La Grande Anse" and "Les Porteuses," as well as "Ti Canotiè," the story of Maximilien and Stèphane, two boys who venture dangerously far out to sea in their canoe and are caught by a current that sweeps them from Martinique toward Dominica. By the time a passing steamer notices the canoe, Stèphane has died. Hearn's novel *Youma* (1890), written in Martinique, is the story of a slave girl who refuses to participate in a slave rebellion. Hearn subsequently published *Two Years in the French West Indies* (1890), a series of impressionistic essays about life in the Caribbean. In later life Hearn lived in Japan, where he became a noted collector of Asian folktales and published a number of books with Japanese subjects.

Christopher Lee

HEMINGWAY, ERNEST MILLER (1899–1961). Ernest Hemingway, winner of the Pulitzer Prize in fiction (1952) and the Nobel Prize in literature (1954), grew up in Oak Park, Illinois. Except when rough water forced

submarines. In "At Sea," however, while he is pursuing escaped German sailors, his intuitive observation of sea scenes partially frees him emotionally and creatively, shortly before he is fatally wounded.

In the posthumously published editorial condensation *The Garden of Eden* (1986), the novel's opening mise-en-scène is a paradoxical merging of sea and land. Bordering a French seaside resort, a tidal canal runs inland to the city of Aigues Mortes, while next to the canal's entrance a jetty projects into the Atlantic. A young American at the hotel with his bride hooks a sea bass at the juncture of canal, sea, and jetty. In an episode symbolically relevant to the couple's cross-sexual role-playing, the fish runs out along the jetty to strain beyond its tip toward the open sea before being forced back to the base of the phallic structure and led into the adjacent canal. Later, thematically related diving and swimming scenes indicate the alienation of husband and wife while defining a superior balance of aggression and submission between the husband and a woman with whom he finds an idyllic symbiosis. Another swimming episode recalls the spirit of Santiago's voyage and Hemingway's Nobel acceptance remarks, as the lovers go out where neither has gone before and view the coastline from a perspective not seen by other swimmers.

Hemingway's many journalistic articles on marine subjects are listed in the following bibliography. The revealing logs he kept of activities aboard the *Pilar* in 1934–1935 and 1936 are unpublished at this writing but may be examined at the JFK Presidential Library, Boston.

FURTHER READING: Baker, Carlos. *Ernest Hemingway: A Life Story.* New York: Scribner's, 1969; Baker, Carlos. *Hemingway: The Writer as Artist.* Princeton: Princeton UP, 1963; Hanneman, Audre. *Ernest Hemingway: A Comprehensive Bibliography.* Princeton: Princeton UP, 1967; Miller, Linda. "The Matrix of Hemingway's *Pilar* Log, 1934–1935," *NDQ* 64, no. 3 (Summer 1997): 105–23; Reynolds, Michael. *Hemingway: The Final Years.* New York: Norton, 1999; Samuelson, Arnold. *With Hemingway: A Year in Key West and Cuba.* New York: Random, 1984; Sylvester, Bickford. "Hemingway's Extended Vision: *The Old Man and the Sea*," *PMLA* 81 (March 1966): 130–38; Sylvester, Bickford. "The Cuban Context of *The Old Man and the Sea*," *The Cambridge Companion to Hemingway.* Ed. Scott Donaldson. New York: Cornell UP, 1996, 243–68.

Bickford Sylvester

[HERBERT, HENRY WILLIAM], "FRANK FORESTER" (1807–1858). Born in England and arriving in America in 1831, Henry William Herbert initiated a career as a writer of romances: his best-known fiction, *Ringwood the Rover*, was serialized in 1839 and published as a "cheap" novel in 1843. Under the name "Frank Forester," he wrote extensively and authoritatively on field sports, which in his day comprised hunting, fishing, and horsemanship. Despite gaining apparent success in both genres, he ended his life with suicide.

Although the subjects of Herbert's fiction range widely, *Ringwood the Rover: A Tale of Florida* marks an extension of the genre of southwest fiction into the Gulf of Mexico and Caribbean.* Herbert followed *Ringwood* with *Guarica, the Charib Bride: A Legend of Hispaniola* (1844) and *Tales of the Spanish Seas* (1847). He capitalized on the war with Mexico in *Pierre the Partisan: A Tale of the Marches* (1848). His settings parallel James Fenimore Cooper's* forays into this area with *Mercedes of Castile* (1840) and *Jack Tier; or, The Florida Reef* (1848). The success of works like *Ringwood* may have inspired Cooper's serial publication of *Jack Tier* in 1846–1848.

William Southworth Hunt has written *Frank Forester: A Tragedy in Exile* (1933).

R. D. Madison

HERNE, JAMES A[HERN]. (1839–1901). James A. Herne was an actor, manager, and playwright whose early reputation as a successful melodramatist was established on the basis of his collaborations with playwright/producer/director David Belasco. Later in his career, however, he made a transition to a more realistic style, winning the approval of William Dean Howells.* He has been hailed, perhaps overly enthusiastically, as the "American Ibsen" for his best-known play, *Margaret Fleming* (first perf. 1891; pub. 1917), which sensitively treats the issue of illegitimacy.

The sea figures prominently in four of Herne's plays. The early *Hearts of Oak* (first perf. 1879 under the title *Chums*; pub. 1940) was written with Belasco and based closely on an English nautical melodrama, *The Mariner's Compass* (1865). It is set on the coast near Marblehead, Massachusetts, and reworks a familiar melodramatic situation of two friends in love with the same woman. Phenomenally popular and much imitated, the play featured special effects, including a lively baby, a cat that stretched on cue, and a shipwreck.* *Drifting Apart* (first perf. 1888; pub. 1940) deals with the havoc wrought by drink in the lives of a Gloucester* fisherman and his wife. Originally titled *Mary, the Fisherman's Child*, it is a temperance play enlivened by the addition of New England local color and an innovative dream sequence representing the death of the child by starvation. Before the revelation that the death has been a bad dream, the drunken fisherman, a role played by Herne, ships out aboard the *Sprite* and is shipwrecked and enslaved by Chinese pirates.*

Early in 1889 Herne had started work on a play originally called *The Hawthornes*, which took on a new form and color after he spent a summer near Lamoine, Maine. When *Shore Acres' Subdivision* (subsequently, *Shore Acres*) opened in 1892 (pub. 1928), it was set at Frenchman's Bay near Bar Harbor and became a huge success for Herne. Partly inspired by the land boom in Maine, the action of the play entails the resistance of Uncle Nat, played by Herne in another starring role, to the sale of the family farm and the marrying off of his niece Helen to the man she loves. The scenes transpire on the farm, in the Berry Lighthouse, where Nat's brother Martin is the keeper, and aboard the trawler *Liddy Ann*. Multiple backdrops display Frenchman's Bay and Mount Desert Island and call for a catboat to be seen sailing lazily among the islands. The short third act shows Nat struggling to light the beacon in the lighthouse,* followed by an extended silent scene of the *Liddy Ann*, with Helen aboard, making her way perilously near the rocks, with the light coming on just in time to guide her way.

The success of *Shore Acres* allowed Herne to build a home at Southampton, Long Island, and "indulge his taste for quiet, and for the sea," according to his daughter Julie. Herne lived near the old whaling port of Sag Harbor, where he set the play of the same name, his last dramatic effort. *Sag Harbor* (first perf. 1899; pub. 1928) featured Herne as Cap'n Dan Marble, whose real-life model was the *Gretchen*'s Captain Peterson, a scallop fisherman on Great Peconic Bay. More than any of Herne's earlier plays, *Sag Harbor* is suffused with its seaside setting. In addition to Cap'n Dan Marble of the sloop *Kacy*, its central characters are mainly associated with the sea: William Turner, agent for the steamer *Antelope*; his son Ben, a boatbuilder; his younger son Frank, a naval seaman; ships' carpenters; and Mrs. Russell, the ancient widow of an old whaling captain. A leisurely plot sets up the brothers as rivals for the same woman and ultimately marries off Cap'n Dan to a woman he has long courted. The play is largely set in a shipyard, showing Shelter Island and Gardiner's Bay, North Haven, and Sag Harbor on a backdrop. The stern of the *Kacy* is onstage, and the opening talk is of boat repairs and scallop fishing. Mrs. Russell reminisces about when there were seventy whalers in the harbor and speaks knowledgeably of whaling. A third-act storm adds typical melodramatic action.

Though never quite escaping the confines of the genres in which he worked, Herne nonetheless advanced the cause of realism in treating maritime subjects and settings, which he used to raise important social issues. In his compassionate handling of troubled characters, he paves the way for Eugene O'Neill.* [*See also* DRAMA OF THE SEA]

FURTHER READING: Edwards, Herbert J., and Julie A. Herne. *James A. Herne: The Rise of Realism in the American Drama*. Orono: U of Maine P, 1964; Perry, John. *James A. Herne: The American Ibsen*. Chicago: Nelson-Hall, 1978.

Attilio Favorini

HERSEY, JOHN [RICHARD] (1914–1993).

The prolific author John Hersey was born in China and moved to the United States in 1925, when his family decided to return. He was educated at Yale and Cambridge Universities and served for a time as secretary to Sinclair Lewis before becoming a journalist. Hersey wrote two maritime novels. *Under the Eye of the Storm* (1967) examines the marriages and the lives of two married couples on a small sailing yacht during a magnificently portrayed hurricane in the coastal waters of Massachusetts and Rhode Island.

Hersey's less-known *A Single Pebble* (1956) is set on a junk being towed up the Yangtze River in the 1920s. Old Pebble is leader of the work gang hauling the junk and its occupants up the river against a rising spring current. He sings songs of the river and classical operatic arias to inspire his crew in their work and to cover the noise of their groans. The story is narrated by the only passenger, a young American engineer who is weakened in body and mind by dysentery and by a crush on the comely young wife of the vessel's owner. He is on his way up the river to plan the destruction of the natural navigational hazards that create the very challenges that make Old Pebble's life meaningful.

Blues (1987), the national best-seller that won for Hersey the Pulitzer Prize, is an extended fictional conversation between a "fisherman" and a "stranger" who are fishing for bluefish off the coast of Cape Cod.* The pair converse philosophically about interconnections between humankind and the natural world and discuss fishing lore and the metaphysics of fishing. Good recipes are included in the book, as well as poems by John Ciardi, James Merrill, Robert Penn Warren, and Elizabeth Bishop.*

Hersey published *Key West Tales* (1993) the year he died. The book is a collection of fifteen tales, including factual reportage and fiction, that present vignettes of famous or fictional people who lived in Key West* and a tapestry of life on the island. In the final years of his life, Hersey and his wife divided their time between Key West and Martha's Vineyard.

James F. Millinger and Jill B. Gidmark

HIGGINSON, THOMAS WENTWORTH (1823–1911). This Harvard graduate and versatile man of letters felt at home in water from his early childhood in Cambridge, Massachusetts. While ministering to the Unitarian church at Newburyport, Massachusetts, he then formed friendships on the Isles of Shoals. Later, he sailed to Fayal in the Azores with his invalid wife and stayed at a fishing village that opened his eyes to the picturesque colorfulness of Europe and the attractions of a life that seemed crude and impoverished, yet somehow salubrious in contrast with New England. In the Civil War, however, Higginson faced his greatest seagoing challenges as colonel of the First South Carolina Volunteers, a regiment of freed slaves whose adventures in Jacksonville, Florida, as well as on the Carolina Sea Islands and tidal rivers he recounted in *Army Life in a Black Regiment* (1870, popularly reprinted in 1997). When a regimental gunboat burned as a consequence of rebel shelling while it was anchored just ashore from Port Royal Island, Higginson drew upon both Robinson Crusoe and Dante to characterize the disaster.

Settling in Newport after the war, Higginson depicted that Rhode Island city as "Oldport," both in his only novel, *Malbone* (1869), and in *Oldport Days* (1873), a collection of nature writings, tales, and sketches. These included a Thoreauvian reflection on the serene pleasures of rowing a wherry and a quietly dreamlike representation of a vessel's catching fire and sinking gently into the sea. A mentor to other writers, particularly women, Higginson provided encouragement to Celia Thaxter* of Appledore, Maine, and Harriet Prescott Spofford of Newburyport, Massachusetts. His most famous protégé, however, was Emily Dickinson,* who displayed a copy of *Malbone* in her parlor when her "safest friend" visited in 1870. [*See also THALATTA*]

Jane Donahue Eberwein

HINE, EPHRAIM CURTISS (1818?–1853). Sailor and author raised in Genoa, New York, Ephraim Curtiss Hine is best known today as the model for the nautical poet Lemsford in Herman Melville's* novel *White-Jacket* (1850). Melville, who was Hine's shipmate on the frigate *United States* during 1843–1844, treats the poet in the novel with a gentle irony; while there is no other record of relationship between the two, the title of one of Hine's novels, *Orlando Melville: or, the Victims of the Press-gang* (1848) is suggestive. Hine's poems, mailed home during his navy service, were published in Auburn, New York, newspapers and collected in a volume, *The Haunted Barque* (1848); they are travel pieces, naval sketches, romantic tragedies, melancholy musings, and other popular types. His novels and short stories include *Roland de Vere; or, The Knight of the Black Plume* (1848), *The Signal; or, the King of the Blue Isle* (1848), and *Wilson McFarland* (1850?).

After leaving the navy, Hine joined the Revenue Cutter Service and died in the shipwreck* of the cutter *Hamilton* off the coast of Charleston, South Carolina. By odd coincidence, another revenue cutter, the *Jefferson Davis*, which made a vain rescue attempt, was captained by William C. Pease, the son-in-law of Valentine Pease, the captain under whom Melville served on the whaleship *Acushnet*.

Thomas Farel Heffernan

THE HISTORY OF CONSTANTIUS AND PULCHERA, OR, CONSTANCY REWARDED (1801). Anonymously authored, *The History of Constantius and Pulchera* is a forty-six page sea romance. The story opens in Philadelphia with sixteen-year-old Pulchera, daughter of a successful merchant, locked in her bedroom. She is due to set sail for France with Monsieur LeMonte, son of a French nobleman and the man her father is forcing her to marry. Her true love, Constantius, has been abducted and reportedly killed by British seamen while attempting to rescue her from being forced to follow her father's will. All hope of rescue exhausted, Pulchera embarks on her voyage with LeMonte.

The sea functions, as it does in ancient Greek romances, as an obstacle to the lovers' union. A few weeks into the voyage, Pulchera and LeMonte's ship is overtaken by a British warship. Taken aboard the latter, Pulchera discovers that Constantius is also a passenger, alive and well. A storm destroys the warship, and from here on the couple must endure shipwrecks* and separations.

The larger part of the narrative focuses, however, on Pulchera. Washed up alone on a beach, she is rescued by an American privateer, forced to pretend she is a sailor by the name of Valorus when again captured by the British, and once more shipwrecked. Pulchera and her fellow sailors struggle to survive a winter in a frozen wilderness before they are finally picked up in the spring by a ship bound for Great Britain. She travels to France, where, having withstood the forces of patriarchal control, British and French imperialism, and nature, she is reunited with Constantius. Monsieur LeMonte releases her from her engagement; Constantius and Pulchera sail for America, where her father, repentant, gives his blessing. They marry and, one assumes, live happily ever after.

As Thomas Philbrick commented in *James Fenimore Cooper* and the Development of American Sea Fiction* (1961), *Constantius and Pulchera* is "[t]he earliest American example of the extensive use of nautical elements in prose fiction. . . . But in spite of all this prolonged and violent nautical action, the author gives almost no sense of the ship, the sailor, or the sea" (29–30).

Ellen Gardiner

HOLMES, OLIVER WENDELL (1809–1894). Oliver Wendell Holmes, a writer and distinguished academic physician, spent his life around Boston. He was the social leader of a group of intellectual luminaries that included Henry Wadsworth Longfellow,* James Russell Lowell,* and Ralph Waldo Emerson. In his day a well-known wit and after-dinner speaker, Holmes is now remembered for a handful of poems, some about the sea.

"Old Ironsides," the poem that made him known, first appeared in a Boston newspaper in 1830. This elegy was his emotional protest against plans to tow the famous frigate U.S.S. *Constitution* to a scrap yard. Instead, says the poem, she ought to set out to sea in a storm, unmanned and under full sail. Republished in newspapers and broadsides* nationwide, the poem galvanized public opinion in favor of preserving the frigate. "The Chambered Nautilus," arguably Holmes' best poem, first appeared in the February 1858 issue of *The Atlantic Monthly*, a magazine that he had named and helped to found. The ode describes a sea creature that expands its beautiful spiral shell to accommodate its physical growth; inspired by the example of this image, the poet then urges the human soul onward to achieve similar spiritual growth.

Other sea-related poems deserve attention. Among his serious poems, "La Maison D'or" (1890) compares life to a sea voyage, and "The Steamboat" (1840) celebrates technology. Among his light verse, "The Old Man of the Sea" (1858) pokes fun at tiresome tellers of sea stories; "A Sea Dialogue"

(1864) contrasts a gabby passenger with a silent seaman; and "Ballad of the Oysterman" (1830) parodies tales of ill-fated lovers.

Critics find Holmes' poetry excessively sentimental for modern taste, but his best verse has the power to charm through forthright feeling, sharp wit, and vivid imagery.

Stephen Curley

HOUGH, HENRY BEETLE (1896–1985). Editor of the *Vineyard Gazette* on the island of Martha's Vineyard from 1920 almost until his death, Henry Beetle Hough was the grandson of a sea captain. He was born and raised in the whaling city of New Bedford, where his newspaper-editor father serialized *Moby-Dick** (1851) in the *Standard* in 1912. That city, Herman Melville,* and especially the rhythms of island life became recurrent themes in Hough's nonfiction books and eight novels. *The New England Story* (1858), set in a contemporary coastal town, depicts a fictional search for the truth about a whaling captain; though *Story* is a conventional romance, the figure of Captain Enoch Adams, the quest theme, and narrative evasions recall aspects of *Moby-Dick*.

Best known for *Country Editor* (1940), Hough drew on family lore as well as research for two books for young readers, *Great Days of Whaling* (1958) and *Melville in the South Pacific* (1960). His historical writings include *Martha's Vineyard, Summer Resort 1835–1935* (1936), *Whaling Wives* (with Emma Whiting, 1953), and *Far Out the Coils* (1985), a personal account of Vineyard history that laments both the cruelty of whaling and the threat of commercial growth.

An active conservationist, Hough was increasingly occupied during his last two decades in battling real estate developers, polluters, and the McDonald's restaurant chain, among other threats to island culture and values chronicled in the autobiographical *Mostly on Martha's Vineyard* (1975), *To the Harbor Light* (1976), and *Soundings at Sea Level* (1980). His collections of essays about Martha's Vineyard include two collaborations with noted photographers: with Alfred Eisenstaedt in *Martha's Vineyard* (1970) and with Alison Shaw in *Remembrance and Light* (1984). These books and the Sheriff's Meadow Foundation, which he founded in 1959 to preserve fragile open spaces, are legacies of Hough's strong sense of nature and of place.

Wesley T. Mott

HOUSTON, JAMES [ARCHIBALD] (1921–). James Houston has made his mark in writing, art, film illustration, film and documentary production, and design. Winner of numerous awards, Houston has written several children's books and novels on the Arctic,* Arctic seas, and the Inuit people.

Houston was born in Toronto in 1921, the son of a clothing importer.

He received extensive art training in Toronto, Paris, and Tokyo. From 1940 to 1945 Houston served in the Canadian* armed forces. From 1949 to 1962 he served the Canadian government in various positions in the Northwest Territories, the Arctic region, and Baffin Island. In 1962 Houston joined Steuben Glass in New York as a designer, where for the past dozen years he has held the title of master designer.

Houston has won three Canadian Library Association Book of the Year awards (1966, 1968, and 1980). His books for young readers generally center on a young boy who struggles against nature and prejudice to survive. Examples include *Eagle Mask* (1966), the story of a boy growing to be a man on a whale hunt, *Tikta'liktak: An Eskimo Legend* (1965), the tale of an Eskimo boy stranded on an ice floe, and *Ghost Paddle* (1972), another coming-of-age account among the Inland River people of the Canadian Northwest. Houston successfully moved to contemporary themes for young readers in the late 1970s. He has written eighteen children's books, most of which he has also illustrated.

Houston has also written serious popular fiction, including such works as *The White Dawn: An Eskimo Saga* (1971), *Ghost Fox* (1977), *Spirit Wrestler* (1980), *Eagle Song* (1983), *Running West* (1989), and most recently, *The Ice Master* (1997). *The White Dawn*, Houston's first novel and his best-known work, is the story of three whalers stranded among the Eskimos. It was a Book-of-the-Month Club main selection in 1971 and released as a motion picture in 1974. In fact, many of the sixteen screenplays that Houston has written are adaptations of his books: *The White Archer* (1967), *Akavak* (1969), and *Ghost Fox* (1979). *Spirit Wrestler* was set on Baffin Island in the 1950s, and *Eagle Song* is a survival story of two survivors of a ship's crew that was attacked by Indians. *The Ice Master*, an exciting tale of Arctic whaling set around Baffin Inland in the 1870s, has received high praise. His 1995 autobiographical memoir, *Confessions of an Igloo Dweller*, was a bestseller. Houston writes of what he knows: ships, the Inuit people, and the dangerous waters of the Arctic. [*See also* JUVENILE LITERATURE]

Boyd Childress

HOWE, TINA (1937–   ). Obie-award-winning playwright Tina Howe often employs sea imagery as metaphoric devices in her plays. Born in Boston and graduated from Sarah Lawrence College, Howe began to have her works professionally produced in the early 1970s; her plays often reflect her love of the New England seashore. For example, a private beach between Marblehead and Gloucester* on the North Shore of Massachusetts is the scene for *Coastal Disturbances* (first perf. 1986; pub. 1987), a romantic comedy. Holly Dancer, a young, aspiring photographer at romantic and professional crossroads, encounters an assortment of characters from her present and past, including two former love interests: a disillusioned lifeguard and a successful New York gallery owner. In a series of brief scenes reminiscent of snapshots, Howe develops Holly's evolving perceptions about love, commitment, and creativity against an ever-changing seascape. Although Howe stresses in her production notes the importance of sustaining the illusion of sand, sky, and ocean, she, like her protagonist, experiences "technical difficulties" in attaining photographic realism, as evidenced in the play's structure.

Through vivid stage imagery, elliptical and overlapping dialogue, and fragmented scenic construction, Howe shows how emotion reflects nature and how women in particular are biologically related to its cycles. She treats the sea as a privileged site for the self-actualization of women. The ocean, with its vast subterranean realm, becomes an alternative reality, where rational and conscious creativity and self-fulfillment can be tempered by the release of emotional and psychosexual energies. With this critically acclaimed play, which was nominated for a Tony award for Best Drama, Howe established her position as an important playwright with both artistic and commercial potential.

The sea, evoked in profuse imagery, figures prominently in Howe's subsequent works, such as *Approaching Zanzibar* (first perf. 1989; pub. 1989), a panoramic road play, and even more significantly in *Pride's Crossing* (1997), which dramatizes the attempts of Mabel Tidings Bigelow, a fictional New England matriarch, to swim the English Channel. [*See also* DRAMA OF THE SEA]

David R. Pellegrini

HOWELLS, WILLIAM DEAN (1837–1920). A native of Ohio, William Dean Howells began to work in his father's printing shop at age nine. A self-taught student of languages and literature, he early entered a career in journalism. After writing a campaign biography of Abraham Lincoln, Howells was appointed American consul to Venice, where he resided during the Civil War. From 1871 to 1881 he was chief editor of *The Atlantic Monthly* and, beginning in 1886, contributed to *Harper's*, moving to New York in 1888. In addition to his journalistic work, Howells wrote numerous novels, stories, plays, poems, travel sketches, and pieces of literary criticism. He also commented on the political events of his time and made himself the spokesperson and promoter of literary realism, becoming America's preeminent man of letters.

Intimately acquainted with Europe, particularly Italy, Howells frequently wrote about the cultural peculiarities of the New World and the Old World, and he occasionally used a transatlantic voyage as setting for his stories. In the romance *The Lady of the Aroostook* (1879) and in the musical farce *A Sea Change; or Love's Stowaway* (1888), young Americans woo each other aboard ships bound for Europe. Part of *Their Wedding Journey* (1871) takes place on board a ship crossing Lake Ontario; part of *Their Silver Wedding Journey* (1899), on a German vessel sailing from New York to Cuxhaven.

Travel by ship is also the topic of four of Howells' contributions to the "Editor's Easy Chair" column in *Harper's Monthly*: he describes a ship and its passengers just returned from Europe (October 1907), the Great Lakes* and their towns and countrysides (April 1908), music on transatlantic vessels (July 1909), and the differences between sea and air travel (January 1911).

Sea voyages and a shipwreck* are central plot twists in *A Woman's Reason* (1883), in which protagonist Helen Harkness, daughter of a bankrupt India trader, awaits the return of her erstwhile fiancé, naval officer Robert Fenton, from China. Howells describes in detail Fenton's efforts to survive on an uncharted coral island in the Pacific, where he and a companion have been abandoned by shipmates after a wreck of the clipper *Meteor*, en route to San Francisco from Yokohama. Helen attempts to survive financially on the rocky Massachusetts Bay shore following her father's death and the presumed death of Fenton. [*See also* OCEAN LINER DRAMA]

Udo Nattermann

HUGHES, [JAMES MERCER] LANGSTON (1902–1967). Langston Hughes, the prolific African American* writer whose work in multiple genres endeared him early in his career to the black American community and later to a broad, international readership, first prepared to set sail in 1922, when he signed on as a messboy aboard the freighter *West Hassayampa*. Hughes' romantic vision of exploring the world as a sailor was shattered, however, when he discovered that the rusty ship he had climbed aboard was bound for nowhere. Towed up the Hudson River to Jones Point, where it was moored among a large group of decommissioned World War I freighters, the *West Hassayampa* merely served as a mother ship and quarters for a crew charged with maintaining the other idle freighters. Although Hughes found his first "experience at sea" somewhat embarrassing, life at Jones Point was nevertheless beneficial to his creative processes; he completed numerous poems, and the experience is humorously recaptured in the first volume of his autobiography, *The Big Sea* (1940).

Armed with letters of recommendation from his superiors that testified to his abilities on shipboard, Hughes left Jones Point in 1923 and signed on to the *West Hesseltine*, bound for Africa. Hughes viewed this departure to sea symbolically: upon leaving the shore, he was also casting off painful memories of his past, such as his experiences with segregation at Columbia University, his many arguments with his father, the poverty of his childhood, and the day-to-day angers generated by racial prejudice. He was also leaving behind the romantic world of books, which had sustained him as a youth in lieu of actual experiences at sea. Fittingly, as the *West Hesseltine* moved past Sandy Hook on the New Jersey shore, Hughes cast overboard the books he had brought on the ship, saving, according to his biographer, only one: Walt Whitman's* *Leaves of Grass* (1855).

Hughes recaptured this and several other sea adventures in poems, short stories, and, most notably, *The Big Sea*, and his fascination with the sea provided material for a number of short stories and poems. In stories such as "Sailor Ashore" (1952) and "Powder-White Faces" (1952), for example, Hughes explored the psychological trauma of racial oppression that dogged black sailors both onshore and at sea. In such poems as "Sea Charm" (1921), "Rising Waters" (1925), "Sea Calm" (1926), "Death of an Old Seaman" (1926), "Fog" (1926), "To Captain Mulzac" (1943), and "Island" (1950), Hughes' skills at rendering symbolism and metaphor from memories of his sea adventures attained their fullest power, transforming the sea into a canvas of words from which to explore themes of love, death, loneliness, sexuality, and racial identity and oppression. [*See also* SEA IMAGERY IN MODERN AND CONTEMPORARY POETRY]

Christopher C. De Santis

HURLBUT, FRANCES [BRINDEL] (1842?–1892). Orphaned by age nine, Frances Hurlbut, née Brindel, left Pennsylvania for Newport (now Marine City), Michigan, to live with her aunt, Emily Ward. Hurlbut's only publication, *Grandmother's Stories* (1889), recounts Aunt Emily's tales of their pioneer family. Two themes dominate: the danger of the untamed Great Lakes,* which destroy ships, lighthouses,* and life; and the virgin region's lure of prosperity, despite danger.

Hurlbut was intimately connected with the Great Lakes, swimming and sailing them from her youth. Her grandfather, Eber Ward, was a sailor and a lighthouse keeper; her uncles, Sam and Eber Brock Ward, were, by 1854, the Lakes' largest shipbuilders. Hurlbut attended Newport Academy, which her aunt established and her uncles financed, graduated from Michigan State Normal School (now Eastern Michigan University), married L. A. Hurlbut, had one child (Florence), and died in Crescent City, a now-deserted lumber town on North Manitou Island.

Donald P. Curtis

HUSSEY, CYRUS W. *See GLOBE* MUTINY.

INGRAHAM, JOSEPH HOLT (1809–1860). Born in Portland, Maine, Joseph Holt Ingraham was a teacher, minister, and popular writer who produced more than 100 novels, 25 in 1845 alone at the peak of his career. Until the late 1840s Ingraham wrote popular historical romances, many about pirates* and sea adventures. After his ordination in 1852 as a minister of the Episcopal Church, Ingraham turned his talents to writing biblically-based fiction.

Little is known about the early years of Ingraham's life. Around 1826 he may have traveled to Buenos Aires, Argentina, on one of his grandfather's merchant ships and worked for a time as a clerk. His novel *Paul Perril, the Merchant's Son* (1847) may be a fictionalized account of his experience in South America.

Ingraham's first book, the nonfiction travel narrative *The South-West* (1835), is based on his 1830 sea and river journey from New England to Natchez, Mississippi, by way of Bermuda, the Bahamas, Cuba, and New Orleans. This detailed work, directed toward an audience of northerners, chronicles his journey and offers a northerner's perspective on the South. His first novel, *Lafitte*: The Pirate of the Gulf* (1836), was tremendously popular; like several of his subsequent works, it was adapted into a stage production. Ingraham's pirate tales and sea adventures include *Captain Kyd; or, The Wizard of the Sea* (1839), *The Dancing Feather* (1842), *Morris Graeme; or, The Cruise of the Sea-Slipper* (1843), *The Midshipman; or, The Corvette and Brigantine* (1844), *The Spanish Galleon; or, The Pirate of the Mediterranean* (1845), and *The Lady of the Gulf: A Romance of the City and Seas* (1846).

Although both his adventure and biblical novels sold well, Ingraham struggled financially throughout his life. He died at age fifty-one from an accidentally self-inflicted pistol wound.

Christina L. Wolak

IRVING, WASHINGTON (1783–1859). The first American to succeed as a professional author, Washington Irving was born in New York City in the last year of the American Revolution. Although he is best known today as the author of "Rip Van Winkle" and "The Legend of Sleepy Hollow" (1819–1820), short tales that depict landlocked life in the sleepy Dutch villages of the Hudson River valley, Irving's literary interests ranged widely. A seasoned traveler, he was especially attracted to narratives of sea voyages, shipwrecks,* and pirate* treasure.

Irving made three round-trip voyages across the Atlantic. His first European tour, 1804–1806, was to London, Bordeaux, Genoa, Messina, Naples, Rome, Geneva, and Paris. In 1815 Irving sailed again to England to oversee family business investments. While there, he wrote most of the pieces for *The Sketch Book of Geoffrey Crayon, Gent.* (1819–1820). In "The Voyage," the second sketch in the volume, he compared daydreaming to taking a sea voyage. The most famous nautical reference in *The Sketch Book* is the figure of Hendrick Hudson, bowling with the silent crew of the *Halfmoon* in a Kaatskill glen. Hudson and the crew figure, too, in the "Storm Ship" frame tale within "Dolph Heyliger" in *Bracebridge Hall* (1822).

Returning to England from a year's tour of Germany and France, Irving wrote *Tales of a Traveller* (1824). "The Money Diggers" section of this collection contains five connected stories about pirates* and buried treasure. In the first tale, "Hell's Gate," Irving's narrative persona, Diedrich Knickerbocker, recalls the thrills and terrors of sailing through "Hell's Gate" channel in Long Island Sound. At flood tide the passage was flat and calm, but at half tide "Hell's Gate" lived up to its name. Associated in local lore with shipwrecks, murder, and pirates' gold, "Hell's Gate" sets the scene for the next tale, "Kidd the Pirate." Kidd starts out as a pirate hunter, then turns pirate, and comes to a pirate's end in London, where he is hanged at Execution Dock. Before he is arrested and hanged, Kidd buries his gold.

Kidd's treasure also figures in "The Devil and Tom Walker." To learn the location of the gold, Walker strikes a bargain with the devil, who demands Walker's soul. The devil makes Walker promise that the gold will be put to the devil's use by being loaned out at usurious rates. In "Wolfert Webber, or Golden Dreams," Webber, who stubbornly farms on Manhattan as the city presses in around him, digs up his land searching for Kidd's treasure. At the local inn, a stranger, perhaps the ghost of one of Kidd's buccaneers, mesmerizes the habitués of the place with tales of freebooting adventures. The final tale in the collection, "The Black Fisherman," returns to the Hell's Gate setting of the first tale. Black Sam has seen a party of ruffians burying what might have been a treasure. Webber talks Sam into taking him to the site, but they are scared off by the sudden appearance of the mysterious buccaneer. At the end of the story, Webber finds that his worthless land is the real treasure, in that it will fetch a handsome price once it is parceled out in city lots.

In 1826 Irving sailed to Madrid, where he researched and wrote *A History of the Life and Voyages of Christopher Columbus* (1828) and *The Voyages and Discoveries of the Companions of Columbus* (1831). Irving saw Columbus* as a quixotic figure: part poet, part realist. He acknowledged Columbus' shortcomings but admired his determination. In *Voyages and Discoveries*, he referred to Vasco Núñez de Balboa's discovery of the Pacific as one of the most important events in the age of exploration.

After returning to America in 1832, Irving continued to write narratives and tales based on voyages or island life. "The Haunted Ship" (1835), subtitled "A True Story as Far as It Goes," is about a ship found adrift off the Bahama banks, its cargo rifled, its decks covered in blood. While the ship is being towed to Boston for refitting, the ghosts of its murdered crew bedevil their living replacements. After refitting, the unlucky ship is sent on a trading mission to South America. During the voyage south, the phantom crew is again seen on the decks and in the rigging. While the ship is riding at anchor off a South American port, and the captain and crew are ashore, a fierce tropical storm comes up. Despite the efforts of the phantom crew, the ship is driven onto the rocks and breaks up.

In *Astoria: or Anecdotes of an Enterprise beyond the Rocky Mountains* (1836) Irving shows how Captain James Cook's accounts of sea otters found along the Northwest Coast* of North America and the fortunes to be made in the fur trade set off a rush of expeditions to the fur-rich coast. Among the most famous of these were the voyages of the *Tonquin** and the *Beaver*.

Financed by John Jacob Astor, the *Tonquin* expedition left New York on 8 September 1810, with a crew of French Canadian* voyageurs, anchored in the Sandwich Islands the following February, reached the Oregon coast in March, and then sailed to Vancouver Island on a trading voyage. The captain's irascible treatment led to bloody fighting; eventually, an explosion of the ship's powder magazine destroyed the vessel, killing all on board. Unaware of the fate of the *Tonquin* and its crew, the *Beaver* sailed from New York on 10 October 1811. Unsure of the status of the settlement at Astoria, Astor ordered Captain Sowle to proceed cautiously. After arriving in the Sandwich Islands without incident, the *Beaver* sailed for Astoria, anchoring off Cape Disappointment on 9 May 1812, safely outside the treacherous bar at the mouth of the Columbia River. In August 1812 the *Beaver* put to sea again on what was supposed to be a voyage up the Northwest Coast to Russian Alaska, arriving in New Archangel (Sitka), where Sowle spent forty-five days "boosing and bargaining" with the Russian commander of New Archangel. Taking on a cargo of sealskins and other furs, the *Beaver* sailed for Canton rather than risk a winter voyage to Astoria. In Canton Sowle's stubbornness caused him to hold out for a higher price than had been offered for his cargo. When prices subsequently fell, and word of the British war with America reached him, Sowle was forced to sit out the war in Canton.

Woolfert's Roost and Other Papers (1855) contains three sea stories: "The Bermudas," "Guests from Gibbet Island," and "The Phantom Island." "The Bermudas," with its frame tale of the "Three Kings of Bermuda," is based on "The Bermuda Pamphlets," a compilation of shipwreck* stories from Jacobean times that may have influenced *The Tempest* (1623). The idea for the tale about the three kings came from Irving's readings in Samuel Purchas' *Purchas His Pilgrimes* (1625). Irving adapted "Guests from Gibbet Island" from a German tale by Jakob Grimm, adding accounts of pirates hanged in chains and hidden treasure. The protagonist of "The Phantom Island" is a romantic Portuguese cavalier who becomes obsessed with discovering the Island of the Seven Cities. [*See also* GHOSTS AND GHOST SHIP LEGENDS; PIRATE LITERATURE]

FURTHER READING: Bowden, Mary Witherspoon. *Washington Irving*. Boston: Twayne, 1981; Hedges, William. *Washington Irving: An American Study, 1802–32*. Baltimore: Johns Hopkins UP, 1965; Roth, Martin. *Comedy and America: The Lost World of Washington Irving*. Port Washington, NY: Kennikat, 1976; Rubin-Dorsky, Jeffrey. *Adrift in the Old World: The Pilgrimage of Washington Irving*. Chicago: U of Chicago P, 1988.

James J. Schramer

ISHMAEL. The narrator of Herman Melville's* *Moby-Dick** (1851) names himself in the novel's well-known opening line, "Call me Ishmael." Through this name, Melville associates his narrator with the Old Testament Ishmael as well as with characters having the same name in nineteenth-century fiction, as in James Fenimore Cooper's* *The Prairie* (1827) and William Starbuck Mayo's* *Kaloolah* (1849). At the beginning of *Moby-Dick*, Melville's Ishmael, like his namesakes, is a wanderer, antisocial and restless; unlike them, however, his alienation is exacerbated by a suicidal despair, which is resolved by his decision to go to sea and by his companionship with the wise and caring Polynesian harpooner Queequeg.* As an American, he represents independent youth, seeking adventure and economic success in unknown realms. He is differentiated from this convention, however, by his questioning mind, spiritual awareness, comic sensibility, and sensitivity to suffering. At sea, Ishmael learns; a whaleship proves his college. His friendship with Queequeg is strengthened as they share the often dangerous work of whaling on board the *Pequod*.* He also enthusiastically commits himself to Captain Ahab's* monomaniacal quest for the white whale; in certain moments, such as when he stands watch for whales at the masthead and once when he takes the helm, he experiences a life-threatening, abstract trance similar to Ahab's obsession.

Increasingly, however, Melville presents Ishmael as observing the behavior of Ahab, his shipmates, the crews of other whaleships, the changing moods of the sea, and all its creatures. As such, he is both a democrat and an Everyman, identified with the novel's diverse characters and committed to perceiving life from diverse perspectives. As the only survivor of the *Pequod*'s destruction by Moby Dick, Ishmael resembles Job's messengers and Samuel Taylor Coleridge's Ancient Mariner, as well as Holocaust memoirists. For Ishmael to be able to tell the story of this traumatic whaling voyage, however, necessitates that he develop an alternative quest to Ahab's, one that seeks knowledge from multiple sources and cultures regarding whales and their lives, one that affirms the value of a continued search for knowledge of all life.

Although literary critics have occasionally condemned Ishmael's open-mindedness as untrustworthy, twentieth-century writers, including William Faulkner,* Ralph Ellison, Thomas Pynchon, Jay Cantor, Peter Benchley,* and David Guterson,* endorse his struggle to know by modeling their narrators or major characters after him.

Elizabeth Schultz

ISLANDS IN THE STREAM (1970). Entitled and published posthumously, this novel by Ernest Hemingway* (1899–1961) consists of three editorially renamed segments about the sea that the author tentatively prepared for a projected novel on the sea, land, and air. In "Bimini," in the mid-1930s, a major painter of seascapes, the lonely father of three sons by two failed marriages, tries to use island seclusion, disciplined work, fishing habits, and emotional detachment to control his remorse over having put art before loved ones. By reliving that distraction, he hopes to fulfill his artistic potential and capture the sea's essence in his painting. In a memorable fishing episode, one visiting son learns that unaccountable loss must be accepted in life, but the artist himself has not fully learned this lesson, so central to his strategy, for he is overcome by the accidental death, shortly, of two of his sons and their mother, compounded by the loss of his remaining son in World War II ten years later.

This added blow is revealed in "Cuba," part two, set in 1944. Too depressed to paint, the artist drives himself obsessively on his boat, searching for German submarines. Yet his creativity persists; in his desperate ruminations ashore, painterly views of the sea recur.

On the artist's next patrol, weeks later in "At Sea," the novel's final section, as he and his crew pursue escaped German sailors through the islands of the Camaguey archipelago, his painter's eye initiates moments of intuitive insight. Two of these are induced by a flight of flamingos, in which the ugliness of individual parts contributes to a beautiful, visual composition (ch. 15). He is moved at last to accept instances of apparent disorder, including by implication his personal losses, as part of a reassuring order that can be sensed by the human mind, even though not understood. Realizing at the chase's end that now nobody could match him as a painter of the sea, he is fatally shot (ch. 21).

For some readers overreliance on human logic is revealed in "At Sea" as the root cause of the artist's difficulty in resigning himself to gratuitous adversity, and it also explains his impairment in relationships and creativity. By "seeing," in the ocean's visible forms, the operation of a natural truth that he feels no need to verify discursively, he has already "painted" the sea that he can never put on canvas. Had he lived, could he have sustained this liberating intellectual humility in his art and in fathering the surrogate sons in his crew? His uncertainty leaves readers to ponder the extent of his progress.

In 1977 the novel was adapted into a film that starred George C. Scott.

Bickford Sylvester

J

JACK TAR. The term "Jack Tar" appears in Anglo-American fiction, drama, poetry, and song during the eighteenth and nineteenth centuries as a generic proper name for an able-bodied seaman. The name "Jack" was used in reference to a common deepwater sailor beginning in the seventeenth century, while "Tar" derives from tarpaulin, the utilitarian tarred canvas made into clothing to protect sailors from weather before the institution of regulation uniforms. From at least the appearance of Ned Ward's satirical look at British naval life, *The Wooden World Dissected* in 1705, "Jack Tar" mariners were consistently associated with the qualities of candor, wry humor, haughtiness, honesty, patriotism, and bravery. Heroic American Tar characters arose with the growth of an American navy, such as those referred to in the title of the plays *The Enterprize, or, A Wreath for American Tars*, produced in Philadelphia in 1803, and *The Naval Frolic, or A Tribute to American Tars* (1812).

Specific characters named Jack Tar and others with names like Tom Haulyard, Ben Block, and Jack Hawser, frequently appeared onstage and in books produced for both seamen and general audiences. "Hawser Martingale" was the pen name of John Sherburne Sleeper,* who wrote *Jack in the Forecastle* (1860); "Harry Halyard"* was the pseudonym of an author who was an important figure in American pre–Civil War sea fiction but whose identity remains unknown. Their mariner characters were usually engaged in one of two activities: at sea bravely winning their country's battles, while on land winning the heart of an innocent lass. A modern treatment of the theme is Jesse Lemisch's *Jack Tar vs. John Bull: The Role of New York's Seamen in Precipitating the Revolution* (1997). [*See also* DRAMA OF THE SEA]

Daniel Finamore

JAMES, HENRY (1843–1916). Henry James made nineteen Atlantic crossings and lived for much of his life in seacoast cities and villages. In his longer fiction, scenes near the English Channel in *What Maisie Knew* (1897) and in Venice in *The Aspern Papers* (1888) and *The Wings of the Dove* (1902, film adaptation 1997) are significant. In James' tales, the sea figures importantly in "A Tragedy of Error" (1864), "A Landscape Painter" (1866), and "The *Patagonia*" (1888), a story modeled on the "ship of fools" concept and set aboard a steamer sailing from America to Europe. A volume of travel essays, *Transatlantic Sketches* (1875), was one of his earliest book publications. The sea is most remarkable in James' writing as a metaphor for living.

James used sea language in his public and private writing in at least four ways: to represent threatening experiences and the uncertainty of life in general with words and images relating to, and representing, tempests, storms, floods, and shipwrecks*; to console others by placing both the consoler and the consoled in the same dangerous or beneficial metaphorical situation, such as being lost at sea or sailing smoothly; to represent a pleasant experience in which one is immersed as if bathing; and to indicate movement through experience under one's own power, as in rowing or captaining a vessel.

In the fiction, for instance, James represents protagonist Lambert Strether's moral breakthrough in *The Ambassadors* (1903; adapted for television in 1977), during Strether's final meeting with Marie de Vionnet, using recurrent water imagery. In *The Awkward Age* (1899), Nanda Brookenham is the novel's "experienced mariner." She exerts influence actively—though quietly—to reorganize the circumstances of her little society.

In critical essays James also employs the language of the sea to represent ideas of living. But now the experience in question is a dimension of the fiction. Like life itself, a good story, he writes in his essay "The New Novel" (1914), makes readers feel as if they were "launched" in a "boat."

Overall, the language of the sea helps James in fiction and nonfiction to advance trivial and serious points having to do with human conduct and human relations. That one of his last letters, written on his deathbed, expresses his hope that he could "keep afloat" (4:784) suggests the fundamental significance of sea language to James.

FURTHER READING: Gale, Robert. *The Caught Image: Figurative Language in the Fiction of Henry James*. Chapel Hill: U of North Carolina P, 1954; James, Henry. *Henry James Letters*. 4 vols. Ed. Leon Edel. Cambridge: Harvard UP, 1974–1984; Stein, Roger B. "Realism and Beyond," *America and the Sea: A Literary History*. Ed. Haskell Springer. Athens: U of Georgia P, 1995, 190–208; Zacharias, Greg W. "The Marine Metaphor, Henry James, and the Moral Center of *The Awkward Age*," *Philological Quarterly* 69 (1990): 91–105.

Greg W. Zacharias

JAVA HEAD (1918). *Java Head* is the finest and most popular novel written by Joseph Hergesheimer (1880–1954), whose fiction and belles-lettres essays enjoyed a wide audience throughout the 1920s. The novel plays out a tale of two nautical families caught in the decline of Salem's seafaring commerce during the late 1840s.

From his "Java Head" mansion, Captain Jeremy Ammidon opposes his son William's decision to modernize the family's Pacific trading fleet and move the business to Boston. From his small dockside cottage, Captain Barzil Dunsack confronts his son Edward's opium habit (a result of many years in China) and the ruin it is bringing to the small family business. Indeed, the meeting of East and West leads to further tragedy. The discovery that William has secretly diversified into opium-running precipitates Jeremy Ammidon's fatal stroke. William's younger brother, Captain Gerrit Ammidon, loses his Manchu wife to suicide by opium overdose; Edward Dunsack loses his sanity. Gerrit, now the guarantor of Barzil Dunsack's business, decides to take his ship and his share of the family inheritance out of the Ammidon company and back to the traditional ways of the old Salem shipmasters. He sails from Salem with a new bride: Barzil Dunsack's granddaughter.

Each chapter is presented from the limited point of view of a different character. Overall, the plot is more impressionistic than dramatic: the novel centers more on what the characters see and experience than what they do. The sea provides a constant backdrop for the complex interactions between fathers and sons, old money and new money, East and West. The novel is based not on Hergesheimer's experience at sea but on his extensive secondary research, including his reading of Joseph Conrad (in particular *Youth* [1898], which interestingly was based on a voyage that Conrad had taken aboard the *Palestine* off Java Head in Malayan waters). Like Conrad's London, Salem is portrayed as the heart of a great commercial empire based on a network of ocean trade routes. Descriptions of the houses and docks of Salem always include the rich harvest of ocean trade, but the destructive consequences—cross-cultural intolerance and opium addiction—loom constantly in the background. At every turn, the characters see evidence that Salem will soon fade into the history of the great age of sail.

Jonathan R. Eller

JEFFERS, [JOHN] ROBINSON (1887–1962). Robinson Jeffers, best known for his verse narratives set on California's rugged northern coast, was born in Pennsylvania. In 1903 he moved with his family to Los Angeles and entered Occidental College, where he studied geology, astronomy, and biblical literature, graduating in 1905. In 1913, after graduate studies in languages and literature, medicine, and forestry, Jeffers married Una Call Kuster. They settled in Carmel, a rural community on the coast below the Monterey Peninsula, where they built Tor House, a stone cottage named after the rocky promontories along the English coast near Dartmoor. Jeffers spent the next five decades at Tor House writing the lyric poems and long

narratives that made him one of America's most popular and most controversial poets of the 1920s and 1930s.

The Pacific Ocean profoundly influenced Jeffers. Its violent coastline
serves not only as the setting of many of his poems but as their inspiration.
Beginning with the publication of his first mature work, *Tamar, and Other
Poems* (1924), Jeffers' poetry explores the tenuous connection between humans and their natural surroundings, particularly the sea. Many of his poems, including "Tamar" (1924), "Continent's End" (1924), and "Cawdor"
(1928), imbue the ocean with maternal characteristics, reminding us that
the sea is the source of life. At the beginning of "Tamar" the maternal sea
resuscitates Lee Cauldwell after his nearly fatal fall from a cliff. "Continent's
End" imagines human life emerging from the ocean's womb in the distant
past and meditates on the more ancient source of both human life and the
ocean. In "Cawdor" the ocean has restorative powers for the ailing Martial,
who remembers humankind's primordial link to the sea and finds nourish-
ment in the broth of mussels collected from its tide pools.

But the sea can also be a destructive force in Jeffers' poetry. The mighty
Pacific crashes against its boundaries and destroys rocks in "Continent's
End," and it represents the source of the storms that punish the coast in
"Cawdor" and "Tamar." Tamar Cauldwell, whose acts of incest lead to her
family's destruction, learns her wildness from the ocean that beats against
Point Lobos near the Cauldwell farm. In "Boats in a Fog" (1925) fishing
boats navigate the thin corridor of safety between the shore's murderous
rocks and the open sea's equally perilous fog as they move toward port. The
boats' movement reflects the precarious existence of all living things and the
creation of beauty out of bitter struggle. "The Purse-Seine" (1937) warns
that industrial cities encircle us, separating us from the natural world, lim-
iting our freedom, and threatening to destroy us, just as the fisherman's net
steadily encloses the fish.

The vast ocean's indifference to human concerns fostered Jeffers' inhumanist philosophy, which radically reconsiders humankind's place in the natural world. In his most famous war poem, "The Eye" (1948), the Pacific is
an immense, timeless, unblinking eye that takes no heed of warships or
airplanes. "Calm and Full the Ocean" (1948) finds solace in nature's indifference to the terrors of war. The Pacific marks the edge of Western civilization in "The Torch-Bearers' Race" (1924), and Jeffers situates himself
within the tradition of Old Testament prophets who warned the earliest
forms of that civilization of their errant ways. His poetry warns against for-
getting the sea's inhuman presence and mistaking life for nature's ultimate
achievement. Jeffers reminds us that the Pacific Ocean is more enduring
than human life.

This inhumanist philosophy, along with Jeffers' criticism of American foreign policy during the 1940s, contributed to a sharp decline in his popularity
after World War II. Although his audience dwindled, he continued to pub-

lish poetry until his death at Tor House in 1962. [*See also* SEA IMAGERY IN MODERN AND CONTEMPORARY POETRY]

FURTHER READING: Bennett, Melba Berry. *Robinson Jeffers and the Sea*. San Francisco: Gelber and Lilienthal, 1936; Brophy, Robert J. *Robinson Jeffers: Myth, Ritual, and Symbol in His Narrative Poems*. Cleveland: Case Western Reserve UP, 1973; Karman, James. *Robinson Jeffers: Poet of California*. San Francisco: Chronicle, 1987.

Gregg Allen Walker

JENNINGS, JOHN EDWARD, JR. (1906–1973). John Edward Jennings Jr., historical novelist, was born in Brooklyn, New York. The son of a surgeon, he began his seafaring in 1925 as a foremast hand aboard a tramp steamer traveling in the eastern Mediterranean and the Black Sea. Jennings attended the Colorado College of Mines and New York University and studied engineering and literature at Columbia University. He was a graduate of the Washington Diplomatic and Consular Institute. During World War II, Jennings was a lieutenant commander in the navy and headed the U.S. Naval Aviation History Unit.

Jennings' prolific writing career began with short stories, magazine serials, and travel narratives. Known for his extensive knowledge of the sea, his novels are grand in scale and noted for accurate historical detail, adventure, exploration, heroism, and romance. Thirteen of his books were considered best-sellers, including his first, *Next to Valor* (1939), which was translated into seven languages and was compared in style to the works of James Fenimore Cooper* and Kenneth Roberts.* *The Salem Frigate* (1946), his most popular novel, was published in a dozen languages and chronicles the lives of two men, a ship's surgeon and a carpenter, the women they love, and life and adventure aboard the U.S. frigate *Essex*.

Among Jennings' other historical sea adventures are *Coasts of Folly* (1942), a tale of freedom and liberation in South America written under the pseudonym "Joel Williams"; *The Sea Eagles* (1950), a story of love, daring, and privateering during the first years of the U.S. Navy; *Banners against the Wind* (1954), a biographical novel about Dr. Samuel Gridley Howe; *Chronicle of the* Calypso, *Clipper* (1955), a race on board a clipper ship bound for California; *The Raider* (1963), exploits of a German naval vessel during World War I. Under the pseudonym "Bates Baldwin," Jennings published *A Tide of Empire* (1952), about a young Irishman voyaging to California in the days of the gold rush.

Among Jennings' notable nonfiction are *Clipper Ship Days* (1952), written for juveniles and detailing the part played by clipper ships in the American merchant marine, and *Tattered Ensign* (1966), the story of the U.S. frigate *Constitution* and the early U.S. Navy. Jennings died on 4 December 1973.

Debra Glabeau

JEWETT, SARAH ORNE (1849–1909). Sarah Orne Jewett was born and raised in South Berwick, Maine, a dwindling shipping and manufacturing center. As a girl she listened to her paternal grandfather's tales of life as a sea captain, skirting the embargo of 1807; some fifty years later South Berwick still reviled the embargo and the war it preceded as the genesis of its economic and social decline. As a teen Jewett felt the literary influence of Harriet Beecher Stowe's* *The Pearl of Orr's Island* (1862), which inspired her to introduce her regional culture to the world. Jewett sought, without Stowe's penchant for sentimentality, to acquaint present with past and urban with rural.

She first reached the pages of a major literary journal with "Mr. Bruce," published in *The Atlantic Monthly* in 1869. The piece engendered a productive relationship with editor James T. Fields and, later, William Dean Howells.* In 1877 Howells encouraged her to arrange a number of her vignettes for publication as a larger work. The result was her first book, *Deephaven* (1877), in which two young, city-bred women explore life in a seaside village in Maine during their summer visit. She followed with *Country By-Ways* (1881) and *A Country Doctor* (1884), possibly modeled on Jewett's father and focusing on a young woman's ambitions to become a doctor despite cultural obstacles.

Considered her finest work, *The Country of the Pointed Firs* (1896) fast became popular. The narrator, a middle-aged writer, spends her summer observing the ebb and flow of Dunnet Landing, Maine, a fictional fishing village. Now well past its glory days, Dunnet has lost its sea trade, and the hamlet sits beyond the last stop of the new railroad, fated to a slow decline. Jewett examines the sea in contrast to the land, as one of two elements that constitute the shoreline rather than an environment of its own; her seafarers relate tales of landfalls, not of blue-water adventures. She quarters her narrators within easy view of both land and water, and from their vantage points we learn of the commingled life of mariner and farmer.

While not the focus of her tales, the sea lingers powerfully in the background of Jewett's work, and the inhabitants of her ocean-weathered villages seem spellbound by its legacy. Unlike the squalor of her much-affected inland settings, her shore communities more often display traces of the wealth of the now-past booming sea trade, and their citizens still show vestiges of robust, sea-tutored constitutions, yet, for all its entrancing power, the sea proves an outdated source of bounty. As its provision of economic sustenance and its primers in hearty character fade into the past, Jewett's sea captains lament their society's decay.

Jewett's women outnumber and outdo her men. While the adventuresome legacy of seafaring dies, leaving the men with limited options and direction, the women press productively on, used to self-sufficiency and perhaps prepared by the years of sea trade for the lack of an active male presence. *The Country of the Pointed Firs*' Almira Todd perhaps best embodies

Jewett's resourceful widow. Having lost her husband to the sea, she perseveres, proving equally deft at harvesting her medicinal herbs and at handling a dory's tiller.

Toward the end of her career, Jewett attempted to join the flood of late nineteenth-century historical fiction with *The Tory Lover* (1901), which chronicles the wartime adventures of a loosely veiled John Paul Jones.* Her final book, it is considered an unfortunate departure from her earlier work, as the genre fails to exploit her strengths of contemplative characterization and observation in repose. In addition to her novels, Jewett published poetry, juvenile* fiction, and over 100 short stories, many of them in collected volumes, most notably *A White Heron* (1886) and *Strangers and Wayfarers* (1890).

Jewett was well traveled, making numerous excursions through Europe and the United States, often in the company of her friend Annie Fields, wife of *The Atlantic Monthly* editor. In 1901 Bowdoin College bestowed an honorary Litt.D. degree upon her, making her the first woman thus honored. In 1902 she sustained head and neck injuries when thrown from a carriage, restricting her activities and hampering her creativity; she published only two short pieces thereafter. In March 1909 she suffered a stroke while visiting Annie Fields' home in Boston. Three months later, having withstood the journey to South Berwick, she died in the house in which she had been born.

FURTHER READING: Blanchard, Paula. *Sarah Orne Jewett; Her World and Her Work*. Reading, MA: Addison Wesley Longman, 1994; Jewett, Sarah Orne. *Best Stories of Sarah Orne Jewett*. Gloucester, MA: Peter Smith, 1990.

John F. Hussey

JEWITT, JOHN RODGERS (1783–1821). An Englishman who served aboard the American merchant vessel *Boston*, John Jewitt became famous as a "captive" of the Indians of Nootka Sound, off the coast of Vancouver Island, British Columbia, when he survived the destruction of his ship and massacre of its crew in 1803. Born in Boston, England, Jewitt apprenticed to his blacksmith father and signed aboard the *Boston* as armourer in 1802 at Kingston-upon-Hull, where the ship had stopped to obtain a cargo. When the ship arrived at Nootka Sound, Captain John Salter proved to be a less than sympathetic negotiator and offended the powerful chief Maquinna, who retaliated by murdering Salter and his crew. Jewitt, though badly injured, was spared because Maquinna appreciated his skills as a blacksmith; another man, sailmaker John Thompson, was spared when Jewitt claimed that Thompson was his father.

Until they were rescued by the Boston ship *Lydia* in 1805, Jewitt and Thompson lived among the indigenous people of Nootka Sound. Jewitt became a favorite of Maquinna, who arranged for his marriage with a high-ranking woman and for the sale among the local tribes of daggers and other items fashioned by Jewitt on the salvaged forge of the *Boston*. Jewitt kept a diary of terse entries during his captivity, which he published in 1807 as *A Journal Kept at Nootka Sound*. He subsequently met journalist Richard Alsop and, with his enthusiastic participation, enlarged the journal into *A Narrative of the Adventures and Sufferings of John R. Jewitt; Only Survivor of the Crew of the Ship* Boston, *during a Captivity of Nearly 3 Years Among the Savages of Nootka Sound, with an Account of the Manners, Mode of Living, and Religious Opinions of the Natives* (1815). After the publication of the *Narrative*, Jewitt spent the rest of his life playing the role of himself as captive, regularly singing his signature song, "The Poor Armourer Boy," and even playing himself in a production of James Nelson Barker's play *The Armourer's Escape* (1817). [*See also* DRAMA OF THE SEA; NORTHWEST COAST]

Mary Malloy

JOHN MARR AND OTHER SAILORS WITH SOME SEA PIECES

(1888). This collection of nineteen poems, written and privately published in twenty-five copies by Herman Melville* (1819–1891), is made up of four disparate parts, all linked by the sea. Following an "Inscription Epistolary" to W. Clark Russell, the British sea-fiction writer, the book proper begins with "John Marr," preceded by a prose introduction and followed by three poems named for, as well as spoken by or addressed to, other individual sailors. The next section, "Sea-Pieces," is the shortest, consisting only of "The Haglets" (pub. 1885 in Boston and New York newspapers in a shorter version as "The Admiral of the White") and "The Aeolian Harp." "Minor Sea-Pieces," the third section, contains twelve poems, most notably "The Tuft of Kelp," "The Maldive Shark," and "The Berg." The book ends with seven brief, numbered stanzas under the title "Pebbles."

John Marr is heavily autobiographical, alluding repeatedly to Melville's days as a sailor in the era before steamships, as it does, for example, in "To Ned," an allusion to Toby Greene of Melville's first book *Typee** (1846). It suggests Melville's current life in "Bridegroom Dick," whose relationship with his wife of many years reflects in some ways that of Melville with his wife, Elizabeth. John Marr is, clearly, a version of Melville himself, a bereaved, lonely man whose neighbors know little of the sea and care even less. The anthropomorphized "Tuft of Kelp," cast ashore by a "lonely" sea, may, paradoxically, be both purer and more bitter for the experience of sea and shore.

Poetic art and philosophical musings are other contexts. "The Aeolian Harp" wails as sea winds pass across its strings, its sound like Ariel's versions of reality in *The Tempest* (1623). The poem goes on to compare this artistic rendering with reality itself, a ship's sighting of a wreck: a drifting, waterlogged lumber schooner, which while it cannot sink, is a perpetually shifting danger to all others. The wailing harp expresses, as language cannot, the awful thoughts evoked by this symbol. As seen in a dream in "The Berg," a vessel of war, as if deliberately steered, crashes headlong into an iceberg and immediately sinks. This disaster, apparently caused by human irrationality, has hardly the slightest effect on the cold iceberg, a symbol of natural and perhaps metaphysical indifference to human events, as is "The Maldive Shark." That poem implies the speaker's horror at instinctual voraciousness, embodied in the ravening white shark.

The seven parts of "Pebbles," evoking the questions and speculations with which Melville was concerned throughout his career, may be John Marr's coming to terms with paradoxicality. It praises the pitiless, implacable, inhuman sea, while finding in the seashore rosemary a symbol of healing. "Pebbles" ends a book that expresses in fewer than fifty pages of mature poetry the results of Melville's lifelong engagement with the sea. [*See also* MELVILLE'S POETRY OF THE SEA]

Haskell Springer

JOHNSON, IRVING [McCLURE] (1905–1991). Irving Johnson grew up on a farm in the Connecticut River valley of Massachusetts. Inspired by Jack London's* novels, he had an unswerving desire to go to sea and work with his hands. Johnson spent summers working aboard yachts along the New England coast. In 1929 he and his friend Charles Brodhead went to Germany and signed on board the four-masted bark *Peking* for an 11,000-mile voyage around Cape Horn* to Chile. Johnson's first book, *Round the Horn in a Square-Rigger* (1932), tells of the storm-beset trip. The book was later republished with an afterword entitled "Forty-Eight Years Later" as *The Peking Battles Cape Horn* (1977; with additions, 1995). Johnson lectured with film footage from the voyage for many years; the footage was made into the narrated film *Around Cape Horn* in 1980.

In 1930 Johnson sailed across the Atlantic on the *Shamrock V*, the fifth of the *Shamrocks* with which Sir Thomas Lipton had attempted to win the America's Cup. It was a wild and stormy trip. Johnson returned home on the schooner *Wander Bird*, where he met his future wife, Electa Search ("Exy," 1909–   ), who was sailing as a college friend of the captain's wife. Johnson's two crossings of the Atlantic are recorded in Shamrock V's *Wild Voyage Home* (1933).

Irving and Exy Johnson dreamed of buying their own vessel and sailing around the world. In 1933 they bought a topsail schooner that they renamed *Yankee*.* With a crew of young men and women, they made three eighteen-month voyages around the world; the first two voyages are narrated in *Westward Bound in the Schooner* Yankee (1936) and *Sailing to See: Picture Cruise in the Schooner* Yankee (1939). Perhaps the best of their books, *Westward Bound* expresses a sense of freshness and wonder because of the uniqueness and uncertainty of what the Johnsons were undertaking.

Johnson joined the U.S. Navy in 1941 and spent three years during World

War II aboard the survey ship *Sumner*, charting the islands and waters of the South Pacific. After the war, he and Exy bought an English prize of war, the last pilot schooner built by the Germans before steam took over. They rigged it as a brigantine, named it *Yankee*, and sailed it four times around the world. Yankee's *Wander World: Circling the Globe in the Brigantine* Yankee (1949) describes the first of these voyages (called the "fourth" voyage). With Lydia Edes, the Johnsons wrote an account of the "sixth" voyage, Yankee's *People and Places* (1955).

The Johnsons' last vessel, the ketch *Yankee*, was designed with folding masts and an extrastrong keel so it could be taken through locks and into waters wracked by strong tides. Aboard this ketch, the Johnsons traversed Europe's inland waterways many times and sailed up the Nile before the Aswan High Dam was built; Yankee *Sails across Europe* (1962) and Yankee *Sails the Nile* (1966) record their adventures.

After selling the *Yankee*, the Johnsons continued their sea explorations on vessels owned by friends. In 1984 *National Geographic* produced a special entitled "Irving Johnson: High Seas Adventurer." [*See also* CIRCUMNAVIGATIONS AND BLUE-WATER PASSAGES; CRUISING LITERATURE]

Mary K. Bercaw Edwards

JOINING THE NAVY, OR ABROAD WITH UNCLE SAM (1895). *Joining the Navy* is an autobiographical travel narrative written by African American* enlisted sailor John Henry Paynter (1862–1947). This work describes Paynter's experiences as a cabin boy, first on the man-of-war *Ossipee* and later on the *Juniata*. After graduating from Lincoln University in Pennsylvania, Paynter had planned to attend medical school at Howard University, but failing eyesight forced him to abandon this plan. Because of limited employment opportunities for educated blacks and because of his desire to travel abroad, Paynter enlisted in the U.S. Navy in 1884.

Paynter's narrative primarily addresses his two years at sea with the navy, ending abruptly with his discharge in late 1885. His detailed observations of everyday life in the navy are mingled with meditations on human nature and the state of race relations in the United States. He often uses descriptions of the sea as metaphors for these reflections.

Paynter's purpose, as stated in his preface, is to inspire "the youths of our race to cultivate a desire for that broad experience which depends so much on travel." His cruise took him from the East Coast of the United States to the Azores, then to the Mediterranean Sea and through the Suez Canal to the Red Sea. In the Eastern Pacific he transferred to the *Juniata* for its homeward journey, returning to the United States by way of the Cape of Good Hope. During his travels, he interacted with Caribbean,* European, Asian, and African cultures. His description of these visits is often conflicted, as his generally pro-American sentiment is tempered by an awareness of his own marginalized status in a country and a navy that subscribe to racial discrimination. A second edition of *Joining the Navy*, published in 1911, contains a foreword by the African American writer and scholar W.E.B. Du Bois.

Charles F. Warner

JONES, JOHN PAUL (1747–1792). Born in Scotland, John Paul went to sea as an apprentice at age twelve. After inheriting property in Virginia, he added "Jones" to his name and became a lieutenant in the Continental navy in 1775. His was the first vessel to fly the Continental flag. After reporting to the commissioners at Paris, Jones raided British ports, harried British shipping, and captured ships, including the warship *Drake*. Given a worn-out merchantman, he renamed it *Bonhomme Richard** in honor of Benjamin Franklin and captured seventeen prizes off the coasts of Ireland and Scotland in 1779. His attack on a large British convoy escorted by the frigate *Serapis** and a smaller warship began a famous naval battle. He refused to surrender even when his outclassed ship was on fire, uttering a line that became famous: "I have not yet begun to fight." Finally victorious, he took enough prisoners to exchange for all the Americans then in British prisons.

After the Revolution, Jones worked to get his crew and himself paid for the prizes they had taken. With Thomas Jefferson's blessing, he briefly commanded the fleet of Catherine the Great in the Russo-Turkish War of 1788–1789. He had just been appointed to negotiate for the release of Americans captured by Algerian pirates when he died in Paris. Jones appears as a character in James Fenimore Cooper's* novel *The Pilot** (1824) and in Herman Melville's* novel *Israel Potter* (1855).

Cooper's biography of Jones, written with the aid of Jones' niece, was printed in his *Lives of Distinguished American Naval Officers* (1846). Samuel Eliot Morison's 1959 biography ignored Cooper's work and reproduced errors coming from the work of Alexander Slidell Mackenzie* (1841), commander of the *Somers*.* Other biographical material is found in Anna De Koven, *Life and Letters of John Paul Jones* (1913), F. A. Golder, *John Paul Jones in Russia* (1927), Lincoln Lorenz, *John Paul Jones* (1943), and Gerald W. Johnson, *The First Captain* (1947). [*See also* FANNING, NATHANIEL]

Kay Seymour House

[JONES, JUSTIN] "HARRY HAZEL" (1814–1889). Justin Jones, who wrote under the pseudonym Harry Hazel, authored more than forty dime novels about Boston, war, life at sea, and other adventure. His career as a fiction writer covered the 1840s and 1850s, for the most part, although he edited a newspaper as early as 1834 and issued a weekly story paper during and after the Civil War.

Little is known of Jones' early life. Born in 1814 in Brunswick, Maine, he was obviously a New England resident, as an early record indicates that he was printer of the weekly *Hartford Pearl and Literary Gazette* from August to October 1834. The following month, the name of the paper was changed to the *Boston Pearl and Literary Gazette*, a venture that survived until September 1835. In 1844 Jones was printer for a children's book, *Sam Squab, the Boston Boy*. That same year, he began to use the name Harry Hazel for a series of short fictional works (all of approximately 100 pages).

Jones preceded the widespread popularity of the dime novel with his fast-paced adventure romances, eighteen of which had a naval or nautical theme. His first sea story was *The Corsair, or the Foundling of the Sea, an American Romance* (1846), followed the next year by *The Pirate's Daughter, or, The Rovers of the Atlantic* and *Fourpe Tap, or, The Middy of the Macedonian: in Which Is Contained the Concluding Incidents in the Eventful Career of Big Dick, King of the Negroes*. Jones continued his adventure writing at a prodigious rate: in 1853 alone, he published six sea tales, including *Flying Yankees* and *Harry Tempest*. His books covered life at sea, the American Revolution, pirates,* smuggling, privateering, and the War of 1812. His last book was *The Doomed Ship* (1864), a tale of shipwreck* and rescue in the Arctic.*

Jones used the name "Harry Hazel" in a story paper he published in Boston as early as 1852. *Harry Hazel's Yankee Blade* promised a new story each week, and Jones was still printing the inexpensive paper during the war. Apart from the Harry Hazel publications, Jones left little record of his life, but his contribution as a dime novelist before 1860, when the genre developed its vast popularity, placed him ahead of his time. [*See also* NINETEENTH-CENTURY PERIODICALS]

Boyd Childress

JOURNALS AND LOGBOOKS. The terms "journal" and "logbook" are often used interchangeably to describe chronological accounts kept during the course of a sea voyage, but important differences distinguish them. A logbook is the official record of a ship's whereabouts and activities, required by law and surrendered to the owners at the end of a voyage. Journals are personal diaries and as such can be kept by anyone on board; they often contain material extraneous to the ship's business, including descriptions of shipboard activities and ports of call, illustrations, poems, song texts, and scientific observations.

The publication of shipboard accounts began in earnest in England in 1697 with the buccaneer William Dampier's *A New Voyage round the World*. Two influential shipboard journals penned by Dampier's associates followed: Woodes Rogers' *A Cruising Voyage round the World* (1712) and Edward Cooke's *A Voyage to the South Sea, and round the World* (1712). These three works inspired Daniel Defoe and Jonathan Swift in the development

of *Robinson Crusoe* (1719) and *Gulliver's Travels* (1726), both of which claimed to be actual shipboard journals.

The official "narratives" of British Naval Expeditions to the Pacific Ocean in the late eighteenth century were among the best-read books of the age in England and America. These works, though based on shipboard accounts and preserving their chronological format, were substantially edited before publication—a process that made native people of the Pacific more exotic and English sailors more heroic. The appearance of Richard Henry Dana Jr.'s* *Two Years before the Mast** in 1840 introduced not only an American perspective of shipboard life but the point of view of the forecastle rather than the quarter deck. Extremely popular, Dana's book inspired a rush of sailor imitators, among them Samuel Leech with his *Thirty Years from Home, or A Voice from the Main Deck* (1843) and *Twenty Years before the Mast* (1845) by Nicholas Isaacs. The manuscript that Dana kept aboard the *Pilgrim* and the *Alert* disappeared with his sea chest on his return to Boston and was painstakingly reconstructed after the voyage, but, in fact, few sailors presented their shipboard accounts to the public without some retrospective editing. Defoe even has Robinson Crusoe explain that portions of his narrative will be more interesting with some postvoyage reflection and gives an example of before and after editing to prove his point. The influence of Dana reached into the world of fiction as well, and James Fenimore Cooper,* Herman Melville,* and Edgar Allan Poe,* among others, experimented with fictional accounts of voyages presented as journals. Melville did not discourage the readers of his early novels from thinking of them as autobiographical shipboard accounts rather than well-researched and elaborately crafted works of fiction.

A number of voyage accounts were published to introduce young men to either the folly or the glory of seafaring, and some became religious treatises. An example of the latter is Mary Chipman Lawrence's journal of a Pacific Ocean whaling voyage with her husband, which was edited by Mrs. Helen E. Brown into *A Good Catch: or, Mrs. Emerson's Whaling-Cruise* (1884). In the middle of the twentieth century, with their authors long dead, a number of journals and logbooks began to be published from manuscripts in museum and library collections. Generally presented without the heavy editorial hand that romanticized the sea voyage for the eighteenth- and nineteenth-century audience, these works describe in detail the daily repetitive tasks and cyclical nature of shipboard life.

The publication of such manuscripts has made available for the first time the perspectives of numerous women, including the aforementioned Mary Chipman Lawrence, whose journal was published as *The Captain's Best Mate* (1966), with valuable additional material provided by editor Stanton Garner; this work is substantially different from Mrs. Brown's 1884 version of Lawrence's experiences. A large number of unpublished manuscript journals and logbooks survive, the most numerous being whaling journals, of which

more than 5,000 are held by maritime museums and libraries. [*See also* VOY-AGE NARRATIVES; WHALING NARRATIVES; WOMEN AT SEA]

FURTHER READING: Forster, Honore. *The South Sea Whaler*. Sharon, MA: Kendall Whaling Museum, 1985; Forster, Honore. *More South Sea Whaling*. Canberra: School for Pacific Studies, 1991; Sherman, Stuart. *The Voice of the Whaleman*. Providence, RI: Public Library, 1965; Sherman, Stuart, et al. *Whaling Logbooks and Journals*. New York: Garland, 1986.

Mary Malloy

[JUDSON, EDWARD ZANE CARROLL], "NED BUNTLINE"

(1823–1886). Edward Zane Carroll Judson, better known by his pseudonym Ned Buntline, was born on the Atlantic coast in Stamford, New York. The family moved to Bethany, Pennsylvania, and then to Philadelphia about the time Judson was a teenager. The docks of this port impressed him, and the feeling that he got the first day aboard ship would stay with him for the rest of his life. Running away to sea, he became a cabin boy for the U.S. Navy, then received his commission in 1838 for his efforts in a drowning rescue. His seagoing gave him the opportunity to explore New York, New Orleans, Charleston, the Caribbean,* and many other ports.

At twenty-one he left the navy to fight in the Seminole War. Living in Cincinnati, Ohio, he established a magazine under the name "Ned Buntline." His intense relationship with the sea determined his choice of name: buntlines are the lines attached to the bottom edges of square sails by which they could be hauled up for furling. This relationship is also responsible for the maritime theme in his writing. His years at sea provided him with material for his many eccentric picaresque stories and adventures. His first story, "The Captain's Pig" (published in *Cruisings, Afloat and Ashore, from the Private Log of Ned Buntline*, 1848), was based on a real event; this story delighted readers with a comic narration of how the captain of his ship was ready to eat the pig he had brought on board, before Buntline tricked the captain and ate the pig himself.

Judson had some legal problems before settling in New York, where he became impressed with the port and its vessels. He would devote almost the rest of his life to writing dime novels, a narrative genre that he is credited with originating. These works were tales of violent action, usually written hastily and sold cheaply as serials, mostly centering on activities at sea.

Judson's relationship with William Frederick Cody, better known as "Buffalo Bill," whom he met during the Civil War, has frequently been overstated. Judson claimed to have invented Cody's nickname and to have devoted his life to writing fiction and nonfiction about Cody's deeds and about the rivers of the plains. The truth is that Judson wrote a mere dozen stories in which Buffalo Bill is the hero and that Cody had acquired his nickname before the two met.

Judson, however, did know rivers as deeply as he knew the sea and en-

joyed fishing and traveling up the Hudson River on his own yacht. Many of the titles of his last books, such as *The Naval Detective's Chase; or, Nick, the Steeple Climber, a Thrilling Tale of Real Life*, published posthumously in 1889, show that late in life he was still focusing on the sea. Judson's rousing and sensational style has been compared to sea yarns of James Fenimore Cooper,* Frederick Marryat, and pulp-fiction writers of his day, as well as to the showmanship and high jinks of P. T. Barnum. Other titles of note in his extensive canon, which today are possessed only by a few large libraries or by nostalgia buffs, include *Elfrida, the Red Rover's Daughter, a New Mystery of New York* (1860), republished as *Andros, the Free Rover; or, The Pirate's Daughter* (1883); *The Shell-Hunter; or, An Ocean Love-Chase: A Romance of Love and Sea* (1858); *Harry Bluff, The Reefer; or, Love and Glory on the Sea* (1890); *Harry Halyard's* Ruin: A True Tale for the Intemperate to Read* (c.1850–1870); and *Long Tom Dart, the Yankee Privateer: A New Naval Story of the War of 1812* (1891).

FURTHER READING: Monaghan, James. *The Great Rascal: The Life and Adventures of Ned Buntline*. New York: Bonanza, 1952; Rosenberg, Jack. *Legends of Ned Buntline*. Berkeley: U of California P, 1969; Russell, Don. *The Lives and Legends of Buffalo Bill: A Study in Heroics*. Norman: U of Oklahoma P, 1929.

Margarita Rigal-Aragón

JUVENILE LITERATURE. The first books written expressly for adolescent readers were intended to shape the morals of the young. However, religious tracts and cautionary tales held little appeal for minds eager for adventure and realism. Young readers in the mid-nineteenth century turned to authors such as James Fenimore Cooper,* who wrote exciting books and lived exciting lives.

Cooper's sea stories, including *The Pilot** (1824), *The Red Rover** (1827), and *The Wing-and-Wing* (1842), were early adopted by young readers as their own; Cooper's books remained on lists for children into the twentieth century. When *Two Years before the Mast** (1840) by Richard Henry Dana Jr.,* was published, children claimed it as well. Herman Melville's* *Redburn: His First Voyage** (1849) was based on Melville's merchant marine experiences. Jack London's* *Cruise of the* Dazzler (1903) and *The Sea-Wolf** (1904) became equally popular.

A little-known American author indirectly inspired Robert Louis Stevenson's *Treasure Island* (1883). James F. Bowman, an editor of the *San Francisco Chronicle*, wrote *The Island Home; or, The Young Castaways* (1851). It served as a model for *The Coral Island* (1858) by Robert Michael Ballantyne, a Scot. The favorite author of young Stevenson, Ballantyne influenced his life and writings.

Realistic stories for children gained acceptance between 1850 and 1900. A flood of books poured out to eager readers. William Taylor Adams,* a New England teacher and children's magazine editor writing as "Oliver Optic," produced over 116 books from 1855 to 1910. At least half of these related to the sea or sailing, beginning with *The Boat Club; a Tale for Boys* (1855). Other Optic titles include *The Sailor Boy; or, Jack Somers in the Navy* (1865), *Cringle and Crosstree; or, the Sea Swashes of a Sailor* (1870), and *The Dorcas Club; or, Our Girls Afloat* (1875).

Series books in the late nineteenth and early twentieth centuries included large numbers of sea tales. Another prolific children's author, Edward L. Stratemeyer, wrote the Ship and Shore series, including *The Last Cruise of the* Spitfire (1894) and, writing as "Arthur M. Winfield," *The Rover Boys on the Ocean* (1899). Some children's authors wrote from personal experience. Charles Fosdick, writing as "Harry Castlemon," drew on his years in the navy when writing *Frank on a Gunboat* (1864) and other books in the Gunboat series.

Pirate* stories held a special fascination for the young. Frank R. Stockton's* *Buccaneers and Pirates of Our Coast* (1898) and *Howard Pyle's* Book of Pirates* (1921) are enduring examples of tales of real pirates. Pyle, who illustrated his books, ranks among the best of American illustrators.

Over 300 magazines for children were started in the United States from 1800 to 1900. About forty were still publishing at the turn of the century. As some ceased publication, new ones began. *St. Nicholas Magazine*, published from 1873 to 1939, introduced children to many authors of sea literature. Tales of shipwrecks* and sea journeys, articles on shipbuilding, sailing, seamanship, sea animals, and weather were all part of the appeal that carried *St. Nicholas* into the twentieth century. London's *Cruise of the* Dazzler appeared there in 1902. Stockton contributed often. Pyle's historical novel in which the pirate Blackbeard is a central character, *Jack Ballister's Fortunes* (1895), was first published there.

Changing attitudes toward children's books were apparent by 1920. Publishers established separate children's departments. Children's Book Week was celebrated nationally in 1922, and the first John Newbery Medal for the Most Distinguished Contribution to American Literature for Children, awarded that year, focused attention on children's literature.

Charles Boardman Hawes was awarded the Newbery Medal posthumously in 1924 for *The Dark Frigate* (1923). His sea stories include *The Mutineers* (1920) and *The Great Quest* (1921). Newbery winner Armstrong Sperry, whose novel *Call It Courage* (1940) received the medal in 1941, sailed by schooner to Tahiti as a young man, and his books *Hull Down for Action* (1945) and *Storm Canvas* (1944) reflect the experience of that and succeeding journeys. When Howard Pease, a writer of adventure stories, needed new material, he shipped out as crew on a freighter. His books *The Tattooed Man* (1926), *Secret Cargo* (1931), and *Black Tanker* (1941) all contain central mysteries. So, too, does *Ice to India* (1955) by Keith Robertson, about a colorful villain, a dangerous mission, and a boy's initiation into seamanship.

The Seashore Book (1912) by E. Boyd Smith offered information through pictures and text of ships, shipyards, shipwrecks, and whaling. *I Like Diving* (1929) by Tom Eadie, a professional diver, and *On the Bottom* (1929) by Edward Ellsberg,* a naval commander, were accounts of the raising of the submarine the *S-51.* Random House in the popular Landmark Series of nonfiction books covered years of naval history, including *Clipper Ship Days* (1952) by John Jennings,* *The* Monitor *and the* Merrimack* (1951) by Fletcher Pratt, *The Sinking of the* Bismarck (1962) by Richard Neuberger, *John F. Kennedy and PT 109* (1962) by Richard Tregaskis, and *Battle for the Atlantic* (1953) by Jay Williams.

By mid-twentieth century the growth of children's libraries and the variety of children's books created an ever-growing population of readers. Picture books for young children, mostly imported from Europe before 1930, increasingly were published in America. New printing methods improved the process. In 1938 the Caldecott Medal for the most distinguished picture book of the year was established.

Holling C. Holling, with his wife, Lucille, wrote and illustrated *Seabird* (1948) and *Pagoo* (1957), the adventures of a hermit crab. Perhaps best known is *Paddle-to-the-Sea* (1941), the story of a carved wooden boat as it travels from the Great Lakes* to the ocean. Holling's full-page watercolor illustrations and Lucille's highly informative border drawings make the books exceptional.

In 1958 the Caldecott Medal was awarded to Robert McCloskey for *Time of Wonder* (1957), a beautiful, highly evocative picture story of an approaching storm on the island where the McCloskey family spent their summers. McCloskey's *Bert Dow, Deep Water Man* (1963) and *One Morning in Maine* (1952) also take place there. *Luther Tarbox* (1977) is a rollicking tale about a lobsterman by Jan Adkins, who, like McCloskey, illustrated his own books. Adkins also produced *The Craft of Sail* (1973) and *Wooden Ship* (1978).

As the age of sail receded into memory, authors based sea fiction on historical events of that era. Cornelia Meigs, descendant of naval heroes, set *The Trade Wind* (1926) just before the American Revolution and *Clearing Weather* (1928) just after. The northern blockade of southern ports during the Civil War is the setting for Stephen Meader's historical novel *Phantom of the Blockade* (1962). Eric Haugaard's *Orphans of the Wind* (1966) is set at the time of the American Civil War. In *The Death of* Evening Star (1972), Leonard Fisher re-created strange events aboard a whaling ship through the diary of a ship's "boy."

Biography and fictional biography chronicle lives of seamen, naval heroes, pirates, and explorers for young readers. In 1956 Jean Latham was awarded the Newbery Medal for *Carry On, Mr. Bowditch* (1955), the story of Nathaniel Bowditch,* who, bound out to sea at the age of twelve, became a scientist, mathematician, and author of the standard guide for modern navigation.

Media coverage popularized some books. *A Night to Remember* (1955) by Walter Lord, about the sinking of the *Titanic*,* was popular with young readers, and *Exploring the* Titanic (1991) by Robert Ballard was published at several reading levels. The round-the-world journey of sixteen-year-old Robin Lee Graham in his sloop *Dove*, covered by *National Geographic*, attracted young readers to *Dove* (1972), which was adapted to film in 1974. *Reading Rainbow*, a television program for children, featured books about the sea, including *The Little Red Lighthouse* and the Great Grey Bridge* (1974) by Hildegarde Swift, *Keep the Lights Burning, Abbie* (1985) by Peter and Connie Roop, and *Sailing with the Wind* (1986) by Thomas Locker.

Gary Paulsen, twice Newbery winner, chronicled a boy's survival at sea in *The Voyage of the Frog* (1989). Theodore Taylor wrote of shipwrecks and sea adventure in *The Cay* (1969), *Timothy of the Cay* (1993), *Teetoncey* (1974), and *The Odyssey of Ben O'Neal* (1977). Katherine Paterson depicted the life of the Chesapeake watermen in *Jacob Have I Loved* (1985).

Traditionally, girls accepted male protagonists, but boys avoided books with girls as main characters. A milestone was reached when boys and girls clamored to read *The True Adventures of Charlotte Doyle* (1990) by Avi, the exciting adventures of a girl's Atlantic crossing. It received the Newbery Medal, as did Scott O'Dell's *Island of the Blue Dolphins* (1960), which also features a female protagonist, a shipwrecked Indian girl who survives for years on a Pacific island.

In the 1980s and 1990s concern for the ocean environment replaced the lure of the sea adventure. *The Voyage of the* Mimi, a television series with computer software, a book, *Voyage of the* Mimi (1985), and curriculum for schools, successfully combined oceanography, adventure, and ecology. Recent juvenile titles on a maritime theme include Steve Schuch's *A Symphony of Whales* (1999), about how 3,000 beluga whales trapped in the Bering Strait were saved, and Joseph Brodsky's poem *Discovery* (1999), about America's earliest explorers: fish, birds, and men.

FURTHER READING: Bingham, Jane. *Fifteen Centuries of Children's Books.* Westport, CT: Greenwood, 1980; Collier, Laurie, and Joyce Nakamura. *Major Authors and Illustrators for Children and Young Adults.* Detroit: Gale 1993; Smith, Myron J., Jr., and Robert C. Weller. *Sea Fiction Guide.* Metuchen, NJ: Scarecrow, 1976.

Ann M. Ouellette

K

KENNEY, SUSAN [McILVAINE] (1941–   ). Born in Summit, New Jersey, Susan Kenney teaches at Colby College and has written two works with nautical themes: *Sailing* (1989) and *One Fell Sloop* (1990). Both are based on her experiences steering boats and her apprehension about sailing. *Sailing* follows middle-aged Sara and Phil Boyd in their purchase and sailing of a twenty-year-old sloop. Though she herself takes no pleasure in sailing, to Sara the boat symbolizes a gift of hope and renewed life that she can give Phil, who is ailing with cancer. To Phil, the boat symbolizes self-discovery and control over his destiny; his final voyage alone is a literal one. Sailing becomes a metaphor for the best the married couple can know about each other and about their relationship. *One Fell Sloop*, set in the waters near a coastal island in Maine's Penobscot Bay, is a nautical mystery that includes a chase and rescue at sea.

Mira Dock

KENT, ROCKWELL (1882–1971). Rockwell Kent, painter, writer, adventurer, graphic artist, and political activist, was born in Tarrytown Heights, New Jersey. He trained as an architect at Columbia University and studied painting under William Merritt Chase, Robert Henri, Abbott Thayer, and Kenneth Hayes Miller. In 1905 Henri introduced the young socialist to the rugged cliffs of Monhegan Island, off the Maine coast. Kent lived there for a time, painting, reading, lobstering, building houses, doing odd jobs, and gaining an affinity for the sea that is reflected in his travels, art, and writing.

He had made two trips to Newfoundland before going to Alaska in 1918. In Resurrection Bay near Seward, Alaska, Kent lived on Fox Island with his nine-year-old son and an old Swede who ran a fox and goat ranch. Kent and his son often rowed the twelve miles from town to the island that winter, nearly swamping amid cross currents and squalls. The result of this Alaskan sojourn was his first book, *Wilderness: A Journal of Quiet Adventure in Alaska* (1920), based on his letters and journals. Two New York shows that exhibited his Alaska artwork initiated his rise to fame.

Kent's next sea adventure took him to Chile, where he bought an old lifeboat for twenty-five dollars, named it *Kathleen* after his wife, and prepared it for a sail round Cape Horn.* Kent eventually attempted the venture in another small sloop, but, due to poor weather, made it only into Franklin Sound. He told that story in his second illustrated book, *Voyaging Southward from the Strait of Magellan* (1924). In 1948 Kent illustrated *A Treasury of Sea Stories* and included an evocative sketch of Joshua Slocum* rounding Cape Horn in the *Spray.*

Kent's best-known illustrated book, *N by E* (1930), chronicles his sail to Greenland in the thirty-three-foot *Direction*, the first yacht from America ever to attempt such a voyage. He describes the boat's stormy wreck in a windswept fjord, his overland trek to seek help for the three-man crew, and his painting in Greenland. The history of the *Direction* as well as some of the story that Kent omitted are told in *The Saga of* Direction: *A Cruising Cutter's First Fifty Years* (1978) by Charles H. Vilas. Later trips to Greenland resulted in two more illustrated books, *Salamina* (1935) and *Rockwell Kent's Greenland Journal* (1962).

During the *Direction* voyage, Kent was finishing one of his most ambitious projects, the three-volume Lakeside Press edition of *Moby-Dick** (1930). When the project began in 1926, editors gave Kent not only his choice of books to illustrate but also carte blanche regarding design details. With its 280 illustrations, the book is considered one of the finest produced in this country and contains the most complex illustrations of Herman Melville's* classic novel. Young William Faulkner* was so impressed with Kent's work that he bought an illustration of Ahab* from him, which remained on the wall of his Rowan Oak library the rest of his life. The drawings induced Sterling Hayden* to run away to sea, subsequently dedicating his autobiography, *Wanderer* (1963), to Kent and to another sailing radical, Warwick Tompkins. Elizabeth Schultz devotes an entire chapter to Kent's illustrations in her book *Unpainted to the Last*: Moby-Dick *and Twentieth-Century American Art* (1995).

Always associated with radical causes, Kent was subpoenaed by Senator Joseph McCarthy in 1953, whose committee was intent on destroying several of Kent's "subversive" books housed in overseas government libraries, including *Wilderness* and *N by E.* This incident and the popularity of abstract expressionist style over Kent's dramatic realism damaged his reputation and reduced his ability to obtain the commercial work that he depended to finance his painting.

More recently, Kent's artistic reputation is on the rise, along with that of other American realists such as Winslow Homer and Edward Hopper. Kent even appears as a character in Jane Urquhart's* novel *The Underpainter*, the fictional memoirs of a minimalist painter who became Kent's friend and also studied under Robert Henri. [*See also* THE ARCTIC; CRUISING LITERATURE]

FURTHER READING: Johnson, Fridolf, ed. *Rockwell Kent: An Anthology of His Works*. New York: Knopf, 1981; Kent, Rockwell. *It's Me O Lord*. New York: Dodd, Mead, 1955; Traxel, David. *An American Saga: The Life and Times of Rockwell Kent*. New York: Harper and Row, 1980.

Doug Capra

KESEY, KEN [ELTON] (1935–   ). Ken Kesey was born in La Junta, Colorado, and soon moved to Oregon, where he now lives. He developed a love of hunting and fishing as a child, and much of his writing employs the lush natural settings and small towns of the Pacific Northwest*as fitting places for discussions of the economic exploitation and potential barbarity of the institutionalized management of natural resources, communities, and people.

Near the end of Kesey's *One Flew over the Cuckoo's Nest* (1962), the protagonist, Randle McMurphy, leads a band of inmates from a mental hospital on a fishing trip off the Oregon coast. This trip provides the inmates with a renewed sense of the "normal" world from which they have been exiled and concludes with their doctor's catching an abnormally large flounder. The trip provides the inmates with a sense of community and freedom that is contrasted with the strictures of the institution from which they have escaped. It has been suggested that the flounder represents, among other possibilities, the inmates' long-denied opportunity to liberate themselves from their problems and to expand their spirits and horizons. The 1975 film adaptation starred Jack Nicholson.

Kesey's later novel *Sailor Song* (1992) is set in a remote fishing village in Alaska and includes a colorful cast of characters, most of whom make their living from fishing. When the son of one of the town's leading citizens invades the community with a Hollywood camera crew intent on filming a famous children's story about a Native American tribe, conflict ensues between those eager for the economic boom that the film will surely provide and those who suspect more sinister motives behind the filmmakers' presence. Much of the book's action takes place on luxurious yachts moving up and down the Alaskan coast. Omnipresent in the novel is a double vision of the sea as both a place of destruction and one of overwhelming fecundity. [*See also* AMERICAN INDIAN LITERATURE OF THE SEA]

Christopher Lee

KEY WEST LITERATURE. Key West, Florida, occupies a singular place in American geography and letters. Though just a tiny island (one mile by three in area, population 25,000, twenty-two feet at its highest point) at the southernmost end of U.S. Highway 1, one of forty-two other dots making up the Florida Keys, its secluded, but strategic, location and its tropical allure have not only inspired a number of notable works, such as Ernest Hemingway's* *To Have and Have Not* (1937) and Wallace Stevens'* widely anthologized poem "The Idea of Order in Key West" (1935), but also aided its development as a literary gathering place and home to many well-known writers over the course of the twentieth century.

The earliest known mention of Key West in literature appears in the journals of naturalist John James Audubon* ("Death of a Pirate," in *Ornithological Biography*, 1832). A minor sea novel by James Fenimore Cooper* is *Jack Tier* (1847), whose protagonist is assigned to a navy ship that spends some time in the waters near Fort Jefferson in the Dry Tortugas, some seventy miles west of Key West. Fort Jefferson, begun as a Mexican War fortification in 1846, was completed on the eve of the Civil War. Soon a federal prison, its most notable inmate was Dr. Samuel Mudd, the doctor who set John Wilkes Booth's broken leg following the Lincoln assassination.

However, the development of Key West in American letters came relatively late. Novelist John Dos Passos, who visited Key West in the early 1920s and was taken by the easy availability of Prohibition-era liquor as well as the bountiful big-game fishing in the nearby Gulf Stream, is generally credited with popularizing the island with other writers. Though Hemingway, who went to Key West at Dos Passos' behest and lived there from 1928 until 1939, has become most synonymous with the place and its rough-and-tumble qualities, other notable residents drawn during the first half of the twentieth century include Stevens, Robert Frost,* Thornton Wilder, Archibald MacLeish,* Elizabeth Bishop,* and Tennessee Williams.*

While many of these writers were content primarily to live in, and enjoy, Key West, a number were to make substantive use of characteristic themes and aspects of the place in their works: a number of the poems in Bishop's first collection, *North and South* (1946), examine tropical sensuality and life on the sea; Stevens' poem is an intense meditation on the interaction between the mythic nature of the tropics and the writer's ordering consciousness; and Hemingway's first "Key West" novel, *To Have and Have Not* (1937), concerns the efforts of maverick Harry Morgan to run rum and Chinese nationals into Cuba. While there is no record of the ill-fated Hart Crane's* ever having lived in Key West, a number of his poems composed in 1930–1932 and intended for publication in a volume entitled *Key West* suggest, at the very least, his intimate knowledge of, and fascination with, the place.

Such constants as the surrounding waters, the relative solitude, the tropical lassitude and languor (and the attendant, inexorable decay), the natural beauties of sun and sea, and the mystical quality of "island-ness" are observed by nearly all the writers who have set work here. As a town situated literally at "the end of the line," as well as at the edge of the continent, Key

West has also attracted its share of drifters and grifters, outlaws and outcasts, immigrants and dreamers. One of the most notorious of the many con men in Key West history, New Deal relief official Julius F. Stone was immortalized in Hemingway's *To Have and Have Not* as latter-day carpetbagger Frederic Harrison. Much of the work produced by writers during the second half of the twentieth century reflects a characteristic sense of cultural diversity, individualism, and, often, outright suspicion of such concepts as governmental regulation, societal convention, even law and order.

Possibly the best-known Key West novel of this era is Thomas McGuane's *Ninety-two in the Shade* (1973), the story of a young man's effort to regain his sense of identity by returning to the quirky, but bountiful, place of his formative years. Perhaps the most ambitious is Thomas Sanchez's *Mile Zero* (1989), a sprawling epic that details the development of the island from its very beginnings, including the lives of slave traders, pirates,* sponge divers, cigar makers, turtlers, shark hunters, and other colorful types who are part of the mythos of the place.

McGuane set another book in Key West, *Panama* (1978). Other contemporary novelists who have made use of the place include Jim Harrison in *A Good Day to Die* (1973), David Kaufelt in *American Tropic* (1986), and Alison Lurie in *The Truth about Lorin Jones* (1988) and *The Last Resort* (1998). Recently, mystery novelists have been drawn to the island, notably James W. Hall (*Bones of Coral* [1991]), John Leslie (*Killing Me Softly* [1994]; *Night and Day* [1995]), Tom Corcoran (*Mango Opera* [1998]), and Laurence Shames (*Mangrove Squeeze* [1998]).

In addition, highly regarded fiction writer Joy Williams (*Escapes* [1989]) has set several of her short stories in Key West, and John Hersey* (*Key West Tales* [1994]) did the same; nonfiction writers Hunter S. Thompson (*A Generation of Swine* [1988]) and Jonathan Raban (*Hunting Mister Heartbreak* [1991]) found much on the island for their idiosyncratic turns of mind to ponder. Many of the country's finest poets, including John Ciardi, John Malcolm Brinnin, James Merrill, Judith Kazantzis, and national laureate Richard Wilbur have lived and set work there over the past half century.

Though writers and residents of every stripe bemoan the ever-increasing pace of development within the fabled city, the ever-growing crowds of tourists, and the ever-diminishing returns from the sea itself, the sun still shines, the Gulf Stream still flows, and the island still rests at the veritable end of the road. So long as these verities hold, there is always likely to be a literature of Key West.

FURTHER READING: Altobello, Patricia, and Deirdre Pierce. *Literary Sands of Key West*. Washington, DC: Starrhill, 1996; Kaufelt, Lynn Mitsuko. *Key West Writers and Their Houses*. Englewood, FL: Pineapple, 1986; Murphy, George, ed. *The Key West Reader*. Key West. Tortugas, 1989; Williams, Joy. *The Florida Keys: A History and Guide*. New York: Random, 1986.

Les Standiford

KING, STEPHEN [EDWIN] (1947–   ). Although Stephen King sets much of his best-selling fiction in Maine, the New England coastal state of his birth and residence, he rarely writes about the sea. King has written dozens of horror, fantasy, and science fiction novels, novellas, short stories, and screenplays, including *Carrie* (1974; film adaptation 1976), *Pet Sematary* (1983; film adaptation 1989), *Tommyknockers* (1987; film adaptation 1993), and *Bag of Bones* (1998). Most of his works are best-sellers, and many have been made into major motion pictures.

"Survivor Type," first published in *Terrors* (1982), then later published in King's short story collection *Skeleton Crew* (1985), describes a ship-wrecked* man who resorts to eating himself. *Storm of the Century* (1999), produced as a television screenplay (1999) prior to publication, focuses on a fictional island and a lighthouse* off the coast of Maine that is hit simultaneously with a massive snowstorm and the appearance of an evil sorcerer named Linoge. King describes tidal storm surges that destroy fishing vessels, the town dock, and the lighthouse. If they will not comply with his wishes, Linoge threatens to force all of the islanders to walk to their death into the sea in the same way that he claims the members of the lost colony of Roanoke Island did.

Perhaps King owes his strongest maritime connection to his pseudonym, Richard Bachman, under which name he published five novels between 1977 and 1984. King created a biography for Bachman in which Bachman served for four years in the Coast Guard and ten years in the merchant marine. Stephen King's natural father served in the merchant marine as well.

Richard J. King

KÖEPF, MICHAEL (1940–   ). Born in San Mateo, California, Michael Köepf is the son of a commercial fisherman. He grew up fishing and draws on his experiences as a commercial fishing-vessel captain for his novel *The Fisherman's Son* (1998). The protagonist, Neil Kruger, is adrift in a raft off the California coast, his fishing boat wrecked and his brother killed by a comber. His recollections while he floats include his mother's displeasure at the fisherman's life, his father's fishing companions being lost at sea, and his own purchase of a fishing boat after his father's death. Dazed with hunger, exposure, and thirst, he imagines himself located by search parties.

An earlier novel, *Save the Whale* (1978), follows a Vietnam veteran whose whale-watching leads him to intrigue and danger from duping well-meaning environmentalists by collecting donations for a bogus Save the Whale campaign.

Mira Dock

L

LAFITTE, JEAN (c. 1780–c. 1826). Jean Lafitte was perhaps the most successful, colorful, and popular of all America-based pirates.* For a short time during the early years of the nineteenth century, he was one of the most powerful men in New Orleans, and when he disappeared around 1821, he sailed directly into myth and legend, becoming the central character in numerous novels, plays, and ballads.

Concerning Lafitte's early years there are conflicting stories. According to one, he was born in southwestern France, possibly Bayonne, and he is thought to have been the "Captain Lafette" of a French privateer that sailed into the Mississippi for repairs and provisions in 1804. More likely, however, Lafitte was born in Port-au-Prince, Haiti, in 1782 and moved to New Orleans after the French were expelled during the Haitian revolution of 1794. Sometime around 1805 he became the joint owner with his brother, Pierre, of a New Orleans blacksmith shop, where he traded in contraband brought in by smugglers and privateers. By 1810 Lafitte had established a base on Grand Terre, a secluded island in the Barataria Bay, and from there he commanded up to a dozen ships, which carried letters of marque from the republic of Cartegena to attack Spanish shipping throughout the gulf. All of the plunder was taken to Grand Terre, where it was loaded onto barges and taken into New Orleans. At the height of Lafitte's reign, up to a barge a day arrived in the city, and his pirated goods became a prominent part of the local merchant economy. Lafitte and his Baratarians were accused of attacking ships of all nations, but according to one report it was only after his smuggled goods threatened to monopolize the import trade that Governor Claiborne issued a warrant for Lafitte's arrest.

Lafitte is best known for his actions during the Battle of New Orleans. On 3 September 1814, three British officers approached Lafitte with an offer of money, lands, a pardon, and a commission if he helped their forces when they attacked New Orleans. Lafitte politely stalled and informed the American forces of the impending attack, offering the support of his followers in return for full pardons. Despite his offer, a combined force of the American army and navy raided Grand Terre on 16 September, seizing all ships, arresting Lafitte's followers, and destroying the settlement. Negotiations between Lafitte and the Americans continued, however, and on 17 December Governor Claiborne formally invited Lafitte and the Baratarians to assist the American forces in return for citizenship and full pardons. According to most historical sources, Lafitte and the Baratarians were crucial in the overwhelming American victory when the battle took place early on 8 January 1815.

Although many of his followers settled down to fish, trap, and trade, Lafitte became restless, and within two years he had established a new pirate base on Campeche, at the site of what is now Galveston, Texas. Again Lafitte and his band were accused of attacking ships indiscriminately, and throughout the gulf they were generally known as pirates, not privateers. On 22 September 1819, sixteen of Lafitte's followers were hanged in New Orleans for piracy, and later that year Lafitte was forced to hang one of his own men in order to pacify the Americans for a raid along the Louisiana coast. In 1821, after an American merchant ship was attacked, a military force sailed into Galveston Bay with orders to destroy Campeche. Rather than fight, Lafitte burned his village and sailed away. For several years more Lafitte sailed with his brother, Pierre, but little is known of their experiences. According to one report, Lafitte turned up in Charleston a decade or so later under the name John Lafflin, and for the next twenty years attempted various ventures, including the manufacture of gunpowder in St. Louis.

Lafitte was known as the "the Gentleman Pirate," and almost immediately following his disappearance in the 1820s popular narratives were published about his adventures. During the 1820s two anonymous novels appeared: *The Memoirs of Lafitte, or The Baratarian Pirate* (1826) and *Lafitte or The Baratarian Chief* (1828). Far more important was Joseph Holt Ingraham's* best-seller, *Lafitte, the Pirate of the Gulf* (1836), which Edgar Allan Poe* attacked in the *Southern Literary Messenger* for its romanticization of the pirate.

Throughout the nineteenth century Lafitte and his pirates continued to appear as a fascinating episode in America's past, and both historical texts and children's books inevitably mentioned their participation in the Battle of New Orleans, while rumors of pirate treasure circulated along the Louisiana coast. In the twentieth century Lafitte and his band appeared in two notable historical novels: Odell and Willard Shephard's *Holdfast Gaines* (1933) and Hervey Allen's *Anthony Adverse* (1946). In the former, Lafitte is depicted as the colorful, larger-than-life figure of romantic lore, while in the latter he is less attractive, more like a Cajun Napoleon of the swamps.

More recently, Lafitte has appeared as a ghostly presence in the Dave Robicheaux novels of James Lee Burke, particularly *Sunset Limited* (1998).

The historical Lafitte perceived himself a gentleman and took great pride in his manners and appearance, fiercely denying that he was a pirate, claiming that he was a merchant who only invested in privateering ventures against the Spanish. Despite his protestations, Lafitte became widely known as a pirate and a smuggler, and the romanticized literary character soon replaced the historical figure.

Daniel E. Williams

LAING, ALEXANDER [KINNAN] (1903–1976). Alexander Laing was the author of over twenty books of nautical fiction and history and a long-time librarian at Dartmouth College. Laing grew up in Great Neck, Long Island, New York, entered Dartmouth in 1921, and left in 1925 before completing his degree. In the fall of 1926 he found a position as a seaman aboard S.S. *Leviathan*; he spent several years working at sea and on the shore before returning to Dartmouth. After joining the faculty there in 1930, Laing earned his B.A. in 1933, as a member of the class of 1925. He was a member of the Dartmouth Sailing Club and served as its commodore in 1956.

Laing's nautical fiction includes *The Sea Witch* (1933), a historical novel set among the clipper ships of 1840s New York, and *Jonathan Eagle* (1955), about a young New England sailor during the early republic. He also wrote several histories, of which the best known include *Clipper Ship Men* (1944), *American Sail: A Pictorial History* (1961), and *Seafaring America* (1974).

Peter H. McCracken

LAKEBOAT (first perf. 1980; pub. 1981). Written by Pulitzer Prize-winner David Mamet (1947–   ), the play *Lakeboat* was inspired by his experience as a ship's steward following his sophomore year in college. Mamet writes frequently about the gritty urban, machismo world of small-time hustlers and about anger and violence between men and women, but *Lakeboat* is his only major play that deals directly with a maritime setting and theme. The play's focus is life aboard the *T. Harrison*, "a steel bulk-freight turbine steamer registered in the Iron Ore Trade" that roams the Great Lakes.* The passengers consist of eight men: two officers, five veteran seamen, and a young college student. The shipmates spend most of their time discussing sex, drinking, sidearms, gambling, and the fate of a shipmate left ashore. They wander the galley, bridge, and deck, conduct fire and evacuation drills, and contemplate the life of a seaman.

The heart of the play, however, examines the binary effects of life upon the Lakes. In one respect, the Lakes are places of isolation and loneliness, where one has too much time to reflect on unfulfilled dreams. At the same time, the confines of the lake boat provide a gathering place where the men can form a sense of community and also experience sharing and acceptance, qualities not available to them ashore. [*See also* DRAMA OF THE SEA]

Brian Knetl

LANE, CARL [DANIEL] (1899–1995). Carl Lane, a nautical writer and illustrator born in New York City, developed his love for the sea while vacationing in Maine, where he eventually settled. Lane wrote *The Fleet in the Forest* (1943), a Great Lakes* historical novel about the construction of Commodore Oliver Perry's Lake Erie fleet during the War of 1812 and a prophetic shipwright's anticipation about an unsettled wilderness lake. Other fiction includes *River Dragon* (1948), a historical children's novel about steamboats, *The Fire Raft* (1951), and *Black Tide* (1952).

A noted sailor, designer, and builder of yachts, Lane revamped the Boy Scouts of America's *Sea Scout Manual*; wrote for several publications, including *Saturday Evening Post, Sea Power*, and *Collier's*; and penned his own authoritative sailing handbooks: *Boatowner's Sheet Anchor* (1941), *The Boatman's Manual* (1943), *How to Sail* (1947), and *The Cruiser's Manual* (1949). [*See also* JUVENILE LITERATURE OF THE SEA]

Donald P. Curtis

LARCOM, LUCY (1824–1893). Lucy Larcom was a prolific and highly regarded writer of descriptive and religious verse, short fiction, and inspirational prose in the second half of the nineteenth century. Born on the Massachusetts North Shore in Beverly, she lived and worked as a young girl in the Lowell mills, taught elementary school in Illinois, and, for eight years, taught at the Wheaton Seminary (now Wheaton College) in Norton, Massachusetts. She retired from teaching in 1863, and, as the protégé of John Greenleaf Whittier,* achieved a considerable literary reputation. Her volumes of poetry include *Similitudes, from the Ocean and the Prairie* (1853), *Poems* (1863), *Hillside and Seaside in Poetry* (1877), and *Wild Roses of Cape Ann* (1880). *Ships in the Mist: And Other Stories* was published in 1860, and the autobiographical *A New England Girlhood*, recounting her life in the mills and as a teacher, in 1889.

Her poems characteristically articulate a faith that God may be found in the contemplation of nature. They rely on images and sentiments that are often trite by contemporary expectations; the frequent images derived from her own life on the Massachusetts coast are no exception. But occasionally, Larcom's precise and colorful observations of the physical and social qualities of her New England environment, particularly in her earlier poems, convey a joyousness that makes reading her a pleasure. [*See also* SEA IMAGERY IN MODERN AND CONTEMPORARY POETRY]

Thomas R. Brooks

LATINO/A LITERATURE OF THE SEA. The body of work that is referred to as Latino/a literature of the United States includes writing produced by Mexican Americans or Chicano/as, Cuban Americans, Dominican Americans, Puerto Ricans on the mainland, and other people of Central and South American heritage living in the United States. The centrality of the sea in such Latino/a literature varies widely, depending on which of these groups is in question.

The sea is most prominent in the writing of Cuban Americans, not just because Cuba is an island but also because of the large number of Cubans who have reached the United States by sea, rather than by land or air. In Mexican American or Chicano/a literature, on the other hand, the sea tends to be less predominant as setting or metaphor, given that Mexican immigrants generally reach the United States by land routes and across the Rio Grande River. Some Mexican American families, further, have lived in the United States for generations, becoming American not through immigration but because the boundaries between the United States and Mexico shifted south with the Treaty of Guadalupe Hidalgo in 1848, leaving many former Mexicans within the new boundaries of the United States. In general, literature by peoples descended from, or connected to, island cultures of the Caribbean* tends to refer more often to the sea than does the literature produced by peoples of Central or South America who have reached the United States primarily by traveling over land.

Historically, Cubans attempting to leave Fidel Castro's regime since 1959 have reached the United States in large numbers by traveling across the ninety miles from Cuba to Florida, either with Castro's permission in large-scale "boat lifts" such as the Mariel boat lift of 1980 or illegally in very small boats or homemade rafts, hence the name "*balseros*," or "rafters." It is estimated that at least one of every four rafters who undertake the passage dies in the attempt. Cuban American literature in which the sea is prominent often depicts these perilous journeys. For example, Achy Obejas' novel *Memory Mambo* (1996), as well as her short story "We Came All the Way from Cuba So You Could Dress like This?" (1994), from her collection by the same title, both open with the protagonists' childhood memories of such crossings.

The sea, as both the physical barrier and the potential bridge between Cuba and the United States paradoxically represents both the possibility of escape and freedom and the danger of death along the way in novels such as J. Joaquín Fraxedas' *The Lonely Crossing of Juan Cabrera* (1993), Virgil Suarez's *Latin Jazz* (1989), and Margarita Engle's *Skywriting* (1995). Fraxedas' *The Lonely Crossing of Juan Cabrera* tells the story of three men who venture the difficult journey on a raft constructed of inner tubes; the political struggle of the would-be exiles is displaced onto a struggle with nature, as the characters face a hurricane, a shark attack, and near starvation. But the sea also represents the only chance of salvation, as the men catch and eat fish for food, and the currents of the Gulf Stream carry the raft closer to the United States. The immensity and power of the sea are also conveyed through the novel's description of rescuers' efforts to scan the ocean's surface for would-be refugees.

The subject of Suarez's *Latin Jazz* is the 1980 Mariel boat lift; powerful scenes describe a sea literally obscured by the number of boats on its surface as they arrive at Mariel Port from Key West* and leave full of escaping Cubans. Once again, the sea is a paradoxical site, threatening the survival of those on the small, overcrowded boats while simultaneously offering the only possibility of reuniting Cuban families. Engle's *Skywriting* envisions the lone *balsero*'s journey from the perspective of the family members he leaves behind. The *balsero*'s mother and half-sister pace Cuba's beaches waiting for news as they imagine the various possible scenarios: hurricanes, sharks, capture by Cuban patrol boats, rescue by the U.S. Coast Guard or by rescue teams of Cuban exiles.

In much literature by Caribbean U.S. Latino/as, references to the sea are part of a larger thematic strand concerning memories of a tropical island homeland that is often set against the urban backdrop of immigrants' existence on mainland U.S. In "Aguantando," from Dominican American writer Junot Diaz's short-story collection *Drown* (1996), the ocean becomes associated with the narrator's childhood memories of rejection and loneliness after his father leaves the family for the United States; other stories in the collection offer a foil for these memories through scenes of gritty New Jersey neighborhoods inhabited by alienated and disoriented immigrant adolescent males. In Puerto Rican writer Judith Ortiz Cofer's collection of essays, poems, and short stories, *The Latin Deli* (1993), and poems such as "Exile" from *Terms of Survival* (1987), the sea is invoked with nostalgia by adult exiles who long to return home and/or with resentment and hostility by children who have grown up in the mainland United States and consider it their "home."

The memory of the sea is at times recuperative, as in Ortiz Cofer's short story "Letter from the Caribbean," in *The Latin Deli*, in which a sighting of dolphins by a woman vacationing on a Puerto Rican beach becomes a magical metaphor for healing. In Cuban American Dolores Prida's play *Beautiful Señoritas* (first perf. 1977; pub. 1991), the memory of the limitless ocean has the power to endure in the face of a grim urban present; more darkly, the ocean seems to represent childhood innocence turned sour when one character ends her life by setting herself on fire and running into the sea.

In several poems from Dominican American Julia Alvarez's collection *The Other Side*/El Otro Lado (1995), the sea is again connected metaphorically to a culture and a language that have been lost and to the cultural transition from the Dominican Republic to the United States. The use of the sea as a metaphor for a sort of cultural "in-between" place, in which immigrants belong fully neither to their home culture nor to their adopted culture and country, is echoed, although not explicitly invoked, in Mexican American Lorna Dee Cervantes' poem "Refugee Ship" (1982). Similarly, in Cristina Garcia's *Dreaming in Cuban*** (1992), the sea figures prominently as a metaphor for the cultural and geographical chasms that divide a Cuban family separated by the aftermath of the 1959 revolution; crossing the ocean, as characters do physically and spiritually, in life and after death, represents their attempts to bridge that gulf in culture and understanding. In *A Place Where the Sea Remembers*** (1993), by Sandra Benìtez, who is of Puerto Rican descent but was raised partially in Mexico and El Salvador, the sea takes on the resonance of a cultural and communal memory, as it witnesses the triumphs and disasters of life in a seaside Mexican town.

The sea in U.S. Latino/a literature is sometimes associated with Spanish colonization, since the first *conquistadores* arrived by sea. This theme is at work, for example, in Rudolfo Anaya's short novel *The Legend of La Llorona* (1984), which is a retelling of the story of "la Malinche," the indigenous woman who translated the Mayan and Aztec languages for Hernán Cortés and thus participated in his conquest of Mexico. The connection of the sea with Spanish conquest is also present, to a lesser degree, in Anaya's better-known work *Bless Me, Ultima*** (1972), in which the protagonist's father's family, named "Márez" (the Spanish word for ocean is "*mar*"), are descended from *conquistadores*. Interestingly, in the latter novel, the *conquistadores*, as well as the sea that brought them, are associated most overtly with an appealing restlessness and limitless freedom; in contrast, the metaphorical role of the sea is more negative in Puerto Rican Gloria Vando's poem "Legend of the Flamboyán" (1993) about the Spanish colonization of Puerto Rico.

In Chicana Gloria Anzaldúa's landmark, genre-crossing volume *Borderlands*/La Frontera: *The New Mestiza* (1987), the sea figures as metaphor for the dissolution of, and escape from, borders and boundaries of a geographical, social, and spiritual nature. In the opening poem, the natural power of the sea to eat away at the shore points out the unnaturalness of political borders. In "A Sea of Cabbages," the metaphorical use of the sea suggests a boundlessness and freedom that contrast sharply with the manual labor performed incessantly by migrant workers. In "*Compaòera, cuando am-bamos*," the sea represents the dissolution of bodily boundaries and perhaps also of cultural constraints against lesbian sexuality. References to the ocean have a similar function in Chicana Emma Pérez's novel *Gulf Dreams* (1996), set in a coastal Texas town; images of the sea at night or sunset serve as a counterpoint to the narrator's childhood memories of picking cotton in the fields during scorching heat and also suggest the potential for liberation from socially imposed restrictions on lesbian desire. [*See also* CARIBBEAN LITERATURE OF THE SEA]

FURTHER READING: Masud-Piloto, Felix. *From Welcomed Exiles to Illegal Immigrants: Cuban Migration to the U.S., 1959–1995*. Lanham, MD: Rowman and Littlefield, 1996; Magill, Frank N., ed. *Masterpieces of Latino Literature*. New York: HarperCollins, 1994; Martìnez, Julio A., and Francisco A. Lomelì, eds. *Chicano Literature: A Reference Guide*. Westport, CT: Greenwood, 1985; McKenna, Teresa. *Migrant Song: Politics and Process in Contemporary Chicano Literature*. Austin: U of Texas P, 1997.

Marta Caminero-Santangelo

LAY, WILLIAM. *See GLOBE* MUTINY.

LE GUIN, URSULA K[ROEBER]. (1929–   ). Born in Berkeley, California, Ursula K. Le Guin earned her B.A. at Radcliffe College in 1951 and her M.A. in French and Renaissance literature at Columbia University in 1952. Author of over fifty books of fiction, short stories, poetry, and criticism, she is usually considered a children's writer of fantasy, but mature readers admire her artful adaptation of ancient myths and Jungian archetypes to contemporary concerns.

Although her works often draw upon the sea for images, metaphors, and titles, only two of them fully develop nautical settings and themes: the first and third novels of her most famous and honored work, *The Earthsea Trilogy*, a saga of an island world where maritime values and pursuits dominate the culture. *A Wizard of Earthsea* (1968) begins the story of Ged, an apprentice wizard whose training replicates the nautical experiences of Christ, Odysseus, Beowulf, and Jonah, as he learns to control sea and wave with his magic spells. He sails from island to island, improving his seamanship, learning the rudiments of boatbuilding, and feeling increasingly comfortable at sea, an attitude that distinguishes him from his evil enemies. In *The Farthest Shore* (1972), a mature Ged sails through Earthsea seeking a rogue wizard and among many adventures encounters the Children of the Open Sea, people who live a simple life on great rafts where they find inner peace and contentment. As a paean to the sea's calming powers, these two novels develop Le Guin's characteristic themes of harmony, wholeness, and self-knowledge.

Le Guin uses a coastal setting in *Searoad: Chronicles of Klatsand* (1991) to dramatize the inner lives of women in a coastal Oregon village during the twentieth century. This collection of related, realistic stories reveals Le Guin's recent interest in feminism and her continuing recognition of maritime settings as a powerful literary resource.

Dennis Berthold

LEDYARD, JOHN (1751–1789). The only American to write an account of Captain James Cook's third voyage to the Pacific Ocean, John Ledyard was born in Groton, Connecticut. After the death of his mariner father and the remarriage of his mother, the young Ledyard was sent to live with his paternal grandfather in Hartford. He attended Dartmouth College for a short time before beginning the extensive travel that would take him to every continent.

Shipping as a sailor from New London to Europe, Ledyard met Captain Cook in London. He signed aboard Cook's expedition as a corporal of marines and set sail for the Pacific in July 1776. Though the British Admiralty required sailors to turn over to them their private accounts of the voyage at its completion, Ledyard and his shipmates John Rickman, Henrich Zimmermann, and William Ellis all published their own accounts of the voyage before the official narrative appeared in 1784. Portions of Ledyard's *A Journal of Captain Cook's Last Voyage to the Pacific Ocean* (1783) are similar enough to Rickman's 1781 book of the same title to have been based largely on it, if the men did not share diaries at sea. There are important differences, however, especially in the description of Cook's death in Hawai'i and in the detailed accounts of fur trading. Ledyard was impressed with the prices that sea otter pelts, purchased incidentally at Nootka Sound, brought at Canton, and his book was largely intended to inspire a mercantile venture on the Northwest Coast.*

Failing to find a voyage sponsor in the newly independent United States, Ledyard sailed to Paris in 1784, where he gained the notice of Thomas Jefferson. With Jefferson's support, Ledyard formed a plan to walk across Siberia, sail from there to Nootka Sound, off Vancouver Island, and then walk across North America to Virginia, but the Empress Catherine refused permission. In 1787 he made the attempt anyway and was apprehended at Irkutsk. Upon his release, Ledyard signed on to explore the source of the Niger River with the Association for Promoting the Discovery of the Interior Parts of Africa, but he died in Cairo before the departure of the expedition. Ledyard had an enthusiastic biographer in Jared Sparks, whose *Life of John Ledyard* was published in 1828.

The Boston vessels *Columbia* and *Washington* left in September 1787 for the voyage that Ledyard imagined and, ultimately, inspired. The *Columbia* returned to Boston from the Northwest Coast and Canton in August 1790, the first American vessel to circumnavigate* the globe and the pioneer in a trade route that would ultimately lead to American annexation of the Oregon Territory. [*See also* VOYAGE NARRATIVES]

Mary Malloy

LEGENDS AND MYTHS. *See* GHOSTS AND GHOST SHIP LEGENDS; GREAT LAKES MYTHS AND LEGENDS.

LEGGETT, WILLIAM (1801–1839). William Leggett was a midshipman-turned-author who helped to develop the sea yarn into popular reading. In the course of his naval service, Leggett contracted yellow fever in the West

Indies and suffered the persecutions of a commander in the Mediterranean for his ability to quote Shakespeare. Following a duel, he was court-martialed and resigned his commission to take up journalism and authorship. His sea stories, collected in *Tales and Sketches by a Country Schoolmaster* (1829) and *Naval Stories* (1834), are deeply influenced by Washington Irving's* sentimentality but also anticipate Edgar Allan Poe's* Gothic sensationalism.

Leggett begins a number of his stories with a false sense of calm or tranquillity and proceeds into a nightmare of grotesque violence; his sea is a pool of primal energies, the placid surface of which is tragically inscrutable. "The Encounter" (1834) ends with a bloody collision at sea, and "The Main-Truck, or a Leap for Life" (1834) climaxes with a father's threatening to shoot his son unless he leaps from the mainmast into the sea. Leggett stories often combine this type of melodrama with a concern for the humane treatment of sailors. His tale "Brought to the Gangway" (1834) opens with a needlessly cruel flogging and ends with a double drowning. Displaying a range of versatility in terms of narrative technique and use of vernacular speech, William Leggett, along with his contemporaries Nathaniel Ames* and John W. Gould,* developed the sea tale into a staple of popular American fiction.

Hugh Egan

LIEBERMAN, LAURENCE [JAMES] (1935–). Four years at the College of the Virgin Islands in the 1960s were critical years for poet Laurence Lieberman, for it was then that he discovered the Caribbean.* Since those formative years, from his home in the Midwest, Lieberman has systematically traveled to nearly every Caribbean island for extended periods, and he is now widely known for his unique narrative poetry recounting those numerous travel adventures. In all his poems, Lieberman epitomizes the stateside traveler in the Caribbean, a sort of exuberant "everytourist," and his poetry is filled with emphatic italics and exclamatory statements.

The Unblinding (1968), his first collection, includes poems written when Lieberman lived in St. Thomas and explored the underwater world. In "The Transvestite" he writes of his desire to transform himself into a sea creature to connect more intimately to the water. In "The Drowning," he likens the sea to a lover. The numerous fish a snorkeler in the Caribbean might encounter are described in colorful detail in "The Coral Reef." "Hands and the Fisherman's Wife" is a moving love poem written from the point of view of the fisherman's wife as she awaits her husband's return. In other poems he writes of the mystery of porcupine puffer fish and tarpon.

In *The Osprey Suicides* (1973), the poet continues his underwater adventures. "Lobsters in the Brain Coral" is a tense record of his pursuit of a twenty-pound "langouste" with a sling spear. He imagines he is part of a dance as the water controls his movements in "The Diving Ballet."

Eros at the World Kite Pageant: Poems 1979–1982 (1983) contains poems about the Caribbean and also about the poet's trip to Japan, including "Ago Bay: The Regatta in the Skies." Here Lieberman appreciates clouds shaped as sailboats in a picturesque cove in Japan. This volume, however, marks a change for Lieberman; henceforth, he focuses more on the individuals and incidents of his Caribbean travels and less on landscape or seascape. In the many volumes of poetry that have followed—his most recent being a collection named for the previously mentioned poem, *The Regatta in the Skies: Selected Long Poems* (2000)—Lieberman describes his activities at festivals, monuments, and intriguing points of interest on nearly all the Caribbean islands. [*See also* SEA IMAGERY IN MODERN AND CONTEMPORARY POETRY]

Erika J. Waters

LIFESAVING LITERATURE. In 1871, spurred to action by a series of sensational wrecks along the New Jersey coast, Congress passed legislation to organize and fund the U.S. Life-Saving Service (1871–1915) on a national scale to create a system of well-dispersed stations with salaried crews on the Atlantic, Pacific, and Great Lakes* coasts. Technological innovations, such as self-bailing lifeboats, networked telegraph communications, and the breeches buoy—a system of ropes, pulleys, and a buoy or life-car that could be used to ferry wreck victims from ship to shore—coupled with routine patrols enabled lifesaving crews to warn vessels to safety with red Coston flares or to respond to shipwreck.* The new system proved unparalleled, reducing the number of drownings while quelling the public's outcry for a solution to the devastating loss of life in shipwreck.

In 1915 the Life-Saving Service was combined with the Revenue Cutter Service (1790–1915), which was charged with enforcing maritime laws, to form the Coast Guard. By this time, the Life-Saving Service had rescued more than 177,000 people from wrecks, helped to prevent countless other maritime disasters, and operated from more than 270 stations. In 1939 the U.S. Lighthouse* Service (1789–1939), responsible for maintaining maritime navigational aids, also merged with the Coast Guard.

Lifesaving crews—local watermen familiar with a district's unique coastal characteristics—were generally hired for the winter storm season. Although the majority of surfmen were white, some crews were racially diverse. For instance, Native Americans from the Wampanoag tribe on Martha's Vineyard and the Shinnecock tribe on Long Island were integral to both volunteer and paid lifesaving efforts. In 1880 the lifesaving crew at Pea Island Station on North Carolina's Outer Banks, under Richard Etheridge's leadership, became the service's first all-black crew.

The Life-Saving Service's success was widely celebrated in contemporary literature and art and, as coastal tourism became increasingly popular, was also reflected in the rise of spectatorship at the scenes of wrecks. Not only would spectators gather to view the aftermath of wrecks, as Henry David Thoreau* vividly describes in his account of the wreck of the *St. John* in *Cape Cod* (1864), but crowds would also turn out to observe lifesaving crews' drills and dramatic rescue efforts. When Thoreau wrote *Cape Cod*, aid to shipwrecked mariners in Massachusetts depended on the volunteer lifeboat crews and charity houses of the Massachusetts Humane Society, one model for the nationally organized lifesaving system. Shipwreck metaphors infuse Thoreau's narrative; in the chapter "The Beach," the narrator explores a dilapidated and seemingly abandoned charity house near the beach.

In comparison, naturalist Henry Beston's* *The Outermost House* (1928) records his experiences while living near the outer beach on the arm of Cape Cod.* Unlike the barrenness of Thoreau's charity house, the nightly presence of Nauset station coastguardsmen walking their assigned patrols to warn ships of danger or to respond to groundings offered Beston companionship as well as a strong sense of protection. Drawing on the history of lifesaving on the cape, in the chapter "Lanterns on the Beach," Beston describes the duties of the coastguardsmen and elaborates on the hardships endured by surfmen in performing their mundane, yet quietly heroic, tasks.

Media representations, from newspapers, to weekly and monthly magazines, fueled public interest in lifesaving by featuring dramatic rescue narratives. For example, "The United States Life-Saving Service" in *Scribner's Monthly* (January 1880) and "The American Life-Saving Service" in *Harper's New Monthly Magazine* (February 1882) educated readers about the history and operations of the service while recounting the details of rescues. Many such essays argued in favor of increased federal funding for the service based on its incredible success. To help readers fully appreciate the romantic drama of lifesaving narratives, articles were often accompanied by illustrations of rescue equipment and surfmen in action. The service's widely circulated annual report documented the yearly activity in each of its thirteen districts as well as featured prose accounts of the most memorable wrecks and rescues. From 1876 to 1889, William D. O'Connor, a professional literary figure and assistant to the general superintendent, compiled the annual report and, through his vivid writing, helped to generate public interest in lifesaving. O'Connor's posthumously published *Heroes of the Storm* (1904) includes many of his most dramatic entries about the surfmen's strength and heroism. In the poem "Patroling Barnegat," published in *Leaves of Grass* (1881), Walt Whitman,* a friend of O'Connor, describes surfmen's dedication in patrolling a beach lashed by a furious gale.

Not all lifesaving literature glamorized the actions and valor of the surfmen. Rebecca Harding Davis,* in a *Lippincott's Magazine* essay "Life-Saving Stations" (March 1876), complicates her praise for the Life-Saving Service in New Jersey by linking the surfmen to questionable wrecking practices and the notorious "Barnegat pirates,"* renowned for luring ships to destruction for profit and famous for their inhospitality. In "The Open Boat" (1897), based on his experiences during the foundering of the *Commodore* off the coast of Florida, Stephen Crane* challenges the national exuberance over the success of lifesaving. Although the correspondent argues that the coast reached by the survivors is protected by houses of refuge rather than fully manned lifesaving stations, the men in the boat experience cycles of hope and despair based on their expectations of rescue by the Life-Saving Service. After they think they see a lifeboat being wheeled along the beach, for instance, their relief turns to disgust when the lifeboat turns out to be an omnibus filled with tourists.

Widespread reporting about the Life-Saving Service also helped to carry its exploits beyond literature to become the focus of great marine epic paintings such as Winslow Homer's *The Life-Line* (1884) and *The Wreck* (1896). In these, as in many of his other seascapes, Homer captures the drama and ambiguous success of humans' efforts to survive at the margin of land and sea in the teeth of elemental forces. [*See also* PYLE, (JOHN) HOWARD]

FURTHER READING: *Annual Report of the Operations of the United States Life-Saving Service, 1875–1914.* Washington, D.C. U.S. Government Printing Office; Noble, Dennis L. *That Others Might Live: The U.S. Life-Saving Service, 1878–1915.* Annapolis, MD: Naval Institute P, 1994; Shanks, Ralph C., and Wick York. *The U.S. Life-Saving Service: Heroes, Rescues and Architecture of the Early Coast Guard.* Ed. Lisa Woo Shanks. Petaluma, CA: Costano, 1996; Weatherford, Carole Boston. *Sink or Swim: Black Lifesavers of the Outer Banks.* Wilmington, NC: Coastal Carolina, 1999.

Daniel W. Lane

LIGHTHOUSE LITERATURE. The literature surrounding lighthouses throughout North America encompasses light stations and lightships on both U.S. coasts, on the Great Lakes,* in the southern Delta area, in Alaska and Hawai'i and across Canada. Much of it, both historical and imaginative, concerns the trials of lighthouse keepers as well as the historical and cultural significance of lighthouses themselves.

In 1939 the government discontinued the U.S. Lighthouse Service, which had governed the maintenance of the country's lighthouses since 1789, and turned over control of the light stations to the Coast Guard. George R. Putnam presents the events of his own career as commissioner of the Lighthouse Service in *Sentinel of the Coasts: The Log of a Lighthouse Engineer* (1937). Other literature detailing the lives of keepers often describes the isolation and heroism of lighthouse crews and their families. Edward Rowe Snow's* *Famous New England Lighthouses* (1945) presents vivid anecdotes of heroic feats of keepers in that region, including Ida Lewis, a revered Rhode Island lightkeeper who alone saved twenty-three people from drowning during her career at Lime Rock. Lewis and other female lightkeepers are described in greater detail in Mary Louise Clifford's *Women Who Kept the Lights: An Illustrated History of Female Lighthouse Keepers* (1993).

In addition to the historical corpus, much imaginative literature involving lighthouses and keepers exists. Herman Melville's* "Agatha" letters (1852) feature Agatha as the daughter of a lighthouse keeper. Earlier this century, Joseph Crosby Lincoln* published the popular *The Woman Haters* (1911), a novel concerning the keepers at the Eastboro Twin Lights, and *Rugged Water* (1924), a novel and subsequent Paramount motion picture (1925) that detailed the experiences of two men at the Setuckit Life Saving Station. More recently, Howard Norman published *The Bird Artist* (1994), an evocative, laconic novel set in the remote hamlet of Witless Bay, Newfoundland. The novel charts the courses of two tormented love relationships and a murder against a backdrop of fogs, squalls, and devouring seas. The two female protagonists are strong and mercurial; one of the male lovers is a sketcher of marsh birds and the other is a seductive, charismatic lighthouse keeper. James Michael Pratt's *The Lighthouse Keeper* (2000) chronicles a saga of three generations weathering storms in a lighthouse off the coast of Massachusetts.

Lighthouses served as the setting for plays in the nineteenth century (e.g., William Busch's *Maid of the Lighthouse* [c.1870]) and throughout the twentieth (e.g., Owen Davis' *Lighthouse by the Sea* [1903], H. Austin Adams' *'Ception Shoals* [1917], Willard Robertson's *The Sea Woman* [1925], Ray Bradbury's* *The Foghorn* [1975], and Jaime Meyer's *Harry and Claire* [1989]). These often include troubled or enigmatic characters. Busch's youthful play is a pseudo-Shakespearean tragicomedy, its Roman setting and aspects of its plot recalling *Cymbeline* (1623). It involves a love affair between Marina, the foster daughter of a lighthouse keeper, and Patricio, whom she rescues from a shipwreck.* Her father, Britano, opposes the match. In the course of the action, Patricio's brother Brutus steals a locket with Marina's picture and attempts to woo her in the person of his brother. Ultimately, the lovers triumph over Brutus' evil designs, and the lighthouse keeper gives his blessing to his daughter's marriage.

'Ception Shoals likewise has Eve, the sexually innocent ward of her Uncle Job, sequestered in a desolate lighthouse off the California coast. She saves a young man on a nearby shoal and falls in love with him. When her uncle attempts to thwart the match, she kills him. Written under the influence of Freudian psychology, the production was most remembered for the entrance of the sultry actress Nazimova (playing Eve) in a dripping wet bathing suit. Davis' *Lighthouse by the Sea* is notable for a sensational scene in which the granddaughter of a lighthouse keeper walks the tightrope of a thin wire to relight the signal. Robertson's *The Sea Woman* presents Molla, a frustrated heroine involved in lighthouse love and death. After losing her innocence, Molla sets fire to the lighthouse, killing herself and the man who made her pregnant. *The Foghorn*, a brief, evocative, two-character drama, is set in a remote lighthouse and features a whalelike sea beast whose cries plaintively echo those of the foghorn.

Harry and Claire brings lighthouse literature into the New Age. Walter

Mitty-esque Harry is a lighthouse keeper, and Claire is the woman he keeps. He plays at being a sea captain and dreams of an alluring shoreside waitress, Elsa, who swims out to make his dreams a reality in the second act. Claire is blind and possessed of somewhat erratic clairvoyance. There are also a hot-air balloonist named Captain Bob and a talking goldfish. Thematically, author Meyer is engaged with the idea of floating free versus being anchored, of trust and disbelief. Structurally, like many examples of the lighthouse drama preceding it, the play is a romance of fantastic figures in quest of their hearts' desires. [*See also* DRAMA OF THE SEA; LIFESAVING LITERATURE]

Melanie Brown and Attilio Favorini

LINCOLN, JOSEPH C[ROSBY]. (1870–1944). Joseph C. Lincoln, the descendant of a long line of a seafarers, was a prolific author of best-selling verses, stories, and novels that portrayed life along the shore of Cape Cod* with nostalgia and humor. The son of Captain Joseph and Emily (Crosby) Lincoln, the author was born in Brewster, a small village that was home port for sea captains, fishermen, innkeepers, shop merchants, and saltworks owners.

After leaving Cape Cod, Lincoln worked for several years as a bookkeeper in Boston before becoming a commercial artist for *The League of American Wheelmen Bulletin* (LAW), in which his first poems were published. These early verses (1896–1898), such as "The Ballade of Miss Polly's Hat" and "Waiting for the Mail," were often brief, rhymed stories reminiscent of his boyhood experiences on Cape Cod. In 1897 Lincoln and his wife, Florence Ely Sargent, moved to New York, where he continued to submit his stories and poems to *Harper's Weekly, Ainslee's*, and *The Saturday Evening Post* while working as editor for a banking magazine. His first critical recognition came with the publication of "The Cod-Fisher" in *Harper's Weekly* (7 July 1900). A lengthy poem evoking spray-soaked fishermen aboard a battered schooner in stormy seas, it was included in Lincoln's first book, *Cape Cod Ballads and Other Verses* (1902). His first novel, *Cap'n Eri* (1904), a story of three Cape Cod sea captains, became an overnight success.

Thereafter, Lincoln devoted himself to writing. Dubbed the "Literary Dean of Cape Cod" by William Dana Orcutt, Lincoln wrote hundreds of short stories, poems, yarns, and more than forty novels about the people and villages of his native coast. *Cape Cod Yesterdays* (1935) contains his personal observations on a vanishing way of life. A bibliography of his work appears in *A Prolific Pencil: A Biography of Joseph Crosby Lincoln, Litt. D.* by Percy Fielitz Rex (1980).

Susan Raidy Klein

LINDBERGH, ANNE MORROW (1906–   ). Anne Morrow Lindbergh was born in 1906 in Englewood, New Jersey. Her father, Dwight Whitney Morrow, was ambassador to Mexico when Charles Lindbergh visited Mexico

City in 1928, soon after he had completed his famous solo transatlantic crossing. Lindbergh and Anne Morrow met in Mexico City, and they married soon after her graduation from Smith College in 1929. Anne Lindbergh quickly developed the skills of an aviator and provided invaluable assistance to her husband in their explorations for new air travel routes. In the course of their voyages by seaplane, the Lindberghs visited many islands and developed a strong knowledge of the sea, which is particularly evident in one of Anne's accounts of their travels, *Listen! the Wind* (1938). Generally a shy and reserved individual, Anne often found the stresses of the couple's fame a challenge, one greatly heightened by the publicity surrounding the kidnapping and death of their first child and the ensuing trial two years later. She recounted these experiences in her five volumes of diaries and letters, covering 1922 to 1944.

Lindbergh found solace and escape in life outside the United States—in part on remote islands, particularly off the coast of Florida. Retreats in the early 1940s and especially in the spring of 1955 provided the foundation for her best-known work, *Gift from the Sea* (1955), in which she uses a similar visit to a beach to explore a woman's relationships with others. Lindbergh found reflections of society's problems in the sea and in seashells found at the beach, and she drew many of her insights from the ocean. *Gift from the Sea* spent eighty weeks on the best-seller list; after fifty-one weeks in the top slot, it was replaced by her collection of poems, *The Unicorn and Other Poems* (1956), a volume that includes a number of poems with a seaside setting. A good recent biography is Susan Hertog's *Anne Morrow Lindbergh: Her Life* (1999).

Peter H. McCracken

LODGE, GEORGE CABOT (1873–1909). Son of Senator Henry Cabot Lodge and acquaintance of Edith Wharton, Henry James,* and his own biographer, Henry Adams, the poet and verse dramatist George Cabot Lodge was well acquainted with the sea. Growing up in the coastal Massachusetts town of Nahant and, as an adult, summering off Nantucket* on Tuckernuck Island, Lodge also served as a gunnery officer aboard the *Dixie* during the Spanish-American War.

Sea-based subjects, symbolism, and imagery resonate throughout Lodge's poetry, notably in his first two published volumes, *The Song of the Wave and Other Poems* (1898) and *Poems, 1899–1902* (1902). Characteristically, Lodge stresses the sea's abstract, metaphysical qualities. In poems such as "Song of the Wave," "Fog at Sea," "The Ocean Sings," and "Ode to the Sea" and in the four-poem sequence "Tuckanuck," the sea is a transcendent, self-exploratory symbol for death, love, and poetic inspiration. Personification and apostrophe frequent Lodge's sea poems; in "A First Word," "the Ocean" beseeches the poet to give voice to her "songs." Because he rejected realism and modernism, Lodge has been criticized for overuse of abstraction and emotional language. Yet some of his poems include more concrete imagery, as in a line describing waves: "the face of the waters was barred with white" ("Song of the Wave"). Although less prominent, the sea in Lodge's later volumes of verse (*The Great Adventure* [1905] and *The Soul's Inheritance and Other Poems* [1909]) remains an underlying, unifying presence in sea-inspired allusions and figurative language.

Retreating to the seashore in failing health, Lodge died on his beloved "Tuckanuck" Island at the age of thirty-six. [*See also* SEA IMAGERY IN MODERN AND CONTEMPORARY POETRY]

Dana L. Peterson

THE LOG OF THE SKIPPER'S WIFE (1979). James W. Balano (1912–1982) edited the seagoing diary of his mother, Dorothea ("Dora") Moulton Balano (1882–1951), the wife of a Maine cargo schooner captain. The resulting "log" covers the days when Dora accompanied her husband in the coasting trade in 1910–1913, including one trip to Brazil.

Dora is presented as an engaging and frank woman who introduces us to life in the aft cabin of a cargo schooner as we rarely see it. Liberated and college-educated, Dora is both curious and critical in examining her relationship with her husband, Captain Fred, his business associates, his crew, and her life as wife of the captain. She describes the dowdiness of his hometown on the coast of Maine in contrast to the cultured life that she longs for. She reveals her desire to get pregnant as well as her husband's sexual appetites and escapades. At the end of the diary, unbeknownst to her husband, Dora is scheming with the vessel's owners to send Captain Fred (and thus her) on a cargo run to France. [*See also* JOURNALS AND LOGBOOKS; WOMEN AT SEA]

James F. Millinger

LONDON, JACK (1876–1916). Born John Griffith Chaney in San Francisco in 1876, Jack London was deserted by his father and raised in Oakland by his mother and his stepfather, whose surname he adopted. London worked at many jobs as a teenager in order to buy a sloop for oyster pirating in San Francisco Bay. He switched to the other side of the law when he joined the fish patrol. London's youthful exploits provide the basis for two juvenile works: *The Cruise of the* Dazzler (1902) and *Tales of the Fish Patrol* (1905).

Although better known for his Klondike fiction, London was a prolific writer of American seafaring fiction and nonfiction. Like his Northland writings, London's sea literature is rooted both in broad personal experience as a sailor and in extensive research on navigation. An avid reader of the seafaring works of James Fenimore Cooper,* Richard Henry Dana Jr.,* Frederick Marryat, Robert Louis Stevenson, Stephen Crane,* and Frank Norris,* London was most strongly influenced by Herman Melville,* Dana, Joshua

Slocum,* and Joseph Conrad. He was reading *Typee** (1846) and *Moby-Dick** (1851) at a time when Melville's writing had fallen from favor. London's sea writings generally sustain the tradition of his literary antecedents; however, he incorporates such varied concerns as social Darwinism, imperialism, environmentalism, socialism, naturalism, and gender and racial issues, thus producing a unique blend of seafaring adventure, brisk narrative, and ideology.

At seventeen, London signed on as a sailor aboard the *Sophia Sutherland*, a three-masted sealing schooner headed for Asia and the Bonin Islands. During this voyage, London plunged into the brutal, but exhilarating, realities of seafaring life. His tenure on the *Sophia Sutherland* satisfied his yearnings for travel and adventure as well as providing a basis for later writing. While at sea, London experienced a typhoon that became the subject of a prizewinning sketch, "Story of a Typhoon off the Coast of Japan" (1893). This early narrative, published in a San Francisco newspaper, revealed the powerful intermingling of sensory detail and human emotion typical of London's later writing.

Unable to find work after returning from this voyage, London tramped across the country. He was jailed for vagrancy in Buffalo. Once he returned to California in 1898, he joined other gold-seekers in boarding ship for the Klondike. Although London found little gold, he gathered substantial raw material for a successful writing career. Capitalizing on his Klondike experience, London published *The Son of the Wolf* (1900), *The God of His Fathers* (1901), *Children of the Frost* (1902), *A Daughter of the Snows* (1902), and *The Call of the Wild* (1903) and *White Fang* (1906).

Established in early adulthood as a writer of realistic and naturalistic fiction, London returned to seafaring as a subject in 1904 with *The Sea-Wolf*,* a novel incorporating the *Ghost*, a microcosmic ship, an Ahab*-like captain named Wolf Larsen,* and a brutalized crew. Once again, London drew on his experiences aboard the *Sophia Sutherland*, but more influential were senior shipmates' "yarns" as well as the published accounts of Captain Alexander McLean, London's model for Larsen.

In *The Sea-Wolf*, London takes on the mythic Nietzschean Superman in Larsen, a brilliant, but sadistic, overreacher whose quest for revenge leads not only to his own alienation and disintegration but also to abuse of his crew. The arrogantly masculine Larsen contrasts with the novel's ultimate survivor, Humphrey Van Weyden, a sissified initiate into shipboard life who is transformed by hard work and exposure to challenging circumstances. London's novel features sharply detailed images of seafaring life as well as the amoral individualism embraced by both captain and crew of the *Ghost*. Van Weyden and Larsen eventually clash over Maud Brewster, a refugee from a shipwreck. Larsen's primitive ruthlessness contrasts with Van Weyden's commitment to love, cooperation, and optimism. Through Van Weyden, London interjects his belief in the socialistic value of collective action as well as a more balanced model of masculinity. *The Sea-Wolf*, the subject of several cinematic productions, remains one of London's most successful novels.

Success with *The Sea-Wolf* enabled London to devote more energy to socialist causes. From 1905 to 1909, his short stories, novels, journalism, and nonfiction recurrently advocated collective action over individualism. Notable during this phase is *Martin Eden** (1909), the story of a meagerly educated sailor driven to reinvent himself as a professional writer. Disillusioned by his literary success, Martin envisions escape to a South Seas paradise. En route, he succumbs to despair and commits suicide by plunging into the sea. Although *Martin Eden* cannot be classified as sea fiction, the sea plays a role in the hero's consciousness.

During this phase of his own career, London also returned to the sea, albeit more optimistically. Between 1906 and 1907, Jack London oversaw construction of a fifty-five-foot, iron-keeled boat named the *Snark*, designed to carry him and his second wife, Charmian (generally considered to be the model for the fictional Maud Brewster), on a projected voyage around the world. To fund the $30,000 project, London offered to write a variety of articles for such major publications as *Cosmopolitan* and *Collier's*. After seven years of planning, London and his crew set sail on 23 April 1907. As time permitted, London served as navigator. Throughout the eighteen-month voyage, the *Snark* was plagued by severe leakage, mechanical breakdown, illness, and crew problems; however, London was welcomed at stops in Hawai'i, the Marquesas, Tahiti, Bora Bora, Penduffryn, and other South Seas ports. After contracting several tropical diseases, London was forced to end the voyage.

Despite his disappointment, London discovered that the *Snark* experience led to an important shift in his fictional concentration. Once attracted to the symbolic wilderness of the Northland, London redirected his attention to the South Seas. A youthful admirer of Melville's *Typee*, London visited Nuka Hiva in the Marquesas Islands. Expecting paradise on earth, he was appalled by the devastating effects of white visitors and commercialism on the natives' health and on the environment. Such stories as "Samuel" (1913), "The Terrible Solomons" (1910), and "The Heathen" (1909) reflect the consequences of white incursions into oceanic culture.

While on the *Snark* voyage, London was so profoundly affected by the spread of leprosy among South Seas islanders that he featured the disease in "Koolau, the Leper" (1909), "The Sheriff of Kona" (1909), and "Goodby, Jack" (1909). Sea writings that draw on the *Snark* voyage include *Adventure* (1911), *South Seas Tales* (1911), *The Cruise of the* Snark (1911), *The House of Pride and Other Tales of Hawai'i* (1912), and *A Son of the Sun* (1912). The novel *The Mutiny of the* Elsinore (1914) draws on London's 1911 voyage from Baltimore to Seattle on the 3,000-ton, four-masted bark *Dirigo*. Overall, these sea-based texts reflect London's attempt to infuse nautical themes with his concern for human justice and environmental and cultural preservation.

London's final years, from 1913 to his death in 1916, were beset by financial, personal, and health problems as well as disillusionment with American socialism. However, a 1915 voyage to Hawai'i restored both health and optimism. During his stay, he read the works of C. G. Jung, whose archetypal theories inform *The Turtles of Tasman* (1916) and *On the Makaloa Mat* (1919), which includes the notable short story "The Water Baby." London also wrote two dog novels, *Jerry of the Islands* (1917) and *Michael, Brother of Jerry* (1917), which draw on his Hawaiian sailing experiences.

London died on 22 November 1916; the exact cause of death is still debated. Such tropical diseases as yaws and dysentery probably contributed to the kidney failure, which was exacerbated by self-administered dosages of morphine, that ended his life at age forty.

FURTHER READING: Bender, Bert. "Jack London in the Tradition of American Sea Fiction." *Sea-Brothers: The Tradition of American Sea Fiction from* Moby-Dick *to the Present.* Philadelphia: U of Pennsylvania P, 1988, 83–98; Labor, Earle, and Jeanne Campbell Reesman. *Jack London.* Rev. ed. New York: Twayne, 1994.

Susan Irvin Gatti

LONG TOM COFFIN. The coxswain of the schooner *Ariel* in James Fenimore Cooper's* novel *The Pilot** (1824), Long Tom is Cooper's quintessential seaman. Coming from the Coffin family of whalers from Nantucket,* Long Tom constantly carries his harpoon and uses it as a weapon. He considers land useful only for drying fish and raising vegetables and teaches other seamen to read the omens of the sea and sky. When his beloved schooner is wrecked in a storm, Long Tom chooses to remain on board. While the bodies of his shipmates are soon washed ashore, the sea never relinquishes Long Tom.

Critics praised Long Tom, some comparing him to Parson Adams as an original addition to literature's fictional characters. T. P. Cooke began his stage career in the role of Long Tom in a dramatic version of *The Pilot* produced in London in 1825.

Kay Seymour House

LONGFELLOW, HENRY WADSWORTH (1807–1882). Henry Wadsworth Longfellow was born in Portland, Maine, at a time when that seaport was second in New England only to Boston in total tonnage engaged in maritime trade. Close to half a century later, in the poem "My Lost Youth" (1855)—his reminiscences of those early days—Longfellow's most vividly rendered memories center on the sparkling waters of Casco Bay: the magical aura of its distant islands and horizons and the exotic mystery of the ships and seamen from faraway places. Despite the focus of Portland's trade on the prosaic commodities of lumber and molasses, these boyhood impressions of the sea as a place of mystery and enchantment find their way into most of the fifty or so poems he wrote in which the sea is a prominent element.

Two of his earliest poems using the sea as setting are also among the best known of his shorter narrative poems. Both use ballad traditions to elevate American subjects to legendary status. Inspired by a then-recent discovery in Massachusetts, "The Skeleton in Armor" (1841) is a lively rendering of a presumed Viking warrior's sea voyage to America. "The Wreck of the *Hesperus*" (1841) interprets the historical sinking of a schooner off Gloucester* as the result of the captain's arrogant disregard of storm warnings.

Longfellow's rendering of the historical deportation of the Acadians in *Evangeline* (1847) situates their village near the sea, which is also the route of their exile. Narrative poems of the sea in *The Seaside and the Fireside* (1850) include "Twilight," on the terror experienced by a fisherman's wife and child during a storm as they await his return from the sea, and "Sir Humphrey Gilbert," which fancies the colonizer's death at sea as the result of collision of his vessel with an iceberg. The longest poem in the "By the Seaside" section of the volume, "The Building of the Ship," while its ship-of-state metaphor has become hackneyed, is a striking portrait a decade before the Civil War of the country's hope that the timbers of Maine and Georgia will remain permanently united in a seaworthy vessel named the *Union*.

Among the miscellaneous poems to appear in *The Courtship of Miles Standish and Other Poems* (1858), "The Phantom Ship" versifies the seventeenth-century legend popularized by Cotton Mather's *Magnalia Christi Americana* (1702) of the specter of a New Haven, Connecticut, ship sent by God to the port to relieve the inhabitants' distress at its sinking. "The Discoverer of the Lost Cape" returns to Norse legend, this time focusing on Arctic* exploration. Longfellow's only poem on the Civil War, "The Cumberland" (1863), commemorates the defeat of that sloop of war by the Confederate* ironclad, *Merrimack*. Later narrative sea poems include "The Musician's Tale: The Ballad of Carmilhan" in Part Second of *Tales of a Wayside Inn* (1872), in which a defiant captain meets his fate in an encounter with a ghost* ship, and "A Ballad of the French Fleet" (1878), which depicts the providential deliverance of Boston from a French attack in 1746. Longfellow used dialogue as a narrative device in sea poems of his final years, "Maiden and Weathercock" (1880) and "The City and the Sea" (1882).

Longfellow's most sustained use of the sea in narrative poetry appears in "The Musician's Tale: The Saga of King Olaf" in the first volume of *Tales of a Wayside Inn* (1863). Olaf returns to Norway from exile to avenge his father's death and to Christianize the country, in response to a challenge from the pagan god Thor. The poem includes descriptions of the construction of Olaf's great battleship, the *Long Serpent,* and the epic sea battle with his enemies, who eventually defeat him. Unwilling to surrender, Olaf the sea warrior leaps with his shield from his ship into the sea and is never seen again.

Longfellow also invoked the sea in many of his lyrical poems, often exploring the metaphorical implications of tides and waves. In both "The Tide Rises, the Tide Falls" (1880) and "August 4, 1856" (1882), the motion of the tides is reminiscent of the cycle of life and death. The rhythmical motion and sound of sea waves suggests the mournful tone of elegy in "Elegiac Verse" (1882) and the transcendent majesty of John Milton's poetry in "Milton" (1875). The motions of water are associated with inward renewal in "Brook and Wave" (1873) and "The Tides" (1875).

The most sustained images of the sea in his lyrical poetry reflect upon human creativity. "Seaweed" (1850) tracks the stages of the creative process—from the excitement of the initial impulse, through the stress of giving it form, to the peace of mind that comes at the end of the struggle to create. Many of these lyrics explore the nature of inspiration. The brilliant reflections of a celestial body on ocean swells represent the poet's flashes of intuition in "The Evening Star" (1850, titled "Chrysaor" in later editions). The crackle of a driftwood fire and the roar of the sea mingle with, and animate, the conversation of old-timers reminiscing on the past in "The Fire of Driftwood" (1850). The glimmer of a ship's lamp and the hushed breath of the sea anticipate the regenerative influence of dawn in "Four by the Clock" (1882). "The Sound of the Sea" (1875) explores the sudden and mysterious origins of inspiration. "Becalmed" (1882) compares a period without inspiration to an ocean calm. The speaker of "The Broken Oar" (1878) sees an analogy between the labor of the rower and the efforts of the poet. The vision of the poet is portrayed as a sea journey to the ends of the earth in "Dedication" (1880). The great poet of the future is depicted in "Possibilities" (1882) as a fearless mariner sailing through uncharted seas.

Longfellow's fascination with the sea, to the end of his life, seems in many respects to refect the attitudes of the landsman gazing wistfully at the sea in "The Secret of the Sea" (1850), haunted by a ballad with mystical implications. In the ballad, another landsman asks an aged helmsman the secret of the beauty of his song. The helmsman replies, "Only those who brave its dangers/ Comprehend its mysteries." [*See also* MONITOR AND MERRIMACK; "PIETAS IN PATRIAM"; SEA IMAGERY IN MODERN AND CONTEMPORARY POETRY]

FURTHER READING: Arvin, Newton. *Longfellow: His life and Work*. Boston: Little, Brown, 1963; Longfellow, Henry Wadsworth. *The Complete Poetical Works of Longfellow*. Ed. Horace E. Scudder. Boston: Houghton Mifflin, 1893; Longfellow, Samuel, ed. *Life of Henry Wadsworth Longfellow*. 3 vols. New York: Greenwood, 1969; Williams, Cecil B. *Henry Wadsworth Longfellow*. Boston: Twayne-G. K. Hall, 1964.

Joseph Flibbert

LONGFELLOW, SAMUEL. *See THALATTA.*

LONGITUDE: THE TRUE STORY OF A LONE GENIUS WHO SOLVED THE GREATEST SCIENTIFIC PROBLEM OF HIS TIME (1995). Written by journalist and science writer Dava Sobel (1947–), *Longitude* is a work of scientific and historical nonfiction that became an international best-seller. A fully illustrated edition by Sobel and William J. H. Andrewes was published in 1998. Andrewes also compiled *The Quest for Longitude* (1996), an illustrated collection of essays by twenty experts. Sobel's interest in history and science continued with *Galileo's Daughter: A Historical Memoir of Science, Faith, and Love* (1999).

Latitude is the distance, either north or south, from the equator. Since before the days of Christopher Columbus,* captains found their ships' latitude by measuring the angular distance from the horizon to either the North Star or the sun at its highest point during the day. Longitude is the distance, either east or west, from the prime meridian (e.g. Greenwich), a great circle. Longitude is more difficult to determine than latitude: the navigator must know the local time aboard his or her ship and simultaneously know the local time at a point on the prime meridian, because time equals east-west distance as a measure of the earth's rotation.

By the turn of the eighteenth century, when pendulum clocks kept time onshore, and "dead reckoning" was the only way to calculate longitude on board, a captain could sail across the Atlantic following a parallel of latitude but would be unsure of the longitude. He could not know for certain the ship's distance from land. The inability to determine longitude accurately resulted in protracted voyages and in shipwreck.* The quest for a means to find longitude at sea involved the greatest scientists of the period, including Galileo, Sir Isaac Newton, Edmund Halley, and Robert Hooke.

Sobel tells the story of 22 October 1707, when weather and navigational error wrecked four British warships and killed 2,000 men. Spurred by this disaster, Parliament enacted the Longitude Act of 1714, which offered up to £20,000 for a solution. Sobel's hero, John Harrison (1693–1776), craftsman and perfectionist, devoted his life to creating a marine timepiece, later named a chronometer, that could function accurately regardless of shipboard motion and temperature variation. Harrison completed the first of five successful marine timepieces in 1735. His third, H-3, took nineteen years to finish. As a result of his work, by 1815 about 5,000 chronometers were keeping time aboard ship. Captain James Cook, Captain William Bligh, and Captain Robert Fitzroy (master of the *Beagle,* on which Charles Darwin sailed) used early chronometers. Though Harrison received grants and financial awards, the Board of Longitude maltreated him and his inventions. He received the balance of his prize money only through the intervention of King George III.

In a lucid, logical style, Sobel weaves history and science into an exciting narrative, enabling readers of all levels of maritime experience to understand and enjoy the eighteenth-century race to discover a means to calculate longitude at sea, an essential chapter in maritime history.

Richard J. King

LONGITUDE 49 (first perf. 1950; pub. 1952). Written by ex-merchant seaman and Maritime Union official Herb Tank (1922–1982), *Longitude 49* is a well-crafted example of agitprop drama set aboard the American tanker *Mackay* docked in Abadan, Iran. Here the "workers" include Brooks, a black union delegate; Maguire, a disillusioned old radical; the country boy Alabama; and Blackie, a drunken ex-prize-fighter simmering with revolutionary fervor. The "capitalists" are represented by an anonymous Captain and Mate, who are concerned that Brooks' distribution of left-wing literature aboard the ship will cause dissension. The villainous Mate shoots Brooks, who had been subduing the inebriated Blackie to prevent him from attacking the officers. A blood transfusion provided by Alabama fails to save Brooks' life. The Captain, who initially encouraged the Mate to trump up a charge against Brooks, now turns on him in the face of solidarity among the crew. The crew's union-inspired strength precludes a more violent reaction, symbolized by Maguire's discarding a gun through a porthole.

Longitude 49 nicely captures the camaraderie of the forecastle and mess-room and is dense with details of the tanker trade. Brooks, the Mate, and the Captain are vaguely reminiscent of Billy, Claggart, and Vere in Herman Melville's *Billy Budd, Sailor* (1924). The resolution of the plot turns on the need to maintain the status quo and on maritime law, though Tank's sympathies are unambiguously with the crew. The play is also reminiscent of Eugene O'Neill's* S.S. *Glencairn** cycle (1919). The original New York production notably featured Sidney Poitier as Brooks. There were also productions at the left-wing Unity Theatre in London, in East Berlin, and in Czechoslovakia. [*See also* DRAMA OF THE SEA]

Attilio Favorini

LOVECRAFT, H[OWARD]. P[HILLIPS]. (1890–1937). Born in Providence, Rhode Island, H. P. Lovecraft subsequently used that seaport and such Massachusetts ports as Salem, Marblehead, and Newburyport (which he refashioned into "Arkham," "Kingsport," and "Innsmouth," respectively) in much of his weird fiction. In doing so, he drew not only upon Salem's importance in the history of the witchcraft hysteria but also upon maritime associations of those various ports.

These associations figure most prominently in "The Shadow over Innsmouth" (1942), a long story in which retired Captain Obed Marsh has established the Esoteric Order of Dagon, a cult involving the sea and the suggestively named Devil Reef at the entrance to Innsmouth harbor. The batrachian appearance of the port's inhabitants, it turns out, is a result of Marsh's return to Innsmouth long before with an aquatic, semihuman mate from the South Seas. Three stories set in Kingsport also touch upon New England's maritime history. "The Terrible Old Man" (1921) concerns a retired captain who preserves the souls of shipmates in bottles. "The Festival" (1925) deals with the survival of ancient rites in caverns connected to the town's harbor. In "The Strange High House in the Mist" (1931), an isolated cottage acts as a sinister gateway to the mysteries of the sea.

Behind much of Lovecraft's fiction lies his so-called Cthulhu Mythos, a pantheon of malign, vaguely defined deities who interact with, and prey upon, the human race. Cthulhu, for instance, is said to reign over the City of R'lyeh, which disappeared beneath the seas and thus presumably contributed to the myth of Atlantis. Dagon (not coincidentally, the Philistine god of the sea) is Cthulhu's subordinate. These deities figure directly in "Dagon" (1919) and "The Call of Cthulhu" (1928), in both of which submerged and fantastic realms rise unexpectedly to the surface of the sea, while in "The Temple" (1925) a disabled German submarine discovers Atlantis.

Lovecraft wrote floridly, making striking use of the sea and of outer space to suggest the loneliness of humanity within an indifferent, if not hostile, universe.

Grove Koger

LOWELL, JAMES RUSSELL (1819–1891). James Russell Lowell, poet, literary and social critic, editor, abolitionist, scholar of comparative literature, Harvard professor, diplomat, and consummate traveler, frequently crossed the Atlantic to visit Britain and the Continent. On 12 July 1851, he sailed from Boston in the bark *Sultana* on his first trip to Europe. As he relates in the section "At Sea" in *Leaves from My Journal in Italy and Elsewhere* (published as part of *Fireside Travels*, 1854), he found the five-week voyage tedious and exasperating, especially the twelve-day calm experienced in mid-Atlantic. The sea's repetitive action put him in mind of William Wordsworth's "Ecclesiastical Sonnets" (1837, published as "Ecclesiastical Sketches" in 1822) and the organ music of J. S. Bach.

The monotony was broken by the appearance of a finback whale and by the crew's harpooning a sunfish. Near the Azores, Lowell was so impressed with Portuguese men-of-war and flying fish that he conjectured how Pedro Calderón, renowned Spanish playwright of the Golden Age, would have rendered such creatures. He was particularly taken with the beauty of a bioluminescent trail of a shoal of fish, with sails by moonlight, and with a cloudless sunrise in midocean. He also took great delight in conjecturing when or whether a sail, an island, or the new shore of the Old World might appear on the ocean-horizon.

In the section "In the Mediterranean" in *Leaves from My Journal*, Lowell wrote warmly and with humor of the chief mate on his voyage, who, he declared, was the best thing he had seen and learned from at sea.

Aspects of the sea, especially its hazards, appear as themes in several of Lowell's poems. In "The Sirens" (1841) Lowell writes of the uninviting nature of the sea, where "A cold and lonely grave,/A restless grave" and "The leaden eye of the sidelong shark" and other dangers ever await the unwary mariner. "On Board the '76" (1865), a poem about a ship crippled in a sea battle, has a vivid description of the damage that pirate* cannon have inflicted on a ship's rudder, scuppers, sails, shrouds, and spars. However, "The Voyage to Vinland" (1868) treats the "unpathwayed seas" as a place of opportunity and exploration, where the doughty Biörn, the son of Heriulf, sees a ship that leads "every way to man's desire,/And ocean the wide gate to manful luck." Poems such as "Seaweed" (1859), "Bon Voyage" (1888), and "The Flying Dutchman" (1869) also include sea themes. [*See also* GHOSTS AND GHOST SHIP LEGENDS; SEA IMAGERY IN MODERN AND CONTEMPORARY POETRY]

Brendan A. Rapple

LOWELL, ROBERT, JR. [TRAILL SPENCE].

LOWELL, ROBERT, JR. [TRAILL SPENCE]. (1917–1977). Robert Lowell, the son of a naval officer, recalled in the poem, "Commander Lowell: 1887–1950" (*Life Studies*, 1959) how his father, in his postnaval life, would boom "Anchors Aweigh" in the bathtub and would frequent the Sunday Yacht Club and the Maritime Museum at Salem, Massachusetts. His mother's death is remembered in "Sailing Home from Rapallo: February 1954" (*Life Studies*), a description of his ocean voyage while accompanying his mother's body from Italy to the United States. His sonnet "To Margaret Fuller* Drowned" (1967) is a tribute to that writer, who was drowned with her husband and child.

In 1946 Lowell published *Lord Weary's Castle*, a collection of poems that includes "The Quaker Graveyard in Nantucket,"* an elegy written to commemorate Lowell's cousin, Warren Winslow, whose naval vessel disappeared during World War II. Often compared to John Milton's "Lycidas," "The Quaker Graveyard" evokes a graphic image of a drowned sailor caught in the dragnet of the ship before the corpse is weighted and once more consigned to the deep. Replete with literary allusions, the poem uses Melvillean references to Ahab* and the *Pequod*ername to depict the gory violence with which Nantucket Quakers captured and processed whales. Ultimately, however, human beings are powerless against the spewing Atlantic, which is engorged with dead sailors. "The Drunken Fisherman," also from *Lord Weary's Castle*, alludes to the spout of the sperm whale and the whale's fury.

Another key maritime influence was the Maine coastal town of Castine, where Lowell and his second wife, author and critic Elizabeth Hardwick, spent many summers. In "Castine Harbor" (1967), the ocean, a mix of hydrogen and oxygen in Lowell's poetic vision, becomes a symbol for marriage. "Castine 1860" (1970) evokes American watercolorist Fitz Hugh Lane's painting a ship in Castine harbor not far from Lowell's barn. In "No Hearing," Lowell watches the frothing breakers and the steamer the *State of Maine*, the training ship for the Maine Maritime Academy in Castine, in dry dock. In 1965 Lowell spent the summer in Castine and wrote "Waking Early Sunday Morning," "Fourth of July in Maine," and "Near the Ocean" (*Near the Ocean*, 1967). "Water," from *For the Union Dead* (1964), describes the granite shore of a nearby lobster town.

The Dolphin, a collection of confessional verse, was published in 1973 and won a Pulitzer Prize in 1974. Dolphin, mermaid,* and fishing images permeate the autobiographical content of the poems. Lowell's dramatic adaptation of Herman Melville's* tale "Benito Cereno"* (*The Old Glory*, 1964) won an Obie award for the best off-Broadway play. Among his translations is *The Voyage and Other Versions of Poems by Baudelaire* (1968). [*See also* SEA IMAGERY IN MODERN AND CONTEMPORARY POETRY]

FURTHER READING: Axelrod, Steven Gould, and Helen Deese. *Robert Lowell: A Reference Guide*. Boston: G. K. Hall, 1982; Hamilton, Ian. *Robert Lowell: A Biography*. New York: Random, 1982; Mariani, Paul. *Lost Puritan: A Life of Robert Lowell*. New York: Norton, 1994; Williamson, Alan. *Pity the Monsters: The Political Vision of Robert Lowell*. New Haven, CT: Yale UP, 1974.

Sally C. Hoople

M _____

MacDONALD, JOHN D[ANN]. (1916–1986). Best known for his creation of tough-guy detective Travis McGee, suspense novelist John D. MacDonald lived for many years in South Florida and set much of his work there. In his novels the sea functions both as a paradisiacal retreat from the commercialized Florida landscape and as an inviting backdrop for evil deeds. McGee himself lives on a houseboat, the *Busted Flush*; his adventures often have seagoing interludes or episodes, including violent climaxes on boats in *The Deep Blue Goodbye* (1964) and *Bright Orange for the Shroud* (1965). MacDonald's greatest sea story, however, entitled *The Last One Left* (1967), is outside the McGee series. This novel features murder at sea, a survivor adrift, betrayal among thieves, and buried loot. Characteristically, MacDonald demonstrates a sure touch with both a variety of high- and low-life characters and the subtropical settings they inhabit. [*See also* KEY WEST LITERATURE]

Philip J. Egan

MacHARG, WILLIAM [BRIGGS] (1872–1951). Born in Chicago, William MacHarg was a journalist, editor, and publisher of *The American Mercury*, as well as a fiction writer. He collaborated with Edwin Balmer (1883–1959) on mystery, romance, and adventure stories, some of which are set in the Chicago and Great Lakes* area. Their best-known novel, *The Indian Drum* (1917), deals with Chicago shipping empires and has its climax in a great winter storm on Lake Michigan. Corrupt ambition, disguise, madness, a purported Native American legend, and shipwrecks* contribute to this story of betrayal, blackmail, restoration, and atonement. Both authors also wrote short fiction, including stories of the Great Lakes, for newspapers and magazines. [*See also* AMERICAN INDIAN LITERATURE OF THE SEA]

Mary DeJong Obuchowski

MACK, WILLIAM P[ADEN]. (1915–   ). Novelist William P. Mack was born 6 August 1915, in Hillsboro, Illinois. His first professional writing experience was in 1931 as an interim reporter on the *San Francisco Daily News*, where his brother-in-law was city editor. He graduated from the U.S. Naval Academy in 1937. When, early in World War II, his destroyer, U.S.S. *John D. Ford*, returned from the American defeat in the Battle of the Java Sea, Mack wrote the official battle reports. Besides many professional articles, Mack has written three books known to every U.S. naval officer and appearing in a number of editions: *Naval Ceremonies, Traditions, and Usage* (1980), *Command at Sea* (1982), and *Naval Officer's Guide* (1964).

His distinguished naval career included assignments as speechwriter for the secretary of the navy and for presidents John F. Kennedy, Lyndon Johnson, and Richard Nixon. As commander, Seventh Fleet, during the Vietnam War, his operations against the North Vietnamese included the mining of Haiphong harbor in 1971. After serving as superintendent of the Naval Academy, Mack retired in 1975 as a vice admiral. Mack collaborated with his son, William P. Mack Jr., on a first novel, *South to Java* (1987), based upon his South Pacific experiences. Writing solo, Mack has produced five more World War II naval novels: *Pursuit of the Seawolf* (1991), *Checkfire!* (1992), *New Guinea* (1993), *Straits of Messina* (1994), and *Normandy* (1995). *Captain Kilburnie* (1998) is a novel of the Nelson era. Mack lives in Annapolis, Maryland.

C. Herbert Gilliland

MACKENZIE, ALEXANDER SLIDELL (1803–1848). Career naval officer, author, and naval historian, Alexander Slidell Mackenzie gained notoriety for his part in quelling the "mutiny"* aboard the *Somers** in December 1842. Mackenzie, who legally changed his last name from Slidell, entered the navy as a midshipman at age twelve, served under the legendary Oliver Hazard Perry, and eventually attained the rank of commander. He was captain of the *Somers*, a brig on her second cruise as a training vessel, when he was told by his first mate that there was an apparent plot by a small group of men to take over the vessel. Although he at first dismissed the story as exaggerated, Mackenzie came to believe the vessel was in danger of mutiny and hanged three of her crew at sea. One of the men executed was eighteen-year-old midshipman Philip Spencer, son of John C. Spencer, President Tyler's secretary of war. When news of the hangings made its way into the press, Mackenzie was both praised and vilified for his action. A court-martial trial cleared him of any misconduct.

In addition to serving in the navy, Mackenzie was an author of travel books as well as naval biographies. His works include *A Year in Spain* (1829), *The American in England* (1835), *Spain Revisited* (1836), *The Life of Commodore Oliver Hazard Perry* (1840), and *The Life of John Paul Jones** (1841). Mackenzie's actions in the *Somers* affair, together with his shrill participation in the debate over the Battle of Lake Erie in the War of 1812, earned him the enmity of fellow author and naval historian James Fenimore Cooper.* Mackenzie was respected and liked, however, by other members of the literary establishment, including Washington Irving,* Henry Wadsworth Longfellow,* and Richard Henry Dana Jr.*

Hugh Egan

MacLEISH, ARCHIBALD (1892–1982). Poet Archibald MacLeish is best known as a winner of three Pulitzer Prizes and as the librarian of Congress from 1939 to 1944. While a student at Yale University, MacLeish began a long friendship with Britain's sea-poet John Masefield. Following service in the army during World War I, MacLeish was a successful trial lawyer. In 1923 he quit the practice of law and moved his family to Paris, where he devoted his time to poetry. While in Paris he met and became friends with Ernest Hemingway,* F. Scott Fitzgerald,* and other authors and artists. His poetry often focused on aspects of nature, on exploration, or on nationalistic or patriotic themes.

Water as a metaphor played an important role throughout MacLeish's career, starting with his first published work, "The Song of the Canoe" (1911). MacLeish wrote another early work using the sea, "Soul-Sight" (1917), while on a troopship steaming toward war service in France. The sea appeared in many of his poems of exploration or discovery: "Land's End" (1927), "Pole Star" (1936), "Evacuation of Troy" (1948), "Ship's Logs" (1962), and *Conquistador* (1932), as a few examples. MacLeish's experiences while living on Anguilla for many summers highlighted his interest in islands and their inhabitants, as explored in "Hebrides" (1976), "Bahamas" (1962), and "Calypso's Island" (1952). Two poems for Hemingway, "Voyage" (1933) and "Poet" (1954), also include sea imagery.

Peter H. McCracken

MARDI AND A VOYAGE THITHER (1849). The third of Herman Melville's* published books, *Mardi*, in its use of symbolism and allegory, its experimentation with fictional forms, and its interest in metaphysical questions, anticipates the later preoccupations of *Moby-Dick** (1851). Like its predecessors *Typee** (1846) and *Omoo** (1847), *Mardi* begins as a conventional travel narrative based loosely on Melville's experiences in the South Pacific. But the narrator soon abandons in midsea a whaling voyage he finds dull and begins a succession of fabulous adventures when he encounters a brigantine adrift on the open sea with two survivors of an attack on it. In a later engagement, one of the survivors, Samoa, helps the narrator to rescue a beautiful and mysterious woman, Yillah, from a canoe where she is about to be offered as a human sacrifice. Proceeding to an archipelago called Mardi, the narrator, now infatuated by Yillah, assumes the persona of a demigod, Taji, and becomes the guest of Media, one of the islands' kings.

The sudden disappearance of Yillah prompts a voyage throughout the archipelago that occupies the remaining two-thirds of the work.

In his quest for the idealized Yillah, Taji is accompanied by Media and three sages: Mohi, a historian; Babbalanja, a philosopher; and Yoomy, a poet. As they journey through the archipelago, the sages debate such matters as death and immortality, faith, fame, kingship, power, evil, and truth—usually displaying the biases of their respective perspectives and often coming to no conclusion. Through these discussions, Melville repeatedly examines the issues of what constitutes authoritative knowledge, the differences between scientific and imaginative renderings of experience, and the relationship between fact and truth. When they come ashore, they scrutinize, often satirically, the islands and their rulers. For example, King Peepi, the ten-year-old-ruler of Valapee, rules entirely by whim; his counselors have flattened noses from bowing to him. Uhia, the ruler of Ohonoo, wants to move his island to the center of the archipelago to consolidate power over all of Mardi. The only ambition of Borabolla, the lord of Mondoldo, who lives from one feast to the next, is to increase his already considerable girth. Later islands such as Dominora (England) and Vivenza (the United States) allow Melville to engage in political satire on topical issues such as England's colonial ambitions and slavery in America.

The discursive structure of *Mardi*, its irreverent tone, and the inconclusive nature of most of the discourse portend the failure of the search for Yillah, called an Albino when first introduced, and prefigure the catastrophe of the search for the more ominous albino in *Moby-Dick*. Toward the conclusion of the narrative, Taji—reminded by an enchantress throughout the journey of the futility of his quest for the evanescent ideal of Yillah—visits Hautia on the isle of Serenia. Failing to overcome the hazards of deep diving for precious pearls, the west-journeying Taji sets off in endless pursuit of the ever-elusive Yillah.

FURTHER READING: Davis, Merrell R. *Melville's* Mardi—*A Chartless Voyage*. New Haven: CT: Yale UP, 1952; Foster, Elizabeth S. "Historical Note" in *Herman Melville*, Mardi *and a Voyage Thither*. Ed. Harrison Hayford et al. Evanston, IL, and Chicago: Northwestern UP, 1970; Moore, Maxine. *That Lonely Game: Melville*, Mardi *and the Almanac*. Columbia: U of Missouri P, 1975.

Joseph Flibbert

MARINE RESEARCH SOCIETY SERIES. Between 1921 and 1934, the Marine Research Society, operating out of the Peabody Museum of Salem, Massachusetts, published twenty-six books on maritime-related subjects. Intended both as entertaining reading and as references for scholars, these volumes or their reprints are standard references for traditional American maritime history scholarship. Subjects included the construction, rigging, and navigation of ships, stories of ships and their voyages, accounts of life at sea, pirates* and shipwreck,* fishing and whaling, marine art, and ship model construction. Most of the society's titles have become classics in their field. The society produced volumes both in regular and in large-paper editions and also distributed a newsletter to members. The society ceased operations after forty years, and its records are held today by the Peabody Essex Museum.

Daniel Finamore

"MAROONED" LITERATURE. Although the theme of the marooned (forcibly abandoned) or castaway (shipwrecked*) sailor is not unknown in American literature, there is little to compare with the stature of the two non-American works: Daniel Defoe's *Robinson Crusoe* (1719) and Johann David Wyss' *The Swiss Family Robinson* (1812–1813). There is instead a handful of what were once widely read factual narratives, primarily from the eighteenth and nineteenth centuries, as well as occasional uses of the theme in imaginative literature.

Not surprisingly, the earliest such accounts in North American maritime history made their way into the literatures of other nations. These include the story of the marooning of Marguerite de La Roque on the "Isle of Demons" off the eastern coast of Canada* in 1542, which soon found a place in the *Heptameron* (1558) of Marguerite of Navarre. More influential was William Strachey's account of the wreck of the *Sea Venture* in the Bermudas in 1609 and of its castaways, *A True Reportory of the Wracke, and Redemption of Sir Thomas Gates Knight* (1625), an apparent source in manuscript for Shakespeare's *The Tempest* (1623). Edward Cooke's *Voyage to the South Sea . . . Wherein Is Given an Account of Mr. Alexander Selkirk* (1712) is important as source material for *Robinson Crusoe*.

The wreck of the *Nottingham Galley* out of London was perhaps the most notorious shipwreck of the eighteenth century in American waters. Bound for Boston, the *Nottingham Galley* ran aground on Boon Island, a rock off the coast of New Hampshire, on 11 December 1710. By the time the survivors were rescued a few weeks later, they had been reduced to cannibalizing the bodies of their dead. The ship's captain, John Dean, and his brother Jasper published their account, *A Narrative of the Shipwreck of the* Nottingham Galley, in 1711. Cotton Mather promptly abridged the narrative in his *Compassions Called For* of the same year. The Deans produced a second version of their account in 1722, and in one form or another their story went through a number of British and American editions, becoming a staple of the "sensational" sea literature so popular at the time.

A number of important American accounts date from the early nineteenth century. One such was a Marylander's narrative of his five years on a barren island off the southwestern coast of South America, *A Journal of the Shipwreck and Sufferings of Daniel Foss* (1816). Another example is *A Narrative of the Sufferings and Adventures of Capt. Charles H. Barnard* (1829). Captain Barnard was collecting sealskins and oil in the Falkland Islands in 1813, when he rescued a party of British castaways. Although he informed them of the war that had recently broken out between their two countries and reached an agreement with them to ignore the hostilities, he subsequently found himself marooned by the Britons. Barnard's courage and resourcefulness enabled his small party to survive a year and a half in the harsh Antarctic climate.

Another American captain, James Riley,* ran his ship aground on the forbidding coast of northwest Africa opposite the Canary Islands on 7 September 1815. Riley described the wreck and the subsequent months of enslavement of his party by Saharawis in *Loss of the American Brig* Commerce (1817). The work proved phenomenally popular, selling a million copies by 1859, and was read by Abraham Lincoln when he was a child.

Fictional use of the castaway theme was made by Edgar Allan Poe* in *The Narrative of Arthur Gordon Pym of Nantucket** (1838) and by James Fenimore Cooper* in *Homeward Bound* (1838), *The Crater* (1847), and *The Sea Lions** (1849). Its fullest imaginative deployment in American literature, however, appears in the works of Herman Melville.* In *Typee** (1846) and *Omoo** (1847), Melville described a situation soon to become familiar in Pacific Island literature, that of the beachcomber who has jumped ship. In "The Encantadas, or, The Enchanted Isles"* (1856) he profiled a grim gallery of voluntary and involuntary exiles in the Galápagos Islands.*

Subsequent use of the theme was made by Jack London* in the climactic scenes of *The Sea-Wolf** (1904); by Charles Nordhoff* and James Norman Hall in *Pitcairn's Island* (1934); by James Gould Cozzens* in his allegorical novel *Castaway* (1934); by Kenneth Roberts* in his fictional account of the ordeal of the crew of the *Nottingham Galley, Boon Island* (1956); by Scott O'Dell in the young adult novel *Island of the Blue Dolphins* (1960); and by Frederic Prokosch in *The Wreck of the* Cassandra (1966). In the harrowing *John Dollar* (1989), Marianne Wiggins describes the moral degeneration of young girls castaway in the Andaman Islands, Bay of Bengal, leading critics to compare it to William Golding's *Lord of the Flies* (1954). [*See also* SEA-DELIVERANCE NARRATIVES]

FURTHER READING: Huntress, Keith, ed. *Narratives of Shipwrecks and Disasters, 1586–1860.* Ames: Iowa State UP, 1974; Leslie, Edward E. *Desperate Journeys, Abandoned Souls: True Stories of Castaways and Other Survivors.* Boston: Houghton Mifflin, 1988; Neider, Charles, ed. *Great Shipwrecks and Castaways; Authentic Accounts of Adventures at Sea.* New York: Harper, 1952; Wharton, Donald P., ed. *In the Trough of the Sea: Selected American Sea-Deliverance Narratives, 1610–1766.* Westport, CT: Greenwood, 1979.

Grove Koger

MARTIN, WILLIAM (1950–   ). History and the sea are the subjects of the fiction of William Martin, contemporary novelist and screenwriter. Born in Cambridge, Massachusetts, and earning a B.A. from Harvard University

(1972) and an M.F.A. from the University of Southern California (1976), Martin has spent much of his life on or near the coastal waters of Massachusetts. He is a member of an old Yankee family, and his work conveys a deep sense of the sea's prominence in shaping New England history, character, and landscape.

Back Bay (1980), the author's first novel, is a work of historical suspense that takes its title from a section of Boston built on a swamp in the nineteenth century to accommodate the newly wealthy merchant class. Told through the eyes of a contemporary history student, Martin's story employs historical detection and marine archaeology to forge present-day links to the thieves, privateers, shipowners, and merchants of Boston's maritime past.

Cape Cod (1991), Martin's fourth novel, turns to a theme of historical intrigue along New England's outermost shoreline. Once again, the sea is a central element in the novel, against which Martin offers detailed views of Cape Cod's* history, waters, and environmental conflicts. From the landing of the *Mayflower* passengers, through the age of sail, and into the present era of whale-watching, the sea mirrors the constancy and change experienced by Cape Codders from one generation to the next.

In a more recent novel, *Annapolis* (1996), Martin moves away from New England but continues to dramatize life at and near the sea, chronicling the perfidies, tragedies, and ambitions that form the history of the nation's naval institution and one of its prominent families. As with his earlier fictional work, Martin's novel is not only about the sea and our relationship with it; it is about our relationship to history itself.

Susan Raidy Klein

MARTIN EDEN (1909). This semiautobiographical novel by Jack London* traces a rough, untutored sailor's development into an accomplished writer. Martin Eden's chance acquaintance with Ruth Morse, a bourgeois student, motivates him to develop his mind in order to be worthy of her love. In so doing, Martin comes to realize that he has a talent and originality far beyond bourgeois conventionality; as he struggles in poverty for recognition as a writer, he becomes increasingly alienated. Therefore, when he does finally receive acclaim and win the acceptance of Ruth's family, he can feel only the hollowness of life and commits suicide.

The sea plays an indirect, albeit significant, role in the novel, almost all of which is set onshore. Martin does go to sea to get money in order to continue writing, but London only briefly, at best, outlines the hardships of the sailor's existence. At the end London also portrays Martin's dream of sailing off to Polynesia to escape the social world, but it is a dream that he lacks the will or energy to bring to reality. As a symbol of the mindless, naturalistic struggle that cannot be overcome by romantic dreams, the sea is an appropriate setting for the novel's ending, where Martin jumps overboard and drowns.

This novel was adapted into film in 1942, starring Glenn Ford.

John Samson

"MARTINGALE, HAWSER." *See* [SLEEPER, JOHN SHERBURNE].

MARY CELESTE. From time to time, ships at sea and even remote light-houses* have been found abandoned for no explicable reason and their crews never found. The half-brig *Mary Celeste* (built 1861) has become the quintessential archetype of these events and their ensuing lore and rationalization.

The *Mary Celeste* was launched as the *Amazon* in 1861. She was renamed the *Mary Celeste* in 1868. On 4 December 1872, she was found abandoned between the Azores and Portugal with her sails still set. The last logbook entry was 24 November, and her last position was given as six miles off the island of Santa Maria. Her boat was gone along with the ship's papers and the captain's chronometer and sextant, but other navigational instruments were still aboard. Nothing else appeared to be missing. There was some trash water in the cabins, but no sign of panic or violence. The vessel carried a cargo of 1,700 barrels of alcohol. The crew consisted of the captain, his wife, his two-year-old daughter, and a crew of seven. They were never found. The *Mary Celeste* was found by the British brigantine *Dei Gratia* and salvaged, but she later struck a reef near Haiti and was lost in 1885.

Popular newspaper accounts spread the story of the *Mary Celeste*. Dozens of legends have accreted to her, and numerous explanations of what happened have been posed. None have answered the question conclusively. Original documents pertaining to the *Mary Celeste* can be found in Charles Edey Fay, Mary Celeste: *The Odyssey of an Abandoned Ship* (1942; reprinted as *The Story of the "Mary Celeste,"* 1988).

Mary K. Bercaw Edwards and Horace Beck

MASON, ARTHUR (1876–1955). Born in Ireland, Mason went to sea at age seventeen to embark on a career that would last twenty-four years. He became a naturalized citizen of the United States in 1899. For much of his career he was engaged in the lumber trade out of various ports from San Francisco to the Pacific Northwest,* where he served as mate and captain on a number of vessels.

When his sea career was over, he worked as superintendent of deck rigging at the Port Newark naval shipyard at the beginning of World War I and then began his decade-long work as a writer. His main contributions to American sea literature include a novel, *The Flying Bo'sun: A Mystery of the Sea* (1920), and a collection of stories, *The Cook and the Captain Bold* (1924). He also published a less successful novel, *Swansea Dan* (1929), and two volumes of autobiography, *Ocean Echoes* (1922) and *An Ocean Boyhood* (1927). *The Flying Bo'sun* and *The Cook and the Captain Bold* are notable for Mason's engaging, plain style, for the inclusion of memorable anecdotes from small commercial vessels during the last years of sail, and for Mason's understated authority as an experienced seaman.

Bert Bender

MASON, F[RANCIS]. VAN WYCK (1901–1978). World War I and II veteran, importer, and ultimately writer, F. Van Wyck Mason was born in Boston on 11 November 1901. He was awarded a B.S. from Harvard University in 1924 after serving briefly with the U.S. Army in France during 1918–1919. After leaving Harvard, Mason operated an importing firm in New York for three years before retiring to become a full-time writer in 1928. In all, he penned fifty-eight novels, including mysteries and historical fiction. Mason also wrote a handful of children's books and, at various times, used the pseudonyms Van Wyck Mason, Geoffrey Coffin, Frank W. Mason, and Ward Weaver. From 1956 to his death in a drowning accident on 29 August 1978, Mason lived in Bermuda with his second wife.

Mason's career as a writer featured numerous historical romances or novels with a nautical setting. Although a few of his mystery novels were set at sea, his love of the sea inspired most of his historical fiction, beginning with his first romance, *Captain Nemesis* (1931). Though reviews were lukewarm, Mason hit the best-seller list with *Three Harbors* (1939), his first in a series of nautical fictional accounts of the American Revolution. Three more novels followed: *Stars on the Sea* (1940), *Rivers of Glory* (1942), and *Eagle in the Sky* (1948). Collectively, these four books took readers from the beginning to the end of the war. Four subsequent novels featured naval warfare, including the posthumously published *Armored Giants* (1980), an uninspired account of the *Monitor* and *Merrimack*.* Other books featured fictional accounts of Sir Francis Drake and Henry Morgan. In 1969 Mason published *Harpoon in Eden*, a story of Nantucket* whaling ships during the 1830s.

Mason never reached the popularity of writers such as Kenneth Roberts,* yet his prolific output attests to his success. From his remote island home, Mason reaped profits from fictional sea stories with historical settings.

Boyd Childress

MASON & DIXON (1997). Thomas Pynchon (1937–   ) refers to the sea extensively in the first 200 pages of his 773-page novel *Mason & Dixon*. Some twenty years after the fact, Rev. Wicks Cherrycoke is recounting a sailing expedition that he undertook in January 1761 aboard the British frigate *Seahorse* and his shipboard encounter with Charles Mason and Jeremiah Dixon, who are ostensibly sailing around the world to regain their "sanity." Images of eighteenth-century nautical life abound, including depictions of sailors with mouths open, with braided hair, wearing strange hats, puffing on pipes, and eating potatoes. Some seamen are described as jealous and loutish and frequently drunk, especially when asked to perform duties high in the masts or below on the lower deck. Others are desperate and dirty, and still others are daring and full of good humor. Once Mason and Dixon begin to map the American territories, the locale shifts from shipboard to the southern part of the United States, and the nautical references cease.

Too little is known about Pynchon's reclusive life to speculate about his penchant for including such detailed seafaring information as, for example, that no sailing ship would come intentionally to the windward side of another. In one significant nautical image, Mason compares the loss of his wife to having lost his anchor, drifting in unknown waters, and trying to reorient himself by aligning his position with celestial bodies and planets.

A voyage backward and forward in time, the novel may have been set in the eighteenth century, but the issues addressed, such as slavery, boundaries, and questions of time and moral responsibility, are of contemporary importance. [*See also V.*]

Ralph Berets

MATHER, COTTON. *See* "PIETAS IN PATRIAM."

MATTHIESSEN, PETER (1927–   ). New York-born Peter Matthiessen has borne the double titles of author and naturalist since the beginning of his professional writing career. Son of an architect father who was also a trustee of the National Audubon Society, Matthiessen has continually demonstrated a deep respect for, and knowledge of, the natural world, which permeates his writing. Having served in the navy 1945–1947, he began writing short stories at Yale University while enrolled in courses in zoology and ornithology. His junior year, 1948–1949, was taken at the Sorbonne, University of Paris. In 1950 he received both his B.A. from Yale and the distinguished *Atlantic* Prize for Best First Story ("Sadie").

In 1951 Matthiessen cofounded the *Paris Review* with Harold L. Humes, and during 1954–1956 he captained a deep-sea charter fishing boat out of Montauk, Long Island, New York. He has been a commercial fisherman and a member of expeditions to wild areas of all five continents, keeping a record of his observations of the natural world in both his fiction and nonfiction. His first nonfiction volume, the encyclopedic *Wildlife in America* (1959), was written after a three-year journey to every then-existing North American wildlife refuge and is in the permanent collection of the White House Library. He was a National Book Awards judge in 1970; he received both the National Book Award for Contemporary Thought and the American Book Award for *The Snow Leopard* (1978). In 1985 he was awarded a gold medal for Distinction in Natural History from the Academy of Natural Sciences. He is a member of the New York Zoological Society and from 1965 to 1978 served as a trustee.

The volumes of Matthiessen's work that depict the marine world are many and encompass diverse locales and themes; a recurring concern is the tension created between the natural world and capitalist forces. *Oomingmak: The Expedition to the Musk Ox Island in the Bering Sea* (1967) chronicles Matthiessen's experiences in a 1964 trip underwritten by the University of Alaska and the Institute of Northern Agricultural Research, whose purpose was the capture of musk ox calves for transfer to Fairbanks, where they would become the source of a permanent North American herd. In the same year he produced the reference *The Shorebirds of North America* with Ralph S. Palmer and artist Robert Verity Clem. In 1970 Matthiessen undertook another of his numerous "remote" journeys, this time as a diver in Australia, accompanying a team attempting to capture the first footage of the great white shark. He chronicled this period in *Blue Meridian: The Search for the Great White Shark* (1971). The film was eventually released under the title *Blue Water, White Death* (1970). He is also the author of a children's book, *Seal Pool* (1972), illustrated by William Pene Du Bois and published in England as *The Great Auk Escape*.

Far Tortuga* (1975) remains Matthiessen's most extensive fictional treatment of the sea and has enjoyed lasting critical acclaim for its singular narrative technique as well as its carefully researched and documented setting. The characters illustrate one of Matthiessen's ongoing concerns: the vanishing breed of "hands-on" fishers, slowly pushed into uselessness by human greed, monolithic corporations, and increasingly mechanized fishing procedures.

More recently, Matthiessen has returned to nonfiction chronicles about the sea and its inhabitants, human and otherwise. His own experience as a commercial fisherman and boat captain informs his study of the vanishing community of eastern Long Island fishermen, *Men's Lives: The Surfmen and Baymen of the South Fork* (1986), adapted into a play, *Men's Lives,** by Joe Pintauro (first perf. 1992; pub. 1994). His murder-mystery trilogy about Edgar J. Watson, pioneer of the Florida Everglades (*Killing Mr. Watson* [1990], *Lost Man's River* [1998], and *Bone by Bone* [1999]), is set in the Ten Thousand Islands region off the coast of southwest Florida. The lushly photographed *Baikal: Sacred Sea of Siberia* (1992) contains his diary of a twelve-day journey along the 400-mile lake that holds one-fifth of the world's fresh water and includes a study of the region's fishing population, wildlife, and encroaching pollution. Matthiessen continues to travel and explore widely, and his work appears in numerous popular publications including *Audubon, The New Yorker,* and *Outside.*

FURTHER READING: Cooley, John. "Matthiessen's Voyages on the River Styx: Deathly Waters, Endangered Peoples," *Earthly Words: Essays on Contemporary American Nature and Environmental Writers.* Ed. John Cooley. Ann Arbor: U of Michigan P, 1994, 167–92; Dowie, William. *Peter Matthiessen.* Boston: Twayne, 1991.

Eric G. Waggoner

MAURY, MATTHEW FONTAINE (1806–1873). The 1855 publication of Matthew Fontaine Maury's *Physical Geography of the Sea* inaugurated the distinct discipline of oceanography, but earlier essays under the pseudonym "Harry Bluff" helped shape reform of the antebellum U.S. Navy. Born in Fredericksburg, Virginia, Maury pursued a career as an officer in the U.S. Navy that led to his appointment as superintendent of the National Observatory in Washington, D.C. Maury's greatest contribution to literature was an oblique one: his research leading to the 1851 publication of his *Whale Chart* and *Explanations and Sailing Directions to Accompany the Wind and Current Charts* inspired Herman Melville's* chapter "The Chart" in *Moby-Dick** (1851).

On the eve of the Civil War, Maury resigned from the U.S. Navy to enter the service of the Confederacy, first as a naval officer and later as a diplomat. In 1868 he returned to the United States to teach at the Virginia Military Institute, where he remained for the rest of his life. Charles Lee Lewis has written *Matthew Fontaine Maury: The Pathfinder of the Seas* (1927).

R. D. Madison

MAYO, WILLIAM S[TARBUCK] (1811–1895). Born in Ogdensburg, New York, William S. Mayo was a successful physician and author of popular adventure fiction. His mother's family had been in the whaling industry for generations, and his father served in the merchant marine and owned a boatbuilding business. Family lore and his father's tales probably contributed to his desire for adventure and influenced his writings about the sea. From 1838 to 1840 Mayo sailed to northern Africa, the Barbary Coast, and Spain; although he reportedly kept notebooks of these journeys, none have been found.

Mayo's fiction satisfied the popular appetite for exotic travel adventure. His travel experience formed the basis of his first novel, the critically acclaimed and best-selling *Kaloolah; or, Journeyings to the Djebel Kumri: An Autobiography of Jonathan Romer* (1849), which focuses on the protagonist's adventures in America, at sea, and in Africa. His second novel, *The Berber* (1850), which features a Barbary pirate,* was based on Mayo's travels and his study of Moorish life and customs. *Romance Dust from the Historic Places* (1851), a collection of miscellaneous writings, also focuses on the sea adventures of captains, pirates, and merchants. Mayo often touched on social issues and the need for reform in his sea fiction. In "The Captain's Story" (1846) and *Kaloolah*, he denounced the harsh treatment of sailors. Also in *Kaloolah* the evils of slavery are represented through a depiction of the brutal conditions aboard a slave ship. *Kaloolah* has been suggested as a source for Herman Melville's* *Moby-Dick** (1851); an article by Cecil D. Eby Jr., published in the *New England Quarterly*, compares the two works (1962).

In 1851 Mayo married into wealth, resigned his medical practice, and pursued private business interests. In 1862 he published a thirty-three-page letter to Abraham Lincoln's secretary of the navy, Gideon Welles, in which he presented his plan for establishing American control of the seas. He did not publish fiction again until his 1871 novel of manners, *Never Again*.

Christina L. Wolak

McCORMICK, JAY W. (1919–   ). Jay W. McCormick was born and grew up in the small Lake Huron port town of Harbor Beach, Michigan. His father was a Great Lakes* ship captain, and the younger McCormick spent considerable time sailing the Lakes with him. After he graduated from the University of Michigan in 1942, he became a reporter for the *Detroit News* and ultimately taught English at Wayne State University.

Of his two published novels, *November Storm* (1943) is the more critically acclaimed and successful because of McCormick's close association with, and knowledge of, its subject. Originally written while he was a senior at Michigan, it won a prestigious Hopwood Award in creative writing from that institution in 1942. The story, considered by some critics to be the best portrayal of life aboard a Great Lakes ship, concerns a teenage boy who takes a job as deckhand on an ore carrier. In this rite of passage, an awkward and naive young man is initiated not only into the life of a sailor but into life as an adult as well. The confined and claustrophobic space of the ship, its own microcosm, forces him into contact with a number of characters, many of whom are deftly drawn. The crew are only ordinary men, but the very ordinariness of their lives brings out desire, pettiness, jealousy, and violence. The dramatic climax of the novel comes when a terrifying autumn storm descends upon the ship in Lake Michigan.

Robert Beasecker

McKENNA, RICHARD [MILTON] (1913–1964). Richard McKenna was a career naval enlisted man whose 1962 novel *The Sand Pebbles* is a classic of naval fiction.*

McKenna's childhood in Mountain Home, Idaho, was enriched by his great habit of reading, but when he entered the navy at age eighteen, he found it difficult to keep that habit alive due to prevailing demeaning assumptions about the interests of enlisted men. Nevertheless, even while serving on U.S. Asiatic Fleet ships such as the *Asheville, Edsall, Luzon*, and *Gold Star*, he managed to keep reading; the flood of good books and educated servicemen he encountered in World War II motivated him to become a novelist.

McKenna retired from the navy as a chief petty officer in 1953. After earning a degree at the University of North Carolina, McKenna began writing science fiction stories such as those later published in *Casey Agonistes and Other Stories* (1973). He published a few naval stories in national magazines and then wrote *The Sand Pebbles*, an instant popular success. McKenna set the novel on a naval gunboat in China in the midst of the Chinese revolution in the 1920s, drawing on tales of his shipmates, on his own long experience as a machinist's mate, and on extensive research into history and anthropology. Perhaps the most unusual feature of McKenna's writing is his ability to evoke the mystery of a young enlisted man's encounter with steam engineering. He also draws a powerful portrayal of the gradual disintegration of a naval crew, paints an authentic picture of U.S. gunboat diplomacy in the era, and outlines convincingly the awakening of his protagonist into the great, mysterious world beyond his ship and the naval service.

Completed portions of McKenna's second novel and other stories were published in *The Sons of Martha and Other Stories* (1967) and in Robert Shenk's *The Left-Handed Monkey Wrench: Stories and Essays by Richard McKenna* (1986).

Robert Shenk

McNALLY, TERENCE (1939–   ). Terence McNally's seriocomic dramas have won him acclaim as one of the most prolific playwrights of the 1990s, one particularly interested in the representation of gay men. Along with other dramatists who portray the healing and redemptive powers of nature for the urban character, McNally uses a popular seaside resort for his pastoral setting. In *Lips Together, Teeth Apart* (first perf. 1991; pub. 1992), the gay colony of New York's Fire Island is the scene in which two married couples—John and Chloe, Sally and Sam—spend the Fourth of July weekend. While siblings Sam and Chloe relive childhood memories, Sally and John attempt to hide their night of passion from their spouses. John and Chloe hide the fact that John has incurable cancer. Sam and a pregnant Sally grapple with her history of miscarriages, Sam's midlife crisis, and the appropriateness of their holding on to the summer house in a gay colony bequeathed to Sally by her brother, who has died of AIDS. McNally's adeptness at humorously drawn characters overrides the occasional melodramatic effect, while his language and imagery achieve a poignant lyricism. This is nowhere more evident than in the memories of the ocean that become significant markers in the life of each character, shared in effusive exchanges that echo the rhythms of the sea.

Sealed off from the ocean's expanse lies the pool, around which the play's action takes place. If the ocean represents, as it does to Chloe, restorative powers of nature, then the pool—man-made, chemically treated, in which neither couple will swim—represents both emotional isolation and the irrational fear of AIDS. Thus, when both couples immerse themselves and share their anxieties and secrets, the water offers absolution. When at the play's conclusion they view, along with their offstage and unseen neighbors, the Independence Day fireworks, the ocean becomes the site for a ritualized, communal experience in which individuals are joined to community and nation. Fire Island, the gay resort, serves as a liminal site mediating between civilization and nature and between the private and social realms.

McNally utilizes the pastoral genre and the recuperative power of water in two other noteworthy plays, *Love! Valour! Compassion!* (first perf. 1994; pub. 1995) and *Dusk* (first perf. 1996; pub. 1996). In the former, nocturnal skinny-dipping represents a healing and rebirth for a community of friends devastated by losses of all kinds, particularly due to AIDS. *Dusk*, the last in a triptych of short plays set on a beach, by McNally, Joe Pintauro, and John Guare, was produced under the title *By the Sea, by the Sea, by the Beautiful Sea* (1996). [*See also* DRAMA OF THE SEA; NANTUCKET CYCLE]

David R. Pellegrini

McPHEE, JOHN [ANGUS] (1931–   ). John McPhee, master craftsman of nonfiction prose in more than twenty books and *New Yorker* articles beyond count, turned his attention to the sea in *Looking for a Ship* (1990). The subject is actually multiple: the decline of the U.S. Merchant Marine, a young mate's frustrating search for his next berth, a tough, honest captain's perspective on fifty years of seafaring, and an old container ship on a voyage down the west coast of South America. But while McPhee amasses facts and details, sorts and resorts them, and listens to the voices of officers and crew, these strands twist together, and the narrative advances and deepens as precise information about the ship and her men accumulates.

Contexts in every aspect of seamanship—navigation, ship handling, pilotage, stowage, storm strategy—the encumbrances of bureaucracy, and the dangers of piracy expand page by page, while extended portraits of Second Mate Andy Chase and Captain Paul Washburn, as well as shorter profiles of half a dozen other officers and seamen, grow incrementally through conversations. McPhee's method is an arduous one, almost like that of a computer programmer piecing together bits of information, inventing possible chains, and testing alternative paths to create an accurate and accessible vision of the daily life of merchant sailors. If the text provides a view more from the bridge than the engine room, as some readers note, that view nevertheless comprehends the whole ship and her men, both afloat and ashore. The closing image of the S.S. *Stella Lykes*, "dead in the water" off Balboa with a fractured hull and power plant down, stands as an emblem of the whole narrative. [*See also* CRUISING LITERATURE]

Robert C. Foulke

MELVILLE, HERMAN (1819–1891). More than any other American author, Herman Melville used the sea as setting and concept to create great literature. With broad-ranging and deep philosophical interests, his books are far more than adventure stories. In his works, Melville struggles with human interactions in a diverse and complex world, the boundaries of knowledge, and the search for truth. Melville's success began with his first book, *Typee** (1846), and continued with *Omoo** (1847). While financial success eluded Melville after these first two books, their reception was a major influence on his continuing to write on maritime subjects. His time at sea inspired his next four books; *Mardi** (1849), *Redburn** (1849), *White-Jacket** (1850), and *Moby-Dick** (1851). Only *Pierre* (1852) is a complete departure from the sea: he returns with "The Encantadas"* (1854), the John Paul Jones* section of *Israel Potter* (1854–1855), and "Benito Cereno"* (1855). Moreover, *The Confidence-Man* (1857) is set on a steamboat, and many of Melville's Civil War poems in *Battle-Pieces* (1866) concern naval warfare. Late in his life, however, he published *Clarel* (1876), an 18,000-line poem of a pilgrimage through the Holy Land with little maritime association, and *Timoleon* (1891), a small collection of nonmaritime poems. Nonetheless, his other late collection of poems, *John Marr and Other Sailors** (1888), and *Billy Budd, Sailor** (1924), the short novel he was working on at the time of his death, exhibit a powerful maritime influence.

Although born to an upper-middle-class family, at age twelve Melville was thrust into poverty when his father, Allan Melvill, went bankrupt and died in delirium in 1832. His mother, Maria Gansevoort Melvill, was left with eight children and no way to make a living. In 1839 Melville (the final "e" was added to the family name in 1832) went to sea in an effort to help support his family. Now age nineteen, he signed on to the full-rigged merchant vessel *St. Lawrence* (1833), Oliver P. Brown, master, for his first sea voyage. Melville sailed from New York to Liverpool and back to New York: the passage to England took twenty-seven days, and the passage home forty-nine days. Melville's fourth book, *Redburn: His First Voyage*, subtitled *Being the Sailor-boy Confessions and Reminiscences of the Son-of-a-Gentleman, in the Merchant Service*, describes in a fictional manner what Melville encountered as he learned the skills of a sailor.

Melville's next major trip was in 1840, when he traveled to Illinois by boat with his friend Eli James Murdock Fly. Their three-day journey by canalboat from Albany to Buffalo may have provided the description of the Erie Canal found in Chapter 54 of *Moby-Dick*, "The Town-Ho's Story." Melville and Fly crossed Lake Erie by steamboat and then, from Detroit, booked passage on a Lake Huron and Lake Michigan steamboat to Chicago. From there, Melville and Fly crossed the prairie to Galena, Illinois, where his uncle Thomas Melvill Jr. had a farm. It is unknown whether Melville actually went up the Mississippi River since the source for his description of "The River," meant to be a part of *The Confidence-Man*, is actually Timothy Flint's *A Condensed Geography and History of the Western States; or, The Mississippi Valley* (1828). However, Melville's time on inland waterways decidedly influenced his tenth book, *The Confidence-Man*, a bleak work of despair set on board the *Fidéle*, a Mississippi River steamboat. The month and route of Melville's return to New York are unknown.

With his family still in financial trouble, Melville embarked from Fairhaven, Massachusetts, on 3 January 1841, for the most influential voyage of his life. He joined the crew of the whaleship *Acushnet* (1840), Valentine

Pease Jr., master, on its maiden voyage. His time on the *Acushnet* is the basis for his account of a whaling voyage in his sixth book, *Moby-Dick*. But the vessel Melville creates in *Moby-Dick*, the *Pequod*,* is a fantastical Nantucket* ship, with belaying pins of sperm-whale teeth and a tiller made from the lower jaw of a sperm whale. Melville, at twenty-one, shipped on the *Acushnet* as a green hand—the same rank he had held on the *St. Lawrence*. However, before his whaling years were finished, Melville had worked his way up to bow oarsman, the position held by Ishmael* in *Moby-Dick*, and then possibly to boatsteerer (harpooneer).

In November 1841 the *Acushnet* spent six days at anchor off Chatham Island in the Galápagos Islands.* The Galápagos, the location of Melville's ten sketches entitled "The Encantadas"* (1854), were called enchanted because the baffling currents in nearby waters were, Melville writes, "so strong and irregular as to change a vessel's course against the helm, though sailing at the rate of four or five miles the hour" (sketch first, "Encantadas"). The *Acushnet* returned to the waters of the Galápagos for the month of January 1842, but the six days at Chatham Island in 1841 were the longest continuous period during which Melville may have had the possibility of going ashore. Surprisingly. Chatham Island is referred to only twice—and then in passing—in "The Encantadas."

When the *Acushnet* reached Nukahiva in the Marquesas Islands in July 1842, Melville and his shipmate Richard Tobias Greene, whom he called "Toby," deserted and made their way to the interior. Melville hurt his leg en route and was forced to remain behind while Toby escaped, hoping to secure medicines for Melville. However, Toby never returned, and Melville learned only years later that he had effected his escape on another Fairhaven whaleship, the *London Packet*.

The embellished story of his adventures on Nukahiva is told in Melville's first book, *Typee*. In reality he spent only one month on the island (9 July–9 August 1842), but he lengthens the time to four months in his narrative. As he did with all his books, in writing *Typee*, Melville interspersed his own adventures with information he found in written sources. Three major sources for *Typee* are David Porter's* *Journal of a Cruise Made to the Pacific Ocean* (1815), Charles S. Stewart's *A Visit to the South Seas* (1831), and George H. von Langsdorff's *Voyages and Travels in Various Parts of the World* (1813).

Melville escaped from Nukahiva on the Australian whaleship *Lucy Ann* (1819), Henry Ventom, master. Now signed as an able seaman, he joined a crew torn by dissent. The *Lucy Ann* was bark-rigged and quite small, only eighty-seven feet long, with a sickly captain and a first mate, James German, who was prone to drink. Additionally, the vessel was inadequately officered. It carried four whaleboats but had only one mate, two illiterate boatsteerers, and a newly shipped boatsteerer who soon turned against the captain. A whaleship carrying four whaleboats would normally carry four mates (or boatheaders) and four boatsteerers (or harpooneers). The captain soon became very ill, and German headed for Tahiti, where the captain was put ashore. In an effort to prevent desertion while yet staying close to the captain, the *Lucy Ann* left port and sailed back and forth off the harbor of Papeete, Tahiti; there, ten men refused duty. These ten men were held on the French frigate *La Reine Blanche*; later, they were taken to a Tahitian "calaboose" (jail). Melville joined the mutineers in their confinement ashore. During his time as a prisoner, Melville was under a doctor's care, and his leg was treated. Roughly three weeks later, in October 1842, Melville escaped to the neighboring island of Eimeo (now Moorea), Society Islands. Melville's passage on the *Lucy Ann*, the mutiny,* and his imprisonment are treated in his second book, *Omoo*.

Melville wandered the island of Eimeo until November 1842, when he joined the Nantucket whaleship *Charles and Henry* (1832), John B. Coleman Jr., master. Melville evidently signed on as boatsteerer and spent five months aboard the *Charles and Henry*, much less than the claim of "the author's own personal experience, of two years & more, as a harpooneer" that he made to his English publisher, Richard Bentley (letter of 27 June 1850). From his time on the *Charles and Henry*, Melville drew the beginning of his third book, *Mardi*.

Discharged at Lahaina, Maui, Melville traveled to Oahu aboard the *Star*, Captain Burroughs, master. During Melville's stay in Honolulu, the *Acushnet* came into port, and Valentine Pease Jr., on 2 June 1843, filed an affidavit taking notice of Melville's desertion eleven months earlier, a federal offense. Six weeks later, Melville enlisted as an ordinary seaman on the American naval frigate *United States* (1797), James Armstrong, master. The frigate sailed under the pennant of Commodore Thomas ap Catesby Jones. Melville was one of approximately 480 men on board.

Melville spent fourteen months on the *United States*, and in that time he witnessed 163 floggings. His absolute hatred of this form of corporal punishment resounds throughout his fifth book, *White-Jacket*, and in his final work, *Billy Budd, Sailor*. Melville's long period at sea ended on 3 October 1844, when the *United States* arrived at Boston. He traveled on the ocean several more times, but never again as a seaman. In 1860 he sailed around Cape Horn* aboard the clipper ship *Meteor* (1852) with his younger brother, Thomas, as captain. Homesick and depressed, however, Melville took a steamer from San Francisco to Panama, crossed the isthmus, and then returned to New York on the steamer *North Star*.

Although unknown to him at the time, an event occurred while Melville was at sea on the *Charles and Henry* that would deeply affect his life. His first cousin Guert Gansevoort was the first lieutenant of the U.S. training brig *Somers** (1842) under the command of Captain Alexander Slidell Mackenzie.* Three men, including the son of the secretary of war, were hanged for mutiny on 1 December 1842. Mackenzie was court-martialed after questions arose as to whether a mutiny had actually been planned. Some claimed that Mackenzie should have waited until the *Somers* reached St. Thomas in the Virgin Islands, a mere two days away, to try the men in a formal military court. Mackenzie was acquitted, but questions remain to this day. The many similarities between the *Somers* incident and *Billy Budd, Sailor* include a suspected mutiny, a "drumhead court" or officers' council controlled by the commanding officer, punishment by hanging, and unresolved questions about the commander's decision. Melville refers directly to the *Somers* in *Billy Budd, Sailor*, suggesting that he was still troubled almost fifty years later by an incident so closely tied to his family.

In his writings, Melville relied not only on his own experience but also very heavily on his reading. "I have swam through libraries," he writes in *Moby-Dick* (ch. 32). Melville consumed books and was consumed by them. As he read, he argued with them, laughed and cried over them, and became fiercely angry with them. The books he owned are filled with notes and jottings done with slashing pen marks and furious periods. Melville's reading, both literary and factual, inspired his writing. An alchemist of words, Melville transformed his often mundane sources. For example, the information in the "Cetology" chapter of *Moby-Dick* (ch. 32) is borrowed nearly verbatim from the "Whales" entry in volume 27 of *The Penny Cyclopaedia of the Society for the Diffusion of Useful Knowledge* (1843). As Melville infused the dry information with his own humor and philosophical ponderings, he transformed it into literature of the highest order.

Both his time at sea and his reading influenced Melville's works, but he might never have achieved greatness had he not met first Evert Duyckinck, at the center of the New York literary world, and then Nathaniel Hawthorne.* Melville initially met Duyckinck as the editor of *Typee*, and although the two men were quite different, remarkably, they became friends. Melville had access to Duyckinck's library, one of the greatest private libraries in the country. Duyckinck wrote to his brother George: "Melville . . . has borrowed Sir Thomas Browne of me and says finely of the speculations of the *Religio Medici* that Browne is a kind of 'crack'd Archangel.' Was ever anything of this sort said before by a sailor?" (letter of 18 March 1848). In August 1850, Duyckinck went to Pittsfield, Massachusetts, to visit Melville, and during this visit a party of ten, seven of whom were literary men, climbed Monument Mountain. Here, for the first time, Melville met Hawthorne. His new book, which he had previously told Duyckinck was "mostly done," took another year to complete. That book was *Moby-Dick*, and Melville's long, philosophical conversations with Hawthorne reshaped the book, subsequently dedicated to Hawthorne. The letter Hawthorne wrote on first reading *Moby-Dick* no longer exists, but Melville's response to it does. Melville calls it "your joy-giving and exultation-breeding letter" and goes on to say: "A sense of unspeakable security is in me this moment, on account of your having understood the book" (letter of [17?] November 1851).

Unfortunately, few others understood, and *Moby-Dick* was never reprinted in Melville's lifetime. Melville spent the next forty years living in obscurity until his death. He wrote only two more full-length works after *Moby-Dick* and worked for nineteen years as a customs inspector. It was a life of aching sadness, depressed and depressing. When he died, he was yet again revising the manuscript he had entitled *Billy Budd, Sailor*. The redemption of his reputation began with the publication of Raymond Weaver's biography, *Herman Melville: Mariner and Mystic*, in 1921 and has continued to this day.

Among the rich and numerous critical, biographical, and/or derivative works that have appeared over the years, even contemporary authors such as Larry Duberstein (*The Handsome Sailor*, 1998) and Frederick Busch (*The Night Inspector*, 1999) have turned to the historical Melville as a significant character in their novels. [*See also* MELVILLE DRAMATIZATIONS; MELVILLE'S POETRY OF THE SEA; MUTINIES; RED RECORD; WHALING NARRATIVES]

FURTHER READING: Bercaw, Mary K. *Melville's Sources*. Evanston, IL: Northwestern UP, 1987; Gilman, William H. *Melville's Early Life and* Redburn. New York: New York UP, 1951; Heflin, Wilson. "*Herman Melville's Whaling Years*." Diss. Vanderbilt University, 1952 (presently being co-edited by Thomas Farel Heffernan and Mary K. Bercaw, forthcoming, Vanderbilt UP); Sealts, Merton M., Jr. *Melville's Reading*. Columbia: U of South Carolina P, 1988; Springer, Haskell, and Douglas Robillard. "Herman Melville," *America and the Sea: A Literary History*. Ed. Haskell Springer. Athens: U of Georgia P, 1995, 127–45.

Mary K. Bercaw Edwards

MELVILLE DRAMATIZATIONS. Herman Melville* (1819–1891), himself influenced by dramatists as diverse as Shakespeare and Douglas Jerrold (British author of popular nautical melodrama), has, in turn, inspired numerous dramatizations of his own work. These include adaptations for stage, film, television, opera, dance, and even mime. The dramatizations are characteristically marked as much with the historical reflection and worldviews of their adapters as with the presumptions of their originals.

The adaptations develop a trend toward dramatizing rather than narrating evident in Melville's own late work, as noted by Harrison Hayford and Merton Sealts, editors of *Billy Budd,* * *Sailor (an Inside Narrative)* (1962). This last novel of Melville has, in fact, been dramatized most frequently, though all but one of these dramatizations were written without knowledge of the scholarly edition that removed what was mistakenly thought of as the historical "preface" to the story and that documented Melville's presumed intention to leave unresolved the contradictions his story raised. Paradoxically enough, the enticement of dramatic irony that allowed Melville to move among various narrative positions has eluded the many dramatizers of the novel, whose adaptations tend to resolve Melville's ambiguities one way or another. Thus, Louis O. Coxe* and Robert Chapman, the first dramatizers of *Billy Budd* (as *Uniform of Flesh* in 1947 and then rev. as *Billy Budd* and perf. on Broadway in 1951), supply the scene of Vere's communicating the death sentence to Billy, which the novel's narrator only conjectures; they show Vere's begging forgiveness and telling Billy that the law is "wrong." At the same time, they eliminate mention of Vere's death, of the erroneous report of the events, and "Billy in the Darbies." In this adaptation, Billy's fate loses some of its implacability, and the drama seems to derive from the development of Vere's conscience.

The libretto by E. M. Forster and Eric Crozier for the Benjamin Britten opera (1951; rev. 1961) narrows the focus of the action by framing the story with a prologue and epilogue delivered by an aged Vere. Their Vere is a more sensitive soul than Melville's, and their Billy less of a radical innocent. The opera employs "Billy in the Darbies" melodramatically before the hanging, rather than in its narrative setting as playing a part in the mythologizing of Billy Budd. Peter Ustinov's 1962 film, in which he took the role of Vere, also seems to place emphasis on Vere as a referee between good and evil, though critical reaction was divided over whether he was a tragic figure, a feelingless Pilate, or a martinet. In various adaptations, Claggart's character is overdetermined as motivated by fear, pride, impotence, or homosexual attraction. A television adaptation in 1952 changed the setting to an American ship during the War of 1812 and featured a prologue presenting Vere as torn between personal feelings and duty to country but ultimately justified in maintaining discipline. This prologue was delivered on television by Admiral William Halsey. By contrast, in a 1969 musicalized stage version, Billy stands in for conscientious objectors, and his mates sing a song entitled "It Ain't Us Who Makes the Wars." Joyce Sparer Adler's *Melville, Billy and Mars* (1989) likewise interprets the novel as being fundamentally antiwar and treats Vere as embodying the tragedy of civilization, which has found it necessary to follow the violent way of Claggart and to sacrifice the peace symbolized by Billy.

*Moby-Dick** (1851) has naturally offered more challenges to dramatization, spurring adapters to experimentation in virtually all dramatic media. None of the three Hollywood films of the novel is considered a classic. A 1926 silent version and a 1930 sound film featured John Barrymore as Ahab* and eliminated Ishmael.* Ahab survives and comes back to marry the girl he left behind. The 1956 film version was written by Ray Bradbury,* directed by John Huston, and starred Gregory Peck as Ahab. The American painter Gilbert Wilson* was fascinated by *Moby-Dick*, having written a libretto and designed stage sets for an opera entitled *The White Whale*, and created a thirty-minute, 16mm film of the novel (1955), narrated by Thomas Mitchell. The experimental Iowa Theatre Lab toured with a mime adaptation of the novel in the 1970s. Charles Olson* wrote *The Fiery Hunt*, a dance drama in four parts, in 1948 for Erik Hawkins of the Martha Graham troupe. The drama features Ahab as protagonist and Ishmael as chorus, depicting the whale as manifestation of the conflict within Ahab's psyche. It was never performed (pub. 1977). Peter Mennin composed *Concerto for Orchestra* (Moby-Dick) in 1952, an ominous and ruggedly virile modal piece that depicts the mystery and obsession behind Ahab's relentless pursuit. The work premiered the same year and was recorded in 1996. In 1996 two operatic versions of *Moby-Dick* were presented. *Moby-Dick: An American Opera* (music by Doug Katsaros; libretto by Mark St. Germain) was produced by the Players Guild of Canton, Ohio, and *Moby-Dick* (music by Paul Flush and John Kenny; libretto by Paul Stebbings and Phil Smith) was produced by American Drama Group Europe and TNT Music Theatre Britain in Volos, Greece. A television adaptation of the novel (1998) featuring Patrick Stewart as Ahab and Gregory Peck (Ahab in the 1956 film) as Father Mapple* did not win wide acclaim. Also in 1998 the Snug Harbor Cultural Center on Staten Island produced the experimental, multimedia *Ahab's Wife* or the Whale* by Ellen Driscoll and Tom Sleigh. This production was less an adaptation than a series of theatrical images inspired by the novel. A similarly adventuresome approach was followed by the avant-garde solo performance artist Laurie Anderson, whose "Songs and Stories from Moby Dick" premiered in 1999.

Two authors have attempted full-fledged stage adaptations. Adler's *Moby-Dick* (1989) emphasizes the magnetic pull on Ishmael of essentially life-destructive Ahab and the opposing influence of life-preserving Queequeg.* The dramatization uses a screen as a backdrop to project slides of Rockwell Kent's* illustrations from the 1930 Random House edition. Orson Welles' *Moby-Dick, Rehearsed* (first perf. in London in 1955; pub. in a rev. version in 1965) uses the device of a rehearsal by an acting troupe of the 1890s to concentrate on the poetry in the novel. Welles focuses on key scenes and emphasizes the great passages of the work. Because of the brevity of the play, characters other than Ahab are not so much developed as introduced. Sometimes lines are assigned to characters other than those Melville designated, and key characters (Fedallah) and scenes (the doubloon scene) are eliminated or greatly truncated. The actor-characters explain the omissions with the complaint "We have been asked to learn enough of it," presumably in school. Yet, the actors are rehearsing in the 1890s, when Melville had been largely forgotten. Like the Coxe/Chapman and Forster/Crozier dramatizations of *Billy Budd*, Welles' stage adaptation of *Moby-Dick* has held the stage since its premiere, notably in an environmental staging in Denver in 1980 by the respected director William Woodman and in revivals in 1996 by the Theatre Workshop of Nantucket* and in 1999 by the Berkshire Theatre Festival in Stockbridge, Massachusetts.

"Benito Cereno"* (1856) has also been notably dramatized. Robert Lowell's* adaptation was initially produced in the 1960s and published in 1965, along with his dramatizations of Nathaniel Hawthorne's* short stories "En-decott and the Red Cross" and "My Kinsman, Major Molineux," under the collective title *The Old Glory* (1965). Lowell shifts his focus from Amaso Delano* as a symbol of America's inability to comprehend evil, perhaps in reaction to the critical view espoused by Yvor Winters that the Africans in revolt themselves symbolized evil. Written and performed during the de-veloping civil rights struggle, Lowell's drama converts the novella into a play on race relations in the 1960s, linking the event on the Spanish ship *San Dominick* to historical conditions in the pre–Civil War United States and to ongoing social conditions in America. Lowell's version ends with the capture of Babo.

Joyce Sparer Adler has also adapted "Benito Cereno" (1990). Her dra-matization differs from Lowell's in adhering more closely to the events of Melville's story. It does not conclude with Delano, Babo, and Benito Cer-eno in the small boat but advances to Melville's ending, in which Cereno and Babo confront each other even in death. The implication drawn by Adler is that neither Cereno nor Babo symbolizes evil. Rather, the evil is shown to be the master–slave relation itself. Adler interprets Melville's story as an implied warning of a possible civil war in the United States.

An operatic version by George Rochberg of *The Confidence-Man* (1857) was produced by the Santa Fe Opera in 1982. Numerous other minor one-act plays, recordings, radio plays, short films, comic books, and plays for children dramatizing Melville's sea novels abound. [*See also* DRAMA OF THE SEA]

FURTHER READING: Adler, Joyce Sparer. *Dramatization of Three Melville Nov-els.* Lewiston, NY: Edwin Mellen, 1992; Coxe, Louis O., and Robert Chapman. *Billy Budd.* New York: Hill and Wang, 1962; Estrin, Mark. "Dramatizations of American Fiction: Hawthorne and Melville on Stage and Screen." Diss., New York University, 1969; Rochberg, George. *The Confidence Man (a Comic Fable).* Bryn Mawr, PA: Theodore Presser, 1982; Smith, Kenneth D. "Dramatic Adaptations of Herman Mel-ville's *Billy Budd.*" Diss., Notre Dame University, 1970; Wallace, Robert K. "Review of *Ahab's Wife or The Whale,*" *Melville Society Extracts* 116 (February 1999): 27–29.

Attilio Favorini and Joyce Sparer Adler

MELVILLE'S POETRY OF THE SEA. Although he spent only a short period of his life at sea, Herman Melville* (1819–1891) was deeply affected by his maritime experiences and made use of them in his fiction, sketches, and poetry. Poems about the sea appeared early in his work, in the novel *Mardi** (1849) as short lyrics that celebrated such subjects as "A Paddle-Chant," a "Battle-Chant of Narvi," and "The Maiden under the Sea." In *Moby-Dick** (1851), he adapted a hymn of the Reformed Protestant Dutch Church to sing "The ribs and terrors in the whale,/Arched over me a dismal gloom" (ch. 9).

Strongly moved by his experience of the Civil War, he wrote his first volume of poetry, *Battle-Pieces and Aspects of the War* (1866). A number of the best poems in the volume were about the sea, war maneuvers, and battles. "The Stone Fleet" told of the whaling ships scuttled in Charleston Harbor by Northern forces to block it as a route for Southern forces. Several poems expressed an elegiac regret for the technological changes in modern warfare and the loss of the old wooden ships: "In the Turret" describes the *Monitor*,* an ironclad ship of war, and "A Utilitarian View of the *Monitor's* Fight" emphasizes this new warfare where "all went by crank,/ Pivot, and screw,/ And calculations of caloric." "The *Temeraire*" puts the narrator in mind of the great days of war before the ironclads. "Battle of Stone River, Tennessee," "Running the Batteries," and "The Battle for the Bay" describe specific naval engagements. The poem "Commemorative of a Naval Victory" depicts the sailor in heroic terms and dwells upon the darker side of war in a powerful image in which "The shark/ Glides white through the phosphorus sea."

Although the long, narrative poem that Melville next published, *Clarel* (1876), has notable imagery of the sea, it is essentially a land-bound narrative, finding its landscapes in the desert and worn-out stony scenes of Palestine. But the volume that followed, *John Marr and Other Sailors with Some Sea-Pieces** (1888), brought the poet back to his beloved element. In varied poetic forms, the book as a whole tells a gripping story of an aged sailor, retired from the sea, who is landlocked and exiled from his dearest experiences. He resorts to memory and, in the introductory piece titled "John Marr," "invokes these visionary ones," calling up the friends he had known and recalling some he had not known to give a picture of more than a century of oceanic experience. There are poems about people like "Tom Deadlight," an ancient sailor dying aboard a British warship in 1810; "Bridegroom Dick," who muses over his past in 1876; and "Jack Roy," a heroic figure who appears in more than one of Melville's works. "The Haglets" and "The Berg" recall the role that fate plays in the destruction of ships and their crews. The power and harshness of the alien sea are invoked in poems where shipwrecks* and rafts are emptied of their human freight. A brief quatrain, "The Tuft of Kelp," summarizes both aspects of the ocean: "All dripping in tangles green,/ Cast up by a lonely sea/ If purer for that, O Weed,/ Bitterer, too, are ye?" The sea allows only a bitter catharsis, but even that is balm to the wounded soul of John Marr, for he can sing, in a brief poem at the end of the book: "Healed of my hurt, I laud the inhuman Sea—/ Yea, bless the Angels Four that there convene;/ For healed am I even by their pitiless breath/Distilled in wholesome dew named rosmarine." Evoking the sea in all its power, inhumanity, and "otherness," John Marr, the sailor/poet, finds comfort and respite from his life ashore.

The last volume that Melville saw through the press, only months before his death, is *Timoleon, Etc.* (1891), a collection more miscellaneous than *John Marr*, but it does contain poems that recall the sea. "Off Cape Colonna" directs attention to the remains of a Greek temple on the foreland of the peninsula, as seen from a passing ship. "The Archipelago" is all about islands, chains, and groups of islands. The title word, as Melville knew, stands for the Aegean Sea, the site of Greek islands, and the poem roves through the archipelagoes of the Sporades and Cyclades, the Polynesian isles and the Marquesan group. All these islands, as he says in the poem, "retain in outline true/ Their grace of form when earth was new/ And primal."

Although Melville left unpublished poems at his death, they contain little about the sea, but one, "The Old Shipmaster and His Crazy Barn" (1922–1924), is about another ancient mariner on land who finds his barn to be like a ship at sea: "In March winds it creaks/Each gaunt timber shrieks like ribs of a craft off Cape Horn."* As Melville found the best subjects for his fiction in the sea, he also found much of his poetic inspiration in it. The poems, much less read than the fiction, display the development of the aging writer's response to the world about him, and these poems of the sea offer a fair, open space for further study of the novelist who became a poet.

FURTHER READING: Robillard, Douglas, ed. *Poems of Herman Melville*. Kent, OH: Kent State UP, 2000; Shurr, William H. *The Mystery of Iniquity: Melville as Poet, 1857–1891*. Lexington: U of Kentucky P, 1972; Stein, William Bysshe. *The Poetry of Melville's Late Years: Time, History, Myth and Religion*. Albany: SUNY P, 1970; Vincent, Howard P., ed. *The Collected Poems of Herman Melville*. Chicago: Hendricks House, 1947.

Douglas Robillard

MEN'S LIVES (first perf. 1992; pub. 1994). Written by Joe Pintauro (1930–), *Men's Lives* is a dramatization based on the nonfiction work titled *Men's Lives: The Surfmen and Baymen of the South Fork* (1986) by Peter Matthiessen* (1927–). Pintauro's play adapts Matthiessen's documentary and chronicles the way of life of the fishing families on the East End of Long Island.

The narrator, "Peter," interacts with members of one particular old fishing family, alive and dead. In a series of nostalgic flashbacks and stories, Peter tries to impart to the audience the purity and beauty of their tenuous existence, threatened by a shortsighted environmentalist bill that would outlaw their method of fishing. The family is descended from fishermen and neither knows any other way of life nor wants it. Alice, the mother, is proud and thrilled with her life in the shack that she inherited; Lee, the charming oldest son, realizes their impending doom but doesn't want to change; William, the youngest, just wants to be a fisherman like his father. Shortly after the bill is passed, Walt, the father, dies of a heart attack, and Lee is killed in an alcohol-related accident. William goes to the city to learn a trade, is reduced to mowing lawns for weekenders, and misses home.

The sea in *Men's Lives* is a powerful presence, a place of history and natural rhythm, one of fear, death, and beauty. The men and women brought up in its cycles live with it and for it and fear suffocation away from it. They would literally rather die than give up their lives. The sea washes up bones and relics, making concrete the cycles of human history. The fishermen's close bonds with one another and their simple harmony are presented in sharp contrast to the sport fishermen and corrupt politicians who distort the environmental threat and extinguish a civilization for their own greed or misguided idealism.

Matthiessen's book includes photo-documentation and a full history of the community from colonial times through the twentieth century. [*See also* DRAMA OF THE SEA]

Gwen Orel

MEREDITH, WILLIAM [MORRIS] (1919–   ). With nine volumes of poetry to his credit, including the Pulitzer Prize-winning *Partial Accounts: New and Selected Poems* (1987) and the National Book Award-winning *Effort at Speech: New and Selected Poems* (1997), William Meredith is also known for his critical studies and translations. While his earliest works were influenced by his experiences as a naval aviator in World War II and the Korean War, his more recent poems draw on his appreciation for the ambiguity of coastal settings.

Many of Meredith's early poems, such as the series "Carrier," "Transport," and "Battlewagon" from *Ships and Other Figures* (1948), incorporate description of naval life and vessels. Through these images, Meredith explores the contrast between the orderliness of ships and their destructive potential, as well as humanity's complex relationships with the sea. Naval themes also appear in later works. For instance, in "The Wreck of the *Thresher*," a poem that appeared in *The Wreck of the* Thresher *and Other Poems* (1964), Meredith reflects on the sudden deaths of a submarine's crew, reminding readers of the ocean's relentless power and warning against overconfidence in technology. Similarly, in "February 14," from *Hazard, the Painter* (1975), the image of a sentry walking off the deck of an aircraft carrier anchors the speaker's musings on the union of spirit and body.

In other Meredith poems, sea imagery evokes less violent observations. In "Rhode Island," for instance, a second poem from the *Hazard* sequence, the speaker views the seashore as a setting for sensual leisure. "Whorls," printed in *Earth Walk: New and Selected Poems* (1970), draws on the imagery of ocean currents to suggest universal spiraling patterns that inform human interaction and observation. [*See also* SEA IMAGERY IN MODERN AND CONTEMPORARY AMERICAN POETRY]

Daniel W. Lane

MERMAID LITERATURE. One might assume that an anatomically impossible creature like a half-fish, half-woman would appear—at least occasionally—in the literature of the fantastic, but a search produces few references to mermaids in American literature. There is no shortage of "mermaid" Web sites, however.

Mermaids seem to have been a European phenomenon, as least as far as literature is concerned. "I have heard the mermaids singing," says J. Alfred Prufrock in T. S. Eliot's* "The Love Song of J. Alfred Prufrock" (1915); "I have seen them riding seaward on the waves." Maybe Eliot/Prufrock did see them, but few other American authors did. The most famous mermaid story, of course, is Hans Christian Andersen's "Little Mermaid" (1846), and Oscar Wilde wrote a story called "The Fisherman and His Soul" (1891), in which a man falls in love with a mermaid he catches in his net. Mermaids appear in the poetry of Shakespeare, John Donne, William Butler Yeats, Matthew Arnold, and Alfred Tennyson, but across the Atlantic, only Emily Dickinson* saw "the mermaids in the basement" of the sea (Poem #520, 1891). Oliver Wendell Holmes* includes mermaids in the last line of his parody "The Ballad of the Oysterman" (1828). The sea nymphs of William Cullen Bryant's* "A Day-Dream" (1860) also have many of the qualities of the mermaid. One contemporary title, Lisa Carey's *The Mermaids Singing* (1998), concerns how myth and truth and the sea's healing powers affect three generations of Irish American women. Perhaps British poets, like other Britons, are closer to the sea than their American counterparts and are therefore more likely to encounter the mer-folk. Christopher Columbus* claimed to have seen "sirens" in the West Indies, but they were probably homely manatees, and 100 years later, in much colder waters, Henry Hudson saw a blue-haired mermaid. For the most part, however, "real" mermaids, as opposed to literary devices, are more common in European waters.

At least some of today's "literature" can be seen on the large or small screen, and there have been a surprising number of movies featuring mermaids. There are *Tarzan and the Mermaids*, made in 1938; *Million Dollar Mermaid*, a 1952 Esther Williams vehicle; and *Mermaids*, a 1990 film with Cher and Winona Ryder that has nothing whatever to do with women with fish tails.

In 1948, however, Glynis Johns starred in a British movie called *Miranda*, in which she actually wore a mermaid tail. She is caught off Cornwall by a fisherman and rescued by a doctor who has to decide whether he wants to stay with her in a cave or introduce her to civilization. She prefers dry land to the sea, except when she gets wet, at which time her tail reappears. Because the movie was such a success in England, Hollywood quickly turned out their own version, called *Mr. Peabody and the Mermaid* (1948), starring William Powell and Ann Blyth. In this number, Mr. Peabody, a proper Bostonian on vacation in the Caribbean,* hooks a mermaid while fishing and brings her home to his hotel. He immediately falls in love with her, and she with him, although she can communicate her feelings only through an adoring gaze, since she cannot talk. After returning to Boston, Peabody tells his tale to a psychiatrist, who informs him that it was only a hallucinatory midlife crisis.

Ann Blyth's mermaid is a peculiar combination of 1940s bathing beauty and traditional mermaid. For most of the film, those who see the mermaid see only her tail, so they derogatorily refer to her as a fish, but there are other references to her as a "sea cow" or a "manatee," revealing that the producers were aware of the mermaid's true lineage. One curious element in this and other mermaid movies is the arrangement of the tail fin. In order for a human in a mermaid outfit to swim, she must move her "tail" up and down, for that is the only way human legs can move. (Of the aquatic vertebrates, only the whales, dolphins, and sirenians use a horizontal tail motion.) But mermaids in movies are not bound by restraints that affect mortals, so despite the cetological orientation of the empennage, the tail structure is usually shown with the scales of a fish.

In *Splash,* a 1984 version of the mermaid-and-mortal love story, the mermaid is played by Darryl Hannah, and her mortal paramour by Tom Hanks. The mermaid arrives in New York, having swum from Cape Cod* to seek her true love. Unfortunately (and inexplicably), she can stay only for six days, but the couple falls into a torrid romance, and while she could not talk at all when they met (like all descendants of Andersen's mermaid), she learns English in an afternoon by watching television at Bloomingdale's. She is placed in a giant fish tank at the American Museum of Natural History (where we see her scales and her horizontal tail), and she escapes. After a chase through the streets of New York, she fetches up at a pier at the South Street Seaport. As the army closes in, she leaps into the East River, and her handsome prince follows.

In 1989 the contemporary apotheosis of the mermaid emerges in a Walt Disney animated film, *The Little Mermaid*. Hans Christian Andersen gets a credit ("based on a story by . . ."), and just as Andersen wrote it, the mermaid falls in love with handsome Prince Eric. Because she is not allowed to visit mortals, she strikes a deal with Ursula the Sea Witch, a marvelous character who has the upper body of a garish woman and an evening dress that terminates in the tentacles of an octopus. In exchange for giving her legs, Ursula takes the mermaid's voice and will take her soul if she cannot get the prince to kiss her by sunset of the third day. The Disney people improvised a "happily ever after" ending, designed to get audiences to leave the theater singing some of the songs written by Howard Ashman and Alan Menken, one of which ("Under the Sea") won an Academy Award.

The mermaid, having made regular appearances throughout the literature and mythology of Europe, remained submerged and invisible throughout most of the American narratives but took to the silver screen like—well, you know.

FURTHER READING: de Rachewiltz, Siegfried W. *De Sirenibus: An Inquiry into Sirens from Homer to Shakespeare*. New York: Garland, 1987; Ellis, Richard. *Monsters of the Sea*. New York: Knopf, 1994; Gachot, Theodore. *Mermaids: Nymphs of the Sea*. San Francisco: Collins, 1996.

Richard Ellis

MERRIMACK. *See MONITOR* AND *MERRIMACK.*

MERWIN, SAMUEL (1874–1936). Born in Evanston, Illinois, Samuel Merwin attended Northwestern University but did not graduate. His literary career began with the publication of two popularly acclaimed novels, *The Short Line War* (1899) and *Calumet "K"* (1901), written in collaboration with his boyhood friend Henry Kitchell Webster. Following the separation of this team, Merwin produced a steady stream of novels into the 1920s, when his interest turned to drama.

Many of his novels draw on Chicago and the greater Midwest for subject matter; three of these, published successively over a span of seven months, make effective use of the Great Lakes* as settings and are of particular interest. In *His Little World: The Story of Hunch Badeau* (1903), the captain of a Lake Michigan lumber schooner loses his ship and its cargo in a storm off Manistee. The rough-and-tumble tactics of a large Chicago timber conglomerate used against a small Lake Michigan lumber company are recounted in *The Whip Hand: A Tale of the Pine Country* (1903). *The* Merry Anne (1904) tells the story of the captain and crew of a lumber schooner who unwittingly run afoul of a Chicago whiskey-smuggling ring in Lakes Michigan and Huron.

Robert Beasecker

MERWIN, W[ILLIAM]. S[TANLEY]. (1927–   ). Born in New York City and educated at Princeton University, W. S. Merwin has lived and worked in France, Portugal, Majorca, New York, and, in later years, Hawai'i. The author of four books of prose and the translator of eighteen books of poetry and prose, Merwin has written thirteen books of poetry, including *A Mask for Janus* (1952), *The Drunk in the Furnace* (1960), *The Lice* (1967), the Pulitzer Prize-winning *The Carrier of Ladders* (1970), *Opening the Hand* (1983), *The Rain in the Trees* (1988), and *Travels* (1992).

Merwin's poetry is distinguished by its close attention to the natural world and to the ways in which language is used to mediate and express the human experience of nature. In his poetic meditations upon the numinous quality of the physical world, Merwin has often focused his artistic eye upon the sea and its shores. The third section of *Green with Beasts* (1956) is centered upon images of the ocean, while the first twelve poems of *The Drunk in the Furnace* constitute a formal sequence of sea poems that includes mythic treatments of the sea, as in "Odysseus," and imaginative explorations of the northern oceans, as in "The Frozen Sea."

In the late 1960s Merwin's sea poetry began to focus upon the degradation of marine environments. "For a Coming Extinction" (*The Lice*), one of his many poems about whales, laments the arrogance that has driven humans to crave mastery over the creatures of the sea. In later poems, such as "Sunset Waters" (*Opening the Hand*) and "Anniversary on the Island"

(*The Rain in the Trees*), seascapes are used to explore the richness and complexity of human family and love relationships. In recent poems, the abiding presence of the sea and shores of Merwin's home landscape of Hawai'i are central to his poetic vision. [*See also* SEA IMAGERY IN MODERN AND CONTEMPORARY POETRY]

Michael P. Branch

METCALF, PAUL [CUTHBERT] (1917–1999). Since his three-volume *Collected Works* was published (1996–1998), Paul Metcalf's writings are widely available. He is probably best understood as a member of the Black Mountain group; although he never attended that experimental North Carolina college, his early work was printed by the Black Mountaineer Jonathan Williams at Jargon Press. Most important, Metcalf was profoundly influenced by the group's dominant figure, Charles Olson.* Living near the college in the early 1950s, Metcalf had contact with Olson and others and also spent time on campus. But his most important connection with Olson was Herman Melville*: Metcalf was his great-grandson, and his parents, especially his mother, Eleanor Melville Metcalf, had been generous to Olson in his scholarly pursuit of Melville from the time he was a graduate student at Harvard.

The Melville influence is most evident and successful in *Genoa* (1965), an Olson-esque pastiche and montage drawing on Melville biography, family history, and writing, particularly *Moby-Dick** (1851), as well as historical documents concerning Christopher Columbus'* voyages and discoveries. Here and elsewhere in the Metcalf canon there are rich allusions to other Olson concerns, such as Mayan civilization. Parts of *The Middle Passage* (1976) are stunning, for example, that on the killer whale Orca. Especially memorable is the epic and musical description of whale copulation, presented in stirring, graphic, and ecologically poetic language. Whales generally and Moby Dick specifically are depicted in *The Wonderful White Whale of Kansas* (1997), in which Melville's Captains Ahab* and Vere (of *Billy Budd** [1924]) are presented as Wizard of Oz–like manipulators of men.

On their own, not as merely those of Melville's descendant, Metcalf's sea writings (and others) offer fertile and easily accessible grounds for research and criticism.

Donald Yannella

MICHENER, JAMES A[LBERT]. (1907–1997). Prolific novelist James A. Michener was rescued as a foundling by a widow living in Doylestown, Pennsylvania. Years later, having taught high school and college, Michener found his nascent career as a textbook editor interrupted by World War II, an experience that altered his life dramatically. As a member of the Naval Reserve, he was posted to the Pacific and ultimately set foot on dozens of its islands, providing him with material for his first and perhaps most satisfying work, *Tales of the South Pacific* (1947).

Tales of the South Pacific is a series of nineteen episodes dealing with the American experience in the Pacific theater of World War II; the book dramatizes the war's impact on Americans and islanders alike. Narrated by a colorless naval functionary, the episodes are set in the New Hebrides, New Caledonia, the Solomon Islands, and Norfolk Island, home of descendants of the *Bounty* mutineers. Only as the book unfolds does it become clear that its plot is building toward an Allied assault, Operation Alligator, on a Japanese-held island. Recurring character Tony Fry, a thoughtful navy lieutenant who will ultimately die in the assault, is implicitly contrasted with Bill Harbison, an extroverted officer whose oft-stated desire for "action" wanes when the assault eventually takes place.

Tales of the South Pacific received the Pulitzer Prize, but its reincarnation as the immensely popular Rodgers and Hammerstein musical *South Pacific*** (1949) led to Michener's fame and made it possible for him to devote the rest of his life to writing. The romantic musical was based on only two of the book's episodes, however, and falsified its generally realistic tone.

Michener followed *Tales of the South Pacific* with other volumes about the Pacific world. These included *Return to Paradise* (1951), essays and stories growing out of his own return to the islands after the war, and *Rascals in Paradise* (1957, written with A. Grove Day), biographical sketches of ten colorful Pacific interlopers, including Captain William Bligh of the *Bounty*. Michener's interest in the Pacific culminated in *Hawaii* (1959), a lengthy chronicle that carries the islands from their creation in volcanic upheaval, through their peopling by Polynesians, American missionaries, and Chinese and Japanese peasants, to the brink of statehood. The novel includes several highly evocative accounts of life at sea but also exhibits what would become an increasing willingness to sacrifice character development to the demands of historical structure. It was made into a motion picture starring Max von Sydow, Julie Andrews, and Richard Harris in 1966.

Michener went on to write about other parts of the globe in equally epic fashion. In *Caribbean*** (1989) he dramatized the history of yet another island world, this time in overtly episodic fashion. [*See also* NORDHOFF, CHARLES AND JAMES NORMAN HALL; PITCAIRN ISLAND]

FURTHER READING: Becker, George J. *James A. Michener*, New York: Frederick Ungar, 1983; Day, A. Grove. *James Michener*. 2d ed. Boston: Twayne, 1977; Hayes, John Phillip. *James A. Michener: A Biography*. Indianapolis: Bobbs-Merrill, 1984; Michener, James A. *The World Is My Home: A Memoir*, New York: Random, 1992; Severson, Marilyn S. *James A. Michener: A Critical Companion*. Westport, CT: Greenwood, 1996.

Grove Koger

MIDDLE PASSAGE (1990). Charles Johnson's (1948–   ) third novel and seventh published book, *Middle Passage* won for its author the National

Book Award in the year of its publication. As Johnson's original working title, "Rutherford's Travels," suggests, the work portrays the adventures of a picaro-like hero who stows aboard the *Republic*, a slave ship bound from New Orleans to the west coast of Africa, plying for the duration of the novel that triangular sea route that is known, at least the segment from Africa to the West Indies, as the Middle Passage. As narrator-protagonist-journalist, freedman Rutherford Calhoun affords the author a perspective of not only the plausible "historical insider" but also the educated, loquacious, philosophical moral voice, seldom reticent about matters anachronistically beyond the nautical setting and the cultural context of the fiction at hand.

Johnson has acknowledged some of his inspirational sources in both print and visual media. Among these are Robert Hayden's* miniature epic "Middle Passage" (1945), quoted by Johnson as epigrammatical introductory material, and historical documents that include accounts of the 1839 *Amistad* uprising. As to literary purpose, Johnson justifiably claims a multigeneric achievement; *Middle Passage* is simultaneously a rousing adventure yarn, a sea story travel account in satirical, allegorical vein similar to Jonathan Swift's *Gulliver's Travels* (1726), and a humor-laden novel of social and moral protest. These qualities are deftly underpinned with a recurrent framework of philosophical rumination about human nature and self-knowledge, an intriguing mediation that ultimately transcends the entertaining fictional narrative. [*See also* AFRICAN AMERICAN LITERATURE; SLAVE NARRATIVES]

Fred M. Fetrow

MIDSHIPMAN LITERATURE. The definition of midshipman literature is tied to the definition and status of the midshipman, which have changed over the years.

In the early years of the United States, a midshipman was a naval officer-in-training, or, as a passed midshipman, a junior officer, at the bottom of the commissioned ranks. He might be as young as nine or older than thirty. With the founding of the U.S. Naval Academy (initially the Naval School) in Annapolis in 1845, its students became naval cadets, who upon graduation spent a period of time with the fleet as midshipmen before advancing to higher rank. Since 1912, Naval Academy students have been called midshipmen; upon graduation they become ensigns (navy) or second lieutenants (marines).

Midshipmen of the pre–Naval Academy sort are important in various works of naval literature set prior to 1845. These are mostly novelizations of the early careers of such naval heroes as Stephen Decatur. From 1851 until the creation of naval Reserve Officers' Training Corps (ROTC) in 1925, the Naval Academy was the only source of U.S. Navy midshipmen, and it remains the primary source today. Hence, American midshipman literature is largely connected with the U.S. Naval Academy. Most such lit-

erature is juvenile literature,* fiction for boys. The novels typically have
young male protagonists either going through the Naval Academy or (if set
prior to 1912) having recently graduated. Many of the authors were associated with the Naval Academy either as staff or graduates. One of the earliest such novels is *Joe Bentley: Naval Cadet* (1889), by H. H. Clark, Naval
Academy chaplain, who later wrote *Midshipman Stanford* (1916). The period from the Spanish-American War (1898) to the end of World War I was
especially fertile, with over two dozen boys' novels featuring midshipmen
published, many in series. All show the lot of the midshipman as wholesomely adventurous. These include series by Cyrus Townsend Brady,* Yates
Stirling, and Edward L. Beach Sr.* and two books by Richmond P. Hobson,
all academy graduates. Harriet Irving Hancock's four Dave Darrin novels,
one for each year at Annapolis, were all published in 1911. Academy professor William O. Stevens produced two in 1912–1913, and the 1920s saw
four juvenile novels from Fitzhugh Green, another graduate.

The best-known author from this period, though the books themselves
are little known today, was Upton Sinclair, who (under the pen name Ensign
Clark Fitch) produced a series of midshipman novels and tales between 1898
and 1903, all following the adventures of young Clif Faraday. These include
Clif, the Naval Cadet, or, Exciting Days at Annapolis (1903). The tales were
published in *True-Blue Magazine*, then republished separately. Academy
graduate Robb White produced *Midshipman Lee of the Naval Academy* in
1938.

George Bruce's *Navy Blue and Gold* (1936) became a very successful
movie (1937), starring Robert Young and James Stewart. *Space Cadet*
(1948), by Academy graduate and major science fiction writer Robert A.
Heinlein, became a television series. Though set in the future, its Space
Academy is clearly based on the Naval Academy. While nearly every other
Naval Academy novel is set in a time roughly contemporary with its publication, *Midshipman Plowright* (1969), by James T. Pole, an academy professor, rather successfully novelizes the school's earliest days in 1845.

The 1980s saw significant new approaches to the old material. Perhaps
the most powerful midshipman novel to date is graduate James Webb's *A
Sense of Honor* (1981), set during the Vietnam War. Conversely, the only
thoroughly comic midshipman novel is graduate David Poyer's* *The Return
of Philo T. McGiffin* (1983). In Anne D. LeClaire's mystery *Every Mother's
Son* (1987), the protagonist must find the cause of her midshipman son's
death. In *Plebe* (1997), graduate Hank Turowski celebrates the value of the
rugged first year at the academy. [*See also* NAVAL FICTION; NAVAL
MEMOIRS]

C. Herbert Gilliland

MISTER ROBERTS (1946, 1948). *Mister Roberts* served as the title for a
novel, a play, and a film based on the stories of Thomas Heggen (1919–
1949), which first appeared in *The Atlantic Monthly, Life,* and *Reader's Di-*

gest, where Heggen was on staff. Heggen's novel (1946) became a best-seller, selling over 850,000 copies. The play (first perf. 1948; pub. 1948) adapted by Heggen and Joshua Logan, was a popular and critical hit, running for three years, a total of 1,157 performances, and winning Tony awards in the first season they existed for Best Play, Outstanding Director, and "Distinguished Performance" or Best Actor for Henry Fonda in his favorite role. The 1955 film won the Academy Award for Best Supporting Actor for Jack Lemmon as Ensign Pulver and nominations for Best Picture and Best Sound.

A college graduate, Heggen served in the navy at Guam, Iwo Jima, and Okinawa, drawing on such experiences for his stories. *Mister Roberts* details the life of the bored, unmotivated crew of the cargo freighter AK 601, the U.S.S. *Reluctant*, serving in the Pacific from just before V-E Day until a few weeks before V-J Day. Oppressed by a rigid, humorless captain and by repetitive tasks, the crew bicker and play practical jokes. Mister Roberts is the ship's cargo officer, who inspires loyalty in the crew and longs for active duty. He knows the ship's men need liberty to distract them from spying on the nurses in an island hospital and from picking fights with one another, but the captain refuses to give it to them.

Aiming for an admiralship, the captain withholds liberty to pressure Mister Roberts into giving up his attempts to get a transfer. The captain's animosity toward Mister Roberts is also fueled by his dislike of "college men." Mister Roberts yields to this pressure and, in a fit of anger, throws overboard the captain's prize palm tree. Unknown to him, the crew forge a transfer letter with the captain's signature and pass it on and award him the "order of the palm." When the crew hear that Roberts has been killed in an attack on his ship by a Japanese suicide plane, Ensign Pulver, formerly a rather immature joker, prepares to step into Roberts' shoes as mediator between the men and the captain, fighting their real enemy, "boredom."

The Pacific in *Mister Roberts* exists as a place far away from action, where men are thrown into contact with one another with little hope of diversion or meaningful experience. All of the action in the play is on the *Reluctant*; warships are offstage. Getting off the ship, either by shore leave or combat duty, is the only route to maturity.

Mister Roberts is of a piece with other coming-of-age stories written after World War II and later filmed, including *South Pacific** (1949), *From Here to Eternity* (1953), and *Bridge on the River Kwai* (1957). A sequel, *Ensign Pulver*, was made in 1964. A brief television series called *Mister Roberts* followed, along with a live television special. Ironically, Heggen died of drowning in his bathtub in 1949. [*See also* DRAMA OF THE SEA]

Gwen Orel

MOBY-DICK, OR THE WHALE (1851). *Moby-Dick* is the sixth sea book written by Herman Melville* (1819–1891) and the first to draw deeply on his Pacific whaling experiences. Impatient with his popular reputation based on *Typee** (1846) and *Omoo** (1847) and dismissive of his rapidly written *Redburn** (1849) and *White-Jacket** (1850), he was determined to pick up where he had left off in *Mardi** (1849), a work boldly experimental in style and an ambitious voyage in the world of mind. Melville's exhilaration and despair during the eighteen months when he was writing *Moby-Dick* are evident in some ten passionate letters to his neighbor Nathaniel Haw-thorne,* to whom he would dedicate the book "In Token of My Admiration for His Genius."

Not a novel in the usual sense, *Moby-Dick* is a book of great plenitude, mixing fiction with factual data on whaling and blending philosophical spec-ulation with high comedy. At the center is a sailor's yarn of the sort told during long night watches at sea. A Nantucket* whaling captain named Ahab,* consumed with anguish at the loss of his leg to an immense white whale known throughout the fisheries as Moby Dick, takes command of the *Pequod** on a monomaniac quest vowing death to Moby Dick. Finally tracked down in the far Pacific, Moby Dick smashes into the hull of the *Pequod*. As Ahab hurls his harpoon at the whale, he is caught in his own line and whisked to his death in the sea. The ship and all boats are lost. One survivor lives to tell the tale ("Epilogue").

Moby-Dick begins with two unexpected preliminaries: a half-comic "Ety-mology" of the word *whale*, followed by a dozen pages of "Extracts" from world literature imaging the massive size and power of Leviathan. They establish the mythic history of whales and warn the reader of the mortal risks to those who encounter them.

With a famously abrupt opening sentence—"Call me Ishmael"*—Melville names the narrator for the 135 chapters of *Moby-Dick*. Biblical connotation marks Ishmael as an outcast man of the wilderness, though the name trans-lates as "whom God hears." As sole survivor of the *Pequod* disaster, Ishmael feels freed from traditional values of landsmen and unafraid to subvert all their comfortable orthodoxies. "Loomings" (ch. 1) is a stunning prologue praising the sea's power to cast spells on the imagination, drawing men away from stifling routines and stirring them to reverie and meditation.

Ishmael recalls his adventure, beginning in New Bedford and Nantucket, when he becomes the bosom friend of a Polynesian harpooner, Queequeg* (chs. 2–21). After they board the *Pequod*, the narrator's interest shifts to Ahab and his crew. The three mates—Starbuck, Stubb, and Flask—are sub-stantial men typifying the New England maritime hierarchy. Among them only Starbuck, a Nantucket islander and Quaker like Ahab, will have the moral stature to attempt, unsuccessfully, to challenge Ahab's obsessive mis-sion. The three harpooners, each assigned to a mate for the chase, are wild and exotic: a Pacific islander, a Native American Indian, and a gigantic black African.

But the captain's presence dominates the ship. Though aware that Ahab is named after an evil Old Testament king (chs. 16, 19), Ishmael is sympathetic to his suffering, signified by Ahab's whalebone leg, and fascinated by his bold defiance of the gods. In a brilliant sequence of chapters (36–40) the narrator turns the deck of the *Pequod* into an Elizabethan theater. In "The Quarterdeck" (ch. 36), a powerfully choreographed scene, Ahab incites the crew by offering a gold doubloon to the first man to sight the white whale. Here he mesmerizes the crew with a black mass ceremony, as later he will temper his harpoon with the blood of his pagan harpooners in the name of the devil (ch. 113).

Many middle chapters in *Moby-Dick* contain graphic accounts of whaling activities. Sometimes referred to as the book's "cetological center," these chapters provide accurate details on such matters as calls from the mast head, lowering the boats, the elaborate equipment of the whaleboats and the duties of the oarsmen, boatheader, and boatsteerer (harpooner), pitchpoling, using the lance, towing the carcass, cutting in, trying out, stowing down, and cleaning up. Such information grounds the novel in reality and foreshadows plot events.

To his own experiences on three Pacific whalers Melville added bits from contemporary whaling accounts, such as those by J. Ross Browne,* whose *Etchings of a Whaling Cruise* (1846) he had reviewed, and the Reverend Henry T. Cheever's* *The Whale and His Captors* (1849). He relied on Thomas Beale's *The Natural History of the Sperm Whale* (1839) and Frederick Debell Bennett's *Narrative of a Whaling Voyage* (1840) and others for factual data. Two whaling pieces were probably germinal to *Moby-Dick*. A widely read magazine story by J. N. Reynolds,* "Mocha Dick: or the White Whale of the Pacific" (1839), offered a concept and a name variant. Owen Chase's* *Narrative* (1821), recounting the true fate of the whaleship *Essex*,* staved by a giant whale in mid-Pacific, served Ishmael as elaborate affidavit (ch. 45) for the coming catastrophe of the *Pequod*. These works and others are openly commented on by Ishmael (ch. 32), providing veracity and ballast for his whaling epic.

Throughout, Melville endows his story with the complexity and reach of classical literature. Ishmael alludes often to both mythological and biblical figures. As with Ahab and Ishmael, the great whale has Old Testament links, made clear in Chapter 81, where Ishmael quotes five verses from Chapter 41 of the *Book of Job* wherein "Leviathan" is presented as the measure of God's power. Thus, Ahab's vengeance against Moby Dick can be read, among other possibilities, as God-defiance, a fascinating theme to Melville in the light of his own revolt against the Calvinism of his youth. Questions of faith and doubt abound in *Moby-Dick*.

Ten or so whale killings occur between the *Pequod*'s unsuccessful first lowering (ch. 48) and its fatal encounter with Moby Dick (ch. 135). Each kill serves as a center for a chapter sequence. Thus, "Stubb Kills a Whale" (ch. 61) is introduced by a preceding chapter explaining the whizzing lines in whaleboats, one of which will ultimately strangle Ahab; the killing is followed by two more technical chapters and capped by a comic scene between Stubb and the black cook. Ishmael has previously ridiculed the images of whales in many famous paintings and prints (chs. 55–57). The killings give him opportunities to lecture on whale anatomy: its blanket of blubber, head, case, brain, spoutings, tail, penis, and so on. Anatomy inevitably slides into philosophy mixed with Ishmaelian high jinks. The chapter on blubber (68) and the exceptional sequence of eight chapters on the sperm whale's massive head (chs. 70, 74–80) focus on two of Ishmael's passions: analogies between great whales and worthy philosophies and his frustrated attempt to read the "mystical brow" of the sperm whale, which in its "dread powers" represents "the Diety." The chapter ends with Ishmael's putting the "brow" before the reader with the challenge: "Read it if you can" (ch. 79).

The major maritime events of the voyage, other than the whale killings, are nine gams or encounters with other whalers. To each ship Ahab has but one question: "Hast thou seen the White Whale?" Their varied responses help define the abnormality of Ahab's quest. Captain Boomer of the *Enderby*, having himself lost an arm to the white whale, is appalled: "ain't one limb enough?" (ch. 100). Captain Gardiner of the *Rachel*, an old Nantucket friend, begs Ahab to assist in the hunt for Gardiner's young son missing since the day before in one of his whaleboats. Ahab's brusque refusal is a measure of his dehumanization (ch. 128). The last of the ships, the ironically named *Delight*, has just lost five of its crew to Moby Dick, but their report only inflames Ahab further (ch. 131).

Ishmael's break from sympathy with Ahab may occur symbolically in a lurid night scene around the tryworks. While flames beneath the pots turn the *Pequod* into a hell-ship, Ishmael at the helm experiences a hallucination that almost leads to capsizing the ship. Stare not too long into the fire, he warns himself, "lest it invert thee" (ch. 96). Ahab's fascination with fire, marked by his scar, at last culminates on the night of a typhoon when corposants blaze at the mast tips. To the terror of the crew, Ahab proclaims the flames to be his father and his god (ch. 119).

Though temporarily captured by Ahab's fiery hunt, Ishmael's personal quest is the sea itself. His early hope that in "landlessness" he will discover "the highest truth" (ch. 23) seems not to be fulfilled, yet the sea brings him self-knowledge, recorded in memorable passages. During a masthead watch in pleasant weather he is lulled into reverie by the rocking ship; then, as he merges with the soul of the "mystic ocean" and experiences transcendence, he is suddenly yanked back to reality by a near fall (ch. 35). On reaching the Pacific, Ishmael writes a love poem to "my dear Pacific" (ch. 111), but the same "mysterious divine Pacific" shortly blasts the *Pequod* with a typhoon that leaves her "bare-poled" (ch. 119), stripped of sails. Ishmael frequently reminds the reader that the sea is and always has been a graveyard and that "green navies and green-skulled crews" lie beneath benign surfaces (ch. 40). The sea can murder the stateliest frigate at will (ch. 58). Cannibal creatures roam beneath gilded waters. Sharks follow whaleships and tear at the carcasses of dead whales. A strange, dreamlike giant squid rises from the deeps with a sucking sound and disappears (ch. 59). Serene, terrible, unknowable, the sea is life itself.

Told by a young man with a riotous imagination and with many varying moods of thought, *Moby-Dick* celebrates the life of men on the sea frontier. The 700 American whalers exploring the Pacific do not deserve the contempt of merchant and naval vessels. Whaling is more than a filthy butchering business; it is a noble and honorable occupation, as perilous as war. Whalemen are descended from a long line of famous heroes and dragon slayers (ch. 82). Although Ishmael praises the American thrust into the Pacific, he insistently questions established traditions, doubts the literal truth of the Bible, challenges the existence of God, and makes comedy out of many sober matters. No wonder that *Moby-Dick* was disconcerting to Melville's contemporaries. Twentieth-century readers have been far more receptive to Ishmael's quest for identity, to his passionate search for the sacred, to his hilarities, to his joy in discontinuities. They have been grateful, above all, for Melville's wonderful gift of language.

The rise to renown of *Moby-Dick* at home and abroad has been a cultural phenomenon. In the 1920s, after decades of neglect, scholarly studies established Melville's great prose epic as a major text, leading to its inclusion in the college canon. Subsequently, through films, dramatic readings, television specials, cartoons, and comics, both the white whale and the half-crazy old sea captain with the ivory leg have become icons of popular culture, familiar to all. Now ranked at the top of American literary works, *Moby-Dick* continues to inspire imaginative responses at the highest levels of art and literature. Composer Laurie Anderson, for one example, premiered her "Songs and Stories from Moby Dick" in October 1999 at the Brooklyn Academy of Music.

FURTHER READING: Bezanson, Walter E. "*Moby-Dick*: Work of Art," *Moby-Dick* by Herman Melville. Ed. Harrison Hayford and Hershel Parker. Norton Critical Edition. New York: Norton, 1967; Bryant, John, ed. *A Companion to Melville Studies.* New York: Greenwood, 1986; Parker, Hershel, and Harrison Hayford, eds. Moby-Dick *as Doubloon: Essays and Extracts (1851–1970)* New York: Norton, 1970; Schultz, Elizabeth A. *Unpainted to the Last:* Moby-Dick *and Twentieth-Century American Art.* Lawrence: UP of Kansas, 1995; Sealts, Merton M., Jr. "Whose Book Is *Moby-Dick?*" *Melville's Evermoving Dawn: Centennial Essays.* Ed. John Bryant and Robert Milder. Kent, OH: Kent State UP, 1997, 58–74.

Walter E. Bezanson

MONITOR AND MERRIMACK. The indecisive, four-hour duel between the two armored vessels U.S.S. *Monitor* (built 1862) and U.S.S. *Merrimack* (built 1855) took place on 9 March 1862, in Hampton Roads, Virginia, and marked a turning point in naval affairs. The Swedish-born inventor John

Ericsson designed and built the U.S.S. *Monitor*, a ship in which much was new and untried. Ridiculed as "a cheese box on a raft," the moderate-draft *Monitor* presented a minimum and impregnable target with great offensive power. Completed only two weeks before the battle, she was commanded by Lieutenant John L. Worden, USN.

Her opponent was originally built in 1855 as the screw frigate U.S.S. *Merrimack*. While in inactive status at the Norfolk Navy Yard in 1860, the U.S. Navy burned and sank her to prevent her capture. Desperate for ships, the Confederate navy raised her, and Lieutenant J. M. Brooke rebuilt her as an ironclad ram. Renamed C.S.S. *Virginia*, she was barely completed when she got under way on 8 March 1862, commanded by Flag Officer Franklin Buchanan, Confederate States Navy. Sinking the wooden ships U.S.S. *Cumberland* and U.S.S. *Congress* and attacking the U.S.S. *Minnesota*, she withdrew after Buchanan was wounded and hospitalized, but, by then, she had clearly demonstrated the inability of wooden warships to defend themselves.

The next morning, 9 March, under the command of Lieutenant Catesby ap R. Jones, CSN, the *Virginia* reappeared. Surprised to find that *Monitor* had arrived during the night to support the Union fleet, *Virginia* (ex-*Merrimack*) engaged *Monitor*. Though they exchanged gunfire at close range, the numerous hits produced only slight damage, further demonstrating the invulnerability of armored ships.

The dramatic action between the *Monitor* and the *Merrimack* has been recorded in more than 100 book-length historical accounts, poems, and contemporary ballads. Some of the more notable of these are Herman Melville's* "A Utilitarian View of the *Monitor*'s Fight" (1866), Charles Clark's "The *Monitor* and *Merrimac* [sic]" (c.1862), A. Van Dyke's "The Great Naval Combat" (c.1862), Elizabeth Porter Beach's "The Last Broadside" (c.1862), and an anonymous poem called "The Turtle" (rpt. in Burton Egbert Stevenson's *Poems of American History* [1922]), which describes the related action of the *Merrimack*'s sinking of the *Cumberland* on 8 March. Popular sheet music, such as G. Weingarten, "Monitor Polka"; V. Tinans, "Ericsson Galop"; and D. Brainard Williamson, "Oh! Give Us a Navy of Iron," was published immediately after the battle, during the Civil War (1861–1865).

For the curious, the final "k" in *Merrimack* is sometimes omitted, in error. The ship was originally named for a river of the same name in New Hampshire and Massachusetts. Further confusion arose in 1898, when the U.S. Navy named another ship the *Merrimac*, using the variant spelling without the "k." Purists on Civil War naval matters watch all spellings very closely.

John B. Hattendorf

MOORE, CHRISTOPHER K. (1957–   ). Christopher Moore has lived on the California coast for over twenty years, using his experiences on diving and fishing boats around the world in two offbeat novels. *Island of the Sequined Love Nun* (1997) focuses on the protagonist's job offer on Alualu Island northwest of Micronesia, his navigation by motorboat through a hurricane to get there, his plan to save the native Shark People from mysterious events, and his escape by canoe and his ensuing weeks lost at sea. *The Lust Lizard of Melancholy Cove* (1999), set in Pine Cove, California, involves a Sea Beast with psychic powers who leaves the ocean and is aided by various characters, including a seascape painter, to find love and happiness.

Mira Dock

MOORE, MARIANNE [CRAIG] (1887–1972). A member of the generation of poets that included T. S. Eliot,* Ezra Pound,* and William Carlos Williams,* Marianne Moore was highly regarded by her contemporaries for poetry that was metrically unique and that characteristically subjected her close observations of the physical world to the transforming power of her poetic imagination. Her impact on American poetry was felt not only through the force of her own comparatively small body of work (approximately 160 published poems) but also through her close ties with other poets and their work.

Many of her poems, particularly the earlier work, use very concrete marine images to ground her sense of the relation between the real and the imagined. See, for example, "The Frigate Pelican," "The Fish," "A Grave," "Sea Unicorns and Land Unicorns," and "Sojourn in the Whale," all published in *Selected Poems* (1935). While the marine imagery in these poems is often startlingly precise, the corporeal world of nature is not ultimately what interests Moore, who views the sea and most things in it as mutable, flexible, the image of change and the ungraspable. Rather, what interests Moore is the way the particular world of the sea informs, shapes, even "charms" our understanding of more abstract concepts such as aesthetics and morality. The short poem "A Jelly-Fish" (1959) exemplifies this superbly when it describes its subject as "Visible, invisible/ a fluctuating charm." [*See also* SEA IMAGERY IN MODERN AND CONTEMPORARY POETRY]

Thomas R. Brooks

MOORE, RUTH (1903–1989). Ruth Moore was born on Gott's Island, Maine, where she lived for thirteen years before moving to the mainland to continue her education. She graduated from New York State College for Teachers in 1925 but did not pursue a teaching career. She worked for a time in New York for the National Association for the Advancement of Colored People (NAACP) and later as an associate editor for *Reader's Digest*. During her lifetime she published fourteen novels and two books of poetry. Her final book, *The Tired Apple Tree* (1990), a collection of poems, was published posthumously. It focuses largely on the inhabitants and legends of coastal Maine, with such pieces as "Skipper McBride," "Remembrance of a Deserted Coastal Village," and an extended narrative poem about English geographer and navigator Richard Hakluyt, entitled " 'For It May Be That Gold Is Not All.' "

Moore began her first novel, *The Weir* (1943), shortly after moving to California. Her characters in this work and in most of her others are Maine islanders and fishermen, much like her own ancestors, who live and die by the sea. Her fine eye for descriptive detail, much of which focuses on the sea environment, and her ear for local dialect place her in the tradition of regional realism. Her second novel, *Spoonhandle* (1946), was made into a film, *Deep Waters* (1948). Despite her belief that physical distance from her native region improved her ability to write about its coast and its people, she returned to Maine in 1947, where she built a house on Mount Desert Island and lived for the remainder of her life. One of Moore's most popular books, *Cold as a Dog and the Wind Northeast* (1958), is a collection of ballads focusing on aspects of maritime myth as diverse as mermaids,* missing fishermen of sunken ships, and the Old Man of the Sea.

Although out of print for many years, several of Moore's books have been reprinted by Blackberry Press in Maine; in 1993 Sanford Phippen edited a collection of Moore's letters, titled *High Cloud's Soaring, Storms Driving Low: The Letters of Ruth Moore.*

Tina M. Aronis

MORRELL, ABBY JANE [WOOD] (1809–1???). The cousin and second wife of Captain Benjamin Morrell,* Abby Jane Wood married the captain when she was fifteen. She accompanied him on the last of his four voyages of commerce and exploration, in the schooner *Antarctic* (1829–1831). Apparently emulating his account of his ventures in his 1832 *Narrative of Four Voyages. . . .*, Abby Jane Morrell "wrote" her own *Narrative of a Voyage to the Ethiopic and South Atlantic Ocean, Indian Ocean, Chinese Sea, North and South Pacific Oceans, in the Years 1829, 1830, 1831* (1833). Actually, though, according to an introductory "Advertisement," her narrative was written and printed before her husband's, but its publication was delayed. The publishing house of Harper touts its ostensible author as an educated woman whose book will be read with pleasure, especially by her countrywomen. But according to Eugene Exman's *The Brothers Harper* (1965), like her husband's book, hers was ghostwritten, apparently from her notes, by Samuel L. Knapp, author of *Lectures on American Literature* (1829).

Whether describing places visited, calling for missionaries to spread Christianity and civilization, declaring its ostensible author a friend of the mariner because she wants to reform him, announcing a belief in what seems racial equality (but declaring that "savages" should learn English because their own languages are too simplistic), or declaring that the Euro-American discoverers of places hitherto unknown to their world should, as a matter of common sense, possess them, Mrs. Morrell's book is a series of self-serving clichés. Its lack of organization compounds the weakness—conchology and reform of seamen, for example, making up one chapter. Because of its mixed authorship, Mrs. Morrell's *Narrative* resists comparison to other sea-related writings by nineteenth-century American women. [*See also* WOMEN AT SEA]

Haskell Springer

MORRELL, BENJAMIN (1795–1839). Benjamin Morrell, sealing captain and explorer, was born in Rye, New York, the son of a shipbuilder. His early experiences included being twice captured by the British during the War of 1812 and spending over two and a half years in prison. Subsequently, he made a number of deep-sea voyages as a sailor on commercial vessels, mostly to the Pacific.

Morrell's only claim to authorship is *A Narrative of Four Voyages to the South Sea, North and South Pacific Ocean, Chinese Sea, Ethiopic and Southern Atlantic Ocean, Indian and Antarctic Ocean. From the Year 1822 to 1831* (1832). It narrates his adventures on his first command, the sealing schooner *Wasp* (1822–1824), and three more voyages, also in schooners. His second wife, his cousin Abby Jane (Wood) Morrell,* accompanied him on the last of these and put her name to a separate account of it (1833). Morrell apparently died of a fever in Mozambique.

Despite Morrell's uneven interpretations of the South Pacific islanders whom he encountered and his sometimes bloody behavior there, his accounts do remain important. More significantly, his assertions of Antarctic* discovery, if true, would make him notable in far-southern exploration. His book is also remembered as one source for details in Edgar Allan Poe's* *The Narrative of Arthur Gordon Pym** (1838).

Morrell's Antarctic claims have been challenged and in some cases proved wrong. His work does evidence an overactive imagination, and one critic even called him "the Baron Munchausen of the Pacific." Morrell's too-frequent errors in position are probably due to carelessness, the lack of a chronometer and therefore having to rely solely on a magnetic compass, and inability (because of weather) to take frequent sun sights. His melodramatic, clichéd, and self-justifying style similarly supports incredulity, but those qualities may be mostly the product of his ghostwriter, Samuel Woodworth, author of the hugely popular poem "The Oaken Bucket" (1818), whose authorship was not revealed until 1965 by Eugene Exman in *The Brothers Harper*.

Haskell Springer

MOWAT, FARLEY [MCGILL] (1921–   ). Farley Mowat is one of Canada's more popular and controversial writers. Born 12 May 1921, in Belleview, Ontario, Mowat graduated from the University of Toronto in 1949. He spent two years during World War II as an infantry officer in the Canadian* army. Before completing his degree, Mowat interned in the Northwest Territories as a biologist, an experience that helped shape his literary career. In 1952 he published his first book, *People of the Deer*, a critique of the nation's policy on Native Americans. Mowat would return to the Arctic* region for later works such as *Top of the World Trilogy* (1976) and other writings about life on the sea and by the sea. He wrote two books at the request of the Foundation Maritime Company, *The Grey Seas Under* (1958) and *The Serpent's Coil* (1961), a thriller about a Newfoundland tug. In 1965 he published *Westviking: The Ancient Norse in Greenland and North America*, a popular history of the Vikings. A pictorial account of Newfoundland's coast, *This Rock within the Sea* (1968), enjoyed brief success, but his 1972 *A Whale for the Killing*, spurred by the death of a fin whale near Mowat's hometown, Burgeo, received considerable international attention. His *The Farfarers: Before the Norse* (2000) describes the transatlantic voyage of a pre-Indo-European people, whom Mowat refers to as the Albans, from Scotland to Newfoundland in the 700s.

Mowat turned his love of the sea for at least two juvenile* books, *Curse of the Viking Grave* (1966) and a twentieth-century pirate tale, *The Black Joke* (1962). His *The Boat Who Wouldn't Float* (1969) won the 1970 Stephen Leacock Medal for humor. This delightful book is the humorous account of a schooner voyage along the coastlines of the Atlantic provinces on the way to Montreal for Expo '67.

Mowat received numerous literary awards and in 1982 was named an officer of the Order of Canada. [*See also* AMERICAN INDIAN LITERATURE OF THE SEA]

Boyd Childress

MR. PENROSE: THE JOURNAL OF PENROSE, SEAMAN (1815).

One of the first novels composed in America, *Mr. Penrose: The Journal of Penrose, Seaman* was written by William Williams (1727–1791) during the thirty years of his adult residency in the colonies, roughly 1745–1775. Born in Bristol, England, where he also died, Williams was sent to sea by his parents because he could not excel as a scholar. He lived for a few years as a castaway in the Caribbean* before settling in Philadelphia, where he made a name for himself painting portraits, landscapes, and theatrical scenes, taught drawing, and gave flute lessons. He painted and ornamented ships for Thomas and James Penrose of Philadelphia, renowned shipbuilders, whom he complimented by using their family name for the hero of his only novel.

When Williams arrived in London from New York, where he had lived for probably half a dozen years, he took with him the completed manuscript, which was published posthumously in a severely bowdlerized edition in four volumes as *The Journal of Llewellin Penrose, a Seaman* by his benefactor Thomas Eagles in 1815. A pirated German translation appeared two years later, followed by a shortened, single-volume edition in English by Eagles' son John in 1826. The original manuscript was discovered by David Howard Dickason, who published it in Williams' own style and idiom, adding an introduction, in 1969.

The novel tells the tale of a Welsh sailor, Llewellin Penrose, who is ship-wrecked,* imprisoned by Spaniards, and deserted by his mates. He lives on the Mosquito Coast of Central America for twenty-seven years, where he dies, having refused repeated opportunities to return to civilization. In the lively, good-humored, and absorbing narrative, Penrose marries and fathers children (including a daughter named "America"), has various misadventures with Native Americans and Europeans, suffers natural disasters, and painstakingly develops a utilitarian personal philosophy against adversity, his modus vivendi.

The narrative resonates to other sea literature. Luta, Penrose's first wife, a comely Native American of seventeen who dies in childbirth, is a "Green Grove" who anticipates both lusty Fayaway in Herman Melville's* Typee* (1846) and the elusive Yillah in his Mardi* (1849). A Scots sailor in Penrose's community hurls his harpoon at a pod of killer whales with the ruthless vigor of Captain Ahab*; when a whale's tail crushes the sailor's canoe, the man disappears. Most significantly, however, Williams' journal is a rousing and realistic travel tale in the tradition of Daniel Defoe's Robinson Crusoe (1719).

Jill B. Gidmark

MRS. CALIBAN (1983). In Rachel Ingalls' (1940–   ) slim, well-written novel, told by a limited third-person narrative voice, a six-foot-seven-inch amphibian humanoid slips into the house and into the loveless, sexless life of a California housewife. Captured in the Gulf of Mexico, his home, "Larry" has been studied and also tortured by staff at a scientific institute. In escaping he has killed the torturers and is being hunted. Dorothy, the protagonist, hides him and over time finds him gentle, gloriously sexual, quite human in some ways, but irrevocably alien in others.

Ingalls persuades the reader that Dorothy's secret life with this supposed "monster" from the deep, despite its early hints of hallucination, is true in an essential way. That truthfulness, complicated as it is by Larry's distance from home, by Dorothy's desire to keep him with her as long as possible, by her husband, his affairs, and other lives intersecting with theirs, makes the story of this odd couple finally one of cataclysmic loss. At the end, Dorothy stands listening to the language of the sea, alone.

Haskell Springer

MURPHY, ROBERT CUSHMAN (1887–1973). Born in Brooklyn, Robert Cushman Murphy graduated from Brown University in 1911. The following year he married Grace E. Barstow and embarked on the whaler

Daisy for the South Atlantic. A naturalist nominally in search of pelagic birds, Murphy proved an able chronicler of shipboard life as well. He published the scientific findings of his trip in *A Report on the South Georgia Expedition* (1914). After several other voyages in pursuit of natural history, he published his masterwork, *Oceanic Birds of South America* (1936). This work is notable for its inclusion of the biographical sketch of Rollo Howard Beck in "The Field Worker" and the synoptic "An Ornithological Circumnavigation of South America," as well as for the many narratives of maritime collecting and lore interspersed throughout the two volumes. A seagoing equivalent to the highly literary *Birds of Massachusetts and Other New England States* by Edward Forbush (1927–1929), Murphy's work builds on centuries of exploration in the South Atlantic and South Pacific Oceans.

Murphy was associated with the American Museum of Natural History from 1921 until his death. An admired raconteur, he was challenged well along in his career to write something more in the narrative vein, and the result was *Logbook for Grace* (1947), a reworking of his diary and letters from the New Georgia voyage on the *Daisy* under the crusty captain Benjamin D. Cleveland (later one of the last skippers of the *Charles W. Morgan*, the world's only surviving wooden whaleship, now docked at Mystic Seaport in Mystic, Connecticut).

Logbook for Grace has the richness of discovery present in Charles Darwin's *Journal*, the humanity and whaling lore of *Moby-Dick** (1851), and the innocent, but tempered, enthusiasm of Jack London's* *The Cruise of the Snark* (1911). A pictorial companion, *A Dead Whale or a Stove Boat*, was published in 1967. Grace E. Barstow Murphy wrote *There's Always Adventure: The Story of a Naturalist's Wife* (1951).

R. D. Madison

"MURRAY, LIEUT." *See* [BALLOU, MATURIN MURRAY].

MUTINIES. Mutiny at sea describes an act of collective insubordination by a crew against their vessel's captain or officers. The term *mutiny* dates back to the sixteenth century, when it was commonly applied to military insubordination; more recent usage generally implies maritime applications. Though U.S. law differentiates between mutiny on a naval vessel and mutiny on a merchant vessel, the implied intent of the word and the illegality of the act remain the same.

Given its dramatic and confrontational nature, mutiny has played a pivotal role in numerous works of American literature. Perhaps the most famous mutiny of all, that aboard the H.M.S. *Bounty* in April 1789, has also inspired the most fiction. A small selection of *Bountyana* historical fiction includes Charles Nordhoff* and James Norman Hall's *Bounty* trilogy (*Mutiny on the Bounty* [1932], *Men against the Sea* [1934], *Pitcairn Island* [1934]), Louis Becke and Walter Jeffery's *The Mutineer* (1898), Eric Wilson's *Adams* *of the* Bounty (1959), and William Kinsolving's *Mister Christian* (1996). Nordhoff and Hall focus on the historical events surrounding the mutiny, the mutineers' eventual arrival on Pitcairn Island,* and Captain Bligh's remarkable 3,618-mile voyage through the South Pacific in an open boat. Kinsolving writes about Fletcher Christian's return to England from Pitcairn and his eventual involvement with the English mass mutinies at The Nore and at Spithead (1797), while Becke and Jeffery suggest an alternative end to Christian's life. *The Last Mutiny* by Bill Collett (1993) describes Captain Bligh's life after returning home.

Events on board the U.S. brig *Somers*,* in which Commodore Alexander Slidell Mackenzie* hanged three men suspected of conspiring to incite mutiny, influenced and inspired considerable analysis in Herman Melville's* *Billy Budd** (1924), which questions what is and is not mutinous action. Herman Wouk's* *The* Caine *Mutiny* (1951) is another classic story of naval insurrection, this time set in World War II. Captain Queeg's* infatuation with trivial regulations and his inability to handle important issues of discipline and command force his crew to relieve him of duty during a raging typhoon.

Edgar Allan Poe's* *The Narrative of Arthur Gordon Pym of Nantucket** (1838) draws its story from the 1824 mutiny on board the Nantucket* whaler *Globe*.* The *Globe* mutiny inspired several books, and Poe probably read *A Narrative of the Mutiny on Board the Whaleship* Globe *of Nantucket* (1828), by William Lay and Cyrus Hussey, two survivors of the mutiny who were marooned* in the Mulgrave Islands. The fictional and factual versions of this story influenced Melville's *Moby-Dick** (1851); Melville includes excerpts from Lay and Hussey's story and another *Globe* story in *Moby-Dick*'s "Extracts."

Jack London's* *The Mutiny of the* Elsinore (1914) highlights the divisions of class; despite knowing nothing of the sea, the upper-class narrator successfully controls a mutiny among the lower-class crew long enough to guide the ship toward Valparaiso and safety. In London's classic novel *The Sea-Wolf** (1904), the brutal Wolf Larsen* attempts, but eventually fails, to maintain total domination of his vessel in the face of physical threats from the crew and intellectual threats from Humphrey Van Weyden, the rich aesthete whom the *Ghost* picks up on its way to the Bering sealing grounds.

Eugene O'Neill's* short play *Ile* (1917) explores the causes of mutiny in the story of an icebound whaling ship in search of oil ("ile," in the captain's vernacular). Like Larsen in *The Sea-Wolf,* Captain Keeney crushes physical threats from the crew, but he cannot halt the intellectual effects of his actions. His wife's descent toward madness causes him to turn toward home, until the ice clears and whales are spotted; O'Neill explores how the two mutinies affect Captain Keeney in different ways.

Middle Passage* (1990), by Charles Johnson, describes mutiny on another hell-ship, this one returning from Africa in 1830 with a cargo of slaves* and the slaves' god in an enormous crate. The intersection of two mutinies and a countermutiny creates conflicts that reflect America's long-standing struggles regarding slavery. Johnson's main characters recall those in *Moby-Dick*. [*See also BLAKE: OR THE HUTS OF AMERICA*]

FURTHER READING: Guttridge, Leonard F. *Mutiny: A History of Naval Insurrection*. Annapolis: Naval Institute P. 1992; Kopley, Richard, ed. *Poe's* Pym: *Critical Explorations*. Durham: Duke UP, 1992; Rose, Elihu. "The Anatomy of Mutiny," *Armed Forces and Society* 8 (1982): 561–74.

Peter H. McCracken

MYTHS. *See* GHOSTS AND GHOST SHIP LEGENDS; GREAT LAKES MYTHS AND LEGENDS.

N

THE NAGLE JOURNAL: A DIARY OF THE LIFE OF JACOB NA-GLE, SAILOR, FROM THE YEAR 1775 TO 1841 (1988). Jacob Nagle (1762–1841) was rarely not "in articles," or not signed aboard some vessel, during a forty-five-year career at sea that took him, via impressment, from the U.S. Navy during the Revolution into nineteen years of service in the Royal Navy. He was present at a remarkable series of historic events. He fought under George Washington at the Battle of Brandywine and spent some time at Valley Forge, then served in highly successful American privateers before being captured and impressed into the British navy. Footloose in London at the end of the war, he volunteered for the First Fleet to Australia and served as a member of Governor Arthur Phillip's boat crew, witnessing most of the historic moments in the first days of landing. Nagle was in the party from the First Fleet that settled Norfolk Island. He also served under Horatio Nelson in the Mediterranean. Nagle then spent more than twenty years of service in the merchant marine. His description of the China trade in the first decade of the nineteenth century is particularly interesting.

Although he served for a time as a master's mate and as a master of prize vessels, his journal, edited by John C. Dann 139 years after Nagle's death, presents a view from before the mast. Through his seaman's eyes, we see the wandering life of the sailor, an expert in the world of vessels on the high seas, but adrift and at the mercy of crimps, prostitutes, innkeepers, and other shady landsmen ashore. However, there are goodhearted landsmen as well as villains and fair masters and mates as well as cruel ones. This journal offers a view from the bottom up and gives a good sense of what one voice from the forecastle thought of the seafaring life in the late eighteenth and early nineteenth centuries. Dann has done an excellent job of preserving the vigorous "oral" quality of Nagle's writing.

James F. Millinger

NANTUCKET. As the whaling capital of the world for portions of the eighteenth and nineteenth centuries, Nantucket Island, fifty square miles and twenty-four miles off the southern shore of Cape Cod,* offered America an early example of how it might conduct itself as an independent world power. Functioning, in effect, as a cultural metaphor, the island would assume an important and enduring role in the American literary tradition.

Prior to the arrival of the island's first English settlers in 1659, Nantucket figured largely in the oral traditions of the region's Native Americans, with a legend linking the island's discovery to the appearance of a giant eagle making its way into the "Nantucket" chapter of Herman Melville's* *Moby-Dick** (1851). In 1676, after the outbreak of King Philip's War on the mainland, the island's Indian interpreter, Peter Folger, became Nantucket's first recognized poet, authoring an anti-Puritan ballad entitled "A Looking Glass for the Times," which would be published posthumously in 1725 and 1763 and is praised in the *Autobiography* (1793) of Folger's grandson, Benjamin Franklin. Another Folger descendant, the Nantucket whaling merchant Timothy Folger, provided Franklin with information used in his map and description of the Gulf Stream (1786). Just prior to the outbreak of the Revolution, Franklin drew upon his long-standing Nantucket connection in a meeting with the British statesman Edmund Burke, whose speech before Parliament, "On Conciliation with the Colonies" (1775), looks to the whale fishery as a quintessential example of how the "recent people" of the American colonies have, in many instances, outstripped the accomplishments of their mother country. Yet another observer who saw Nantucket as central to an appreciation of colonial America was St. John de Crèvecoeur, whose *Letters from an American Farmer* (1782) provides an in-depth description of a Quaker whaling community that epitomizes what the American people are all about.

In the immediate aftermath of the Revolution, which destroyed most of Nantucket's whaling fleet and removed London as a market for the island's oil, Britain and France offered Nantucketers an array of economic incentives if they would whale from an adopted shore. Thomas Jefferson's *Observations on the Whale-Fishery* (1788) recounts these developments and suggests policies that would enable America to regain its former glory as the world's whaling leader. As it turned out, Nantucket would emerge from the political and economic chaos of the War of 1812 as the booming capital of a fishery that had grown to include the Pacific Ocean.

During this period, the exploits of the Nantucket whalemen brought national and international attention to the island. The *Narrative* of the *Essex** disaster (1821), written by the first mate, Owen Chase,* describes the sinking of a Nantucket whaleship by its supposed prey and the incredible horrors suffered by the survivors. Two other Nantucket whalemen, William Lay and Cyrus Hussey, recounted their experiences in *The Globe Mutiny** (1828), telling how Samuel Comstock led a brutal mutiny* before ultimately dying at the hands of natives in the Mulgrave Islands. In 1835 the island whale oil merchant Obed Macy published his *History of Nantucket*, providing not only an account of the island's rise as a whaling port but also selections from a variety of island poets, most notably Peter Folger and an eighteenth-century Quaker whaleman, Peleg Folger.

In the meantime, a host of American writers looked to the island and these works for inspiration. In 1824 James Fenimore Cooper* established the genre of American sea fiction with the publication of *The Pilot,** a novel featuring the Nantucketer Long Tom Coffin,* a giant of a man in the same mythic mold as Natty Bumppo of Leatherstocking fame. Even though *The Pilot* is primarily set in the English Channel, Cooper inserts a recreational whale hunt into his narrative, drawing attention to the fact that the Nantucket whale fishery has created a distinctly American breed of sailor. Joseph C. Hart's* *Miriam Coffin, or The Whale-Fishermen* (1834) strives to make the same point, describing Nantucket as "this American Island" in its portrayal of the rise and fall of the female whaling merchant Miriam Coffin. Edgar Allan Poe's* *The Narrative of Arthur Gordon Pym of Nantucket** (1838) draws not only on the narratives of Nantucket whalemen but also on Hart's whaling novel (as would Herman Melville*) in his account of a Nantucketer's "extraordinary series of adventures." Following in the footsteps of Hart, whose mother was a Coleman from Nantucket, two other New Yorkers with island backgrounds published highly successful novels that looked to Nantucket as the breeding ground for their heroic protagonists: *The Adventures of Harry Franco* (1839) by Charles Frederick Briggs* and *Kaloolah* (1849) by William Starbuck Mayo.*

While these novels tended to exalt the island's status as a whaling port, the poet John Greenleaf Whittier* was more interested in its role as an exemplary Quaker community in his ballad "The Exiles" (1841). Whittier concludes his stirring account of how Thomas Macy and his family first settled on the island with a four-stanza tribute to the island as a Quaker abolitionist enclave of freedom and tolerance. A year after the publication of Whittier's poem, an escaped slave by the name of Frederick Douglass* delivered his first speech before a white audience at the Nantucket Atheneum. Douglass' *Narrative* (1845) ends, appropriately enough, with this speech on Nantucket.

Although a plethora of nineteenth-century writers and intellectuals went to Nantucket and recorded their impressions (including Daniel Webster, John James Audubon,* Ralph Waldo Emerson, and Henry David Thoreau*), it would be left to Melville, who appears not to have visited the island prior to writing *Moby-Dick* (1851), to provide the definitive account of Nantucket in its whaling heyday. Although written well after the island had surrendered its whaling preeminence to New Bedford, Melville's "Nantucket" chapter combines Burke's sense of the fishery's global scope with Cooper's conception of the whaleman as a rugged individual to portray the Nantucketer as an unstoppable, all-conquering hero: "For the sea is his; he owns it, as Emperors own empires" (ch. 14). The summer after the publication of *Moby-Dick*, Melville visited Nantucket for the first time, writing a series of letters to Nathaniel Hawthorne,* known today as the "Agatha letters," which contain stories and scenes collected during his trip. Melville would subsequently write an unpublished novel entitled *The Isle of the Cross* (the manuscript of which has never been found), which may have drawn upon this material; echoes from this visit are also detectable in Melville's book-length poem *Clarel* (1876).

Even as Nantucket fell into a century-long economic decline with the loss of the whaling industry, the island maintained a reputation for literary sophistication. In addition to works of poetry, highlighted by the collection *Seaweeds from the Shores of Nantucket* (1853), island authors such as Frederick Coleman Sanford, in a series of articles published in local and regional newspapers entitled "The Nantucket Sea Kings," helped to promote and inevitably romanticize Nantucket's whaling legacy. In the meantime, Nantucketers caught up in the exodus to the west brought a decidedly island perspective to an ever-evolving national literature, of which Martha Summerhayes' *Vanished Arizona, Recollections of the Army Life of a New England Woman* (1908) is a prime example. The Nantucket roots of Ernest Hemingway's* mother would have a profound influence on that writer, who traveled to the island with her as a boy and subsequently read Melville's *Moby-Dick* while still in high school, ultimately moving to the old whaling port of Key West* and turning to the sea as a major source of inspiration.

The increasing popularity and influence of *Moby-Dick* throughout the twentieth century ensured that Nantucket would always be something more than an island summer resort when it came to the American literary imagination. Robert Lowell's* seminal poem "Quaker Graveyard in Nantucket" (1946) begins where *Moby-Dick* ends, with the sinking of the *Pequod*.* Proclaiming that "this is the end of whale road," Lowell—a conscientious objector during World War II—brings a sense of outrage, horror, and loss to a meditation on Nantucket's brutal and pious Quaker whaling heritage. John Steinbeck,* who had grown up in the whaling town of Monterey, California, wrote much of *East of Eden* (1952) while on Nantucket, ultimately moving to the old whaling port of Sag Harbor, New York, where he wrote his last novel, *The Winter of Our Discontent* (1961), about a defunct whaling town beset by the challenges of becoming a summer resort. From the local humorist Nathaniel Benchley, whose novel *The Off-Islanders* (1961) brings issues of national and international importance to bear on a Nantucket-like place, to the dramatist John Guare, Nantucket remains, in the words of Joseph C. Hart, "this American Island." [*See also* AMERICAN INDIAN LITERATURE OF THE SEA; LIGHTHOUSE LITERATURE; NANTUCKET CYCLE; WHALING NARRATIVES]

FURTHER READING: Crosby, Everett U. *Nantucket in Print*. Nantucket, MA: Tetaukimmo, 1946; Philbrick, Nathaniel. " 'Every Wave Is a Fortune': Nantucket Island and the Making of an American Icon," *New England Quarterly* (1993): 434–47; Philbrick, Nathaniel. *Away Off Shore, Nantucket Island and Its People, 1602–1890*. Nantucket, MA: Mill Hill, 1994.

Nathaniel Philbrick

NANTUCKET CYCLE. New York playwright John Guare (1938–   ) is best known for *The House of Blue Leaves* (1971) and *Six Degrees of Separation* (1990), but three of Guare's dramas mark the only substantial sequence of American sea plays other than that written by Eugene O'Neill.* *Women and Water, Gardenia*, and *Lydie Breeze* form what has sometimes been called the "Nantucket* Cycle." In his Author's Notes to *Women and Water*, Guare refers to this group as a "series of plays tracing the lives of a group of idealists in the 19th century" (3). A fourth play, *Bulfinch's Mythology*, meant to be third in the historical sequence, is as yet unpublished and unperformed.

Women and Water is first in the series, though last written (first perf. 1984–1988 in various drafts; pub. 1990). It opens in 1864 at the Civil War Battle of Cold Harbor (Union lines) and introduces us to a quartet of characters whose intertwined stories are carried through to the end of the cycle. Joshua Hickman is a Secret Serviceman spying on Ulysses Grant at the behest of President Lincoln, Amos Mason is a Union private, Lydie Breeze is a nurse, and Dan Grady is a crafty sergeant who controls medical supplies and exchanges them for personal profit. The play is so crammed with incident, spectacle, and twists of plot as to more than earn the playwright's own designation of it as a melodrama.

While most of the action is given over to forging the relationships of these characters, the play is rich in sea ambience. There are references to the Walt Whitman* poem "On the Beach at Night Alone" (1859) and flashbacks to a horrifying tale of mutiny* and murder aboard the whaler *Gardenia*, to the time of Lydie's birth (1841) on board the ship, and to a maritime pageant on Nantucket* where Lydie wears a mask of Neptune and carries a gardenia.

In act 2, at Lydie's urging, the men abandon the war effort and accompany her back to Nantucket, where, through the device of a buried ship's log and a flashback to the *Gardenia*'s 1857–1861 voyage, the details of the slaughter of the ship's black crew members are revealed. Ultimately, the four idealists burn all the logs of the *Gardenia*, and the play ends with an incantation "erasing" the books of the Bible from the Apocalypse back through the "uncreation" of Eve in Genesis.

Perhaps overburdened by the author with the task of retrospectively justifying the action of the plays that follow it in the cycle, *Women and Water* suffers from a superfluity of incident and self-conscious poeticism. The play's extensive religious and literary allusions—from Noah's Ark to *Moby-Dick** (1851)—strain for coherence.

Far more successful is *Gardenia* (first perf. and pub. 1982). The first act is set in June 1875 on the beach at Nantucket, immediately retrieving motifs from the previous play: Joshua recites Whitman, Lydie fumes over the demise of her gardenia, and their Utopia has been given the backflowing name "Aipotu." The plot in the first act revolves around the device of a money bag stolen by Dan from two robber barons on their way to bribe President Grant, and Guare turns it into an analogue of *The Tempest* (1623), in which the men argue over who is to be Prospero while comporting themselves like the comic trio of Caliban, Stephano, and Trinculo. Lydie wavers symbolically between a liberated Ariel and an imperiled Miranda. When she swims naked in the ocean, it is one of several instances in the cycle where "women" and "water" images converge in a complex trope of passion, poetry, freedom, and danger.

In act 2 it is 1884, and the setting is Charlestown Prison in Boston, where Joshua is serving a sentence for having murdered Dan in a drunken quarrel. Now the sea images recede before those of confinement, execution, and cell-like depths.

Far more concentrated and fleshed out than *Women and Water*, *Gardenia* strikes a careful balance between the sensational story of who shall possess Lydie and an almost allegorical investigation of the theme of government. Guare seems to be urging that the exercise of political power in the absence of personal integrity and true self-possession is a harrowing spectacle.

Lydie Breeze (first perf. and pub. 1982), the most openhandedly poetic play of the cycle, returns the action to Nantucket in 1895. Visible are the Hickman house and an overturned rowboat on the beach. Now the action is dominated by the generation following the original quartet of idealists. The plot, which almost perfunctorily describes the final foiling of Amos Mason's political ambitions, recedes before a lush poeticism ("Swim into my torso. Swim into my breasts . . . Take me to the sea," a character says to her lover) and symbolism. Lydie's daughter Gussie, who has been likened to the figurehead on a ship by Joshua (the only one of the four original idealists to appear in this play), meets a man named Rock. But, in opposition to the *Mayflower* voyage, they sail off together to the East, toward Europe, recollecting the backflowing linguistic turns in the previous two plays. *Lydie Breeze* ends with Joshua's reading Whitman to his daughter Lydie on the beach, evoking with satisfying symmetry Prospero's lesson to Miranda near the start of *The Tempest*.

Evocations of such leviathans as Shakespeare, Eugene O'Neill,* and Henrik Ibsen, along with waves of biblical and mythological allusions undocumented here, are both the strength and the weakness of the Nantucket cycle. [*See also* DRAMA OF THE SEA]

FURTHER READING: Bryer, J. R., ed. *The Playwright's Art*. New Brunswick, NJ: Rutgers UP, 1995; King, Bruce, ed. *Contemporary American Theatre*. New York: St. Martin's, 1991; Savran, David, ed. *In Their Own Words: Contemporary American Playwrights*. New York: Theatre Communications Group, 1988.

Attilio Favorini

THE NARRATIVE OF ARTHUR GORDON PYM OF NANTUCKET (1838). *The Narrative of Arthur Gordon Pym of Nantucket* is the only complete, novel-length work by Edgar Allan Poe* (1809–1849). In it, Arthur Gordon Pym relates a series of wild adventures that he experienced at sea, dating his adventures from June 1827 to March 1828.

Each of Pym's adventures has little or no relation to the others, and each one occurs on a different vessel. In the first, he takes his sloop *Ariel* on a nearly disastrous midnight cruise off the coast of Nantucket*; then, as a stowaway aboard the brig *Grampus*, he undergoes extreme privations and danger from savage mutineers. When the brig is wrecked by a storm, Pym and a few companions drift southward on the wrecked hulk for more than 1,000 nautical miles. After enduring starvation, cannibalism, and sharks, Pym is rescued with one other survivor by the schooner *Jane Guy*, whose captain he persuades to explore the southerly areas of the Antarctic,* where the entire ship's crew is killed by the natives of an island. Pym, his companion, and a captured native escape in a canoe, which is carried still farther south into warm, milky waters. His narration ends abruptly as the canoe plunges toward a gigantic, shrouded white figure at the South Pole.

The first portion of the novel appeared in the 1837 January and February issues of the *Southern Literary Messenger*. In the novel's preface, Pym states that he had permitted a "Mr. Poe" to publish the earlier part of the adventures in the *Southern Literary Messenger* but adds that subsequently he decided to relate the narrative himself. A note at the end announces Pym's death and elucidates "facts" that "have, beyond doubt, escaped the attention of Mr. Poe."

Other features of the novel tend to confuse time periods and narrative voices. There are occasional discrepancies in calendar dates. Sections of digressive material, which Poe copied more or less directly from various sources, interrupt the adventures to discourse on nautical maneuvers and stowage, the Galápagos* tortoise, the nestling habits of albatross and penguins, and earlier voyages into south polar waters. Occasionally, the tale makes use of loglike daily entries aboard ship as a narrative device.

There is an odd structural symmetry to the episodic, seamed narrative. The preface and final note are equal in length, as are the first and last "voyages" in the sloop *Ariel* and the frail canoe. The adventures in the brig

Grampus balance the adventures in the schooner *Jane Guy*. The central section, which is the longest, includes the adventures on the hulk of the wrecked *Grampus*.

In *Pym*, as in Poe's other sea tales, the situation of being at sea provides the setting for an account of terrifying adventures that the narrator has endured and survived. Pym confronts life-threatening dangers at sea: each vessel in which he voyages is fragile and unstable; each captain and crew prove to be irresponsible and rebellious; and in each adventure Pym experiences extreme self-consciousness and a sense of helplessness and surging terror, but his irrational, frenzied activity somehow enables him to survive. The final image of the huge white figure concludes Pym's narrative enigmatically, perhaps echoing the completely white world of "Captain Adam Seaborn's" *Symzonia** (1820), a fictional rendering of a recent theory claiming that the earth's poles were hollow and habitable.

Poe used at least twenty sources for *Pym*, a number of which are nonfiction accounts of the sea: a manual of seamanship, stories of maritime disasters from the 1806 *Mariner's Chronicle*, the 1836 *Remarkable Events and Remarkable Shipwrecks,** the 1832 *Narrative of Four Voyages*, attributed to Captain Benjamin Morrell,** and Jeremiah Reynolds'** writings that urged U.S. exploration of south polar regions. Poe may have used such sources to impart a tone of authenticity and to pique the curiosity of contemporary readers who were interested in expanding the territorial domain of the United States into the area of the South Pole. Additional sources Poe used for *Pym* are still being discovered. [*See also* MUTINIES]

FURTHER READING: Kopley, Richard, ed. *Poe's* Pym: *Critical Explorations*. Durham, NC: Duke UP, 1992; Pollin, Burton R., ed. *The Imaginary Voyages: The Narrative of Arthur Gordon Pym, the Unparalleled Adventure of One Hans Pfaall, the Journal of Julius Rodman. By Edgar Allan Poe*. Vol. 1 of *Collected Writings of Edgar Allan Poe*. 4 vols. Boston: Twayne, 1981.

Joan Tyler Mead

NAVAL FICTION. Most American authors who have written good naval fiction have drawn, in part, on personal experience. For instance, dissatisfied with the portrait of nautical life in Sir Walter Scott's *The Pirate* (1821), James Fenimore Cooper* penned a more realistically detailed portrait of ships and the sea in *The Pilot** (1824), basing his descriptions partly on his own three years as a midshipman in the U.S. Navy. This novel, which features Revolutionary War hero John Paul Jones,* was the first of Cooper's many nautical romances. In contrast, *White-Jacket** (1850), a semiautobiographical novel that author Herman Melville* based on his yearlong enlisted service aboard the American frigate *United States*, is a kind of social criticism. The book realistically manifests the harsh, often unjust conditions of the American bluejacket. Melville's other work of naval fiction, *Billy Budd*,

*Sailor,** written just before Melville's death and published posthumously in 1924, goes beyond realism. The artificial situation posed by Melville in this dark chronicle—in which Captain Vere of a seventy-four-gun British naval vessel is apparently forced to condemn the "innocent" Billy Budd, a seaman who has struck his superior officer dead—is clearly allegorical.

In *Mutiny on the* Bounty (1932), Charles Nordhoff* and James Norman Hall (not naval veterans but both World War I pilots) brought to life the cruelty of William Bligh of H.M.S. *Bounty*, a cruelty that, on a voyage to the South Seas that took place in the late eighteenth century, had provoked Bligh's first mate Fletcher Christian and most of his crew to mutiny.* The two sequels to this work, *Men against the Sea* (1934) and *Pitcairn's Island** (1934), trace fictionally the further history of Bligh and the mutineers.

Nordhoff and Hall based their work on extensive historical research; so did naval officer and author Edward Ellsberg.* In *Captain Paul* (1940), Ellsberg sketched adeptly the brilliant sea battles of the Revolutionary War hero John Paul Jones. Besides the battles, Ellsberg gets across the huge difficulties that were imposed by self-serving bureaucrats and profiteers who wouldn't give Jones the ships or the orders he deserved. Yet another researcher who wrote of the navy was army veteran Francis van Wyck Mason.* Among many works of historical fiction, Mason sketched Confederate* naval* adventures such as those in *Proud Flags* (1951) and *Our Valiant Men* (1956).

Most of the best naval fiction has been written since 1940. In 1941 Marcus Goodrich's* *Delilah* appeared to rave reviews. The novel is set on the coal-burning destroyer *Delilah* in the Philippines in 1916–1917 (a destroyer like the one in which Goodrich had served) as the United States clings to an increasingly precarious neutrality. The ship's mission is to head off a Moro uprising on a remote island. An exceptional novel twenty years later concerning the same general period was written by a former naval chief petty officer, Richard McKenna.* In *The Sand Pebbles* (1962) the protagonist is an enlisted man enraptured with steam engineering but disdainful of main-deck naval life. Besides accurately picturing the navy of the Yangtze Patrol, in which the author had served, and the historical situation of American gunboat diplomacy, McKenna convincingly portrays the psychology of a crew under great stress and the growth of a young enlisted man into awareness of the great world outside his engine room.

The novels written about World War II are just as adventure-filled but somewhat less philosophical. The best, Herman Wouk's* 1951 novel *The* Caine *Mutiny*, convincingly pictures the coming-of-age of an immature young officer on an inglorious destroyer-minesweeper in the Pacific (the kind of vessel in which Wouk had spent the war) who supports a quasi-mutiny against his paranoid skipper, the infamous Captain Queeg.* The real villain of the novel, however, is the novelist Torn Keefer, in whom Wouk pictures presciently an intellectual contempt for the military that flowered only in the Vietnam era but (as the novel would seem to suggest) had been latent for decades.

Of the other naval fiction about World War II, some of the best has been written by career mariners such as Captain Edward L. Beach,* whose classic submarine novel *Run Silent, Run Deep* (1955) had a fine sequel, *Dust on the Sea* (1972). Beach portrays dramatic submarine attacks with flair and with meticulous technical accuracy but also realistically portrays a commander's troubles with subordinates and superiors. Also drawing on deep personal experience is *Away All Boats** (1954), a novel by a career merchant mariner who joined the navy on the outbreak of the war; Kenneth Dodson's description of operations aboard an amphibious ship that takes part in many wartime invasions is autobiographical. Recently, following a naval career that concluded with a tour as superintendent of the Naval Academy, Admiral William P. Mack* has written several novels about destroyer operations in the war. His first book, *South to Java* (1987), succeeds in picturing such episodes as the dramatic 1942 destroyer attack against Balikpapan, in which Mack himself had participated.

Many other wartime novels are worth mentioning. James Michener's* *Tales of the South Pacific* (1947), begun while Michener was a naval administrative officer in the Pacific, has some naval content, though it paints the atmosphere of the time and place more thoroughly than the naval profession. Journalist Harry Homewood wrote submarine novels such as *Silent Sea* (1981) and *Final Harbor* (1982), which succeed in telling good stories and also accurately reflect the technical side of the submarine war that Homewood knew. John Clagett's portrait of blood-thumping service on PT boats in *The Slot* (1957) is highly authentic, though his later novel *Papa Tango* (1982), about a main character who had been tragically burned beyond recognition in a PT encounter (as Clagett himself had been), is, in many ways, more interesting. Journalist James Bassett's novel *Harm's Way* (1962), based on Bassett's staff duty with Admiral William Halsey in the Pacific, reflects the view from the flag bridge better than that from the main deck.

Set in a different naval service are Sloan Wilson's* three Coast Guard novels, based on his wartime command of three different ships. The best of these is *Ice Brothers* (1979), which has as its subject the arduous "Greenland Patrols," and *Pacific Interlude* (1982), in which the protagonist has difficulties skippering a gasoline tanker in the Pacific.

Although they may picture an occasional malcontent, profiteer, or weak commander, all the novels just mentioned generally portray the navy and the war effort in a positive light. In sharp contrast is the little-known, but excellent, *Goodbye to Some* (1961), an antiwar novel by wartime navy pilot Gordon Forbes about flying navy Liberator bombers in the far Pacific at the war's end. Although his buddies are always joking, the protagonist Iverson is personally terrified when he flies his 2,000-mile patrol missions, and he considers many of his fellow pilots to be glory-seeking daredevils. The book offers uniquely compelling portraits of the interaction of a group of somewhat immature young pilots and of piloting a large aircraft in combat. A mildly antiwar book with a different subject is Jan de Hartog's* 1966 novel *The Captain*, in which a Dutch tugboat skipper concludes his account of disastrous convoy voyages to Murmansk by advising his son to become a civilian, not a military pilot. This novel offers an interesting view of the British navy from the bridge of a civilian vessel.

Not all American naval fiction recounts deeply serious, death-defying events. Some of it is very humorous, like Thomas Heggen's *Mister Roberts** (1946). Here the officer protagonist, beloved by the crew, desperately wants to get into the fighting but must deal instead with interminable backwater cruises and an imperious, incompetent captain. Heggen himself did manage to participate in several wartime invasions aboard an assault transport. William Brinkley's* 1956 *Don't Go Near the Water* is another comic novel about the war. Brinkley had served as a naval public affairs officer, and naturally, wartime public affairs is the focus of Brinkley's writing. More comprehensive in terms of naval characters and operations but just as humorous are the stories of Admiral Daniel Gallery,* especially the collections *Now Hear This* (1965) and *Stand By-y-y to Start Engines* (1966), stories set in the postwar navy of the 1950s.

Many other novelists have written naval fiction about events since World War II. Michener's brief, but elegiac, *The Bridges at Toko-Ri* (1953), about carrier pilots in the Korean War, is one of the few decent novels about naval aviators, despite its author's not having been a pilot. The ex-naval aviator Stephen Coonts has written several books, beginning with *The Flight of the Intruder* (1986), that inimitably capture the experience of jet flying in the Vietnam era, just as the surface naval expert David Poyer* has written a series of excellent novels of modern frigate and destroyer duty during the Cold War, beginning with *The Med* (1988) and *The Gulf* (1990). Poyer also penned a good comic novel about the Naval Academy, *The Return of Philo T. McGiffin* (1983), his first major success. Another academy graduate, Marine Corps veteran (and later secretary of the navy) James Webb gives a lively, if controversial, academy portrait, *A Sense of Honor* (1981), begun while Webb was teaching English at that institution. Finally, there have been several novels about nuclear submarines. Most of them—like Edward L. Beach's* 1978 *Cold Is the Sea*—are written by authors with nuclear submarine experience.

There is one significant exception: Tom Clancy's* *The Hunt for Red October* (1984), like most of his subsequent fiction, is based not on personal experience but on extensive technological research and on Clancy's own longtime naval and military interest. Clancy's work suggests you don't have to have been in the navy to write good naval fiction. But obviously it helps.

Robert Shenk

NAVAL MEMOIRS. Since the nineteenth century, many authors have written naval memoirs or other personal accounts of naval service that have significance beyond the historical or the naval.

In *Journal of a Cruise* (1815), for example, Captain David Porter* traced in lively prose his highly successful raids in the *Essex* upon the British whale fishery in the Pacific during the War of 1812. Charles Nordhoff (grandfather of the coauthor of *Mutiny on the* Bounty of the same name) wrote in *Man-of-War Life* (1855) a highly readable account of his teenage enlisted cruise to China and Japan aboard the American ship of the line *Columbus*. This book was commercially more successful than James Fenimore Cooper's* *Ned Myers; or, A Life before the Mast* (1843), a memoir of Myers' life taken down by his friend Cooper that has a partially naval subject and is less strident than Herman Melville's* semiautobiographical novel *White-Jacket** (1850), although all these books manifest the harsh (indeed, often life-threatening) circumstances of the American bluejacket.

Other older works of note are Frederick Palmer's *Autobiography of George Dewey* (1913) and Captain William Harwar Parker's *Recollections of a Naval Officer, 1841–1865* (1883), about an American naval officer who became the superintendent of the Confederate States Naval Academy. But the gem of all these older accounts is Rear Admiral Charles E. Clark's memoir, *My Fifty Years in the Navy* (1917). When the Civil War broke out, and he with other Naval Academy midshipmen* had to choose between the Union and Confederacy, Clark chose the Union. Through his subsequent career he saw a great variety of shipboard duty, much of it historically important: he was with Farragut at the Battle of Mobile Bay, was present at the bombing of Valparaiso, and was the captain of the *Oregon* as that vessel helped to batter the Spanish fleet into submission at Santiago during the Spanish-American War. Clark's charming memoir puts the best light upon a naval ethos in which the relation of officer to enlisted was sometimes conceptualized as that of father to son, though it often resembled (in its customary floggings, poor pay, and other oppression) that of master to slave.

In the twentieth century, a number of authors wrote autobiographically about their naval duty. Most of these works are about World War II, although there are exceptions: Admiral Daniel Gallery's* humorous memoir *Eight Bells and All's Well* (1965) traces his naval career from 1917 to 1960, and William J. Lederer's sometimes hilarious recollections, *All the Ships at Sea* (his first book, written in 1950, while he was a navy captain), reaches back to his enlisted service in the 1920s.

Of literary-quality memoirs about World War II itself, a few are by naval professionals, such as *Under the Red Sea Sun* (1946), in which Admiral

Edward Ellsberg* masterfully recounts his recall to do naval salvage work, and *Submarine* (1952), a partly autobiographical and somewhat amateurish book by which Captain Edward L. Beach* initiated his writing career. Commander Edward Peary Stafford's two engaging recollections, *Little Ship, Big War: The Saga of DE 343* (1984) and *Subchaser* (1988), are also worth noting.

Other memoirs have been written by academics, looking back. Among these is Alvin Kernan's *Crossing the Line* (1994). Here a literary expert portrays memorably his youthful and enterprising enlisted experience as an aviation ordnanceman, service in which Kernan participated in highly significant events: he was on the *Enterprise* during the Battle of Midway and later was on the carrier *Hornet* when it was sunk. In Samuel Hynes' *Flights of Passage* (1988), a literature professor captures well his youthful experience as a Marine Corps pilot, both during flight training and in the midst of the Pacific War. Historian Louis R. Harlan's memoir *All at Sea* (1996) narrates convincingly a young man's coming-of-age as an officer aboard a small amphibious craft that deployed to several theatres of war. Perhaps the most philosophical of all these reflective works is English professor Robert Edson Lee's delightful *To the War* (1968), in which the author attempts to come to terms with his "on the fringe" wartime experience as a "hull repair specialist."

Of course, many other American authors had naval service in the war and described it at less than book length. Of special note are James Michener's* *The World Is My Home: A Memoir* (1992), which devotes some ninety pages to his official duties (and many unofficial activities) while an administrative officer in the South Pacific, and Sloan Wilson's* memoir *What Shall We Wear to This Party?* (1976), which devotes similar space and some fine description to his service in the U.S. Coast Guard, including arduous patrol duty in the North Atlantic and successive command of three Coast Guard vessels.

Selections from these works, from some of the full-length memoirs mentioned earlier, and from short autobiographical recollections of writers such as Louis Auchincloss, Russell Baker, Ben Bradlee, Alex Haley,* Samuel Eliot Morison, Carl Rowan, Lewis Thomas, C. Vann Woodward, and Herman Wouk* appear in Robert Shenk's edited *Authors at Sea: Modern American Writers Remember Their Naval Service* (1997), a compendium of naval service during World War II.

Robert Shenk

NELSON, JAMES L. (1962–   ). Born in Lewiston, Maine, James L. Nelson, a former professional square-rig sailor, traces his love of the sea to his earliest memories, when he chose boats and model ships for boyhood toys. Nelson attended the University of Massachusetts-Amherst and the University of California-Los Angeles (UCLA), earning his B.A. in motion picture and television production from UCLA in 1986. After two years as an assistant editor for a Hollywood television production company, Nelson succumbed to his nautical wanderlust and spent five years serving aboard sailing ships, including the *Golden Hinde*, the *Lady Washington*, and the Revolutionary War-era replica H.M.S. *Rose*.

Drawing upon his firsthand knowledge of tall-ship sailing, Nelson has authored the Revolution at Sea Saga, a series of historical novels depicting the American naval struggle during the Revolutionary War. *By Force of Arms* (1996) introduces protagonist Isaac Biddlecomb, American smuggler and sea captain. Drawn into the escalating maritime conflict not by patriotic zeal but by the lure of economic gain, Biddlecomb suffers the loss of his ship and her illicit cargo to a Royal Navy revenue cutter and the indignity of capture and before-the-mast servitude aboard a British brig. Escape follows, but, now having been bloodied by King George's forces, Biddlecomb joins the Revolutionary cause. At the behest of General Washington, he raids and captures British gunpowder stores on Bermuda in *The Maddest Idea* (1997) and delivers the badly needed powder to Washington's army, bolstering the general's siege of Boston. The third book of the cycle, *The Continental Risque* (1998), finds Biddlecomb participating with the newly formed Continental navy in its 1776 amphibious raid upon the British armory at New Providence, Bahamas. In *Lords of the Ocean* (1999), Biddlecomb commands the Continental brig of war *Charlemagne*. He transports Dr. Benjamin Franklin across the wintry North Atlantic to France, raids the English coast, and escalates the colonial war.

Self-consciously endeavoring to join the ranks of C. S. Forester and Patrick O'Brian, Nelson nevertheless forgoes his forerunners' stylized tones. His dialogue aims for the patterns of contemporary speech, stressing the immediacy, rather than the arcane distance, of his subject matter. Unlike Forester's Horatio Hornblower and O'Brian's Jack Aubrey, Isaac Biddlecomb is not bred to the naval service, and Nelson's nonperiod diction supports his main character's newcomer status by allying him, as a fellow neophyte, with the reader.

John F. Hussey

NEMEROV, HOWARD [STANLEY] (1920–1991). Howard Nemerov was born in New York City and died in University City, Missouri. He served as a pilot with the Royal Canadian* Air Force before joining the U.S. Air Force for the last two years of World War II. Upon discharge, he worked as associate editor of the literary serial *Furioso* (1946–1951) and completed his first book of poems, *The Image and the Law* (1947). One of the poems in this collection, "The Soldier Who Lived through the War," uses sea imagery to establish both Nemerov's politics and aesthetics. In 1978 his *Collected Poems* (1977) earned Nemerov the Pulitzer Prize and a National Book Award. Ten years later, he was named poet laureate of the United States

(1988–1990). His images and themes of the sea, infusing his novels, short stories, essays, poetry, and plays, celebrate the sea as the giver of life and expose its perils and threat of death.

Nemerov's fiction includes short stories of the bizarre and grotesque collected in *A Commodity of Dreams and Other Stories* (1959), in which is embedded the archetypal sea journey. Growth, development, and becoming are present in the expansion of ocean waves, in sea life, in journeys across the sea, and most importantly in the metamorphosis of the sea into an intentional voice.

Sea imagery figures importantly in all of Nemerov's writing. "The Pond" (1966), as microcosm, depicts love's labor's lost and found and creation and death in water and, by extension, in the sea. The spirit of the pond is an avenging one, reenacting the ancient myth of castration and recalling Venus rising from the sea. The poem ends with a paradox that asserts that life and death coexist in the pond, and such antithesis applies as well to the larger sea world. The sea is shrunk to a goldfish bowl in "Goldfish" (1962), and the sea swells to macrocosm in "Hope" (1973). This poem depicts Lady Hope withstanding a terrific storm at sea even as fishermen on a wharf remain oblivious to the sea's turbulent power, capable of capsizing and sinking their ships. The final stanza affirms that Lady Hope will succeed in treading the perils of the deep because she balances her way with an unsinkable anchor.

In *Journal of the Fictive Life* (1981), Nemerov recounts dreams and interprets them as part of the creative process. The final dream in "Three Dreams on the Same Theme" occurs on an ocean liner in distress; the dreamer realizes that the sea bestows freedom upon him. Nemerov's sea imagery can reinterpret creation and liberation. The title character in "The Mud Turtle" (1967), exemplifying the opposing forces of Nemerov's sea imagery, journeys from the mud deep below the underwater of the sea to the light of the mountaintop only to return again to the bottom of the deep. The turtle embodies contraries such as sloth and speed, courage and cowardice, existing in a habitat of both mud and gemstone.

Nemerov uses irony as one conscious rhetorical strategy, and such strategies limit excesses of emotion and celebrate the authority of wit in his sea imagery. His poems present oblique slants on his subjects that surprise his readers and challenge their unexamined perspectives. His poem "Make Love Not War" (1960), which concludes with a focus on sands of the sea, entered popular culture as a slogan on bumper stickers.

Readers delight in discovering comic shifts that unveil Nemerov's wit and lead one to encounter another world. Intertextually and metaphorically, his work abounds with images of the sea: its harbors, tides, creatures of the deep, and experiences on and of the sea. The title of his poem "I Only Am Escaped Alone to Tell Thee" (1955) echoes the messengers who inform Job of the destruction of his family and his possessions; Herman Melville* had used these very words to preface the epilogue of *Moby-Dick** (1851). [*See also* SEA IMAGERY IN MODERN AND CONTEMPORARY PO-ETRY]

William E. Tanner

NICKERSON, THOMAS (1805–1883). At fifteen years old, Thomas Nickerson was the youngest member of the crew of the Nantucket* whale-ship *Essex** when she was rammed and sunk by a whale in the Pacific Ocean, 20 November 1820. In 1876, fifty-five years after the appearance of first mate Owen Chase's* account of the disaster, Nickerson, then the proprietor of a boardinghouse on Nantucket, sent his own narrative of the *Essex* to the professional writer Leon Lewis, then living in Penn Yan, New York. For reasons unknown, Lewis never edited the account, eventually lending Nick-erson's notebook to a neighbor, who died with it in his possession. Not until 1980 did the narrative come to the attention of Nantucket whaling expert Edouard Stackpole, who confirmed that it was a previously unpub-lished account of the *Essex*. In 1984 the Nantucket Historical Association published an edition of Nickerson's narrative edited by Helen Winslow Chase and Edouard Stackpole. An unabridged edition of the narrative is included in *The Loss of the Ship* Essex, *Sunk by a Whale: First-Person Accounts*, edited by Thomas Philbrick and Nathaniel Philbrick (2000). Nathaniel Phil-brick draws heavily on Nickerson's narrative in his book *In the Heart of the Sea: The Tragedy of the Whaleship* Essex. (2000). [*See also* SHIPWRECK LITERATURE; WHALING NARRATIVES]

Nathaniel Philbrick

NINETEENTH-CENTURY PERIODICALS (1828–1933). First and foremost in the popular dissemination of maritime-related stories in America was *Harper's New Monthly Magazine* (1850–1853). While this is by no means the earliest or the most specialized periodical relating to maritime affairs, it brought to the American masses a tremendous assortment of marine-related articles and illustrations. Within the first six months of pub-lication, there appeared articles on sailors being attacked by sharks, the story of the storm-tossed steamer *Hibernia* and her mad cook, shore-whaling off the Cape of Good Hope, and a notice of the U.S. Congress passing legis-lation forbidding the flogging of sailors in the navy.

December 1851 saw illustrated articles on Henry Grinnell's American Arctic* Expedition in search of Sir John Franklin and on the Boston Tea Party. There also appeared a brief announcement about the squadron being sent from New York to Japan under Matthew Calbraith Perry* to initiate trade, the famed Japan Expedition. In January 1854 the maritime history of Dutch and English relations with Japan formed a thirteen-page article di-rectly related to the Perry expedition. That March, the Grinnell Expedition was again featured with an illustrated follow-up article based on the experiences of Elisha Kent Kane, doctor in the U.S. Navy, as published in his book *The U.S. Grinnell Expedition in Search of Sir John Franklin: A Personal Narrative* (1853).

In March 1856, two extraordinary articles appeared in *Harper's New Monthly*. The first, a twenty-five-page piece entitled "Commodore Perry's Expedition to Japan," gave Americans their first glimpse of the inhabitants of "that strange country." There were illustrations of Japanese merchants, peasants, and regents as well as street scenes and architecture, in addition to a portrait of Perry himself. The next article, "The Story of the Whale," was on a subject equally strange and remote to most Americans. It combined cetology with whaling history, descriptions of technology, curious events both real and imaginary, and a romantic description of life at sea away from "licentious civilization" (466).

Harper's also produced an illustrated weekly, *Harper's Weekly, a Journal of Civilization* (1857–1916). Published in New York, it was a powerful organ of public opinion, forming the basis for illustrated history books. The most dramatic illustrations often accompanied the shortest stories. For instance, the cover illustration for 25 June 1864, the "Burning of the Steamer *Berkshire*, on the Hudson River, on the Night of June 8, 1864," is based on six short paragraphs, and the large and terrifying wood engraving "Parrot on a Rampage" is based on a single paragraph describing how, in a storm, a monstrous Parrot gun broke loose from its stays onboard the U.S. steamer *Richmond* off Mobile (14 May 1864). An impressive two-page illustration from 13 February 1864 of "The United States Sloop of War *Richmond* on Blockade Duty, off Mobile" gave the public a dramatic look at the nature of naval activities during the Civil War. This story was supported by another two-page illustration, "A Story of the Sea, Incidents in the Life of a Sailor," which had as its focal vignette, naturally, a shipwreck,* and is surrounded by other vignettes of "Heaving the Lead," "Furling Sail," and "In a Foreign Port" (12 March 1864). Shipwrecks were often recorded and pictured in every illustrated newsweekly of the nineteenth century; likewise, many new vessels, especially those incorporating unique naval architecture, received special notice.

There were other illustrated magazines, such as the weekly *Frank Leslie's Illustrated Newspaper* (1855–1891), published in New York and hyped as "The Pictorial and Literary History of the Times." Some of its marine-related articles were decidedly historical and literary. In the issue of 7 January 1871, Harriet Prescott Spofford's eight-column article, "Some Legends of the New England Coast: The True Account of Captain Kidd," decries the activities of New England coastal treasure-seekers and then fully describes the life and times of this merchant-captain-turned-pirate, including his trial and hanging.

As in any free-press journal of the American Union, *Leslie's* has its editorial side as well. The issue of 21 January 1871 devotes a column and a half to upholding the good name of the Civil War admiral David Dixon Porter, who came under attack by General Benjamin Franklin Butler over a private letter he had written in wartime condemning the actions of General Ulysses S. Grant. Other marine-related articles from 1871 include "Winter Life among the Wreckers" (18 February), an illustrated story of the American storeships *Supply, Saratoga*, and *Hunter* en route to Havre to supply foodstuffs to war-torn France (18 March), the explosion of the ferryboat *Westfield* (12 August), and a charming little cover story, "The Belle of the Voyage," which highlights the attentions that a beautiful woman may obtain from the captains of transatlantic voyages (8 April). Many interesting whaling stories appear in this publication.

America's first illustrated newsweekly, *Gleason's Pictorial Drawing-Room Companion* (1851–1854), which later became *Ballou's Pictorial Drawing-Room Companion* (1854–1859), featured an exalted view of a busy Boston harbor as its masthead. Like *Frank Leslie's Illustrated Newspaper*, these periodicals are a combination of literature, history, current events, and valuable knowledge. Within the latter category one could find such articles as the 28 January 1854 two-page spread "Minute Representation of an American Line-of-Battle-Ship, with Full Explanation of Its Parts." This includes two superb views: an exterior broadside view delineating the sails, rigging, hull, and structural components of the vessel and an interior cutaway showing the arrangements of the various decks and the activities therein.

Steamships are another frequent highlight. Saturday, 4 March 1854, features a two-page illustration of "The Collins Fleet of New York and Liverpool American Mail Steamers." A week later, it is a U.S. mail steamer entering the port of Havana, Cuba. This latter illustration is part of a larger article about Havana, which includes a bird's-eye view of the city and harbor. The same issue has a half-page illustration of the steamer *Eastern City*. The 18 March cover story is about the "New Steamship *William Norris* of Philadelphia." Other steam vessels featured in 1854 include the Philadelphia iceboat (25 February), the Royal Navy flagship *Duke of Wellington* (22 April), river steamers *Missouri* and *Humboldt* (15 April), the U.S. mail steamship *John L. Stephens* (1 April), the *Himalaya* of Great Britain, "the largest steamship in the world" (18 March), the royal mail steamship *America* (17 June), the steam yacht *Sayed Pacha*, built for his highness the grand admiral of the Egyptian fleet (10 June), the U.S. steam frigate *Fulton* (24 June), and the "very artistic and pleasing model of maritime grace and beauty," the French screw-steamer *Laromiguere* (3 June). Other miscellaneous marine-related articles included a tribute to Nathaniel Bowditch* (25 March) and an article on Caribbean* underwater archaeology conducted by James A. Whipple upon the Spanish ship-of-the-line *San Pedro Alcantara* in the waters off the Venezuelan island port of Coche, which includes a detailed illustration of a diver with helmet, air supply, and a diving bell (24 June 1854).

Periodicals specifically written for and about sailors and maritime affairs include *The Sailor's Magazine, and Naval Journal* (1828–1933), published by the Seamen's Friend Society in New York, and *The Friend* (1843–1925), first published by Samuel C. Damon, seamen's chaplain, Honolulu. Both magazines were created expressly to promote temperance, Christianity, and the development of a "bond of union," whereby sailors could be rescued from "the fangs of monsters in wickedness" (*Sailor's Magazine, and Naval Journal*, September 1828). Articles include poetry, a naval journal, classified advertising, disasters, reports of various seamen's bethels,* and the Seamen's Friend Society, as well as features on sailors' Sabbaths at sea and narrative accounts of all sorts. Other periodicals of a similar nature include *The Sea Bird, Devoted to the Best Interests of Sea Men and Their Families* (1857–1860), published in New York by the Mariner's Family Industrial Society, and *Sheet Anchor* (1843–1847), published in Boston by Jonathan Howe. Much like the *Sailor's Magazine* and *The Friend*, the *Sheet Anchor* has standard columns relating to seamen's homes in various cities and ports, poetry and verse, temperance and disasters. It also has book reviews, advertisements, and an obituary column. Whaling-related stories, oil prices, and other whale-fishery matters are frequent.

Literary magazines such as *The Knickerbocker, or New York Monthly Magazine* (1833–1865), published in New York by John A. Gray, contain occasional articles or stories relating to maritime affairs. Some fairly important maritime writings appear in *The Knickerbocker*, such as J. N. Reynolds,* "Mocha Dick, or the White Whale of the Pacific: A Leaf from a Manuscript Journal" (May 1839), one of Herman Melville's* sources for *Moby-Dick** (1851). A very informative article from the point of view of marine affairs in nineteenth-century periodicals appeared in the March 1859 issue. Entitled "Seamanship of *The Atlantic Monthly*," its author, Duncan McLean, asserts that an article called "Men of the Sea," from the January 1859 issue of *The Atlantic Monthly*, which describes sailors as degraded, was written out of inexperience, ignorance, and stupidity. His own assertion that "the seamen of our day have not degenerated" seems more in keeping with publications such as *Harper's* and *Leslie's*, where the activities of ships and sailors are extolled rather than bemoaned.

Scribner's Monthly Illustrated Magazine for the People (1870–1930), published in New York by Charles Scribner's Sons, features the work of prominent authors and illustrators of its time, though not every issue has items of maritime merit. Some examples include "Ocean Passenger Travel" by John H. Gould (April 1891), which outlines both the history of transatlantic steam navigation, including record passages, as well as the comforts and vagaries of the typical passage from the viewpoint of the traveler. An item of particular interest in this article is the bill of fare as described for first cabin, second-cabin, and steerage passengers. In the same issue is a story called "Where the Ice Never Melts; The Cruise of the U.S. Steamer *Thetis* in 1889" by Robert Gordon Butler, describing the perils of Arctic* navigation and shipwreck. The *Thetis* had been sent to the Alaskan Arctic for the purpose of building the U.S. government-sponsored house of refuge at Point Barrow, as well as to stand by to help any vessels of the whaling fleet there that may have gotten into difficulty.

By the first half of the nineteenth century, whaling had become such a large and complex industry that in 1843 a newspaper was published in New Bedford entitled *Whalemen's Shipping List and Merchants' Transcript* (1843–1914). Its stated purpose is to provide information to "ship owners and merchants, and not less so to the parents and wives, the sisters, sweethearts, and friends of that vast multitude of men, whose business is upon the mighty deep" (*Whalemen's Shipping List and Merchants' Transcript*, March 1843, p. 8). Every issue lists port of registry, rig, tonnage, captains, owners, dates of departure and arrival, cargo, and miscellaneous comments for every vessel engaged in the industry. It is the primary source for Alexander Starbuck's *History of the American Whale Fishery* (1878). [*See also* CONFEDERATE NAVAL FICTION; COOPER, JAMES FENIMORE; DAVIS, REBECCA HARDING; JUVENILE LITERATURE; LIFESAVING LITERATURE; MELVILLE, HERMAN; PIRATE LITERATURE; POE, EDGAR ALLAN]

FURTHER READING: Exman, Eugene. *The Brothers Harper*, New York: Harper, 1965; Kouwenhoven, John A. *Adventures of America, 1857–1900: A Pictorial Record from* Harper's Weekly. New York: Harper, 1938; Lomazow, Steven. *American Periodicals: A Collector's Manual and Reference Guide*. West Orange, NJ: Steven Lomazow, 1996; Mott, Frank Luther. *A History of American Magazines*. 5 vols. Cambridge: Harvard UP, 1930–1968.

Michael P. Dyer

NORDHOFF, CHARLES, the elder (1830–1901). A journalist, Charles Nordhoff was born in Erwitte, a village in Westphalia, Prussia. At five, he emigrated with his parents to Ohio, where they died. Left an orphan in the care of a family in Cincinnati, he was apprenticed to a printer at age thirteen. After serving a year, he ran away. He became a compositor for a Philadelphia newspaper and then enlisted in the navy in 1845, joining the ship of the line U.S.S. *Columbus* on her world voyage to establish full diplomatic relations with China and to make America's first attempt to open Japan. Returning home in 1847, Nordhoff joined merchant vessels sailing to Europe, the Far East, and Australia. After shifting to New England whaling and fishing, he came ashore in 1854 to begin a journalistic career.

He began by publishing nonfiction: graphic descriptions of sea life. The first to appear was *Man-of-War Life* (1855), a description of the navy from an enlisted man's point of view. This book was followed with *The Merchant Service* (1855) and *Whaling and Fishing* (1856). These three were collected as *Nine Years a Sailor* (1857) and later retitled *Life on the Ocean* (1874). His grandson and namesake republished selections as *I Served in Windjam-*

mers (1941). A fourth book, *Stories of the Island World* (1857), included descriptions of Madagascar, Java, Iceland, Ceylon, and New Zealand.

In 1857 Nordoff became an editor for Harper Brothers and then managing editor of William Cullen Bryant's* *New York Evening Post*, 1861–1871. In 1868 he published his only volume of fiction, *Cape Cod* and All Along the Shore*, a collection of pieces from *Harper's* and *The Atlantic Monthly*. He became Washington correspondent for James Gordon Bennett's *New York Herald* from 1874 until 1890 and published several books on politics. At his death in 1901, he was considered one of the foremost American journalists. His grandson, the younger Charles Nordhoff,* in collaboration with James Norman Hall, continued the tradition of maritime writing.

John B. Hattendorf

NORDHOFF, CHARLES [BERNARD] the younger (1887–1947) **AND JAMES NORMAN HALL** (1887–1951). Writers Charles Nordhoff and James Norman Hall were born the same year but worlds apart, Nordhoff in London of American parents and Hall in Colfax, Iowa. They met during World War I as members of the Lafayette Flying Corps, whose history they subsequently detailed in written collaboration.

For their next project the two chose to produce a collection of travel pieces about the South Pacific, and they embarked for Tahiti early in 1920. Nordhoff went on to the Cook Islands, and Hall to the Tuamotu Archipelago; their account of their travels, *Faery Lands of the South Seas*, appeared the following year (1921). Both men continued living on Tahiti but at first pursued separate writing careers. By 1912, however, the two had resumed collaboration, first on a juvenile* novel about the Lafayette Flying Corps and then on a trilogy of novels about what they would help to make one of the most famous events in maritime history.

Inspired by a historical account of the mutiny* aboard the H.M.S. *Bounty* on 27 April 1789, Nordhoff and Hall undertook to re-create the mutiny in fictional terms. If their first volume succeeded, they intended to treat subsequent events in further novels, and succeed it did. *Mutiny on the* Bounty (1932) was a best-seller and inspired a memorable motion picture in 1935, starring Charles Laughton as Captain William Bligh and Clark Gable as First Mate Fletcher Christian, the mutineers' leader. Other film versions were released in 1962 and 1984, the latter with Mel Gibson and Anthony Hopkins.

Nordhoff and Hall followed *Mutiny on the* Bounty with *Men against the Sea* and *Pitcairn's Island* (both 1934). The former elevates Bligh, the ostensible villain of the first volume, into a heroic figure who guides his tiny boat of loyalists for well over 3,000 miles across the Pacific to the island of Timor in the East Indies. The latter dramatizes the violent fate of the *Bounty* mutineers on Pitcairn Island,* southeast of the Tuamotus, and is the least historical of the trilogy due to the paucity of information available. Although occasionally marred by problems of tone and, in the final volume, structure, the *Bounty* trilogy is popular fiction of a very high order. As testament to the enduring interest of the saga, William Kinsolving came out with *Mister Christian* in 1996, a fictional tale in which Fletcher Christian escapes Pitcairn Island, frees an Englishwoman from debauched privateers and finds love with her on a deserted island, finds his way to England, and survives as a fugitive between decks in the sea battles of the Napoleonic Wars.

Nordhoff and Hall continued to write, both independently and in collaboration, Hall four times more prolific than Nordhoff, but nothing they produced subsequently could match the dramatic appeal of their most famous saga. Hall produced a pendant volume in *The Tale of a Shipwreck** (1934), in which he discusses not only the *Bounty* but also a voyage to Pitcairn and the wreck of his own schooner on the return trip. Hall's rollicking yarn *Doctor Dogbody's Leg* (1940) was reprinted as a Heart of Oak Classic by Henry Holt in 1998. Together the two wrote *The Hurricane* (1936), *The Dark River* (1938), and *No More Gas* (1940), all minor works with a Pacific island setting; *Botany Bay* (1941), a grim, but far more substantial, novel about the infamous Australian penal colony; and *Men without Country* (1942), a slight adventure novel about prisoners who escape the penal colonies of French Guiana and sail across the Atlantic to offer their services to the Free French. In *Lost Island* (1944) Hall bade fictional farewell to the idyllic Pacific world he saw vanishing and in *The Far Lands* (1950) to the Pacific of the distant past.

Nordhoff died in California in 1947. Hall died in 1951, leaving an unfinished autobiography, *My Island Home* (1952). Hall's grave in Tahiti overlooks Matavai Bay, where the *Bounty* once anchored.

FURTHER READING: Briand, Paul L., Jr. *In Search of Paradise: The Nordhoff–Hall Story.* New York: Duell, Sloan, and Pearce, 1966; Hall, James Norman. *My Island Home: An Autobiography.* Boston: Atlantic Monthly-Little, Brown, 1952; Hall, James Norman. *The Tale of a Shipwreck.* Boston: Houghton Mifflin, 1934; Roulston, Robert. *James Norman Hall.* Boston: Twayne, 1978.

Grove Koger

NORRIS, [BENJAMIN] FRANK[LIN] (1870–1902). Although his short life was adventurous enough, including trips to Africa's Transvaal and Cuba during the Spanish-American War, Frank Norris' disposition to set two of his less successful novels partly at sea probably arose from his familiarity with the San Francisco Bay Area, where his family settled in the 1880s. Norris' first novel, *Moran of the* Lady Letty (1898), centers on the encounter of the wealthy and genteel Ross Wilbur and Moran Sternersen, the daughter of the captain of the ship that rescues him. She succumbs to Wilbur and slips into a role submissive to her lover, however committed she has been to winning, to being one of the surviving fittest in life's brutal struggle.

Here Norris is less concerned with individual psychology or roles than with large ideas, the irresistible forces that determine the course of personal lives. The sea serves more as a setting than as a naturalistically determining factor.

Moran is a melodramatic novel that begins predictably with the protagonist, a former Yale crewman, being shanghaied* when he leaves an upper-crust social gathering and ventures near the infamous waterfront. Spirited away by the infamous Captain Kitchell and his small crew of shark-hunting Chinese, who throughout are drawn in the racist terms of the period, Wilbur and his new mates encounter the derelict bark *Lady Letty*. Kitchell's hopes for salvage rights are dashed when the surviving daughter of the owner is discovered aboard. Following are fishing adventures and a battle with another Chinese crew for the ambergris prize carried by a dead sperm whale. In the contest Moran falls in love with Wilbur, is murdered by the thieving Chinese for the ambergris loot, and is allowed to drift out to sea through the Golden Gate in conventional Viking fashion.

Norris achieves a more fundamental naturalism in *A Man's Woman* (1900). The first two chapters trace the Darwinian struggle across the Arctic* ice floes of polar explorer Ward Bennett and his suffering crew after their ship, the *Freja*, has been crushed by shifting packs. Reduced to animal instincts, the surviving crew and even the dogs are thoroughly brutalized in their struggle against the elements. Bennett, his chief engineer, Richard Ferris, and the crew finally meet the whaleships they have been searching for. Their failed attempt to reach the North Pole has been in progress for four years before they return. The remaining 90 percent of the novel takes place in the United States, where Bennett is put in contrast to, and conflict with, Lloyd Seabright, a wealthy and self-reliant nurse. Drawn to Ferris before the journey, she is disappointed by his broken spirit, the result of losing his hands to frostbite. Lloyd's desire to preserve what she can of her professional integrity and to be an independent woman suffers when she converses with Bennett. Ferris dies, and Lloyd admits her love for the harsh and brutal Bennett. She nurses him through the typhoid that he has contracted in his attempt to aid his comrade Ferris. She realizes that the Arctic explorer must play his manly part to her maternal instinct, and so he leaves with her blessing for another attempt to conquer nature and the elements.

Raw and flawed, *A Man's Woman* is a vigorously naturalistic rendering. Norris focuses on the qualities that allow the hero to prevail against incredible odds rather than depicting the failure of victimized naturalistic protagonists such as he would with the farmers in *The Octopus* (1901).

FURTHER READING: Dillingham, William. *Frank Norris: Instinct and Art*. Athens: U of Georgia P, 1969; Graham, Donald. *The Fiction of Frank Norris*. Austin: U of Texas P, 1978; Graham, Donald, ed. *Critical Essays on Frank Norris*. Englewood Cliffs, NJ: Prentice-Hall, 1980; Pizer, Donald. *The Novels of Frank Norris*. Bloomington: Indiana UP, 1966.

Donald Yannella

THE NORTHWEST COAST. Stretching from the Columbia River north
to Yakutat Bay, Alaska, the Northwest Coast is a region of rugged mountains
and dense forests. From ancient times, the sea provided abundant natural
resources as well as the easiest means of travel for trade and communication.
The literature that grew up on the Pacific Ocean coast of North America is
consequently infused with salt water.

In anthropological terms, the Northwest Coast is the native home of more
than a dozen groups of people, related through cultural characteristics but
not sharing a common language. Northwest Coast Indians were expert mariners, regularly taking their large cedar dugout canoes on trading or warring
expeditions along 1,000 miles of coastline and effectively harvesting the
abundant stocks of fish, roe, shellfish, and sea mammals that lived along
their coast. According to native tradition, humans were first discovered in a
clamshell on the beach by Raven, the primary character of Northwest Coast
Indian legend. Numerous stories describe historic and mythic relationships
between people and sea creatures, and rituals still survive that honor the
animals harvested for human consumption.

Though Captain James Cook was not the first European to arrive on the
Northwest Coast, the description of his arrival in 1778 was the first to appear
in print. *A Voyage to the Pacific Ocean, Undertaken by the Command of His
Majesty, for Making Discoveries in the Northern Hemisphere* (1784) described
in detail the native people and landscape of the region. The official narrative
was actually preceded by several unofficial accounts, including John Rickman's *Journal of Captain Cook's Last Voyage* (1781), an account in German
by Henrich Zimmermann, *Reise um die Welt* (1781), William Ellis' two-
volume *Authentic Narrative of a Voyage Performed by Captain Cook and
Captain Clerke* (1782), and *A Journal of Captain Cook's Last Voyage to the
Pacific Ocean* (1783) by the American John Ledyard.* Several of the men
who were with Cook when he reached the Northwest Coast, on the third
of his voyages to the Pacific, made subsequent visits for which Admiralty
accounts were published. These include George Dixon's *A Voyage round
the World; but More Particularly to the Northwest Coast of America* (1789),
James Colnett's *A Voyage to the South Atlantic and round Cape Horn* into
the Pacific Ocean, for the Purpose of Extending the Spermaceti Whale Fisheries*
(1798), and George Vancouver's *A Voyage of Discovery to the North Pacific
Ocean, and round the World; in Which the Coast of Northwest America Has
Been Carefully Examined and Accurately Surveyed* (1798).

Americans followed closely in the wake of Cook, with an important trade
that brought manufactured goods to the Northwest Coast from Boston and
sea otter pelts from British Columbia and Alaska to Canton. The competitive
American entrepreneurs who sponsored trading voyages were less willing to
share the results of their endeavors through publication than the British
government, which used the publications to document their claims to territory.

The Englishman John Jewitt* described the capture of the ship *Boston* in his popular *Narrative of the Adventures and Sufferings of John R. Jewitt* (1815), but, for the most part, American shipboard accounts remained unpublished until the twentieth century. There were some exceptions, and Northwest Coast passages are included in the following: Archibald Campbell's *Voyage around the World* (1825), Captain Richard J. Cleveland's *Narrative of Voyages and Commercial Enterprises* (1842), Peter Corney's *Voyages in the Northern Pacific* (1896), Edmund Fanning's* *Voyages to the South Seas, Indian and Pacific Oceans, China Sea, North West Coast, Feejee Islands, South Shetlands, & c.* (1838), Ebenezer Johnson's *A Short Account of a Northwest Voyage* (1798), Benjamin Morrell's* *A Narrative of Four Voyages in the South Seas and Pacific Ocean* (1832), Samuel Patterson's *Narrative of the Adventures and Sufferings of Samuel Patterson, Experienced in the Pacific Ocean, and Many Other Parts of the World* (1817), and the accounts of the Astoria venture, most notably Washington Irving's* *Astoria: or Anecdotes of an Enterprise beyond the Rocky Mountains* (1836), but also including Gabriel Franchere's *Rélation d'un Voyage à la Côte du Nord-ouest de l'Amérique* (1820), Ross Cox's *Adventures on the Columbia River* (1831), and *Adventures of the First Settlers on the Oregon or Columbia River* (1849) by Alexander Ross.

Among recent publications of eighteenth- and nineteenth-century shipboard manuscript accounts are John Boit's *Log of the* Union (1981), Joseph Ingraham's *Journal of the Brigantine* Hope *on a Voyage to the Northwest Coast of North America, 1790–1792* (1971), Stephen Reynolds' *Voyage of the* New Hazard *to the Northwest Coast, Hawai'i and China, 1810–1813* (1938), and several publications edited by Frederick Howay, including *The Voyages of the* Columbia *to the Northwest Coast 1787–1790 and 1790–1793* (1941).

Charles Wilkes described the region between Puget Sound and the Columbia River in detail in his *Narrative of the United States Exploring Expedition** (1844), and James G. Swan was among the first of the permanent settlers to publish an account, entitled *The Northwest Coast; or, Three Years' Residence in Washington Territory* (1857). As the region began to be populated by immigrants from the eastern United States, Europe, Asia, and Africa, the maritime trades maintained their economic supremacy, and several authors incorporated them into novels. In addition to his history of the port of Seattle, *Northwest Gateway* (1941), and his biography of *Peter Skene Ogden: Fur Trader* (1967), sailor-author Archie Binns* incorporated maritime themes into *You Rolling River* (1947), *The Timber Beast* (1944), and especially the powerful novel *Lightship* (1934). The maritime industries continue to inspire writers, and the modern fishery in Puget Sound is the setting for David Guterson's* *Snow Falling on Cedars* (1994). Theodore Roethke, the dean of Northwest poets, celebrates the sea in a number of poems, including "The Whale" (published in *I Am! Says the Lamb* [1961] but composed much earlier). [*See also* AMERICAN INDIAN LITERATURE OF THE SEA; CANADIAN LITERATURE OF THE SEA]

FURTHER READING: Barcott, Bruce, ed. *Northwest Passages: A Literary Anthology of the Pacific Northwest from Coyote Tales to Roadside Attractions.* Seattle: Sasquatch, 1994; Malloy, Mary. *Boston Men on the Northwest Coast: The American Fur Trade 1788–1844.* Fairbanks: U of Alaska P, 1998; Silveira de Braganza, Ronald Louis, et al. *The Hill Collection of Pacific Voyages.* San Diego: U of California P, 1974.

Mary Malloy

THE NORTHWEST PASSAGE. Beginning in 1497, the search for a practical water route to the Orient through North America spawned numerous European exploratory expeditions. John Cabot was the first to seek the Northwest Passage when in 1497 England commissioned him to chart a route to the Pacific that bypassed Spanish possessions in North America. His limited exploration of the Newfoundland coast inspired the voyages of Martin Frobisher in 1576, Henry Hudson in 1610–1611, and Edward Parry in 1819–1820, among those of countless other explorers, many of whom never returned. Not all searches were confined to the Arctic* region. James Cook discovered the Sandwich Islands (modern-day Hawaiian Islands) en route to search for a western entrance to the Northwest Passage in three voyages from 1776 to 1779. Other explorers, including René Robert Cavelier, de la Salle, Major Robert Rogers, and the team Meriwether Lewis and William Clark, sought a freshwater route through America, traveling over networks of rivers led by native guides. Lewis and Clark reached the Pacific Ocean in 1806, culminating a two-year journey chronicled in the eight-volume *The Original Journals of the Lewis and Clark Expedition* (1904–1905), edited by R. G. Thwaites, which ended thoughts of a commercially viable Northwest Passage through the continental United States. Finally, in 1905 Roald Amundsen became the first man to navigate a ship safely through the ice-clogged waters of the Arctic Ocean. In his two-volume work *The North West Passage* (1908), Amundsen concluded that his route was impractical for both commercial and military passage.

Early publications of significance on the Northwest Passage include Arthur Dobbs' *An Account of the Countries Adjoining to Hudson's Bay* (1744), on an expedition captained by John Middleton (1741–1742), which contributed to further expeditions into the northern waters as well as to further literature on the topic. Major Robert Rogers, leader of Rogers Rangers, a team of guerrilla fighters during the colonial era, sent expeditions through Lake Michigan and Lake Superior into the western rivers in search of the Northwest Passage shortly after Dobbs' expedition. Rogers published a book chronicling these journeys in *A Concise Account of North America* (1765), as well as in a play, *Ponteach: or the Savages of America* (1766) to capitalize financially on his experiences. Herman Melville* mentions the

Northwest Passage in the "Extracts" section opening *Moby-Dick** (1851), as well in Chapter 24, where reference is made to Cook and George Vancouver's searches for the passage in the Pacific Northwest.

The Northwest Passage, like *Moby-Dick*, evokes a sense of mystery and exploration and the relentless search for the truth. Inspired by the accounts of Dobbs and Rogers, Kenneth Roberts'* historical novel *Northwest Passage* (1936) is the story of the legendary Major Rogers' raids on French/Indian outposts in Canada and his subsequent search for the Northwest Passage. Roberts' novel inspired the MGM film *Northwest Passage* (1940), directed by King Vidor, which, along with the novel, rekindled interest in the legendary route. A recent study, Ann Savours' illustrated *The Search for the North West Passage* (1999), is a gripping chronicle charting the search for the Northwest Passage from the Elizabethan age to the middle of the twentieth century.

The mythic lure of the Northwest Passage continues to manifest itself in modern explorers, as on 22 July 1958, when the U.S. submarine *Nautilus* led a voyage navigating beneath the ice in the Arctic region. On 25 August 1969, the commercial oil tanker *Manhattan* (1961), aided by Canadian* icebreakers, completed its journey through the Arctic waters, leading its owners to exclaim that the Northwest Passage had been conquered. The *Manhattan*'s hull was breached by an iceberg at one point and was icebound at another, yet her mission was touted as a success despite its obvious commercial impracticality. The expeditions of the *Nautilus* and the *Manhattan* are testament to the enduring interest in the Northwest Passage and its mystical intrigue to contemporary explorers.

An illustrated contemporary account is James P. Delgado's *Across the Top of the World: The Quest for the Northwest Passage* (1999).

Nathaniel T. Mott

O _____

OCEAN LINER DRAMA. A number of plays and musicals take place during ocean crossings. Two famous American musicals are set on glamorous ocean liners from Prohibition New York to liberated France. *Anything Goes* (1934), featuring music and lyrics of Cole Porter, was based on books by Guy Bolton, P. G. Wodehouse, Howard Lindsay, and Russell Crouse. The coauthored title by Bolton and Wodehouse, a comedy about a shipwreck,* became unproducible after the real-life sinking of the S.S. *Morro Castle* on 8 September 1934, and required revisions by Lindsay and Crouse. Nightclub singer Reno Sweeney, originally played by Ethel Merman, is the entertainment on the cruise. Also onboard are two stowaways: Sweeney's friends Billy Crocker, who wants to be near Hope Harcourt, the debutante he loves, and Moon-Face Mooney, Public Enemy Number Thirteen, who is escaping the long arm of the law. Their romantic and criminal misadventures involve the female passengers, including Reno's backup singers, and the sturdy crew of the ship. The classic Porter score includes "I Get A Kick Out of You," "You're the Top," "Blow, Gabriel Blow," "Anything Goes," the sea chantey "There'll Always Be a Lady Fair," and a crew song. Film versions in 1936 and 1956 jettisoned several Porter songs and most of the book.

Based on Anita Loos' 1925 novel of the same title, *Gentlemen Prefer Blondes* (1949) features music by Jules Styne and lyrics by Leo Robin. The show is mostly set on board the *Ile de France*, which is taking Lorelei Lee, played by Carol Channing in a star-making turn, and her chum and nominal chaperon Dorothy Shaw to France, courtesy of her rich friend button tycoon Gus Esmond. On board, Lorelei and Dorothy meet the American Olympic team en route to the 1924 Paris Olympics. Sir Francis Beekman loses a diamond tiara to Lorelei, and Henry Spofford falls in love with Dorothy.

After a series of complications, the musical ends with the two couples happily wed. The 1953 film version starred Marilyn Monroe and Jane Russell.

Another musical features an infamous ocean liner in a minor role. *The Unsinkable Molly Brown* (1960), with music and lyrics by Meredith Wilson and book by Richard Morris, is loosely based on the life of the famous Denver socialite. It traces the heroine's rise from poverty in the Colorado silver mines to life among the elite in Monte Carlo. Brown's heroism during the sinking of the *Titanic** finally wins over the snobs of Denver and wins back her husband. The score's break-out hit was Molly's anthem "I Ain't Down Yet." The Broadway production was a triumph for Tammy Grimes, as the 1964 film version was for Debbie Reynolds.

The infamous ocean liner moved center stage in *Titanic** (1997, stage; 1997, 1999, 2000 films), with book and lyrics by Peter Stone and music by Maury Yeston. In act 1 the crew exults in staffing the largest moving object in the world, the first class toasts their prosperity and the wonders of technology, the second class explores exciting new social options, and the third class anticipates the opportunities that await in America. The act 1 finale is instrumental, with the stage converted to a moonless sea and a model of the ship sailing toward the iceberg. The tone of act 2 is darker, moving from doubt, to horror and panic, then finally to acceptance and elegy. The act opens with the crew waking up the passengers when the ship collides with the iceberg and moves through the boarding of the lifeboats, to the reflections of those left on board, including the ship's architect, who reviews his drawings and envisions the final moments before the ship sinks. An epilogue turns to the survivors aboard the S.S. *Carpathia*, who remember the dead. A stunning finale reunites the living and the dead in a visionary restaging of the ship's disembarking. The original Broadway production featured a cast of forty-three and an ingenious set by Stewart Laing which showed several decks of the ship simultaneously in a variety of flexible arrangements.

On a lighter note, *At Home Abroad* (1935) was a lighthearted revue featuring music by Arthur Schwartz and lyrics by Howard Dietz. The around-the-world cruise of Otto and Henrietta Hatrick served as an excuse for a series of songs and sketches featuring Beatrice Lillie, Ethel Waters, Eleanor Powell, Reginald Gardiner, and Eddie Foy Jr. in a variety of exotic settings. Under the direction of Vincent Minnelli, Lillie repeated her classic sketch about a tongue-tied London shopper and also played a Russian ballerina, a geisha girl, and the wife of an Alpine guide; Waters sang "Hottentot Potentate," "Thief in the Night," and "Loadin' Time"; and Powell played a high-hatted, tap-dancing Eton boy and a Samoan beauty.

An ocean crossing is also featured in the nonmusical play *Our Hearts Were Young and Gay* (1946). Adapted by Jean Kerr from the 1942 book of the same name by Cornelia Otis Skinner and Emily Kimbrough, the play depicts the European adventures of the original coauthors. Acts 1 and 2 take place aboard ship. After evading Cornelia's parents and learning how to deal with the ship's staff, the young women overcome their fear of shipwreck, unwittingly catch a stowaway, win a talent competition, share their sink with the eccentric British ladies from next door, and meet two college men. Act 3 brings their adventures to a dizzying end in Paris. [*See also* DRAMA OF THE SEA; RICE, ELMER]

FURTHER READING: Green, Stanley. *Broadway Musicals: Show by Show*. Milwaukee, WI: Hal Leonard, 1985; Leonard, William Torbert. *Theatre: Stage to Screen to Television, Volume 2: M–Z*. Metuchen, NJ: Scarecrow, 1981.

Brian T. Carney

OGILVIE, ELISABETH [MAY] (1917–   ). Born in Roxbury, Massachusetts, and soon thereafter uprooted to Maine, Elisabeth Ogilvie gained critical and popular attention for her first novel, *High Tide at Noon* (1944). The novel and its sequels, *Storm Tide* (1945) and *The Ebbing Tide* (1947), centered on the Bennetts, a family presiding over a small island off the coast of Maine. During the next four decades, in penning a prolific stream of low-key romantic novels, mysteries, and juvenile fiction, Ogilvie became known for her lyrical, pleasant descriptions of Maine's islands and coastal fishing villages.

While primarily a storyteller in the tradition of domestic women's fiction, Ogilvie's novels emanate with the distinct flavor of daily life along the Maine coast and its environs. Fishing lore and the minutiae of coastal life provide the lifeblood for most of her forty books, which include such appealing titles as *Becky's Island* (1961), *Waters on a Starry Night* (1968), *The Dreaming Swimmer* (1976), the autobiographical *My World Is an Island* (1954), and *The Summer of the Osprey* (1987). Ogilvie's Jennie Glenroy series relates the adventures of the daughter of a nineteenth-century shipbuilder. Her juvenile fiction includes *Come Aboard and Bring Your Dory* (1969).

Ogilvie currently lives in the Maine of her fiction, where she writes, fishes, wanders the coastline, and paints boats. [*See also* JUVENILE LITERATURE]

Brian Anderson

THE OLD MAN AND THE SEA (1952). This short novel by Ernest Hemingway* (1899–1961) received the Pulitzer Prize in 1953 and special recognition in Hemingway's Nobel Prize Award in 1954. It was adapted into a film in 1958 that starred Spencer Tracy. Perhaps the only major American novel entirely about another culture, it has no American characters, except for two uncomprehending tourists who appear once.

Santiago,* an aged, hand-line fisherman in Cojimar, just east of Havana, is known as "El Campeón" (the Champion) for his physical prowess. But in September 1950, he has not taken a fish in eighty-four days, eschewing the smaller marlin near shore while seeking the rare giants in the depths of the Gulf Stream. Manolin, his youthful apprentice, has been forced by his parents to work with a fisherman who markets average fish. Santiago persists alone, without income, depending for bait and food upon the continuing assistance of Manolin.

On the eighty-fifth day Santiago hooks a 1,500-pound marlin 600 feet down in the mile-deep sea. With the huge fish lashed alongside his skiff, Santiago sails back to Cojimar, battling sharks that follow a fearless mako in stripping away all the marketable meat. Arriving home on the night of his third day at sea, exhausted and despondent, the old man sleeps without his recurrent dream of lions. But when he awakes in the morning, Manolin shares with him a fictional plan to fish together again, thereby obliquely reminding his tutor of a champion's commitment to his destined role. Despite their unspoken knowledge that the severely injured Santiago, near death, will fish no more, the old man returns to sleep, this time dreaming of the lions; Manolin, the succeeding champion, watches reverently by his cot.

Although sometimes lamented for its celebration of aggression or attacked as an unconvincing departure from Hemingway's hardheaded empiricism, this novel is widely regarded as his most consummate realization of a discernible natural order embracing human affairs. The old man's resolution, to the death, parallels that of the marlin's and the mako's, suggesting that the sea sanctions the sacrificial behavior of individual creatures responsible for the round of contact between species. The hero's numinous impression that time momentarily stops at the marlin's death indicates that the slaying of a respected adversary is a timeless necessity, one mystery Hemingway found in the bullring.

These and other devices unobtrusively empower a sea narrative notably similar to *Moby-Dick** (1851) in epistemological focus. With this work Hemingway's canon achieves circular completion.

Toni D. Knott

OLIVER, MARY (1935–   ). A popular and highly acclaimed American poet, recipient of both the Pulitzer Prize and the National Book Award, Mary Oliver has composed numerous lyric poems set on coastal Cape Cod.* Born in Cleveland, Ohio, Oliver began writing poems when a teenager. After briefly attending Ohio State University, Oliver transferred to Vassar College, alma mater of one of her favorite poets, Edna St. Vincent Millay. After graduation, Oliver again echoed Millay's career by settling in Provincetown, Massachusetts, at the tip of Cape Cod.

Some of Oliver's cape poems straightforwardly, yet eloquently, depict that coast's native flora and fauna. A few poems, for example, convey the inspiring physical beauty of sea creatures, from the majestic ("Humpbacks," 1983), to the meek ("Whelks," 1992). In "Mussels" (1979) and "Clamming" (1986), the poet vividly describes the creatures she harvests from the sea for food. Some of these poems do more than chronicle the common-place, offering philosophical and spiritual insights realized during daily coastal walks. In "Starfish" (1986), for instance, the speaker learns how to love the earth, despite its limitations, by watching starfish flourish in their seemingly inhospitable sea habitat. In "The Sea" (1983) and "The Hermit Crab" (1990), the poet acknowledges that land-dwelling life forms not only began in the sea but will also return there. Several of Oliver's cape poems, including "Clam Man" (1978) and "The Waves" (1986), feature portrayals of characteristic aspects of that coast's folklife.

Most of these poems, as well as other of her related cape writings, appear in the collection *New and Selected Poems* (1992). [*See also* SEA IMAGERY IN MODERN AND CONTEMPORARY POETRY]

Ted Olson

OLMSTED, FRANCIS ALLYN (1819–1844). Francis Allyn Olmsted, author of *Incidents of a Whaling Voyage to Which Are Added Observations on the Scenery, Manners and Customs, and Missionary Stations of the Sandwich and Society Islands* (1841), was twenty years old when he graduated from Yale University in the fall of 1839. Despite the urgings of his friends, on 11 October of that year he shipped aboard the New London whaleship *North America*, Nathaniel Richards, master, on a voyage to the Pacific Ocean. In the preface to *Incidents of a Whaling Voyage*, Olmsted describes shipping aboard a whaler in hopes of overcoming illness, a chronic disorder of his nervous system, in the warm and mild tropics. With a penchant for moralizing and an acute skill for observation, he embarked as a convalescent passenger when he was well enough to do so. He claims to have kept both a journal and a sketchbook, but there is no indication that either has survived in public collections.

In the *New York Review* (October 1841), an anonymous review of *Incidents of a Whaling Voyage* decried Olmsted's book, saying that "it bespeaks for him no promise of success as a narrator of the adventures and perils of the sea" (535). The reviewer compares Olmsted's work to that of Richard Henry Dana Jr.* and James Fenimore Cooper,* the luminaries of American sea literature in those years. Olmsted appears lackluster because of his pose as spectator rather than participant. However, after the manner of Thomas Beale, Olmsted's aspiration was to write a description of whaling "proportionate to its adventurous character and importance," and in this he succeeds. He makes no pretense at any point to being a sailor, and he offers the reader solid observations of life aboard an American whaleship. Likewise, his illustrations are the first pictures of whaling to appear in an American whaling narrative. Neither Cooper nor Dana attempted to illustrate their works, but Olmsted felt that the illustrations were more important than the text itself for accuracy. There are three full-page whaling scenes, one full-page view of the *North America*, one unique view of pulling teeth from the jaw of a sperm whale, and two midpage vignettes: one of whale craft, including harpoons, and one a pattern of cutting-in showing how the blubber was removed from the whale.

Perhaps his own training in the medical profession at Yale inspired Olmsted to emulate so closely the efforts of Thomas Beale, a surgeon on the British whaleships *Kent* and *Sarah and Elizabeth* between 1830 and 1833. Beale's *The Natural History of the Sperm Whale* (1839) is a work of singular importance to whaling historians and cetologists. Olmstead acknowledges that some of the statistical data in his chapters on whales and whaling were acquired after his return, and, like Beale, he quotes large passages from other scholars of the day.

Similar to Beale's lengthy descriptions of the inhabitants of various Pacific island groups, Olmsted digresses from his whaling narrative text to take a light-duty anthropological view of the natives of the Hawaiian Islands, paying special attention to missionary activities. His observations and comments on these islands and Tahiti constitute half the text. [*See also* WHALING NARRATIVES]

Michael P. Dyer

OLSON, CHARLES [JOHN] (1910–1970). The poet Charles Olson was born and raised in the inland city of Worcester, Massachusetts, but the family always spent summers in the fishing port of Gloucester*; widowed in 1935, his mother provided a permanent base there for Olson. It thus became the location where much of Olson's work on Herman Melville* was done, which culminated in the provocative *Call Me Ishmael* (1947). This study of *Moby-Dick** (1851), expanded from Olson's earlier straightforward "Lear and *Moby-Dick*," published in *Twice a Year* (1938), draws on Karl Brandt's *Whale Oil: An Economic Analysis* (1940) as well as sources available to Melville. It emphasizes Melville's prescient understanding of the relationship between the commercial activity of whaling in the "space" of the Pacific Ocean and conquest and settlement of the American West. Olson also authored the dance-play *The Fiery Hunt* (1977), a dramatized debate between Melville's Ahab* and Ishmael,* focusing on their conflict over the fate of the white whale.

The Maximus Poems (vol. 1, 1960; vol. 2, 1968; vol. 3, 1975) were begun literally as letters to the Gloucester poet Vincent Ferrini* and continued as such from "exile" in Washington, D.C., and Black Mountain College, North Carolina, until Olson took his family to settle in Gloucester permanently in 1957. The poet then began to trace episodes in Gloucester history in great detail. In this epic, two volumes of which were published in Olson's lifetime and one posthumously, fishermen's tales of the sea have their place, sometimes as heard conversation, sometimes via the local writer James B. Connolly. Olson himself ventured to sea on only one occasion, a three-week swordfishing cruise in July 1936. It was, as one might expect, a momentous experience for him, recorded fully in his diary and published in *Olson: The Journal of the Charles Olson Archives*, no. 7 (Spring 1977): 3–42.

The unifying theme of the later Maximus poems is Gloucester as a pivot in the westward migration of peoples from the cradle of civilization in the Near East. The city's delay in accepting modern habits, retaining the values of courage and trust exhibited by fishermen, is embodied in the symbol of Cape Ann as an island of refuge that the nation turned its back on as it moved inland in its tainted "progress." [*See also* CREELEY, ROBERT; MELVILLE DRAMATIZATIONS; METCALF, PAUL]

FURTHER READING: Butterick, George F. *A Guide to the Maximus Poems of Charles Olson*. Berkeley: U of California P, 1978; Charters, Ann. *Olson/Melville: A Study in Affinity*. Berkeley, CA: Oyez, 1968; Clark, Tom. *Charles Olson: The Allegory of a Poet's Life*. New York: Norton, 1991; Maud, Ralph. *Charles Olson's Reading: A Biography*. Carbondale: Southern Illinois UP, 1996.

Ralph Maud

OLSON, [MERLE THEODORE] TOBY (1937–   ). Poet and novelist Toby Olson was born in Berwyn, Illinois, but spent much of his childhood moving around the United States. This constant movement instilled a theme of travel into his work, particularly his novels. He spent four years as a medical corpsman in the navy, from 1957 to 1961, then earned a degree at Occidental College in 1965. In 1975, after more moving around the country, he began teaching English at Temple University. Olson does much of his writing at home on Cape Cod,* in North Truro, Massachusetts. His novel *Seaview* (1982) describes the cross-country drive of a couple trying to return to Cape Cod before the death of the terminally ill wife. *At Sea* (1993), which takes place in North Truro, recounts the investigation of a murder on Cape Cod. In *Dorit in Lesbos* (1990), the protagonist takes a meditative cruise in waters around Huntington Harbor, California, and Panama and uncovers a family secret on the Greek isle of Lesbos.

Peter H. McCracken

OMOO (1847). Herman Melville's* second novel and sequel to *Typee** (1846), *Omoo* traces the wanderings of the narrator, whom the men call Typee, and Doctor Long Ghost. They begin as discontented sailors on board the *Julia* (the *Lucy Ann* in real life), become involved in a mutiny,* and are put in custody on Tahiti. They travel about Tahiti and Eimeo, observing the natives' customs, which, Typee laments, have been ruined by the advent of Western culture, particularly the missionaries. At the end, Typee determines to go to sea again and sails off in the *Leviathan*, as Melville does in the *Charles and Henry*.

In the section at sea, which constitutes the first third of the novel, Melville deepens the criticism of the tyranny of shipboard conditions he had begun in *Typee*. Poorly provisioned and beset by illness, the crew is commanded by the ineffectual Captain Guy and his drunken, bullying mate Jermin. As the situation on board deteriorates, Typee and Long Ghost attempt to mediate the conflict between Jermin and the men, but to no avail. In these scenes Melville condemns the harshness of the officers' rule and portrays, as he would do so fully in *Moby-Dick* (1851), the wild variety of sailors. Officials of any sort are depicted as either weak and useless or evil and vindictive. The mutineers receive only condemnation by the British consul Wilson, and before their incarceration on Tahiti they are imprisoned on a French frigate, symbolic of the larger imperialist powers threatening the men and the South Seas. [*See also THE RED RECORD*]

John Samson

O'NEILL, EUGENE [GLADSTONE] (1888–1953). Eugene O'Neill, America's preeminent playwright, winner of the Nobel Prize (1936) and four Pulitzer Prizes (1920, 1922, 1928, 1957), was born in the Barrett Hotel, New York City, son of the actor James O'Neill and his wife, Mary Ellen (Ella) Quinlan.

O'Neill was always attracted to the sea, beginning from his summers spent in New London, Connecticut, where his father bought Monte Cristo Cottage, overlooking the Thames River, which flows into the Atlantic. To this day, the cottage resounds to foghorns and sea noises. From an early age O'Neill had his own rowboat and later a motor dory. As a child he was photographed sitting reading on a rock overlooking the water, now commemorated by a statue near the railway station.

After hospitalization for tuberculosis at Gaylord Farms, Connecticut (1912), he returned to a boardinghouse in New London, where he swam so frequently that swimming became his most important permanent physical activity. Most of his matrimonial residences overlooked the sea, at the old Coast Guard station at "Peaked Hill Bar," Massachusetts; at "Spithead," Hamilton, Bermuda; at the specially built "Casa Genotta," Sea Islands, Georgia; in rented quarters at Puget Sound, Washington; in San Francisco hotels; and in the remodeled "Point o' Rocks," Marblehead, Massachusetts. His only residences lacking a sea view were Chateau du Plessis in France and "Tao House" overlooking the San Ramon valley of California. There in a world of then-unpopulated mountains, in a swimming pool apparently suspended in space, he reexperienced the rapturous and devastating experiences of his earlier life.

Attempting to escape his first marriage to Kathleen Jenkins, O'Neill went briefly to Honduras in May 1910 with the financial help of his father. After returning to New York in June 1910, he shipped aboard the Norwegian windjammer *Charles Racine* as a working passenger bound for Buenos Aires. He worked briefly on the German vessel *Timandra* and returned to New York in May 1911 on board the *Ikala*, soaking up the forecastle experience he was later to use in numerous plays. In July 1911 he shipped aboard the

S.S. *New York* for England as able seaman, returning on her sister ship, S.S. *Philadelphia*; for many years he sported a sweater with that name.

O'Neill made extensive use of his sea experiences throughout his dramatic career, beginning with the one-act *Thirst* (first perf. 1916; pub. 1914), where three people die on a raft, followed by another one-act, *Warnings* (written 1913; rev. into the scenario *S.O.S.*, 1917; pub. 1914), concerning a wireless operator who goes deaf, with disastrous results; this play recalls Joseph Conrad's *The End of the Tether* (1913). The one-act *Fog* (first perf. 1917; pub. 1914) is also concerned with a raft of survivors, saved by the supernatural cry of a dead child that brings about their rescue.

Most importantly, the four one-acts of the S.S. *Glencairn** cycle re-create aspects of forecastle life. *Bound East for Cardiff* (first perf. 1916; pub. 1916) deals with the death of an injured seaman. *In the Zone* (first perf. 1917; pub. 1918) evokes the wartime possibility of submarine attack and a sailor disappointed in love. *The Long Voyage Home* (first perf. 1917; pub. 1919) shows the broken dream of a shanghaied sailor, while *Moon of the Caribbees* (first perf. 1918; pub. 1918), usually played first, sums up O'Neill's attitude toward shipboard life with a romantic and experiential introduction to this series, a microcosm of human existence. *Ile* (first perf. 1917; pub. 1919) portrays a gentle wife driven into insanity as she sails with her whaler husband. *The Rope* (first perf. 1918; pub. 1919) has a prodigal son theme that looks ahead to O'Neill's first Broadway success. *Where the Cross Is Made* (first perf. 1918; pub. 1919), which includes buried treasure and insanity, has one hallucinatory scene depicting the return of drowned sailors; this play was cut down from the unfinished four acts of *Gold* (first perf. 1921; pub. 1921).

O'Neill's first Broadway success, *Beyond the Horizon* (first perf. 1920; pub. 1920) is also a "sea play," about two brothers who reverse roles. The poetic younger brother renounces his escapist sailing vessel voyage, marrying the love of his older brother and ruining the family farm. He dies of tuberculosis, as the older one returns as a hardened sea-dog entrepreneur. *The Personal Equation* (no perf.; pub. 1988) has importance in its portrayal of the familial and political plot of a second engineer and his anarchist son, who attempts to destroy the vessel, only to end up as a brain-damaged vegetable.

Anna Christie (first perf. 1921; pub. 1922), a successful play, concerns Chris Christophersen, the master of a coal barge, his daughter, Anna, formerly a prostitute, and Matt Burke, a shipwrecked* sailor overwhelmed with Anna's beauty. Eventually, they plan to marry. Here there is a repetition of the situation of *Moon of the Caribbees*, where the sea, in the tropics or off a foggy New England coast, exercises a mysteriously emotional and curative influence on the characters. Anna and Matt discover love and the necessity of marriage and companionship.

The Hairy Ape (first perf. 1922; pub. 1922) combines forecastle and political drama in eight scenes. This time O'Neill's central character, Yank, is a stoker who celebrates his strength and importance as a man who makes a vessel move. As before, the forecastle, or stokehole in this play, is a universe in itself, populated by men who epitomize the history of the sea. In a stage set that evokes a prison, Yank celebrates his physical force as the source of power in a mechanized world, while Paddy the old Irishman regrets the passing of a simpler, romantic world where the pure strength of men was the motive force of sailing ships. Then it was man against the elements rather than man at the "bottom," the mechanistic servant of filthy, polluting machines. Ridiculing Paddy's sea chanteys and evocations of the world of sail, Yank celebrates his work in the stokehole in sexually charged words of rape as he shovels coal into the furnace that drives the ship. On deck the purity of the sea is shown in contrast to the exploitative and discontented universe of wealth. When those two worlds clash in the stokehole, as the passenger Mildred visits what she perceives as a zoo, Yank's certainty is destroyed. His pride in his mechanistic cosmos is lost, and after experiencing his total lack of political power, he submits to the fatal embrace of a gorilla, finding in such a death a pessimistic fulfillment. The play was adapted for film in 1944.

In *The Fountain* (first perf. 1922; pub. 1926) the sea is the motivating force of discovery in the voyage of Christopher Columbus* and Ponce de Leon. The *Santa Maria*, carrying corrupt and self-aggrandizing European colonists, brings oppression and disaster to Puerto Rico. Nonetheless, it leads Ponce de Leon to experience the purity of the world's three major religions when he discovers in Florida the fountain of tripartite knowledge together with Beatriz, an evocation of Dante's Beatrice. The play concludes by celebrating the salvific power of love.

The affirmative image of the sea as escape from civilization and the joy of primitivism come into fatal contrast with New England culture in *Diff'rent* (first perf. 1920; pub. 1922). In this play, the whaler Caleb experiences sex in a Pacific island community, only to be forced to pay for it through suicide after rejection by the puritanical New England woman he has continued to love. Later the musical motif of the trilogy *Mourning Becomes Electra* (first perf. 1931; pub. 1931) is "Shenandoah," a chantey expressing "the brooding rhythm of the sea." In *The Haunted*, Orin Mannon tells of Lavinia's discovery of sexual freedom in the sea-surrounded world of "The Happy Isles" in the Pacific Ocean, while Christine's beloved in *The Homecoming* and *The Haunted* is the master of a sailing vessel.

The sea is also a world of competition, trade, adultery, and disaster in "The Calms of Capricorn" (written 1931; no perf.; no pub.), one of three surviving portions of O'Neill's aborted cycle "A Tale of Possessors, Self-Dispossessed," the others being *More Stately Mansions* (first perf. 1961; pub. 1982) and *A Touch of the Poet* (first perf. 1957; pub. 1957). In "The Calms" scenario, O'Neill develops the central theme of relentlessly possessive economic ambition and self-destruction within the Harford family when the sailing vessel *Dream of the West* is becalmed off gold-rush San Francisco, foiling the captain from surpassing the record of the clipper *Flying Cloud*.

Finally, in his most poignant and complex work, the posthumously performed *Long Day's Journey into Night* (first perf. 1956; pub. 1956), O'Neill, in the persona of the autobiographical character Edmund Tyrone, conveys the psychic and emotional importance of the sea as the source of experiences that took him beyond himself, suspending him between earth and heaven, making him part of the sea, realizing life in a moment of "ecstatic freedom." These events are recalled as a trinity of experiences. The first occurs on a sailing vessel, when he is lying on the bowsprit, looking back on the sails, and finds himself in unity with the vessel, the elemental ocean, and the moon and the stars. He recalls a second moment of affinity while sitting in the crow's nest of an American Line steamer at dawn, with smoke pouring from its funnels, when he identifies with the journey of life, individual fulfillment, and "the last harbour." Finally, swimming extraordinarily far out, he recounts his experience of beatitudinous revelation beyond the normal limits of humanity, momentarily glimpsing the secret of existence and becoming it. He returns to the mundanity of land-bound life, where he feels himself a permanent stranger, while his images of the sea permanently burn themselves into the reader or playgoer's experience. The play was adapted into film in 1962 (starring Katharine Hepburn and Jason Robards) and 1996. [*See also* DRAMA OF THE SEA; HALLET, RICHARD MATTHEWS; SEA MUSIC; SHANGHAIING]

FURTHER READING: Bogard, Travis, ed. *Eugene O'Neill: Complete Plays*. 3 vols. New York: Library of America, c.1988; Bogard, Travis, ed. *The Unknown O'Neill: Unpublished or Unfamiliar Writings of Eugene O'Neill*. New Haven, CT: Yale UP, 1988; Gelb, Arthur, and Barbara Gelb. *O'Neill*. New York: Harper and Row, 1974; Manheim, Michael, ed. *The Cambridge Companion to Eugene O'Neill*. New York: Cambridge UP, 1998; Ranald, Margaret Loftus. *The Eugene O'Neill Companion*. Westport, CT: Greenwood, 1984; Sheaffer, Louis. *O'Neill; Son and Artist*. Boston: Little, Brown, 1973.

Margaret Loftus Ranald

"OPTIC, OLIVER." *See* [ADAMS, WILLIAM T.].

THE ORDINARY SEAMAN (1997). Francisco Goldman's (1955–) second novel, *The Ordinary Seaman* has been described as a modern parable of America's hidden immigrant culture. Son of a Jewish American father and Catholic Guatemalan mother, Goldman populates his fiction with characters who serve as projections of a self that is culturally divided. *The Ordinary Seaman* is essentially a story about *liminality*, that space, like the sea itself, where one's perceptions or situation blends with, or crosses over into, the perceptions or situations of others.

The novel centers on Esteban, a nineteen-year-old Nicaraguan between adolescence and manhood, communism and capitalism, first and second love. An ex-Sandinista guerrilla, he signs on as a sailor without seaman's papers and is transported, with a makeshift crew of fourteen other desperate *Centroamericanos* from varied backgrounds, to the urban jungle of a remote pier in a desolate Brooklyn shipyard. Abandoned, in political, legal, and personal limbo, they become virtual prisoners on a ship that never sails, the broken-down, rat-infested *Urus*. A cavernous freighter crippled by fire damage, stripped for parts, and lacking even the most basic provisions for human habitation, this vessel becomes a death trap.

A "greenhorn" undergoing a rite of passage, Esteban had been encouraged by a surrogate father-figure to jump ship in a foreign land to escape a megalomanic captain with no regard for his ship or crew beyond their usefulness. Goldman uses the uniquely privileged position of the sea captain to illustrate the corrosive effects of unbridled egoism, which not only skews the moral compass but jeopardizes life itself.

Victor Verney

OUT OF MY DEPTHS: A SWIMMER IN THE UNIVERSE (1983). Following the tradition of early American colonizers who struggle to conquer a new and wealthy land of freedom, Paul West (1930–   ) offers in this book a first-person narrative meditation in which the aim is to conquer the whole universe. The protagonist, presumably West himself, has been for more than thirty years trying to learn how to swim. Eventually, he succeeds. Swimming in the book is a metaphor for apprehending life and death; the complete narration becomes an allegory for human existence.

As Edgar Allan Poe* had in *Eureka* (1847), West in *Out of My Depths* has written a prose poem that joins old and new literary, philosophic, and scientific orientations. West's expansive novel echoes Homer's *Odyssey* in the ninth-century B.C., Galileo Galilei's *Discourse on Things That Float* (1612), Henry David Thoreau's* *Walden* (1854), Samuel Beckett's *Molloy* (1951), and Jacques Derrida's more contemporary deconstructionism, among other works.

West presents his self-contemplation in five chapters. "Sea Fever," the first, shows his desperation at being unable to swim and proposes that the reader take a trip into the depths of the mind. "A Trough in Time," the second chapter, is the beginning of the journey; here the protagonist learns how to float and focuses attention on the important aspects of existence. Chapters 3 and 4, "Old-Style Backstroke" and "Breaststroke to Dive," represent the first stages of acquiring the ability to swim as well as seizing an awareness about life and death. In "My Tutor Shows Me How," which closes the book, the narrator finally comprehends natural order and becomes a true "swimmer in the universe."

Margarita Rigal-Aragón

P _____

PALATINE. The 1738 wreck of the English ship *Princess Augusta* on Block Island, off the Rhode Island coast, is the initial source of the "Palatine" legend. The *Princess Augusta* was en route from Rotterdam to Philadelphia, carrying over 300 immigrants from the Rhine Palatinate of Germany ("Palatines"). More than 200 of the Palatines, as well as the captain, died on the voyage from typhoid or exposure; the first mate, Andrew Brook, became master. Caught in heavy snow and high winds off Point Judith, Brook made the decision to head for Philadelphia, attempting to pass between Block Island and Montauk Point. On 27 December 1738, the vessel struck "the Hummocks," the northernmost spit of Block Island. The islanders took off the more than 100 people remaining on the vessel, but the captain refused to remove their belongings. Captain Brook and his crew removed their own belongings and the ship's tackling, then unbent the ship's sheet anchor and allowed the vessel to drift off. Four days after the *Princess Augusta* struck, it was blown ashore and broke up. In a process called "wrecking," some islanders salvaged the immigrants' chests, which contained gold, silver, and pewter.

For seventy-five years after, islanders and nonislanders claimed to have seen the "Palatine Lights" in all seasons and in varying magnitudes and intensity. Some thought they saw lines, spars, and rigging ablaze in the lights. The legend maintains that the lights, a symbol of the guilt of those who did not help the Palatines, were seen until the last of the participants died.

John Greenleaf Whittier* learned of the legend from his friend Joseph P. Hazard of Newport, Rhode Island. His poem "The Palatine" was published in *The Atlantic Monthly* in January 1867 and subsequently as part of his collection *The Tent on the Beach* (1867). In Whittier's version, the islanders use false lights to draw the ship to its death, then strip the ship of its valuables and burn it, leaving the survivors to die on the beach; each year, on the anniversary of the wreck, the burning ship appears. Only much later, in 1876, did Whittier write a letter to the Block Islanders apologizing for his historical errors.

William Gilmore Simms* also wrote a poem on the legend entitled "The Ship of the Palatines," first published in the *Ladies' Companion*, edited by William W. Snowden, in July 1843 and reprinted in *Poems Descriptive, Dramatic, Legendary and Contemplative* in 1853. Simms claims that the tradition upon which the legend is founded is still current. Unlike Whittier, Simms knew that the passengers, not the ship, are called Palatines. His poem's evil is wrought by the captain and crew, who kill the passengers for their wealth, then burn the ship. Again, the burning ship appears on each anniversary until the sons of all the men involved are dead. Although Simms claims in his headnote not to have tampered with the facts, he nevertheless dramatically alters the setting from Block Island to the Carolina banks. [*See also* GHOSTS AND GHOST SHIP LEGENDS]

Mary K. Bercaw Edwards

PARETSKY, SARA (1947–   ). V. I. Warshawski, the protagonist in all of Sara Paretsky's mysteries to date, is a private investigator in Chicago who pursues criminals. In some of her exploits, Warshawski traces them to the wharves, marinas, and beaches of the city; in several cases, as in *Blood Shot* (1988), she nearly loses her life on the shore of Lake Michigan. In *Deadlock* (1984), Warshawski investigates the death of a cousin whose body has been found floating near the wharf of the grain company that employed him. Her search leads her to travel aboard a Great Lakes* freighter, narrowly avoiding being blown up along with it as it passes through the Soo locks; she later barely escapes death at the hands of the ship's owner when she confronts him aboard his sailboat on Lake Michigan.

Critical episodes of the short story "Three-Dot Po" in *Windy City Blues* (1995) take place along the icy waters of Belmont Harbor, where, while jogging in winter, Warshawski finds a body, tracks the murderer, and, but for the help of a golden retriever named Po, almost drowns. The introduction to *Windy City Blues* is subtitled "A Walk on the Wild Side: Touring Chicago with V. I. Warshawski," which begins with a description of a blue heron and presents a tour of the city, focusing on the lakefront. In this uncharacteristically poetic passage, Paretsky offers Lake Michigan as a metaphor for both the untamable and the nurturing in nature and in human relationships.

Mary DeJong Obuchowski

THE PATHFINDER (1840). This fourth novel in James Fenimore Cooper's* (1789–1851) Leatherstocking Series, *The Pathfinder* is set in the Lake Ontario region during the French and Indian War. In addition to detailing his hero Natty Bumppo's failed attempts at romance, Cooper delineates for the first time the characteristics of sailing on the Great Lakes,* a region he learned during his service in the Navy just before the War of 1812. Cooper creates a young Lakes sailor, Jasper Western, who commands the *Scud*, a vessel designed and rigged to handle the difficult conditions on the Lakes. When Western is accused of treason, his command is given to an experienced saltwater seaman, Charles Cap, who voices the typically condescending attitude of ocean sailors for Lake men during the early nineteenth century. Cap's boasted saltwater skills prove unequal to the task of handling the vessel in a freshwater gale, however, and Western reassumes command, proving Cooper's point that on the frontier new conditions demand new technology, new methods, and new attitudes.

Victoria Brehm

PEQUOD. Ishmael,* the narrator of Herman Melville's* *Moby-Dick* (1851), chooses to go to sea for a three-year voyage on the fictional Nantucket* whaleship *Pequod*, choosing that vessel over the *Devil-Dam* and the *Tit-bit*. Ishmael tells us the *Pequod* "was the name of a celebrated tribe of Massachusetts Indians, now extinct as the ancient Medes" (ch. 16). The *Pequod* is based, in part, on the historical whaleship *Acushnet*, on whose maiden voyage Melville sailed, leaving New Bedford on 3 January 1841. The *Pequod*, in contrast, leaves Nantucket on Christmas Day (ch. 22).

The *Pequod* is, in many ways, a fantastical ship, with its belaying pins made of sperm-whale teeth and its tiller made from the lower jaw of a sperm whale. It has become, like its captain, a "cannibal of a craft, tricking herself forth in the chased bones of her enemies" (ch. 16). There are discrepancies within Melville's text concerning the *Pequod*: the whaleship first has a tiller (chs. 16, 96, 123) but later a wheel (chs. 61, 118). The whalemen sleep mostly in hammocks (ch. 29 and frequently elsewhere) but occasionally in bunks (chs. 27, 64). Melville several times mentions that there are thirty men on board (chs. 123, 126, 134), but there are actually roughly forty-five individually designated. The source for the sinking of the *Pequod* by a sperm whale at the end of *Moby-Dick* was Melville's reading of Owen Chase's* *Narrative of the Most Extraordinary and Distressing Shipwreck* *of the Whale-Ship* Essex,* *of Nantucket* (1821). In the *Pequod*, Melville created a grim, trophy-studded vessel, which haunts the reader's mind.

Mary K. Bercaw Edwards

PERCIVAL, JAMES GATES (1795–1856). Though he often mentioned the ocean in his poetry, James Gates Percival made little use of direct observation. As state geologist for Connecticut, he mapped the landforms along the Atlantic and Long Island Sound. But in verse he seldom drew on this knowledge. He followed instead the practices of his eighteenth-century predecessors, preferring to write of the abstract and the grand. His 110-line poem "Sea Pictures" (1823) describes ocean winds as "softly breathing o'er the marble main," with the result that "they smooth its billows to a liquid plain." The speaker in the 1,075-line "The Wreck" (1823) works to present not actualities of the sea but, as he puts it, the sea's "beauty and sublimity." Such verse was lauded in its day but was less esteemed once William Cullen Bryant* and Henry Wadsworth Longfellow* began to publish.

Percival is perhaps best remembered as a geologist and an assistant to Noah Webster.

Bernard F. Engel

THE PERFECT STORM (1997). A work of creative nonfiction by Sebastian Junger (1962–   ) subtitled *A True Story of Men against the Sea, The Perfect Storm* recounts the 1991 October storm off the coast of Nova Scotia where natural forces combined to create what meterologists termed "the perfect storm" because its conditions could not possibly have been worse.

Junger focuses on the six doomed crew members of the *Andrea Gail*: Bobby Shatford, Alfred Pierre, David Sullivan, Michael "Bugsy" Moran, Dale Murphy, and Captain Billy Tyne. The *Andrea Gail*, out of Gloucester,* Massachusetts, is a swordfishing boat, also called a longliner, and she is set to make one more fishing trip for the season, putting out in late September. Junger explores the personal moments of the crew before the ill-fated voyage and interweaves information throughout the narration, about fishing the Grand Banks, the men's personal lives, other great storms, *Moby-Dick** (1851), and the technical aspects of the storm itself. Junger also recounts successful rescue operations for the crew of the *Satori*, another vessel that is a victim of the storm, as well as stories of other rescue attempts. Although *The Perfect Storm* is nonfiction, the narrative skill of Junger and his tremendous description of the Atlantic Ocean in the throes of a gigantic storm induce a novelistic tone. A film version was released in 2000. [*See also* GLOUCESTER; SHIPWRECK LITERATURE]

Frank Rotsaert

PERRY, COMMODORE MATTHEW [CALBRAITH] (1794–1858). Commodore Matthew Perry served a long and distinguished career in the U.S. Navy, which began in January 1809, when he was commissioned as a midshipman. Perry is best known for commanding an 1853 expedition of four vessels, including the steam frigates *Mississippi* (built 1841) and *Susquehanna* (built 1850), on a mission to break Japanese isolationism and secure trading privileges for the United States. A return to Japan the following year, with a larger military force, formally secured these privileges on 31 March 1854 by the Treaty of Kanagawa. In Chapter 24 of *Moby-Dick** (1851), Herman Melville* alludes briefly to the isolationism of Japan, believing that when Japan becomes open to trade, a whaleship should receive the credit.

Perry and his Japanese expedition inspired widespread patriotism and a greater interest in Asia. The John Luther Long story *Madame Butterfly* (1898), the David Belasco play *Madame Butterfly* (first perf. 1900), and the Giacomo Puccini opera *Madama Butterfly* (first perf. 1904) explore the potentially tragic implications of cultural conflict in eighteenth-century Japan. Perry's 1853 mission provides the setting for the Steven Sondheim/David Prince production of *Pacific Overtures* (first perf. 1976), a moderately successful Broadway musical chronicling the social changes resulting from the American incursion. Perry documented his experiences in *Narrative of the Expedition of an American Squadron to the China Seas and Japan. Performed in the Years 1852, 1853 and 1854 [Under the Command of Commodore M. C. Perry, United States Navy, by Order of the Government of the United States]* (1856). [*See also SOUTH PACIFIC*]

Nathaniel T. Mott

[PETERSON, CHARLES JACOB], "HARRY DANFORTH," "J. THORNTON RANDOLPH" (1819–1887). Charles Jacob Peterson was an editor, publisher, and historian, born in Philadelphia, where he worked all his life. Once he acquired an ample fortune, he and his wife purchased a mansion in Newport, Rhode Island, enjoyed its summer beach and coastal activities, and in 1866–1867 voyaged to Europe.

While founding, editing, and contributing to his popular *Peterson's Magazine* and managing a publishing house, Peterson wrote poetry, novels, and historical chronicles. One slim story has a sea setting, "The Disguised Frigate" in *Sartain's Union Magazine of Literature and Art* (April 1851). His *Cruising in the Last War* (1850) treats sea activity during the Mexican War.

Only Peterson's patriotic histories of American military and naval heroes have stood the test of time. Although emphasis in many of his books is placed on land heroes, Peterson does justice to sea figures as well, treating them exclusively in his best-known and most influential book, *A History of the United States Navy, and Biographical Sketches of American Naval Heroes from the Formation of the Navy to the Close of the Mexican War* (1852). In its preface, Peterson admits that the lives of well-known American naval captains and the American navy have been amply treated by historians and authors, notably James Fenimore Cooper.* He asserts that his work is unique because it combines history and biography, that his sources include old magazines and newspapers, and that only the inaccuracy of available data forced him to exclude treatment of American privateers.

The book itself is divided into two unequal parts. The first briefly sketches early sea activity and the growth of sea power to oppose Great Britain, Tripoli, and Mexico. The longer, second part extols thirty-six naval heroes. Sketches include John Paul Jones,* Oliver H. Perry, and Matthew C. Perry,* hero at Vera Cruz and negotiator of a pact that opened up Japan to Western commerce. One unattractive subject is Jesse Duncan Elliott, whose delay in aiding Oliver Perry on Lake Erie against the British in 1813 Peterson tries to explain away but cannot. Peterson's favorite subjects are Stephan Decatur, hero at Tripoli during and after the War of 1812; Isaac Hull, commander of "*Old Ironsides*" against the British frigate *Guerrière*; and Charles Stewart, a success against French privateers, Tripolitan pirates,* and the British from 1800 to 1815.

Robert L. Gale

PHELPS, ELIZABETH [STUART] (1844–1911). Growing up in Andover, Massachusetts, Elizabeth Phelps was a lifelong resident of New England and had a summer home in Gloucester.* She was a staunch feminist who participated in causes that ranged from temperance to conditions of factory workers. Though the main theme in her fifty-seven books is the plight of women, three titles contain connections to the sea. *The Story of Avis* (1877), set on the coast, is about a young artistic woman whose career suffers due to her marriage and who longs to fit her expression to the voice of the sea; the woman's conflicts are described in rich sea imagery. *An Old Maid's Paradise* (1879) describes two women who attempt to live independently on the seashore. *Jack the Fisherman* (1887) focuses on an alcoholic fisherman who tries to rise above his lot in life.

Mira Dock

PHIPS, WILLIAM. *See* "PIETAS IN PATRIAM."

"PIETAS IN PATRIAM: THE LIFE OF HIS EXCELLENCY SIR WILLIAM PHIPS" (1697, 1702). Author Cotton Mather (1663–1728) himself never voyaged extensively at sea, yet his life was shaped by maritime experience. A Boston native and a minister, Mather was surrounded by sea culture and exhorted sailors to lead godly lives and to take lessons from maritime tragedies. In 1724 his favorite son, Increase, was lost at sea.

Mather selects the life of William Phips (1651–1695) for the most extensive biography in his *Magnalia Christi Americana: or, The Ecclesiastical History of New-England* (1702); it is also the most maritime. One of America's earliest self-made men, Phips rose from poverty and obscurity to become one of the most powerful men in the colonies. His success was funded entirely by the treasure he recovered from a Spanish wreck.

Unlike Mather's lives of John Winthrop and William Bradford, his life of Phips shows not a religious man of self-sacrifice but an ambitious figure driven by secular gain. Mather notes that Phips' primary virtue was his capacity for change. Phips' greatest transformation was his rise from poor sheepherder on the Maine frontier, to Boston's first royal governor. Unwilling to set aside his ambitions, Phips outfitted a frigate and sailed for the Caribbean,* where he had heard tales of sunken Spanish treasure. Although his first two expeditions failed, Phips prevailed upon James II in 1686 to underwrite a third expedition, which proved to be wonderfully successful. After locating the sunken wreck, Phips returned to England with more than £50,000 in Spanish treasure. For his efforts, Phips received not only £16,000 of the booty but also a knighthood and a commission as a high sheriff.

Upstart sea captain and treasure hunter, Sir William was named first royal governor of Massachusetts, but his years as governor were unremarkable. He returned to Boston in May 1692 during the Salem witch hysteria, and after appointing a court of oyer and terminer, he left for the frontier to focus on problems with Native Americans. When he returned in the late summer, the Salem executions had already taken place, and the witch hysteria had reached its peak. With even his own wife being accused, Phips sought advice from the leading ministers, and, on their recommendation, he stopped the trials and released the remaining suspects. Yet the colony was fractured with political factionalism, and Phips quarreled openly and sometimes violently with members of the opposition. In 1694 he returned to London to answer their charges of corruption and misconduct in office. Before he could clear his name and while planning yet another treasure-hunting expedition, Phips died in London in 1695.

As sailor, treasure-hunter, and soldier, Phips was consumed with material success; Mather struggles to place his secular ambitions within the greater context of New England's spiritual quest.

Daniel E. Williams

THE PILOT (1824). James Fenimore Cooper's* (1789–1851) professed purpose in writing this, the first sea novel in English, was to portray shipboard life accurately and to honor the naval heroes of the Revolution. At the time, *The Pilot* successfully challenged the authenticity of Sir Walter Scott's *The Pirate* (1821).

The action of the book takes place in the North Sea, where two Continental vessels, a frigate and a schooner, send a party ashore to retrieve a mysterious pilot known only as Mr. Gray. His speech betrays his Scottish origins, which causes some distrust among the Americans. It also partly explains his hatred of England and his devotion to freedom.

The pilot and the American vessels have been sent to capture important English citizens to use as hostages. This mission perfectly suits two young American officers whose fiancées are being held in an old abbey, where their loyalist guardian has taken them. Cooper's attempt to incorporate young women and a love plot into a historical novel largely taking place at sea requires choreography in blending public duty and private desires. Once aboard ship, it is one of the women, in fact, who calls attention to a British frigate approaching through the fog.

With the exception of one treacherous coward, a lawyer named Dillon, characters on both sides of the war are likable, although the upper-class characters are less interesting than the common seamen and soldiers. The titular hero, obviously based on the historical figure John Paul Jones,* is petulant and moody some of the time and comes alive only when ships and lives are in peril. The memorable episodes in the book take place at sea. In the first, the pilot uses his intimate knowledge of the waters of the North Sea to extricate the Continental frigate from some shoals during a fierce storm that blows a sail from the boltropes. In the second, the Americans battle a British cutter, then board and capture it after Long Tom Coffin* uses his harpoon to pin the British commander to the mast of his own ship. Finally, the pilot defeats one British frigate and then skillfully outsails another while escaping to safety.

FURTHER READING: Cooper, J. Fenimore. *Lives of Distinguished American Naval Officers.* Philadelphia: Carey and Hart, 1846; Philbrick, Thomas. *James Fenimore Cooper and the Development of American Sea Fiction.* Cambridge: Harvard UP, 1961.

Kay Seymour House

PIRATE LITERATURE. The earliest accounts of pirates were published by ministers and magistrates who used the authority of print to reinforce their public condemnations of both piracy and pirates. One of the first was Edward Randolph, surveyor-general of customs in the American colonies during the last decade of the seventeenth century. In his 1696 report, "A Discours about Pyrates, with Proper Remedies to Suppress Them," Randolph complained that illegal commerce was not only allowed but encouraged by colonial officials, including the royal governors, specifically citing the Bahamas, South Carolina, Pennsylvania, Massachusetts, and Rhode Island as being pirate havens, though noting that active measures were being initiated to suppress piracy in American waters. Broadside* proclamations calling for the arrest of some of the most troublesome pirates were published by colonial governors, listing the crimes and contraband of the pirates.

Some of the most interesting accounts were published after the pirates were captured and condemned. Ministers, including Cotton Mather, published accounts of the last moments of pirates confronting death at the gallows. A familiar genre adapted from English criminal narratives, these accounts usually included the minister's execution sermon, his dialogue with the pirates as they prepared for death, and their dying speeches. Intended to terrify readers, the ministers inevitably focused attention on the uncertainties of death rather than on the iniquities of life. In such publications as *Faithful Warnings to Prevent Fearful Judgments* (1704), *Instructions to the Living, from the Condition of the Dead* (1717), *Useful Remarks: An Essay upon the Remarkables in the Way of Wicked Men* (1723), and *The Converted Sinner* (1724), Mather depicted pirates as repentant sinners who approached their deaths warning both spectators and readers not to follow their bad examples.

Not all pirates were so contrite. John Quelch, who was executed on 30

June 1704, with five of his crew, considered himself a privateer rather than a pirate; he had attacked nine Portuguese ships off the coast of South America without knowing that England and Portugal had signed an alliance. According to the narrative published after his execution, *An Account of the Behavior and Last Dying Speeches of the Six Pirates* (1704), Quelch died demanding to know what crimes he had committed. His final warning was for captains to be cautious about bringing treasure into New England, declaring that they would be hanged for it.

Two decades later William Fly was even more defiant. From the time he was brought into Boston harbor to the moment he was executed less than two weeks later on 12 July 1726, Fly exhibited nothing but obstinacy and blasphemy. Although others of his crew confessed, offering details of their mutiny* and subsequent piracies, Fly refused to acknowledge his guilt, claiming he was falsely accused. Despite Cotton Mather's considerable efforts, when led to the gallows, Fly not only refused to humble himself by uttering a final confession but also reproached the hangman for not understanding his trade; with his own hands he adjusted the rope that launched him into eternity. His final words reproached captains to treat their crews well. Ministers Cotton Mather and Benjamin Colman both published accounts of Fly, depicting the pirate as a hardened sinner on the road to hell. Mather's *The Vial Poured Out upon the Sea* (1726) and Colman's *It Is a Fearful Thing to Fall into the Hands of an Angry God* (1726) equally transformed the pirate's defiance into damnation.

In addition to execution sermons, the most common pirate publications were the published proceedings of pirate trials, which often appeared together. While the ministers addressed the spiritual transgressions of the pirates, the trial accounts reproduced in print their criminal prosecutions, offering explicit evidence and testimony to reinforce the passing of sentence. A mixture of both narrative text and legal document, the trial accounts include the depositions of the accusers and the accused, often offering unusually rich detail about pirate life. In such accounts as *The Trials of Eight Persons Indited for Piracy* (1718), *The Trials of Thirty-Six Persons for Piracy* (1723), *The Tryals of Sixteen Persons for Piracy* (1726), and *The Trials of Five Persons for Piracy* (1726), the captains and crews of the plundered ships testify how they were captured and robbed, sometimes listing the confiscated items and their value, while the pirates declare their innocence, testifying that they were "forced men," though the accounts often include the final confessions of the condemned men as proof of their guilt.

The two most remarkable publications about pirates in the Americas were published in Europe. In 1678 Alexandre Olivier Exquemelin published *De Americaensche Zee-Rovers*, which was published in London six years later as *Bucaniers of America* (1684). Exquemelin, who lived among the buccaneers of Tortuga and Hispaniola, offers a vivid and often bloody account of pirate pillage and cruelty. Several of the most notorious buccaneers and their exploits are described, including Henry Morgan and his sacking of Panama City in 1671.

The most important of all pirate publications was Captain Charles Johnson's *A General History of the Robberies and Murders of the Most Notorious Pyrates* (London, 1724). Mistakenly believed to have been written by Daniel Defoe, Johnson's work gathered together court proceedings, newspaper accounts, and personal testimony to create the most comprehensive and graphic account of pirates ever published. The bloody careers of the most notorious pirates in American waters are described in detail, including those of Henry Avery, Edward Teach, Stede Bonnet, Samuel Bellamy, George Lowther, Edward Low, and William Kidd. Johnson even includes chapters on the two most notorious female pirates, Mary Read and Ann Bonny, when they sailed the Caribbean* with John Rackam and his crew. Johnson's remarkable compendium remains the standard source for 1690–1725, the period historians call the "golden age of piracy."

Focus on this golden age, however, has led to a misleading assumption that pirates disappeared from American waters by the 1730s. If the number of publications about them is any indication, pirates were thriving a century later. Throughout the eighteenth century any criminal activity at sea, particularly mutiny and murder, was labeled piracy, and trial and execution narratives of such crimes were often published. While outwardly similar in convention to the narratives published by the Puritan ministers, these later publications focus less on the pirate's preparations for death and more on his transgressions in life. In 1769, the year that Joseph Andrews was executed, three different accounts were published, all describing his brutal murder of the captain, mate, cabin boy, and two passengers on board the sloop *Polly* (*The Last Dying Speech and Confession of Joseph Andrews, A Narrative of Part of the Life and Adventures of Joseph Andrews*, and *An Account of the Trial of Joseph Andrews*). Equally sensational, "The Confession of Alexander White, Pirate" was published as part of America's first criminal magazine, *The American Bloody Register* (1784). In his unusually explicit account, White admits that his love for a woman of higher rank led him to commit murder and mutiny.

Throughout the late eighteenth and early nineteenth centuries, the narratives became more graphic, romanticized, and sentimentalized, blurring the lines between myth and reality and indicating that even as pirates became less of an actual threat, they were becoming more popular as fictional characters. In the popular *A Narration of the Captivity of John Fillmore* (1790), for example, the narrator vividly describes how he and several other "forced men" killed the notorious pirate John Phillips and took over his ship in 1724. Although Fillmore died before the narrative was published, and although the story was related indirectly sixty-six years after the events, the printer nevertheless makes use of Fillmore's first-person voice to describe Phillips and his pirate crew.

Perhaps the most poignant and thrilling of pirate narratives published during the nineteenth century are tales of victims and survivors. In 1822 Barnabas Lincoln published the *Narrative of the Capture, Sufferings and Escape of Capt. Barnabas Lincoln and His Crew*, an account of the horrid treatment he and his crew received after they had been taken by Mexican pirates in December 1821 off Key Largo. For more than a month the pirates ransacked the American ship and abused its crew, finally leaving them marooned* on a desolate island. Daniel Collins' *Narrative of the Shipwreck of the Brig* Betsy *and Murder of Five of Her Crew by Pirates* (1825) describes how his ship was wrecked when it ran aground off the coast of Cuba and how Collins and six others rowed to a small island in their longboat, where they were met by several local fishermen. Their joy was short-lived, however, for the fishermen sold them out to a group of cutthroat pirates, who butchered five of the survivors before Collins escaped into a mangrove swamp. The most affecting and popular of the pirate captivities was Lucretia Parker's *Piratical Barbarity, or The Female Captive* (1825). Similar to the narratives of Lincoln and Collins, Parker's book describes her experiences after her ship was attacked by a group of murderous pirates. A helpless captive, Parker watched the captain and crew being murdered, while begging for their lives.

The most popular of all pirate captivities were the tales of Americans captured by Barbary Coast pirates and sold into slavery. During the last decades of the eighteenth century, a dozen or more American ships were captured, and, according to one estimate, over 150 Americans were enslaved. In response to the public outrage, writers began to treat the theme of enslaved Americans in both novels and plays. In one of her first efforts on the American stage, Susanna Rowson* wrote and produced a comic opera, *Slaves in Algiers*, in 1794. Three years later Royall Tyler published his novel, *The Algerine Captive** (1797), and John Foss followed with an excellent firsthand account of the capture of an American ship by Barbary Coast corsairs, *A Journal of the Captivity and Sufferings of John Foss, an American, Several Years a Prisoner in Algiers* (1798).

On the heels of these were two fictionalized accounts, *Humanity in Algiers or, the Story of Azem, by an American Late a Slave in Algiers* (1801) and *The History of the Captivity and Sufferings of Mrs. Maria Martin Who Was Six Years a Slave in Algiers* (1801). Following Rowson on the stage were Maria H. Pinckney's *The Young Carolinians, or Americans in Algiers* (1818), Mordecai Noah's *The Siege of Tripoli* (1820), Jonathan S. Smith's *The Siege of Algiers* (1823), and J. S. Jones' *The Usurper, or Americans in Tripoli* (1841). Understandably, both novels and plays dramatized strong nationalistic and libertarian themes.

American print culture never produced the likes of Long John Silver or Captain Hook, but during the first part of the nineteenth century several historical pirates gained brief textual fame. Jean Lafitte* was certainly the most famous, generating several novels and plays; Samuel Tully, Cornelius

Wilhelms, and Charles Gibbs also gained notoriety when their narratives were published. Less than a week after he was executed for murder, mutiny, and piracy in December 1812, Tully was resurrected in print when *The Life of Samuel Tully* was published. Similarly, when Wilhelms faced the gallows in 1839, a remarkably sensational account was published, the *Life and Execution of Wilhelms, the Braganza Pirate!*, to exploit the excitement caused by his crimes and condemnation. Charles Gibbs achieved even greater literary effect; in addition to ephemeral publications, such as *The Pirate's Advice to Those Who Witnessed His Awful End* (1831), Gibbs' life and crimes were fictionalized in several collections of criminal biographies.

As printing technologies improved, the popular press led to an explosion of both publications and readers; stories about pirates thrived. In both the *Record of Crimes in the United States* (1833) and *The Lives of the Felons* (1847) pirates were centrally featured along with murderers, robbers, and counterfeiters.

The first American pirate anthology, *The Pirates' Own Book*, was published by Charles Ellms* in 1837. Rivaling Johnson's *General History* in popularity, the book was such a success that it was reprinted seven more times during the next two decades and is available today in an unabridged Dover reproduction (1993). Herman Melville* mentions it in *Redburn** (1849). Similar in manner and almost as popular was *The Pirate's Almanac* (1844).

By the middle of the nineteenth century the marketplace was flooded with hundreds of cheap pamphlet novels about exotic adventurers, many of whom were outlaw heroes who were often depicted sympathetically. Alongside such stock character types as highwaymen and frontiersmen, pirates often appeared as romantic swashbucklers. As bold, masterless men, pirates personified many of the most positive qualities in the American myth of the free individual. In *The Florida Pirate* (1823), for example, the anonymous author depicts the adventures of a courageous black captain who chooses piracy over slavery. In a competitive, often ruthless world, piracy provided an alternative that seemed less deceitful than many of the more lawful professions, such as Samuel Judah describes in *The Buccaneers* (1827). Filled with scenes of war and plunder, Judah's popular historical novel characterizes piracy as a justifiable means of dealing with an unjust world.

Two of the most interesting popular novels from the antebellum period describe the heroic adventures of two female pirate captains, Maturin Murray Ballou's* *Fanny Campbell, the Female Pirate Captain* (1845) and Lorry Luff's *Antonita, The Female Contrabandista* (1848). In both, the protagonists exceed their male crews in courage, skill, and even virtue. [*See also* BEHRMAN, S. N.; BROADSIDES; DRAMA OF THE SEA; WOMEN AT SEA]

FURTHER READING: Cordingly, David. *Under the Black Flag.* New York: Random, 1995; Cordingly, David, ed. *Pirates: Terror on the High Seas.* Atlanta: Turner, 1996; Cordingly, David, and John Falconer. *Pirates: Fact and Fiction.* New York:

Cross River, 1992; Creighton, Margaret S., and Lisa Norling, eds. *Iron Men, Wooden Women: Gender and Seafaring in the Atlantic World, 1700–1920*. Baltimore: Johns Hopkins UP, 1996; Rediker, Marcus. *Between the Devil and the Deep Blue Sea*. Cambridge: Cambridge UP, 1987; Reynolds, David S. *Beneath the American Renaissance*. New York: Knopf, 1988.

Daniel E. Williams

THE PIRATE'S DAUGHTER (1997). This modern epic adventure on the high seas tells the story of protagonist Wilson Lander, a man trapped in a directionless existence. Led by tarot cards to a young woman who is a seasoned sailor, he joins her on the maiden voyage of an experimental, high-tech sailboat. Piracy* and intrigue take Lander to Africa, where he becomes embroiled in slavery, war, and gambling and eventually gains self-awareness.

Author Robert Girardi (1961–   ) was born in Virginia, grew up in Athens and Paris, and returned to the United States as a teenager with his family. His inspiration for this, his second novel, is his discovery that piracy still plagues the seas today.

Mira Dock

PITCAIRN ISLAND. Discovered by the British in 1767, Pitcairn is a tiny volcanic island (2.5 square miles or 6.5 square kilometers) located in the South Pacific at 25° 4' S., 130° 6' W. The island was colonized in 1790 by nine mutineers* from the British naval vessel H.M.S. *Bounty*, six Tahitian men, nine Tahitian women, and a baby girl. The colony was discovered in 1808 by Nantucket* sealing captain Mayhew Folger aboard the *Topaz* of Boston and became a British possession in 1839.

The story of its discovery was first published in the United States in Amasa Delano's* *Narrative* (1817). The best modern account of Folger's discovery is Walter Hayes' *The Captain from Nantucket** (1996). The first comprehensive account of the *Bounty* mutiny and Pitcairn was by Englishman John Barrow (1831), first published in the United States as *A Description of Pitcairn's Island* (1833). Other early accounts are Thomas Boyles Murray's *Pitcairn: The Island, the People, and the Pastor; with a Short Account of the Mutiny of the* Bounty. (1854), appearing in America as *The Home of the Mutineers* (1854); Diana Belcher's *The Mutineers of the* Bounty (1871); and Rosalind Amelia Young's *Mutiny of the* Bounty (1894).

The story concerns the *Bounty*'s captain, Lieutenant William Bligh, and his intended voyage to the Pacific to bring breadfruit plants back to the British colonies in the West Indies, his fateful five-month stop in Tahtiti and the crew's attraction to life there, and the subsequent mutiny led by Fletcher Christian. Christian took the *Bounty* to Pitcairn, where he established a settlement. In 1808 it was discovered that only one of the original fifteen English and Polynesian men was left alive, John Adams (alias Alexander

Smith), who lived there with four women and a number of children and teenagers.

This intriguing chronicle spoke to the romantic movement in literature and served as inspiration for creative literature both in Britain and in the United States, beginning with Mary Russell Mitford's *Christina, the Maid of the South Seas* (London, 1811; no American ed.). *Christina*, a narrative poem in five cantos, is a tale of love, with the fictional heroine the orphaned daughter of Fletcher Christian and his Tahitian wife, casting Christian as a romantic hero. It was read in manuscript and corrected by James Burney, who had sailed with James Cook, and was read as well by Samuel Taylor Coleridge, who corrected the proofs. It was by all accounts popular in the United States. Lord Byron's *The Island* (1823) casts Fletcher Christian as a hero, the ideal of romantic rebellion in his desire for a Paradise on earth. British travel writer Dea Birkett's *Serpent in Paradise* (1998) paints a disillusioned picture about becoming acquainted with what she had envisioned would be an idyllic South Pacific retreat.

Significant nineteenth-century American literature using the story includes William Cullen Bryant's* "A Song of Pitcairn's Island" in his *Poems* (1832), which emphasizes the peaceful and religious serenity of life on remote Pitcairn. Nathan Welby Fiske's *The Story of Aleck* (1829; rev. and reissued as *Aleck*, 1845 and later eds.) focuses on the lone surviving mutineer. Mark Twain's short story "The Great Revolution in Pitcairn" in *The Stolen White Elephant* (1882) was probably based on the story of Englishman Joshua Hill, an 1833 arrival to Pitcairn who tried to take over the island but was ousted by the British.

Twentieth-century American literature includes Jack London's* "The Seed of McCoy," in *South Sea Tales* (1911); Charles Nordhoff* and James Norman Hall's *Pitcairn's Island* (1934; part of the *Bounty* trilogy); and William Kingsolving's *Mister Christian* (1996). American film adaptations of the story include the classic *Mutiny on the* Bounty (1935), which starred Charles Laughton as a sadistic, elderly Bligh and Clark Gable as a dashing Fletcher Christian; *The Women of Pitcairn Island* (1957); *Mutiny on the* Bounty (1962); and *The* Bounty (1984), starring Mel Gibson and Anthony Hopkins. Australian John Toohey published *Captain Bligh's Portable Nightmare* (1999), a largely factual and highly imaginative account. A description of the discovery of the wreck of the *Bounty* at Pitcairn by Luis Marden appears in the December 1967 issue of *National Geographic*. Today, thirty-eight of Christian's descendants live on Pitcairn. [*See also* CLEMENS, SAMUEL LANGHORNE]

Edward J. Lefkowicz

A PLACE WHERE THE SEA REMEMBERS (1993). A novel written by the Mexican American author Sandra Benítez (1941–   ) first published in 1993, this short collection of unified tales opens with Remedios, a local *curandera*, or healer, in the small coastal village of Santiago, Mexico, waiting at the edge of the sea for "the one blue wave that will bring a corpse to shore" (2). The identity of this corpse is not disclosed until the penultimate chapter of the book, and the reader is forced to wonder what the connection might be between this unidentified body and the small cast of characters whose dreams and tragedies are rendered so poignantly in the staccato rhythms and poetic prose of the chapters that make up this fablelike narrative. Remedios forms the spiritual nexus for both the individuals and their respective stories, which, in the end, cohere into a mosaic-like vision of the mysterious ineffable connection between humankind and the sea. "It is stories that save us," Remedios avers (103).

The sea itself is a constant physical and symbolic backdrop in Benítez's dark tale, which resonates with a mythic import that is as quietly, but insistently, understated as the pained lives of the impoverished villagers who inhabit Santiago. At times, as in the "César Burgos" chapter devoted to a local fisherman who has lost his wife and two of his three sons in a tragic bus accident, the sea is a place for new beginnings in which to forget the "heartbreak on the shore" (88), where a father can hope for his remaining son that "the sea might turn the boy into himself again" (92). But the sea also represents death, as the first page of the novel promises and the final page affirms. [*See also* LATINO/A LITERATURE OF THE SEA]

Peter F. deCataldo

PLATH, SYLVIA (1932–1963). Sylvia Plath was born in Boston, and her family moved to Winthrop, Massachusetts, a seaside suburb, in 1936, where she lived until they moved inland to Wellesley in 1942. Her childhood by the Atlantic was significant in developing her nautical consciousness, and she makes many references to the sea in her poems.

"Full Fathom Five" (1958) deals with a sea god who is both father and muse. Winthrop plays a significant role in two 1959 poems, "Point Shirley" and "Man in Black." In both, the speaker returns to her childhood home by the sea. In the first, the sea is a devouring natural force; in the second, it forms a macabre setting for the appearance of a ghostly figure, threatening and austere. "The Bull of Bandylaw" (1959) takes a mythic approach to the sea in forceful animal imagery. Plath uses her knowledge of the Massachusetts coast in "Green Rock, Winthrop Bay" (1958), "Suicide off Egg Rock" (1959), "Magnolia Shoals" (1959), "The Baby Sitters" (1961), and "Mussel Hunter at Rock Harbor" (1958). Of these, "Suicide off Egg Rock" is the strongest; here, Plath renders a gritty beach scene and an alienated man with great empathy.

Plath doesn't always regard the sea as hostile or threatening. A poignant image occurs at the end of "Tulips" (1961), where the convalescent speaker begins to feel emotions again after having closed herself off. These feelings arouse tears, which, like the sea, are warm and salty. Plath's move to England with her husband, Ted Hughes, gave rise to poems with European seaside settings, notably the bleak "Berck-Plage" and the mythic "Medusa" from 1962. In the last months of her life, personal, psychic, and familial matters preoccupied her, but the sea appears in "Contusion" (1963), where the speaker notes how obsessive the sea becomes as it spills over rocks. [*See also* SEA IMAGERY IN MODERN AND CONTEMPORARY POETRY]

Claire J. Keyes

POE, EDGAR ALLAN (1809–1849). Edgar Allan Poe, best known for his tales of Gothic horror, was a writer of poetry, short and long fiction, an unfinished drama, criticism, literary theory, essays, and a "cosmological prose poem." His more than seventy short fictions include "ratiocinative" tales, comical pieces, hoaxes, imaginary landscape sketches, and science fiction.

Poe's use of nautical lore in his writing was informed by his own experiences at sea as well as his use of authentic maritime materials. He observed the workings of vessels during transatlantic and coastal passages, and he experienced being at sea in severe weather. As a child he crossed the Atlantic twice with his foster parents, the Allans. The first crossing, in 1815, when he was six, was a rough voyage of thirty-seven days from Norfolk to Liverpool; in 1820 he returned to New York in another transatlantic passage, this one lasting thirty-six days. Between March and May 1827, he traveled on coastal vessels between Richmond, Norfolk, and Baltimore. After he joined the army in May 1827, his battery was moved by brig from Boston through severe gales off Cape Cod* to Charleston, South Carolina, en route to nearby Fort Moultrie. A year later Poe's battery was moved, again by vessel, from Charleston to Fortress Monroe, Old Point Comfort, Virginia.

For his source material, Poe took considerable information from Benjamin Morrell's* *Narrative of Four Voyages* (1832), Jeremiah Reynolds'* *Address on the Subject of a Surveying and Exploring Expedition to the Pacific Ocean and South Seas* (1836), chronicles of maritime disasters at sea, and other nautical materials. Occasionally, he copied the source directly, although he is not always accurate in his own descriptions of shipboard activity or in conveying nautical information.

His three sea tales, "MS. Found in a Bottle" (1833), *The Narrative of Arthur Gordon Pym of Nantucket** (1838), and "A Descent into the Maelstrom" (1841), are accounts of miraculous survival in realistic maritime settings. The unnamed voyager in "MS." sets sail from Java, and when the ship founders in a storm, he is somehow transferred from the deck of one ship to the rigging of another. Pym embarks from Nantucket and voyages past a number of actual places while he escapes a number of near deaths, though he ends in a fantasized Antarctica.* In "Maelstrom" an old sailor relates his return from the depths of a giant whirlpool that lies off the coast of Norway.

Several other tales contain references to the sea. Much of "The Oblong Box" (1844) takes place aboard a coastal packet ship that is lost in a spectacular shipwreck* off Ocracoke Inlet. The sea is a felt presence surrounding Sullivan Island in "The Gold Bug" (1843), and "The Premature Burial" (1844) culminates in a dream aboard a sloop anchored in the James River. There are sweeping descriptions of oceans from the elevated perspectives of balloon trips in "Hans Pfaall" (1835) and "The Balloon Hoax" (1844). Sailors appear in "King Pest" (1835), "The Murders in the Rue Morgue" (1841), and "The Thousand-and-Second Tale of Scheherazade" (1845). Sealike metaphors occur in "Four Beasts in One" (1836, "The sea of people"), in "William Wilson" (1839, "The vortex of thoughtless folly"), and in "The Man of the Crowd" (1840), whose narrator gazes out at "the tumultuous sea of human heads."

Most of the sea imagery in the poetry is indeterminate and suggestive. Death rules in "The City in the Sea" (1845), where all animation is fixed or suspended, and the sea is "hideously serene." "Annabel Lee" (1848) concludes with the incantatory lines "In her sepulchre there by the sea—/ In her tomb by the side of the sea." Other images include "A dark unfathomed tide" ("Imitation," 1827), "o'er the starry sea" ("Al Aaraaf," 1829), "o'er a perfumed sea" and "On desperate seas" ("To Helen," 1831), "the chill seas/Around the misty Hebrides!" ("The Valley of Unrest," 1845), "the solemn sea" ("To One in Paradise," 1834), "Some tumultuous sea" ("To F—," 1835), and "seas without a shore" ("Dreamland," 1844)

Stephen Marlowe's contemporary novel *The Lighthouse at the End of the World* (1995) is a fictional speculation on what may have happened to Poe in the final week of his life, told from the perspectives of Poe and of his fictional detective C. Auguste Dupin. Dominick Argento's* opera *The Voyage of Edgar Allan Poe* (1976) presents Poe's nightmarish life and demise as a sea voyage. In 1999 the Pierpont Morgan Library, New York City, mounted "Poe: The Ardent Imagination," an exhibition commemorating the 150th anniversary of Poe's death.

FURTHER READING: Poe, Edgar Allan. *Collected Writings of Edgar Allan Poe.* Ed. Burton R. Pollin. Boston: Twayne, 1981; Poe, Edgar Allan. *The Complete Works of Edgar Allan Poe.* Ed. James A. Harrison. 17 vols. New York: AMS, 1965, 1979; Poe, Edgar Allan. *The Letters of Edgar Allan Poe,* rev. ed. Ed. John Ward Ostrom. 2 vols. New York: Gordian, 1966; Silverman, Kenneth, *Edgar A. Poe: Mournful and Never-Ending Remembrance.* New York: HarperCollins, 1991; Thomas, Dwight, and David Jackson, eds. *The Poe Log: A Documentary Life of Edgar Allan Poe, 1809– 1849.* Boston, G. K. Hall, 1987.

Joan Tyler Mead

PORTER, DAVID (1780–1843). The son of a veteran of the American Revolution, David Porter was born in Boston and grew up in Baltimore. He began his naval career as a midshipman in 1798 and became master commandant in 1806. In the War of 1812, Porter was captain of the frigate *Essex* (1799) and harassed the British whale fishery in the Pacific. Though losing his ship in 1814 in a battle with the British ships *Phoebe* and *Cherub*, Porter became a national hero. After the war he worked as navy commissioner, commander of the West India Squadron, commander of the Mexican navy, consul-general to the Barbary States in Algiers, and U.S. chargé d'affaires to the Ottoman empire, where he remained resident until the end of this life. Two of his children, David Dixon Porter and the adopted David Glasgow Farragut, would also become well-known naval officers.

Porter recounted his adventures of the War of 1812 in *Journal of a Cruise Made to the Pacific Ocean* (1815), which documents his seafaring abilities, chronicles his fight against the British, and, supported by masterful drawings from Porter's own hand, depicts his exploration of the Marquesas and the Galápagos Islands.* His patriotic struggle was eulogized by Washington Irving* in "Biographical Memoir of Captain David Porter" (*Analectic Magazine*, September 1814) and by Philip Freneau* in the poem "On the Capture of the United States Frigate *Essex*" (1815). James Fenimore Cooper* summed up Porter's achievements in the *History of the Navy* (1839), while Herman Melville* criticized Porter's treatment of Marquesan natives in *Typee* (1846) but also drew inspiration for his sketches called "The Encantadas"* (1856) from Porter's description of the Galápagos Islands. The zoologist William Beebe* praised Porter's geographic and biological observations in *Galápagos, World's End* (1924). Porter wrote another travel book, *Constantinople and Its Environs* (1835), which collects his experiences in Turkey and contains his professional assessment of the country's navy.

A good recent study is *The U.S.S.* Essex *and the Birth of the American Navy* by Frances Diane Robotti and James Vescovi (1999), a patriotic tribute to the early navy.

Udo Nattermann

PORTER, KATHERINE ANNE (1890–1980). Callie Russell Porter was born in Indian Creek, Texas, into a poor family and died in Silver Spring, Maryland, early assuming her paternal grandmother's name. Living in Mexico, New York, Paris, Germany, and Washington, D.C., Katherine Anne Porter concentrates on personal conflict in her writing regardless of its setting. She won the National Book Award and the Pulitzer Prize in fiction in 1966.

Porter's most significant use of the sea in her writing is in *Ship of Fools* (1962), which took her twenty years to produce. She began the novel in 1941, although her ideas for it took shape even a decade earlier, the result of two events. The first was her 1931 sea voyage from Vera Cruz, Mexico, to Bremerhaven, Germany; the second was her 1934 reading of Sebastian Brandt's fifteenth-century allegory *Das Narrenschiff*, from which she took the title of her novel.

The journey in *Ship of Fools*, a motif common in Porter's work, is a literal voyage; in fact, Porter explained that the novel's episodic plot was informed by the very movement of ships and the motion of waves. In particular, the plot centers on international travelers going from Mexico to Germany in 1931 aboard the German freighter *Vera* ("truth"). The passengers, trapped between the unhappy world they left behind and the happiness they antic-ipate at their destination, are suspended without the security of land.

The close quarters of the *Vera* serve Porter's thematic purpose. Wilhelm Freytag, one of the passengers, reveals part of that purpose when he observes that most passengers behave as if they are still onshore. On ship, behaviors and actions seem intensified in a negative way. Given that distortion, Porter examines the polarities that define human existence, an existence divided between the novel's central characters on the upper deck and Spanish de-portees on the lower deck or steerage. Throughout their journey, the upper-deck characters essentially view those below with varying degrees of pity, fear, and disgust. Their failure to move beyond their self-serving isolation accounts for the novel's pessimism. Porter's travelers are morally desolate, and they end their voyage unchanged.

Jeraldine R. Kraver

POUND, EZRA [LOOMIS] (1885–1972). Ezra Pound was born in Hailey, Idaho. As an expatriate living in Europe, Pound's experiments with translation and poetic form resulted in his vivid translation of the eighth-century Anglo-Saxon poem "The Seafarer" (1911) and in the imagist style of his long poem, the *Cantos* (1970). The *Cantos* juxtaposes precise, but dissimilar, images under the premise that the interaction between them will help create meaning. Some of these images take just half of a poetic line to deliver; others take many pages. For this reason, the *Cantos* is variously called obscure, incoherent, or a masterpiece of the twentieth century.

The *Cantos* takes the epic sea traveler Odysseus as its recurring protagonist as he navigates vast seas of philosophy, history, literature, and even politics. The poem begins with Odysseus traveling to the underworld to meet the dead soothsayer Tiresias. Tiresias tells Odysseus, just as he did in Homer's *Odyssey*, that he will return home over dark seas, losing all companions. But Pound's Odysseus never returns, and Pound never finishes his poem. Nev-ertheless, the *Cantos* sets out upon a tremendous journey through time, with particularly long stops in medieval China, colonial America, and mod-ern Europe.

During the literary journey of the *Cantos*, Pound simply touches upon a few details of any one of the given subjects that he treats, then changes subjects. He models this approach, in part, on what he knows of the sailing technique of Hanno, ancient Carthaginian sailor who explored uncharted waters by always keeping in rough relation to whatever shoreline was available. Pound likewise changes the points of topical reference as his images unfold—"in periplum," a phrase taken from *periplus*, the Greek term for the standard navigational technique used in the ancient world.

Pound's advocacy of fascism during World War II resulted in his imprisonment outside Pisa, Italy. His experiences of fear, lament, and regret in Pisa led to a mental breakdown. During some of his most trying personal moments, he calls out through his *Cantos* to Kuanon, Chinese goddess of Mercy and patron deity to those who travel by sea.

Robert E. Kibler

POYER, DAVID [ANDREISSEN] (1949–   ). David Poyer graduated from the U.S. Naval Academy in 1971 and is a naval reserve captain, experienced sailor, and underwater diver. Poyer adapted his active-duty navy experiences to write best-selling sagas of naval fiction. *The Med* (1988), *The Gulf* (1990), *The Circle* (1992), *The Passage* (1995), *Tomahawk* (1997), and *China Sea* (2000) chronicle the adventures of protagonist Dan Lenson from the time he reports to his first ship after graduating from the Naval Academy in Annapolis through his career in the surface-ship navy. These books, in the tradition of Joseph Conrad and Herman Wouk,* study human conflict aboard Lenson's vessels at sea during modern naval battles and raging storms.

Poyer has also used his diving background in a series of novels that chronicle the adventures of commercial diver Tiller Galloway. In *Hatteras Blue* (1989), Galloway discovers gold on a sunken German U-boat off the Carolina coast. *Louisiana Blue* (1994) and *Bahamas Blue* (1991) follow Galloway's struggle to avoid the temptation of drug-running, which had earlier landed him in jail. Galloway is in his element underwater rather than ashore awaiting his next diving job. Working in the depths of the sea, where the community is small and the camaraderie is usually tight, helps Galloway survive dry-land evils and resolve personal conflict.

The sea is home to Poyer's characters. Substantial problems occur onshore; at sea they get resolved or forgotten as the sea tests the characters. On the water, failure means death, whether on the bridge of Lenson's warship or in the depths of Galloway's latest dive.

Joseph Navratil

PUEBLO (first perf. 1971; pub. 1970). Using documentary materials, playwright Stanley Greenberg (1945–   ) dramatizes the 1968 North Korean attack on, and capture of, the American surveillance vessel the U.S.S. *Pueblo*. Aesthetically, the play unfolds as a dream, in the style of a memory play. Commander Lloyd Mark Bucher is on trial, and a court of inquiry is investigating his surrender of the *Pueblo*, as he recollects the moments preceding his capture at sea. Many early scenes depict the excitement, romance, and danger of the attack at sea; the sights and sounds of a vessel under siege create the tension and thrill of a game of hide-and-seek.

Most important to Greenberg, however, is presenting the play from inside Bucher's head. Greenberg reaches for tragic dimensions when Bucher, in the interest of his men's safety, must act in violation of those military codes in which he firmly believes. He surrenders his ship with no attempt to fight or flee and signs a confession stating that he was involved in espionage inside Korean waters. Bucher's surrender and complicity with his captors raise issues that touch on the functional flaws of military bureaucracy. The play interprets the abandonment of the *Pueblo* as a lack of efficiency. Also revealed is the unwillingness of military bureaucracy to take responsibility for its own tactical decisions, especially in leaving Bucher unaware of the inherent dangers of his mission. Ultimately, Bucher is presented as a man who is sacrificed by a system that he is committed to serving. [*See also* DRAMA OF THE SEA]

Brian Knetl

THE PUMP HOUSE GANG (1968). *The Pump House Gang* is a collection of essays by Tom [Thomas Kennerly] Wolfe (1931–   ) that profiles individuals or groups who have broken away from mainstream U.S. culture, especially from its rules for establishing status. The eponymous first essay entitled "The Pump House Gang" focuses on a group of surfers and their cohorts from Windansea beach in La Jolla, California. This piece portrays a surfing lifestyle and ethos defined by youth and liberation from the dominant culture's concerns and responsibilities.

A particular relationship to the ocean is, of course, a key aspect of this subculture; in order to be accepted, one must feel and understand the power and mystery of "the Oh Mighty Hulking Pacific Ocean" (21). Facing, riding this powerful and mysterious force establishes and helps maintain one's immunity from mainstream preoccupations. The essay includes a brief profile of director Bruce Brown, whose exceedingly popular surf film *The Endless Summer* (1966) both represented and helped popularize the image of surfing and the surfing lifestyle as liberation from daily obligations and restrictions.

Byron Caminero-Santangelo

PYLE, [JOHN] HOWARD (1853–1911). Howard Pyle was one of America's foremost artists of children's books, and he exerted a dramatic influence on generations of book illustrators. Pyle was born in Wilmington, Delaware. Until attending art school, he was an admittedly mediocre student. A visit to Chincoteague Island, Virginia, in 1876 inspired a submission of drawings and an article to *Scribner's Monthly Magazine* (April 1877) that described the island, its people, and the annual wild pony roundup. His publishing and illustrating career began with the acceptance of this article and two short children's works. Medieval English legends provided the source for most of his work; his tales of King Arthur and of Robin Hood are classics and are still in print many decades later.

A turning point in Pyle's early career came with " 'Wreck in the Offing!' " (*Harper's Weekly*, 9 March 1878, p. 202), depicting a frightened man at the door of a lifesaving* station, pointing to the storm outside. Unlike his previous "idea sketches" for magazines, Pyle convinced Harper's editors to allow him to create the final illustration, and the editors published it as a double-page spread. "North Folk Legends of the Sea" (*Harper's Monthly Magazine*, January 1902), written and illustrated by Pyle, featured some of the earliest successful color magazine reproductions. Pyle produced numerous other sea-related stories and pictures throughout his career; many were collected in the posthumous *Howard Pyle's Book of Pirates* (1921), which recounts the escapades of various cutthroats in dramatic stories and illustrations. Pyle's single visit to Europe ended with his untimely death in Florence, Italy. [*See also* JUVENILE LITERATURE; PIRATE LITERATURE]

Peter H. McCracken

Q

QUEEG, CAPTAIN. Lieutenant Commander Philip Francis Queeg is the fictional captain of the U.S.S. *Caine*, the nearly obsolete minesweeper-destroyer that serves as the scene of action for Herman Wouk's* World War II novel *The* Caine *Mutiny* (1951). Queeg relieves another captain from command of the *Caine* early in the novel; it soon becomes apparent to the officers and crew that he is both paranoid and a petty tyrant. Queeg severely punishes his men for the least infraction and proves himself a coward in battle. His inept handling of the *Caine* during a typhoon nearly sinks the ship and prompts the ship's executive officer to remove him from command, an action supported by another officer on duty as well as the helmsman. Subsequently, the executive officer is court-martialed for mutiny,* but an excellent lawyer secures a "not-guilty" verdict for him by casting aspersions on Queeg for his irrational and vindictive actions as captain of the *Caine*. Wouk adapted his novel into a play, *The* Caine *Mutiny Court-Martial*, in 1954, the same year that the film starring Humphrey Bogart was released.

Christopher Lee

QUEEQUEG. Queequeg is the fictional Polynesian harpooner in Herman Melville's* *Moby-Dick** (1851). Acknowledging the multinational, multiracial composition of crews in the nineteenth-century American whaling industry, Melville assigned several Asian, African, and Native American characters, including Queequeg, important roles in his novel. A native of an imaginary South Pacific island, Queequeg epitomizes the "noble savage"; he is a king's son as well as a cannibal. Despite his outlandish dress and mysterious tattoos and despite his commitment to a pagan faith, Melville assures his readers, primarily through his narrator Ishmael,* of the rare nobility of Queequeg's character. His skills as a harpooner are superb, and he expresses a dauntless courage, a ferocious energy, and a lively dedication to the ship's enterprise in both the hunting and the processing of whales.

Throughout *Moby-Dick*, however, other virtues make Queequeg a mentor and a model for young Ishmael. Repeatedly shown helping others, he acts independently, counter to self-interest or social convention, as revealed by his perilous dives, first, into the Atlantic to rescue a young man who has taunted him for his unusual appearance and, later in the novel, after the sinking head of a whale to rescue a fellow harpooner. Not only do his good-heartedness, generosity, and integrity mitigate Ishmael's initial cynicism, but his coffin proves Ishmael's life buoy at the novel's conclusion.

Literary critics increasingly identify Queequeg as the hero of *Moby-Dick* and associate him with Melville's vision of a nation free from slavery and racism.

Elizabeth Schultz

R

RATIGAN, WILLIAM O. (1910–1984). Born to a Great Lakes* steamboat engineer in Detroit and later adopted by an Ottawa tribe chief, William Ratigan called Michigan his home. This Great Lakes historian's writings celebrate ordinary Americans who made big names for themselves. His books are seasoned with Lakes poetry, often his own. He is best known for *Soo Canal!* (1954), a historical novel about the famous waterway's construction, and *Great Lakes Shipwrecks* and Survivals* (1960, 1969, 1977), which dramatically retells the Lakes' worst disasters. Highly respected, each edition commemorates a lost boat: the *Bradley*, the *Morrell*, and the *Edmund Fitzgerald.**

Ratigan's work includes "Hiawatha and America's Mightiest Mile" (1955), an essay that marvels at the relationship between Henry Wadsworth Longfellow's* poem and the Soo Canal; *Adventures of Captain McCargo* (1956); *Highways over Broad Waters; The Long Crossing* (1959); and a 1958 children's folktale trilogy: *Blue Snow, Adventures of Paul Bunyan and Babe*, and *Tiny Tim Pine.* [*See also* JUVENILE LITERATURE]

Donald P. Curtis

THE RAVEN (1995). Peter Landesman (1965–) is a journalist and a painter whose first novel, *The Raven*, is based on written accounts of a historical tragedy off the southern coast of Maine. On 29 June 1941, thirty-six people aboard a forty-four-foot pleasure cruiser, the *Raven*, departed in deep fog from Rehoboth for a day of deep-sea fishing and picnicking in Casco Bay. They were never again seen alive, and the *Raven* was never found. Bodies of the fourteen women, charred and bloated, were eventually hauled up from the sea by a lobsterman and his nine-year-old son, as was the captain's body, naked and roped to a cask. Bodies of the remaining men were not recovered. Landesman's evocative and haunting account of the rumors and conflicting details surrounding the craft's disappearance seeks to resolve the mystery fictionally.

Landesman's immersion in the lore of the sea, his accurate regional geography, and his historical record give the work verisimilitude. His book is highly descriptive, with frequent nuance of color expressed in movement of waves and in interplay of light and fog. The sea itself—the most prominent feature of a poetic, yet realistic, drama—infuses the lives of all the inhabitants of the coastal town, from a college student who physically comes of age in a wooded swimming hole near Great Island, to the aged fishermen of Bailey Island who refuse to learn to swim because they know that battling the sea would prolong the agony of death by water. Another character, a hack historian, is modeled on the historical figure Edward Rowe Snow.* The narrative follows a half dozen such characters over forty-four years, whose lives the tragedy irrevocably changes; it ends with a flashback aboard the *Raven* in the voice of the captain, who helplessly observes the transformation of a pleasure party into chaos and death.

Jill B. Gidmark

THE RECOGNITIONS (1952). The first novel by William Gaddis (1922–1998), *The Recognitions* is a wildly convoluted work that circuitously follows the lives of several interconnected characters. The first major incident takes place on board the *Purdue Victory*, where Camilla Gwyon dies in her stateroom from complications of appendicitis. The surgeon who botched her operation is not really a doctor but a counterfeiter trying to elude his pursuers. The ship had set sail from Boston, bound for Spain as Camilla dies, but the rest of the sea journey is of little concern to Gaddis.

A second important shipboard incident takes place when Otto, another forger, is headed back to New York on a banana boat, trying to disguise who he is and what he is up to. Near the end of the novel, Otto is again on a banana boat, the *Island Trader*, headed for the Caribbean* port of Tibiezza. Otto is constantly one step ahead of getting caught, but he always manages to escape. Gaddis seems primarily interested in demonstrating that fraud and deception are the modern world's most effective means of survival.

A Mr. Yak is later introduced as another character who disguises his identity and uses the sea as a means of eluding detection. He sails around the world like the Flying Dutchman, never able to make port. Near the end of the novel, Father Martin dies from poisoning aboard ship, perhaps signifying that sea life is synonymous with corruption and death. The final sea-related incident occurs when the *Ever Lasting Mercy* docks in Naples, and the surviving offspring of the original central characters are in a position to sort out their sordid relationships and responsibilities.

The sea provides a backdrop of uncertainty against which many of the characters have to define themselves. Much like James Joyce and Thomas Pynchon, Gaddis uses setting and atmosphere to delineate his characters' states of mind. In this vein, the sea becomes associated with the unconscious, a frequent literary conceit. [*See also MASON & DIXON; V.*]

Ralph Berets

THE RED RECORD (1895). At the close of the nineteenth century, the National Seamen's Union of America (NSUA) issued a harrowing, twenty-two-page pamphlet called *The Red Record*, outlining sixty-four cases of shipboard brutality and murder. The goal was to alert the general public and lawmakers to the physical abuse of working seamen by ships' officers. Though rarely mentioned specifically, the pamphlet was widely read by sailors and maritime authors and provides historical context for a number of contemporary literary works, such as Herman Melville's* *Billy Budd, Sailor** (begun late 1880s; pub. 1924) and Jack London's* *The Mutiny of the* Elsinore (1914), which examine on-ship violence between ranks.

Prior to publication of *The Red Record*, the NSUA had made several substantiated claims regarding abuse of seamen by officers. Though the U.S. Revised Statute 4611 had specifically abolished "flogging" aboard vessels of commerce in 1850, the NSUA charged that ship's officers got around such tight language by substituting crueler methods of punishment, such as the withholding of food, beatings with handspikes and lashes, physical torture, and murder. Without prohibitory federal legislation, they claimed, case-specific legal opinion had given ship's officers unchecked disciplinary latitude. As a result of these claims, a study was undertaken by the U.S. Treasury Department, and a bill was introduced in 1895 in the House of Representatives that forbade masters, mates, or other officers from abusing or unnecessarily endangering seamen.

The Red Record outlined instances of mistreatment and identified certain officers as notorious and habitual abusers, indicating that the courts were not disposed to treat the complaints of working seamen seriously. Citing the Eighth Amendment that bars cruel and unusual punishment as its legal justification, the NSUA, over the signature of General Secretary T. J. Elderkin, originally published *The Red Record* as a supplement to its house organ, *The Coast Seamen's Journal*, in order to make its complaints a matter of public record.

A thoroughgoing, contemporary account is Stephen Schwartz's *Brotherhood of the Sea: A History of the Sailors' Union of the Pacific 1885–1985* (1986).

Eric G. Waggoner

THE RED ROVER (1827). James Fenimore Cooper's* (1789–1851) second sea novel, *The Red Rover* opens in Newport, Rhode Island, in 1759, where young Harry Wilder and his companions, Dick Fid and Scipio Africanus, await berths. Fid and S'ip hire out aboard the *Dolphin*, pirate* ship of the protagonist Red Rover, while Wilder becomes captain of the *Royal*

Caroline, which sets out to sea shadowed by another vessel and beset by storm. Abandoned by his crew, Wilder and his three female passengers are rescued by the mysterious pursuer, the *Dolphin*. Fid and S'ip, happily re-united with their leader, recount having rescued him as a small boy adrift at sea. The Red Rover seizes a British cruiser, the *Dart*, and through re-markable coincidence Wilder is discovered to be Henry de Lacy, the long-lost son of one of the three female passengers. Moved by this reunion and by Wilder's noble spirit, the Red Rover spares him from the vengeance of the pirate crew. He sets his crew on land with all their booty, sends Wilder and the hostages away aboard the *Dart*, and remains alone on his ship with his cabin boy. From a distance Wilder watches the *Dolphin* catch fire and burn as a small boat appears to put off from the sinking ship.

The novel then leaps forward twenty years, to Newport in 1779, where the Red Rover and Captain Henry de Lacy meet again, now as two heroic captains of the Continental navy. Wounded, clutching an American flag, the Red Rover utters dying words of triumph.

The Red Rover was adapted for the stage by Samuel Chapman in 1828.

Brad S. Born

REDBURN: HIS FIRST VOYAGE (1849). *Redburn*, the third novel writ-ten by Herman Melville* (1819–1891), is based on Melville's first sea voy-age, a journey from New York to Liverpool in 1837. The novel's narrator, Wellingborough Redburn, is an adolescent New Yorker whose middle-class family has fallen on hard times. Filled with romantic visions of seafaring, he joins an American merchantman as ship's boy and is rapidly disillusioned through repeated encounters with the brutal realities of shipboard life.

On the voyage out, Redburn's ideal of manhood is challenged by Jackson, a sickly, diabolical, and misanthropic slacker who corrupts the entire crew. During six weeks in Liverpool, Redburn encounters the inhumanity of the British class system as he helplessly observes an impoverished mother and three children starve to death in a basement. Harry Bolton, an aristocratic young Englishman, introduces Redburn to the vices of London and later dies on a whaling cruise. On his return voyage, Redburn describes how the Irish immigrants suffer from cholera, starvation, and other miserable con-ditions in steerage.

Although Melville considered the book a potboiler, it presents a vivid picture of transatlantic voyage* and a moving portrayal of a young man's initiation into the moral complexities of a world governed by greed and commercialism.

Dennis Berthold

REYNOLDS, J[EREMIAH]. N. (1799?–1858). Details of the life of J. N. Reynolds are sketchy, and his lingering reputation today is mainly the result of his influence upon major works of Edgar Allan Poe* (*The Narrative of*

Arthur Gordon Pym* [1838]) and Herman Melville* (*Moby-Dick** [1851]). Reynolds, who was born in Cumberland County, Pennsylvania, raised in Clinton County, Ohio, and attended Ohio University for three years, first came to the public's attention in 1825 as a staunch proponent of an Antarctic* exploring expedition that might authenticate the existence of the so-called Symmes Hole as postulated by John Cleves Symmes in 1818. According to this theory, which was popularized by 1820 in a fantasy-fiction, *Symzonia, A Voyage of Discovery** (published by one "Adam Seaborn" in 1820 but usually thought to be written by Symmes himself or possibly by Reynolds), the earth was hollow and "habitable" at the poles. Reynolds' determination to prove this theory bordered, at times, on the obsessive.

During the 1820s Reynolds petitioned Congress for funds to explore and chart the Antarctic, but the early interest of John Quincy Adams' administration was replaced by the indifference of Andrew Jackson's, and Reynolds managed to secure only enough money to fund a combined voyage of discovery and sealing in southern waters under the command of Captains Nathaniel Palmer and Benjamin Pendleton. This "American Antarctic Exploring Expedition" set out in 1829 with Reynolds himself aboard but reached no farther south than the Palmer Peninsula. Four years later, Reynolds returned to Boston aboard the U.S. frigate *Potomac* and wrote an account of his travels on this vessel, *Voyage of the* Potomac (1833). He then renewed his efforts to launch a full-scale expedition to the Antarctic and was asked to present his case before the Congressional Committee on Naval Affairs. In 1836 Congress finally approved the funding necessary for the polar expedition, the U.S. Exploring Expedition* of 1838–1842 (better known as the Wilkes Expedition), but Reynolds himself was excluded from participating in the voyage, an exclusion that Poe labeled "shameful" and "scandalous."

Reynolds' bitterness over this slight led him to withdraw from public attention except for occasional contributions to magazines and periodicals, the most famous of which, "Mocha Dick" (1839), is an acknowledged source of Melville's masterpiece. [*See also* NINETEENTH-CENTURY PERIODICALS]

Peter F. deCataldo

RICE, ELMER (1892–1967). Born Elmer Reizenstein, the playwright Elmer Rice is best known for his realistic and expressionistic dramas of urban life. However, he turned to the sea for two of his plays.

Between Two Worlds (first perf. 1934; pub. 1935) takes place on the S.S. *Farragut*, traveling from New York to Cherbourg and serving as a microcosm of the larger world and a means for keeping the characters together. The action centers on Kovolev, a Soviet motion-picture director, whose virility and charm are in contrast to Margaret Bowen, an American heiress who feels her life is worthless. The other Americans on board either share

Margaret's feelings of uselessness or are ignorant, frivolous, complacent, and materialistic. Rice's attack is both broad, targeting Hollywood and racial prejudice, and more narrowly focused, attacking American complacency and Soviet conformity. The title serves double duty: the forty-two passengers are literally suspended on the ocean between two worlds, just as the best hope for the world is suspended between the individually imperfect systems of capitalist democracy and communism.

The Grand Tour (first perf. 1951; pub. 1952) combines an ill-fated affair with a love song for Europe, especially Paris, and an exploration of the tensions between morality and money. The play opens with Nell Valentine, a schoolteacher from Bridgeport, Connecticut, making arrangements for a European vacation paid for by the substantial insurance policies she had on her deceased father. On an ocean liner to Europe she meets Raymond Brinton, a banker from Minneapolis whose wife is divorcing him. After a whirlwind courtship in Paris and Chartres, Ray and Nell decide to marry when his divorce is final. After Ray reveals that he has embezzled money from his bank to finance his family's plush, upwardly mobile life, a bank official tells Nell that Ray will not be prosecuted if he returns the money. Knowing that Ray does not have enough money, Nell uses her own money to repay the bank. She also realizes that Ray still loves his wife and leaves him. In the final scene, she breaks down while showing slides of her vacation to her students in Bridgeport, blaming her tears on hay fever.

Although both plays had short runs on Broadway and are not ranked among Rice's best work, they reveal solid construction, a sense of theatrical flair, a concern for broad social and political issues, and an appreciation for ocean travel. [*See also* DRAMA OF THE SEA; OCEAN LINER DRAMA]

Brian T. Carney

RICH, ADRIENNE [CECILE] (1929–   ). The author of twenty books of poems and four prose works, Adrienne Rich was born in Baltimore. "Diving into the Wreck" (1972), a poem frequently anthologized, contains her fullest, most dramatic reference to the sea. In this poem, the speaker gives up her old notions of power because they don't seem to apply where the sea is the controlling element. Attempts to gain power over the sea appear useless to Rich's diver, who has to move differently in the sea and adjust. This crucial understanding makes further discoveries possible, and a merging of powers, both masculine and feminine, occurs. This merging forms the major action of the poem and leads to the diver's understanding of his/her androgynous nature. The sea proves a valuable context for a developing consciousness.

An earlier reference to the sea may be found in "Shooting Script," Part I (1969–1970), where Rich uses the sea chiefly as a metaphor of change. Observing the surf on a rocky coastline, the poet notes how the elements of rock and wave naturally affect and transform each other. Wave and rock compose a type of conversation that this montagelike poem parallels to human interaction. The sea forms the setting for the eighth of Rich's "Love Poems" (1974–1976). Here, the poet rejects the possibility of suicide by drowning; such a willed death is not something for which she is suited. In the self-reflective "Solfegietto" (1985–1988), the ocean represents all that is vast and unknowable.

A resident of Santa Cruz, California, since 1984, Rich makes reference to the Pacific Ocean in her long poem "An Atlas of the Difficult World" (1990–1991). Even though she lives within two miles of the coast, she finds in this poem that the earth is more compelling. Rich has no deep affinity for the sea. In the same poem, she finds the sea lacking as an instructor about how to live one's life. Ultimately, the sea, for Adrienne Rich, is its own entity, often violent and mainly separate from human concerns. [*See also* SEA IMAGERY IN MODERN AND CONTEMPORARY POETRY]

Claire J. Keyes

RICHARD, MARK (1955–   ). Author of the sea novel *Fishboy* (1993), Mark Richard (pronounced ree-SHARD) has been, at different times in his life, disc jockey, newspaperman, photographer, and private investigator. As a young man, Richard took time off from his study of journalism at Washington and Lee University to work on fishing boats up and down the eastern seaboard. In 1989 he published a collection of short stories, *The Ice at the Bottom of the World*, for which he was awarded a PEN/Hemingway prize and a Whiting Foundation grant. Included in this volume is the story "Fishboy," an early version of what would become Richard's first novel. Most recently, Richard has published a second volume of stories, *Charity* (1998), in which the sea is only tangential.

Fishboy is a surrealistic account told by a young stowaway who jumps aboard a coastal fishing trawler manned by a haunted, homicidal crew. Spun with a dreamy, beyond-the-grave lyricism, Fishboy's yarn is full of Gothic violence, dark humor, and insistent anatomical detail. As part of his own story, Fishboy passively records the stories of his shipmates, each of whom suffers some paranoid torment. Together, Fishboy's narrative and these interior tales constitute an allusive anthology of bleak fables and fish stories. With its heightened rhetorical performance as well as its emphasis upon shared myths of guilt and redemption, *Fishboy* contains echoes of the King James Bible, the literary South, and, above all, sea authors such as Herman Melville,* Edgar Allan Poe,* and Peter Matthiessen.*

Hugh Egan

RICKETTS, EDWARD F[LANDERS]. (1897–1948). Edward F. Ricketts, marine biologist and ecologist, was John Steinbeck's* collaborator on *Sea of Cortez* (1941) and the model for "Doc," protagonist of Steinbeck's Monterey novels *Cannery Row* (1945) and *Sweet Thursday* (1954), and for

"Friend Ed," one of four principal characters in Steinbeck's play-novelette *Burning Bright* (1950). Born on the west side of Chicago, Ricketts was haphazardly educated at Illinois State Normal School and the University of Chicago. He took no undergraduate degree but completed ten quarters of zoology.

In 1923 Ricketts moved to California, where he became owner of a biological supply house, Pacific Biological Laboratory, eventually situated on the Monterey waterfront in the area known as "Cannery Row." Ricketts' business involved collecting marine organisms for sale to college and university laboratories. He found in California's intertidal zones a relatively unstudied flora and fauna, and his research led to his time-honored handbook, *Between Pacific Tides* (1939), now in its fifth revised and updated edition. Originally written with junior author Jack Calvin,* *Between Pacific Tides* is both ecological and inductive in its method, with animals grouped according to their characteristic habitats and in order of their commonness—a revolutionary approach in 1939 and one still relevant.

Ricketts was as passionately interested in the arts and humanities as in the sciences, and his lab became a magnet not only for biologists at work at Stanford University's nearby Hopkins Marine Station but also for artists, political radicals, and intellectuals of every stripe. Jungian psychologist Joseph Campbell and writer Henry Miller were among the habitués of Pacific Biological, and the work of the reclusive poet Robinson Jeffers,* who also lived nearby, was one of many topics for discussion. Ricketts' most enduring impact, however, was on Steinbeck, who from 1930 until 1936 was almost constantly in his company. Five years younger than Ricketts, Steinbeck was profoundly influenced by the marine biologist's ecological vision—as may be seen in the social principles of mutual interdependence advanced in Steinbeck's *The Grapes of Wrath* (1939).

In 1940 Steinbeck and Ricketts chartered Captain Tony Berry and his purse seiner, the *Western Flyer*, for an expedition to Mexico's Gulf of California, also known as the Sea of Cortez, where they spent six weeks collecting marine organisms. The scientific results of the expedition included the description of more than fifty species previously unknown to science, as well as significant range extensions for many known organisms; specimens collected by Ricketts and Steinbeck are preserved at the California Academy of Science in San Francisco.

The published result of the voyage was Steinbeck and Ricketts' *Sea of Cortez* (1941). The second half of the book is scientific treatise: an annotated phyletic catalog and bibliography of the species encountered and illustrations of the organisms. This portion of *Sea of Cortez* is largely the marine biologist's, although Steinbeck worked at the collecting and sorting of animals and helped review the scientific literature. The first half of the book, the "Log from the Sea of Cortez," combines marine biology, mysticism, humor, adventure, and speculative metaphysics in a remarkable account of the expedition. Apparently, Steinbeck wrote the "Log" from Ricketts' expedition journal and unpublished essays, using a scheme of organization and collaboration developed by both men.

Ricketts' coauthorship of the "Log" was obscured after his death, when Viking Press dropped the scientific portion of *Sea of Cortez* and published *The Log from the Sea of Cortez* (1951) as a "new" book, with Steinbeck's name alone on the cover and in the headers. Ricketts' name remained on the title page, and Steinbeck's eulogy, "About Ed Ricketts," served as preface to the volume. Although this publishing gambit was, in part, an attempt to increase sales and bring Ricketts' ideas to a wider audience, it encouraged the now-widespread misconception that the biologist was responsible solely for the excised scientific treatise on the marine organisms and that *The Log from the Sea of Cortez* was Steinbeck's alone.

Ricketts served as the model for "Doc," protagonist of Steinbeck's novel *Cannery Row* (1945). Marine biologist and tide-pool philosopher, half goat and half Christ, "Doc" is high priest to the dispossessed bums and whores of Monterey's waterfront. In 1954, Steinbeck published a sequel to *Cannery Row*, *Sweet Thursday*, a lighter and more sentimental comedy about Doc's courtship of a prostitute named Suzy.

Ricketts was also the basis for "Friend Ed," a character in Steinbeck's poorly received play-novelette *Burning Bright* (1950). "Friend Ed" appears variously in three acts as a circus clown, farmer, and finally a freighter captain who is confidant to Joe Saul, an aging man who fears that he is sterile but longs for a child. Saul's cherished wife, Mordeen, becomes pregnant by another man, Victor, to give Saul the child he craves. When Victor threatens to betray his fathership of the child to Saul, "Friend Ed" in his freighter captain persona stabs Victor to death and tosses him overboard. After the murder, when Saul receives incontrovertible medical evidence of his sterility, "Friend Ed" persuades him to forgive Mordeen and accept the child as a gift of love, then sails away on his ship.

Ricketts died in 1948 of injuries received when his car was struck on the railroad tracks in Monterey by the Del Monte Express. His death preempted a second scientific expedition that he and Steinbeck had been planning, to the Queen Charlotte Islands off the coast of British Columbia.

FURTHER READING: Astro, Richard. *John Steinbeck and Edward F. Ricketts: The Shaping of a Novelist*. Minneapolis: U of Minnesota P, 1973; Astro, Richard. *Edward F. Ricketts*. Boise: Boise State UP, 1976; Hedgpeth, Joel W. *The Outer Shores, Part 1: Ed Ricketts and John Steinbeck Explore the Pacific Coast* and *The Outer Shores, Part 2: Breaking Through*. Eureka, CA: Mad River, 1978.

Susan F. Beegel

RIESENBERG, FELIX (1879–1939). Felix Riesenberg was one of the most important figures in American literature of the sea during the 1920s and 1930s; his literary contributions were preceded by many years of firsthand sea experience during the final transitional years from sail to steam. Following the example of his father, a German sailor who went to sea at age thirteen, Riesenberg went to sea in 1895 at age sixteen. In 1898 he made his first of many Cape Horn* passages, sailing as an ordinary seaman aboard the *A. J. Fuller*, under the command of Charles M. Nichols. Later he began his career in steam as a cadet on the ocean liner *St. Louis*. He navigated the airship *America* in the Wellman Polar Expedition of 1906–1907 and eventually commanded the New York state school ship, U.S.S. *Newport*, from 1917 to 1919 and then again from 1923 to 1924.

His experience on the *Newport* coincides with his publishing two manuals of seamanship that were widely used for years, *The Men on Deck* (1918) and *Standard Seamanship for the Merchant Service* (1922). Also in 1918 he published the first of two autobiographical works, *Under Sail*, an account of his experiences aboard the *A. J. Fuller* intended to inform his readers of "that phase of our sea life that formed and forged the link between the old and the new present of the America of steam and steel" (10–11). This was also his goal in his most important and still very readable novel *Mother Sea* (1933), in which his central character Clyde Nicholson recalls Captain Charles Nichols of the *Fuller*. Riesenberg was an associate editor and wrote a regular column for the *Nautical Gazette*. In 1931 he coauthored a sea novel, *Maiden Voyage*, with Archie Binns* and in 1937 published *Living Again: An Autobiography*, a work focused on, among other things, his sea experience during the transitional years between sail and steam.

Bert Bender

RILEY, JAMES (1777–1840). While on a voyage from Gibraltar to the Cape Verde Islands during the summer of 1815, Captain James Riley and his crew of the brig *Commerce* were shipwrecked on the barren coast of the western Sahara, where they were soon enslaved by wandering Bedouins. The Americans were bought and sold several times until Riley convinced an Arab trader to buy him and four others as a speculative investment, pledging his life that he and his companions could be ransomed for a considerable profit. The trader agreed to take them north across the desert to a European consul or merchant, and for the next three months the small group suffered great hardship as they journeyed to Mogodore, where the Americans were finally ransomed by William Wilshire, the British consul general. Riley returned to the United States and in 1817 published *An Authentic Narrative of the Loss of the Brig* Commerce.

A popular best-seller during the early decades of the nineteenth century, this narrative of shipwreck* and enslavement caused an immediate sensation, and for a short period of time Riley became one of the best-known men in the United States. Translated into French and German in 1818, the book was republished in six other editions from 1818 through 1859. Nearly a million copies of the book are said to have sold before the Civil War. According to his biographers, Abraham Lincoln read Riley's narrative as a child, and the book, a graphic account of white men enslaved by dark men, helped to convince him that slavery was morally wrong. For over a century Riley's narrative was forgotten, but in 1965 it was edited by Gordon H. Evans and published under the title *Sufferings in Africa: Captain Riley's Narrative*.

Riley assisted in publishing another North African shipwreck and captivity narrative, Judah Paddock's *A Narrative of the Shipwreck of the Ship* Oswego *on the Coast of South Barbary*, in 1818. James Feminore Cooper* used Paddock's work as a source for *Homeward Bound* (1838). Riley also assisted one of his crew, Archibald Robbins, in publishing his narrative *A Journal Comprising an Account of the Loss of the Brig* Commerce (1818).

Upon his death in 1839 during a return voyage to Africa, Riley was buried at sea. Later, in 1851, *Sequel to Riley's Narrative: Being a Sketch of Interesting Incidents in the Life, Voyages, and Travels of Capt. James Riley* was published twice in Ohio, one edition by A. R. Wright in Springfield and a second by George Brewster in Columbus. Although little known, Riley's narrative remains one of the most important books in antebellum print culture.

Daniel E. Williams

"RINGBOLT, CAPTAIN." *See* [CODMAN, JOHN].

RIVER-HORSE: THE LOGBOOK OF A BOAT ACROSS AMERICA (1999). In a style reminiscent of Samuel Clemens* and Paul Theroux,* William Least Heat-Moon [William Trogdon] (1939–   ) captures what it was like to traverse America from the Atlantic to the Pacific before the age of rail when the nation's waterways were its highways. The 5,000-mile voyage from Elizabeth, New Jersey, in Newark Bay, through a portion of Lake Erie, through the Columbia River in northwest Oregon, is aboard a twenty-two-foot outboard-powered C-dory. There is some urgency in the narrative, propelled by his desire to make the journey in a single year, but what emerges over more than 500 pages is a pleasantly ambling, yet comprehensive, travel narrative composed of vignettes on, and contemplations about, America's inland waterways.

The book bears few of the markers of maritime literature. The river is neither a boundary nor a conduit into a deep unknown, life on Least Heat-Moon's vessel presents little deprivation, and shoreside comforts are always near. Yet the overarching theme is that the lakes, rivers, and oceans of the world are all one, an idea that prompts the author to find meaning in pouring a bottle of Atlantic water into the Pacific Ocean upon completing his journey. It also prompts an appendix urging readers to support environmental endeavors to clean up inland waters. The work, with *Blue Highways:*

A Journey into America (1982) and *PrairyErth: A Deep Map* (1991), forms a trilogy, but only *River-Horse* focuses on the water. [*See also* AMERICAN INDIAN LITERATURE OF THE SEA; GREAT LAKES LITERATURE]

Daniel M. Albert

[ROARK, GARLAND], "GEORGE GARLAND" (1904–1985). Born in Groesbeck, Texas, Garland Roark spent the first two decades of his work life on the advertising staffs of various retail stores in Texas, promoting everything from groceries to jewelry. In 1946 he launched a new career as a writer of popular fiction with the publication of his first novel, *Wake of the Red Witch*, whose principal character, Sam Rosen, is transformed by the treachery and duplicity of those around him in a relentless search for sunken treasure. The novel was made into a film starring John Wayne in 1948. Over the next twenty-five years, Roark produced an average of a book a year, most of them works of historical sea fiction set in the nineteenth century. In 1951 Roark published *Doubtful Valley* under the pseudonym "George Garland," the first of six novels of western lore that he wrote under that name.

His works of sea fiction include *Fair Wind to Java* (1948), also made into a movie (1953); *Rainbow in the Royals* (1950), adventures sailing to California during the early years of the gold rush; *Star in the Rigging; A Novel of the Texas Navy* (1954), an account of the contributions of a small naval fleet to Texas' battle for independence in 1835; *The Outlawed Banner* (1956), naval action of the Civil War; and *The Lady and the Deep Blue Sea* (1958), a narrative of a clipper race.

Roark wrote as a historical features columnist for the *Houston Chronicle* in the early 1960s. He died in Nacogdoches, Texas, on 9 February 1985.

Joseph Flibbert

ROBERTS, KENNETH [LEWIS] (1885–1957). Chronicling the lives of Maine coastal families in most of his distinguished historical novels of the eighteenth and early nineteenth centuries, Kenneth Roberts acquired and put to use an impressive and detailed knowledge of nautical matters. Even when most of the action takes place on land, as it does in *Arundel* (1930), the scenes that he sets on shipboard reflect this knowledge. In *Rabble in Arms* (1933), which concerns the events leading up to the Revolutionary War Battle of Saratoga, a memorable part of the story is devoted to Benedict Arnold's construction of a fleet of American ships on Lake Champlain that engaged a more powerful British fleet at the Battle of Valcour Island and bought needed time for the American forces.

Most directly maritime of all Roberts' novels are *The Lively Lady* (1931) and *Captain Caution* (1934). Both works take place during the War of 1812 and recount the adventures of American civilian mariners who resourcefully augmented the undersized American navy with privateers, took the war to Great Britain, and helped turn the tide of affairs. These books are rich in details of shipbuilding, shipboard life, and naval tactics.

The early nineteenth-century events of the rebellion in Haiti led by Toussaint L'Ouverture and America's breaking of the power of the pirates* of Tripoli are joined in *Lydia Bailey* (1947). Relatively little of the novel's action takes place on the sea, but American naval tactics at Tripoli, as seen from the land, are the subject of some dramatic chapters. *Boon Island* (1956) relates the events leading up to the 1710 shipwreck* of the *Nottingham Galley* on a desolate island off the Maine coast and the twenty-four-day ordeal of the survivors. [*See also* SEA-DELIVERANCE NARRATIVES]

Lawrence I. Berkove

ROBERTSON, MORGAN (1861–1915). Son of a Great Lakes* captain, Morgan Robertson was born in Oswego, New York, on Lake Ontario. He wrote popular sea fiction with the authoritative voice of an expert seaman. Sailing from 1877 to 1886, he first shipped out on a Great Lakes vessel before exploring the oceans. Coinciding with the transition from sail to steam propulsion, Robertson's time at sea was spent on both vessel types. His fresh- and saltwater voyages familiarized him with much of the globe, and by age twenty-one, Robertson had risen from cabin boy to first mate.

Robertson held many jobs—jeweler, watchmaker, inventor, cowboy, swimming instructor—before, at age thirty-six, he tried his hand at writing, the craft that was to occupy him for the rest of his life. His fourteen books, numerous short stories, and articles are almost all connected to the sea or the Great Lakes. He wrote with a remarkable degree of technical accuracy and creative energy. Technological changes that he witnessed fueled his imagination about the future and inspired his speculative fiction, such as *Futility: Or, The Wreck of the* Titan (1898). This novel, with its famous Atlantic liner *Titan*, wrecked on an iceberg one April night, eerily prefigures the wreck of the *Titanic** in 1912. Some of his work, including *Down to the Sea* (1905), is comic, ranging from lighthearted to mordant. Often his writing conveys his Darwinian ideas and mystical beliefs, as in *Where Angels Fear to Tread* (1899). Praised for his breezy style and his clever plots, Robertson's use of precise sea terminology has drawn both acclaim and criticism.

Ever on the verge of making his fortune, Robertson died nearly impoverished, standing up and staring seaward from a cheap room in Atlantic City. Royalties from his books later made his widow financially independent. Robertson's best-known works include *Masters of Men* (1901), *Shipmates* (1901), and *Sinful Peck* (1903).

Donald P. Curtis

A ROMANCE OF THE SEA-SERPENT (1849). This novel by Eugene Batchelder (1822–1878) is one of the stranger works of American sea literature. Written in six sections called "Coils," it opens on the yacht *Hope* as protagonist Dick Forbes and other "beaux and belles" are sailing to Nahant, Massachusetts, summer resort for the Boston elite, from several weeks at Newport, Rhode Island, a city just becoming the new center of beaumonde fashion. While those on board are recounting stories of the sea serpent, the title character slithers on shore at Nahant, eats a few people, and terrorizes many others, then returns to the sea near the yacht. He listens to the stories about him and, in response to those who are skeptical, attacks and eats them in ironic spite.

The scene then shifts, in parody of John Milton's *Paradise Lost* (1667), to a gathering of the denizens of the deep, presided over by "His Snakeship." He tells the others that he is taking a vacation, since he has been invited to several soirees in Newport, which crave the presence of royalty, and to a Harvard commencement, where he is to receive an honorary doctorate. The serpent goes to Cambridge, where he attacks a proctor, escapes to Newport, where he literally crashes the largest ball, and is chased back to sea. Dick Forbes leads a grand attack and vanquishes him and his watery cohorts. Batchelder appends 100 pages detailing the speculations about, and reports of, the existence of sea serpents. The whole is a lighthearted satirical jab at fashionable seaside society and the contemporary fascination with sea monsters.

A second edition of the work was published the same year under the title *A Romance of the Sea-Serpent, or, The Ichthyosaurus (by Wave); Also a Collection of the Ancient and Modern Authorities, with Letters from Distinguished Merchants and Men of Science.* [*See also* ALBEE, EDWARD; GHOSTS AND GHOST SHIP LEGENDS; MERMAID LITERATURE]

John Samson

ROWSON, SUSANNA H[ASWELL]. (1762–1824). Born in Portsmouth, England, Susanna H. Rowson became an actress, educator, prolific writer in several genres, and notably the author of *Charlotte Temple* (1791), America's first best-selling novel. Rowson's father, William Haswell, was a lieutenant in the British Royal Navy, and her childhood and adolescence were marked by personally and politically traumatic ocean passages that she later recalled in numerous novels and other writings. In these works the ocean consistently figures as a medium of both crisis and communication, a marker for the far-reaching social, economic, and cultural disruptions and transformations of the Revolutionary period.

Rowson's mother, Susanna, died giving birth to her, and she was left behind in England in her first year of life, when her father voyaged to Nantasket, Massachusetts, to serve as a collector of royal customs revenue. In 1766, when Rowson was five, he returned to take her to America. The crisis-ridden translatlantic crossing that ensued is vividly dramatized in her autobiographical novel, *Rebecca, or the Fille de Chambre* (1792). The novel recounts how Rowson's ship was nearly sunk in a hurricane and blown far off course, her experience of severe rationing and near starvation, and the ship's final disaster running aground in an ice storm near Lovell's Island entering Boston harbor.

Rowson's second transatlantic crossing, at age sixteen in 1778, was marked by political as well as personal crisis. After her father was made a prisoner of war during the Revolution, Rowson's family had their property confiscated and lived in extreme poverty and internal exile for over two years before sailing back to England penniless, as part of a prisoner exchange. Problematic crossings figure as emblematic rites of passage in several of Rowson's other novels: *Victoria* (1786), *Mary, or the Test of Honour* (1789), *Charlotte Temple*, and *Reuben and Rachel; or, Tales of Old Times* (1798).

On her third and final transatlantic passage in 1793, Rowson returned to America as a thirty-one-year-old author and actress. She remained in the United States the rest of her life, becoming an American citizen in 1802. In key works written soon after her return to the post-Revolutionary United States, such as the play *Slaves in Algiers: or, A Struggle for Freedom* (1794) and the song "The Sailor's Landlady" (1794, also referred to as "America, Commerce, and Freedom"), Rowson develops explicit links between seafaring, the violent political crises of the time, and the liberal doctrine of commerce as the primary means of social improvement in the post-Revolutionary era.

In *Charlotte Temple*, Charlotte's loss of "innocence" during the transatlantic passage allegorizes the loss of political "virtue" that was a key concept in Republican political theory of the era. Similarly, the communication of ideas and goods in maritime commerce is explicitly linked to Revolutionary ideals of liberty in *Slaves in Algiers* and brings about democratic bounty and well-being in "The Sailor's Landlady." In this song, one of the most popular of the 1790s, American sailors celebrate the wealth created by oceangoing commerce, singing:

> Then drink round my boys, 'tis the first of our joys
> To relieve the distress'd, clothe, and feed 'em.
> 'Tis a duty we share, with the brave and the fair,
> In this land of commerce and freedom.

Second only to her emphasis on women's experience, the transatlantic passage and maritime commerce figure in Rowson's novels and other writings as key sources of personal and political iconography. [*See also* OCEAN LINER DRAMA; WOMEN AT SEA]

Philip Barnard

RUDLOE, JACK [J.] (1943–   ). Born in New York, Jack Rudloe moved to Florida as a boy and began his self-education as a marine biologist. In 1964 he founded the Gulf Coast Specimen Company of Panacea, Florida, which collects marine specimens for laboratories around the world. A few years later he began writing personal narratives that blend science and philosophy as they explore contemporary problems of marine ecology.

Inspired by an early correspondence with John Steinbeck,* Rudloe's works combine concrete descriptions of the coastal environment's ecological diversity with philosophical speculations on life and death, coastal development, and the struggle between the human desire for knowledge and nature's need to exist untouched. His first books, *The Sea Brings Forth* (1968) and *The Erotic Ocean* (1971), focus on specimen collecting. *The Living Dock at Panacea* (1977), a more autobiographical work, describes a year in the life of the dock in front of his home on Dickerson Bay. *The Time of the Turtle* (1978) traces the life cycle of the sea turtle, and *The Wilderness Coast* (1988) describes numerous forays after rare sea creatures. Rudloe has contributed articles to such naturalist periodicals as *Audubon, National Geographic,* and *Natural History,* many of them coauthored with his wife, Ann Rudloe.

Dennis Berthold

S

SAMUELS, SAMUEL (1823–1908). Samuel Samuels was the most famous of the packet-ship masters, eventually commanding the renowned *Dreadnought* (1853). Packets sailed on a set schedule, regardless of whether or not their cargo holds were full. Almost all that is known of Samuels comes from his autobiography, *From the Forecastle to the Cabin*, published by Harper and Brothers in 1887. Samuels states that the purpose of his autobiography is to keep young men from running away to sea—"I would not commit my memoirs to paper if I felt that they would, in the slightest, tend to induce a boy to become a sailor" (2)—but his stories are such rollicking fun that they prove a strong temptation. At age eleven, Samuels ran away from home. He had devoured the works of James Fenimore Cooper* and Frederick Marryat, and these inspired him to go to sea. As he struggles to become a sailor, his early misadventures are both humorous and cautionary. On numerous occasions, he barely escapes beatings.

Samuels suffers from seasickness his first three years at sea. Another sailor attempts to cure him by having him swallow a bit of raw pork tied to a rope yarn and then yanking the yarn—a treatment also attempted in Frederick Pease Harlow's* *The Making of a Sailor* (1928). Later, Samuels is shanghaied*—drugged and forcibly shipped—on a full-rigged ship bound for Liverpool. Despite his troubles, Samuels, with the kindness of other sailors, learns the skills of the seaman and soon becomes an officer and then a captain by age twenty-one. Samuels encounters pirates,* brawls, floggings, and countless storms, and each story is more incredible than the last. His greatest adventure is rescuing a Scandinavian woman from a Turkish harem. Well known for his nonviolent treatment of sailors, Samuels was not afraid to ship even the toughest sailor. He states: "I never rejected a crew . . . on account of their bad character. I generally found among these men the toughest and best sailors" (266).

The full-rigged ship *Dreadnought* was built specifically for Samuels, and her speed coupled with the reputation of her captain led to her fame in both song and story. As Ralph D. Paine notes in his introduction to the 1924 edition of *From the Forecastle to the Cabin*, the *Dreadnought* maintained "an astonishing consistency of performance for a vessel under sail" (xv). There are many versions of the song "Dreadnought," a sign that it was sung often and in many locations. It is mentioned in Rudyard Kipling's *Captains Courageous** (1897), when Captain Disko Troop sings "this ancient, ancient ditty" to "a most dolorous tune, like unto the moaning of winds and the creaking of masts" (ch. 4). Kipling's description is intriguing. By 1897 the *Dreadnought* was not ancient, since the vessel had been built only in 1853; however, the old Engish tune to which it is sung (also the tune of the naval ballad "The Flash Frigate") is.

Samuels' book tells an appealing story, but, unlike Harlow's *The Making of a Sailor* or Richard Henry Dana's* *Two Years before the Mast** (1840), it is not strictly accurate. Samuels is too often the hero. [*See also* SEA MUSIC]

Mary K. Bercaw Edwards

SANDBURG, CARL [AUGUST] (1878–1967). Carl Sandburg, poet, historian, journalist, novelist, labor organizer, folksinger, and collector of American dialect, was born to Swedish immigrant parents in Galesburg, Illinois. Sandburg early understood the beauty, power, and destructiveness of water. He experienced the sea through service in Puerto Rico during the Spanish-American War and as a foreign correspondent in Sweden from late 1918 to early 1919. Residence in Milwaukee from 1907 to 1912 and in Chicago from 1912 through the early 1940s provided regular contact with Lake Michigan. In his poem "North Atlantic" in *Smoke and Steel* (1920), Sandburg alludes to his sea-loving, seagoing ancestry.

Approximately thirty Sandburg poems make significant reference to the Great Lakes* or the sea. Short, imagistic poems such as "Fog" in *Chicago Poems* (1916) present bodies of water as sources of pure aesthetic beauty. In "The Harbor," also from *Chicago Poems*, Lake Michigan offers seagulls an aesthetically liberating and sustenance-providing environment far better than that available to the downtrodden poor in Chicago's ghettos. Poems like "Young Sea" from *Chicago Poems*, "The Sea Hold" from *Cornhuskers* (1918), and "Far Rockaway Night till Morning" and "Flying Fish" from *Smoke and Steel* portray the oceans as wise, loving companions and complements to men, even those who know that their chosen professions will ultimately lead to their deaths at sea.

"North Atlantic" and "Bones" from *Chicago Poems* present the sea as an elemental, cosmic power adopting many roles and faces, ever calling to men and eliciting moods from dream, to adventure, to desperate loss. In other poems, like "Under" from *Chicago Poems*, the sea is an unconscious and uncaring primal power. It makes clear human insignificance in the cosmic order. Poems like "Docks" from *Chicago Poems* and "Sea Wash" from *Smoke and Steel* portray the seas as great and endlessly restless bodies whose eternal motion and change capture and reflect the ebb and flow of the universe. Sandburg often presents the seas as age-old sources of death and life. In "Baltic Fog Notes," for example, from *Smoke and Steel*, Sandburg presents life at sea as joyful, rigorous, full of adventure, and compelling, offering an attractive alternative to life and death ashore.

Sandburg's early poetry contains the most frequent and most central references to the sea and the Great Lakes. Ultimately, Sandburg's explorations make it clear that his dominant usage of the sea is aesthetic rather than philosophical. For him, the land, not the sea, provided the major inspiration. [*See also* SEA IMAGERY IN MODERN AND CONTEMPORARY POETRY]

Philip A. Greasley

SANTAYANA, GEORGE [JORGE AUGUSTÍN NICOLÁS RUIZ DE] (1863–1962). The Spanish-born American idealist-philosopher George Santayana drew on his frequent Atlantic crossings in forming concepts of the world and himself. He also used shipboard experience when developing abstract argument and inventing the analogies, metaphors, and imagery that make his writing accessible to the public. He wrote in *Persons and Places* (1944) that, because his family included blue-sea merchants, he early learned to think of the world as dominated by salt water. This means, he said, that we find ourselves living in a treacherous wasteland, a world of forces not interested in us.

His maritime voyaging may seem to have had an inauspicious beginning, but he found it invigorating. He writes in *Persons and Places* that he was deathly ill for three days when, still a child, he was taken on a small ore ship running from Bilbao to Cardiff. But, he says, seasickness "purges the system of its poisons" (130). He recovered quickly, and the experience was one of those later causing him to write a paean to the physical and spiritual coziness of life at sea and its lesson that, subject to forces though we are, we may be led by them to understand our place in the universe.

At age nine he was taken on the first of his many crossings of the Atlantic. This was a twelve-day trip from Liverpool to Boston, beginning 4 July 1872. The ship was the Cunard liner *Samaria*, a 3,000-ton "old tub" of a steamer that, like many ships of its day, used auxiliary sails (this *Samaria* is not to be confused with the later 20,000-ton liner of the same name). Though Santayana was again thoroughly seasick, a young Irishwoman took care of him. He made his first crossing without a family member or friend in June 1882, when he was nineteen, sailing from New York to Antwerp on his way to Spain, his youth prodding him to take the cheapest ships rather than the most direct. He does not name this ship but says that it was a "second-rate" vessel of the Red Star Line (204). He was again "dreadfully" seasick, but a

"Mrs. X" and her nineteen-year-old daughter looked after him. Writing of this experience, he reflects that the nightmare of seasickness will pass and leave the sufferer stronger for having endured it. By 1912, established as a Harvard professor of philosophy and an idealist poet, Santayana could afford travel on newer, larger liners. He crossed the ocean in January of that year on the *Olympic* (built 1911), sister ship of the *Titanic*.* At 46,000 tons, the *Olympic* was big enough to ride out the wintry gales of the North Atlantic without troubling its passengers.

In his acceptance of mal de mer, Santayana shows a strength of will that appeared again in his ultimate reflections on his travels, *My Host the World* (1953). He first observes, "Ideals are relative to the will." That is, they may be altered by intellect and temperament. The intermingling of delight in the physical and the mental or spiritual appears in his summary of the causes for his "passion for travel." He says that these are aesthetic (love for change and the picturesque), satirical (recognition that "the gods" laugh at this world), and love of contrast (especially as travel exposes the dullness of life at home). The traveler must use the brain, must be accurate in sense impressions, and should be "an artist recomposing what he sees." The goal is not to collect exotica but to arrive at a "corrected view of the truth" (33–35).

Understanding himself as a voyager, Santayana seeks answers to such puzzles as the reason for pairing our bodies with what he terms spirit, a uniting of irreconcilables. Spirit is perhaps superior yet can exist only in a body. He also thinks philosophy should give humankind a set of clear, rational aims. In both argument and statement, he draws on the sea. The dangers of ocean travel, he says, present to us the perils inherent in all existence. He speaks of intellectual failures as wrecks and compares the world to a cockleshell adrift on an overmastering force.

Several pieces in *Soliloquies in England and Later Soliloquies* (1923) muse on the importance of seawaters or use maritime settings. "Praises of Water" reflects on the hypothesis that all life began in the oceans, concluding that living creatures still have a "watery core" that compels them to flow through life. The title of "The Voyage of the Saint Christopher" alludes both to Columbus* and to the patron saint of travelers, St. Peter. The poet sets out on a sea voyage hoping to find heaven. His own faults and foibles and those of his shipmates bring on two mutinies,* in which most of the crew go ashore.

Santayana lived out his last eleven years in Rome. He remained the voyager, though his seas were now those of the intellect and the imagination. To the end, memories of shipboard days informed his reflections on existence and destiny.

Bernard F. Engel

SANTIAGO. In *The Old Man and the Sea** (1952) by Ernest Hemingway* (1899–1961), Santiago, an elderly Cuban fisherman known as "El Campeón" (the Champion), captures a giant marlin after a heroic struggle and exhausts his remaining strength battling sharks that consume the marketable meat. Injured and dying, he retains his resolution at the novel's end; the old man's mystical vision at the moment of the marlin's death signifies that he has participated in a timeless natural order giving his struggle transcendent meaning.

Santiago's epiphany culminates unions with nature experienced by a succession of protagonists in Hemingway's middle period, when he moved from existentialism to a combined romantic and religious mysticism. Santiago possesses rare characteristics necessary for attunement to the Gulf Stream, nature's microcosm in the novel. Indomitable, intuitively perceiving the natural purpose of his special calling, he willingly extends himself against nature's forces in order, paradoxically, to perpetuate its processes. In this, he matches the instinctive behavior of the charismatic carnivores he encounters: the marlin and the mako shark, champions of their species. Santiago's voyage is not a quest but a pilgrimage, the ritualized vocational routine of an initiate, and so is the recurrent dream of his identification, when a youthful sailor, with lions he observed on an African beach. Santiago's name and vocation associate him with St. James, as do parallels between his voyage and the legend of Santiago de Compostela.

Santiago's origins add credence to his portrayal as humanity's link to nature. His blue eyes are the color of the sea and of the marlin and mako sharing his relation to them. Furthermore, like Gregorio Fuentes, Hemingway's boatman and partial model for Santiago, the old man is from the Canary Islands. His eye color, common in that Spanish province, suggests that Santiago's heritage not only unites the old and new Hispanic worlds but includes Continental racial and ethnic mixtures. Moreover, as amateur oceanographers like Hemingway have long known, the Gulf Stream and the Canary Current are part of a series of surface currents circling the North Atlantic, waters that perpetually connect the sites of Santiago's seaborne discovery of his role and his crowning, seaborne reenactment of that role. That, with his implied panethnicity, further demonstrates his suitability as a representative human among the species and forces of nature.

David R. Goodman

SARGENT, EPES (1813–1880). A Boston newspaperman and son of a Gloucester* sea captain, Epes Sargent is best remembered as the author of the lyrics of one of the best-known nautical songs of the nineteenth century. In addition to *American Adventures by Land and Sea* (1841) and other works meant for a schoolhouse audience, Sargent was the author of several historical romances, a few comic pieces, two books on spiritualism, and a number of poems and sonnets. But his fame rests on the single poem, "A Life on the Ocean Wave," which was set to music by Henry Russell and published about 1838. The song was an instant hit, not only among the public ashore who were inspired by its romantic imagery of the jaunty sailor class but by seafarers, who longed to live the life it described. The poem later appeared in Sargent's anthology *Songs of the Sea with Other Poems* (1847), but it was as song lyrics that it continued to be reprinted into the twentieth century. [*See also* SEA MUSIC]

Mary Malloy

SCENES ON LAKE HURON (1836). Written anonymously by "a North American," *Scenes on Lake Huron: A Tale; Interspersed with Interesting Facts in a Series of Letters* purports to be the description of an autumn 1822 voyage taken by schooner from Green Bay, Wisconsin, to Detroit. According to the author in his introduction, the main purpose of this fictionalized travelogue, besides describing the scenery of that portion of the Great Lakes* and its dangerously changeable weather, was to defend the reputation and promote the intrepidity and skill of Lakes sailors from their ocean-going colleagues, who maintained that the former were "no seamen at all." The narrative, in the form of letters to an unnamed friend and signed "M," provides graphic examples to counter such beliefs. Copyright records in the Library of Congress suggest that the author of this book may be one A. J. Matsell, a small New York City publisher during the 1820s and 1830s who specialized in religious and philosophical works and about whom scant additional biographical information is available.

Robert Beasecker

SCHOOLCRAFT, HENRY ROWE (1793–1864). Born in upstate New York, Henry Rowe Schoolcraft was trained as a glassmaker. Like many Americans of his age, however, as a young man Schoolcraft went west, where his knowledge of mineralogy led eventually to his appointment to the 1820 expedition to the shores of Lake Superior led by Lewis Cass. In 1822 Schoolcraft became Indian agent at Sault Ste. Marie, Michigan, where he met and married Jane Johnston, granddaughter of the Chippewa chief La Pointe. They gathered the material that would form the basis of his most important work, *Algic Researches* (1839), the earliest collection of American Indian stories in the United States, revised and reprinted as *The Myth of Hiawatha* (1856) in the wake of the success of Henry Wadsworth Longfellow's* narrative poem *The Song of Hiawatha* (1855).

Not surprisingly, Schoolcraft's adaptations of his Great Lakes* material were influenced by the romantic novel and read like a cross between James Fenimore Cooper* and Nathaniel Hawthorne.* Schoolcraft has come under fire from anthropologists for his ethnocentric interpretation of his Native American sources. Nevertheless, he saved much indigenous material that otherwise would have been lost, and his animist portraits of Great Lakes fauna and watercraft provided the underpinnings for one of America's greatest epics.

Mentor Williams has edited *Narrative Journal of Travels* (1953) and *Indian Legends* (1955). [*See also* AMERICAN INDIAN LITERATURE OF THE SEA]

R. D. *Madison and Victoria Brehm*

SEA-DELIVERANCE NARRATIVES. Sea-deliverance narratives are as old as human experience on water. A "sea-deliverance" story is one told by a survivor of an experience in which the sea is not only the stage on which it takes place but also a player in the drama. The experience is often terrifying, sometimes violent and cruel, sometimes an adventure, but always transforming. Those who live to tell the tale of sea deliverance are possessors of profound new knowledge and are now compelled to tell their story. In the telling of it, their re-creation allows others to experience it vicariously. The narrators describe their sea deliverance in the language and culture of their particular time and place, but the story itself is universal and timeless. Like the archetypal hero of a hundred cultural myths, the sea deliverance hero passes through a process of separation from the known world, of trial upon the sea, of transformation, and of return to the safety of the shore, driven now to re-create the experience for others so that they may be likewise transformed by the power of the story.

American sea deliverance has a rich background in the ancient mythology of the Middle East and of Greece, in Irish and Norse mythology, in the Bible, and in British literature, especially of the Renaissance. In America the wellspring of sea deliverance is in accounts, narratives, and poems of Atlantic-crossing experiences of early explorers and travelers. In American sea-deliverance literature, the archetypal voyage* is combined with a search for a New World, a new Jerusalem, a lost Eden where youth may be recovered and a golden age re-created.

The *Log of Christopher Columbus* (1492–1493), for example, is a sea-deliverance narrative as well as a daily record of the expedition. Columbus'* account of a violent storm on the return voyage has the basic elements of a sea-deliverance narrative, including his attempt to preserve the story of his voyage by sealing a parchment copy in waxed cloth inside a cask and heaving it overboard. The shipwreck* of Sir Thomas Gates' *Sea Venture* in the Bermudas in 1609 was the occasion for a sea-deliverance poem, "Newes from Virginia" (1610) by Richard Rich. William Strachey's "True Reportory of the Wracke, and Redemption of Sir Thomas Gates" (1625) was read by Shakespeare and influenced his writing. Henry Norwood's "A Voyage to Virginia" (1732) describes famine and death on board the ill-fated *Virginia Merchant*. John Josselyn's *Account of Two Voyages* (1639) includes his poem "And the Bitter Storm Augments," on sailing into a violent storm at sea.

For these early writers and their audiences, the sea experience was an example of God's providence. The narrative re-created the events dramatically so that the audience not only understood the meaning of the story intellectually but also experienced it emotionally and spiritually. The storms, shipwrecks, famine, and pirates* of sea life are drawn so as to illustrate the reality of the Christian life. What in the nature of the sea is terrifying and disorienting is made comprehensible. The sea voyage and deliverance are metaphors for spiritual pilgrimage. The hero's journey is to an understanding of God's providence, and his narrative is a call to faith for the audience who hears or reads it.

Among American seventeenth- and early eighteenth-century writers, the providential sea deliverance is especially well developed, and it reinforces a sense of uniqueness not only among New England's Puritans and Pilgrims but also among Maryland's Catholics. William Bradford of Plymouth Plantation in 1620 and Father Andrew White, an English Jesuit en route to Maryland in 1633, both record instances of providential sea deliverance in their voyages. Three generations of New England's Mather family used the sea-deliverance story as moral exemplum. Richard Mather's *Journal* for 1635 records a dramatic escape from a storm on his original Atlantic crossing, and both his son Increase in his *Essay for the Recording of Illustrious Providences* (1684) and grandson Cotton in *Magnalia Christi Americana* (1702) devote entire chapters to sea-deliverance narratives. Richard Steere's long poem *A Monumental Memorial of Marine Mercy* (1684) creates a psychological portrait of passengers and crew caught in a violent storm as well as an extended metaphor for the Christian's passage from ignorance to truth. Anthony Thatcher's 1635 letter describing his shipwreck and loss of his family is especially poignant. Philip Ashton's *Ashton's Memorial** (1725) relates his capture and eventual escape from pirates, and the *Narrative* (1760) of Briton Hammon, a black slave from Marshfield, Massachusetts, recounts his shipwreck and capture first by Indians and then by the Spanish and then escape to, and combat with, the British navy before returning to his master thirteen years later. The conflicting and antagonistic accounts by John Dean (1711) and Christopher Langman (1711) of the shipwreck of the *Nottingham Galley* and subsequent cannibalism on Boon Island constitute one of the more infamous incidents of early New England maritime history, addressed in a contemporary novel by Kenneth Roberts.*

In the eighteenth century, as the American colonies became a maritime country, the taste of the age evolved away from providence as a controlling aesthetic. Neo-classicism and the concept of the sublime created a new distance and point of view from which the mysterious and explosive power of nature could be viewed within an ordered whole. Sea-deliverance literature reflected these changing aesthetic attitudes, and the expanding commercialism and nationalism of the new nation subsumed the early sense of uniqueness developed in providential writings in a larger vision of manifest destiny to exploit the blessings of nature in a new continent. The sea was at once a protector of the new nation and a reminder of the explosive power of nature. J. Hector St. Jean de Crèvecoeur's chapter on Nantucket* in his *Letters from an American Farmer* (1782) represents the new aesthetic and new nationalism of the American sea literature. The ocean for Crèvecoeur represents both unbounded opportunity and protection from the oppression and corruption of Europe. His New Man, the American, asserts himself on the ocean as well as on the prairies or in the forest.

Philip Freneau's* poetry likewise saw oceans as American lakes on which to proclaim American virtue and patriotism. His poetry of the sea is, in part, like "The British Prison Ship" (1780), patriotic and heroic. He also saw the sea from a more reflective and tragic point of view, and these poems evoke the transience not only of life at sea but of all human life. The power and timelessness of the ocean are contrasted again and again in Freneau with the vulnerability and transience of human life. Poems such as "The Argonaut" (1788), "Hatteras" (1789), and "The Wanderer" (1790) evoke the poignancy of sea experience, its essential loneliness and separation from society; in that way Freneau's nascent romanticism elevates sea experience to a metaphor for all human experience.

The fullest literary use of sea deliverance came in the American romanticism of the early nineteenth century, a period paralleled by America's greatest maritime commercial power. The three decades before midcentury produced Washington Irving's* "The Voyage" in *The Sketch Book of Geoffrey Crayon, Gent.* (1819); James Fenimore Cooper's* *The Pilot*(1824) and other maritime novels; Richard Henry Dana's* *Two Years before the Mast** (1840); Edgar Allan Poe's* *The Narrative of Arthur Gordon Pym of Nantucket** (1838); and most significantly, Herman Melville's* sea novels, culminating in *Moby-Dick** (1851).

Despite the decline of sailing ships in the later nineteenth century, sea-deliverance themes continue to find expression in American literature in, for example, the naturalism of Stephen Crane's* "The Open Boat" (1898) and Jack London's* *The Sea-Wolf** (1904) and in twentieth-century novels such as Herman Wouk's* *The* Caine *Mutiny* (1951), Ernest Hemingway's* *The Old Man and the Sea** (1952), and more recently, Peter Matthiessen's* *Far Tortuga** (1975) and Charles Johnson's *Middle Passage** (1990). In their metaphorical and symbolic use of the ocean in combination with a spiritual "voyage" as a central concern, both T. S. Eliot's* "The Dry Salvages" (1941) and Robert Lowell's* "The Quaker Graveyard in Nantucket" (1945) are poems very much in the sea-deliverance tradition. [*See also* "PIETAS IN PATRIAM"]

FURTHER READING: Huntress, Keith, ed. *Narratives of Shipwrecks and Disasters, 1586–1860*. Ames: Iowa State UP, 1974; Springer, Haskell, ed. *America and the Sea: A Literary History*. Athens: U of Georgia P, 1995; Wharton, Donald, ed. *In the Trough of the Sea: Selected American Sea-Deliverance Narratives, 1610–1766*. Westport, CT: Greenwood, 1979.

Donald P. Wharton

THE SEA HORSE (first perf. 1974; pub. 1974). The title of this two-character play by Edward J. Moore (1935–   ) refers to a dive in an unnamed central California seaport town, the scene for a pivotal encounter between the lonely tavern owner and the charming ne'er-do-well commercial seaman who drifts in and out of her life. This grittily realistic character study was an early success for the acclaimed off-Broadway Circle Repertory Theatre and won, for Moore, the Vernon Rice Drama Desk Award for Outstanding New Playwright in 1974. [*See also* DRAMA OF THE SEA]

David R. Pellegrini

SEA IMAGERY IN MODERN AND CONTEMPORARY POETRY.

Throughout the ages, the immensity, power and mystery of the sea have provided a rich subject and background for poetry in narratives of self-discovery and social and political commentary, lyrical evocations of love and loneliness, and philosophical meditations on the meaning of life. Although not as significantly a maritime nation as is, say, Great Britain, the United States, defining itself early on geographically in terms of the Atlantic and Pacific Oceans, shares in the heritage of the significance of the sea. Modern and contemporary American poets often employ the sights and sounds and images of the sea in evocative ways, finding in the sea paradoxical images of eternity and mortality, unity and disintegration, significance and meaninglessness.

This paradoxical response to the sea appears in the poetry of the first truly American poets, Walt Whitman* and Emily Dickinson,* who both highlight the sea's protean nature. The sea is a major metaphor in "Sea Drift," a section of *Leaves of Grass* (1859). Here the sea, though reminding Whitman of death, becomes more significantly the voice of democracy, defining the individual self and establishing the possibility of communication among people to create a living nation. The sound of the waves in "Out of the Cradle Endlessly Rocking" (1859) allows the lone speaker to know himself and his purpose in life; in "Out of the Rolling Ocean the Crowd" (1865, 1881), the speaker's surging, rhythmical lines express aurally what the poem presents intellectually: the ocean waves as an image of union with others and with the spirit of the universe.

In contrast, Emily Dickinson's taut, gemlike musings by the inner self reveal a sense of separation from the natural world. The sea in "I started early" (#520, 1890), for example, seems the beautiful, but dangerous and overpowering Other, seeking to efface individual consciousness. Her submerged metaphors of the sea, as in this poem, are often sexual; here a female speaker is both attracted to, and seeks to escape from, a male sea. Yet for Dickinson, too, the sea as an image of eternity offers the possibility of a transcendent union of the self with a greater being, as in "My River runs to thee" (#162, 1890) or "Wild Nights" (1890), with its image of a boat ecstatically merging with the sea.

The social and political stance that underlies much of Whitman's poetry is part of a broader tradition in American poetry, from the ship-of-state metaphors in the poems of Ralph Waldo Emerson, through several important twentieth-century poets. Ezra Pound* in *The Pisan Cantos* (lxxiv–lxxxiv of *The Cantos*, 1948), for example, views the sea mainly as a means of commercial interaction, while William Carlos Williams* uses the boats in "The Yachts" (1935) to critique the American class structure, personifying the yachts as members of the wealthy classes sailing heedlessly over the drowning poor. In a more general indictment of civilization, Louise Bogan contrasts the refreshing wildness of the sea with the sterility and destructiveness of shore life in her poem "Putting to Sea" (1968). Writing against the backdrop of World War II in "The Quaker Graveyard in Nantucket"* (1946), Robert Lowell* describes the sea as irredeemably contaminated by the ferocity of human beings toward one another.

For African American writers, our inhuman deeds also contaminate the sea; Robert Hayden* portrays the sea as the burial place for the dead and dying enslaved Africans en route from Africa to America ("Middle Passage," 1946); Michael S. Harper* even more radically declares the waters of Charleston Harbor eternally polluted by America's actions during the American Revolution, when 500 African slaves destined for American auction blocks were taken from their slave* ship and purposefully drowned so that they would not be used by the British ("American History," 1970).

From a feminist perspective, Adrienne Rich* also depicts the sea as the final resting place of our wrecked ship of state; more importantly, it is the neutral element that may teach us to transform our society. In "Diving into the Wreck" (1973), the narrator enters the sea, where she must learn to live in new ways, without the power and control so necessary to a patriarchal American civilization. Mary Mackey's "Don't Tell Me the Sea Is a Woman" (1976) denies the traditional gendering of the sea by men. Olga Broumas speaks especially to the transformative powers of the sea with poems such as "Walk on Water" and "Mercy" (from *Perpetua* [1989]) and "Bride" and "Sea Change" (from *Pastoral Jazz* [1983]); sea imagery frequently infuses her work.

The sea, then, provides a fertile context for poets to explore the public relationship of the self to society. Following the current of the more mystical poems of Whitman and the private musings of Dickinson and other nineteenth-century poems such as "The Chambered Nautilus" (1858) by Oliver Wendell Holmes,* twentieth-century poets often examine the emotional life. In the first imagist poems, H. D.* suggests a comparison between the fragile, imperfect, but enduring, seaside vegetation and human suffering and endurance (*Sea Garden* [1916]). T. S. Eliot* in "The Love Song of J. Alfred Prufrock" (1922) turns his emotionally enervated narrator seaward for a redeeming vision of singing mermaids*—only, however, to be denied the vision, wakened instead by human voices to the deadness of this world.

For Hart Crane* in "Voyages" (1930), the sea, first an eloquent setting for love, in essence becomes love itself. The theme of love occupies Robinson Jeffers,* too; his long, narrative poems, outside the mainstream of modern American poetry but echoing Crane in their emotional intensity, rely heavily on images of the mysterious and violent Pacific along the California coast to create the atmosphere appropriate to stories of human passion.

Babette Deutsch in "Earliness at the Cape" (1957) explores, in her comparison of dawn to the blades of a shell opening, the sharp pain that pleasure gives. Forging a raw narrative of a young man's encounter with a shark, James Dickey* in "The Shark's Parlor" (1968) exposes youth's desire for blood, for control, and an older man's realization of the encounter as a spiritual awakening into the meaning of death. In contrast, the absence of sharks in "Tide Turning" (1982) by John Frederick Nims releases the narrator to an inebriating sense of joy and freedom and camaraderie with both his shipmates and the sea.

Contemplating the sea often leads poets to the deeper philosophical and religious questions of the meaning of life, and twentieth-century poets are no exception. Eliot's *The Waste Land* (1922) provides tantalizing glimpses of the sea's redemptive power; in the later, deeply religious poetry of "The Four Quartets" (1940–1942) and "Marina" (1943), the serenity of the sea offers hope and grace. Sometimes poets find themselves almost overwhelmed by the destructive power of the sea, leading them to question the very meaning and value of life. The relentless natural forces of the sea depicted by Robert Frost* in "Once by the Pacific" (1928) presage not only our individual human end but the end of the world itself; in "Neither Out Far nor in Deep" (1936) the sea yields up no answers to life's mystery.

Paradoxically, perhaps, this absence of gods, this indifference of the world to us, can make the world more meaningful. Wallace Stevens* discovers in the sea a perfect metaphor for the ever-changing nature of reality, the chief subject of his poetry. In "Sunday Morning" (1915), in the image of an island—the living, dying natural world—he finds the true meaning of beauty. In "The Idea of Order at Key West*" (1934), the singer, walking beside the sea, finds inspiration in the ever-changing natural world but also gives meaning and order to its chaotic physicality. Elizabeth Bishop* discloses in poems set beside the sea the haunting indifference of the world to us. When, for example, the narrator in "At the Fishhouses" (1955) dunks her hand in the ice-cold water, meaning suddenly crystallizes around the realization that meaning is undiscoverable.

Other contemporary poets, not struggling quite so hard for meaning, find spiritual solace in the sea. Theodore Roethke, whose central subject is the natural world, finds the sea emotionally restorative; the incessant ebb and flow of the sea in "The Rose" (1964) create a meditative calm, allowing the important questions of life to surface, enabling a new sense of self to emerge. Similarly, Mary Oliver* describes the feeling of perfection that the ocean, as both the genesis of life on earth and an image of life's conclusion, brings to those who contemplate its incessant tidal motions. In an intricate and objective series of descriptions of seashells, those discarded habitats of sea creatures, May Swenson in "Some Small Shells from the Windward Islands" (1967) reminds us of the world's mystery.

Yet contemplating the sea's creatures also sometimes helps poets relieve the weight of the world's inscrutability. Inheriting Eliot's spiritual vision, Stanley Kunitz in his long meditative poem "The Wellfleet Whale" (1983) first describes the whale in terms of the divine Other, an incarnation of the inexplicable, but inspiring, mysteries of life. By the end of the poem, the beached and dying whale has become an image of ourselves, partaking of mortality. While Kunitz's final vision of the whale seems a diminished empathy, other poets realize the fully redemptive power of simply being in the presence of such magnificent sea creatures. This is the case with the seals in an early poem by Daniel G. Hoffman, "The Seals of Penobscot Bay" (1954); playful, serene, in dramatic contrast to the dark, treacherous human world, they bring delight to the eyes of the narrator watching from the deck of his destroyer. Or, to look at this another way: if, as in "Who Knows Where the Joy Goes" (1984) by May Sarton, we kill the dolphins, if we lose the wild things of the world, we are diminished, left friendless and alone. In his call to solidarity with wild animals thoughtlessly plundered by power-hungry nations, Gary Snyder* ends his poem "Mother Earth: Her Whales" (1974) with a lyrical vision of whales plunging and rising in the sparkling light of a revitalized earth.

The intellectual pursuit of order within eros, politics, and religion in the present moment is the focus of W. H. Auden, whose poetry tends toward the jubilant and lyrical. Auden wrote such occasional poems as a eulogy for Henry James* (1941) and a birthday poem for Marianne Moore* (1967). Among his shorter poems on a nautical theme are "Doom is dark and deeper than any sea-dingle" (1930), "O Love, the interest itself in thoughtless Heaven" (1932), "Now through night's caressing grip" (1935), "Look, stranger, at this island now" (1935), "The Waters" from "The Quest" (1940), "Atlantis" (1941), and "Fleet Visit" (1951). His masterpiece, arguably, is "The Sea and the Mirror: A Commentary on Shakespeare's *The Tempest*" (1944).

Powerful and alluring, the voice of the sea resounds for modern and contemporary American poets as well as for ancient ones, calling them to things of the physical and spiritual world. In a variety of voices, employing a variety of images of the sea, these poets highlight the sea's power to calm, enchant and mystify—and also to destroy.

FURTHER READING: Solley, George C., and Eric Steinbaugh. *Moods of the Sea: Masterworks of Sea Poetry*. Annapolis: Naval Institute P, 1981; Welland, Dennis. "Twentieth Century Poetry," *America and the Sea: A Literary History*. Ed. Haskell Springer. Athens: U of Georgia P, 1995, 260–88.

Nancy Prothro Arbuthnot

THE SEA LIONS (1849). The last of the sea novels of James Fenimore Cooper* (1789–1851) and the second to last of his books, *The Sea Lions* reflects both the historical context in which it was published and Cooper's mature philosophical and literary thought. In contrast to his earlier sea fiction characterized by stock romantic improbabilities, *Sea Lions*, published in the same year as Herman Melville's* *Redburn*,* reflects the realistic vogue in nautical literature of the 1840s inspired by the immense popularity of Richard Henry Dana's* *Two Years before the Mast** (1840). At the same time, the novel explores issues of spiritual quest and identity probed in a darker vein two years later by Melville (who reviewed *Sea Lions*) in *Moby-Dick** (1851).

The story centers on a sealing expedition on a vessel named the *Sea Lion* to an island north of Antarctica.* The voyage is financed by a mercenary lay deacon from the Sag Harbor area of Long Island, Ichabod Pratt, and undertaken by Roswell Gardiner, a young, competent, but overly confident seaman. Pratt had learned of the location of an immense rookery on this island from Thomas Daggett, a dying sailor, whose nephew from Martha's Vineyard, Captain Daggett, outfits a rival ship identical in dimensions and name to Gardiner's, intending to shadow Gardiner to the secret location. Gardiner's journey to the island and search for a pirate* treasure in the West Indies, also revealed by the dying older Daggett, are complemented by a quest for spiritual truth. That quest is partly the result of the rejection of Gardiner's marriage proposal by Deacon Pratt's niece, Mary, whose orthodox Christian beliefs clash with Gardiner's liberal Unitarian views.

During the voyage south, Daggett proves to be both a capable adversary and a propitious collaborator, especially in a storm off the Carolina coast and a whale hunt off Brazil. But faithful to his responsibilities to Pratt, Gardiner eludes Daggett off Cape Horn,* only to be rejoined by him on the seal island after a successful harvesting season. Delayed in their departure by Daggett's greed, both vessels become icebound by a fierce winter that eventually claims Daggett and his crew as its victims. In the midst of the awesome spectacle of nature's magnitude, power, beauty, and mystery, the ever-resourceful Gardiner is humbled and undergoes a transcendent experience. Aided by the preachments of a pious shipmate, Stimson, passages from a Bible provided to him by Mary, and a sighting of the Southern Cross, Gardiner is converted to an orthodox Christianity that allows him to win Mary's hand when he returns safely to Long Island. In this manner, Gardiner's spiritual transformation is made to accommodate Cooper's own more conservative religious views.

Most notable among the many sources Cooper used to authenticate his narrative are Edmund Fanning's* accounts of his sealing voyages and Charles Wilkes' descriptions of the Antarctic* region in *Narrative of the United States Exploring Expedition* (1845). [*See also* U.S. EXPLORING EXPEDITION]

Joseph Flibbert

SEA MARKS (first perf. 1971; pub. 1982). From 1959 to 1962 playwright Gardner McKay (1932–   ) starred in the television series *Adventures in Paradise*, in which he played Adam Troy, a sailor who traveled the seas in his schooner *Tiki*. He later turned to playwriting.

His works include *Sea Marks*, a two-character play that charts the romance between Colm Primrose, an Irish fisherman from the Western Islands, and Timothea Stiles, a woman from Wales who works for a publisher in Liverpool. They become acquainted through a series of letters, which Timothea excerpts into a volume of poetry called *Sea Marks*. After their brief affair in Liverpool, Colm rejects both a new wardrobe and his literary success, returning to the sea and continuing his correspondence with Timothea. The climax of the play comes during Colm's speech to a ladies' club describing his relationship with the sea and mourning the drowning death of his foster father. [*See also* DRAMA OF THE SEA]

Brian T. Carney

SEA MUSIC. In the narrowest sense, "sea music" refers to music sung or played by people who work in the maritime trades: deepwater and coastal merchant sail, fishing, whaling, or the navy. The term is frequently expanded to include the music of coastal communities and members of occupations dependent on the sea for their livelihood, music sung and played by emigrants and passengers, and songs of river, lake, and canal life and work. Folk and popular music based on nautical themes written by non-seagoing people and even the nonnautical music that sailors heard in port and then took to sea can also be considered "sea music."

Sailors' music enjoyed a heyday during the nineteenth century. Songs from this period can be roughly divided into two types: songs for work and songs for pleasure. The term "chantey" (also spelled "chanty," "shanty," or "shantey") refers specifically to work songs sung at sea to accompany various shipboard tasks: heaving up to the anchor, hauling lines to raise and adjust sails, pumping ship, and "tossing the bunt" when furling square sails. "Chantey" is always pronounced with the soft "sh" sound, and this spelling is favored by those who connect the term to the French command, "Chantez" (sing!). The etymology of the term is uncertain, as it has not been found in print before the mid-nineteenth century; consequently, it is unlikely to have come into general use before the early nineteenth century. There is limited evidence for the use of nautical work songs in English before the nineteenth century, although Roger Abrahams in *Deep the Water, Shallow the Shore* (1974) and others provide evidence for a significant work song tradition among people of African descent along the eastern and southern coasts of the United States and in the Caribbean.* These songs were used especially for cargo handling and rowing as well as for other nonmaritime tasks. See, for example, the compact disc by the Menhaden Chanteymen, *Won't You Help Me to Raise 'Em: Authentic Net-Hauling Songs from an African American Fishery* (1990).

The inauguration of the Black Ball Line, scheduled transatlantic packet service, in 1818 signaled economic changes that eventually reduced the size of crews on merchant ships. Smaller crews and the mixing of sailors from various cultures aboard ship (including, importantly, African Americans,* West Indians, and Irish) resulted in the flowering of the chantey tradition. "Blow the Man Down," "Shenandoah," "Rio Grande," "Hanging Johnny," and "Sally Brown" are among the best-known chanteys today, but hundreds of others existed. Chanteying was largely confined to square-rigged merchant vessels and was little used or nonexistent on naval vessels, fishing schooners, and fore-and-aft-rigged coastal traders. The chantey tradition reached its peak in the second half of the nineteenth century and slowly died, as a working genre, with the decline of commercial sail in the early twentieth century. However, in the West Indies and aboard fishing vessels, songs were still used to lighten work into the 1950s and 1960s.

Chanteys share a number of characteristics. The rhythm of shipboard work generally dictates the form of the song, thus setting the tempo or indicating where the pulls or pushes ("hauls" and "heaves" to sailors) are to come. Chanteys are often classified according to the jobs at which they are used (halyard chanteys, capstan chanteys, pumping chanteys) because of the necessity of matching the rhythm of the music with the motions involved in the work. They also provide entertainment and relief from the monotony of long, laborious tasks by incorporating music into the work.

The songs vary greatly in performance. Depending on the task at hand, a given song may be shortened, lengthened, quickened, or slowed. As tools to help accomplish work, they are valued for their efficacy rather than their beauty. Some claim that a chantey is "as good as ten men on a line." While some chanteys have story lines, often the lyrics are drawn from a common repertoire of couplets and rhymes that can be used interchangeably in a large number of songs. Any chantey might have numerous versions of both melody and lyrics.

In many crews, a few individuals would quickly be identified as the favored song leaders, or "chanteymen," early in a voyage. Their qualifications included a good repertoire, the ability to set the rhythm and "feel" of the song to help the men most effectively combine their efforts, a sense of which song would suit the mood of the crew, and an ability to improvise new lyrics. This last qualification often related to another essential function of the chantey: without officially complaining, it allowed the crew to voice opinions about their treatment by the officers, the condition of the vessel, or the quality of their food all within earshot of the captain or mates. While complaints in chantey lyrics were general in nature, application to the specific problem mentioned would be obvious. This served as an important emotional and social release for the crew while making their viewpoint known to the officers.

Also related to the "complaint" aspect of chanteys were the few ceremonial songs, such as "The Dead Horse," "Leave Her, Johnny, Leave Her," or "Salt Horse," which were sometimes sung at specific points in the voyage. Chanteys such as "Shenandoah" or "Rolling Home" could be reserved for raising anchor in the last port of call on a voyage, when the ship was homeward bound.

In their off-duty hours, sailors sang what they referred to as "main-hatch songs," "fo'c's'le songs," or "forebitters" (when off-watch, the foremast hands would often gather at the forebitts, posts near the bow used for mooring the ship). This repertoire included naval ballads, love songs, patriotic songs, minstrel songs, sentimental songs, occupational songs such as whaling and fishing ballads, and other popular music of the time. Dance tunes and songs from a variety of cultures also found their way into the repertoire of American sailors. Some sailors collected songs, while others made their own and wrote them down in diaries or journals, sometimes performing them for their shipmates.

Deepwater sailor songs were occasionally published in popular music collections in the late nineteenth century, but entire collections of American sailor songs by folk-music scholars did not appear until the 1924 publication of *Roll and Go: Songs of American Sailormen* by Joanna Colcord.* Later collections include Frank Shay's *Iron Men and Wooden Ships* (1948), William Main Doerflinger's *Shantymen and Shantyboys* (1951), folksinger Burl Ives' *Sea Songs of Sailing, Whaling, and Fishing* (1956), the posthumous publication of *Chanteying aboard American Ships* (1962) by Frederick Pease Harlow,* Gale Huntington's *Songs the Whalemen Sang* (1964), and Abrahams' *Deep the Water, Shallow the Shore*. Harlow's work is the single most authoritative source on the practice of chanteying. Its exact and vivid descriptions of chanteys at work are derived from the author's own experience on nineteenth-century square-riggers during the heyday of chanteying. Another comprehensive work is *Shanties from the Seven Seas* (1961) by Englishman Stan Hugill (1906–1992). It is the single most extensive collection of chanteys and, like Harlow's book, is informed by the author's own experience.

The inland waterways of America had their own musical traditions. Meriwether Lewis and William Clark, working their way up the Missouri River, had a French Canadian* fiddler with them who played for Native Americans to "break the ice" of cross-cultural contact. Rafts carrying a variety of products down the Ohio and Mississippi Rivers and their tributaries often carried fiddlers, and river transport played an important role in the sharing of repertoire among musicians in those regions. Show music, popular music, and tunes to accompany fashionable dances such as waltzes or schottisches were taken to the interior by steamboats. Roustabouts working on riverboats sang at their work and frequented dances and social events along the rivers. Workers on canal barges developed a repertoire of songs, and sailors on the Great Lakes* used some chanteys as well as a repertoire of ballads about their trade.

Ballads and nautical songs were sung by inland traditional singers for generations after any direct contact with the sea, and nautical imagery and metaphor played an important role in nineteenth-century religious music. This practice continued into the twentieth century with bluegrass and gospel music. Popular-music songwriters in the twentieth century have continued to compose material on nautical themes, from the Broadway musical *Showboat* (1927), to the Beach Boys' "Surfin' USA" (1963).

Some singers and songwriters of the "folk revival" starting in the 1950s turned their attention to traditional maritime music. Throughout his entire career, rock and bluegrass guitarist and banjo player Jerry Garcia included sea music and other traditional music in his solo and ensemble, electric and acoustic repertoires; his compact disc *Shady Grove* (1996) includes "Off to Sea Once More," "Jackaroo," and "The Handsome Cabin Boy." In 1969 Crosby, Stills, and Nash recorded "Wooden Ships," a parable of rival political castaways trying to survive on a desert island, and, in 1982, the popular "Southern Cross," about the hope and freedom of life on the water. Gordon Bok and Canadians Stan Rogers and Gordon Lightfoot are among the better-known folk maritime songwriters. Gordon Lightfoot's "The Wreck of the *Edmund Fitzgerald*"* (1976), written in the form of a traditional nautical ballad, achieved considerable radio airplay on pop stations in the 1970s and 1980s. Far from a dying art form, both traditional and contemporary sea music has experienced a significant revival in the late twentieth century. [*See also* SAMUELS, SAMUEL; SHORE LEAVE MUSICALS]

FURTHER READING: Abrahams, Roger. *Deep the Water, Shallow the Shore.* Austin: American Folklore Society, U of Texas P, 1974; Colcord, Joanna. *Roll and Go: Songs of American Sailormen.* Indianapolis: Bobbs-Merrill, 1924, Rev. ed., New York: Norton, 1938; Doerflinger, William Main. *Shantymen and Shantyboys.* New York: Macmillan, 1951; Harlow, Frederick Pease. *Chanteying aboard American Ships.* Barre, MA: Barre Gazette, 1962; Hugill, Stan. *Shanties from the Seven Seas.* London: Routledge and Kegan Paul, 1961. Repub. Mystic, CT: Mystic Seaport, 1994.

Craig Edwards and Robert Walser

THE SEA SERPENT; OR, GLOUCESTER HOAX (first perf.?; pub. 1819). The versatile William Crafts (1787–1826), a South Carolina lawyer and public official, wrote essays, poems, and dramatic criticism for the *Charleston Courier*. In rhyming couplets full of witty allusions, his play *The Sea Serpent* describes what happens when a gullible Captain Jonathan sights a sea monster off the coast of a small New England fishing town. The wily mayor quickly spreads the news and offers a reward for the creature's capture, hoping to swell the town coffers. What supposedly resembles a monstrous snake is finally caught, but it turns out to be only an albacore. Other characters include two scientists, a pair of lovers whose marriage depends on the monster's being caught, a painter with a vivid vision of the serpent, and a number of skeptical fishermen. [*See also* DRAMA OF THE SEA]

Brian T. Carney

THE SEA-WOLF (1904). This novel by Jack London* (1876–1916) traces the development of the narrator, the effete literary critic Humphrey Van Weyden, through his encounter with the brutish Wolf Larsen.*

Crossing San Francisco Bay in a fog, Van Weyden's ferry is sunk, and he is picked up by Wolf's sealing schooner *Ghost*. Wolf determines to keep "Hump" on his crew to make a man of him. Life at sea is a Darwinian struggle in which Hump's idealistic values are put to the test. Of those on board, Wolf is the fittest, London's version of Nietzsche's superman, for he possesses amazing physical prowess as well as a developing intellectual knowledge, both of which buttress his materalist outlook. Hump has risen to become first mate when the *Ghost* picks up Maud Brewster, a shipwrecked poetess with whom Hump immediately feels an affinity that blossoms into love. Threatened by Wolf, Hump and Maud set out in a small boat and land on an island, where they eventually reencounter Wolf, ravaged apparently by a brain tumor, and they finally overcome him. They declare their mutual love and are rescued.

This sea experience is for Hump a proving ground in his development; his values are challenged, and through the rigors of nautical life he grows into vigorous, yet still virtuous, manhood.

The novel was adapted for film several times: 1920, 1926, 1930 (with dialogue by S. N. Behrman*), 1941 (starring Edward G. Robinson), 1958 (with the title *Wolf Larsen*), and 1997.

John Samson

"SEABORN, ADAM." *See SYMZONIA.*

"SEAFARER." *See* BARKER, BENJAMIN.

SEARLS, HENRY HUNT "HANK," JR. (1922–   ). Novelist and author of nonfiction and short fiction, Hank Searls was born in San Francisco 10 August 1922. Graduated from the U.S. Naval Academy in 1944 with the wartime-accelerated class of 1945, he remained an active-duty naval officer until 1954. He served in the Pacific as a gunnery officer on U.S.S. *Washington* and later with air photo reconnaissance squadrons mapping Labrador and Newfoundland. Indeed, it was at 20,000 feet in a B-24 flying over Newfoundland that Searls began writing, initially detective and aviation short fiction.

His thrillers often involve aviation or aquatic themes; he wrote novelizations of the movies *Jaws 2* (1978) and *Jaws: The Revenge* (1971). *Kataki* (1987) fictionalizes George Bush's World War II experiences as a navy pilot in the Pacific. Also set in World War II, *The Hero Ship* (1969) involves an American carrier heavily damaged by kamikazes, inspired by the near sinking of the U.S.S. *Franklin*, which Searls witnessed. In the early 1970s Searls and his wife sailed the South Pacific, a voyage he made use of in *Overboard*

(1977), where a man and wife try to resolve relational differences while sailing the South Pacific. *Sounding* (1982) is a remarkable modern counterpart to *Moby-Dick** (1851), with a whale-protagonist as a thoroughly developed character yet still "very like a whale."

Perhaps Searls' best-known book is the nonfiction *The Lost Prince: Young Joe, the Forgotten Kennedy* (1969), about the Kennedy brother whose plane was shot down over France on a special mission during World War II.

C. Herbert Gilliland

SEASCAPE WITH SHARKS AND DANCER (first perf. 1984; pub. 1974). The setting of this play by Don Nigro (1949–   ) is a beach house on Cape Cod.* A struggling writer, Ben, has just fished a young woman, Tracy, out of the Atlantic Ocean. Ben presumes that she was drowning, but Tracy insists that she was dancing. As Tracy warms herself in Ben's beach house with hot chocolate, the two share childhood memories, tell stories, discuss the general pattern of their lives, and argue. After some time of confinement together, however, the two draw together and become lovers. Two months pass, and they continue to live together, but without any growth in the relationship, ostensibly due to Tracy's fear of attachment. Through nightmares and stories, she illuminates her belief that attachment leads to disappointment and pain.

The sea reflects Tracy's view of an uncaring world. She describes the sea as dirty and dead, as a habitat for sharks that are unblinking, vacant, and disinterested creatures despite their awareness of human presence. Her actions throughout the play, including her decision to abort the baby that she and Ben conceive, demonstrate her personal inability to bond while at the same time she tries to elicit a caring relationship from Ben. [*See also* CO-LUMBUS PLAYS; DRAMA OF THE SEA]

Brian Knetl

SECOND SKIN (1964). *Second Skin*, written by John Hawkes (1925–   ), is a phantasmagoric, apparitional novel that focuses on a psychologically unstable narrator who recites his tale from a floating island off the coast of New England. It is difficult to differentiate the factual from the real in this novel, since we experience the point of view of the central character, Skipper. Skipper is an ex-navy officer whose life is filled with tragedy, including the apparent suicides of his father, his wife, and his daughter. He describes his journey on the floating island as one of survival against the greatest of odds. His ship is called *Peter Poor*, but the hallucinatory style of the novel makes it difficult to tell whether this ship is the one he was on while in the navy or while sailing with his family.

Many allusions to *The Tempest* (1623) can easily be identified, but the purpose they serve remains elusive. Like much of Hawkes' other fiction, *Second Skin* is dominated by dream imagery. The sea plays a significant role in this novel because much of the action is set on the floating island, and much of the dream imagery involves the sea.

Ralph Berets

SEMMES, RAPHAEL (1809–1877). A naval officer first in the United States and then in the Confederate navy, Raphael Semmes wrote two books on his naval adventures. The first, *Afloat and Ashore during the Mexican War* (1851), is an account of his service during that conflict. In the early portion of the work, the only part concerned with the sea, Semmes relates his service during the naval blockade of Vera Cruz. After the surrender of that city, he became attached to a party sent to rescue an American midshipman* accused of spying. The remainder of the book contains his observations on the country and people and his recounting of the American army's victorious march to Mexico City.

Unlike *Afloat and Ashore*, Semmes' second work, *Memoirs of Service Afloat during the War between the States* (1869), is essentially a tale of the sea. Semmes' voyages in the *Sumter* and the *Alabama** and his return to the postwar South as well as his arguments for the Confederacy's position are the major topics of this book. In this second effort Semmes is a far more self-conscious literary artist. He employs foreshadowing to heighten dramatic tension: when he describes the christening of the *Alabama*, for example, he also predicts her later demise off the coast of France. His depiction of the battle between the *Hatteras* and the *Alabama* is, like the engagement itself, brief but exciting. Semmes' descriptions of storms at sea lend drama to his narrative of the perils faced by the crews of the privateers, and his explanations of the effect of weather and ocean currents on shipping and seamanship are clear and illuminating.

Although Semmes' first work was a best-seller, his second attracted little attention outside the South because of the author's partisan approach to his material. Despite the lack of public enthusiasm, Semmes' *Memoirs* is a literary accomplishment. [*See also* CONFEDERATE NAVAL FICTION; NAVAL MEMOIRS]

Anna E. Lomando

SERAPIS. In 1779 a large new frigate named the H.M.S. *Serapis* boasted the copper sheathing introduced by the British in their navy at the beginning of the American Revolution. Rated at forty-four guns, the *Serapis* actually carried fifty: a main battery of twenty eighteen-pounders on a lower deck, twenty nine-pounders on an upper gundeck, and ten six-pounders on the quarterdeck. Commanded by Captain Richard Pearson, the *Serapis* was convoying a fleet of forty-four sail off Flamborough Head on the east coast of England when she was attacked by the smaller *Bonhomme Richard** of forty-four guns under the command of John Paul Jones.*

In the historic sea battle that followed on 23 September, Captain Pearson was forced to surrender. He later claimed in his court-martial that he had been attacked by two American frigates. Acquitted and complimented on his actions, Pearson was knighted by King George III, while Jones got nothing for his victory. Jones turned the *Serapis* over to the French, who refitted her and sent her to the Indian Ocean, where she was destroyed by fire when a sailor dropped a flaming torch into a tub of brandy.

Kay Seymour House

SHANGHAIING. In the second half of the nineteenth century, as the U.S. Merchant Marine began to change from sail to steam and from American to foreign personnel, it became increasingly difficult to find a crew for a sailing vessel. As the best and most profitable routes went to steamships, new technology made it possible to build massive, iron-hulled sailing vessels for carrying bulk cargoes cheaply. Often poorly manned and maintained, these vessels developed a reputation for brutality under their "bucko mates," and few experienced sailors were willing to sign on under such conditions.

It was possible to get men through trickery: saloon owners, prostitutes, and boardinghouse keepers often cooperated to create a debt that a man could not pay off except by signing aboard a ship and surrendering his advanced wages. Under more desperate situations, shipowners turned to "crimps," men and women who would forcefully abduct men using drugs or violence. By the time a man woke from the opium or chloroform that had been slipped into his drink or cigar, he was on a ship headed to Shanghai, China. Though the practice of "shanghaiing" was known to have occurred from New York, Boston, Philadelphia, and Baltimore, the most notorious ports were on the West Coast. San Francisco led the pack, with the ship-jumping inducements of the goldfields leaving many ships shorthanded, but Portland, Oregon, and Port Townsend, Washington, were not far behind.

Paddy West and other well-known crimps were celebrated in several chanteys, but, for the most part, shanghaiing became a more popular theme in twentieth-century movies than it was in nineteenth-century novels. The most famous appearance of a crimp in literature is the Liverpool thug who brings a corpse on board the *Highlander* in Herman Melville's* *Redburn** (1849). Shanghaiing occurs in Samuel Samuels'* *From the Forecastle to the Cabin* (1887). Frank Norris* includes a shanghaiing episode in *Moran of the* Lady Letty (1898), reportedly based on the experiences of a San Francisco coastguardsman, and a hapless S.S. *Glencairn** crewman is shanghaied in London in Eugene O'Neill's* play *The Long Voyage Home* (perf. 1917; pub. 1919). A number of factual accounts of being shanghaied were written by sailors, including James H. Williams, whose autobiographical writings were collected in 1959 as *Blow the Man Down! A Yankee Seamen's Adven-*

tures under Sail. A good history of the practice can be found in *Shanghaiing Days* (1961) by Richard H. Dillon.

Mary Malloy

SHIP OF GOLD IN THE DEEP BLUE SEA (1998). Blending a harrowing account of the September 1857 foundering of the S.S. *Central America* during a storm off the Carolina coast with a chronicle of engineer Tommy Thompson's recent efforts to locate the wreck and recover its treasures, this nonfiction narrative by Gary Kinder (1946–   ) examines the intricacies and technology of deep-sea exploration and shipwreck* archaeology.

When the *Central America*, a three-masted side-wheel steamer, left Panama on its scheduled passage to New York, it carried nearly 600 passengers and crew, many returning east from the Californian goldfields with vast sums of both registered and undeclared stores of gold, estimated at up to twenty-one tons. Using eyewitness testimony and newspaper coverage of the sinking to provide the historic underpinnings of his narrative, Kinder dramatizes the heroic efforts of Captain Herndon and company to save the sinking vessel. Although 149 passengers and crew were rescued by passing vessels, hundreds drowned when the steamer with its stock of gold ultimately foundered.

Moving the narrative forward more than a century, Kinder introduces Thompson, an innovative engineer whose training, experimentation, and marketing skills enable him, with the financial backing of the Columbus*-America Discovery Group, to search for, locate, and recover the *Central America*'s riches from a depth of more than 8,000 feet. Kinder's narrative combines the drama of high-risk adventure with the carefully orchestrated, scientific approach to exploration and recovery efforts in a deep-sea environment as well as accounts of the legal challenges over the ownership of the wreck and its contents.

Daniel W. Lane

THE SHIPPING NEWS (1993). A novel by E[dna]. Annie Proulx (1935–   ), *The Shipping News* was awarded the 1993 National Book Award in fiction and the 1994 Pulitzer Prize in fiction. Proulx, who lived in Vermont and Newfoundland at the time of writing *The Shipping News*, has since moved to Wyoming.

Consumed by feelings of inadequacy and failure, unemployed and recently widowed newspaperman R. G. Quoyle leaves Mockingburg, New York, and sets out with his aunt and two young daughters for Quoyle's Point, the isolated site of his dead grandparents' home on Omaloor Bay in Newfoundland. Quoyle has a job as a reporter, covering car wrecks and the "shipping news" for the *Gammy Bird*, a sensationalist newspaper in the fishing village of Killick-Claw.

Throughout the novel, Quoyle wrestles with the problems of his new life, including the logistical difficulties of commuting across the bay and paying for the renovation of the decaying house on Quoyle's Point. As he forges a new identity and develops self-reliance, Quoyle helps a local boatbuilder to craft a wooden rodney to replace his own poorly designed, secondhand boat, a lopsided craft that he uses in his daily crossings of the bay. The perils and pains that Quoyle endures in piloting his rickety boat and in building its replacement recall the canoe-building follies of Robinson Crusoe, in that the boat represents both the instrument and the impediment to his escape from Quoyle's Point. In a metaphorical coda to Quoyle's personal journey of sacrifice and renewal, a storm sweeps the ancestral house into the bay. In turn, Quoyle is able to shed the weighty, artificial connections to the house and its hard-living, incestuous former occupants.

Quoyle's name, as Proulx points out in the first chapter's epigraph, is an obsolete, alternative spelling for a coil of rope. Proulx builds on this nautical motif through other character names, including Quoyle's love interest Wavey, and through subsequent chapter epigraphs, which are mostly explanations of various sailing knots and other terms taken from Clifford W. Ashley's *The Ashley Book of Knots* (1944) and Gershom Bradford's *The Mariner's Dictionary* (1972; first pub. as *A Glossary of Sea Terms*, 1927).

The novel derives much of its energy and humor from the quirky, seagoing culture of Newfoundland. Among the Killick-Claw residents Quoyle encounters are Dawn, a young college graduate with a degree in pharology (the study of lighthouses* and signaling), and Nutbeem, the foreign-news editor who plans to escape the harsh winters of Newfoundland by sailing to Florida, a plan thwarted when his boat is destroyed by a merry drunken mob at his going-away party.

Although a self-conscious "headlinese" narrative style and Quoyle's initial sense of alienation give *The Shipping News* a postmodern veneer, the hero's spiritual and physical awakening, set against the unforgiving sea-bound environment of Newfoundland, recalls earlier works like Daniel Defoe's *Robinson Crusoe* (1719) and Jack London's* *The Sea-Wolf* (1904), in which a sea journey serves as an impetus for character transformation and redemption. As several critics have noted, the icy and stormy waters uniting the diverse residents of Killick-Claw can be seen as an embryonic fluid for the rebirth of the urban-bred and malaise-ridden Quoyle. Proulx's sea imagery and her depiction of the relationship with the sea in her coastal Newfoundland characters infuse this rich novel.

Brian Anderson

SHIPWRECK LITERATURE. Shipwrecks have always been a popular subject in American literature. For early settlers, the perilous voyage* from Europe to America was a providential test, and disasters at sea were interpreted as signs of divine disfavor. Living in a world rife with typological significance, survivors and observers of shipwrecks could not avoid making a connection between a journey at sea and the journey of life, so maritime tragedies were perceived as jeremiads that warned people not to stray from the righteous path. Yet shipwreck accounts also carried a promise of deliverance; no matter how devastating the disaster, someone always survived to tell the tale, and the survivors could not help but see God's hand in their survival.

One of the first to collect shipwreck accounts in order to discern a pattern of divine dispensation was Increase Mather, whose *Essays on the Recording of Illustrious Providences* (1682) included a number of maritime misadventures. Many were borrowed from James Janeway's popular English collection, *Mr. J. J.'s Legacy to His Friends* (1675), but Mather also included several accounts he collected from American sources, of which Anthony Thatcher's account of 1635 and Ephraim How's account of 1676 were especially important. Similarly, both Cotton Mather and William Shurtleff exploited shipwreck as a providential call for repentance. On 11 December 1710, the *Nottingham Galley* was cast up on the rocks of Boon Island, off the coast of Massachusetts, and Captain John Dean and his crew remained stranded on the barren rocks for three weeks, suffering great misery and deprivation before resorting to cannibalism. In London, Dean published a narrative of the shipwreck, *A True Account of the Voyage of the* Nottingham Galley (1711), but the story was too compelling to set aside. In *Compassions Called For* (1711) Mather used the Dean text to supplement his call for reform, and a quarter century later in *Distressing Dangers and Signal Deliverances* (1727) Shurtleff also made use of the Dean text as an illustration of divine power.

The most popular of all early American shipwreck narratives was Jonathan Dickinson's *God's Protecting Providence Man's Surest Help and Defense in Times of Greatest Difficulty and Imminent Danger* (1699). Frequently republished in both England and America and translated into German and Dutch, Dickinson's narrative reached nearly thirty separate editions. While on a voyage from Port Royal to Philadelphia, Dickinson and twenty-three others were shipwrecked off the central coast of Florida during a fierce storm on the night of 23 September 1696. For three months the survivors struggled up the coast until they finally reached Charleston on 26 December, but not before several of the party had died from hunger and exposure. While stressing divine mercy for their deliverance, Dickinson offered a straightforward account of their ordeals and endurance.

In *The Wonderful Providence of God* (1730), William Walling narrated how he survived eight days on a floating wreck, and both Joseph Bailey in *God's Wonders in the Great Deep* (1749) and Nathanael Peirce in *An Account of the Great Dangers and Distresses and the Remarkable Deliverance of Capt. Nathanael Peirce* (1756) relate how they survived on the hulks of ships that had foundered during storms. One of the most harrowing of such narratives is Barnabas Downs' *A Brief and Remarkable Narrative of the Life and Extreme Sufferings of Barnabas Downs* (1786). Shortly after setting sail, Downs' privateer, the brig *Arnold*, was wrecked during a terrible snowstorm near Plymouth Harbor on 26 December 1778. During the first night sixty of the crew died, and two days later the nearly frozen Downs was thought to be dead when the rescuers finally reached the *Arnold*.

Two of the most interesting narratives from the late eighteenth century were Daniel Saunders' *A Journal of the Travels and Sufferings of Daniel Saunders* (1794) and Benjamin Stout's *Narrative of the Loss of the Ship* Hercules (1800). Unlike the earlier providential accounts, these are highly developed texts detailing the experiences of the captains and crews after they ran aground while on distant voyages. Saunders, a seaman on board the *Commerce* bound for Bombay, was part of a group of seventeen sailors who, after wrecking on the Arabian coast, struggled along the desert shore for over a month with little food or water, only nine surviving the ordeal. Less concerned with the spiritual significance than with the physical experience, Saunders closely describes the hardships he endured and his interaction with the Arabs he encountered. Reflecting the changes in the post-Revolutionary literary marketplace, the printer attempted to exploit the exotic setting by adding an ethnographic appendix on Arabian culture. Stout's narrative was set in an equally alien world and even less concerned with providential lessons. While sailing from India to England, Stout and his crew were wrecked on the South African coast during a storm in June 1796, and for several weeks they traveled through the country until they reached the Cape of Good Hope. Although fearing the local tribes, Stout and his crew were kindly treated; he ironically describes the Dutch and English colonists as being less civilized than the natives.

One of the most significant developments in the shipwreck genre was the advent of large anthologies. In 1804 Archibald Duncan published his multivolume *The Mariner's Chronicle* in London, which anthologized nearly thirty different accounts (including the Dean, How, and Stout narratives). Two years later the Duncan text was pirated in Philadelphia, and in 1813 Andrus and Starr, two Hartford printers, again published it, under the title *Remarkable Shipwrecks*. In addition to all of Duncan's original material, they added an account of an 1809 shipwreck and a patriotic series of sketches describing naval battles between English and American ships during the War of 1812. As an indication of both the genre's and the book's popularity, the printers included a twenty-eight-page list of subscribers, a total of nearly 5,000 names. The Philadelphia printer Matthew Carey was equally interested in exploiting the genre's popularity, and in 1810 he published two separate collections, *Narratives of Calamitous and Interesting Shipwrecks* and *Interesting Narratives of Extraordinary Sufferings and Deliverances*. Taking half of his material from Duncan and gathering the other half from various sources, including an Indian captivity narrative, Carey published eight narratives in each of his texts, and it is likely that the success of one encouraged him to publish the other.

During the 1830s three other popular anthologies were published, each subsequently reprinted several times. The first was an edition of *The Mariner's Chronicle*, by Deacon Durrie, Henry Peck, and Lorenzo Peck, published in New Haven, Connecticut, in 1834. Borrowing freely from Duncan, the printers added a number of other accounts of shipwrecks that had occurred since 1804, especially several recent steamboat explosions as well as descriptions of whales, polar bears, icebergs, maelstroms, pirates, and famous sea battles. Demonstrating the advancements in printing technology, the Durrie and Peck text was stereotyped, included twenty-five engravings, and ran nearly 500 pages. Equally ambitious was R. Thomas' 1835 collection, *Interesting and Authentic Narratives of the Most Remarkable Shipwrecks*. Similarly based on Duncan but also drawing from many later shipwrecks (particularly the tragic 1833 account of the *Amphitrite Convict Ship*, in which only 3 of 136 survived), the Thomas text was perhaps the most popular of all antebellum shipwreck anthologies. Similar to the Durrie and Peck and the Thomas texts was Charles Ellms'* *Shipwrecks and Disasters at Sea* (1836). The author of several other well-liked collections, including *The Pirates' Own Book* (1837), Ellms catered to a popular audience and compiled material from a variety of sources in order to reach a mass market.

Perils at Sea, published as the fourteenth volume in Harper's "Boys and Girl's Library" (1852), was intended as a juvenile* book and marketed to school districts. The collection contained eight accounts that, according to the publisher's preface, were chosen for their piety and fortitude in suffering.

While shipwreck anthologies sold well in the literary marketplace, a number of separate accounts also attracted large audiences. *A Narrative of the Shipwreck and Unparalleled Sufferings of Mrs. Sarah Allen*, for instance, was printed in at least three editions between 1816 and 1817. While on a voyage from New York to New Orleans, Allen's ship sprang a leak and sank along the Florida Gulf coast; for nearly a month she and other survivors wandered along the desolate coast until they were discovered by Indians. An even more exotic tale of being shipwrecked and stranded was *A Journal of the Shipwreck and Sufferings of Daniel Foss*, a fictional Robinson Crusoe-type narrative published in two editions during 1816. Supposedly, Foss was the only survivor of a ship that foundered in the Antarctic,* and for five years he lived alone on a barren island.

One of the most widely known and important single narratives was Owen Chase's* *Narrative of the Most Extraordinary and Distressing Shipwreck of the Whaleship* Essex* (1821), from which Herman Melville* borrowed for the climactic scene in *Moby-Dick* (1851). But the story of a whaleship being sunk by a sperm whale was only a part of the Chase narrative. After their ship was sunk, the *Essex* survivors remained at sea in three open boats for over three months. Not only were the bodies of the dead cannibalized, but the cabin boy was shot for food. Melville was given a copy of the Chase narrative by Lemuel Shaw, his father-in-law, but he also encountered the story in several of the anthologies. The Thomas collection included an abbreviated narrative of the *Essex* tragedy, and Durrie and Peck's *The Mariner's Chronicle* contained Captain George Pollard's version of the events, a brief account that had originally been published in London. Other contemporary versions of the *Essex* tragedy were published in 1824 by Thomas Chapple, who remained on Henderson Island, and in 1831 by Daniel Tyerman and George Bennett, who discussed with Pollard the events surrounding the *Essex*.

Perhaps the most important of all antebellum narratives was James Riley's* *An Authentic Narrative of the Loss of the Brig* Commerce (1817). In August 1815 Captain Riley and his crew were shipwrecked off the coast of what is now Western Sahara, and they were finally ransomed to the English consul in Mogadore by Arab traders. Returning to the United States a year later, Riley wrote an extensive account of his shipwreck and captivity, which remained a steady seller for many years.

Riley's text was actually a part of a larger genre of Barbary Coast captivity narratives. From the 1790s to about 1820, a score of narratives, plays, and ballads was published depicting English and American sailors, usually shipwrecked, in captivity along the North African coast. In *Horrors of Slavery; or, The American Tar in Tripoli* (1808), William Ray recounted the year and a half he spent in captivity after his ship foundered on the Barbary Coast. Similarly, in the fictionalized *History of the Captivity and Sufferings of Maria Martin* (1809), Martin related experiences during the five years she was a slave in Algiers after her husband's ship ran aground.

Though occasional accounts were published throughout the remainder of the nineteenth century, and though shipwrecks continued to be featured as a dramatic device in numerous plays and novels, the shipwreck genre declined as the newspaper business burgeoned. For particularly sensational or tragic events, however, shipwreck narratives continued to be printed, both individually and in collections, and thus they continued to remain a common adventure plot in popular literature.

In more serious forms of literature shipwreck narratives exerted an equally profound influence. Scholars of Edgar Allan Poe* have found several sources for his *Narrative of Arthur Gordon Pym of Nantucket** (1838) in the literature of sea disasters, particularly his use of both cannibalism and the maelstrom. Sailors casting lots to see who might be killed and eaten so that those remaining might survive appeared as early as the Janeway and Mather texts and also in *Strange News from Plymouth: Or, a Wonderful and Tragical Relation of a Voyage from the Indies* (London, 1684). Similar incidents can also be found in the narratives about the wrecks of the *Nottingham Galley* (1710), *Peggy* (1765), and the *Essex* (1822), all of which were widely published in the various anthologies. Poe is thought to have used the wreck of the *Tonquin** (1807) as described in Washington Irving's* *Astoria* (1836) and to have borrowed from texts about the shipwrecks of the *Betsy* (1756), the *Centaur* (1782), the *Sidney* (1806), and the *Polly* (1811). As an editor and reviewer, Poe probably received copies of the Thomas, Ellms, and Durrie and Peck anthologies during the 1830s.

Later authors of the nineteenth and twentieth centuries treated shipwrecks in quite different ways. In "A Tragedy of the South Atlantic," a whaling story from Thornton Jenkins Hains'* 1903 collection, *The Strife of the Sea*, the events of the *Essex* tragedy reveal not natural theology but an awe-inspiring, if ruthless, Darwinian world. Stephen Crane's* naturalistic short story "The Open Boat" relates his 1897 experiences during the shipwreck of the *Commodore*, which went down with a shipment of arms bound for Cuba. Morgan Robertson's* 1898 novel, *Futility: Or, the Wreck of the* Titan, eerily predicts a *Titanic**-like disaster when a supposedly unsinkable ship fatally collides with an iceberg. Jack London's* *The Sea-Wolf** (1904) opens with Wolf Larsen's* rescuing Humphrey Van Weyden in a move that critic Bert Bender (in *Sea-Brothers* [1988]) sees as pulling the shipwreck survivor from the world of romanticism to one in which only the fittest survive.

Later, in Archie Binns'* novel *Lightship* (1934), images of Darwinian struggle augment the traditional motif of the sea voyage as quest for knowledge. Using various accounts of the *Nottingham Galley* wreck, Kenneth Roberts* wrote the novel *Boon Island* (1956) as a survival tale, and the book was popular enough to be republished several times in the United States and translated into nine different languages. More recently, the shipwreck that ends Peter Matthiessen's* 1975 novel *Far Tortuga** suggests an awareness of the natural world and the tenuous place of humans within it.

The sinking of the *Titanic** is one of the most enduring inspirations for modern shipwreck literature, most prominently in Walter Lord's *A Night to Remember* (1955), a best-selling novel adapted to an award-winning film (1958). The *Titanic* provided the name and inspiration for both the 1997 Tony-winning Broadway musical and the 1998 Oscar-winning film. Langston Hughes* in *The Book of Negro Folklore* (1958) documents a folk story about an African American* named Shine, who worked on board and survived the disaster. No person of color was allowed to sail on the *Titanic*; world heavyweight boxing champion Jack Johnson, among others, was refused passage.

In the opening chapter of *Cape Cod** (1864), Henry David Thoreau* describes his feelings as he contemplates the 1849 wreck of the Irish brig *St. John*. Studying the wreckage and the bodies of the immigrants, he stoically meditates about the peaceful sea, which had so recently displayed its deadly power. Shipwreck literature from Homer's *Odyssey* to Paul Gallico's *Poseidon Adventure* (1969; film adaptation starring Gene Hackman and Ernest Borgnine, 1972) illustrates the danger of being deceived by the ocean's grand stillness. [*See also* SEA-DELIVERANCE NARRATIVES]

FURTHER READING: Bender, Bert. *Sea Brothers: The Tradition of American Sea Fiction from* Moby-Dick *to the Present.* Philadelphia: U of Pennsylvania P, 1988; Cox, Edward Godfrey. *A Reference Guide to the Literature of Travel.* Seattle: U of Washington P, 1935; Huntress, Keith. *A Checklist of Narratives of Shipwrecks and Disasters at Sea to 1860.* Ames: Iowa State UP, 1979; Huntress, Keith. *Narratives of Shipwrecks and Disasters.* Ames: Iowa State UP, 1774; Landow, George P. *Images of Crisis: Literary Iconology, from 1750 to the Present.* Boston: Routledge and Kegan Paul, 1982; Springer, Haskell, ed. *America and the Sea: A Literary History.* Athens: U of Georgia P, 1995.

Daniel E. Williams and Arnold Schmidt

SHORE LEAVE MUSICALS. A number of American musicals involve sailors on shore leave. The most famous of these is *On the Town* (1944), with music by Leonard Bernstein, lyrics and book by Betty Comden and Adolph Green, and choreography by Jerome Robbins. The original cast featured Comden and Green as Ozzie and Claire and Nancy Walker as Hildy.

Based on the ballet *Fancy Free* (1944) by Bernstein and Robbins, the musical traces the adventures of three sailors on a twenty-four-hour shore leave during World War II. Excitable Ozzie meets effervescent anthropologist Claire at the Museum of Natural History. Naive Chip meets the brassy cabdriver Hildy. Gabey searches for the elusive Miss Turnstiles, a beautiful woman whose picture he has seen on the subway. After an elaborate chase through several nightclubs and Coney Island, the three couples sadly part company at the Brooklyn Navy Yard. They are replaced narratively by three new sailors ready for a day of adventure during the song "New York, New York." A 1949 movie adaptation featured Frank Sinatra, Gene Kelly, Vera Allen, and Betty Garrett; the musical was staged on Broadway in 1999. In 1999 George Wolfe mounted a short-lived production of *On the Town* at the New York Shakespeare Festival.

Hit the Deck! (1927), with music by Vincent Youmans, lyrics by Clifford Grey and Leo Robin, and book by Herbert Fields, was based on Hubert Osborne's successful 1922 "sea-goin' comedy" *Shore Leave*, not to be confused with *Kiss Them for Me* (1945), a play by Luther Davis based on Frederic Wakeman's novel *Shore Leave* (1944). It remained largely faithful to the original, although the heroine's name was changed from Connie to Looloo. Looloo, a successful Newport, Rhode Island, coffee-shop owner, is so smitten with sailor Bilge Smith that she follows him to China and spends her inheritance to salvage a scow for him after his navy career is over. The popular hits from the score were "Sometimes I'm Happy" and "Hallelujah." The musical had an elaborate Hollywood history. The 1930 RKO film *Hit the Deck* was unmemorable. It was revamped in 1936 as *Follow the Fleet,* a vehicle for Fred Astaire and Ginger Rogers that retained the basic plot but substituted a score by Irving Berlin. Finally, a 1955 remake of *Hit the Deck* featured Youmans' original score and a reworked story line.

Dames at Sea (1968) is an affectionate spoof of early Hollywood musicals like *The Gold Diggers of 1933* (1933) and *42nd Street* (1933). The music is by Jim Wise, with lyrics and book by George Haimsohn and Robin Miller. The six actors in the cast play a number of roles, including Broadway star Mona Kent; "Hard Luck" Hennessey, a down-on-his-luck producer; blond chorine Joan; Dick and Lucky, sailors on leave who happen to be an aspiring songwriter and a song-and-dance man; Ruby, an aspiring dancer just off the bus from Centerville, Utah. The characters are brought together through a series of happy coincidences, but their hopes for mounting their show "Dames at Sea" are dashed when their theatre is slated for demolition. They decide to produce the show on Dick and Lucky's battleship: "Dames at Sea" at sea! Mona convinces the Captain, an old boyfriend, to go along with the plan but is forced to drop out of the show when she gets seasick. Ruby steps into the role and becomes an instant star; a similar fortune awaited Bernadette Peters in the Ruby Keeler role. The musical ends with a triple wedding. The score consists of lively spoofs of standard Hollywood and Broadway love songs and production numbers.

Ankles Aweigh (1955) featured music by Sammy Fain, lyrics by Dan Shapiro, and book by Guy Bolton and Eddie Davis. An old-fashioned revue, it featured a workable book that was long on gags and coincidence, a lovely tap-dancing chorus line, funny comedians, and some great songs. The thin plot describes the honeymoon of a Hollywood starlet and a navy pilot that is continually interrupted by the studio and navy top brass. The score included the jaunty "Walk like a Sailor." [*See also* DRAMA OF THE SEA]

FURTHER READING: Comden, Betty, and Adolph Green. *The New York Musicals of Comden and Green*. New York: Applause, 1997; Green, Stanley. *Broadway Musicals; Show by Show*. Milwaukee, WI: Hal Leonard, 1985; Leonard, William Torbert. *Theatre: Stage to Screen to Television, Volume II: M–Z*. Metuchen, NJ: Scarecrow, 1981.

Brian T. Carney

SIEGEL, ROBERT HAROLD (1939–   ). Growing up in the Midwest, Robert Harold Siegel also spent time on Long Island's Jones Beach, cruised the Caribbean,* and currently sails and whale-watches off the coasts of Maine, New Hampshire, and California. His *Whalesong* trilogy is based on his underwater swimming in Lake Michigan. This fantasy cycle chronicles humpback whales and creates a fictional whale culture. Book One, *Whalesong* (1981), recounts the youth and adulthood of a mythical whale, Hruna, who takes a Lonely Cruise and then the Plunge, a mystical journey in which he experiences the Whale of Light. Book Two, *White Whale* (1991), recounts the life of Hruna's offspring, Hralekana-Kolua, whose experiences include establishing friendship with a human boy, mating, and becoming gravely injured attempting to save his friend's ship. In Book Three, *The Ice at the End of the World* (1994), Hralekana-Kolua recovers, battles the mythical Kraken, rejoins his pod, and leads them through danger to new krill beds.

Siegel's poems, many about bodies of water, sailors, whales, and water creatures, appear in the collections *The Beasts & the Elders* (1973) and *In a Pig's Eye* (1980).

Mira Dock

SIGOURNEY, LYDIA [HOWARD HUNTLEY] (1791–1865). Lydia Sigourney, the "sweet singer of Hartford," was one of the most famous literary women in nineteenth-century America. Her interest in the ocean and the sailing life came from her many excursions along the New England coast and a trip to Europe in 1840. She collected her poems about sailors and the ocean in a volume entitled *The Sea and the Sailor* (1845). Other editions were published as *Poems for the Sea* and *Poetry for Seamen*. Meant to be a "companion to the voyager," her poems are reminders of the blessings of home; many of the poems depict the sad farewells and the blissful reunions so common to the seafaring life. Sigourney's poetry also has a strong evangelical theme: it contains many prayers for the safety of sailors and reminds readers that the wonders of the sea are the work of God. [*See also* SEA IMAGERY IN MODERN AND CONTEMPORARY POETRY]

Karen Woods Weierman

SIMMS, WILLIAM GILMORE (1806–1870). William Gilmore Simms was born in Charleston, South Carolina, where he spent most of his life. He was, with the exception of Edgar Allan Poe,* the most significant author of the antebellum South. Beginning as a lawyer, Simms soon turned to his true love, writing, and became a prolific author, penning more than eighty volumes. Two-thirds of these are devoted to poetry, drama, short stories, and novels and romances; the remainder, to history, geography, biography, and miscellaneous nonfiction. A major editor and reviewer, Simms was an outspoken advocate of the South and its institutions, in particular, slavery and secession. His support of these positions permeated his fiction, his essays, and his lectures and won him a term as a state legislator but prevented objective evaluation of Simms' work until well into the twentieth century. Financial losses during the Civil War required increased literary effort, which probably hastened his death.

Simms wrote almost 2,000 poems, the majority dealing with nature. Because he was a romantic and a Charlestonian, Simms used the sea as his subject for some; sea imagery appears occasionally in others. His most ambitious undertaking in this genre, the long, dramatic poem *Atalantis, a Story of the Sea: In Three Parts* (1832), tells of a sea fairy who escapes the advances of a sea demon and marries a mortal. Critics find the work heavily indebted to Lord Byron.

Simms' one novel-length work of the sea is *The Cassique of Kiawah: A Colonial Romance* (1859). The story, set in seventeenth-century South Carolina, recounts both life aboard a pirate* ship and American Indian warfare. Although one of his favorites, the romance is largely unknown because it was omitted from the definitive edition of Simms' works, first published in the 1850s and reprinted several times thereafter. [*See also* PALATINE]

Norman E. Stafford

SISTER WATER (1993). Nancy Willard's (1936–   ) novel depicts the lives of Jessie and Henry Woolman and their daughters, Martha and Ellen, in the Great Lakes* region. Devastated by her husband's death, Ellen is courted by wealthy developer Harvey Mack, who wants to acquire her father's property. Sam Theopolis, hired as companion for the widowed and confused Jessie, eases into the family's life. When Sam is charged with the drowning death of an unidentified "water woman," Martha's son-in-law, Elmer, defends him. Things took grim for Sam until two Pawquacha Indians present new evidence, and surprising outcomes result.

Willard employs water imagery to link nature and spirit, the living and the dead. Skilled in water occupations from ancestral times, the Pawquachas of Drowning Bear, Wisconsin, have access to the spirit world through springs feeding the Huron River and Lake Michigan. When needed, they bring evidence from the dead to the living. If threatened, they change into river creatures. A network of underground streams, representing the invisible unity of all things, connects the Great Lakes. Henry Woolman's protection of one such stream flowing through his Ann Arbor basement museum first draws Jessie to him. In contrast, Harvey Mack hopes to bury the stream under a sumptuous mall. The "water woman" is associated with death, and Sam's openhearted exchange of gifts with her in the graveyard leads to his mistaken arrest for murder. It was Harvey who, having ignored her warning appearance in his aquarium videotape, has a drunken encounter with her that causes her death and ultimately will result in his own. Ellen learns that the Pawquacha water woman has stories to mend hearts, and with her mythic aid, she envisions a mighty river. On one bank, her father helps her husband, Mike, upstream toward death. On the other, children throng downstream into life. Ellen joins the children.

Janet Ray Edwards

SLAVE NARRATIVES. Beginning in the eighteenth century and flourishing through the three decades before the Civil War, autobiographical narratives written by freed or fugitive slaves depict both the literal and metaphorical significance of the sea in the lives of their authors.

Early narratives by Briton Hammon (1760) and Olaudah Equiano* (1789), while primarily documentary in their approach, also suggest metaphorical possibilities. (Within this entry, with one exception, specific titles of the narratives are omitted because they are all lengthy and can be easily accessed using the word "narrative.") Hammon's narrative recounts his shipwreck* en route from Plymouth to Jamaica, his eventual escape from Havana to London, his service aboard several British naval and merchant ships, and his final return to New England. Adopting the pattern of the sea-deliverance* tale, a popular colonial form of spiritual autobiography, Hammon interprets his deliverance from shipwreck and his safe return home as a sign of Providence.

Equiano similarly portrays his safe return from many sea voyages as a sign of God's favor. His narrative is the first, and one of only a few, to describe the horrors of the Middle Passage. With his first owner, a British naval lieutenant, Equiano spent six years aboard gunships in the Mediterranean Sea; for his next owner, a Philadelphia merchant, Equiano worked aboard several ships in the West Indies trade. After purchasing his freedom and settling in London, he embarked on additional voyages to the Mediterranean, the West Indies, Greenland with the 1773 Phipps Expedition, and Honduras. While his narrative never romanticizes the sea, it frequently credits his independence and status in life to the knowledge and skills he gained aboard ships. By invoking religious imagery to portray his life as a seagoing pilgrimage, he further asserts the value of his autobiography.

The function of the sea as an avenue for advancement or escape emerges in several nineteenth-century narratives as well. The account of Charles Ball (1836), for example, describes his work as both cook and seaman in the American navy, which gave him the knowledge, as well as the inspiration offered by free black seamen with whom he worked, to escape to Philadelphia aboard a coastal trader. Moses Grandy's narrative (1844) similarly documents how the sea provided a means of escape. As a slave bargeman in the tidewater region, Grandy was hired out to run the British blockades that precipitated the War of 1812. By splitting his earnings with his owner, Grandy finally was able to buy his freedom. After moving to Boston, he shipped out on several coastwise voyages and two trips to the Mediterranean, thereby earning enough money to purchase his wife's freedom as well. Yet another account of escape by sea appears in the narrative of Harriet Jacobs (1861), who, after a seven-year confinement in a dark attic hideaway, finally escaped her master by bribing the captain of a Northern-bound vessel. Her description of the voyage is brief but memorable, recalling her exhilaration as the ship set sail on Chesapeake Bay.

The image of ships sailing out of Chesapeake Bay is central to Frederick Douglass'* *Narrative of the Life of Frederick Douglass an American Slave* (1845), the most familiar example of the genre. In his famous apostrophe to the ships, Douglass fashions the sea and the outward-bound vessels upon it into an emblem of liberty. Combining popular romantic imagery of the unfettered ocean as symbolic of natural freedom with patriotic sentiment that celebrated the country's golden age of sail, Douglass employs romantic maritime nationalism to advance his appeal for the liberation of fellow African Americans.*

Narratives by Lunsford Lane (1842), Henry "Box" Brown (1849), James W. C. Pennington (1849), and Henry Bibb (1850) also use romantic sea imagery to endorse abolitionism and resistance. Rather than documenting actual voyages, these writers go to sea metaphorically, using imagery of the wild, unruly sea to suggest slaves' natural yearning for freedom and elemental right to resistance. Literal slave mutiny* is addressed in Solomon Northup's narrative (1853), which recounts his aborted mutiny plot on a coastwise slaver.

Except for Equiano's early account, John Thompson's narrative (1856) provides the most extensive treatment of the sea in the slave narrative tradition. Combining literal experience with seagoing metaphor, Thompson crafts a strong indictment of slavery and endorsement of slaves' yearning for freedom. Fearing pursuers after he had escaped by land, Thompson took to the sea as a cook on a whaling vessel. Drawing on this experience, his narrative describes in concrete detail the tools and techniques of the whaling industry. Thompson also turns this cetological material to metaphysical use. Adapting the tradition employed by Hammon and Equiano, he ends his narrative with a sermon about a Christian seafarer on a metaphorical ship whose rigging and instruments provide the means of safe passage from earth to heaven. Fusing this nautical image of a Christian's pilgrimage with that of a fugitive slave's progress, Thompson ends his narrative with a metaphysical conceit proclaiming both spiritual and political liberation. [*See also BLAKE; MIDDLE PASSAGE; SEA-DELIVERANCE NARRATIVES*]

FURTHER READING: Andrews, William L. *To Tell a Free Story: The First Century of Afro-American Autobiography, 1760–1865.* Urbana: U of Illinois P, 1988; Bolster, W. Jeffrey. *Black Jacks: African American Seamen in the Age of Sail.* Cambridge: Harvard UP, 1997; Farr, James Barker. *Black Odyssey: The Seafaring Traditions of Afro-Americans.* New York: Peter Lang, 1989; Malloy, Mary. *African Americans in the Maritime Trades: A Guide to Resources in New England.* Sharon, MA: Kendall Whaling Museum, 1990; Schultz, Elizabeth. "African-American Literature," *America and the Sea: A Literary History.* Ed. Haskell Springer. Athens: U of Georgia P, 1995, 233–59.

Brad S. Born

SLAVE SHIP (1966). Written by Amiri Baraka [LeRoi Jones] (1934–   ), the play *Slave Ship* was first produced by the Spirit House Movers and Players Theatre Company in 1967 at the Chelsea Theatre, New York City. It traces the historical Middle Passage taken by slaves from West Africa to the New World and their experiences once they arrive on American soil. The first half of the play is set in the hold of a slave ship on the Middle Passage. The inhabitants of the hold curse each other and curse the African gods, and some even kill themselves and their own children. After their arrival in the New World, the slaves participate in Nat Turner's uprising but are defeated when Tom, an old plantation slave, betrays the uprising for a pork chop from his master. After being defeated, the slaves regroup and hold a celebration, which involves a mixture of Yoruba chanting and dancing, in which the audience is invited to participate. The severed head of Tom is thrown into the midst of the revels, exciting the slaves to greater exuberance and frenzy. The play briefly shifts back to the hold of the ship so the audience can hear the "killed white voice" of their captors.

Baraka evokes the sensation of the sea through sound effects and the "sea smells" simulated through the use of incense. The shouts of the white sailors and the ship's captain establish the ship's route on the Middle Passage. [*See also* AFRICAN AMERICAN LITERATURE OF THE SEA; DRAMA OF THE SEA; *MIDDLE PASSAGE*; SLAVE NARRATIVES]

David Jortner

[SLEEPER, JOHN SHERBURNE], "HAWSER MARTINGALE"

(1794–1878). An author and journalist from New England, John Sherburne Sleeper first went to sea in 1809 as a cabin boy and assumed his first command in 1821. By 1825 he was captain of an East Indiaman, and he spent much of his career in merchant service out of Boston. After retiring from the sea in 1830, he began working in the printing industry, publishing and editing several newspapers in Lowell and Boston. Using the pseudonym "Hawser Martingale," Sleeper published several books that fictionalized his adventures at sea. His early stories, serialized in the newspapers he edited, focused on the deadly combination of drunkenness and mutiny* at sea; given the opportunity, Sleeper rarely failed to preach moral reform and temperance. When he avoided moralizing, Sleeper's humor could illustrate the vitality and comedic aspects of life at sea.

Sleeper's first book, *Tales of the Ocean* (1842), is a collection of stories that draw from his time as a sailor. One story, "Impressment of Seamen," was the source for the incident in Herman Melville's* *White-Jacket** (1850) in which White Jacket, threatened with flogging, considered hurtling himself at Captain Claret and sending them both into the ocean. In Sleeper's story, the flogged sailor actually threw himself and the captain overboard. Sleeper's other works include the autobiographical *Jack in the Forecastle* (1860) and the novel *Mark Rowland* (1867), which includes the story of a sperm whale's ramming a whaler.

Peter H. McCracken

SLOCUM, JOSHUA

(1844–1909?). Joshua Slocum, the first single-handed circumnavigator and author of the classic *Sailing Alone around the World* (1900), was born in Nova Scotia. At sixteen he left home to work as a deepwater sailor and by 1869 commanded his first vessel. In 1871 he married Virginia Walker, who, along with their children, sailed with him until she died in 1884. About two years later he married his cousin Henrietta ("Hettie") Endicott, and for their wedding trip the couple went to sea on the *Aquidneck*, which he owned. On this inauspicious voyage, Captain Slocum killed a man in putting down a mutiny,* and the uninsured ship was wrecked in Brazil and was a total loss. From its wreckage, however, Slocum built a thirty-five-foot "canoe" and sailed the *Liberdade* 5,500 miles to Washington, D.C. Hettie never again accompanied him to sea.

By that time the age of sail was almost over, as was Slocum's career as a merchant captain on sailing vessels. He tried authorship, publishing *The Voyage of the* Liberdade in 1890 but making no money on it. When in 1892 a retired whaling captain gave him the hulk of an old oyster sloop named *Spray*, Slocum rebuilt it and tried fishing for a time. By 1894 he had published another book, *Voyage of the* Destroyer *from New York to Brazil*, recounting the sad story of his commission to deliver to Brazilian authorities an iron gunboat built by John Ericsson, designer of the Civil War *Monitor*.* The boat sank in harbor in Bahia, and Slocum went unpaid. The book, too, was a financial failure.

His next venture, the boldest till then, was to take the *Spray* on the world's first single-handed circumnavigation.* In April 1895 he left Boston harbor, reportedly with only $1.50 in cash. Sailing without a chronometer and altering his planned course at times to avoid various threats, including piracy, Captain Slocum crossed and recrossed the Atlantic and struggled through the Straits of Magellan into the Pacific. Thence he sailed to Australia, through the Coral Sea and the Indian Ocean, around the Cape of Good Hope, and, crossing the Atlantic once again, ended his 46,000-mile voyage in the United States on 27 June 1898.

Sailing Alone around the World, serialized in 1899–1900 and published as a book in 1900, is a classic of nautical literature not only because of its pioneering tale of seamanship but more so because of Slocum's distinctive character and voice. His practical realism about the sea and its dangers and his immense, but understated, skill as a seaman, combined with his appreciation not only for the *Spray* but for natural and human beauty, make his account engaging to sailors and armchair adventurers alike. An easy literary concord results from his remarkable competence with both tiller and pen. Slocum's love of his vessel, narrative skill, modesty, honesty, realism, and dry wit account for the book's reprinting in every decade since its appearance. Once he had shown the appeal of what he had done, others followed in similar ventures and wrote about them, making Slocum the inaugurator of a genre: solo circumnavigation accounts. Not only was *he* imitated, but many replicas of *Spray* have been built.

Despite excellent proceeds from the book and from lecturing, Slocum was not happy. He made solitary trips in the *Spray* to winter in the Caribbean.* Among the incidents of his life at this time was a charge of rape during a lecture stop in New Jersey. It was medically disproved, but he spent over a month in jail. Not long afterward he delivered a rare Caribbean orchid to President Theodore Roosevelt.

Finally, at age sixty-five, Slocum made perhaps his boldest plan: to sail the *Spray* to South America, up the Orinoco and Rio Negro, to the still mysterious sources of the Amazon, down the Amazon to the sea, and back to New England. He left in stormy weather; neither he nor his boat was ever seen again. A court finally declared him officially dead as of the day he set sail: 14 November 1909.

FURTHER READING: Slocum, Victor. *Capt. Joshua Slocum: The Life and Voyages of America's Best Known Sailor.* New York: Sheridan House, 1950; Spencer, Ann. *Alone at Sea.* New York: Doubleday, 1998; Teller, Walter M. *Joshua Slocum.* New Brunswick, NJ: Rutgers UP, 1971; Teller, Walter M. *The Voyages of Joshua Slocum.* New Brunswick, NJ: Rutgers UP, 1958.

Haskell Springer

SMITH, EDGAR NEWBOLD (1926–   ). A descendant of a maritime family, Edgar Newbold Smith graduated from the U.S. Naval Academy in 1948. Best known as a collector of naval prints, Smith compiled *American Naval Broadsides*: A Collection of Early Naval Prints, 1745–1815* (1974). A collector's catalog of 117 prints accompanied by a chronological narrative, the work focuses on the American navy under sail, with particular emphasis on events of the American Revolution, the early federal period, and the War of 1812.

In 1976 Smith, an avid sailor, undertook an unprecedented journey to the high Arctic* on his forty-three-foot sloop *Reindeer*, with a crew of six. They sailed north from Reykjavik, Iceland, to their northernmost destination, Moffen Island, a small atoll inhabited by walruses at 80° north latitude, which brought them to within 600 miles of the North Pole. The homeward journey retraced the route taken by the Vikings past the eastern coast of Greenland through Denmark Strait, with its treacherous fogs, pack ice, and violent squalls. *Reindeer* was the first American sailing yacht to navigate the strait. *Down Denmark Strait* (1980) is Smith's vivid account of the 10,500-mile journey.

Brian Sateriale

SMITH, JOHN (1580–1631). Although born in Lincolnshire, England, Captain John Smith initiated many traditions in American literature, among them geography, autobiography, and history.

A True Relation (1608), his earliest account of his experiences in the Chesapeake Bay region of Maryland and Virginia, is the first book in English written entirely in America. Besides recounting his Virginian explorations in several works, he reported on a 1614 voyage to the coast of New England (which he named) in *A Description of New England* (1616). His magnum opus, *The Generall Historie of Virginia, New-England, and the Summer Isles* (1624), an extended compilation of earlier writings by Smith and others, was followed by a work of exceptional value to students of early American seafaring: *A Sea Grammar* (1627). An expansion of Smith's own *An Accidence or the Path-way to Experience Necessary for All Young Sea-men* (1626), *A Sea Grammar* is based largely on a manuscript glossary of maritime terms by Henry Mainwaring and is the earliest handbook for seamen in English. Like Smith's other writings, *A Sea Grammar* is infused with the personality of the great adventurer and proponent of New World colonization. His experiments with naval dialogue foreshadow a demand for realism in maritime language and seamanship, while his own character provided a ready-made prototype for the larger-than-life romantic sailor-hero that has dominated American literature of the sea since its inception.

At the time of his death, Smith was working on a book he described as "my history of the sea." If any of the manuscript exists, it remains undiscovered. Smith's extant writings have been edited and introduced by Philip Barbour in *The Complete Works of Captain John Smith (1580–1631)*, 3 vols. (1986). A useful synopsis of Smith's life and works is Everett Emerson's *Captain John Smith* (1993).

R. D. Madison

SNIDER, CHARLES HENRY JEREMIAH (1879–1971). A Canadian* born in Sherwood, Ontario, Charles Snider first sailed the Great Lakes* at age eleven and later worked in its merchant marine. During a fifty-year career at the *Toronto Telegram*, Snider researched, explored, and became a master historian of the Great Lakes, even navigating, as his own skipper, the routes of the early Lakes explorer René Robert Cavelier, de la Salle. Noted for locating eleven vessels sunk in the War of 1812, Snider wrote extensively on that era. His knowledge of marine craft, terms, technology, and history permeates his work.

Snider's *The Story of the* Nancy *and Other Eighteen-Twelvers* (1926) presents the Lakes' darkly mysterious, yet romantically picturesque, nature. Other works include a weekly newspaper column, "Schooner Days," *In the Wake of the Eighteen-Twelvers* (1913), *Under the Red Jack* (1928), and *Tarry Breeks and Velvet Garters* (1958), a fictional Great Lakes adventure set during the days of French sail.

Donald P. Curtis

SNOW, EDWARD ROWE (1902–1982). A prolific producer of maritime history and lore for popular consumption, Edward Rowe Snow was born in Winthrop, Massachusetts. He graduated from Harvard University and earned a master's degree in history from Boston University. Among his ninety-seven books are *Great Storms and Famous Shipwrecks* of the New England Coast* (1943), *Famous New England Lighthouses* (1945), *Great*

Gales and Dire Disasters (1952), *The Vengeful Sea* (1956), *Piracy,* * Mu-tiny,* * and Murder* (1959), *New England Sea Tragedies* (1960), *True Tales of Buried Treasure* (1960), *True Tales of Terrible Shipwrecks* (1963), *Astounding Tales of the Sea* (1966), *Incredible Mysteries and Legends of the Sea* (1967), *Great Atlantic Adventures* (1970), *The Islands of Boston Harbor, 1630–1971* (1971), and *Ghosts,* * Gales and Gold* (1972).

Many of his titles include stories recycled from earlier books or from news-paper columns he wrote for Boston-area newspapers. Well known in New England as a raconteur, Snow did not hesitate to tell his own story in his books. He was proud of his seafaring ancestry and included a chapter about his mother in his book *Women of the Sea* (1962). The daughter of Captain Joshua Nickerson Rowe, Alice Rowe Snow spent some fifteen years at sea with her parents aboard the schooner *Village Belle*, the brig *J. Bickmore*, and the bark *Russell*. As the "Flying Santa," Snow began, in 1936, to fly Christmas presents to lighthouse keepers around New England, many of whom figured in his books. The character of the hack historian Leslie Ev-erett Dove in Peter Landesman's *The Raven** (1995) is modeled on Edward Rowe Snow. [*See also* WOMEN AT SEA]

Mary Malloy

SNYDER, GARY [SHERMAN] (1930–   ). Born in San Francisco, Gary Snyder grew up among the forests, mountains, and shores of the Pacific Northwest.* A graduate of Reed College (1951), Snyder first went to sea during the summer of 1948 and later spent eight months from September 1957 to April 1958 as an engine wiper on the oil tanker *Sappa Creek* as it roamed the Persian Gulf, the Mediterranean, and the Pacific. During the late 1950s and most of the 1960s, Snyder studied Zen Buddhism in Japan, beginning a lifetime of devotion to Buddhist principles.

A prominent voice in the San Francisco renaissance and the modern eco-logical movement, Snyder has published sixteen books of poetry and prose to date. Reflecting a lifetime of thought and writing, *Mountains and Rivers without End* (1996) gathers thirty-nine sections composed over a forty-year period into a long poem in the tradition of Walt Whitman,* Ezra Pound,* and William Carlos Williams.* Inspired in large part by Snyder's awareness of the planetary water cycle and by his Buddhist belief that everything finally interconnects, *Mountains and Rivers* interweaves prehistory, geology, Na-tive American culture, East Asian aesthetics, ecology, and global mythology into a major statement of wisdom and compassion. Many sections are awash in intermingled land- and waterscapes: among others, "Boat of a Million Years" moves among the seas and shores of the Middle East; "Haida Gwai, North Coast . . ." describes the chaotic juncture of land, river, and ocean at Naikoon Beach in the Queen Charlotte Islands; and "Afloat" glides along in an ocean kayak where the sea, sky, and ice meet in Glacier Bay, Alaska. Throughout the long poem, mountains interpenetrate with rivers and lands with waters. Desert landscapes reveal ancient seas that preexisted there. Beneath the concrete of modern cities ancient watercourses still run.

On the English Department faculty at the University of California at Davis since 1985, Snyder lives with his family in the watershed of the South Yuba River in the Sierra foothills of northern California. [*See also* SEA IMAGERY IN MODERN AND CONTEMPORARY POETRY]

Anthony Hunt

SOLO CIRCUMNAVIGATIONS. *See* CIRCUMNAVIGATIONS AND BLUE-WATER PASSAGES.

SOMERS. A naval brig of 266 tons, named after naval hero Richard Somers, the U.S.S. *Somers* (built 1842) was the site of an important mutiny* in 1842, the consequences of which were that three Americans were hanged from her yardarm by command of Captain Alexander Slidell Mackenzie.* On 26 November 1842, the *Somers* was returning from her second cruise, a training mission of naval apprentices, when Mackenzie was informed by his first lieutenant Guert Gansevoort (Herman Melville's* first cousin) that there was apparently a plot by a small group of men to take over the vessel and turn her into a pirate.* The ringleader of the alleged conspiracy was eighteen-year-old acting midshipman Philip Spencer, the son of John C. Spencer, President Tyler's secretary of war. Although he at first treated the story with ridicule, Mackenzie arrested Spencer later that same day. When confronted, Spencer admitted to speaking of taking over the ship but claimed it was in jest. Over the next two days some suspicious incidents on board, including a mysterious rush aft and gatherings of men speaking in low tones, convinced Mackenzie that a full-blown mutiny was indeed evolving and that immediate action needed to be taken. On 1 December 1842, Mackenzie executed Spencer along with boatswain's mate Samuel Cromwell and seaman Elisha Small.

The *Somers* arrived in New York two weeks later, and the hangings became the subject of intense national discussion. Amid wildly conflicting reports, Mackenzie was praised or condemned with equal vigor by newspapers in New York, Boston, and Washington. His critics, among them Spencer's father and James Gordon Bennett of the *New York Herald*, were outraged that Mackenzie had engaged in such extreme action when, in fact, no overt act of mutiny ever occurred, no trial was held to determine the validity of the accusation, and no chance was given the three accused men to refute the charges against them. According to some, young Philip Spencer might have been engaged in an elaborate role-playing game. Mackenzie's supporters, who included sailor-lawyer Richard Henry Dana Jr.,* Horace Greeley of the *New York Daily Tribune*, and other members of the Whig press who supported a strong navy to combat piracy,* commended Mackenzie for acting swiftly and even heroically. A naval court-martial trial was convened in New York the following February, during which Mackenzie stood accused of murder, oppression, conduct unbecoming an officer, and other specifications. Witnesses were heard, and Mackenzie submitted his own written version of events. He was eventually acquitted on all counts.

The verdict did not put the matter to rest. The trial transcript, *Proceedings of the Naval Court Martial in the Case of Alexander Slidell Mackenzie*, was printed in 1844 with an eighty-page review by James Fenimore Cooper.* Cooper, once a navy man himself and at that time a naval historian as well as renowned author of the sea and the American frontier, concluded that Mackenzie acted with needless haste and panic and had been taken in by dubious impressions rather than the solid, verifiable facts. The *Somers* incident eventually made its way into some of America's enduring literature. Herman Melville, who felt a warm family loyalty toward his cousin Gansevoort, refers to the *Somers* affair in *White-Jacket** (1850), *Billy Budd** (1924), and his poem "Bridegroom Dick" (1888). The *Somers* continued her service in the navy until 1846, when, in a squall off the coast of Veracruz during the Mexican War, she sank, losing thirty-nine men.

FURTHER READING: Egan, Hugh. "Introduction," *Proceedings of the Naval Court Martial in the Case of Alexander Slidell Mackenzie*. Delmar, NY: Scholars' Facsimiles and Reprints, 1992; Hayford, Harrison, ed. *The* Somers *Mutiny Affair*. Englewood Cliffs, NJ: Prentice-Hall, 1959; McFarland, Philip. *Sea Dangers: The Affair of the* Somers. New York: Schocken, 1985.

Hugh Egan

SOUTH PACIFIC (1949). The musical *South Pacific* began life as *Tales of the South Pacific* (1947), a collection of interwoven short stories by James Michener* based on his experiences in World War II. The volume opens with a detailed description of vast ocean and gracefully nodding coconut palms, and its concern throughout is with both the beauty and the peril of the sea. The collection won the Pulitzer Prize in 1948.

Broadway producer and director Joshua Logan brought the stories to the attention of Richard Rodgers and Oscar Hammerstein II, who fashioned the material into the musical *South Pacific*. The team combined three of Michener's tales: "Our Heroine," which details the romance between Nellie Forbush, a nurse from Little Rock, Arkansas, and French planter Emile de Becque; "Fo' Dolla," which introduces the character Bloody Mary and tells of the tragic love affair between her daughter Liat and Lieutenant Joe Cable; and "A Boar's Tooth," which features the comic exploits of Seabee Luther Billis. The stories are connected by both plot and theme. Nellie and Luther are friends who star in the Thanksgiving show, and Cable and de Becque go on a dangerous mission together to escape their romantic troubles. Both romances are hampered by prejudice. Nellie initially turns away from Emile when she discovers he has had children by a Polynesian woman; Joe realizes he can never marry Liat.

The original production starred Mary Martin as Nellie, Ezio Pinza as Emile, and Juanita Hall as Bloody Mary. The score features such Rodgers and Hammerstein classics as "There Is Nothing like a Dame," "Some Enchanted Evening," "I'm Gonna Wash That Man Right outta My Hair," "Bali Hai," and "You've Got to Be Carefully Taught," a powerful protest against racial prejudice. Under Logan's direction, the staging was noted for using cinematic dissolves between scenes. The musical won the Pulitzer Prize and eight Tony awards. Also under Logan's direction, it was adapted into a film starring Mitzi Gaynor and Rossano Brazzi (1958). Although the stage production was able to summon up the sea only through the dazzling costume and set designs by Motley and Jo Mielziner, the movie's sumptuous cinematography takes full advantage of the South Pacific setting, reinforcing the beauty and danger of the tropical locale, especially the lure of the exotic and elusive island of Bali Hai. [*See also* DRAMA OF THE SEA]

Brian T. Carney

SPARTINA (1989). Writer John Casey (1939–   ) spent four years on tiny Fox Island in Narragansett Bay, Rhode Island, an experience on which his novel *Spartina* is based. But Casey, graduate of Harvard University, Harvard Law School, and the Iowa Writers' Workshop at the University of Iowa, is not Dick Pierce, the fisherman-protagonist of this book.

Pierce digs for clams, sets lobster pots, and works aboard other men's vessels while trying to earn enough money to complete the building of his own fishing boat, the *Spartina-May*. He is a native of southern Rhode Island who is left with only one acre after his family's land was sold to pay his father's hospital bills. Wracked with bitterness, Pierce resents the building of summer cottages on land formerly his and verbally attacks many of the summer people and pleasure sailors. The novel concerns not only the building of Pierce's boat but also his affair with Elsie Buttrick, the manipulative daughter of summer people who has come back to Rhode Island to work as a Natural Resources officer, and his relationship with his oft-ignored and sullen wife, May Pierce.

Casey planned *Spartina*, the winner of the 1989 National Book Award, as part of a projected "Rhode Island trilogy," to consist of two novels and a collection of nine short stories. The novel evokes Rhode Island in the days when Galilee, Rhode Island, was a major fishing port, and people made their living from the sea. Although published in 1989, it depicts Rhode Island more as Casey experienced it when he first moved to Fox Island in 1968. The major metaphor of the novel is spartina, the "smart grass," which, according to Casey, closes itself against the salt of the salt marshes but allows in the water. By the end of the novel, Pierce likens himself to spartina, shutting himself against bitterness.

Mary K. Bercaw Edwards

STEAMING TO BAMBOOLA: THE WORLD OF A TRAMP FREIGHTER (1982). In his author's note to *Steaming to Bamboola*, Christopher T. Buckley (1948–   ), son of William F. Buckley Jr.,* writes, "The ship, the people, and the events are real. The names of the ship and her crew were changed." Buckley's book reveals his vision of America's seafarers during the Vietnam War, misfits of the late 1970s and early 1980s who go to sea to escape problems on land. He shows us the alcohol, drugs, sex, and violence of their lives as they work aboard the fictional tramp steamer *Columbianna* in America's "Fourth Arm of Defense" during those turbulent years. His view of the ship's crew is marred by his attention primarily to deck personnel; we see very little of the men in the engine room. The character sketches of the crew are interspersed with short studies of some institutions (Sailor's Snug Harbor), leading personalities (union president Paul Hall), and history connected with the U.S. Merchant Marine.

James F. Millinger

STEINBECK, JOHN [ERNST] (1902–1968). John Steinbeck, winner of the 1962 Nobel Prize in literature, was born in Salinas, California. As a child, he divided his time between his family's home in the rich agricultural land of the Salinas valley and their summer cottage in Pacific Grove, where he spent many happy hours exploring the shoreline of Monterey Bay. As a writer, he divided his talents between these two environments, the California land and his "home ocean." To the general public, Steinbeck is best known for his great social reform novel of the Dust Bowl disaster, *The Grapes of Wrath* (1939; film adaptation 1940), and for stories of California farmworkers and ranchers such as the play-novelette *Of Mice and Men* (1937; film adaptations 1939, 1992) and the short story "The Red Pony" (1937; film adaptation 1949). To aficionados of sea literature, he is best known as the coauthor, with marine biologist Edward F. Ricketts,* of the nonfiction work *Sea of Cortez* (1941) and as author of the Monterey novels *Cannery Row* (1945; film adaptation 1982) and *Sweet Thursday* (1954), though his sea connections are far more extensive than these three works.

Steinbeck attended Stanford University sporadically from 1919 until 1925. In between bouts at school he moved about restlessly, working with Mexican laborers on a sugar beet plantation, helping to build irrigation canals and dams, and sailing from Los Angeles to New York City on board the freighter *Katrina*, with stops in Panama City and Havana. Steinbeck never completed a college degree but majored in English and took a series of creative writing courses. He also pursued his interest in the sea by enrolling for a 1923 summer session at Hopkins Marine Station, studying marine ecology and participating in field trips and collecting expeditions. After leaving Stanford, Steinbeck took a job as caretaker of a Lake Tahoe cabin in order to write full-time.

In 1929 his parents gave him and his soon-to-be wife, Carol Henning, use of the beach house in Pacific Grove rent-free. The next ten years would be Steinbeck's most productive decade as an author. His first book, *Cup of Gold* (1929), was a romantic historical novel about the adventures of the buccaneer Sir Henry Morgan, drawn, in part, from Steinbeck's Caribbean* experiences aboard the *Katrina*. *Tortilla Flat* (1935; film adaptation 1942), a comic novel about the lives of poor Mexican American *paisanos* in the coastal town of Monterey, brought Steinbeck widespread acclaim. Several short story collections and the play-novelette *Of Mice and Men* were also products of these years.

The Pacific Grove years were dynamic, in part, because of Steinbeck's intense and influential friendship with marine biologist Ricketts, whose laboratory and biological supply house were not far from the author's cottage. A pioneering early ecologist and author of the classic handbook *Between Pacific Tides* (1939), Ricketts contributed greatly to the biological and ecological cast of Steinbeck's thought, just as the "salon" atmosphere of his lab contributed to the creative energy at large in the Monterey area during the 1930s. Steinbeck would later immortalize Ricketts as "Doc" in the novels *Cannery Row* and its sequel *Sweet Thursday*, both bittersweet comedies capturing the magical quality of these years pursuing art, philosophy, beer, women, and marine biology by the sea.

As the Great Depression deepened, so did Steinbeck's commitment to the plight of migrant workers exploited by California's almost feudal system of agriculture, with *In Dubious Battle* (1936) and the Pulitzer Prize-winning *The Grapes of Wrath* the most notable results. *Grapes* also brought Steinbeck enough wealth to finance, for himself and Ricketts, a biological expedition to collect marine organisms from the intertidal zones of Mexico's Gulf of California, also known as the Sea of Cortez. In 1940 Steinbeck and Ricketts chartered Captain Tony Berry and his purse seiner the *Western Flyer* for six weeks of exploring the Gulf faunal provinces. The resulting "voyage of discovery," Steinbeck and Ricketts' *Sea of Cortez* (1941), is an enduring contribution both to literature of the sea and to marine biology. The first half of the book, "Log from the Sea of Cortez" (published separately under that title in 1951), is a narrative account of the expedition combining marine biology, ecology, mysticism, humor, adventure, and speculative metaphysics. The second half is an annotated phyletic catalog and bibliography of the marine fauna encountered, including more than fifty species unknown to science and significant range extensions for many known organisms.

With the outbreak of World War II, Steinbeck shifted his energies to writing propaganda for the war effort. His saltiest endeavor was a story line for a 1944 Alfred Hitchcock film titled *Lifeboat*, treating a cross-section of Americans (a female war correspondent, a millionaire businessman, various merchant seamen including an African American* and a socialist labor organizer, an army nurse, a young mother and baby) thrown together in an open boat with a German submarine commander after both their freighter and the submarine sink in an Atlantic convoy fray. Shortly after completing the screen story, Steinbeck went to work as a war correspondent in North Africa and Europe; his dispatches are collected in *Once There Was a War* (1958). He also divorced his first wife and married Gywndolyn Conger. These distractions may be why Steinbeck abandoned his open boat story to Hitchcock and his screenwriters, who would publish their version of "Lifeboat" in *Collier's* (13 November 1943). The film (1944), starring Tallulah Bankhead and William Bendix, was a popular success, but Steinbeck was outraged both by Hitchcock's turning his black character, a man of "dignity, purpose, and personality," into "a stock comedy Negro" and by the film's swipes at the merchant seamen's union.

When the war was over, Steinbeck turned his attention to the sea once more, publishing *The Pearl* (1947; filmed as *La Perla*, 1945), a parable garnered from his Sea of Cortez expedition, about a Mexican oyster fisherman who finds a valuable pearl that brings evil to his family. Working with Ricketts, Steinbeck planned a scientific expedition to the Queen Charlotte Islands off the coast of British Columbia, but Ricketts' untimely death in 1948 spelled an end to their collaboration. In addition to the Cannery Row novels, Steinbeck memorialized Ricketts as "Friend Ed" in the play-novelette *Burning Bright* (1950), where he appears as captain of a "little freighter" like *Katrina*.

After purchasing a summer home in the historic whaling community of Sag Harbor, New York, with his third wife, Elaine Anderson Scott, Steinbeck produced *The Winter of Our Discontent* (1961; filmed for television, 1983), his only Atlantic seaboard novel. Set in a fictional town called Old Harbor, this novel treats the moral decline of Ethan Hawley, a grocer's assistant descended from whaling captains, and with him the moral decline of contemporary America. Steinbeck's *Travels with Charley in Search of America* (1962), a nonfiction account of his drive across the United States with his pet poodle, helped to bring Steinbeck the Nobel Prize in that year. Its memorable maritime scenes include Steinbeck's opening battle at Sag Harbor to secure his twenty-two-foot cabin cruiser *Fayre Eleyne* in the teeth of Hurricane Donna and his reunion with the Pacific after the cross-country drive.

Steinbeck never lost his interest in marine science. In 1961 he was invited by oceanographer Willard Bascom to become historian for the Mohole Project, an attempt to drill a hole from the bottom of the sea through to the earth's mantle. Steinbeck accompanied geologists, petrologists, zoologists, oceanographers, and engineers aboard the drilling barge *CUSS I* off San Diego and wrote about the experience for *Life* magazine ("High Drama of Bold Thrust through Ocean Floor," 14 April 1961) and *Popular Science* ("Let's Go after Neglected Treasures beneath the Sea," September 1966). Although the Mohole Project was unsuccessful in reaching the earth's mantle, it did result in new technology for exploiting undersea mineral wealth. Such interests were not incompatible with Steinbeck's concerns about marine conservation: overfishing, poisoning of nearshore waters with sewage and industrial runoff from rivers, and dumping atomic waste in the sea. These subjects are discussed in a number of his works, including his last published book, the essay collection *America and Americans* (1966).

At Steinbeck's death, his family scattered his ashes into the Pacific from a cliff on Monterey's Point Lobos overlooking Whalers Bay, a cove where he had played as a child.

FURTHER READING: Astro, Richard, and Joel W. Hedgpeth, eds. *Steinbeck and the Sea*. Sea Grant College Program Publication ORESU-W-74–004. Corvallis: Oregon State UP, 1975; Beegel, Susan F., Susan Shillinglaw, and Wesley N. Tiffney Jr., eds. *Steinbeck and the Environment: Interdisciplinary Approaches*. Tuscaloosa: U of Alabama P, 1997; Benson, Jackson. *The True Adventures of John Steinbeck, Writer*. New York: Viking, 1984.

Susan F. Beegel

STEVENS, WALLACE (1879–1955). Wallace Stevens is one of the most influential American poets of the twentieth century, whose central concern is with the relationship of the human imagination and the world of physical reality. Stevens grew up in Pennsylvania and attended Harvard College and then New York Law School, graduating in 1903; he spent most of his career in Hartford, Connecticut, as an insurance executive. At the same time he was writing poems, publishing his first lyrics in 1914 and his first book in 1923. Thereafter he published a collection of poems every few years, winning the National Book Award in Poetry for 1950 and 1954 and the Pulitzer Prize in 1955.

Early in his law career Stevens traveled a good deal in Florida, a landscape and seascape that dominate his first two collections, *Harmonium* (1923) and *Ideas of Order* (1936). In several important poems throughout his career, Stevens explores his major theme, the relationship between imagination and reality, through sea imagery. His first long, narrative poem, "The Comedian as the Letter C" (1922), establishes the sea as a place of spiritual discovery. "The Idea of Order at Key West"* (1934) dramatizes the interplay of the self and the world: a female figure walking beside the sea sings a song that both reflects the inarticulate sounds of the waves and attempts to give meaning to those sounds; at the same time, physical reality is changed by the song. Later poems utilize sea imagery to present a merging of the self and the world. "Prologues to What Is Possible" (1952) uses an extended metaphor of a figure alone at sea in a boat to describe the state of mind of being at one with the world. Similarly, the sea voyage in "The Sail of Ulysses" (1954) becomes a metaphor for discovering a way of being that fluidly connects reality and the human imagination, so long in contention in Stevens' earlier poems. [*See also* SEA IMAGERY IN MODERN AND CONTEMPORARY POETRY]

Nancy Prothro Arbuthnot

STOCKTON, FRANK [FRANCIS] R[ICHARD]. (1834–1902). Best known for his short story "The Lady or the Tiger?" (1882), Frank R. Stockton lived in the eastern United States and wrote variously for both children and adults. His interest in the water was more thematic than topical. For one thing, the novel that begins his most famous series, *Rudder Grange* (1879), involves a family's life aboard a Hudson River canalboat only at the beginning. The family vacates when the boat floods, but the spirit of the novel's eponymous boat goes with them.

Elsewhere, Stockton's use of the nautical topics is wide-ranging: *The Merry Chanter* (1890) has a heroine in control of a ship; *The Adventures of Captain Horn* (1895) is set on the coast of Peru; and *Kate Bonnet: The Romance of a Pirate's* Daughter* (1902), Stockton's last novel, is about an unrepentant pirate who is eventually hanged. Stockton's short stories include those collected in *Afield and Afloat* (1900). Notable are "The Skipper and El Capitan," in which love and war are resolved when the captain of a Spanish steamer marries the daughter of an American schooner skipper, and "The Landsman's Tale," in which a skipper tells of a foundering ship whose crew chooses to rescue the ship's library over other provisions.

Peter J. Kratzke

STODDARD, ELIZABETH [DREW BARSTOW] (1823–1902). Iconoclastic novelist, short story writer, essayist, and poet, Elizabeth Stoddard was born in the coastal town of Mattapoisett, Massachusetts, the daughter of its foremost shipbuilder and maritime merchant. Both the fluctuations of her father's maritime fortunes and the constant presence of the sea during her childhood had an impact upon her later writing. Although Stoddard moved to New York after her 1852 marriage, she returned regularly to Mattapoisett during her summers to commune with the sea.

Her journals and letters reveal a familiarity with the sea based on her ocean walks and reveries and her subsequent subjective identification with its moods. From her earliest published poems and stories, Stoddard invokes the sea to project intense feeling, associating it in poems such as "House by the Sea" and "House of Youth" (1855) with loss and grief and in "My Own Story" (1860) with a tempestuous eroticism. The sea plays a critical role in all three of her novels, *The Morgesons* (1862), *Two Men* (1865), and *Temple House* (1867), each of which is set in a coastal community resembling Mattapoisett. In *The Morgesons*, a pioneering novel describing a young woman's defiance of conventional gender and religious attitudes as well as her attempt to shape herself in terms of her intelligence and sexuality, Stoddard's partially autobiographical heroine Cassandra increasingly discovers a sense of personal power projected by the sea. Less complex in symbolic and psychological terms than *The Morgesons*, Stoddard's other novels represent the sea as an arbitrary natural force interrupting and disturbing human affairs, responsible for brutally destroying life as well as bringing newcomers to a community.

Stoddard's biographer, James Matlack, maintains that only in her response to the sea did she approach an acknowledgment of divinity.

Elizabeth Schultz

STONE, ROBERT [ANTHONY] (1937–). A distinguished, award-winning novelist, Robert Stone turned to nautical fiction in his fifth book, *Outerbridge Reach* (1992). Born in New York to a family of tugboaters, he served from 1955 to 1958 as a radioman and journalist in the U.S. Navy. His sailing voyages in the Mediterranean and Antarctica* are reproduced as vivid seascapes in his sea novel. An enthusiastic yachtsman, Stone lives in Connecticut.

Outerbridge Reach is based on a failed solo circumnavigation* race in 1969 by one Donald Crowhurst, who faked his logs, became lonely and depressed, and drowned, apparently by walking into the ocean pursuing a religious vision. Nicholas Tomalin and Ron Hall published *The Strange Voyage of Donald Crowhurst* (1970), which Stone borrows from but does not directly credit.

Stone's novel explores the effects of single-handed circumnavigation on Owen Browne, his wife Anne, and Ron Strickland, a documentary filmmaker recording the experience. Owen is an Annapolis graduate in his forties who sells yachts in New York. When his company's millionaire owner mysteriously disappears, Owen replaces him in a round-the-world race, despite his inexperience sailing alone. The tension between Owen, Anne, and Ron grows as they prepare for the race. After Owen leaves, Anne and Ron become lovers. Owen's poorly constructed boat fails him, and he fakes his log in a mad attempt to win by deceit. Morally, intellectually, and physically bereft, he plunges overboard rather than face failure. Anne breaks off her affair, destroys the film, and seeks to restore family honor by entering a sailing race.

Outerbridge Reach demonstrates the sea's continuing symbolic presence as a place of escape, potential regeneration, moral purity, and psychological challenge, all themes imaged in its powerful dust jacket and title page reproduction of Rockwell Kent's* illustration "Hail and Farewell."

Dennis Berthold

STONE, WILLIAM LEETE (1792–1844). William Leete Stone was a journalist and writer whose career as a newspaperman largely overshadowed his work as a historian. Born in New Paltz, New York, Stone had little formal schooling in advance of his employment with several upstate New York newspapers. By 1821, Stone had purchased, sold, and failed in several newspapers across the area before becoming co-owner of the *New York Commercial Adventurer*. A Federalist and a Mason, Stone vigorously supported the construction of the Erie Canal, advocated emancipation, and opposed woman's rights and woman suffrage.

In addition to his newspaper interests, Colonel Stone, as he was known, wrote several books on history, including *Life of Joseph Brant* (1838), *Life and Times of Red Jacket* (1841), *The Poetry and History of Wyoming* (1841), *Uncas and Miantonomoh* (1842), and *Border Wars of the American Revolution* (1843). At the time of his death, Stone had written seven chapters of a biography of American Indian leader Sir William Johnson, also called *Sa-go-ye-wat-ha*, or Red Jacket. Stone's son, also named William Leete Stone, completed and published this biography (1866) after his father died, including in it a memoir about his father.

Stone wrote two brief travel accounts on the Erie Canal, but there is little in his background to explain two peculiar maritime essays that he wrote in the 1830s. In the first, "The Wreck of the Dead" (*Atlantic Souvenir* [1831]: 164–93), Stone tells the story of a shipwreck* in the Gulf of Saint Lawrence. Set in 1828, the tale follows the survivors of the wreck, who turn to cannibalism before they finally freeze to death. This eerie story seems out of place in the magazine, which published largely light literature and travel stories. Stone's other sea story, "The Spectre Fire-Ship" (*Knickerbocker* [1834]: 361–70), is even more bizarre. Set in 1785, the piece also focuses on a shipwreck. The narrator is rescued on board the *El Dorado*, under the command of a captain consumed by the fear of the devil, who appears on a "fire ship." When the *El Dorado* encounters the fire ship, the captain disappears. No sailor ever signed aboard the ship again. Stone wrote for other contemporary periodicals, such as the *American Monthly Magazine*, but nothing matches these two sea tales for interest and curiosity.

Many years after his father's death, the junior Stone, oddly, published "The Spectre Fire-Ship" in *Potter's American Monthly* (16 [1881]: 498–501), a briefer version than his father's. He gives no rationale for republishing the story, though he does mention that his father got the facts firsthand from one Noah Stone of Oxford, Connecticut, who had them from an eyewitness. The son also published essays on pirates* and life on the high seas.

Boyd Childress

STOWE, HARRIET BEECHER

STOWE, HARRIET BEECHER (1811–1896). Harriet Beecher Stowe is internationally famous for her antislavery best-seller *Uncle Tom's Cabin* (1852). In the summer of 1852, still living in Brunswick, Maine, where she wrote *Uncle Tom's Cabin*, Stowe began her romantic Maine idyll *The Pearl of Orr's Island* (1862). The first half of *The Pearl of Orr's Island* appeared in serialization in Theodore Tilton's *Independent* beginning in January 1861. Simultaneously serializing *Agnes of Sorrento* (1862) for *The Atlantic*

Monthly, by April 1861 Stowe was unable to maintain both stories. *The Pearl of Orr's Island* ceased publication with the 4 April 1861 issue of *Independent*, resumed in December, and was finally completed in the 24 April 1862 issue.

Living in Brunswick gave Stowe the opportunity to become closely acquainted with the citizens of nearby Orr's Island. Regional dialect and "painterly" descriptions of the Maine locale provide the backdrop for her coming-of-age novel about Mara Lincoln and Moses Pennel, two children orphaned on Orr's Island by shipwrecks.* The Orr's Islanders' lives are intertwined with the sea, whether the author is discussing local waters or far-flung oceans. Captain Kittridge, a neighbor of Mara and Moses, is retired from a deepwater sailing career and brings the spice of exotic lands to the islanders' simple lives through his tall tales and travel souvenirs. Stowe chronicles the rhythm of island life through the comings and goings of fishermen, storms, shipwrecks, funerals, and ship launchings.

The sea would never be such a focus for Stowe in any other novel. Some slighter maritime references appear in some of her stories. "The First Christmas of New England" includes a description of Cape Cod,* particularly Plymouth harbor, where the *Mayflower* anchors. The Pilgrims spend Christmas Eve aboard a festively decorated ship and Christmas Day working on land. In "Deacon Pitkin's Farm," a young man leaves college, family, and sweetheart to join the crew of a merchant ship and returns seven years later. Both stories appear in *Deacon Pitkin's Farm*, published in London (1875), and in *Betty's Bright Idea*, a similar collection published in New York a year later.

In *The Pearl of Orr's Island*, the reader catches glimpses of how unfamiliar the maritime world was for Stowe. For a good portion of the second half of the novel, Moses Pennel is building a vessel in which he hopes to make his fortune. Although Stowe gives a fairly detailed description of launch day, she never identifies what type of vessel Moses is building. Stowe also has Moses toy with the idea of christening the vessel the *Sally Kittridge*, after Captain Kittridge's daughter and Mara Lincoln's close friend, an issue that she never resolves. Despite these shortcomings, *The Pearl of Orr's Island* captures the character of island life in the first half of the nineteenth century and the impact of the sea on such a community.

Margherita M. Desy

THE SURVIVOR OF THE EDMUND FITZGERALD* (1985). The second and best known of Canadian* author Joan Skelton (Kurisko)'s (1929–   ) three novels, *The Survivor of the* Edmund Fitzgerald chronicles the short, but significant, friendship between two people who meet in the wilderness north of Lake Superior.

Clara Wheatley, a terminally ill wife and mother, opposes her family's urgings to continue treatment and isolates herself in a cabin to await death. The journal she writes there, laced with Native American myth and imagery, becomes the text of the novel. She evaluates her life, struggling to derive a personal sense of self-worth. Clara's process of discovery, marked by feminist insight that comes from negotiating the conflict between pleasing others and fulfilling her own dreams, is accelerated after her realization that she is not alone.

Gene Amort (French for "*trouble at death*"), a young, talented, and successful artist seeking refuge from fans in a superficial art community, stows away on the *Edmund Fitzgerald*, once the greatest of Lakes freighters and a symbol in the novel of technology. In a fierce Lake Superior storm, Gene realizes that the boat is sinking and clambers into a lifeboat at the crucial moment. The disaster's sole survivor, Gene is riddled with guilt as he washes up on the beach near Clara's cabin.

Befriending each other, they jointly come to an understanding of their own mortality, an awareness of the limits of technology, and a need for closure. Clara helps Gene see that saving himself was an act of heroism, not cowardice. Gene helps the pain-stricken Clara commit her most independent act—suicide—in the seclusion of a nearby inlet. [*See also* AMERICAN INDIAN LITERATURE OF THE SEA; GREAT LAKES LITERATURE]

Caroline J. McKenzie and Donald P. Curtis

SYMMES, JOHN CLEVES. *See SYMZONIA.*

SYMZONIA; A VOYAGE OF DISCOVERY (1820). Most scholars believe that "Captain Adam Seaborn," the author of this fictional, first-person narrative, is the pseudonym of army officer and amateur geographer Captain John Cleves Symmes (1780–1829). Symmes claimed that the earth was hollow and accessible by "holes in the poles," basing his theory on sea captains' reports of southern voyages. Granted an audience before Congress, Symmes built interest for the eventual U.S. Exploring Expedition* of 1838–1842.

In *Symzonia* Captain Seaborn constructs *Explorer*, a sail-and-steam ketch designed for seal hunting and Antarctic* exploration that is capable of sixteen knots. Despite a mutinous third mate, Seaborn sails beyond the Antarctic Circle, through warmer waters, and into the earth, proving Symmes' theory. Seaborn discovers a benevolent, Utopian society that he names Symzonia. Through Seaborn's descriptions of Symzonia, the author raises questions about nineteenth-century manifest destiny, exploration, materialism, slavery, and government. Symzonians have invented aircraft, clothes made from spider webs, and jet-propelled ships that can sail within four points of the wind. To protect their society, they ask Seaborn to leave. He sails back to the exterior and on to Canton, China, to trade sealskins. Seaborn convinces the sailors to swear to be silent about their discovery, and he returns home only to lose all of his new wealth onshore. Seaborn claims that he is forced to reveal his findings and publish this narrative in order to earn money for his family and for another voyage to the interior.

Symzonia, along with the works of Jeremiah N. Reynolds,* a disciple of Symmes and an activist for Antarctic exploration, influenced the maritime writings of Edgar Allan Poe,* particularly "MS. Found in a Bottle" (1833) and *The Narrative of Arthur Gordon Pym of Nantucket** (1838). *Symzonia* is one of the earliest American works of science fiction and Utopian fiction.

Richard J. King

T _____

TAYLOR, JAMES BAYARD (1825–1878). James Bayard Taylor, born in Chester County, Pennsylvania, launched his career as a travel writer with *Views Afoot* (1846), an account of a walking tour of Europe, and soon became probably the most popular and prolific American travel writer of his time. His accounts usually emphasize inland areas, but two have significant sections on sea travel. *A Visit to India, China, and Japan in the Year 1853* (1855) recounts a hurried trip leading him to Shanghai, where he was appointed a master's mate by Commodore Matthew Perry* on the voyage to open Japan to the Western world. Though Taylor sailed from Gibraltar across the Mediterranean and then from Suez to Bombay, he says little about the journey except to describe the British fortress at Aden, and even less about the subsequent journey from Calcutta to Shanghai.

He reports the journey to Japan more fully, though he was obliged to give his trip notes to the navy and depends heavily on memory for this early account of American encounters with Japan. His narrative also describes visits to the Loo-Choo Islands (now the Ryukyu), the Bonin group, and the Marquesas, mentioning in his narrative Herman Melville's* *Typee* (1846). When negotiations with Japan begin, Taylor does not find Perry's aggressive tactics at all offensive but contrasts what he considers the forthrightness and firmness of Perry with the duplicity and dissimulation of the Japanese. Despite the brevity of his career as a naval officer, Taylor asserts that promotion in the navy should not be based on seniority and that corporal punishment should be maintained.

In the summer of 1857, as part of a plan to describe for a volume entitled *Northern Travels* (1858) both a day in which the sun did not rise and a day in which it did not set, he sailed up the coast above Norway into the Arctic* circle. Again he writes little about the sea, admiring sunsets and a glacier, finding the maelstrom more famous than dangerous, and thinking the descendants of the Vikings an unimpressive lot.

James L. Gray

TEN NOVEMBER (first perf. 1987; pub. 1987). Inspired by the Gordon Lightfoot song "The Wreck of the *Edmund Fitzgerald*,"* playwrights Steven Dietz (1958–   ) and Eric Bain Peltoniemi (1949–   ) have dramatized the mysterious 10 November 1975 sinking of the S.S. *Edmund Fitzgerald* (1958) on Lake Superior through songs, stories, and Coast Guard reports. The play has several foci. First, the authors touch on the personal stories of the twenty-nine sailors aboard the *Fitzgerald* and their life on the sea. The bitter debates and interrogations surrounding the vessel's sinking are examined. Theories, some humorous, are offered regarding the cause of the disaster. The specific events of the *Fitzgerald* on its final voyage are told in detail, as are the stories of family members of some of the perished sailors.

The real interest of the drama, however, is the destructive and majestic power of not only Lake Superior, dubbed "the graveyard of ships," but of nature in a broader sense. The play examines the ways in which humans arrogantly attempt to control nature through technology and the futility that results. As one sailor in the play observes, "[W]hen the lake wants you, she takes you." Lake Superior is presented as a living entity, relishing her infamous mythology, impossible to suppress, and capable of causing a grief that must be dealt with by mourners left ashore. [*See also* DRAMA OF THE SEA; GREAT LAKES LITERATURE]

Brian Knetl

THALATTA: A BOOK FOR THE SEA-SIDE (1853). Published by Ticknor, Reed, and Fields in Boston, this collection of poems was apparently intended for vacation reading. Although the book's title page gave no indication of editorship, bibliographers ascribe it to Samuel Longfellow (1819–1892), brother of the famous poet, and his Harvard Divinity School classmate Thomas Wentworth Higginson* (1823–1911). The title allusion to the Greek word for the sea in Xenophon's writings is picked up by the anthology's second poem as translated from Heinrich Heine.

Among the 127 poems collected are a passage from Homer, songs from Shakespeare, Scottish ballads, and translations from Spanish as well as German. Even so, *Thalatta* heavily features works by nineteenth-century English and American writers of varying degrees of prominence, and readers would have felt comfortable in perusing the book among friends. Samuel Taylor Coleridge, William Wordsworth, John Keats, George Gordon Lord Byron, Thomas Hood, Charles Kingsley, Sir Walter Scott, Elizabeth and Robert Browning, and Thomas Moore appear in company with John Greenleaf Whittier,* James Russell Lowell,* Henry David Thoreau,* Felicia Hemans, and many other writers, including both editors and the publisher

James T. Fields. Six poems by Henry Wadsworth Longfellow* exceed the number allotted to any other poet except "Anonymous."

There is no evident chronological, national, or formal principle of organization. Edgar Allan Poe's* "Annabel Lee," for instance, turns up between Alfred Lord Tennyson's " 'Ask Me No More' " and Anne Whitney's "Bertha." Yet there seem to be loose tonal or thematic groupings, as where "The Wreck of the *Hesperus*" appears among several lyric or narrative poems relating to storms. The overall impression is that this is a book to be picked up, leafed through, and read from in the manner suggested by Caroline Sheridan Norton in the opening poem, "Prelude," whose speaker invites us to take "some volume of our choice, Full of a quiet poetry of thought" (1) for summer recreation by the shore. [*See also* SEA IMAGERY IN MODERN AND CONTEMPORARY POETRY]

Jane Donahue Eberwein

THAXTER, CELIA [LAIGHTON] (1835–1894). Celia Thaxter was born in Portsmouth, New Hampshire, to Thomas and Eliza Laighton, who moved to the Isles of Shoals, nine miles off the coast of New Hampshire, when Celia was five years old. They eventually settled on the largest of the islands, Appledore, where they built and operated a summer resort hotel beginning in 1848. In 1851 Celia married Levi Thaxter Jr. and a few years later moved to the mainland, settling in Newtonville, Massachusetts. She returned to Appledore each summer, helping to manage the hotel and entertain prominent literary guests, including Nathaniel Hawthorne,* Henry David Thoreau,* Richard Henry Dana Jr.,* James and Annie Fields, Lucy Larcom,* and Sarah Orne Jewett.* James Russell Lowell's* "My Appledore Gallery" (1854) and John Greenleaf Whittier's* "Lines on Leaving Appledore" (1864) commemorate visits made by the poets to the Shoals. Thaxter began an ardent correspondence with Whittier in the 1860s, which continued for the remainder of her life.

The first of her published poems, "Land-locked" (1861), which appeared in *The Atlantic Monthly*, expresses an islander's longing from the mainland for her insular paradise. Thereafter, much of her poetry rhapsodizes the rigors and the simple beauty of island life. Her first published volume of verse, *Poems* (1872), explored facets of island life that would recur in subsequent collections, *Drift-Weed* (1879) and *The Cruise of the* Mystery *and Other Poems* (1886). These include narrative accounts of island legend and history ("The Spaniards' Graves at the Isles of Shoals" [1865], "The Wreck of the *Pocahontas*" [1868], "The Cruise of the *Mystery*" [1886]) and descriptive reflections of the islands' flora ("Rock-Weeds" [1868], "Seaside Goldenrod" [1874], "Flowers in October" [1874]), often exploring the paradox of thriving vegetative life under inhospitable, windswept conditions. Thaxter's enthusiasm for island bird life is the subject of numerous poems, including "The Sparrows" (1874), "Nestling Swallows" (1875), "Medrick and Osprey" (1875), and "The Sandpiper" (1894). The destructive power of storms lashing the islands often finds a countervailing calm in such poems as "A Summer Day" (1862), "Leviathan" (1876), "Contrast" (1876), and "November Morning" (1886).

In addition to her poetry, Thaxter published a series of five essays on the islands in issues of *The Atlantic Monthly* from 1869 to 1873, collected as a book, *Among the Isles of Shoals* (1873). These sketches vividly narrate island history and are drawn from a variety of oral and written sources, including older residents, town records, journals, and even one of Cotton Mather's illustrations of providential intervention among Shoals fishermen. With Thoreauvian acuity, she records the cycle of the seasons—the late arrival of summer, the lingering fall, the bone-chilling and desolate winter, and the slow return of spring birds and vegetation—with consistent reference to the dominant influence of the surrounding sea on the island world. Her nostalgic recollections of childhood pleasures and pastimes on White Island, where her father served as lighthouse* keeper before the move to Appledore, make clear the reason for her lifelong passion for island life.

In "A Memorable Murder" (1875) Thaxter recounts the gruesome details of the murder in March 1873 of two Norwegian immigrant women on the island next to Appledore called Smuttynose. Contemporary Massachusetts author Anita Shreve offers a fictionalized account of this crime, *The Weight of Water* (1997), in which Thaxter appears as a minor character.

Thaxter died on Appledore Island on 26 August 1894. Thaxter's *An Island Garden* (1893) continues to find an appreciative readership among both amateur and professional gardeners. [*See also* SEA IMAGERY IN MODERN AND CONTEMPORARY POETRY]

FURTHER READING: DePiza, Mary Dickson. *Celia Thaxter: Poet of the Isles of Shoals.* Ann Arbor: UMI, 1969; Thaxter, Celia. *The Poems of Celia Thaxter.* Ed. with an introduction by Sarah Orne Jewett. Boston and New York: Houghton Mifflin, 1896; Thaxter, Rosamond. *Sandpiper: The Life and Letters of Celia Thaxter.* Rev. ed. Francestown, NH: Wake-Brook, 1963.

Joseph Flibbert

THEROUX, PAUL [EDWARD] (1941–   ). Paul Theroux was born in Medford, Massachusetts, and received his B.A. from the University of Massachusetts in 1963. Having taught in Malawi, Uganda, and Singapore, he is a prolific novelist and travel writer who divides his time between wintering in England and summering on Cape Cod,* a lifestyle that he describes in his essay "Summertime on the Cape," collected in *Sunrise with Seamonsters: Travels and Discoveries 1964–1984* (1985). The title piece concludes the collection and takes its name from an impressionist painting by J.M.W. Turner; it recounts Theroux's island-hopping around Cape Cod in his skiff *Goldeneye.* Theroux followed the publication of his first novel, *Waldo,* in 1967 with twenty more, over a dozen nonfiction books, short story collections, and children's books. One of his most successful works, *The Mosquito Coast* (1981), was adapted into a film (1986) starring Harrison Ford.

Theroux's travel books have at times met with critical reaction. One reviewer commented that Theroux had mastered writing but not traveling. *Kingdom by the Sea: A Journey around Great Britain* (1983) was Theroux's first travel book and appeared after he had lived in Britain for eleven years. He sailed the entire British coastline and recorded his observations in a largely negative manner, writing that Britons faced the sea as a way of turning their backs on their homeland. *Sailing through China* (1984) chronicled a trip down the Yangtze River with a group of wealthy tourists. Theroux presented a dismal and pessimistic view of China, stating that the Chinese people were oppressed by a life of agriculture and industry. A third travel book, *The Happy Isles of Oceania: Paddling the Pacific* (1992), followed Theroux's divorce and his fear of being diagnosed with cancer. It chronicled the eighteen months that he navigated the Pacific islands in a kayak from New Zealand and Australia to Hawai'i. Considered by some to be Theroux's best travel book, it is also perhaps his most adventurous.

Theroux's journeys transport him by rail and by boat. His chronicles of adventures at sea, on rivers, and around the British Isles establish him as a best-selling travel writer.

Boyd Childress

THOREAU, HENRY DAVID (1817–1862). Henry David Thoreau is most often associated with his birthplace and home, Concord, Massachusetts, and the woods, ponds, and streams in the vicinity of the town. But he frequently made excursions to other places, and often these travels took him to the seaside. The longest of these interludes was the seven months he spent living on Staten Island in New York, working as a tutor to William Emerson's son (Ralph Waldo Emerson's nephew) and unsuccessfully pursuing a writing career. He returned briefly to New York in the summer of 1850, to search the beach of Fire Island for the remains of Margaret Fuller,* who had perished in the wreck of the *Elizabeth*. In July 1851 he spent a week walking the Massachusetts coast, from Plymouth to Hull. Several times he sailed from Boston to Bangor, Maine, as prelude to inland travels. Near the end of his life, in 1861, he ventured west to Minnesota, in an unsuccessful bid to relieve his tuberculosis; on the return trip he and a companion took a steamer from Milwaukee up Lake Michigan and then across Lake Huron. Thoreau also made many visits to the Massachusetts shore, including four trips to Cape Cod,* ocean experiences that proved most important to his writing.

Thoreau was fascinated by watercraft of all types, writing in his *Journal* in March 1860 that a boat vastly expanded his experience of the world. Water plays a large role in much of his writing, in the form of rivers in *A Week on the Concord and Merrimack Rivers* (1849), ponds in *Walden*

(1854), and both streams and lakes in *The Maine Woods* (1864). In *Walden* Thoreau remains pondside, and yet the sea plays an important figurative role in the work; throughout he invokes nautical metaphors, most often as a means of describing or advocating transcendentalist mental voyaging. The literal sea appears in *Cape Cod* (1865) and occasionally in the *Journals*. Thoreau visited the cape in 1849, 1850, 1855, and 1857, excursions that added up to about a month at the seashore. Immediately following his first visit, he undertook to read everything he could find about Cape Cod and to compose a lecture about his trip, which he soon was giving to appreciative audiences. He returned to the cape, in part, for more material, but though his second and third journeys are incorporated in what would become the book *Cape Cod*, the narrative follows the path of the initial trip, with asides on the next two visits. The 1857 trip is chronicled only in the *Journal*. The first four chapters of *Cape Cod* were published in *Putnam's Magazine* in three successive issues in the summer of 1855. The book, however, wasn't published till after Thoreau's death.

Though some critics, such as Joseph Wood Krutch and Walter Harding, claim that *Cape Cod* is Thoreau's "sunniest" work, a sort of holiday book, recent commentators have focused more on the work's dark vision of nature, in contrast to Thoreau's thinking about nature in his other writing. In *Cape Cod*, nature, specifically the ocean, is an indifferent and dangerous power, described as "savage," its buffeting waves likened to hungry wolves. The book opens with the chapter "The Shipwreck,"* in which Thoreau bears witness to the tragedy of bodies washed ashore, torn and rent by the sea in the aftermath of the wreck of the *St. John* off Cohasset.

Wreckage haunts the rest of his journey, as he repeatedly comes upon evidence of the sea's devastating effect on human enterprise. But though he describes the destructive shore as a vast and chaotic morgue, Thoreau is more impressed than appalled by the ocean. He is not taken aback by the merciless sea but claims he sympathizes with the wind and the waves, that their power is simply evidence of nature's laws. He insists in the first chapter that the shore's "beauty was enhanced by wrecks . . . and acquired thus a rarer and sublimer beauty still." The heaving ocean draws Thoreau, partly because it is so strange to his landsman's eyes, but more for the way it indifferently takes human and other animal life. The profligacy of death along the seashore is for Thoreau a redemptive sign of the health and appetite of nature. So he wanders the beach in appreciation rather than fear, not only accepting but celebrating the wild and blunt ocean.

FURTHER READING: Bonner, Willard. *Harp on the Shore: Thoreau and the Sea.* State U of New York P, 1985; Harding, Walter. *The Days of Henry Thoreau.* New York: Dover, 1982; McIntosh, James. *Thoreau as Romantic Naturalist.* Ithaca, NY: Cornell UP, 1974.

Capper Nichols

TITANIC. Built in Belfast, Northern Ireland, in 1912, the R.M.S. *Titantic* and its wreck have become an important international legend of the twentieth century. On the evening of 14 April 1912, the *Titanic*, essence of modernity and technological achievement, was steaming across the Atlantic from Southampton to New York on her maiden voyage. On board, her passengers and crew were oblivious to an iceberg's presence and the impending destruction and death. When the *Titanic* struck the iceberg in the North Atlantic, her steel hull was opened below the waterline for a length of 300 feet. The inrush of water, with which the pumps and system of hull subdivision could not cope, doomed the ship. There were not enough lifeboats to save all of the 2,201 people on board. There was provision for only 1,178 people, though some of the lifeboats lowered were not filled to capacity. Almost 1,500 people, passengers and crew, perished in the most appalling circumstances imaginable. The sinking of *Titanic* had a traumatic effect in both the United States and Europe. The great ship, a signifier of the civilized world, lay fractured on the ocean floor, having plunged through two miles of freezing water with American millionaires and immigrant poor on board. It was a mighty blow to the self-confidence of the age.

Logan Marshall's *Sinking of the* Titanic *and Great Sea Disasters* (1912) was the first book-length publication about the disaster. Feelings of loss, bewilderment, and blame were among emotions expressed in a cathartic outpouring of popular verse. Wellesley College English professor Katharine Lee Bates, who had composed "America the Beautiful" in 1893, published her poem "The *Titanic*" in *Current Literature* (June 1912). Although most of the ensuing popular verse was doggerel, it did achieve considerable social, cultural, and historical significance.

Entrepreneurs flooded an eager market with mementos. Commemorative postcards were especially popular as they combined a high level of memorialization with low cost. The publication of specially composed *Titanic* sheet music was another commercial endeavor. In the United States the first published song appeared on 25 April 1912; within twelve months, more than 100 *Titanic* songs had been published in America. Over half of these were published by the Washington, D.C., firm of H. Kirkus Dugdale, which organized a promotion whereby members of the public submitted lyrics, and company hacks set them to music.

The generally ephemeral *Titanic* sheet music and songs contrast with *Titanic* narrative ballads of folk tradition. Relating strongly to, and informed by, the emigrant and immigrant experience, together with the experience of racial exclusion, *Titanic* songs appear in vernacular oral culture, not only in English but also in Yiddish, Hebrew, Czech, Swedish, Danish, German, and Dutch. For many years the late D. K. Wilgus, American folklorist, studied the *Titanic* traditional ballad complex with all its rich diversity of tradition in the United States, Ireland, and other parts of Europe. These investigations were discussed in an unpublished paper he delivered to the American Folklore Society on 3 November 1977. Wilgus believed that the *Titanic* disaster contributed more songs than any other disaster, or perhaps any other event, in American history.

Artists and writers also expressed the catastrophic event in terms of their individual imagination. For the English novelist and poet Thomas Hardy, the destruction of *Titanic* was a dramatic confirmation of his view that humankind existed at the whim of nature. The collision of ship and iceberg precisely reflected Hardy's sense of humanity being victimized by destiny, powerfully expressed in his poem "The Convergence of the Twain" (1912). The monumental dimension of the disaster and its meanings were also refracted through the imagination of the German expressionist artist Max Beckman in his painting *The Sinking of the* Titanic (1912).

For many in 1912, the loss of the *Titanic* was richly symbolic. For some, the event called into question the established order of things and the presence of a good and merciful God. For others, it confirmed belief in divine retribution for human conceit and arrogance. It seemed to demonstrate the folly of vanity and the presumption that nature could be a conquest of science; it shattered popular faith in the supremacy of technology, progress, and privilege.

The *Titanic* became the subject of messages and meanings from the sublime to the tacky: literature, popular verse, vaudeville, religion, songs, music, opera, dance, drama, art, film, cartoons, jokes, fantasy, graffiti, advertising, satire, politics, pornography, propaganda, science fiction, romantic fiction, exhibitions, and cultural discourse. Walter Lord's *A Night to Remember* (1955) is the most famous, although not the most accurate, American book on the disaster; it was adapted to film in 1958. Daisy Corning Stone Spedden's *Polar: The* Titanic *Bear* (1994) is the best known of juvenile* books on the topic.

Titanic, or rather Titanicism, was an international cultural phenomenon even before the remains of the ship were located on the seabed in 1985 by a joint American-French expedition headed by Robert D. Ballard. Despite the magnitude of other twentieth-century horrors, the *Titanic* has achieved the status of ultimate disaster symbol, or root metaphor, in our cultural consciousness.

The year 1997, eighty-fifth anniversary of the sinking of *Titanic*, was a vintage year for Titanicism. By June 1997 it was possible to have checked out a $6 million *Titanic* exhibition in Memphis, Tennessee, become a secret agent in a *Titanic* CD-ROM, attended a "*Titanic* at Home" international convention in Belfast, visited thousands of *Titanic* sites on the Internet, experimented with a *Titanic* cookbook, and flown to New York for the $10 million Tony award-winning Broadway hit Titanic: *A New Musical* by Peter Stone and Maury Yeston. Although dubbed by a British newspaper as the

"Sing As You Sink Show," this musical extravaganza succeeded, not least because of its elaborate tilting and tiered set and dramatically upbeat songs.

Released in the United States at the end of 1997 and directed by James Cameron, the blockbuster movie *Titanic* was the most expensive film to date, at an estimated cost of over $200 million. To save some money, only one side of a full-sized reconstruction of *Titanic* was built at the Mexican beach town of Rosarito. Nevertheless, in the completed film the resurrected *Titanic* is a spectacular success. The ship is the real star of the movie, which garnered Golden Globe awards and swept the 1998 Oscars. Cameron has remarked that the film is a metaphor for the inevitability of death. The film is also a manifestation of Titanicism, with its key characteristics of profit, pleasure, and memorialization. The film is rich cinematographic entertainment, simulated reality powerfully projecting the vulnerability of life and its dreams in a capricious and uncertain world.

Beyond popular culture, the *Titanic* engages the imagination of more reputable artists, writers, and composers in whose creative work the tragedy takes on meanings that transcend the event itself. Poets, particularly Irish poets such as Louis MacNeice, Derek Mahon, and Anthony Cronin, have explored *Titanic* themes. Internationally, perhaps the most compelling contemporary poem is "The Sinking of the *Titanic*" by Hans Magnus Enzensberger. Translated from German into English by the poet in 1981, this long and complex poem is an extended metaphorical discourse on human loss and the foundering of Western society. English novelist Beryl Bainbridge's *Every Man for Himself* (1996), short-listed for the 1996 Booker Prize and winner of the 1996 Whitbread Novel Award, is a dark and brittle tale of failed hopes and social fracture on board the flawed ship. Erik Fosnes Hansen's *Psalm at Journey's End*, a massive best-seller in its original Norwegian edition (1990) and translated into English (1997), focuses on the lives of *Titanic*'s musicians and connects their doomed world to the looming upheavals of the early twentieth century. The *Titanic* is depicted by American author Cynthia Bass in *Maiden Voyage* (1996), a coming-of-age novel. American short story writer Bailey White combines gentle and fleeting memories of age with the recollected experiences of youth; the ship is luminously observed in her folksy southern collection of domestic vignettes *Mama Makes Up Her Mind, and Other Dangers of Southern Living* (1993).

The cataclysmic failure of *Titanic* was, and remains, a paradigm for the inevitable human failure of flaunted technology, emblematic of the death of an era. *Titanic* symbolizes and prefigures human fears and anxieties about the precariousness of existence, the frightening possibilities of science, the failures of technology, and the indulgence of vanity at the beginning of the twenty-first century. As the twentieth century drew to a close, there was a feeling that, in a way, we had caught up with the *Titanic* and were re-creating the future. *Titanic* is our fin de siècle. [*See also* CUSSLER, CLIVE; OCEAN LINER LITERATURE; SHIPWRECK LITERATURE]

FURTHER READING: Biel, Steven. *Down with the Old Canoe.* New York: Norton, 1996; Eaton, John P., and Charles A. Haas. Titanic, *Triumph and Tragedy.* Wellingborough: Patrick Stephens, 1986; Enzensberger, Hans Magnus. *The Sinking of the* Titanic. London: Carcanet, 1981; Foster, John Wilson. *The* Titanic *Complex.* Vancouver: Belcouver, 1997; McCaughan, Michael. *Titanic.* Cultra: Ulster Folk and Transport Museum, 1982; McCaughan, Michael. *The Birth of the* Titanic. Belfast: Blackstaff, 1998.

Michael McCaughan

TO GILLIAN, ON HER 37TH BIRTHDAY (first perf. 1983; pub. 1984). Set on Nantucket,* this play by Michael Brady (1949–) deals with the aftermath of title character Gillian's death during a boating accident on rough waters two years earlier. Her husband, David, who had attempted suicide on the first anniversary of her death, still has difficulty with his grief and guilt. Through ministrations of family and friends, as well as visions of his deceased wife on the dunes near their beach house, David begins to accept Gillian's death and proceed with his life. In 1996 a film version was released starring Michelle Pfeiffer, Peter Gallagher, and Claire Danes. [*See also* DRAMA OF THE SEA]

Brian T. Carney

TO HAVE AND HAVE NOT (1937). The main plot of this novel by Ernest Hemingway* (1899–1961) deals with a Key West* charter-boat captain's trips across the Florida Strait to Havana. Economic depression in the United States and political oppression in Cuba have widened the gap in both countries between those who have material means and those who have almost none. Hemingway's allusion is to St. Matthew 13:12: "For whosoever hath, . . . shall have more . . . : but whosoever hath not, from him shall be taken away even that he hath." One consequence of the pervasive misery is that the ninety-mile stretch of ocean between the deprived populations, a legal and a physical gulf, is exploited by the desperate as well as the greedy on both sides, in violent smuggling and revolutionary schemes. Cheated out of his honest livelihood, the self-sufficient captain gambles on covert ventures to feed his family. But by the end of a disastrous third trip he has lost everything.

"A man alone" has no chance (ch. 23), the captain concludes in a dying utterance at first seen to show Hemingway abandoning apolitical individualism for socialist collectivism. But if a person alone has no chance of gaining anything beyond wretched survival, neither do people banded together. Following a scene of human carnage on the captain's boat in the middle of the Gulf Stream, a school of two-inch fish mills frantically around recurrent drops of blood in the water (ch. 20). The little fish of the human community, scrambling for minimum subsistence on both shores, mirror a mode of existence in marine species living collectively and by implication governing life within all such species in the natural world.

Moreover, the materially favored but morally deprived "haves" of the novel's subplot are equally desperate emotionally, and the anxiety-ridden affluent ashore have their counterparts, too, beneath the boat, in a complex marine microcosm. Anxious dissatisfaction emerges as nature's imperative for those who struggle together as well as those who struggle alone, for "haves" and "have-nots" alike. Thus, the sea's portrayal in the novel urges alert readers to look beyond materialist interpretations of the captain's last words.

The novel was adapted into a film starring Humphrey Bogart and Lauren Bacall in 1944.

Bickford Sylvester

TONQUIN. A ship of 269 tons built in New York City in 1807, the *Tonquin* was commanded on its maiden voyage by Edmund Fanning,* who later gained fame through the publication of his journals. The vessel did not become a literary icon, however, until a later voyage. In September 1810 John Jacob Astor sent a party of men on the *Tonquin* to the mouth of the Columbia River to establish a trading post for his Pacific Fur Company. Under the command of Captain Jonathan Thorn, the ship arrived in March 1811; part of the company was left ashore at the new post, Astoria, and the ship continued north along the coast to Vancouver Island to trade. In July 1811 the *Tonquin* was captured by Northwest Coast* Indians, and a battle ensued during which the ship's powder magazine was set alight. The vessel exploded, killing all on board.

The incident, the location of which is not clear, was first described in print by one of the men, Gabriel Franchere, who had remained at the Columbia River. Franchere's book, *Rélation d'un Voyage à la Côte du Nordouest de l'Amérique,* was published in French in 1820 (Eng. trans., 1854). Franchere was especially critical of Thorn but described the whole enterprise as fraught with management problems and not well conceived or supported by Astor. Franchere's shipmate Ross Cox told a similar story in his *Adventures on the Columbia River* (1831).

John Jacob Astor hired Washington Irving,* one of the most popular authors of the day, to write his version of the story, and Irving's *Astoria: Or Anecdotes of an Enterprise beyond the Rocky Mountains* appeared in 1836. Irving got most of his information about the *Tonquin*'s voyage from Franchere and Cox, though he also had access to Astor's business records and correspondence between Astor and Thorn. Irving's account of the explosion of the *Tonquin* became a model for subsequent authors, and over the next several decades exploding ships were incorporated into a number of sea novels. Miles Wallingford, the hero of James Fenimore Cooper's* *Afloat and Ashore* (1844), contemplates setting the magazine alight when his ship is captured on the Northwest Coast, and the explosion of the *Jane Guy* in Edgar Allan Poe's* *The Narrative of Arthur Gordon Pym** (1838) is influenced by the *Tonquin* tragedy.

Mary Malloy

TRAVEN, B. *See THE DEATH SHIP.*

*TUNING THE RIG: A JOURNEY TO THE ARCTIC** (1990). This firsthand account of a contemporary sea voyage in the mid-1980s relates the trials, the pains, and a few of the delights of a writer who ships as a deckhand on an oceanographic sailing expedition to observe the behavior of whales in the Northwest Atlantic. The Danish 144-foot oak barquentine *Regina Maris* (1908), having seen difficult service on four oceans, found new life in 1975 as a research vessel. She makes it safely on the two-month voyage from Boston to Greenland and back, to study humpback whales and other wildlife, which the book chronicles. Author Harvey Oxenhorn (1951–1990) uses ship parts to name sections of the book and log information for his chapter headings.

Oxenhorn, who had taught the works of Joseph Conrad and Herman Melville* at Tufts and Stanford before joining the faculty of Harvard University's Kennedy School of Government, is aboard the *Regina Maris* on his inaugural voyage in his thirtieth year and returns to Boston a different person. He writes more about human than whale behavior, for Oxenhorn has all of the problems of the green "boy" on sailing vessels of old, including an immovable captain with whom he cannot relate, living conditions that he cannot tolerate, and a ship's discipline against which he rebels. He grows to accept the interdependence of shipmates, nine women and twenty-one men from seventeen to sixty years of age, in their confined universe; a vessel at sea brings them to understand a unique code of service.

In retrospect, Oxenhorn finds that he has tuned himself to that universe just as sailors adjust the rigging of stays and shrouds to support the towering masts. His insightful narration is written with an ecological consciousness for the history of whaling and a deep appreciation for the beauty and the terror of being at sea and the problems that humans have had for centuries in adjusting to life at sea. He may have had Richard Henry Dana Jr.'s* coming-of-age saga *Two Years before the Mast** (1840) in mind, though Oxenhorn reveals a depth of emotional response to his sea experience that Dana, writing a century and a half earlier, could not.

Oxenhorn was killed in a car accident in the Berkshires, miles from the ocean, just after the book's publication.

James F. Millinger

"TWAIN, MARK." *See* [CLEMENS, SAMUEL].

TWO YEARS BEFORE THE MAST (1840). This autobiographical account of life aboard a merchant vessel was written by Richard Henry Dana Jr.* (1815–1882) and is based on his voyage from Boston to California and back, 1834–1836. Promising a "voice from the forecastle," Dana's book is a combination of realistic detail and lyrical impressionism. Enormously popular when first published, *Two Years* helped to change the course of American sea literature, both fiction and nonfiction, away from the romanticism of James Fenimore Cooper's* early sea novels, toward more gritty and authentic portrayals of nautical life. Herman Melville* so admired the work that he called Dana his "sea brother" and engaged Dana in correspondence as he was writing *Redburn** (1849), *White-Jacket** (1850), and *Moby-Dick** (1851). A work with continuing and multifaceted appeal, *Two Years* was originally praised by Ralph Waldo Emerson, William Cullen Bryant,* Edgar Allan Poe,* and others as a documentary exposé of the hardships of a sailor's life, while this century's appreciation turns more on Dana's symbolic voyage of identity.

Partly as an attempt to cure his ailing eyesight, Dana left behind his Harvard education and Brahmin upbringing on 14 August 1834, sailing for California aboard the hide-carrier *Pilgrim*. His record of the voyage out, much of it in the form of dated diary entries, is filled with landmark initiations and immersions. After a bout of seasickness, Dana stands his first watch, reefs his first sail, twice crosses the equator, and keeps his "trick" at the helm during the rough weather of Cape Horn.* With particular pride Dana reports that he and Ben Stimson, another young man from a privileged family, move from steerage to the forecastle to join the regular sailors. He now feels "one of them."

The life of the sailor had its own horrors, however, and in one of his most compelling passages, Dana describes the flogging of a shipmate by the sadistic Captain Francis Thompson. Dana vows afterward that, once home, he will do what he can to redress the wrongs suffered by common sailors. Dana kept his promise: as a Boston lawyer he regularly represented sailors in their grievances against captains and owners. Descriptions of California, its history and people, along with the work of hide curing and collecting, make up the long middle portion of *Two Years*. Once overeager to join ranks with the common sailor, Dana is haunted with the memory of the flogging and the tedium of his California work, which convince him to return home as soon as possible. He uses his influence to secure a berth aboard the *Alert*. In the record of his return voyage, roughly the final third of the book, Dana creates particularly memorable portraits of sea, sky, and sail, including a lyrical description of the *Alert* as seen from the perspective of the flying jib-boom. Upon entering Boston harbor on 22 September 1836, Dana registers the complexity of his emotions by recording a certain "indifference" and "apathy" at the moment he had looked forward to for over a year (ch. 36). Given the fact that he knew he was returning home to the prescribed routines of Boston gentility, this ending has a special poignancy.

Dana wrote *Two Years* while he was in law school; Harper's published it some three and half years after the *Alert*'s return. Dana's book contract, negotiated by his father, Richard Henry Dana Sr.,* and the poet William Cullen Bryant,* was for $250 and twenty-five free copies. Dana Sr. turned down Harper's initial offer for 10 percent of the sales after the first 1,000 copies sold. Given the popularity of *Two Years*, this was an unfortunate choice for the young author. Dana estimated that the book earned some $50,000 before the copyright ran out. In 1859 Dana made a nostalgic return to California and eventually appended a chapter, "Twenty-Four Years Later," to later editions.

Reading interest in *Two Years* was immediate, reinforced by the discovery of gold in California. The book also fed an East Coast appetite for stories of the "common man" in post-Jacksonian America. Today Dana's work is recognized more for its rich ambiguities than for its literal certainties. As much as *Two Years* is a realistic description of sea life, it is also a narrative search for identity and exhibits the tensions of Dana's dual allegiance to the worlds of land and sea.

The book was adapted into a 1946 film that starred Alan Ladd. [*See also* THE RED RECORD]

FURTHER READING: Gale, Robert. *Richard Henry Dana, Jr.* New York: Twayne, 1969; Lawrence, D. H. *Studies in Classic American Literature*. New York: Thomas Seltzer, 1923; Philbrick, Thomas. Introduction. *Two Years before the Mast*. Richard Henry Dana Jr. New York: Penguin, 1981, 7–29.

Hugh Egan

TYPEE (1846). Herman Melville's* (1819–1891) first novel, *Typee* was, in his day, his most popular. The novel opens on board the whaler *Dolly*, with Melville's narrator discontented and longing for the romantic Marquesas Islands. When they land at Nukuhiva, the narrator and his friend Toby jump ship and eventually make their way into the valley of the feared Typees, whose lives and customs they are surprised to find may be superior to the "civilized" life they have left behind. Toby disappears, and Tommo, as the natives have christened the narrator, further observes and happily participates in the culture of the Typees until anxiety over being tattooed and over knowing that the Typees are cannibals leads Tommo to flee to another whaler anchored offshore.

Although the passages at sea form only the frame of the novel, they are nevertheless significant for the book and for issues that Melville would raise more fully in later novels. Life on board the *Dolly*, Tommo complains, is sterile and harsh, and the tyrannical Captain Vangs abuses the crew. Lacking any power to redress these wrongs, Tommo can escape only in moments of reverie at the thrill of sailing and in his dreams of the exotic wonders of the South Seas. Melville also parallels shipboard life with the larger historical situation of the European powers' imperialistic incursion into Polynesia; Tommo's situation on board thus represents the political and social realities of Western culture, which an individual can escape only temporarily.

John Samson

U

UPDIKE, JOHN [HOYER] (1932–   ). John Updike is the author of over fifteen novels and an impressive body of shorter fiction, poetry, and criticism, much of which has been published in *The New Yorker*. Born in Pennsylvania, he has lived on the Massachusetts coast since 1957. His fiction typically chronicles the suburban and rural mores of late twentieth-century America, often with gentle satire; "Rabbit" Angstrom, the protagonist of four of Updike's best-known novels (1960–1990), epitomizes the strengths and weaknesses of white American middle-class culture.

Several of his novels are infused by the environment of their coastal settings, notably *Couples* (1968), in which the fictional Tarbox was perceived as Updike's own Ipswich, Massachusetts, and *The Witches of Eastwick* (1984). In one collection of critical essays, he likens writing criticism to "hugging the shore," where the writer can "always come about and draw even closer to the land," while writing fiction and poetry is like "sailing the open sea," with its "beautiful blankness all around" (*Hugging the Shore*, 1983, p. xv). Another essay from that collection, "Going Barefoot," appears in *Cape Cod* Stories*, edited by John Miller and Tim Smith (1996).

Thomas R. Brooks

URQUHART, JANE (1949–   ). Jane Urquhart was born near Lake Nipigon, Ontario, north of Lake Superior, where she spent the first five years of her life. Vivid memories of extended time on the north shore of Lake Superior drew her back to that locale in the early 1990s, when she began *The Underpainter* (1997). She had worked briefly for the Royal Canadian* Navy, Halifax (1971–1972), but more important to her creativity were her summers on the south shore of Lake Ontario in an old frame cottage situated on Loughbreeze Beach, where large sections of each of her novels have been composed. In a letter to the author, Urquhart emphasized the necessity of having the sound of the lake in her ears in order to write well.

While the nineteenth century, her travels in Europe, her Irish heritage, and the British writers Emily Brontë and Robert Browning figure more prominently in her fiction, the Great Lakes* form a compelling undercurrent. History and memory, landscape infusing the human psyche, obsessive love, and estrangement are her common themes. Her first novel, *The Whirl-pool* (1986), is set on the Canadian side of Niagara Falls during the summer of 1889 and has two narrative threads. In the first, an undertaker's widow maintains the family business, servicing "floaters" and other bodies whose deaths result from mishaps with the falls. In the second, a military historian's research obsession blinds him to the eros developing between his wife and a young Canadian poet, simultaneously drawn to each other and to the falls. The poet's suicidal plunge into the adjacent whirlpool emphasizes the book's central theme of passion and destruction.

Two short stories in *Storm Glass* (1987) focus importantly on water. In the title story, a bedridden older woman, gazing through her window at the lake, begins to resolve a long-standing rift with her husband by contemplating, in a new way, the colored glass shards that storms have thrown upon the beach. In "The Boat" remnants of a pleasure craft washed up on an ocean beach provide several days' activities for a couple and their visiting grandchildren and haunt their dreams at night.

Admiral Francis Beaufort and his wind scale figure slightly in the two tumultuous love affairs in *Changing Heaven* (1990). Rockwell Kent* is a minor character in *The Underpainter*, which spans seven decades in the life of an American minimalist artist who paints his Canadian mistress in the reflected light of Lake Superior. *Away* (1993), Urquhart's most dazzling use of the sea and its pull on the human psyche, opens with a young Irishwoman dragging a half-drowned sailor from the water. He dies in her arms but not before she has become possessed, "away," with love for him. She marries someone else, survives the potato famine and an Atlantic crossing, and dies mysteriously in a vast Canadian lake. Three generations of her female descendants are subsequently haunted by mystical longings for what they cannot possess.

Jill B. Gidmark

U.S. EXPLORING EXPEDITION. From 1838 through 1842 a U.S. naval squadron under the command of Lieutenant Charles Wilkes in the flagship *Vincennes* traveled over 87,000 miles around the world on the largest government-sponsored exploring expedition ever undertaken. Expedition members included scientists, artists, and more than 400 crew, who explored Pacific islands, Australia, New Zealand, the Hawaiian Islands, the Oregon territory, and California. Among the participants were naturalists

Titian Ramsey Peale and Charles Pickering and geologist James Dwight Dana. Many uncharted islands were encountered, and Antarctica* was established to be a continent. Significant contributions were made in the fields of botany, zoology, geology, anthropology, and navigation, launching the United States' sponsorship of scientific research; natural history collections and ethnological specimens from the expedition formed the foundation of the Smithsonian Institution.

In addition to Wilkes' five-volume *Narrative of the United States Exploring Expedition* (1844), nineteen other volumes of official scientific studies were prepared. Many hundreds of additional books and papers were published about experiences, discoveries, and experiments made on the voyage. Unofficial reminiscences and musings were published by officers and crew members, such as the narrative *Twenty Years before the Mast* (1890) by mizzen-topman Charles Erskine and a volume of poetry and song by U.S. Navy surgeon James C. Palmer entitled *Thulia: A Tale of the Antarctic* (1843). Following the voyage, accusations of misconduct at sea led to a court-martial and reprimand for Wilkes.

Daniel Finamore

V

V. (1963). *V.* is the first published novel of Thomas Pynchon (1937–). One of the main characters, Benny Profane, spends time aboard the ship the U.S.S. *Scaffold* with his old shipmates, the Whole Sick Crew. Part of Profane's voyage leads him through the sewers of New York City. The rats who live in the sewer system control the city's waterways and are being tutored in, among other things, Austin Knight's *Modern Seamanship* (1901). A minor character, Pig Bodine, behaves insubordinately, knocking people over whenever the ship rolls from side to side. Later, in dry dock, the *Scaffold* is described as a great squid with colored tentacles. When Profane travels to Malta aboard the *Susanna Squaducci*, he spots a xebec, a small, three-masted Mediterranean vessel. This ship is identified as the H.M.S. *Egmont* and displays a prominent figurehead of Astarte, the goddess of sexual love.

Pynchon's fiction employs both historical events and myth; at times it is difficult to distinguish between the two. Although the ships in *V.* are described in detail, whether they are factual or fictional is not clear. Among this reclusive author's other fiction, only *Mason & Dixon** (1997) includes references to the sea and seafaring.

Ralph Berets

VIDAL, GORE [EUGENE LUTHER] (1925–). Gore Vidal was born in West Point, New York, attended Philips Exeter Academy in New Hampshire, and served in the army during World War II. A novelist, playwright, and essayist, he occasionally employs maritime settings in his work. In *Empire* (1987), for example, the sea is an important venue for the expansion of America's geopolitical presence in the Caribbean* and the Pacific. In an early homosexual novel, *The City and the Pillar* (1948), the merchant marine provides the protagonist and other characters a vehicle for self-discovery.

Williwaw (1946), a sea story set in the Aleutians, is Vidal's first novel, published shortly after his discharge from the army. Based in large measure on his wartime experience, this readable, occasionally suspenseful novel captures in realistically vivid detail the voyage of a small vessel from its home port to an outlying post in the chain. The book's title alludes to a vicious Aleutian storm. Descriptions of high seas caused by winds in excess of 100 miles an hour, a broken mast, and chaos in general are convincing and engaging as Vidal traces the interactions of crew members and a few passengers. Tensions run high, as does paranoia, and there are superficial, yet effective, types such as a jaded skipper, an ambitious officer, salty crew members, and less-seasoned, less-committed draftees waiting for the war, or at least their tours in Alaska, to end.

Vidal captures a certain amoral pragmatism in the almost naturalistic death of the chief in charge of the engine room when, during a rather heated exchange with one of the mates, he falls overboard into the icy waters after being struck by a hammer tossed to, or thrown at, him. The mate's failure to report a "man overboard" is treated with the naturalistic impersonality or detachment reminiscent of Theodore Dreiser's clinically detached rendering of Clyde Griffith's panicked, yet unemotional, response to Roberta's drowning in *An American Tragedy* (1925).

Donald Yannella

A VIEW FROM THE BRIDGE (first perf. 1955; first pub. 1957). Written by Arthur Miller (1915–   ) and originally produced with the title *From under the Sea, A View from the Bridge* was first seen in New York in 1955 as a one-act at the Coronet Theatre, directed by Martin Ritt. The current two-act version of the play was originally staged in London in 1956 and published in 1957. Chicago's Lyric Opera presented the world premiere of the opera, composed by William Bolcom, in 1999.

The play tells the story of Eddie Carbone, an Italian American longshoreman, and his relationship with his family, including his niece, Catherine. When his cousins Marco and Rodolpho arrive from Italy to work on the docks, the burgeoning romance between Rodolpho and Catherine angers Eddie. Ultimately, Eddie betrays his cousins to the immigration authorities, and Marco kills Eddie in a street fight. Miller connects the lives of the longshoremen to the sea through the use of the narrator, the lawyer Alfieri. Alfieri sets the tone of the play when he compares Red Hook, Brooklyn, to Sicily. Red Hook is the "slum on the seaward side of Brooklyn Bridge . . . the gullet of New York swallowing the tonnage of the world" (6).

Throughout the play, the immigrant cousins are referred to as "submarines" because they "come in under the water" (27). In addition, the play vividly evokes the conditions of longshoreman labor, suggesting comparison with Budd Schulberg's *On the Waterfront*, a play that was published in 1955 and won an Academy Award for Best Screenplay. Schulberg based his drama on a series of articles that ran in the *New York Sun* in the late 1940s under the title "Crime on the Waterfront," by Malcolm Johnson, a series that won a Pulitzer Prize in journalism and that was published along with other reporting by Johnson under the title *Crime on the Labor Front* (1950). *On the Waterfront* was also released as a film (1954) directed by Elia Kazan and starring Marlon Brando, Karl Malden, and Lee J. Cobb. [*See also* DRAMA OF THE SEA]

David Jortner

VOLLMANN, WILLIAM T[ANNER]. (1959–). William T. Vollmann's very ambitious project is a seven-novel series entitled *Seven Dreams: A Book of North American Landscapes*, which interweaves history, myth and legend, imagination, illustrations, and personal travel experience to chronicle the "symbolic history" of North American colonization. The three published volumes of *Dreams* span from mythic Inuit seascapes, to 1990s Quebec, with North Atlantic voyages, cartography, vessels, ports, and other sea-based motifs integral to the novels' complex plots and rich, metaphoric terrain. Seacoasts, tides, currents, waves, islands, fish, aquatic plants, sea mammals, and water gods dominate the multiple points of view.

The first volume of *Seven Dreams, The Ice-Shirt* (1990), centers on the c. A.D. 1000 journey to "Vinland" by the Norse and their subsequent clashes with the Micmac Indians in Newfoundland. Vollmann's account—which includes his observations of contemporary Arctic* and North American seacoast locales—is particularly notable for its depiction of icebound seas. *Fathers and Crows* (1992), the second novel, focuses on efforts by seventeenth-century Jesuits to convert the Hurons in southern Canada. It also charts Samuel de Champlain's frustrated attempts to find a water passage to China through the Canadian* wilderness, during which he encounters the "Sweetwater Sea" (Lake Huron). Although the sea is not a consistent presence in this work, two aquatic motifs—the "Stream of Time" and the water demon Gougou—serve multiple symbolic purposes. *The Rifles* (1994), the third published part of *Seven Dreams*, follows Admiral John Franklin's final, failed attempt to establish the Northwest Passage* in 1845, which saga Vollmann juxtaposes with his own journey to the Arctic Circle and the Resolute Bay area.

Among Vollmann's other works is the autobiographical, illustrated travelogue *The Atlas* (1996), which includes descriptions of the Arctic and of islands in the Northwest Territories and other sea references. Vollmann's interest in the sea is also shown in an article that he published in the 1998 issue of *Civilization*, "Melville's Magic Mountain," where he muses about

the writing of *Moby-Dick** (1851) and other aspects of Herman Melville's*
life. [*See also* GREAT LAKES LITERATURE]

Dana L. Peterson

VONNEGUT, KURT, JR. (1922–   ). Kurt Vonnegut was born in Indianapolis but soon moved east, eventually settling in Cape Cod,* Massachusetts, in 1951, where he lived for twenty years. His essay "Brief
Encounters on the Inland Waterway" (first pub. in *Venture* in 1966) is a
description of a trip from Massachusetts to Florida on the Kennedy family
yacht *Marlin*. In his novels, Vonnegut generally uses the beauty of sea settings as an ironic backdrop for his comments on the potential absurdity and
inhumanity of the grand myths of history, science, and progress. He uses
various island settings to suggest both community and startling disconnect-
edness.

Vonnegut's novel *Cat's Cradle* (1963), set in the future, centers on a
religion called "Bokononism," which is practiced only on a small island in
the Caribbean.* Central to the novel is a material called "ice-nine," a form
of ice with a melting point of 114.4° Fahrenheit that instantly freezes any
water that it touches. When a character in the novel who has died from
swallowing ice-nine slides into the waters of the Caribbean, the oceans of
the earth freeze, ending all life.

Another novel, *Galápagos* (1985), set 1 million years in the future, is the
story of a luxury cruise liner, the *Bahia de Darwin*, which embarks in 1986
on "The Nature Cruise of the Century" just as World War III breaks out.
The ship's passengers include a schoolteacher, a con man, a computer genius, and an American businessman. When the ship is wrecked in the Galápagos Islands,* the passengers are the only survivors of the war. They form
the gene pool from which future humans evolve. These creatures who evolve
are called "fisherfolk," and they have flippers, beaks, and small brains.

Christopher Lee

THE VOYAGE (1990, first perf. 1992). *The Voyage* is an opera in three
acts, a prologue, and an epilogue, with music by Philip Glass (1937–   ) and
libretto by David Henry Hwang (1957–   ). Commissioned by New York's
Metropolitan Opera to commemorate the 500th anniversary, of the voyage
of Christopher Columbus,* it was premiered by the Met 12 October 1992
and remounted in 1996; the libretto was published by the Metropolitan
Opera Guild in 1992.

In the prologue, set in the present, Hwang emphasizes the metaphor of
voyage in the imagination of a wheelchair-bound scientist, modeled after
twentieth-century physicist Stephen W. Hawking (b. 1942), who travels
freely among the planets, following his vision despite faulty equipment.

Act 1 takes place 15,000 years ago, as a spaceship from another world
and its crew frantically prepare for an emergency landing on earth. The ship's

Commander, the First Mate, and the Doctor recall both positive and negative aspects of their own home planet and also observe the life-sustaining qualities in things they see before them: vegetation, oxygen, water, forms of native society, and intelligence. As the act ends, the crew and the natives express fear and fascination with each other.

In act 2, set on day thirty-two of the historic voyage, most of the literal references to the sea occur: solitude, dawn, memories, faith, prayers, the vanishing horizon, madness, and hazy vision. Details of life on board the *Santa Maria* are expressed as the First Mate orders the crew to hoist, pump, and pray. Queen Isabella and the Spanish court at Granada are represented as memories. The chorus offers riches and position to Christopher Columbus,* and the Queen quotes from Scripture for encouragement, bidding Columbus farewell as he sets out for the Indies. On the thirty-second day of the voyage the crew has lost faith in Columbus; solitude crushes him, but a dreamlike vision of Isabella renews his faith in his expedition. The act climaxes with the First and Second Mates' sighting land.

Act 3 is set in 2092 and presents another Commander and Crew, this time in a space station, about to embark on an exploration for the origin of life. The Epilogue finds Columbus on his deathbed in 1506. Pondering the journey ahead, he maintains that the passion for exploration is more significant than the individuals who do it; he is transported to the stars.

Other opera composers have used the Columbus theme, notably Darius Milhaud with *Christophe Colombe*, which he launched at the Berlin State Opera in 1930. The work's self-contained first half, *The Discovery of America*, was staged by the San Francisco Opera in 1968.

Paul Goldstaub

VOYAGE NARRATIVES. Voyage narratives have always been prolific and powerful in Western culture because they represent its centrifugal tendencies in pure and graphic form; they are the core of sea literature.

Within the varied array of writing about the sea, ships, and seamen, the voyage narrative constitutes a central and clearly definable genre. Some of its features emerge as early as Noah's encounter with the Flood or Jonah's descent to the bottom of the sea in the belly of a whale. The wanderings of Odysseus established a narrative pattern that has persisted for nearly three millennia, from the *Argonautica* and the *Aeneid* in the ancient world, through the *Inferno*, to modern retellings by James Joyce and Nikos Kazantzakis. Some strands of narrative, like deception of the crew and immobilization during a storm, reappear regularly throughout this broad span of literary history, from the Bible, to Christopher Columbus,* Herman Melville,* and Joseph Conrad.

Larger organizing principles like quest patterns and Utopian themes structure many of the voyage narratives collected by Richard Hakluyt in the closing decades of the sixteenth century, Lemuel Gulliver's voyages in the eighteenth century, and the Caribbean* epics of Ernest Hemingway,* Peter Matthiessen,* and Derek Walcott* in the twentieth century. Other shore genres have gone to sea and established their own maritime variants, including the picaresque romance exploited by Daniel Defoe, Henry Fielding, and Tobias Smollett and the sea bildungsroman, whose young heroes are initiated in the pages of Sir Walter Scott, Frederick Marryat, James Fenimore Cooper,* Richard Henry Dana Jr.,* Melville, and Conrad.

All of these literary continuities and many more suggest that unique qualities in the sea experience may, in part, account for the shape and persistent themes of voyage narratives. Sea voyages are inevitably linear in structure, with clear beginnings, middles, and ends; even whaling or fishing cruises have departures and landfalls, the navigator's essential points of reference in an otherwise trackless waste of water. The ocean retains no imprint of past events on its surface, though its bottom may be littered with historical relics. Add volatility to this surface, which may mirror the sky one day and mount raging obstacles the next, and the images of uncertainty that narratives need emerge from the experience itself. Force a microcosm of human society to endure these vicissitudes in a confined space for a long period of time, and the formula for tension and conflict at the heart of narratives is complete. These elements belong naturally to the experience of voyaging, without literary invention or elaboration, and need only to be refined and ordered by the writer.

Thus, it is not surprising that historical and literary voyage narratives often have a common structure, similar episodes, and shared themes of alienation, endurance, and transformation. Voyages naturally represent a reaching out into the unknown, a test of human ingenuity and skill, and an emblem of the course of human life. In America throughout much of the nineteenth century, such elements were associated with romance, a dominant narrative pattern that insisted on the ulterior meaning of events. In preceding centuries, sea deliverance,* the earliest form of American voyage narrative, had treated the difficult Atlantic crossing as a test of faith as well as human endurance; surviving the storms and reaching the New World were a sign of God's grace. That vision of divine intervention in an ocean crossing is as old as Columbus,* who vowed to undertake a pilgrimage if he survived a fierce gale on his first voyage back to Europe from America.

Later, the Middle Passage on slave ships became a demonic inversion of the voyage of deliverance, detailing a more horrific crossing from freedom into perpetual bondage. The theological overtones of voyaging faded, but the loading of surface events with metaphysical significance has remained endemic in many American voyage narratives to this day. Such voyages may begin with purposes as simple as fishing, whaling, or racing a yacht, but they end up as quests and acquire the trappings of romance. As Ahab* prepares the *Pequod** for his obsessive pursuit in *Moby-Dick* (1851), the minutest details of a whaleship's preparations are transformed into rituals. On a much smaller scale, Santiago's* overreaching in Hemingway's *The Old Man and the Sea** (1952) finds expression in a formulaic motif, "I went out too far." Captain Raib's final turtling voyage in Matthiessen's *Far Tortuga** (1975) is marked by signs and omens throughout and has become a quest for knowledge before its disastrous finale. In Robert Stone's* *Outerbridge Reach* (1992), partly based on the psychological disintegration of a single-handed sailor in the 1968 race around the world, protagonist Owen Browne's quest to live in virtual reality collapses as voices and silences evade his control. In such ways voyages that begin with simple and direct purposes gain metaphysical dimensions that overwhelm their protagonists.

To be sure, the sea romance began as a simpler form in America, and transformations in protagonists' lives were often more transparent and benign. The first triad of James Fenimore Cooper's* dozen sea novels, written in the 1820s, had more conventional themes reflecting American patriotism, the delicate beauty of ships, and the opposed valences of male life at sea and companionship with females ashore. After the lapse of a decade during which Cooper wrote his *History of the Navy* (1839), the eight novels and one biography of the 1840s were more realistic about life on board ships and more concerned with its connection to the politics and economics of life ashore, drawing closer to the social context at the heart of the novel. Some traditions that bridged the gap between the sea romance and the more realistic portrait of life on ships persisted into the twentieth century. The most important of these is the rite of passage or initiation of a youngster at sea. The paradigm in its simplest form appears in Rudyard Kipling's *Captains Courageous** (1897), wherein a boy of the privileged class is suddenly deprived of his advantages and thrust into a menial position on board a sailing ship where he must not only earn his keep but learn to master a new and entirely foreign world.

The sea initiation has a long ancestry in Western culture, stretching back as far as Telemachus, and in America it reappears as the central story in many of Cooper's novels, in Melville's *Redburn** (1849) and *White-Jacket** (1850), and, with more depth and menace, in Jack London's* *The Sea-Wolf** (1904). This same pattern is the source of narrative power in Dana's *Two Years before the Mast** (1840), where it is joined inextricably with another persistent characteristic of voyage narratives: meditation. The meditation in itself is a form of writing native to the experience of seafaring, with a heritage from the *Odyssey*, through Richard Hakluyt, to Melville, Conrad, Hilaire Belloc, Jan de Hartog,* and many others. Seafaring, through its loneliness in a vast surrounding ocean, promotes inner reflection of a kind that is seldom possible in a busy life ashore, and thoughtful mariners have always succumbed to its power as they try to sustain themselves in a beautiful, but alien, world. In American voyage narratives, both Dana and Melville's Ishmael* set a pattern for meditation that has been repeated in subsequent journals and novels.

In addition to the self-discovery of the initiation pattern, voyage narratives provide an extraordinary setting for microcosmic anatomies of society. Cooper's later novels are very much concerned with the social context of seafaring, and Dana, both in *Two Years* and in his subsequent legal work, sought to define and establish a reasonable role for sailors both on board ship and ashore.

Americans have always been uneasy with the rigid and autocratic command structure of shipboard life, and the infamous *Somers** affair of 1842 led Cooper and Dana into opposite camps in a prolonged political and literary dispute about the conduct of her captain, Alexander Slidell Mackenzie*; Henry Carlisle* retells the story of this obscure mutiny,* execution at sea, and court-martial in *Voyage to the First of December* (1972). Melville anatomized naval discipline in both *White-Jacket** (1850) and the posthumous *Billy Budd, Sailor: An Inside Narrative** (1924). Charles Nordhoff* and James Norman Hall revisited the most notorious mutiny of the eighteenth century in their *Bounty* trilogy (1932–1934), and Herman Wouk* invented a plausible modern mutiny in *The* Caine *Mutiny* (1951).

The anatomy of shipboard life also appears in other forms that have nothing to do with mutinies. In *Looking for a Ship* (1990), John McPhee* creates a detailed portrait of contemporary life in the merchant marine. Using a tradition that goes back to Noah, Katherine Anne Porter* loads a whole civilization on board a passenger vessel in *Ship of Fools* (1945). Here American use of the voyage narrative comes full circle, reversing the sea deliverance to the New World by recrossing the Atlantic on the eve of Europe's disintegration in World War II. [*See also* SLAVE NARRATIVES]

FURTHER READING: Bender, Bert. *Sea-Brothers: The Tradition of American Sea Fiction from* Moby-Dick *to the Present.* Philadelphia: U of Pennsylvania P, 1987; Carlson, Patricia Ann, ed. *Literature and Lore of the Sea.* Amsterdam: Rodopi, 1986; Foulke, Robert. *The Sea Voyage Narrative.* New York: Twayne, 1997; Philbrick, Thomas. *James Fenimore Cooper and the Development of American Sea Fiction.* Cambridge: Harvard UP, 1961; Springer, Haskell, ed. *America and the Sea: A Literary History.* Athens: U of Georgia P, 1995.

Robert C. Foulke

THE VOYAGE OF THE NARWHAL (1998). Andrea Barrett (1965–   ) is the author of five novels and a collection of short stories that won the National Book Award for Fiction in 1996. Her *The Voyage of the* Narwhal combines fact and fiction to explore mid-nineteenth-century fascination with the Arctic.* The sea functions throughout the novel to represent human intrigue with nature and to provoke the crew into a battle for their lives.

Having had his work from a previous voyage appropriated by the captain, protagonist Erasmus Darwin Wells, a naturalist, is given a second chance to advance scientific knowledge. Erasmus' dream is compromised by having to choose between promises to his sister, Lavinia, to protect the captain, Zeke, who is also her fiancé, and saving the lives of his crewmates. Erasmus must wait for Zeke to return from a solo expedition or lead his crewmates to safety, which is further complicated by his increasingly tumultuous relationship with Zeke and feelings of ostracism from the crew. Erasmus is also confronted by injured and disgruntled crewmates who refuse to spend another year trapped in ice floes.

Erasmus' decision to save his crewmates haunts him until Zeke miraculously returns home, having been saved by the Esquimaux. Zeke, in a quest for glory, is willing to exploit the people who helped him, which precipitates Erasmus' final act of bravery: returning a motherless boy to his Arctic home. Erasmus also comes to terms with his relationship to nature and to the Esquimaux.

Caroline J. McKenzie

VUKELICH, GEORGE (1927–1995). "[I]t was good to be on the Great Lakes,"* wrote George Vukelich in 1955 to the editor of the *Milwaukee Journal*, after a spell as an ore boat deckhand. This sentiment pervades much of his work, including his only novel, *Fisherman's Beach* (1962); collections of his newspaper columns, *North Country Notebook, Vol. 1* (1987) and *Vol. 2* (1993); his dozen film documentaries, among them *Wild River Country* (1968) and *The Last Menominee* (1965); two decades of radio broadcasts; and numerous short stories and poems, including "The Bosun's Chair" (1960) and "Song of the Ouisconsing" (1953).

Born and raised near Milwaukee, Vukelich was influenced by the Great Lakes from youth. He explored and fished the Lake country with his father, regarding the outdoors as a place of worship. Inspired by Henry David Thoreau* and John Muir, Vukelich revered the Lakes, and his writing often concerns their preservation. His Lakes fiction is vivid and historically accurate.

Donald P. Curtis

W _____

WALCOTT, DEREK [ALTON] (1930–   ). Winner of the 1992 Nobel Prize in literature, Derek Walcott identifies in his life and work two primary inspirations: the Caribbean* Sea and his mixed-race heritage. Born and raised in the harbor city of Castries, St. Lucia, grandson of two white men and two black women, Walcott was from birth immersed in the patois and simple life of the island fishermen. Walcott also enjoyed a privileged British education in St. Lucia and at the University of the West Indies in Jamaica that steeped him early and thoroughly in the classics. He lived in Trinidad for many years, directing the Trinidad Theatre Workshop from 1959 to 1976. He has since divided his time among Boston, New York City, and St. Lucia. Both a poet and a playwright, Walcott has called the Caribbean the "theatre of the sea" and conceived the mission of his theatre company to produce Shakespeare and sing calypso with equal gusto.

The sea is only an occasional focus of Walcott's drama. *The Sea at Dauphin* (1954), a one-act play that Walcott acknowledged to be modeled on John Millington Synge's *Riders to the Sea* (1904), centers on two ragged fishermen, Afa and Gacia, preparing their rowboat for the day's work. An old, drunken peasant, Hounakin, a recent widower, begs to go with them but is refused because Afa believes he wants to drown himself. Later, the fishermen return to a chorus of women on the beach singing a dirge for Hounakin, who has leaped off high rocks into the sea. Daniel Defoe's *Robinson Crusoe* (1719) had a profound impact on Walcott in its theme of a shipwrecked* sailor who adapts to island life. Crusoe's appraising gaze and creative possession of the island, along with his solitary despair, gave Walcott the theme for his two-person play *Pantomime* (1978), in which the roles of an English hotel owner in Tobago and his black handyman are both comically and tragically reversed. In *Odyssey: A Stage Version* (1993) Walcott counterpoints Homeric and Caribbean themes, interspersing Odysseus' protracted wanderings with commentary by the blind singer Billy Blue. Proteus, the Old Man of the Sea, ghosts,* and mermaids* are among the cast.

Walcott's treatment of the sea is far more thoroughgoing in his poetry. In such poems as "The Harbour," from his first collection, *In a Green Night: Poems 1948–1960* (1962), his island and the sea are vantage points for meditation on the passing of youth and love. In "Origins," from the same collection, the sea is the source of all living things. In *The Castaway and Other Poems* (1965) and *The Gulf* (1970), Walcott foregrounds the Crusoe myth. The title poem in *The Castaway* tells of intense isolation; a green wine bottle choked with sand, its message obliterated, is emblem of a futile attempt at communication from the outside world. In "Laventville," also in the Crusoe vein, the sea is a nagging presence the narrator is afraid to face. Images of the castaway occur in "Crusoe's Island" and "Crusoe's Journal." "Homecoming: Anse La Raye," from *The Gulf*, exposes in its sea imagery the poignancy of the West Indian's continued sense of alienation. Although Walcott's autobiographical poem *Another Life* (1973) contains some sparkling maritime lyricism, particularly in Chapters 9, 13, and 18, the Caribbean people take center stage. In "Names," from *Sea Grapes* (1976), Walcott connects his racial history and identity with that of the sea, a bond that is made more explicit in "Sainte Lucie," from the same collection.

The Star-Apple Kingdom (1979) contains, with the exception of *Omeros* (1990), Walcott's most famous and most autobiographical sea poem, "The Schooner *Flight.*" Shabine, the speaker, is a seaman, a poet, and a reprobate, cast out of his native Trinidad but voicing, with Walcott, ambiguity about his mixed-race heritage, a fierce love for the physical beauty of his island, and a profound and essential affinity for the sea. In the same volume, "The Sea Is History" extols the sea as first principle of civilization and memory. "The Lighthouse"* and "A Latin Primer" in *The Arkansas Testament* (1987) evoke both the frigate bird and language of the sea, seminal ideas that return in *Omeros* (1990). "Gros-Ilet," "The Whelk Gatherers," "The Light of the World," and "Oceano Nox" in the same collection are lyrical celebrations of his Caribbean Sea and people. Images of sea creatures and the ocean infuse newer poetry collected in *The Bounty* (1997). Painting the Caribbean Sea is discussed in his essay "On Hemingway*" (*What the Twilight Says: Essays* [1998]).

Omeros is an evocative, extended modern epic poem set in St. Lucia that ostensibly takes place in the space of a single day. Figuratively, though, the poem spans 300 years and several continents and oceans. An elaborate cast of "wounded" characters is led by a group of simple Caribbean fishing people with derivative Greek names. The title character is a shape-shifter whose incarnations include Homer, the sea, and Walcott himself. A sea-swift, loaded with symbolism, figuratively stitches up the wounds of the world by joining two hemispheres together. The supremacy and eternity of the sea, source of healing for the wounds of all the characters, are celebrated in a final scene of baptism and new life. [*See also* DRAMA OF THE SEA; SEA IMAGERY IN MODERN AND CONTEMPORARY POETRY]

FURTHER READING: Bayer, William, ed. *Conversations with Derek Walcott*. Jackson: UP of Mississippi, 1996; Brown, Stewart. *The Art of Derek Walcott*. Chester Springs, PA: Dufour, 1991; Hamner, Robert D., ed. *Critical Perspectives on Derek Walcott*. Washington, DC: Three Continents, 1993; King, Bruce. *Derek Walcott: A Caribbean Life*. Oxford: Oxford UP, 2000; Terada, Rei. *Derek Walcott's Poetry: American Mimicry*. Boston: Northeastern UP, 1992.

Jill B. Gidmark

WARNER, WILLIAM W[HITESIDES]. (1920–   ). Naturalist-author William W. Warner was born in New York City. From 1944 to 1946, he served in the U.S. Navy, where he rose to the rank of lieutenant, junior grade, and was awarded a Navy Commendation Medal.

Warner is primarily known for his nonfiction work *Beautiful Swimmers: Watermen, Crabs and the Chesapeake Bay* (1976), an ethnographic chronicle of the crabbing culture of the Chesapeake. While painstaking in its scientific descriptions of crabs and crabbing technology, *Beautiful Swimmers* engages the lay reader with Warner's humorous flourishes and his anthropologist-like attention to the rich detail of the lives of Chesapeake watermen. The book captured the 1977 Pulitzer Prize in general nonfiction and the Phi Beta Kappa Award in science.

His second book, *Distant Waters: The Fate of the North Atlantic Fishermen* (1983), grew out of his research trips aboard several North Atlantic trawlers. The work examines the impact of the giant vessels on the Atlantic fishing industry and serves as both a critical assessment and an homage, since such trawlers later fell out of use after the enactment of fishing quotas.

Warner has been active in various conservation organizations, including the Rachel Carson* Trust for the Living Environment and the Chesapeake Bay Foundation. In 1988 he retired from a lengthy career of government service, most notably as an information officer in Latin America and as a research associate and administrator for the Smithsonian Institution.

Brian Anderson

WHALING NARRATIVES. Whalemen often kept their shipboard accounts in the form of a logbook or journal, which was more or less a personal narrative of the seaman's voyage. Commonly elaborated ashore into a more coherent narrative, the most interesting examples offer a detailed view of shipboard life, describing not only the writer's experiences through the voyage but his emotional reaction to those experiences.

American whalemen were often on their ships for two or three years, and life in the ship's universe and in the ship's ports of call, particularly in the Pacific and Arctic,* was noteworthy for its unique aspects. Shipboard life included not only the business of whaling but also other ship duties. Numerous diversions were necessary to make life in cramped and otherwise uncomfortable quarters bearable; scrimshaw and other artistic endeavors, songs, and plays were all recorded.

Because most whalemen before the mast were not well educated, most whalemen's journals had little literary pretense and even less literary merit. Journals descriptive of disasters were the earliest type of American journal to be published. These include Owen Chase's* *Narrative of the Most Extraordinary and Distressing Shipwreck* of the Whale-Ship* Essex* (1821), William Lay and Cyrus M. Hussey's *A Narrative of the Mutiny,* on Board the Whaleship* Globe* (1828), Horace Holden's *A Narrative of the Shipwreck, Captivity, and Sufferings of Horace Holden and Benj. H. Nute* (1836), Elisha Dexter's *Narrative of the Wreck and Loss of the Whaling Brig* William and Joseph (1842), Thomas Spencer's *Narrative of the Events Attending the Massacre of Part of the Crew Belonging to the Whaleship* Triton, *of New-Bedford, by the Natives of Sydenham's Island* (1848), Alonzo Sampson's *Three Times around the World* (1867), Charles S. Taber's *A Narrative of a Shipwreck in the Fiji Islands 1840* (1894), and Thomas I. Jenkins' *Bark* Kathleen *Sunk by a Whale* (1902). A number were published for pecuniary reasons, such as J. C. Mullett's *Five Years on the Pacific Ocean* (1858).

Descriptions of exotic life, particularly in the Pacific, were also popular. Representative examples are Francis Allyn Olmsted's* *Incidents of a Whaling Voyage* (1841), William Torrey's *Torrey's Narrative: or, the Life and Adventures of William Torrey, Who . . . Was Held a Captive by the Cannibals of the Marquesas* (1848), Edward T. Perkins' *Na Motu: or, Reef-Rovings in the South Seas* (1854), Charles L. Newhall's *Adventures of Jack* (1859), and James H. Woodhouse's *Autobiography of Captain James H. Woodhouse* (1897).

An often-published genre of American whaling literature was the reform narrative. Some were consciously modeled after Richard Henry Dana Jr.'s* *Two Years before the Mast* (1840); J. Ross Browne's* *Etchings of a Whaling Cruise* (1846) is perhaps the best example. Others include Stephen Curtis' *Brief Extracts* (1844), Rev. Henry T. Cheever's* *The Whale and His Captors* (1849), George Whitfield Bronson's *Glimpses of a Whalemen's Cabin* (1855), and Daniel Weston Hall's *Arctic* Rovings* (1861). A subcategory included whalers who had found religion or who had recovered from alcoholism, including Joseph Gatchell's *The Disenthralled* (1843), Reuben Delano's *The Wanderings of Reuben Delano* (1846), and George L. Colburn's *Scraps from the Log Book of George Lightcraft* (1847). Some women at sea, wives or daughters of whaling masters, kept journals, but none were contemporarily published.

Imaginative literature sometimes took the form of a whaling journal: Herman Melville's* *Moby-Dick* (1851) is the best-known example. Melville's sources included Owen Chase's *Narrative* (cited earlier) and Jeremiah N. Reynolds'* "Mocha Dick," a story of a white whale first published in the

Knickerbocker (1839). Other novelists used the form of a whaling journal, including Charles M. Newell in *Leaves from an Old Log. Péhe-Nú-e* (1877). Newell, a sometime whaling master, consciously drew on *Moby-Dick*. English author Frank T. Bullen, who had sailed on an American whaler, used the experience for his *Cruise of the "Cachalot"* (1898).

Film adaptations of whaling narratives include *Down to the Sea in Ships* (1922, 1949). [*See also* HART, JOSEPH C.; JOURNALS AND LOG-BOOKS; WOMEN AT SEA]

FURTHER READING Busch, Briton Cooper. *"Whaling Will Never Do for Me": The American Whaleman in the Nineteenth Century*. Lexington: U of Kentucky P, 1994; Forster, Honore. *The South Sea Whaler*. Sharon, MA: Kendall Whaling Museum, and Fairhaven, MA: Edward J. Lefkowicz, 1985; Forster, Honore. *More South Sea Whaling*. Canberra: Research School of Pacific Studies, Australian National U, 1991; Hohman, Elmo P. *The American Whaleman*. New York: Longmans, 1928; Miller, Pamela. *And the Whale Is Ours: Creative Writing of American Whalemen*. Boston: Godine, 1979; Sherman, Stuart C. *The Voice of the Whaleman with an Account of the Nicholson Whaling Collection*. Providence, RI: Providence Public Library, 1965.

Edward J. Lefkowicz

WHITE, E[LWYN]. B[ROOKS]. (1899–1983). Best known for his articles in *The New Yorker* and his children's books, E. B. White reflected significantly upon his relationship with the sea in two important essays, "The Years of Wonder" and "The Sea and the Wind That Blows." The first, written on 13 March 1961 and originally appearing in *The New Yorker*, recounts his time aboard the steamer *Buford* in 1923. White began the round-trip voyage from Seattle to Siberia as a passenger but became a crew member once on board, thus experiencing the sea in a new way. "The Sea and the Wind That Blows" was written in the winter of 1963 and originally published in *Ford Times*. It addresses his lifelong affection for the sea and his lasting relationship with it, even in old age. Both works were reprinted in *Essays of E. B. White* (1977).

Raised on the Maine coast, White sailed for pleasure during his boyhood. Through adulthood he maintained his connection to the sea by building, operating, buying, and selling various watercraft. White's family has maintained an interest in the sea and in traditional boats. Prior to his death in 1997, his son, Joel White, was a craftsman and master designer of wooden sailboats at the Brooklin Boat Yard, in Brooklin, Maine, which he owned and operated. Douglas Whynott's *A Unit of Water, a Unit of Time: Joel White's Last Boat* (1999) is a reverent portrait chronicling White's effort, while battling cancer, to complete his final design, the W-76, a wooden racing boat. Whynott's earlier book, *Giant Bluefin* (1995), focuses on tuna fishing on Massachusetts Bay and the politically charged conflicts between the fishermen and conservationists.

Hillary Frey and Mira Dock

WHITE-JACKET (1850). Based on his experiences in the U.S. Navy, Herman Melville's* (1819–1891) protagonist White-Jacket narrates the voyage of a young man on the *Neversink* as it cruises from Hawai'i, around Cape Horn,* to its home port. Melville's subtitle, *The World in a Man-of-War*, indicates that Melville also attempts to present a full portrait of all aspects of life on board: he describes the various stations, from the maintop to the gundeck, and positions, from the highest officers to the lowest men. Melville's narrator takes an activist position relative to this society, frequently lashing out against the abuses suffered by the sailors. He provides particularly graphic and outraged indictments of the practice of flogging and, more generally, of the arrogation of power by the officers. As the novel proceeds, White-Jacket becomes increasingly concerned with the extent to which life on a man-of-war is bound up with death.

In contrast, from his position in the maintop under the tutelage of seasoned sailors like Jack Chase, White-Jacket comes to appreciate much that is positive about naval life. Jack and other sailors spin their yarns, telling of adventures and exotic locales, and White-Jacket relishes his superior position in the maintop. He comes to feel a sense of development or accomplishment from his experiences as a sailor.

The sea figures prominently in one major scene, one of the most dramatic in all of Melville's writing. Near the end, White-Jacket, plagued by his absurd and impractical jacket throughout the voyage, becomes tangled in it and falls from the maintop into the sea. There he feels the approach of death, rips off the jacket, and surfaces with a new sense of freedom. Springing back into the maintop, he optimistically feels a predestined sense of being "homeward-bound." [*See also THE RED RECORD*]

FURTHER READING: Anderson, Charles R. *Melville in the South Seas*. New York: Columbia UP, 1939; Samson, John. *White Lies: Melville's Narratives of Facts*. Ithaca, NY: Cornell UP, 1989; Vincent, Howard P. *The Tailoring of Melville's* White-Jacket. Evanston, IL: Northwestern UP, 1970.

John Samson

WHITMAN, WALT[ER] (1819–1892). Walt Whitman was born in West Hills, near Huntington on northwestern Long Island. With almost two centuries of ancestral residence on the island and some seafaring tradition in his family, Whitman was naturally attuned to the ocean and its related occupations. Not until 1848 did he venture for any extended period of time beyond the islands now constituting New York City. Even then, his short stay that year in New Orleans placed him on the Mississippi River and the Gulf of Mexico. Whitman returned to New York in the same year, via the Mississippi River, the Great Lakes,* and the Hudson River. On his return, he remained in and around Brooklyn for several years.

Publication of early editions of Whitman's repeatedly revised life's work, *Leaves of Grass* (1855 through 1891–1892), his positions as writer and newspaper editor, and his building ventures provided some money and opportunities for more travel. He visited Ralph Waldo Emerson in Boston and stayed for extended periods in Civil War camps with his brother George. During the Civil War, Whitman held government clerkships in Washington, D.C., so he could nurse sick and wounded Civil War soldiers. In early 1865 he was discharged from one federal government position for the purported obscenity of some of his writings, but intervention by supporters led to his transfer to another government position. Heat prostration in 1872 and a paralytic condition in 1873 led Whitman to move to his brother's home in Camden, New Jersey. From that time until his death, Camden would remain Whitman's point of return.

From his earliest days, Whitman knew, loved, and lived in close proximity to the sea, the shore, and their related activities. He wrote of these throughout a literary career that spanned five decades. One cannot read many pages of Whitman's poetry or prose without encountering references to the sea and those who sail it. In some instances, these references are direct and literal; in others, they allow Whitman to advance larger concepts. "Mannahatta" (1860, 1881) describes the sea-borne life and economy of Manhattan Island. "Song of Joys" (1860, 1881) devotes pages to describing lobstering, mackerel fishing, boating, and whaling. "Salut au Monde" (1856, 1881) has a half-page catalog of "the sail and steamships of the world." However, not all Whitman's literary references to the sea are celebratory. The 1855 edition of *Leaves of Grass* includes an extended narration on a strong swimmer in the ocean, rammed by eddies into the rocky shore, bloodied, battered, drowned, and ultimately carried off by the tide.

Whitman's poetry also portrays American sea history, fostering new myths of heroism for American democracy. For example, "Song of Myself" (1855, 1881) narrates John Paul Jones'* signal naval victory over the British *Serapis* during the American Revolution; the Americans engaged and victoriously boarded the British *Serapis* from their own sinking vessel, the *Bonhomme Richard.** This poem also details the heroic rescue of passengers aboard the drifting and rudderless steamship the *San Francisco*, en route from New York on 23–24 December 1853; the rescuing captain tacks relentlessly for days to stay with the foundering ship and chalks a message to its passengers, making clear his determination to save them.

Whitman's funeral ode for Abraham Lincoln, "O Captain! My Captain!" (1865–1866, 1881) mingles nautical imagery with allusions to the victory of Admiral Nelson's British fleet over Napoleon's larger French and Spanish fleet off Trafalgar, Spain, on 21 October 1805. Whitman's poem represents Lincoln as saving the Union in the same selfless way that Horatio Nelson secures control of the sea for Britain, rendering sea-borne invasion impossible. Both national heroes die pursuing their victories. Although no direct reference to Nelson is made, the parallels are unmistakable.

Sea and seashore references also describe Whitman's personal and poetic biography. "Starting from Paumanok" (1860, 1881) provides an idealized version of the poet's past, while in "Out of the Cradle Endlessly Rocking" (1859, 1881–1882) the sea and its tides, two birds, and a tale of life and death relate Whitman's awakening pact with an integrated vision of his poetic destiny as a singer of both life's pains and joys. Whitman's poem "Facing West from California's Shores" (1860, 1867) uses a classical vision of the western seas to suggest his own impending death. "Old Age's Ship and Crafty Death's" (1890, 1891–1892) parallels Alfred Tennyson's poem "Ulysses" (1842) in its determination to continue the good fight in the face of advancing age and declining resources.

Much more important, however, are Whitman's poems that use references to physical seas to advance larger concepts. Whitman portrays land as the realm of apparent certainty and stasis, while he presents oceans as reflecting the reality of uncertain outcomes, ongoing change, and the unremitting ebb and flow of manifold and often apparently conflicting universal forces. On that basis, sea voyages* and voyagers in Whitman's poetry are readily associated with reality, aspiration, adventure, and heroism. Similarly, in poems such as "In Cabin'd Ships at Sea" (1871), Whitman compares his poetry in *Leaves of Grass* to the voyage of a sailing ship. His poems attempt to capture the realities of both sea and shore, poetically reflecting their multifaceted rhythms, tones, and ever-changing forces. On that basis, he hopes sailors' experiences will attune them to his poetry's worldview as well as its undulations, pulsations, and "liquid flowing syllables." Whitman broadens this comparison in the poems constituting "Fancies at Navesink" (1885, 1888–1889). There, he associates life with poetic aspirations and despairs, ships, voyages, ebbing and rising tides, the undulations of waves, and God's plan.

Believing in correspondences between human and natural realms, Whitman equates the hopes, dreams, and risks of a poetic venture, an extended voyage of discovery to exotic, largely unknown locales, and the heroic adventure by which the soul seeks to know itself and achieve oneness with God. Whitman sees the unity of all time and place and the perfectibility of all. The preface to the 1855 edition of *Leaves of Grass* makes clear his belief that poetry should move from the physical realm to spiritual implications. "Crossing Brooklyn Ferry" (1856, 1881) and "Passage to India" (1871, 1881) do just that. In the former poem, the sights and sounds of the short ferry ride from Manhattan to Brooklyn give way to a vision of the perfection of all times and places and to acceptance of the cosmos and human nature. In "Passage to India," temporal, physical, geographical journeys and links are portrayed as analogous to the human soul in search of itself and God.

In sea voyages, literary ventures, life itself, and the spiritual journey of the soul, Whitman sees and affirms the ebb and flow of cosmic forces. The rising tides of youth, aspiration, and success are balanced against the ebbing tides of age, literary and philosophical uncertainty, life reversals, calamities at sea, and death. The "Sea Drift" section of *Leaves of Grass* includes such sea poems as "Out of the Cradle Endlessly Rocking" (1859, 1881), "As I Ebb'd with the Ocean of Life" (1860, 1881), "To the Man-of-War Bird" (1876, 1881), and others. It embeds this vision of antithetical cosmic forces in marine settings and situations. These poems begin with expressions of mutability, loss, destruction, and death in all realms. Flotsam and jetsam, debris, and sea drift mark the scene and testify to the enormity of destructive forces. Ultimately, however, these poems surmount the apparent victory of death and destruction, reasserting the life-supporting principle of complementary opposition. Fuller, richer life in all its aspects arises out of loss and death. The lifeless sea drift and debris provide the seeds for "man elate over death."

Whitman's poetry rebels against nineteenth-century poetic conventions and limitations. In rejecting then-current poetic forms, it relies on rhythmic repetition, not syllable counting, for poetic regularity. The repetitive, yet ever-changing, rhythm of ocean waves and tides provides both analogy to, and inspiration for, Whitman's poetic revolution. Such rhythm has induced at least three notable composers to set texts of Whitman to music. Howard Hanson wrote a short choral work about a grand voyage on the high seas as an explicit metaphor for life's voyage to death and, presumably, to eternity in his *Symphony No. 7*, subtitled "Sea Symphony" (1974), which uses three fragments from *Leaves of Grass*: "Lo the Sea! The Unbounded Sea," "The Untold Want, by Life and Land Ne'er Granted," and "Joy, Shipmate, Joy!" Ralph Vaughan Williams' much longer *A Sea Symphony* (1907) uses such Whitman poems as "A Song for All Seas, All Ships" and "On the Beach at Night Alone." Composer John Adams has set "The Wound-Dresser" for baritone voice and orchestra (1989, 1992). [*See also* SEA IMAGERY IN MODERN AND CONTEMPORARY POETRY]

FURTHER READING: Allen, Gay Wilson. *A Reader's Guide to Walt Whitman.* Syracuse, NY: Syracuse UP, 1997; Bradley, Sculley, Harold W. Blodgett, Arthur Golden, and William White, eds. *Leaves of Grass: A Textual Variorum of the Printed Poems.* New York: New York UP, 1980; Flibbert, Joseph. "Poetry in the Mainstream," *America and the Sea: A Literary Biography.* Ed. Haskell Springer. Athens: U of Georgia P, 1995, 109–26; LeMaster, J. R., and Donald D. Kummings, eds. *Walt Whitman: An Encyclopedia.* New York: Garland, 1998.

Philip A. Greasley

WHITTIER, JOHN GREENLEAF (1807–1892). A Quaker abolitionist and poet, John Greenleaf Whittier epitomizes the poet of rural life. With his New England contemporaries, however, he had little relish for straying far from the reach of the sea breeze. Sea motifs and imagery enter his earliest poetry from unexpected sources, such as Vikings in "The Norsemen" (1841) and Voyageurs in "The Bridal of Penacook" (1844). But even earlier than these he had written "The Slave-Ships" (1834), based on horror stories of the Middle Passage. "The Ship-Builders" (1846) reinforces Whittier's contention that ships should be constructed only for moral purposes, specifically abjuring the opium and slave trades.

"Skipper Ireson's Ride" (1857), like most legendary material, gains power in proportion as it strays from history. "The Dead Ship of Harpswell" (1866), "The Palatine"* (1867), and "The Three Bells" (1872) follow in the same folkloric vein: Whittier frequently wrote from oral sources without the constraint of formal history, a technique that drew criticism on more than one occasion. His late poems "The Bay of Seven Islands" (1882) and "To a Cape Ann Schooner" (1886) celebrate, respectively, Whittier's "home" waters of Massachusetts and their craft, in this case a vessel named after Whittier himself. [*See also* GHOSTS AND GHOST SHIPS; SEA IMAGERY IN MODERN AND CONTEMPORARY POETRY; SLAVE NARRATIVES]

R. D. Madison

WILKES, CHARLES. *See* U.S. EXPLORING EXPEDITION.

WILLIAMS, TENNESSEE [THOMAS LANIER] (1911–1983). Winner of four New York Drama Critics' Circle Awards and two Pulitzer Prizes for his plays, Tennessee Williams is most identified with the American South. He was born in Mississippi and spent his early childhood there until the family settled in St. Louis in 1918. Although many of his plays are set in New Orleans or along the Mississippi Delta, his works range geographically from desert, to jungle, to mountain, and to sea.

Williams' first transatlantic crossing was on the S.S. *Homeric* in 1928, accompanying his grandfather on a summer trip to Europe. A violent bout of seasickness clouded the first days of that voyage, but he was to make many pleasurable crossings after earning recognition on Broadway. Among the ships mentioned in his *Memoirs* (1975) are the *Queen Mary*, the *Vulcania*, the *Andrea Doria*, and the *Ile de France*. The early 1940s brought visits to Provincetown on Cape Cod,* Acapulco, Key West,* and Havana, all providing opportunities for his favorite recreation, swimming. Ultimately, he bought a house in Key West.

Williams' first produced play was set in a seaport. This one-act, *Cairo! Shanghai! Bombay!* (first perf. 1935; not pub.), presented by amateurs in a residential garden in Memphis, where he was spending a summer with his grandparents, shows funny and touching interactions between sailors and ladies of the night. Sailors are mentioned or appear as minor characters in a number of Williams' plays, often evoking a sense of rootlessness and/or erotic activity. Tom, the character whose memories reconstruct the action of *The Glass Menagerie* (first perf. 1944; pub. 1945; film adaptations 1950, 1987, 1993; television 1966, 1973), has abandoned his mother and sister to become a "merchant sailor." In *The Rose Tattoo* (first perf. 1950; pub.

1950; film adaptation 1955), the teenaged Rosa falls for a sailor named Jack, who has just come home on leave after three months at sea; Rosa's mother particularly objects to the tightness of Jack's navy pants. The opportunistic drifter Chance Wayne in *Sweet Bird of Youth* (first perf. 1959; pub. 1959; film adaptation 1962, 1987; television 1989) mentions that he went into the navy because that was the uniform that looked best on him. Sailors carouse in a bar in the screenplay *One Arm* (first perf. 1948; pub. 1954), and a yacht is used for filming a pornographic movie. Violet of *Small Craft Warnings* (first perf. 1972; pub. 1972) is drawn to "drunk sailor boys." In Williams' most directly autobiographical play, *Something Cloudy, Something Clear* (first perf. 1981; pub. 1995), the character of the author (named August) has two homosexual encounters with a drunken merchant seaman.

Among the authors admired by Williams, Hart Crane* exerted an influence related to the sea. Hart Crane and his mother appear as the two characters in the one-act *Steps Must Be Gentle* (first perf. 1980; not pub.), speaking to each other in a "hypothetical communication" fifteen years after the poet's death. Tormented by his mother's inability to countenance his homosexuality and making a choice to "rest at the floor of the sea," Crane had leaped to his death from the deck of the steamship *Orizaba* about twelve hours north of Havana. According to his *Memoirs*, Williams specified in his will that he be buried at sea near the probable site of Crane's bones. His language in that passage bears striking similarities to that of Blanche DuBois in the final scene of *A Streetcar Named Desire* (first perf. 1947; pub. 1949; film adaptation 1951, 1997; television 1984, 1995, 1998), when she fantasizes about death on the ocean and burial at sea. A similar, though pared-down, version of ocean burial is recounted in *The Night of the Iguana* (first perf. 1961; pub. 1969; film adaptations 1964, 2000) when the Costa Verde hotel proprietor Maxine tells how her husband, Fred, had been dropped in the sea, as he requested on his deathbed. In the same play, Shannon's notion of suicide is to take "the long swim to China." In *Sweet Bird of Youth*, a last resort for Chance Wayne also would be to swim out until sharks and barracudas take him for live bait.

The sea is crucial to the action or atmosphere of several plays. One of the most vivid passages in *Suddenly Last Summer* (first perf. 1958; pub; 1958; film adaptation 1959; television 1993) is Mrs. Venable's recollection of her voyage with her son Sebastian on a four-masted schooner to the Galápagos* (called the Encantadas*), inspired by the sketches of Herman Melville,* where they watch newly-hatched sea turtles make their desperate dash across the sand to the sea while attacked by flesh-eating birds. In Catherine's account of her last moments with Sebastian, she wants to go toward the sea for safety, to the waterfront and docks where a taxi might be found, but Sebastian makes the fatal mistake of heading uphill away from the sea, only to be attacked by a birdlike flock of cannibalistic children.

Sweet Bird of Youth is set in a Gulf Coast hotel overlooking a vast stretch of water. Chance Wayne has come "back to the sea" as a kind of refuge and remembrance of a lost youth when he and his girlfriend used to find privacy on Diamond Key, an offshore sandbar that would be inundated at high tide. Minnie's yacht, on the other hand, serves as a mecca of depravity. In *The Night of the Iguana*, the lure of the still-water beach below the hotel motivates the exits and entrances of various characters who go, and return from, swimming. Most importantly, the nonagenarian Nonno makes it clear that he is urgently drawn to the sea, which he calls "the cradle of life." If life began in the sea, as he claims, then his death near the sea at the end of the play suggests the centrality of the sea in the circular process of life. In *The Milk Train Doesn't Stop Here Anymore* (first perf. 1964; pub. 1964), the so-called Angel of Death Christopher Flanders also refers to the sea as the cradle of life, as well as of civilizations. The play is set in a villa that is supposedly inaccessible except by water, on "the oldest sea in the Western world," the Mediterranean.

Williams often used sea sounds for theatrical effect. Sea or gulf winds blow through many of the hitherto mentioned plays as well as *Summer and Smoke* (first perf. 1947; pub. 1964; film adaptation 1961; television 1972). The boom of the surf punctuates the action in *The Milk Train Doesn't Stop Here Anymore* and *Something Cloudy, Something Clear*. *Small Craft Warnings*, set in a bar above "the Pacific, the world's greatest ocean," employs both the wind and the boom. Fish-eating seabirds flap and swoosh over the scene throughout the one-act *The Gnädiges Fräulein* (first perf. 1966; pub. 1967), which is set on Cacaloony Key and calls for a color scheme emphasizing the grayish white color of pelicans. The one-act *Lifeboat Drill* (first perf. 1981; not pub.) is set in a first-class stateroom aboard the *Queen Elizabeth II*.

Other plays contain at least passing references to the sea. In *Camino Real* (first perf. 1953; pub. 1953; film adaptation 1964), the plaza of a surrealistic tropical seaport is dominated by the luxury hotel *Siete Mares* (Seven Seas) and the fleabag Ritz Men Only; the proprietor of the latter stands in the doorway and metaphorically hawks a vacancy as "a little white ship to sail the dangerous night in." In *The Two-Character Play* (first perf. 1975; pub. 1969), a brother and sister reminisce about swimming off the Gulf Coast that "connects with a sea" and that could itself be called a sea because of its gulls and tides. References to a yacht, deck, and northern lights evoke the sea in *In the Bar of a Tokyo Hotel* (first perf. 1969; pub. 1970). Ernest Hemingway* appears in *Clothes for a Summer Hotel* (first perf. 1980; pub. 1983) and talks about his story "Sea Change." In *The Notebook of Trigorin* (first perf. 1981; pub. 1997), the sea is evoked indirectly in Nina's recitation of Treplev's monodrama and perhaps even in her last-act confession that she has given her child, a "sea gull" like herself, to a couple who took the baby to America. [*See also* DRAMA OF THE SEA]

FURTHER READING: Leverich, Lyle. *Tom. The Unknown Tennessee Williams.* New York: Crown, 1995; Roudané, Matthew C., ed. *The Cambridge Companion to Tennessee Williams.* Cambridge: Cambridge UP, 1997; Williams, Tennessee. *Memoirs.* New York: Doubleday, 1972.

Felicia Hardison Londré

WILLIAMS, WILLIAM CARLOS (1883–1963).

Although modern poet, novelist, and essayist William Carlos Williams once said that all of his art came out of the work-yard of his lifelong home in Rutherford, New Jersey, where he practiced medicine, that is not altogether true. He also traveled upon, and wrote about, the sea. In 1909 he departed from Philadelphia on a second-class ocean liner, the S.S. *Marquette,* for a twelve-day trip across the Atlantic. Williams recalled several moments from this first sea voyage in his book of prose and poems entitled *The Descent of Winter* (1928). Williams and his wife, Floss, took a second trip to Europe in 1924, on the S.S. *Rochambeau* out of New York. He would recall this crossing two years later in the opening passages of his second novel, *A Voyage to Pagany* (1928).

He also traveled in 1931 to Nova Scotia on the steamship S.S. *Voyageur.* The steamer made its way up the Saint Lawrence River as far as St. Anthony's, Newfoundland, and then looped back again. Williams had vowed to swim in the northern waters, so took a dip off Greenly Island, Newfoundland, but the water was too cold for him, and overall the trip was an alienating one. The fog, the weed strands, the midges, and the poverty in the small fishing villages were to contribute to Williams' growing sense of the sea as something alien, deathlike, and deeply tragic.

An early long poem, "Spring and All" (1923), includes a section wherein the sea's many watery arms enviously enclose a young girl's body. A later poem, "The Yachts" (1935), depicts the same alien sea waves, tearfully reaching for the vibrant, youthful yachts whose sharp prows slip easily past them. Many of the titles in *Poems 1929–1935* incorporate a sense of the sea: "The Sea Elephant," "Flowers by the Sea," "The Sun Bathers," and "Nantucket."* The Nova Scotia trip was the source for one of the best-known sea poems in the volume, "The Cod-Head." The sight and smell of hundreds of codfish heads in various states of decay on the strand and bobbling in the waters were Williams' inspiration. An important theme in the poem is sacrifice.

The alien sea also figures powerfully in *Paterson* (1946–1958), Williams' famous long poem. At the end of Book IV, entitled "Run to the Sea," the protagonist emerges from the sea, a place that is "not our home," and turns toward the land, just as Williams, perhaps, in a less grand way, always returned to his work-yard in Rutherford. [*See also* SEA IMAGERY IN MODERN AND CONTEMPORARY POETRY]

Robert E. Kibler

WILSON, GILBERT [BROWN] (1907–1991). Having studied in the 1930s to be a muralist, from the 1940s through the 1960s Gilbert Wilson worked in diverse media to interpret *Moby-Dick** (1851) visually, with the intention of bringing Herman Melville's* novel to the attention of the American common people. In the early 1940s, while working with Rockwell Kent* on a mural, Wilson read *Moby-Dick* for the first time, in the edition that Kent had illustrated. He took exception to Kent's interpretation of the novel and especially with Kent's portrayal of Captain Ahab.* The result was a lifelong obsession with painting the scenes and characters in the book, concentrating on Ahab and the white whale. During this period, he created over 300 dramatic paintings inspired by the novel, which became the basis for a film adaptation of *Moby-Dick* (1955).

In addition, he wrote a libretto, entitled *The White Whale* (c.1965), designing a stage set and scenes for an operatic version of the novel. To begin the opera, Wilson envisioned a cosmic backdrop, against which an image of the whale would appear. This fusion of sea and cosmos he returned to again for one of his final projects, his design for the ceiling of the Frankfort, Kentucky, post office (c.1970). Although never realized as a mural, Wilson's painting of Moby Dick, swimming among stars, planets, and galaxies, projects a wondrous and mysterious interpretation of Melville's whale and of the sea. [*See also* MELVILLE DRAMATIZATIONS]

Elizabeth Schultz

WILSON, SLOAN (1920–   ). Sloan Wilson was a Coast Guard officer before he became a novelist and a yachtsman before he gained a commission in the Coast Guard. He came to regard his Coast Guard experience as more educative than his B.A. from Harvard; the latter two of the three novels that he based on this seagoing service rival in quality his better-known novels, *The Man in the the Grey Flannel Suit* (1955) and *A Summer Place* (1958).

In early 1942 Wilson merely had to pass an examination to get a commission; consequently, upon his first reporting aboard the Coast Guard cutter *Tampa*, the ship's executive officer ridiculed his lack of experience. But after several months escorting convoys on the Greenland Patrol, Wilson was proficient enough to command the small trawler *Nogak*, which was engaged in the same kind of work. He would base the novel *Ice Brothers* (1979) upon this arduous service. Later, Wilson skippered an army supply ship from Long Beach to various ports in the South Pacific, a cruise that supplied the basis for his first novel, *Voyage to Somewhere* (1947). Contracting pneumonia, Wilson had to relinquish this ship, but later he was given command of a gasoline tanker. He wrote *Pacific Interlude* (1982), his most directly autobiographical novel, about this experience.

All these novels manifest authenticity in their descriptions of naval and seagoing trials. Readers of *Pacific Interlude*, for example, participate fully in the fear of their gasoline tanker being blown literally to bits by a stray spark or bullet and understand the disintegrative effect this fear has on the ship's young officers and green crew. Wilson saved some of his most compelling descriptions of his formative Coast Guard days for his 1978 autobiography, *What Shall We Wear to This Party?*, some eighty pages of which describe his exhausting initiation aboard small ships in the ice, cold, and storms of the North Atlantic.

Robert Shenk

WOLF LARSEN. The brutal and eloquent captain of the sealing-schooner *Ghost* in *The Sea-Wolf** (1904), a novel by Jack London* (1876–1916), Captain Wolf Larsen rescues effete writer Humphrey Van Weyden from drowning after a ferry accident and then forces him to work on board his vessel. Shipboard isolation allows Larsen to test his notions of survival of the fittest.

According to Larsen, men are no more than bits of yeast devouring each other. Van Weyden—the specimen in this experiment—feebly objects, citing bookish clichés about morality and spirituality. But Larsen, the biggest bit of yeast on his own ship, demonstrates that Van Weyden's vaguely defined ideals are inadequate to explain the rough life at sea. Larsen's demonstrations are vivid and sometimes painful. At one point, for instance, he chokes Van Weyden until he loses consciousness just to illustrate the instinct for survival at any cost. Larsen's bleak philosophy is self-taught, though sometimes he asserts that he would be happier had he, like his equally brutish but intellectually illiterate brother "Death" Larsen, never opened a book. Ironically, Larsen teaches Van Weyden the tenacity and sailing skills he needs to stand on his own feet and eventually overcome his oppressor.

London intended Wolf Larsen's demise to debunk the philosophy of crass materialism that London had learned about from reading Herbert Spencer and Friedrich Nietzsche. However, many readers continue to find Larsen's pragmatism more compelling than Van Weyden's idealism. The novel, they believe, loses vitality and integrity when it shifts its focus from Larsen to a conventional love relationship between Van Weyden and a woman writer, Maud Brewster, conveniently rescued from another accident at sea. Regardless of London's intent, Wolf Larsen remains one of the most memorable characters in all of sea fiction.

Stephen Curley

WOMEN AT SEA. Women's sea narratives exist in far fewer numbers than narratives written by men. Nevertheless, it has always been possible to find women at sea. Most often they have traveled aboard ship as passengers, servants, or slaves. The overwhelming majority of these women left no record of their experiences at sea, but there are glimpses of them in naval and customs records, in men's logbooks and journals, and especially in the memorials of other female seafarers.

Women before 1700 would have been unable to set down their own experiences at sea. William Bradford did not acknowledge the women and children aboard the *Mayflower* in *Of Plimoth Plantation* (1856). However, Jonathan Dickinson's narrative of the shipwreck of the *Reformation* on the coast of Florida, *God's Protecting Providence* (1699), recounted the sufferings of his wife, infant son, and female slaves, although he seldom referred to them by name.

Janet Schaw, a Scottish gentlewoman, recorded her real sympathy for the penniless indentured servants living in crowded and unsanitary conditions belowdecks as she traveled in relative comfort on the *Jamaica Packet* on the eve of the American Revolution. The spoiled rations they were given scarcely diverted starvation, and their few possessions were ruined in a violent storm. The cries of the afflicted women spilled onto the pages of her private diary, published much later as *Journal of a Woman of Quality* (1934).

English women forged the path for Americans to follow. Lady Mary Wortley Montagu's travel narratives, the missionary activities of the Messrs. Judson in Burma, even cross-dressing accounts of female marine Hannah Snell and Royal Navy shipwright Mary Lacy were published in America after 1790. These and other European publications influenced the development of American women's travel narratives, missionary accounts, and sea stories.

Shipwreck* narratives written by women began to be published in America after 1800. In an extreme example, Ann Saunders aboard the drifting *Mary Francis* drank the blood of her dead fiancé and butchered corpses for distribution to the living while praying earnestly for rescue (*Narrative of the Shipwreck and Sufferings of Miss Ann Saunders . . .* [1827]). As in other shipwreck narratives by men and women published during the Second Great Awakening, Saunders presented her rescue from the gruesome ordeal as an example of divine providence and a religious exhortation to unredeemed sinners.

The majority of women's shipwreck narratives printed in America before 1830, however, concern European women shipwrecked or taken by pirates* off the coast of North Africa. Although these are almost certainly spurious, verified accounts of Englishwomen captives in North Africa go back to the seventeenth century. Two publications, *History of the Captivity and Sufferings of Maria Martin* (c.1806) and *Authentic Narrative of the Shipwreck and Sufferings of Mrs. Eliza Bradley* (1820), went into at least ten editions each before the Civil War. They employ some of the conventional literary techniques of the Indian captivity narrative and the Gothic novel. The books parallel genuine accounts published during this period by American seamen captured by Barbary pirates or shipwrecked on the inhospitable Sahara coast and enslaved by wandering tribesmen.

By convention, a woman went to sea because of a man, and she almost always forsook the sea when united with her true love. *The Female Marine* (1815) tells of the adventures of one Lucy Baker or Lucy Brewer* on the *Constitution* during the War of 1812, who went to sea disguised as a man to escape life in a brothel after being abandoned by her lover. Like the real-life heroine, Deborah Sampson, who served in Washington's army and published an embellished account of it, this fictional heroine was an active patriot. Her naval career in the fighting top contrasted with the passive roles usually relegated to eighteenth- and nineteenth-century women.

Military and civil records show that a few women did masquerade as seamen, only admitting the deception when forced to by circumstance. Susannah Stark's recent study of *Female Tars* (1997) points to real economic advantages for the successfully disguised female sailor as well as for the unofficial contingent of wives and mistresses who sometimes accompanied British and French naval vessels into battle during the Napoleonic Wars. Documentable American examples are extremely rare. As a literary device, masquerading as a man and going to sea certainly offered adventurous women a chance to escape restrictive social conventions and embrace a life of relative freedom. Lucy Brewer, disguised as "George" of the *Constitution*, patronized the brothel from which she had lately escaped. "George" also championed a defenseless girl by offering to fight a duel with her assailant, although later Lucy is supposed to have married the girl's brother.

Journal keeping and letter writing were common among middle-class women and men in the nineteenth century. As travel and relocation increasingly separated loved ones, diaries or journals became long, chronological letters to be read by distant family and friends as a way of sharing experiences. Mary Brewster cited separation as a compelling incentive at the beginning of her long journal aboard the whaler *Tiger*. The pleasure that she and her husband would take in rereading it later on seemed even sweeter (*"She Was a Sister Sailor"* [1992]). For religious women, journeys as recorded in their journals were infused with spiritual significance. In a century of unprecedented change, some women and men believed that they personally witnessed unique events that it was their duty to describe for posterity.

Women travelers included female missionaries and teachers as well as ladies accompanying male relatives to assignments overseas. During the nineteenth century, captain's wives joined their husbands on board vessels with increasing frequency. Some, particularly the wives of whaling captains, visited little-known Pacific islands and, in cities like Hong Kong, Calcutta, Cape Town, Honolulu, and Singapore, created permanent English-speaking communities for congenial female society. Captain's wives sometimes encountered old acquaintances on shore and happy was the reunion that brought with it recent news from home.

In 1829 Abby Jane Morrell,* at twenty already a seasoned mariner's wife, was determined to accompany her husband, Captain Benjamin Morrell* of the schooner *Antarctic*,* to the Pacific. Her *Narrative of a Voyage . . .*

(1833) followed her husband's *Narrative of Four Voyages* (1832), attracting better sales; their 1829–1831 expedition aboard the *Antarctic* is unique for being recorded in print by both a captain and his wife. Although she followed the well-established masculine form, Abby Jane's perspective is distinctly feminine. Reflections on female missionaries in India and the Pacific show her fervent admiration of English and American women active in God's service. Unfortunately, both her book and her husband's were ghostwritten, so the amount of credit that either deserves may never be clear.

Thirty years later, the wife of an American official in China, Mrs. H. Dwight Williams, declared that travel by sailing ship was usually uninteresting. Returning to America, however she was outraged to be taken prisoner when the *Jacob Bell* was captured and burned by the Confederate commerce raider *Florida*. This unexpected denouement, told in the last chapter of *A Year in China* (1864), exhibited the perfidy of the Confederate navy to sympathetic Northern readers. Mrs. Williams berated Captain Maffit and his crew for plundering her possessions but solicited his advice on marine insurance.

Manuscript diaries, letters, and journals reflect the true nature of shipboard routine. Long periods of monotony were occasionally punctuated by violent storms, sickness, injury, or sudden death. Women passengers, including the captain's wife, were kept by class divisions and social custom aft of the mainmast and discouraged from talking to common sailors. A visit from the captain's wife would have intruded on the sailors' privacy and undermined discipline by shortening the social distance between forecastle and cabin. For female passengers on long sea voyages and especially for the captain's family, virtual isolation could be the result.

Since the 1930s, several manuscripts from the days of sail preserved in public and private collections have been edited and published by family members, historical societies, and popular presses. Social historians in the 1960s found that women's experiences at sea provided windows on both women's history and sea history. Not only did they illustrate how individual women interpreted, negotiated, and sometimes circumvented society's rules, but they added subtleties of gender to the interplay of class and power in a vessel's masculine hierarchy. More manuscripts have been published since 1990 than ever before, as readers discover an interest in the mundane topics that nineteenth-century women authors who wrote about the sea avoided as commonplace and even vulgar.

Women diarists include the lively Ruth Bradford, en route to China on the *Julia S. Tyler*, who disdained seasickness and laughed at being tossed out of her bunk during storms but was laid low by the common shipboard malaise of boredom (*Maskee!* [1938]). Many captains' wives had much to do. Some of them cleaned their own quarters, did their own laundry, and cared for their children, and almost all of them sewed. Dorothea Balano particularly hated doing laundry and cursed the task in her journal on board the schooner *R. W. Hopkins* (*The Log of the Skipper's Wife** [1978]). She also treated marital sex with disarming candor in her diary and wrote bitterly of the pregnancy she aborted at her husband's insistence. Reading, journal keeping, and letter writing regularly occupied women at sea. To Mary Chipman Lawrence of the whaler *Addison*, even old letters from home were welcome reading (*The Captain's Best Mate* [1966]).

Eliza Williams became pregnant twice during a single long voyage of the whaler *Florida*. The captain of a vessel served as physician to the crew and midwife when necessary; Thomas Williams safely delivered both babies (*One Whaling Family* [1964]). In contrast, Martha Smith Brewer Brown, wife of the master of the whaler *Lucy Ann*, longed for her husband when she delivered their son in Honolulu. He was whaling in the Arctic,* and Martha was befriended during her confinement by another whaling wife, Mrs. Slumon Gray (*She Went A-Whaling* [1993]).

Grown-up children who went to sea were among the last to write memoirs of the great days of sail. Children did not suffer the same restrictions as adult women, often having the run of the vessel and becoming favorites of the crew. The authors recalled childhood amusements and embarrassments, the thrill of storms, the fun of exploring, the kindness of the sailors. In these nostalgic reminiscences, Mother was always beautiful and gentle, Father always tall and capable. For Lucy Brown Reynolds in *Drops of Spray from Southern Seas* (1896), the loss of her mother after a lingering illness on board the *Cadet* seemed to symbolize both the loss of childhood innocence and the inevitable demise of seafaring. For Alice Rowe Snow of the bark *Russell* (*Log of a Sea Captain's Daughter* [1944]), the parent who died was her father, Captain Joshua Rowe. A few men wrote about childhood experiences at sea, but in this form of sea literature with its roots in the Colonial Revival, women set the example.

During the nineteenth century, women's literature presented life at sea positively or as morally instructive. Ultimately, these books reinforced social expectations about class divisions and women's roles. Even in recently published diaries women usually like to be at sea in spite of danger, discomfort, and occasional marital discord. Unpublished manuscripts, though, are often more ambiguous or even negative: some women hated the sea. When Harriet Bliven abruptly left the whaler *Nautilus* for home, her husband, continuing her journal, was inconsolable. Joan Druett's 3 monographs, *Petticoat Whalers* (1991), *Hen Frigates* (1998), and *She Captains: Heroines and Hellions of the Sea* (2000), compiled from many published and unpublished sources listed in her bibliographies, present a balanced composite of the best, the worst, and the routine in family life at sea during the age of sail.

Of all the captains' wives who took command of a vessel, Mary Patten's story, told in *Hen Frigates*, is perhaps best known. In 1856 the slight young woman took command of the *Neptune's Car* after her husband succumbed to brain fever. She navigated safely around Cape Horn* in gales that made other vessels turn back, while also tending to her husband, and remained in her clothes for over fifty days straight. In San Francisco she received adulation from the press and public, becoming a reluctant example for woman's rights activists. Joshua Patten soon died, however. Mary Patten developed tuberculosis and died within a few years of her husband.

As woman's rights became more of a reality after World War I, women's prospects began to change. Electa Johnson, the wife of Irving Johnson,* became his partner and coauthor during global sailing adventures aboard their schooner *Yankee** (*Westward Bound in the Schooner* Yankee [1936]). Tania Aebi became the first American woman and the youngest individual to sail alone around the world. Her memoir, *Maiden Voyage* (1989), is a woman's coming-of-age story. While men, especially her father, form a large part of her narrative on land, Aebi confronted the sea independently, wrestling with it until the sea became a mentor teaching competence and understanding.

Women slowly began to enter modern maritime industries after the social upheavals of the 1960s and 1970s. Pragmatically, some wanted wages higher than those offered for traditional women's occupations. They also responded to the personal challenge, the elation of adventure, the sense of freedom on the water, the camaraderie of shipmates, the love of a spirited vessel, the communion of self with the sea—the same qualities attractive to men.

Some of these pioneers have written books. Nancy Taylor Robson (*Woman in the Wheelhouse* [1985]) served as a deckhand and later a licensed mate aboard tugboats until grounded by pregnancy. Leslie Leyland Fields continued shore fishing off Kodiak, Alaska, even after the birth of her child altered her relationship to the work. *The Entangling Net* (1997) weaves her story with those of other women fishermen on the Alaska coast. Linda Greenlaw spent eighteen years as a commercial fisherman, the first fifteen on swordfishing boats; she tells her story in *The Hungry Ocean* (1999). Deborah Doane Dempsey, the first woman to receive a seagoing master's license, commanded the *Lyra*, a government-chartered transport, during the Persian Gulf conflict. Later she received a presidential commendation for preventing that same ship from grounding off the Carolina coast (*The Captain's a Woman* [1998]).

Men still play a role in women's life and work at sea, although an ambiguous one. Some women face a tough time gaining acceptance from male shipmates who resent female intrusion. They reluctantly put up with insults in order to fit in. Others encounter subtle resistance from traditional authorities. Marriage and children skew the balance of work and home. Dempsey's husband, also a seagoing master, proved to be her lasting mentor and supporter. Robson's husband and most frequent captain encouraged her advancement from deckhand to mate, and Fields married into a fishing family, but motherhood fundamentally altered their priorities, dividing their loyalties between home and the sea in a way that nineteenth-century captain's wives would understand.

Families who serve the sea have always striven for a balance between work and home, with society frequently determining where the balance point should be in terms of gendered responsibilities. During the last twenty years, studies of eighteenth- and nineteenth-century women at sea have been published right along with contemporary women's sea narratives. Women's sea literature has always reflected time and place, social values and concerns, no less so than during this era of debate on the nature of gender and the status of women. [See also CIRCUMNAVIGATIONS AND BLUE-WATER PASSAGES; CRUISING LITERATURE; JOURNALS AND LOGBOOKS; SEA-DELIVERANCE NARRATIVES; WHALING NARRATIVES]

FURTHER READING: Creighton, Margaret S., and Lisa Norling, eds. *Iron Men, Wooden Women: Gender and Seafaring in the Atlantic World, 1700–1920*. Baltimore: Johns Hopkins UP, 1996; Druett, Joan. *Hen Frigates*. New York: Simon and Schuster, 1998; Druett, Joan. *Petticoat Whalers*. New York: HarperCollins, 1991; Druett, Joan. *She Captains: Heroines and Hellions of the Sea*. New York: Simon & Schuster, 2000; Robinson, Jane. *Wayward Women*. New York: Oxford UP, 1990; Stark, Suzanne J. *Female Tars*. Annapolis, MD: Naval Institute P, 1996.

Karen Alexander

WOOLSON, CONSTANCE FENIMORE (1840–1894). One of the first American realists, Constance Fenimore Woolson began her career writing about the Great Lakes,* including an early story, "Margaret Morris" (1872), which is the first shipwreck* fiction of the Lakes. She set more than a dozen stories on islands or in frontier settlements, most featuring strong women characters whose facility with small boats and bravery in the face of gales served as inspiration for her readers as well as for herself. Miss Jonah of "Ballast Island" (1873) is the first description of a woman lighthouse* keeper in Lakes fiction and the model for many of Woolson's later protagonists: strong, lonely women who draw their strength from the wildness of the maritime landscape and the promontories or islands where they make their homes.

With local-color writing becoming popular in eastern magazines at the time, Woolson delineated many other regional types in her work: missionaries, teachers, explorers, mixed-blood natives, and military personnel at Fort Mackinac. Seven of her Lake stories were collected in *Castle Nowhere: Lake-Country Sketches* (1875), a volume that explores the "false lights" not only of the shipwrecker of the title story, but of religion and society as well. Her 1882 novel *Anne* became a national best-seller that inspired sentimental pilgrimages to Mackinac Island for decades.

When Woolson left the Lakes in the late 1870s, she moved to Florida and became one of the first authors on the post-Reconstruction South; the remainder of her career was spent in Europe.

Victoria Brehm

WOUK, HERMAN (1915–   ). Herman Wouk, author of the best-selling sea novel *The Caine Mutiny* (1951) and other works about the navy in World War II, was born in New York City, eldest son of Russian Jewish immigrants. Educated at Columbia University, Wouk spent the years before World War II working in the entertainment industry and trying to write for the stage. After the Japanese attacked Pearl Harbor, Wouk obtained a commission in the U.S. Navy. Service in the Pacific aboard the destroyer-minesweepers U.S.S. *Zane* and U.S.S. *Southard* gave him firsthand experience of navy life and combat at sea.

Upon his discharge in 1945, he married and began his career as a writer. While at sea, he had begun a story about the radio industry; his mentor from Columbia, the philosopher Irwin Edman, helped him secure a publisher, and *Aurora Dawn* (1947) became a Book-of-the-Month Club selection. Good fortune continued for Wouk when his second novel, *The City Boy* (1948), a story of a young Jewish boy in New York City, received similar popular acclaim.

Wouk's third novel, *The Caine Mutiny*, based loosely on some of his own experiences in the Pacific, became the most popular sea novel emerging from America's World War II experience. Unlike most war novels, however, *The Caine Mutiny* contains no descriptions of conflict; rather, it is a study of the transformation of a young civilian into a naval officer and of the problems of maintaining military discipline during wartime. Wouk stresses the importance of officers and crew working together to overcome the natural elements and the skills and courage required to command a warship both in peace and in times of combat. In keeping with his unusual approach, Wouk focuses on the need for men to show presence of mind not only when their ship is under attack from enemy forces but also when the sea itself becomes their enemy. In fact, the mutiny* occurs when the infamous Captain Queeg* is unable to act during a monsoon that threatens to capsize the *Caine*. The novel's climactic scene, the court-martial of the mutineers who rebelled against the martinet commander Captain Queeg, became the source for Wouk's only successful Broadway play, *The Caine Mutiny Court-Martial* (1954), and the novel served as the basis of an Oscar-winning film (1954), starring legendary actor Humphrey Bogart as Queeg.

In 1964, after completing three more novels and a nonfiction work on his Jewish faith, Wouk undertook a project that would occupy him for the next fourteen years: a study of the causes and consequences of World War II. Published as two novels, *The Winds of War* (1971) and *War and Remembrance* (1978) tell the story of the impact of the war on a navy family named the Henrys. Major sections of each novel detail the submarine war in the Pacific and various major sea battles, particularly Midway and Leyte Gulf. Wouk's careful scholarship is evident in his accounts of these pivotal engagements. Wouk's descriptions of submarine warfare are particularly detailed; he is able to capture the tension and fear that submariners experience when they lose the element of surprise, which makes them a suitable foe for more heavily armed warships. He is also able to give brief but compelling portraits of the role of the aircraft carriers in the war, detailing both the strategic impact of their ascendancy in naval warfare and the human dimensions of the transformation wrought upon the navy as the battleships and their venerated commanders reluctantly gave way to younger men who fought the war in the skies above the ocean.

In the early 1980s both *The Winds of War* and *War and Remembrance* were made into television miniseries, appearing in 1983 and 1988; Wouk assisted in writing the screenplay for both. Concurrently, he turned his attention to his Jewish heritage and the history of the nation of Israel, publishing three novels on these subjects during the next decade.

FURTHER READING: Beichman, Arnold. *Herman Wouk: The Novelist as Social Historian*. New Brunswick NJ: Transaction, 1984; Darby, William. *Necessary American Fictions: Popular Literature of the 1950s*. Bowling Green: Bowling Green State UP, 1987; Mazzeno, Laurence. *Herman Wouk*. New York: Twayne, 1994; Milne, Gordon. *Ports of Call: A Study of the American Nautical Novel*. Lanham, MD, and New York: UP of America, 1986.

Laurence W. Mazzeno

Y ———————————————

YANKEE. Irving Johnson* and his wife, Electa, gave the name *Yankee* to three different vessels (built 1897, 1911, and 1959). The first was built as a deep-sea pilot schooner by the Dutch government in 1897 and named the *Loodschooner 4*. Later named the *Texel*, she was bought by the Johnsons in 1933 and renamed *Yankee*. The Johnsons sailed their topsail schooner three times around the world with a crew of young men and women. Their first voyage is recounted in *Westward Bound in the Schooner* Yankee (1936). The tale of their second voyage, which included baby son Arthur and first mate Sterling Hayden,* is told in the picture book *Sailing to See: Picture Cruise in the Schooner* Yankee (1939). The schooner *Yankee* was sold in 1941 and later wrecked in Nova Scotia.

After World War II the Johnsons bought another vessel, the *Duhnen*. Taken as a prize of war by the British, it was the last pilot schooner the Germans had built (in 1911) before steam took over. The Johnsons bought the vessel in 1946 and rigged it as a brigantine before sailing it four times around the world. The first of these voyages (called the "fourth" voyage) is recorded in Yankee's *Wander World: Circling the Globe in the Brigantine* Yankee (1949). The next voyage is narrated by one of the crew, Donald M. Green (as told to Jessie L. Beattie), in *White Wings around the World* (1953). The tale of the "sixth" voyage is told by Irving and Electa Johnson and Lydia Edes in Yankee's *People and Places* (1955). The crew for the final voyage of the brigantine included Christopher Sheldon and his future wife, Alice Strahan, who served as the doctor on board the *Yankee*. (Sheldon later bought the *Albatross*, Ernest K. Gann's* former vessel, which had been rerigged for the film version of his book *Twilight for the Gods* [1956], and took it to sea with a crew of troubled boys, as depicted in the 1995 film *White Squall*. The *Albatross* was tragically lost in a white squall in 1961;

Alice, the cook, and four boys drowned.) The brigantine *Yankee* was sold in 1958 and later wrecked on a reef in Rarotonga, Cook Islands.

The third *Yankee* was designed jointly by Olin Stephens and Irving Johnson and built in a Dutch yard in 1958–1959. So it could be taken through locks and into dangerous waters, it was rigged as a ketch and included an extrastrong keel, shallow draft, centerboards, and folding masts. The Johnsons sailed the ketch *Yankee* across Europe and up the Nile before the Aswan High Dam was built. Their adventures are recorded in Yankee *Sails across Europe* (1962) and Yankee *Sails the Nile* (1966). The ketch *Yankee* was sold in 1975 and continues to sail. In all their years at sea under the Johnsons, the *Yankee*s had no deaths and no serious injuries. [*See also* CIRCUMNAVIGATIONS AND BLUE-WATER PASSAGES]

Mary K. Bercaw Edwards

YARNS. *See* GHOSTS AND GHOST SHIP LEGENDS; GREAT LAKES MYTHS AND LEGENDS.

Literary/Historical Timeline

c.1000	Viking contact at L'Anse aux Meadows, Newfoundland
1441	African slave trade begins
1492	Christopher Columbus' first voyage to the New World; the *Santa Maria* runs aground on Haiti
1497	John Cabot sails from England to the Atlantic coast of North America
1542	Spanish explorer Juan Rodriguez Cabrillo on coast of California
1614	John Smith explores the New England coastline
1620	The *Mayflower* drops anchor off Provincetown, Cape Cod, on 21 November
1630	The *Arbella* (a.k.a. *Arabella*) arrives at Salem, Massachusetts, on 12 June to establish a Puritan colony
1768–1769	Captain James Cook commences three scientific expeditions to the Pacific under British navy auspices
1769	San Francisco Bay reached by land in an expedition led by Gaspar de Portola
1773	Boston Tea Party on 16 December, in response to the Tea Act of Parliament
1775	The siege of Boston on 17 June, as the Revolutionary War begins
1779	The American *Bonhomme Richard 42*, commanded by Commodore John Paul Jones, captures the British *Serapis 44*, commanded by Captain Richard Pearson, on 23 September
1784	Voyage of the *Empress of China* opens United States–China trade
1787	The departure from Boston of the *Columbia* and the *Washington*, first American vessels around Cape Horn

1792	The *Columbia* enters the Columbia River on second voyage to the Pacific
1801–1805	The Barbary Wars, culminating in defeat of Algiers by a U.S. naval force led by Stephen Decatur in 1805
1803–1806	Captain Meriwether Lewis and Captain William Clark lead an expedition overland to the Pacific coast and back
1807–1809	President Thomas Jefferson signs the embargo on all foreign trade: enacted 22 December 1807; lifted 1 March 1809
1808	Importation of slaves becomes illegal on 1 January per 2 March 1807 Act of Congress
1811	John Jacob Astor's Pacific Fur Company founds the first American settlement on the West Coast at Fort Astoria, now Astoria, Oregon
	The explosion of the *Tonquin* at Vancouver Island
1812	Naval battle between the British frigate *Guerriere 38*, commanded by Captain Dacres, and the American frigate *Constitution 44*, commanded by Commodore Hull, off Nova Scotia
1812–1814	Captain David Porter commands the first U.S. Naval Expedition to the Pacific
1813	Battle of Lake Erie
1815	Battle of New Orleans
1817	Cabotage Act forbidding the carrying of goods between American ports by foreign-built or -registered vessels
1818	Establishment of the Black Ball Line, which began the transatlantic packet service, in which vessels sailed on a schedule full or not full
1820	First American missionaries to Hawai'i
	Sinking of the whaleship *Essex* by an enraged sperm whale
1821	First landing on the Antarctic continent by Captain John Davis of the American sealing vessel *Huron*, on 7 February
1825	The Erie Canal opens on 26 October
1834	Richard Henry Dana Jr. leaves Boston as an ordinary seaman on the brig *Pilgrim*, bound for California
1838	The U.S. Exploring Expedition leaves Norfolk, Virginia, under the command of Charles Wilkes for a four-year scientific circumnavigation, on 14 August
1839	African slaves seize the schooner *Amistad* en route to a Cuban plantation, on 1 July
1841	Herman Melville leaves New Bedford, Massachusetts, on the whaleship *Acushnet*, on 3 January
1842	Wilkes expedition returns, and Smithsonian Institution is established with the expedition's collection
	Three men hanged for mutiny on board the *Somers*

1845	U.S. Naval Academy founded
1846–1848	War with Mexico
1849	The California gold rush begins
1853–1855	Elisha Kent Kane's two exploring expeditions to the Arctic
1854	Commodore Matthew Perry arrives in Japan
1858	First transatlantic cable (1,950 miles long), from Ireland to Newfoundland
1859	Discovery of petroleum in Pennsylvania leads to the decline of whaling
1861	Attack on Fort Sumter on 12 April initiates the war between the North and the South
1861–1865	The Civil War
1862	Battle of the *Monitor* versus the *Merrimack*
1862–1863	Siege of Vicksburg
1864	Battle of *Alabama*, the most successful Confederate commerce raider of the Civil War, commanded by Captain Raphael Semmes, against the Union ship *Kearsarge*, commanded by Captain Winslow
1866	Second transatlantic cable
1867	The United States purchases Alaska and Hawai'i
1869	First transcontinental railroad, obviating the necessity of sailing around Cape Horn or transporting cargo and passengers across the Isthmus of Panama
	Suez Canal opens (100 miles long)
1875	Frederick Pease Harlow sails to the Far East on board the *Akbar*
1877–1880	The American navy's oceanographic ship *Blake*, with Alexander Agassiz, carries out research in the Caribbean Sea, the Gulf of Mexico, and along the Florida coast
1881–1883	Adolphus Greely, later a founder of the National Geographic Society, conducts weather and tidal observations on Grinnell Land as part of an international Arctic expedition
1895	Joshua Slocum sails from Boston to Gloucester, beginning the journey for the first solo circumnavigation of the globe, 24 April
1898	Spanish-American War
	The *Maine* is torpedoed in Havana harbor on 15 February
1903	Department of Commerce and Labor established
	The Pacific cable completed between San Francisco and Hawai'i
1909	Robert E. Peary reaches the North Pole accompanied by his black servant Matthew Henson and a party of Eskimos
1910	Eugene O'Neill first goes to sea
1912	The transatlantic steamship *Titanic* is sunk by an iceberg

1914	Cape Cod Canal opens (7.5 miles long)
	Panama Canal opens (51 miles long)
1914–1918	World War I
1915	Revenue Cutter Service and Life-Saving Service merge to form the Coast Guard
1920	Merchant Marine Act of 1920 (also called the Jones Act), re-authorizes the Cabotage Act and states that the United States must develop and maintain a merchant marine to carry the greater part of its commerce and to serve as a naval and military auxiliary in time of war
1924	The bark *Wanderer*, last square-rigged whaler to depart from New Bedford, wrecks on Cuttyhunk Island soon after departure
1925	Return of schooner *John R. Manta*, last New Bedford vessel to make a whaling voyage
1932	Saint Lawrence Waterway Treaty signed
1935	Transpacific air service established
1936	Merchant Marine Act of 1936 (a.k.a. Bland-Copeland Act): the United States had to maintain an adequate U.S. flag fleet in for-eign commerce for both national defense and commercial pur-poses
1939	Regular transatlantic air service established
1941	Japan attacks Pearl Harbor 7 December; Japan captures Guam, Wake Island, and invades the Philippines
1942	Naval battles of Coral Sea and Midway
1944	D-Day Allied invasion of Normandy, 6 June
1958	First United Nations conference on the Law of the Sea called to define territorial seas and establish international standards for ocean resource management
1959	Opening of Saint Lawrence Seaway
1960	Second United Nations conference on the Law of the Sea
1972	Marine Mammals Act bans killing of whales and importation of all whale products
1978	Panama Canal turned over to Panama
1982	Third United Nations conference on the Law of the Sea
1985	An expedition led by Dr. Robert Ballard of the Woods Hole Oceanographic Institution locates the wreck of the *Titanic*
1989	The oil spill in Prince William Sound, Alaska, by the *Exxon-Valdez*
1995	Collapse of cod, haddock, and flounder stocks forces the closing of George's Bank, one of the world's most fertile fishing grounds

Selected Bibliography

Auden, W. H. *The Enchafèd Flood: Or The Romantic Iconography of the Sea*. New York: Random, 1950.

Bender, Bert. *Sea-Brothers: The Tradition of American Sea Fiction from* Moby-Dick *to the Present*. Philadelphia: U of Pennsylvania P, 1988.

Bercaw [Edwards], Mary K. *Melville's Sources*. Evanston, IL: Northwestern UP, 1987.

Bolster, W. Jeffrey. *Black Jacks: African American Seamen in the Age of Sail*. Cambridge: Harvard UP, 1997.

Boon, Kevin Alexander. *Reading the Sea: New Essays on Sea Literature*. New York: Ft. Schuyler P, 1999.

Busch, Briton Cooper. *"Whaling Will Never Do for Me": The American Whaleman in the Nineteenth Century*. Lexington: UP of Kentucky, 1994.

Carlson, Patricia Ann. *Literature and Lore of the Sea*. Amsterdam: Rodopi, 1986.

Creighton, Margaret S., and Lisa Norling, eds. *Iron Men, Wooden Women: Gender and Seafaring in the Atlantic World, 1700–1920*. Baltimore: Johns Hopkins UP, 1996.

Dana, Richard Henry, Jr. *The Seaman's Friend: A Treatise on Practical Seamanship*. Mineola, NY: Dover, 1997.

Ellis, Richard. *Men and Whales*. New York: Alfred A. Knopf, 1991.

Falconer, William. *A Universal Dictionary of the Marine*. London: T. Cadell, 1769.

Foulke, Robert. *The Sea Voyage Narrative*. New York: Twayne, 1997.

Frank, Stuart M. *The Book of Pirate Songs*. Sharon, MA: Kendall Whaling Museum, 1998.

Gidmark, Jill B. *Melville Sea Dictionary: A Glossed Concordance and Analysis of the Sea Language in Melville's Nautical Novels*. Westport, CT: Greenwood, 1982.

Goode, George Brown. *The Fisheries and Fishery Industries of the United States*. 7 vols. Washington, DC: Government Printing Office, 1887.

Harland, John. *Seamanship in the Age of Sail: An Account of the Shiphandling of the Sailing Man-of-War, 1600–1860. Based on Contemporary Sources*. Annapolis: Naval Institute P, 1984.

Hugill, Stan. *Shanties from the Seven Seas: Shipboard Work-Songs and Songs Used as Work-Songs from the Great Days of Sail.* London: Routledge and Kegan Paul, 1961.

Huntress, Keith. *Narratives of Shipwrecks & Disasters, 1586–1860*, Ames: Iowa State UP, 1974.

Kemp, Peter, ed. *The Oxford Companion to Ships and the Sea.* Oxford: Oxford UP, 1976.

Kent, Rockwell. *N by E.* Hanover, NH: UP of New England, 1930.

Lange, Alexander. *Seafaring America.* New York: American Heritage, 1974.

Malloy, Mary. *Boston Men on the Northwest Coast: The American Fur Trade, 1788–1844.* Fairbanks: U of Alaska P, 1998.

McFarland, Philip. *Sea Dangers: The Affair of the* Somers. New York: Schocken, 1985.

Miller, Pamela A. *And the Whale Is Ours: Creative Writing of American Whalemen.* Boston: David R. Godine, 1979.

Neeser, Robert Wilden. *American Naval Songs and Ballads.* New Haven, CT: Yale UP, 1938.

Philbrick, Thomas. *James Fenimore Cooper and the Development of American Sea Fiction.* Cambridge: Harvard UP, 1961.

Raban, Jonathan. *Passage to Juneau: A Sea and Its Meanings.* New York: Pantheon, 1999.

Santraud, Jeanne-Marie. *La Mer et le Roman Américain dans la Première Moitié du Dix-Neuvième Siècle.* Paris: Didier, 1972.

Skallerup, Harry R. *Books Afloat and Ashore: A History of Books, Libraries, and Reading among Seamen during the Age of Sail.* Hamden, CT: Archon, 1974.

Sealts, Merton M., Jr. *Melville's Reading.* Rev. and enlarged ed. Columbia: U of South Carolina P, 1988.

Sherman, Stuart C., et al. *Whaling Logbooks and Journals 1613–1928: An Inventory of Manuscript Records in Public Collections.* New York: Garland, 1986.

Smith, Myron J., Jr., and Robert C. Weller. *Sea Fiction Guide.* Metuchen, NJ: Scarecrow P, 1976.

Smyth, W. H. *The Sailor's Word-Book: An Alphabetical Digest of Nautical Terms.* London: Brassey's, 1998.

Solley, George C., and Eric Steinbaugh. *Moods of the Sea: Masterworks of Sea Poetry.* Annapolis: Naval Institute P, 1981.

Springer, Haskell, ed. *America and the Sea: A Literary History.* Athens: U of Georgia P, 1995.

Starbuck, Alexander. *History of the American Whale Fishery, from Its Earliest Inception to the Year 1876.* Repr., 2 vols., with a new preface by Stuart C. Sherman. New York: Argosy Antiquarian, 1964.

Stein, Douglas L. *American Maritime Documents, 1776–1860: Illustrated and Described.* Mystic, CT: Mystic Seaport Museum, 1992.

Stein, Roger B. *Seascape and the American Imagination.* New York: Whitney Museum of American Art/Clarkson N. Potter, 1975.

Thomas, Tony. *The Cinema of the Sea: A Critical Survey and Filmography, 1925–1986.* Jefferson, NC: McFarland, 1988.

Tyng, Charles. *Before the Wind: The Memoir of an American Sea Captain.* New York: Viking, 1999.

Van Dorn, William G. *Oceanography and Seamanship*. New York: Argosy, 1974.

Vincent, Howard P. *The Tailoring of Melville's* White-Jacket. Evanston, IL: North-western UP, 1970.

Vincent, Howard P. *The Trying-Out of* Moby-Dick. Boston: Houghton-Mifflin, 1949.

Wharton, Donald P. *In the Trough of the Sea: Selected American Sea-Deliverance Narratives, 1610–1766*. Westport, CT: Greenwood, 1979.

Wilmerding, John. *American Marine Painting*. 2d ed. New York: Abrams, 1987.

Index

Page numbers in **bold type** refer to main entries in the encyclopedia.

The Editorial Board

EDITOR

JILL B. GIDMARK is Morse-Alumni Distinguished Professor of Literature and Writing at the University of Minnesota, General College, Minneapolis, where she has taught since 1978. She is the author of *Melville Sea Dictionary: A Glossed Concordance and Analysis of the Sea Language in Melville's Nautical Novels* (1982). She has presented at national and international conferences and published essays on Herman Melville's *Clarel*, Derek Walcott's *Omeros*, and other nineteenth- and twentieth-century American literature. Her coauthored article on a minor historical figure in *Omeros* won the 1997 Robert A. Miller Prize. Gidmark annually coordinates sessions on Literature of the Sea for conferences of the College English Association. In 1999 she cochaired with Mary K. Bercaw Edwards a special conference for the Melville Society on Melville and the Sea at Mystic Seaport Museum, and in 2000 she organized and chaired a panel on Literature of the Sea at an international conference of the Hemingway Society in Bimini, Bahamas. She is currently editing a special issue of *The Critic* on sea literature.

BOARD MEMBERS

MARY K. BERCAW EDWARDS earned her Ph.D. in English from Northwestern University in 1984. She worked with Harrison Hayford, general editor of the Northwestern-Newberry edition of *The Writings of Herman Melville*, and was a contributing scholar to four volumes of the series. In addition to her scholarly work, she sailed around the world at the age of sixteen in a thirty-eight-foot ketch. Her book *Melville's Sources* was published in 1987. Bercaw Edwards is currently coediting *Melville's Whaling Years* with Thomas Farel Heffernan. She teaches Literature of the Sea for the Williams College–Mystic Seaport Maritime Studies Program and in the graduate program at Wesleyan University. In 1999 she was the program cochair and the on-site logistics coordinator for the Melville and the Sea conference. She also works at Mystic Seaport, where she sets sails on the 1882 full-rigged ship *Joseph Conrad* and the 1841 whaleship *Charles W. Morgan.*

ATTILIO FAVORINI is Founding Chair of the Department of Theatre Arts at the University of Pittsburgh. He founded the Three Rivers Shakespeare Festival and served as its Producing Director for thirteen years. He is a former editor of *Theatre Survey* and the author of four plays, including *Steel/ City,* published by the University of Pittsburgh Press in 1976. Ecco Press has published an anthology of documentary drama under his editorship entitled *Voicings* (1995). He has also written on the narrative structure of *Billy Budd* and on the sea plays of John Guare. In 1986 he sailed around the world as Dean of the Semester-at-Sea program sponsored by the University of Pittsburgh.

JOSEPH FLIBBERT earned his Ph.D. from the University of Illinois. Until his death in 1999, he was Professor of English at Salem State College, where he had also served as chairperson and as director of graduate studies in English. He taught graduate and undergraduate courses on American sea literature for more than twenty years. The author of *Melville and the Art of Burlesque* (1974), he also contributed a chapter, "Poetry in the Mainstream," to *America and the Sea: A Literary History* (1995) and an essay on Nathaniel Hawthorne to *Salem: Cornerstones of a Historic City* (1999). He lectured extensively here and abroad on topics in American and sea literature. He was a founding member and past president of the Nathaniel Hawthorne Society.

R. D. MADISON is Professor of English at the U.S. Naval Academy, where he has led seminars in maritime subjects ranging from *The Tempest* to Joseph Conrad. He has edited several volumes of nineteenth-century maritime and military literature, including Thomas Wentworth Higginson's *Army Life in a Black Regiment* (1997). He has also written a prizewinning play, *Prospect for Freedom: Frederick Douglass and John Brown,* and a sonnet cycle, "Tuckahoe," about the Eastern Shore origins of Frederick Douglass. His collection of *Bounty* narratives is forthcoming.

MARY MALLOY teaches Maritime Studies at the Sea Education Association in Woods Hole, Massachusetts. She received her Ph.D. in American Civilization from Brown University and is the author of *Boston Men on the Northwest Coast* (1998) and other works of maritime history. With her husband, Stuart Frank, she has performed traditional songs from American sailing ships on four continents.

About the Contributors

JOYCE SPARER ADLER, North Bennington, VT.

PARKER BISHOP ALBEE JR., University of Southern Maine.

DANIEL M. ALBERT, Sea Education Association.

KAREN ALEXANDER, University of New Hampshire.

BRIAN ANDERSON, Seabrook, TX.

DAVID D. ANDERSON, Michigan State University.

NANCY PROTHRO ARBUTHNOT, U.S. Naval Academy.

TINA M. ARONIS, Salem, MA.

PHILIP BARNARD, University of Kansas.

ROBERT BEASECKER, Grand Valley State University.

HORACE BECK, Ripton, VT.

SUSAN F. BEEGEL, Williams College-Mystic Seaport Maritime Studies Program.

BERT BENDER, Arizona State University.

RALPH BERETS, University of Missouri-Kansas City.

LAWRENCE I. BERKOVE, University of Michigan-Dearborn.

DENNIS BERTHOLD, Texas A&M University-College Station.

WALTER E. BEZANSON, Emeritus, Rutger's University.

BRAD S. BORN, Bethel College (KS).

MICHAEL P. BRANCH, University of Nevada-Reno.

VICTORIA BREHM, Grand Valley State University.

ROGER J. JIANG BRESNAHAN, Michigan State University.

THOMAS R. BROOKS, Wheaton College (MA).

MELANIE BROWN, University of Minnesota-Minneapolis.

BYRON CAMINERO-SANTANGELO, University of Kansas.

MARTA CAMINERO-SANTANGELO, University of Kansas.

DOUG CAPRA, Seward, AK.

BRIAN T. CARNEY, University of Pittsburgh.

JEFFREY CASS, Texas A&M International University.

BOYD CHILDRESS, Auburn University Library.

MATTHEW D. CHILDS, U.S. Naval Reserve.

GAIL H. COFFLER, Suffolk University.

WILLIAM CRISMAN, Penn State-Altoona.

STEPHEN CURLEY, Texas A&M University-Galveston.

DONALD P. CURTIS, Toledo, OH.

PETER F. DECATALDO, CUNY-New York.

DEAN DEFINO, SUNY-Binghamton.

ED DEMERLY, Henry Ford Community College.

CHRISTOPHER C. DE SANTIS, Illinois State University.

MARGHERITA M. DESY, U.S.S. Constitution Museum.

MIRA DOCK, Portland, OR.

MICHAEL P. DYER, Kendall Whaling Museum.

JANE DONAHUE EBERWEIN, Oakland University.

CRAIG EDWARDS, Mystic Seaport Museum.

JANET RAY EDWARDS, University of Maryland-Baltimore County.

MARY K. BERCAW EDWARDS, Williams College-Mystic Seaport Maritime Studies Program.

HUGH EGAN, Ithaca College.

PHILIP J. EGAN, Western Michigan University.

JONATHAN R. ELLER, Indiana University.

RICHARD ELLIS, New York, NY.

BERNARD F. ENGEL, Michigan State University.

MATTHEW EVERTSON, Arizona State University-Tempe.

ATTILIO FAVORINI, University of Pittsburgh.

FRED M. FETROW, U.S. Naval Academy.

DANIEL FINAMORE, Peabody Essex Museum.

JOSEPH FLIBBERT, Salem State College.

ROBERT C. FOULKE, Skidmore College.

DOREEN FOWLER, University of Kansas.

LISA FRANCHETTI, Washington, DC.

HILLARY FREY, Lingua Franca.

ROBERT L. GALE, University of Pittsburgh.

ELLEN GARDINER, University of Mississippi.

CAROLYN ADELE GARDNER, Mariners' Museum Research Library.

SUSAN IRVIN GATTI, Indiana University of Pennsylvania.

JILL B. GIDMARK, University of Minnesota-Minneapolis.

C. HERBERT GILLILAND, U.S. Naval Academy.

DEBRA GLABEAU, Marblehead, MA.

PAUL GOLDSTAUB, SUNY-Binghamton.

DAVID R. GOODMAN, Los Angeles, CA.

GLENN S. GORDINIER, Mystic Seaport Museum.

GLENN GRASSO, Williams College-Mystic Seaport Maritime Studies Program.

JAMES L. GRAY, Indiana University of Pennsylvania.

PHILIP A. GREASLEY, University of Kentucky.

JOHN B. HATTENDORF, Naval War College.

THOMAS FAREL HEFFERNAN, Adelphi University.

BETSY S. HILBERT, Miami-Dade Community College-Kendall.

SALLY C. HOOPLE, Castine, ME.

KAY SEYMOUR HOUSE, American Antiquarian Society.

ANTHONY HUNT, University of Puerto Rico-Mayagüez.

JOHN F. HUSSEY, U.S. Naval Academy.

ROBERT IMES, Southgate, MI.

DAVID JORTNER, University of Pittsburgh.

CLAIRE J. KEYES, Salem State College.

ROBERT E. KIBLER, Valley City State University.

RICHARD J. KING, Williams College-Mystic Seaport Maritime Studies Program.

SUSAN RAIDY KLEIN, Sandwich, MA.

BRIAN KNETL, University of Pittsburgh.

TONI D. KNOTT, Cullowhee, NC.

GROVE KOGER, Boise Public Library.

PAUL KOSIDOWSKI, Milwaukee Repertory Theatre.

PETER J. KRATZKE, University of Texas-San Antonio.

JERALDINE R. KRAVER, University of Texas-San Antonio.

DANIEL W. LANE, University of Delaware.

LINDA LEDFORD-MILLER, University of Scranton.

CHRISTOPHER LEE, University of California-Los Angeles.

EDWARD J. LEFKOWICZ, Providence, RI.

ANNA E. LOMANDO, Penn State University-New Kensington.

FELICIA HARDISON LONDRÉ, University of Missouri-Kansas City.

ELLEN L. MADISON, Westerly, RI.

R. D. MADISON, U.S. Naval Academy.

MARY MALLOY, Sea Education Association.

RALPH MAUD, Vancouver, Canada.

LAURENCE W. MAZZENO, Alvernia College.

MICHAEL McCAUGHAN, National Museums and Galleries of Northern Ireland.

PETER H. McCRACKEN, University of Washington.

CAROLINE J. McKENZIE, Toledo, OH.

JOAN TYLER MEAD, Marshall University.

JAMES F. MILLINGER, Chebeague Island, ME.

NATHANIEL T. MOTT, Tinton Falls, NJ.

WESLEY T. MOTT, Worcester Polytechnic Institute.

UDO NATTERMANN, University of Indianapolis.

JOSEPH NAVRATIL, U.S. Navy.

CAPPER NICHOLS, University of Minnesota-Minneapolis.

MARY DEJONG OBUCHOWSKI, Central Michigan University.

TED OLSON, East Tennessee State University.

GWEN OREL, Alabama Shakespeare Festival.

ANN M. OUELLETTE, Rockport, MA.

STEVEN H. PARK, University of Connecticut.

DAVID R. PELLEGRINI, University of Pittsburgh.

DANA L. PETERSON, Minneapolis, MN.

NATHANIEL PHILBRICK, Egan Institute of Maritime Studies.

THOMAS PHILBRICK, University of Pittsburgh.

MARGARET LOFTUS RANALD, CUNY-Queens College.

JULIUS ROWAN RAPER, University of North Carolina-Chapel Hill.

BRENDAN A. RAPPLE, Boston College.

MARGARITA RIGAL-ARAGÓN, University of Castilla-La Mancha, Spain.

KENNETH A. ROBB, Bowling Green State University.

DOUGLAS ROBILLARD, Metairie, LA.

FRANK ROTSAERT, Siena Heights University.

JOHN SAMSON, Texas Tech University.

BRIAN SATERIALE, University of Pittsburgh.

ARNOLD SCHMIDT, California State University-Stanislaus.

JAMES J. SCHRAMER, Youngstown State University.

ELIZABETH SCHULTZ, University of Kansas.

JOHN T. SHAWCROSS, University of Kentucky.

ROBERT SHENK, University of New Orleans.

HASKELL SPRINGER, University of Kansas.

NORMAN E. STAFFORD, Arkansas State University.

LES STANDIFORD, Florida International University.

CHRISTOPHER STEN, George Washington University.

FREDERICK STONEHOUSE, Marquette, MI.

WILLIAM A. SULLIVAN, Winthrop University.

BICKFORD SYLVESTER, University of British Columbia.

WILLIAM E. TANNER, Texas Woman's University.

VICTOR VERNEY, Des Moines, IA.

ERIC G. WAGGONER, Arizona State University-Tempe.

GREGG ALLEN WALKER, University of Kansas.

ROBERT WALSER, University of London.

CHARLES F. WARNER, U.S. Naval Academy.

ERIKA J. WATERS, University of the Virgin Islands.

KAREN WOODS WEIERMAN, Worcester State College.

LEE F. WERTH, Cleveland State University.

DONALD P. WHARTON, Plymouth State College.

DANIEL E. WILLIAMS, University of Mississippi.

MELINDA F. WILLIAMS, Texas Woman's University.

RICHARD J. WILLIAMSON, Muskingum College.

CHRISTINA L. WOLAK, University of Nevada-Reno.

DONALD YANNELLA, Barat College.

MICHAEL W. YOUNG, Robert Morris College.

GREG W. ZACHARIAS, Creighton University.